GENERAL THEORY OF LAW AND STATE

BY
HANS KELSEN

TRANSLATED BY
ANDERS WEDBERG
Assistant Professor of Philosophy in the University of Stockholm

THE LAWBOOK EXCHANGE, LTD.
Clark, New Jersey

ISBN-13: 978-1-58477-717-5 (paperback)
ISBN-10: 1-58477-717-6 (paperback)

ISBN-13: 978-1-886363-74-8 (cloth)
ISBN-10: 1-886363-74-9 (cloth)

Lawbook Exchange edition 2007, 2009

Reprinted with permission from the Hans Kelsen-Institut.

THE LAWBOOK EXCHANGE, LTD.
33 Terminal Avenue
Clark, New Jersey 07066-1321

*Please see our website for a selection of our other publications
and fine facsimile reprints of classic works of legal history:*
www.lawbookexchange.com

Library of Congress Cataloging-in-Publication Data

Kelsen, Hans, 1881-1973.
  General theory of law and state / by Hans Kelsen : translated by
Anders Wedberg.
      p. cm.
  Originally published: Cambridge : Harvard University Press, 1945.
  Includes bibliographical references and index.
  ISBN 1-886363-74-9 (alk. paper)
    1. State, The. 2. Law--Philosophy. 3. International law.
  4. Natural law. I. Title.

K252.K45 1999
340'.1--dc21
                                       9832334
                                            CIP

Printed in the United States of America on acid-free paper

GENERAL THEORY OF
LAW AND STATE

BY

HANS KELSEN

TRANSLATED BY
ANDERS WEDBERG
Assistant Professor of Philosophy in the University of Stockholm

CAMBRIDGE · MASSACHUSETTS
HARVARD UNIVERSITY PRESS
1945

PRINTED AT THE HARVARD UNIVERSITY PRINTING OFFICE
CAMBRIDGE, MASSACHUSETTS, U.S.A.

PREFACE

THE PRESENT BOOK is intended to reformulate rather than merely to republish thoughts and ideas previously expressed in German and in French.* The aim has been a double one: first, to present the essential elements of what the author has come to call the "pure theory of law" in such a way as to bring it near to readers who have grown up in the traditions and atmosphere of the Common Law; secondly, to give to that theory such a formulation as to enable it to embrace the problems and institutions of English and American law as well as those of the Civil Law countries, for which it was formulated originally. It is hoped that this reformulation may have resulted in an improvement.

The theory which will be expounded in the main part of this book is a general theory of positive law. Positive law is always the law of a definite community: the law of the United States, the law of France, Mexican law, international law. To attain a scientific exposition of those particular legal orders constituting the corresponding legal communities is the design of the general theory of law here set forth. This theory, resulting from a comparative analysis of the different positive legal orders, furnishes the fundamental concepts by which the positive law of a definite legal community can be described. The subject matter of a general theory of law is the legal norms, their elements, their interrelation, the legal order as a whole, its structure, the relationship between different legal orders, and, finally, the unity of the law in the plurality of positive legal orders.

Since the aim of this general theory of law is to enable the jurist concerned with a particular legal order, the lawyer, the judge, the legislator, or the law-teacher, to understand and to describe as exactly as possible his own positive law, such a theory has to derive its concepts exclusively from the contents of positive legal norms. It must not be influenced by the motives or intentions of lawmaking authorities or by the wishes or interests of individuals with respect to the formation of the law to which they are subject, except in so far as these motives and intentions, these wishes and interests, are manifested in the material produced by the lawmaking process. What cannot be found in the contents of positive legal norms cannot enter a legal concept. The general

* ALLGEMEINE STAATSLEHRE (1925); THÉORIE GÉNÉRALE DU DROIT INTERNATIONAL PUBLIC (1928); REINE RECHTSLEHRE (1934). As to other publications, see the List of Publications at the end of this book.

theory, as it is presented in this book, is directed at a structural analysis of positive law rather than at a psychological or economic explanation of its conditions, or a moral or political evaluation of its ends.

When this doctrine is called the "pure theory of law," it is meant that it is being kept free from all the elements foreign to the specific method of a science whose only purpose is the cognition of law, not its formation.* A science has to describe its object as it actually is, not to prescribe how it should be or should not be from the point of view of some specific value judgments. The latter is a problem of politics, and, as such, concerns the art of government, an activity directed at values, not an object of science, directed at reality.

The reality, however, at which a science of law is directed, is not the reality of nature which constitutes the object of natural science. If it is necessary to separate the science of law from politics, it is no less necessary to separate it from natural science. One of the most difficult tasks of a general theory of law is that of determining the specific reality of its subject and of showing the difference which exists between legal and natural reality. The specific reality of the law does not manifest itself in the actual behavior of the individuals who are subject to the legal order. This behavior may or may not be in conformity with the order the existence of which is the reality in question. The legal order determines what the conduct of men ought to be. It is a system of norms, a normative order. The behavior of the individuals as it actually is, is determined by laws of nature according to the principle of causality. This is natural reality. And in so far as sociology deals with this reality as determined by causal laws, sociology is a branch of natural science. Legal reality, the specific existence of the law, manifests itself in a phenomenon which is mostly designated as the positiveness of law. The specific subject of legal science is positive or real law in contradistinction to an ideal law, the goal of politics. Just as the actual behavior of the individuals may or may not correspond to the norms of positive law regulating this behavior, positive law may or may not correspond to an ideal law presented as justice or "natural" law. It is in its relation to the ideal law, called justice or "natural" law, that the reality of positive law appears. Its existence is independent of its conformity or nonconformity with justice or "natural" law.

The pure theory of law considers its subject not as a more or less imperfect copy of a transcendental idea. It does not try to comprehend

* Cf. my paper *The Function of the Pure Theory of Law* in 2 Law: A CENTURY OF PROGRESS, 1835–1935; CONTRIBUTIONS IN CELEBRATION OF THE 100TH ANNIVERSARY OF THE FOUNDING OF THE SCHOOL OF LAW OF THE NEW YORK UNIVERSITY (1937) 231–241.

the law as an offspring of justice, as the human child of a divine parent. The pure theory of law insists upon a clear distinction between empirical law and transcendental justice by excluding the latter from its specific concerns. It sees in the law not the manifestation of a superhuman authority, but a specific social technique based on human experience; the pure theory refuses to be a metaphysics of law. Consequently it seeks the basis of law — that is, the reason of its validity — not in a meta-juristic principle but in a juristic hypothesis — that is, a basic norm, to be established by a logical analysis of actual juristic thinking.

Much traditional jurisprudence is characterized by a tendency to confuse the theory of positive law with political ideologies disguised either as metaphysical speculation about justice or as natural-law doctrine. It confounds the question of the essence of law — that is, the question of what the law actually is — with the question of what it should be. It is inclined more or less to identify law and justice. On the other hand, some theories of jurisprudence show a tendency to ignore the borderline separating a theory of legal norms regulating human behavior from a science causally explaining actual human behavior, a tendency resulting in confusing the question as to how men legally ought to behave with the question as to how men actually do behave and how they probably will behave in the future. The latter question can be answered, if at all, only on the basis of a general sociology. To become merged in this science seems to be the ambition of modern jurisprudence. Only by separating the theory of law from a philosophy of justice as well as from sociology is it possible to establish a specific science of law.

The orientation of the pure theory of law is in principle the same as that of so-called analytical jurisprudence. Like John Austin in his famous *Lectures on Jurisprudence*, the pure theory of law seeks to attain its results exclusively by an analysis of positive law. Every assertion advanced by a science of law must be based on a positive legal order or on a comparison of the contents of several legal orders. It is by confining jurisprudence to a structural analysis of positive law that legal science is separated from philosophy of justice and sociology of law and that the purity of its method is attained. In this respect, there is no essential difference between analytical jurisprudence and the pure theory of law. Where they differ, they do so because the pure theory of law tries to carry on the method of analytical jurisprudence more consistently than Austin and his followers. This is true especially as regards such fundamental concepts * as that of the legal norm on the one hand,

---

* Cf. my article *The Pure Theory of Law and Analytical Jurisprudence* (1941) 55 HARV. L. REV. 44–70.

and those of the legal right and the legal duty on the other, in French
and German jurisprudence presented as a contrast between law in an
objective and law in a subjective sense; and, last but not least, as regards
the relationship between law and State.

Austin shares the traditional opinion according to which law and
State are two different entities, although he does not go so far as most
legal theorists who present the State as the creator of the law, as the
power and moral authority behind the law, as the god of the world of
law. The pure theory of law shows the true meaning of these figurative
expressions. It shows that the State as a social order must necessarily
be identical with the law or, at least, with a specific, a relatively centralized legal order, that is, the national legal order in contradistinction to
the international, highly decentralized, legal order. Just as the pure
theory of law eliminates the dualism of law and justice and the dualism
of objective and subjective law, so it abolishes the dualism of law and
State. By so doing it establishes a theory of the State as an intrinsic
part of the theory of law and postulates a unity of national and international law within a legal system comprising all the positive legal orders.

The pure theory of law is a monistic theory. It shows that the State
imagined as a personal being is, at best, nothing but the personification
of the national legal order, and more frequently merely a hypostatization of certain moral-political postulates. By abolishing this dualism
through dissolving the hypostatization usually connected with the ambiguous term "State," the pure theory of law discloses the political
ideologies within the traditional jurisprudence.

It is precisely by its anti-ideological character that the pure theory
of law proves itself a true science of law. Science as cognition has always
the immanent tendency to unveil its object. But political ideology veils
reality either by transfiguring reality in order to conserve and defend it,
or by disfiguring reality in order to attack, to destroy, or to replace it by
another reality. Every political ideology has its root in volition, not in
cognition; in the emotional, not in the rational, element of our consciousness; it arises from certain interests, or, rather, from interests other
than the interest in truth. This remark, of course, does not imply any
assertion regarding the value of the other interests. There is no possibility of deciding rationally between opposite values. It is precisely
from this situation that a really tragic conflict arises: the conflict between the fundamental principle of science, Truth, and the supreme
ideal of politics, Justice.

The political authority creating the law and, therefore, wishing to
conserve it, may doubt whether a purely scientific cognition of its products, free from any political ideology, is desirable. Similarly, the forces

tending to destroy the present order and to replace it by another one believed to be better will not have much use for such a cognition of law either. But a science of law cares neither for the one nor for the other. Such a science the pure theory of law wishes to be.

The postulate of complete separation of jurisprudence from politics cannot sincerely be questioned if there is to be anything like a science of law. Doubtful only is the degree to which the separation is realizable in this field. A marked difference does indeed exist in this very feature between natural and social science. Of course, no one would maintain that natural science runs no danger at all of attempts by political interests to influence it. History demonstrates the contrary, and shows clearly enough that a world power has sometimes felt itself threatened by the truth concerning the course of the stars. But the fact that in the past natural science had been able to achieve its complete independence from politics is due to the powerful social interest in this victory: the interest in that advance of technique which only a free science can guarantee. But social theory leads to no such direct advantage afforded by social technique as physics and chemistry produce on the acquisition of engineering knowledge and medical therapy. In social and especially in legal science, there is still no influence to counteract the overwhelming interest that those residing in power, as well as those craving for power, have in a theory pleasing to their wishes, that is, in a political ideology.

This is especially true in our time, which indeed "is out of joint," when the foundations of social life have been shaken to the depths by two World Wars. The ideal of an objective science of law and State, free from all political ideologies, has a better chance for recognition in a period of social equilibrium.

It seems, therefore, that a pure theory of law is untimely today, when in great and important countries, under the rule of party dictatorship, some of the most prominent representatives of jurisprudence know no higher task than to serve — with their "science" — the political power of the moment. If the author, nevertheless, ventures to publish this general theory of law and State, it is with the belief that in the Anglo-American world, where freedom of science continues to be respected and where political power is better stabilized than elsewhere, ideas are in greater esteem than power; and also with the hope that even on the European continent, after its liberation from political tyranny, the younger generation will be won over to the ideal of an independent science of law; for the fruit of such a science can never be lost.

The author was able to prepare this book only because he was privileged to come to the United States and to work during two years at Harvard University. This opportunity he owes above all to the generous help of the Rockefeller Foundation, to which he wishes to express his sincere gratitude.

He gratefully acknowledges the considerable assistance rendered by the Bureau of International Research whose grant aided him in the elaboration of that part of the book which concerns the theory of international law.

Grateful acknowledgment is also made to the Committee on Translation and Publication of a 20th Century Legal Philosophy Series of the Association of American Law Schools, which provided the funds for the translation.

The author is greatly indebted to Professor Jerome Hall for many valuable suggestions and for reading the proofs.

Finally thanks are due to Dr. Anders Wedberg for his valuable help in making the English translation of the main part of the book, which was later revised by the author, and to Dr. Wolfgang Kraus for translating the monograph, *Die Philosophischen Grundlagen der Naturrechtslehre und des Rechtspositivismus* (1929) which appears in the Appendix under the title "Natural Law Doctrine and Legal Positivism."

H. K.

Berkeley, California.
April, 1944

CONTENTS

Nomodynamics

PART TWO: THE STATE

APPENDIX

NATURAL LAW DOCTRINE AND LEGAL POSITIVISM

PART ONE
THE LAW

NOMOSTATICS

I. THE CONCEPT OF LAW

A. LAW AND JUSTICE

a. Human Behavior as the Object of Rules

LAW is an order of human behavior. An "order" is a system of rules. Law is not, as it is sometimes said, a rule. It is a set of rules having the kind of unity we understand by a system. It is impossible to grasp the nature of law if we limit our attention to the single isolated rule. The relations which link together the particular rules of a legal order are also essential to the nature of law. Only on the basis of a clear comprehension of those relations constituting the legal order can the nature of law be fully understood.

The statement that law is an order of human behavior does not mean that the legal order is concerned only with human behavior; that nothing but human behavior enters into the contents of legal rules. A rule that makes murder a punishable delict concerns human behavior which has the death of a human being as its effect. Death itself, however, is not human behavior but a physiological process. Every rule of law obligates human beings to observe a certain behavior under certain circumstances. These circumstances need not be human behavior, they may be, for instance, what we call natural events. A rule of law may oblige neighbors to lend assistance to the victims of an inundation. Inundation is not a human behavior, but it is the condition of a human behavior prescribed by the legal order. In this sense, facts which are not facts of human behavior may enter into the contents of a legal rule. But they may do so only as related to human behavior, either as its condition or as its effect.

It might seem as if this applied only to the laws of civilized peoples. In primitive law, animals, and even plants and other inanimate objects are often treated in the same way as human beings and are, in particular, punished.* However, this must be seen in its connection with the

---

* In antiquity there was in Athens a special court whose function it was to condemn inanimate things, for instance a spear by which a man had been killed. Demosthenes, *Oration against Aristocrates*, 76 (English translation by J. H. Vince, 1935, p. 267): "There is also a fourth tribunal, that at the Prytaneum. Its function is that, if a man is struck by a stone, or a piece of wood or iron, or anything of

animism of primitive man. He considers animals, plants, and inanimate objects as endowed with a "soul," inasmuch as he attributes human, and sometimes even superhuman, mental faculties to them. The fundamental difference between human and other beings, which is part of the outlook of civilized man, does not exist for primitive man. And he applies his law also to non-human beings because for him they are human, or at least similar to man. In this sense primitive law is an order of human behavior, too.

However, besides law there are other orders of human behavior, such as morals and religion. A definition of law must specify in what respects law differs from these other orders of human behavior.

b. Scientific and Political Definition of Law

Any attempt to define a concept must take for its starting-point the common usage of the word, denoting the concept in question. In defining the concept of law, we must begin by examining the following questions: Do the social phenomena generally called "law" present a common characteristic distinguishing them from other social phenomena of a similar kind? And is this characteristic of such importance in the social life of man that it may be made the basis of a concept serviceable for the cognition of social life? For reasons of economy of thought, one must start from the broadest possible usage of the word "law." Perhaps no such characteristic as we are looking for can be found. Perhaps the actual usage is so loose that the phenomena called "law" do not exhibit any common characteristic of real importance. But if such a characteristic can be found, then we are justified in including it in the definition.

This is not to say that it would be illegitimate to frame a narrower concept of law, not covering all the phenomena usually called "law." We may define at will those terms which we wish to use as tools in our intellectual work. The only question is whether they will serve the theoretical purpose for which we have intended them. A concept of law whose extent roughly coincides with the common usage is obviously — circumstances otherwise being equal — to be preferred to a concept which is applicable only to a much narrower class of phenomena. Let

---

that sort, falling upon him, and if someone, without knowing who threw it, knows and possesses the implement of homicide, he takes proceedings against these implements in that court." Cf. also PLATO, THE LAWS, 873, and ARISTOTLE, ATHENENSIUM RES PUBLICA, cap. 57. In the Middle Ages it was still possible to bring a lawsuit against an animal, for instance a dog or a bull which had killed a man, or locusts which had caused damage by eating up the crop; and in due process of law the court condemned the accused animal to death, whereupon the animal was executed in exactly the same way as a human being. Cf. KARL VON AMIRA, THIERSTRAFEN UND THIERPROCESSE (1891).

us take an example. Even since the rise of Bolshevism, National Socialism, and Fascism, one speaks of Russian, German, and Italian "law."
Nothing would prevent us, however, from including in our definition of
a legal order a certain minimum of personal freedom and the possibility
of private property. One result of adopting such a definition would be
that the social orders prevailing in Russia, Italy and Germany could no
longer be recognized as legal orders, although they have very important
elements in common with the social orders of democratic-capitalistic
States.

The above-mentioned concept — which actually appears in recent
works on legal philosophy — also shows how a political bias can influence the definition of law. The concept of law is here made to correspond
to a specific ideal of justice, namely, of democracy and liberalism.
From the standpoint of science, free from any moral or political judgments of value, democracy and liberalism are only two possible principles
of social organization, just as autocracy and socialism are. There is no
scientific reason why the concept of law should be defined so as to exclude the latter. As used in these investigations, the concept of law has
no moral connotation whatsoever. It designates a specific technique of
social organization. The problem of law, as a scientific problem, is the
problem of social technique, not a problem of morals. The statement:
"A certain social order has the character of law, is a legal order," does
not imply the moral judgment that this order is good or just. There are
legal orders which are, from a certain point of view, unjust. Law and
justice are two different concepts. Law as distinguished from justice is
positive law. It is the concept of positive law which is here in question;
and a science of positive law must be clearly distinguished from a philosophy of justice.

c. The Concept of Law and the Idea of Justice

To free the concept of law from the idea of justice is difficult because
both are constantly confused in non-scientific political thought as well
as in general speech, and because this confusion corresponds to the
ideological tendency to make positive law appear as just. If law and
justice are identified, if only a just order is called law, a social order
which is presented as law is — at the same time — presented as
just; and that means it is morally justified. The tendency to identify
law and justice is the tendency to justify a given social order. It is a
political, not a scientific tendency. In view of this tendency, the effort
to deal with law and justice as two different problems falls under the
suspicion of repudiating altogether the requirement that positive law
should be just. This requirement is self-evident; but what it actually

means is another question. At any rate a pure theory of law in no way opposes the requirement for just law by declaring itself incompetent to answer the question whether a given law is just or not, and in what the essential element of justice consists. A pure theory of law — a science — cannot answer this question because this question cannot be answered scientifically at all.

What does it really mean to say that a social order is a just one? It means that this order regulates the behavior of men in a way satisfactory to all men, that is to say, so that all men find their happiness in it. The longing for justice is men's eternal longing for happiness. It is happiness that man cannot find as an isolated individual and hence seeks in society. Justice is social happiness.

1. Justice as a Subjective Judgment of Value

It is obvious that there can be no "just" order, that is, one affording happiness to everyone, as long as one defines the concept of happiness in its original, narrow sense of individual happiness, meaning by a man's happiness what he himself considers it to be. For it is then inevitable that the happiness of one individual will, at some time, be directly in conflict with that of another. Nor is a just order then possible even on the supposition that it is trying to bring about not the individual happiness of each, but the greatest possible happiness of the greatest possible number of individuals. The happiness that a social order can assure can be happiness in the collective sense only, that is, the satisfaction of certain needs, recognized by the social authority, the law-giver, as needs worthy of being satisfied, such as the need to be fed, clothed, and housed. But which human needs are worthy of being satisfied, and especially what is their proper order of rank? These questions cannot be answered by means of rational cognition. The decision of these questions is a judgment of value, determined by emotional factors, and is, therefore, subjective in character, valid only for the judging subject and therefore relative only. It will be different according to whether the question is answered by a believing Christian, who holds the good of his soul in the hereafter more important than earthly goods, or by a materialist who believes in no after life; and it will be just as different according to whether the decision is made by one who considers personal freedom as the highest good, i.e. by liberalism, or by one for whom social security and the equality of all men is rated higher than freedom, by socialism.

The question whether spiritual or material possessions, whether freedom or equality, represents the highest value, cannot be answered rationally. Yet the subjective, and hence relative judgment of value by which this question is answered is usually presented as an assertion of an objective and absolute value, a generally valid norm. It is a peculiarity of the human being that he has a deep need to justify his behavior, the expression of his emotions, his wishes and desires, through the function of his intellect, his thinking and cognition. This is possible, at least in principle, to the extent that the wishes and desires relate to means by which some end or other is to be achieved; for the relationship of means to end is a relationship of cause and effect, and this can be determined on the basis of experience, i.e. rationally. To be sure, even this is frequently not possible in view of the present state of social science; for in many cases we have no adequate experience which enables us to determine how certain social aims may best be attained. Hence, this question as to the appropriate means is also frequently determined rather by subjective judgments of value than by an objective insight into the connection between means and end, that is, between cause and effect; and hence, at least for the moment, the problem of justice, even as thus restricted to a question of the appropriate means to a generally recognized end, cannot always be rationally answered. The issue between liberalism and socialism, for instance, is, in great part, not really an issue over the aim of society, but rather one as to the correct way of achieving a goal as to which men are by and large in agreement; and this issue cannot be scientifically determined, at least not today.

The judgment by which something is declared to be the appropriate means to a presupposed end is not a true judgment of value; it is — as pointed out — a judgment concerning the connection between cause and effect, and, as such, a judgment about reality. A judgment of value is the statement by which something is declared to be an end, an ultimate end which is not in itself a means to a further end. Such a judgment is always determined by emotional factors.

A justification of the emotional function by the rational one, however, is excluded in principle in so far as it is a question of ultimate aims which are not themselves means to further ends.

If the assertion of such ultimate aims appears in the form of postulates or norms of justice, they always rest upon purely subjective and hence relative judgments of value. It goes without saying that there are a great many such subjective judgments of value, very different from one another and mutually irreconcilable. That, of course, does not mean that every individual has his own system of values. In fact, very many individuals agree in their judgments of value. A positive system of values is not an arbitrary creation of the isolated individual, but always the result of the mutual influence the individuals exercise upon each other within a given group, be it family, tribe, class, caste, profession.

Every system of values, especially a system of morals and its central idea of justice, is a social phenomenon, the product of a society, and hence different according to the nature of the society within which it arises. The fact that there are certain values generally accepted in a certain society in no way contradicts the subjective and relative character of these judgments of value. That many individuals agree in their judgments of value is no proof that these judgments are correct. Just as the fact that most people believe, or used to believe, that the sun turns around the earth, is, or was, no proof of the truth of this idea. The criterion of justice, like the criterion of truth, is not dependent on the frequency with which judgments about reality or judgments of value are made.

Since humanity is divided into many nations, classes, religions, professions and so on, often at variance with one another, there are a great many very different ideas of justice; too many for one to be able to speak simply of "justice."

2. Natural Law

Yet one is inclined to set forth one's own idea of justice as the only correct, the absolutely valid one. The need for rational justification of our emotional acts is so great that we seek to satisfy it even at the risk of self-deception. And the rational justification of a postulate based on a subjective judgment of value, that is, on a wish, as for instance that all men should be free, or that all men should be treated equally, is self-deception or — what amounts to about the same thing — it is an ideology. Typical ideologies of this sort are the assertions that some sort of ultimate end, and hence some sort of definite regulation of human behavior, proceeds from "nature," that is, from the nature of things or the nature of man, from human reason or the will of God. In such an assumption lies the essence of the doctrine of so-called natural law. This doctrine maintains that there is an ordering of human relations different from positive law, higher and absolutely valid and just, because emanating from nature, from human reason, or from the will of God.

The will of God is — in the natural law doctrine — identical with nature in so far as nature is conceived of as created by God, and the laws of nature as expression of God's will. Consequently the laws determining nature have, according to this doctrine, the same character as the legal rules issued by a legislator: they are commands directed to nature; and nature obeys these commands, the laws of nature, just as man obeys the laws issued by a legislator.* The law created by a legis-

* BLACKSTONE, COMMENTARIES ON THE LAWS OF ENGLAND, Introduction, §§ 36–39: "Law, in its most general and comprehensive sense, signifies a rule of action; and

lator, i.e. by an act of will of a human authority, is positive law. Natural law, according to its specific doctrine, is not created by the act of a human will; it is not the artificial, arbitrary product of man. It can be and has to be deduced from nature by a mental operation. By carefully examining nature, especially the nature of man and his relations to other men, one can find the rules which regulate human behavior in a way corresponding to nature and hence perfectly just. The rights and duties of man, established by this natural law, are considered to be innate or in-born in man, because implanted by nature and not imposed or conferred upon him by a human legislator: and in so far as nature manifests God's will, these rights and duties are sacred.

However, none of the numerous natural law theories has so far succeeded in defining the content of this just order in a way even approaching the exactness and objectivity with which natural science can determine the content of the laws of nature, or legal science the content of a positive legal order. That which has so far been put forth as natural law, or, what amounts to the same thing, as justice, consists for the most

---

is applied indiscriminately to all kinds of action, whether animate or inanimate, rational or irrational. Thus we say, the laws of motion, of gravitation, of optics, or mechanics, as well as the laws of nature and of nations. And it is that rule of action, which is prescribed by some superior, and which the inferior is bound to obey. Thus when the Supreme Being formed the universe, and created matter out of nothing, He impressed certain principles upon that matter, from which it can never depart, and without which it would cease to be. When He put the matter into motion, He established certain laws of motion, to which all movable bodies must conform. . . . This, then, is the general signification of law, a rule of action dictated by some superior being: and, in those creatures that have neither the power to think, nor to will, such laws must be invariably obeyed, so long as the creature itself subsists, for its existence depends on that obedience. But laws, in their more confined sense, and in which it is our present business to consider them, denote the rules, not of action in general, but of *human* action or conduct: that is, the precepts by which man, the noblest of all sublunary beings, a creature endowed with both reason and free will, is commanded to make use of those faculties in the general regulation of his behavior." — "As man depends absolutely upon his Maker for everything, it is necessary that he should in all points conform to his Maker's will. This will of his Maker is called the law of nature. For as God, when He created matter, and edued it with a principle of mobility, established certain rules for the perpetual direction of that motion; so, when He created man, and endued him with free will to conduct himself in all parts of life, He laid down certain immutable laws of human nature, whereby that free will is in some degree regulated and restrained, and gave him also the faculty of reason to discover the purport of those laws. . . . He has laid down only such laws as were founded in those relations of justice, that existed in the nature of things antecedent to any positive precept. These are the eternal, immutable laws of good and evil, to which the Creator Himself in all His dispensations conforms; and which He has enabled human reason to discover, so far as they are necessary for the conduct of human actions."

part of empty formulas, like *suum cuique*, "to each his own," or meaningless tautologies like the categorical imperative, that is, Kant's doctrine that one's acts should be determined only by principles that one wills to be binding on all men. But the formula, "to each his own," does not answer the question as to what is everybody's own, and the categorical imperative does not say which are the principles that one ought to will to be binding on all men. Some writers define justice by the formula "You shall do the right and forbear from doing the wrong." But what is right and what is wrong? This is the decisive question, and this question remains without answer. Almost all the famous formulas defining justice presuppose the expected answer as self-evident. But this answer is not at all self-evident. In fact, the answer to the question as to what is everybody's own, as to what is to be the content of the general principles binding on all men, as to what is right and what is wrong — the answer to all these questions is supposed to be given by positive law. Consequently all these formulas of justice have the effect of justifying any positive legal order. They permit any desired positive legal order to appear just.

When the norms claimed to be the "law of nature" or justice have a definite content, they appear as more or less generalized principles of a definite positive law, principles that, without sufficient reason, are put forth as absolutely valid by being declared as natural or just law.

Among the so-called natural, inborn, sacred rights of man, private property plays an important, if not the most important, role. Nearly all the leading writers of the natural law doctrine affirm that the institution of private property corresponds to the very nature of man. Consequently, a legal order which does not guarantee and protect private property is considered to be against nature and, hence, cannot be of long duration. "The moment the idea is admitted into society, that property is not as sacred as the laws of God, and that there is not a force of law and public justice to protect it, anarchy and tyranny commence. If 'THOU SHALT NOT COVET,' and 'THOU SHALT NOT STEAL,' [rules presupposing the institution of private property] were not commandments of Heaven, they must be made inviolable precepts in every society, before it can be civilized or made free." * It was John Adams who wrote these sentences, expressing thereby a conviction generally accepted at his time. According to this theory, a communistic organization which excludes private property and recognizes only public property, a legal order which reserves ownership of land and other agents of production to the community, especially to the State, is not only against nature and hence unjust, but also practically not maintainable.

* 6 WORKS OF JOHN ADAMS (1851) 9.

It is, however, hardly possible to prove this doctrine; history shows besides legal orders instituting private property others that recognize private property, if at all, only to a very restricted extent. We know of relatively primitive agricultural societies where the most important thing, the land, is not owned by private persons, but by the community; and the experiences of the last twenty-five years show that a communistic organization is quite possible even within a powerful and highly indus-trialized State. Whether the system of capitalism based on the principle of private property, or the system of communism, based on the principle of public property, is better, is another question. In any case, private property is historically not the only principle on which a legal order can be based. To declare private property as a natural right because the only one that corresponds to nature is an attempt to absolutize a special principle, which historically at a certain time only and under certain political and economic conditions has become positive law.

It does happen, even if less frequently, that the principles put forth as "natural" or "just" run counter to a definite positive law. Socialism too has been advocated by the specific method of the natural law doc-trine and private property has been declared as being directed against nature. By this method one can always maintain and apparently prove opposite postulates. Whether the principles of natural law are pre-sented to approve or disapprove a positive legal order, in either case their validity rests on judgments of value which have no objectivity. A critical analysis always shows that they are only the expression of certain group or class interests. Accordingly, the doctrine of natural law is at times conservative, at times reformatory or revolutionary in character. It either justifies positive law by proclaiming its agreement with the natural, reasonable, or divine order, an agreement asserted but not proved; or it puts in question the validity of positive law by claiming that it is in contradiction to one of the presupposed absolutes. The revo-lutionary doctrine of natural law, like the conservative, is concerned not with the cognition of positive law, of legal reality, but with its defense or attack, with a political not with a scientific task.*

---

* Roscoe Pound, An Introduction to the Philosophy of Law (1922) 33f., says: "The conception of natural law as something of which all positive law was but declaratory, as something by which actual rules were to be measured, to which so far as possible they were to be made to conform, by which new rules were to be framed and by which old rules were to be extended or restricted in their application, was a powerful instrument in the hands of the jurists and enabled them to proceed in their task of legal construction with assured confidence." A "powerful instru-ment" indeed! But this instrument is a mere ideology, or, to use a term more familiar to jurists, a fiction.

3. The Dualism of Positive and Natural Law *

Natural law doctrine is characterized by a fundamental dualism between positive and natural law. Above the imperfect positive law, a
perfect — because absolutely just — natural law exists; and positive
law is justified only insofar as it corresponds to the natural law. In this
respect the dualism between positive law and natural law so characteristic of the natural law doctrine resembles the metaphysical dualism of
reality and the Platonic idea. The center of Plato's philosophy is his
doctrine of the ideas. According to this doctrine — which has a thoroughly dualistic character — the world is divided into two different
spheres: one is the visible world perceptible with our senses, that which
we call reality; the other is the invisible world of the ideas. Everything in this visible world has its ideal pattern or archetype in the other,
invisible world. The things existing in this visible world are only imperfect copies, shadows, so to speak, of the ideas existing in the invisible
world. This dualism between reality and idea, an imperfect world of
our senses and another perfect world, inaccessible to the experience of
our senses, the dualism between nature and super-nature, the natural and
the super-natural, the empirical and the transcendental, the here and
the hereafter, this reduplication of the world,† is an element not only
of Plato's philosophy; it is a typical element of every metaphysical, or,
what amounts to the same thing, religious interpretation of the world.
This dualism has an optimistic-conservative or a pessimistic-revolution-
ary character according to whether it is claimed that there is agreement
or contradiction between empirical reality and transcendental ideas.
The purpose of this metaphysics is not — as is that of science — rationally to explain reality, but rather emotionally to accept or reject it.
And one is free to choose the one or the other interpretation of the
relationship between reality and ideas since objective cognition of ideas
is not possible in view of the transcendentalism involved in their very
definition. If man had complete insight into the world of ideas, he
would be able to adapt his world and especially his social world, his
behavior, to its ideal pattern; and since man would become perfectly
happy if his behavior corresponded to the ideal, he would certainly be-

---

* Cf. the Appendix.
 † In his criticism of Plato's doctrine of ideas, Aristotle (*Metaphysica* 990 b)
says: "But as for those who posit the Ideas as causes, firstly, in seeking to grasp the
causes of the things around us, they introduced others equal in number to these, as
if a man who wanted to count things thought he could not do it while they were
few, but tried to count them when he had added to their number. For the Forms
are practically equal to or not fewer than the things. . . ."

have in this way. He, and hence his own empirical world, would become entirely good. Hence there would be no empirically real world at all in distinction to a transcendental ideal world. The dualism between this world and another world, as a result of man's imperfection, would disappear. The ideal would be the real. If one could know the absolutely just order, the existence of which is asserted by the doctrine of natural law, positive law would be superfluous, nay, senseless. Faced by the existence of a just ordering of society, intelligible in nature, reason, or divine will, the activity of positive law makers would be tantamount to a foolish effort at artificial illumination in bright sunshine. Were it possible to answer the question of justice as we are able to solve problems of the technique of natural science or medicine, one would as little think of regulating the relations among men by an authoritative measure of coercion as one thinks today of forcibly prescribing by positive law how a steam engine should be built or a specific illness healed. If there were an objectively recognizable justice, there would be no positive law and hence no State; for it would not be necessary to coerce people to be happy. The usual assertion, however, that there is indeed a natural, absolutely good order, but transcendental and hence not intelligible, that there is indeed such a thing as justice, but that it cannot be clearly defined, is in itself, a contradiction. It is, in fact, nothing but a euphemistic paraphrase of the painful fact that justice is an ideal inaccessible to human cognition.

4. Justice and Peace

Justice is an irrational ideal. However indispensable it may be for volition and action of men, it is not subject to cognition. Regarded from the point of view of rational cognition, there are only interests, and hence conflicts of interest. Their solution can be brought about by an order that either satisfies one interest at the expense of the other, or seeks to achieve a compromise between opposing interests. That only one of these two orders is "just" cannot be established by rational cognition. Such cognition can grasp only a positive order evidenced by objectively determinable acts. This order is the positive law. Only this can be an object of science; only this is the object of a pure theory of law, which is a science, not metaphysics, of the law. It presents the law as it is, without defending it by calling it just, or condemning it by terming it unjust. It seeks the real and possible, not the correct law. It is in this sense a radically realistic and empirical theory. It declines to evaluate positive law.

One statement a theory can make, however, on the basis of experience: only a legal order which does not satisfy the interests of one at the expense of another, but which brings about such a compromise between the opposing interests as to minimize the possible frictions, has expectation of relatively enduring existence. Only such an order will be in a position to secure social peace to its subjects on a relatively permanent basis. And although the ideal of justice in its original sense as developed here is something quite different from the ideal of peace, there exists a definite tendency to identify the two ideals, or at least to substitute the ideal of peace for that of justice.

5. Justice and Legality

This change of meaning of the concept of justice goes hand in hand with the tendency to withdraw the problem of justice from the insecure realm of subjective judgments of value, and to establish it on the secure ground of a given social order. "Justice" in this sense means legality; it is "just" for a general rule to be actually applied in all cases where, according to its content, this rule should be applied. It is "unjust" for it to be applied in one case and not in another similar case. And this seems "unjust" without regard to the value of the general rule itself, the application of which is under consideration. Justice, in the sense of legality, is a quality which relates not to the content of a positive order, but to its application. Justice in this sense is compatible with and required by any positive legal order, be it capitalistic or communistic, democratic or autocratic. "Justice" means the maintenance of a positive order by conscientious application of it. It is justice "under the law." The statement that the behavior of an individual is "just" or "unjust" in the sense of "legal" or "illegal" means that the behavior corresponds or does not correspond to a legal norm which is presupposed as valid by the judging subject because this norm belongs to a positive legal order. Such a statement has logically the same character as a statement by which we subsume a concrete phenomenon under an abstract concept. If the statement that certain behavior corresponds or does not correspond to a legal norm is called a judgment of value, then it is an objective judgment of value which must be clearly distinguished from a subjective judgment of value by which a wish or a feeling of the judging subject is expressed. The statement that particular behavior is legal or illegal is independent of the wishes and feelings of the judging subject; it can be verified in an objective way. Only in the sense of legality can the concept of justice enter into a science of law.*

* Cf. *infra*, pp. 47 ff.

B. The Criterion of Law (Law as a Specific Social Technique)

If we confine our investigation to positive law, and if we compare all those social orders, past and present, that are generally called "law," we shall find that they have one characteristic in common which no social orders of another kind present. This characteristic constitutes a fact of supreme importance for social life and its scientific study. And this characteristic is the only criterion by which we may clearly distinguish law from other social phenomena such as morals and religion. What is this criterion?

a. Direct and Indirect Motivation

It is the function of every social order, of every society — because society is nothing but a social order — to bring about a certain reciprocal behavior of human beings: to make them refrain from certain acts which, for some reason, are deemed detrimental to society, and to make them perform others which, for some reason, are considered useful to society.

According to the manner in which the socially desired behavior is brought about, various types of social orders can be distinguished. These types — it is ideal types that are to be presented here — are characterized by the specific motivation resorted to by the social order to induce individuals to behave as desired. The motivation may be indirect or direct. The order may attach certain advantages to its observance and certain disadvantages to its non-observance, and, hence, make desire for the promised advantage or fear of the threatened disadvantage a motive for behavior. Behavior conforming to the established order is achieved by a sanction provided in the order itself. The principle of reward and punishment — the principle of retribution — fundamental for social life, consists in associating conduct in accordance with the established order and conduct contrary to the order with a promised advantage or a threatened disadvantage respectively, as sanctions.

The social order can, however, even without promise of an advantage in case of obedience, and without threat of a disadvantage in case of disobedience, i.e. without decreeing sanctions, require conduct that appeals directly to the individuals as advantageous, so that the mere idea of a norm decreeing this behavior suffices as a motive for conduct conforming to the norm. This type of direct motivation in its full purity is seldom to be met with in social reality.

In the first place, there are hardly any norms whose purport appeals directly to the individuals whose conduct they regulate so that the mere idea of them suffices for motivation. Moreover, the social behavior of individuals is always accompanied by a judgment of value, namely, the idea that conduct in accordance with the order is "good," whereas that contrary to the order is "bad." Hence, conformity to the order is usually connected with the approval of one's fellow men; non-conformity, with their disapproval. The effect of this reaction of the group to the conduct of individuals in accordance or at variance with the order, is that of a sanction of the order. From a realistic point of view the decisive difference is not between social orders whose efficacy rests on sanctions and those whose efficacy is not based on sanctions. Every social order is somehow "sanctioned" by the specific reaction of the community to conduct of its members corresponding to or at variance with the order. This is also true of highly developed moral systems, which most closely approach the type of direct motivation by sanctionless norms. The only difference is that certain social orders themselves provide definite sanctions, whereas, in others, the sanctions consist in the automatic reaction of the community not expressly provided by the order.

b. Transcendental and Socially Organized Sanctions

The sanctions provided by the social order itself may have a transcendental, that is, a religious, or a social-immanent character.

In the first place, the sanctions provided by the order consist in advantages or disadvantages that are to be applied to the individuals by a superhuman authority, a being characterized more or less as godlike. According to the idea that individuals have of superhuman beings, in the beginnings of the religious development, they exist, not in a hereafter different from the here, but closely connected with men in the nature surrounding them. The dualism of the here and the hereafter is still unknown to primitive man.* His first gods probably are the souls of the dead, particularly dead ancestors, that live in trees, rivers, rocks, and especially in certain animals. It is they who guarantee the maintenance of the primitive social order by punishing its violation with death, sickness, unluckiness in hunting and in similar ways, and by rewarding its observance with health, long life, and luck in hunting. Retribution does indeed emanate from divinity but it is realized in the here. For nature is explained by primitive man according to the principle of retribution. He regards natural events only with respect to the advantage or disadvantage connected with them, and he interprets the advantageous events as reward, the disadvantageous as punishment inflicted upon him by the personal and superhuman beings whom he imagines as existing within or behind the natural phenomena. The

---

* Cf. my SOCIETY AND NATURE (1943), pp. 24ff.

earliest social order has a completely religious character. Originally, it knows no sanctions other than religious ones, that is, those emanating from a superhuman authority. Only later, at least within the narrower group itself, do there appear, side by side with the transcendental sanctions, sanctions that are socially immanent, that is to say, organized, sanctions to be executed by an individual determined by the social order according to the provisions of this order. In relations between different groups, blood revenge appears very early as a socially organized reaction against an injury considered unjustified and due to a member of a foreign group.

The group from which this reaction issues is a community based on blood relationship. The reaction is induced by fear of the soul of the murdered person. It seems that the latter cannot revenge himself upon his murderer, if he belongs to a foreign group. Hence, he compels his relatives to carry out the revenge. The sanction thus socially organized is itself guaranteed by a transcendental sanction. Those who fail to revenge the death of their relative upon the foreign murderer and his group are threatened with sickness and death by the soul of the murdered man. It seems that blood revenge is the earliest socially organized sanction. It is worthy of note that originally it had an inter-tribal character. Only when the social community comprises several groups based on blood relationship does blood revenge become an intra-tribal institution.

In the further course of religious development, the divinity is conceived of as appertaining to a realm very different from the here, and far removed from it, and the realization of divine retribution is put off to the hereafter. Very often this hereafter is divided — corresponding to the two-fold character of retribution — into a heaven and a hell. In this stage, the social order has lost its religious character. The religious order functions only as a supplement and support to the social order. The sanctions of the latter are exclusively acts of human individuals regulated by the social order itself.

c. Punishment and Reward

It is a fact well worth noting that of the two sanctions here presented as typical — the disadvantage threatened in case of disobedience (punishment, in the broadest sense of the term), and the advantage promised in case of obedience (the reward), in social reality the first plays a far more important role than the second. That the technique of punishment is preferred to that of reward is seen with especial clarity where the social order still has a distinctly religious character, i.e., is guaranteed by transcendental sanctions. Primitive peoples' behavior conform-

ing to the social order, especially the observance of the numerous prohibitions called "taboos," is determined principally by the fear that
dominates the life of such peoples. It is fear of the grievous evil with
which the superhuman authority reacts against every violation of traditional customs. If violations of the social norms are much less frequent
in primitive societies than in civilized societies, as some ethnologists
report to be the case, it is chiefly this fear of the revenge of the spirits,
fear of a punishment that is of divine origin but takes place here, that is
responsible for this effect of preserving social order. The hope of reward
has only a secondary significance. And even in more highly developed
religions, where divine retribution is no longer or not only realized here,
but in the hereafter, the idea of a punishment to be expected after death
holds first place. In the actual beliefs of mankind, fear of hell is much
more alive, and the picture of a place of punishment is much more concrete, than the usually very vague hope of a future paradise where our
virtue shall find its reward. Even when the wish-fulfilling phantasy of
individuals is not limited by any restrictions, it imagines a transcendental
order the technique of which is not entirely different from the technique
of the empirical society.

This may be due to the fact that religious ideology always more or
less mirrors actual social reality. And in this, as far as the organization
of the group is concerned, essentially only one method of bringing about
socially desired behavior is taken into account: the threat and the application of an evil in case of contrary behavior — the technique of
punishment. The technique of reward plays a significant role only in
the private relations of individuals.

d. Law as a Coercive Order

The evil applied to the violator of the order when the sanction is
socially organized consists in a deprivation of possessions — life, health,
freedom, or property. As the possessions are taken from him against his
will, this sanction has the character of a measure of coercion. This does
not mean that in carrying out the sanction physical force must be applied. This is necessary only if resistance is encountered in applying
the sanction. This is only exceptionally the case, where the authority
applying the sanction possesses adequate power. A social order that
seeks to bring about the desired behavior of individuals by the enactment of such measures of coercion is called a coercive order. Such it is
because it threatens socially harmful deeds with measures of coercion,
decrees such measures of coercion. As such it presents a contrast to all
other possible social orders — those that provide reward rather than
punishment as sanctions, and especially those that enact no sanctions at

all, relying on the technique of direct motivation. In contrast to the orders that enact coercive measures as sanctions, the efficacy of the others rests not on coercion but on voluntary obedience. Yet this contrast is not so distinct as it might at first sight appear. This follows from the fact that the technique of reward, as a technique of indirect motivation, has its place between the technique of indirect motivation through punishment, as a technique of coercion, and the technique of direct motivation, the technique of voluntary obedience. Voluntary obedience is itself a form of motivation, that is, of coercion, and hence is not freedom, but it is coercion in the psychological sense. If coercive orders are contrasted with those that have no coercive character, that rest on voluntary obedience, this is possible only in the sense that one provides measures of coercion as sanctions whereas the other does not. And these sanctions are only coercive measures in the sense that certain possessions are taken from the individuals in question against their will, if necessary by the employment of physical force.

In this sense, the law is a coercive order.

If the social orders, so extraordinarily different in their tenors, which have prevailed at different times and among the most different peoples, are all called legal orders, it might be supposed that one is using an expression almost devoid of meaning. What could the so-called law of ancient Babylonians have in common with the law that prevails today in the United States? What could the social order of a negro tribe under the leadership of a despotic chieftain — an order likewise called "law" — have in common with the constitution of the Swiss Republic? Yet there is a common element, that fully justifies this terminology, and enables the word "law" to appear as the expression of a concept with a socially highly significant meaning. For the word refers to that specific social technique of a coercive order which, despite the vast differences existing between the law of ancient Babylon and that of the United States of today, between the law of the Ashantis in West Africa and that of the Swiss in Europe, is yet essentially the same for all these peoples differing so much in time, in place, and in culture: the social technique which consists in bringing about the desired social conduct of men through the threat of a measure of coercion which is to be applied in case of contrary conduct. What the social conditions are that necessitate this technique, is an important sociological question. I do not know whether we can answer it satisfactorily. Neither do I know whether it is possible for mankind to emancipate itself totally from this social technique. But if the social order should in the future no longer have the character of a coercive order, if society should exist without "law," then the difference between this society of the future and that of the present day would be immeasurably greater than the difference between the United States and ancient Babylon, or Switzerland and the Ashanti tribe.

e. Law, Morality, Religion

While recognizing law as the specific social technique of a coercive order, we can contrast it sharply with other social orders which pursue in part the same purposes as the law, but by quite different means. And law is a means, a specific social means, not an end. Law, morality, and religion, all three forbid murder. But the law does this by providing that if a man commits murder, then another man, designated by the legal order, shall apply against the murderer a certain measure of coercion, prescribed by the legal order. Morality limits itself to requiring: thou shalt not kill. And if a murderer is ostracized morally by his fellow men, and many an individual refrains from murder not so much because he wants to avoid the punishment of law as to avoid the moral disapprobation of his fellow men, the great distinction still remains, that the reaction of the law consists in a measure of coercion enacted by the order, and socially organized, whereas the moral reaction against immoral conduct is neither provided by the moral order, nor, if provided, socially organized. In this respect religious norms are nearer to legal norms than are moral norms. For religious norms threaten the murderer with punishment by a superhuman authority. But the sanctions which the religious norms lay down have a transcendental character; they are not socially organized sanctions, even though provided for by the religious order. They are probably more effective than the legal sanctions. Their efficacy, however, presupposes belief in the existence and power of a superhuman authority.

It is, however, not the effectiveness of the sanctions that is here in question, but only whether and how they are provided for by the social order. The socially organized sanction is an act of coercion which an individual determined by the social order directs, in a manner determined by the social order, against the individual responsible for conduct contrary to that order. This conduct we call "delict." Both the delict and the sanction are determined by the legal order. The sanction is the reaction of the legal order against the delict, or, what amounts to the same thing, the reaction of the community, constituted by the legal order, to the evil-doer, the delinquent. The individual who carries out the sanction acts as an agent of the legal order. This is equivalent to saying that the individual who carries out the sanction acts as an organ of the community, constituted by the legal order. A social community is nothing but a social order regulating the mutual behavior of the individuals subject to the order. To say that individuals belong to a certain community, or form a certain community, means only that the individuals are subject to a common order regulating their mutual behavior. The legal sanction is thus interpreted as an act of the legal community; while the transcendental sanction — the illness or death of the sinner or punishment in another world — is never interpreted as a reaction of the social group, but always as an act of the superhuman, and therefore super-social, authority.

f. Monopolization of the Use of Force

Among the paradoxes of the social technique here characterized as a coercive order is the fact that its specific instrument, the coercive act of the sanction, is of exactly the same sort as the act which it seeks to prevent in the relations of individuals, the delict; that the sanction against socially injurious behavior is itself such behavior. For that which is to be accomplished by the threat of forcible deprivation of life, health, freedom, or property is precisely that men in their mutual conduct shall refrain from forcibly depriving one another of life, health, freedom, or property. Force is employed to prevent the employment of force in society. This seems to be an antinomy; and the effort to avoid this social antinomy leads to the doctrine of absolute anarchism which proscribes force even as sanction. Anarchism tends to establish the social order solely upon voluntary obedience of the individuals. It rejects the technique of a coercive order and hence rejects the law as a form of organization.

The antinomy, however, is only apparent. The law is, to be sure, an ordering for the promotion of peace, in that it forbids the use of force in relations among the members of the community. Yet it does not absolutely preclude the use of force. Law and force must not be understood as absolutely at variance with one another. Law is an organization of force. For the law attaches certain conditions to the use of force in relations among men, authorizing the employment of force only by certain individuals and only under certain circumstances. The law allows conduct which, under all other circumstances, is to be considered as "forbidden"; to be legally forbidden means to be the very condition for such a coercive act as a sanction. The individual who, authorized by the legal order, applies the coercive measure (the sanction), acts as an agent of this order, or — what amounts to the same — as an organ of the community constituted thereby. Only this individual, only the organ of the community, is authorized to employ force. And hence one may say that law makes the use of force a monopoly of the community. And precisely by so doing, law pacifies the community.

g. Law and Peace

Peace is a condition in which there is no use of force. In this sense of the word, law provides for only relative, not absolute peace, in that it deprives individuals of the right to employ force but reserves it for the community. The peace of the law is not a condition of absolute absence of force, a state of anarchy; it is a condition of monopoly of force, a force monopoly of the community.

A community, in the long run, is possible only if each individual respects certain interests — life, health, freedom, and property of everyone else, that is to say, if each refrains from forcibly interfering in these spheres of interest of the others. The social technique that we call "law" consists in inducing the individual to refrain from forcible interference in the sphere of interests of others by specific means: in case of such interference, the legal community itself reacts with a like interference in the sphere of interests of the individual responsible for the previous interference. Like for like. It is the idea of retribution which lies at the base of this social technique. Only in a relatively late stage of evolution is the idea of retribution replaced by that of prevention. But then it is a change only of the ideology justifying the specific technique of the law. The technique itself remains the same.

Thus forcible interference in the sphere of interests of another constitutes on the one hand an illegal act, the delict, and on the other hand, a sanction. Law is an order according to which the use of force is generally forbidden but exceptionally, under certain circumstances and for certain individuals, permitted as a sanction. In the rule of law, the employment of force appears either as a delict, i.e. the condition for the sanction, or as a sanction, i.e. the reaction of the legal community against the delict.

Inasmuch as forcible interference in the sphere of interests of individuals is permitted only as a reaction of the community against prohibited conduct of the individual, inasmuch as forcible interference in the sphere of interests of the individual is made a monopoly of the community, a definite sphere of interests of the individuals is protected. As long as there exists no monopoly of the community in forcible interference in the sphere of interests of the individual, that is to say, as long as the social order does not stipulate that forcible interference in the sphere of interests of the individual may be resorted to only under very definite conditions (namely, as a reaction against illegal interference in the sphere of interests of the individuals, and then only by stipulated individuals), so long is there no sphere of interests of the individuals protected by the social order. In other words, there is no state of law which, in the sense developed here, is essentially a state of peace.

h. Psychic Compulsion

The view that coercion is an essential element of law is often falsely interpreted to mean that the effectiveness of the legal sanction is part of the concept of law. The sanction is said to be effective if the individuals subjected to the law — in order to avoid the evil of the sanction — behave "lawfully," or if the sanction is executed in case its condition, the delict, has been fulfilled. An expression of this view is the frequently heard statement that law is an "enforcible" rule or, even, a rule which is actually "enforced" by a certain authority. Typical is the well-known definition given by Holland: "A law in the proper sense of the term is . . . a general rule of external human action enforced by a sovereign political authority." * That is to say, it is of the essence of a legal rule that the sanction it prescribes is executed by the proper organ. But such is the case only if an individual does not behave lawfully, if he "violates" the legal rule. In other words, the sanction to be executed by the organ is provided for only in those concrete cases where the conduct which the legal order tries to bring about has not been "enforced" and, thus, has proved not to be "enforcible." It is only for this case that the sanction is provided.

Let us use the term "subject" to denote the individual who does or does not obey the law, the term "organ" to denote the individual who executes the sanction and by so doing applies the law. If one describes the law as an "enforcible" or "enforced" rule of human behavior, then a distinction must be made between the behavior of the subject, and the behavior of the organ. In his definition, Holland seems to refer to the behavior of the organ. However, those who speak of the "enforcement" of law usually have in mind rather the behavior of the subject: the fact that the subject is compelled to obey the rule of law. They are referring, not to the coercive measure which the organ actually executes, but to the subject's fear that the measure will be taken in case of non-obedience, of unlawful conduct. The "coercion" which they have in mind is thus a psychic compulsion, resulting from the idea men have of the legal order. This idea is "coercive" if it furnishes a motive for the behavior desired by the legal order. So far as this psychic compulsion goes, the law does not differ from moral or religious norms. For moral and religious norms, too, are coercive insofar as our ideas of them make us behave in accordance to them.

* Sir Thomas Erskine Holland, The Elements of Jurisprudence (13th ed. 1924) 41f.

i. The Motives of Lawful Behavior

The attempt to make this "psychic compulsion" an essential element of the concept of law is open to a further serious objection. We do not know exactly what motives induce men to comply with the rules of law. No positive legal order has ever been investigated in a satisfactory scientific manner with a view to answering this question. At present, we do not even have at our disposal any methods which would enable us to treat this sociologically and politically highly important problem in a scientific way. All we can do is to make more or less plausible conjectures. In all probability, however, the motives of lawful behavior are by no means only the fear of legal sanctions or even the belief in the binding force of the legal rules. When the moral and religious ideas of an individual run parallel to the legal order to which he is subject, his lawful behavior is often due to those moral and religious ideas. Benefits which are in no way determined by the legal order but in fact connected with lawful behavior may also be a motive for conduct conforming to the law. A man fulfills his legal duty to pay his debts very often not because he wishes to avoid the sanction provided by the law against an individual who does not pay his debts, but because he knows that if he carefully pays his debts his credit will increase; whereas if he does not pay his debts, he will lose his credit. The advantage of credit is not provided by the legal order as a reward for fulfilling one's duties. It is a benefit connected in fact with lawful behavior; and it is very often the wish to have such benefit which is the motive of lawful behavior. From the fact that people, by and large, behave in accordance with the rules of law, it would be gratuitous to conclude that this is caused by the psychic compulsion which the idea of the legal order, the fear of its sanctions, exercises. That a legal order is "efficacious," strictly means only that people's conduct conforms with the legal order. No specific information is thereby given about the motives of this conduct and, in particular, about the "psychic compulsion" emanating from the legal order.

j. Arguments against the Definition of Law as Coercive Order

1. Eugen Ehrlich's Theory

The doctrine according to which coercion is an essential element of law is very often disputed, especially from a sociological point of view. The typical argument is a reference to the fact that men obey the legal order, fulfill their legal duties in many cases — if not mostly — not because of fear of the sanctions provided for by the legal order, but for other reasons. Thus, for instance, Eugen Ehrlich, one of the founders of the sociology of law, says:

It is quite obvious that a man lives in innumerable legal relations, and that, with few exceptions, he quite voluntarily performs the duties incumbent upon him because of these relations. One performs one's duties as father or son, as husband or wife, does not interfere with one's neighbor's enjoyment of his property, pays one's debts, delivers that which one has sold, and renders to one's employer the performance to render which one has obligated oneself. The jurist, of course, is ready with the objection that all men perform their duties only because they know that the courts could eventually compel them to perform them. If he should take the pains, to which, indeed, he is not accustomed, to observe what men do and leave undone, he would soon be convinced of the fact that, as a rule, the thought of compulsion by the courts does not even enter the minds of men. Insofar as they do not simply act instinctively, as indeed is usually the case, their conduct is determined by quite different motives: they might otherwise have quarrels with their relatives, lose their positions, lose custom, get the reputation of being quarrelsome, dishonest, irresponsible persons. The jurist ought to be the last person of all to overlook the fact that that which men do or leave undone as a legal duty in this sense often is something quite different from, occasionally is much more than, that which the authorities could ever compel them to do or leave undone. The rule of conduct, not infrequently, is quite different from the rule that is obeyed because of compulsion (*Zwangsnorm*).*

The statement that the individuals subject to the legal order conform their behavior to this order not merely because they wish to avoid the disagreeable effects of the sanctions provided for by the order, is undoubtedly correct. But this statement is not at all irreconcilable with the doctrine that coercion is an essential element of law. This doctrine does not refer to the actual motives of the behavior of the individuals subjected to the legal order, but to its content, to the specific means used by the legal order to bring about a certain behavior of the individuals, to the specific technique of this social order. The doctrine that coercion is an essential element of law does not refer to the actual behavior of the individuals subjected to the legal order, but to the legal order itself, to the fact that the legal order provides for sanctions and that by this very fact and only by this fact, that is, by this specific social technique, is it distinguished from other social orders. If an individual — against his instinctive impulse — refrains from murder, adultery, theft, because he believes in God and feels himself bound by the Ten Commandments, and

---

* EUGEN EHRLICH, GRUNDLEGUNG DER SOZIOLOGIE DES RECHTS (1913); quotation from English translation, FUNDAMENTAL PRINCIPLES OF THE SOCIOLOGY OF LAW (1936) 21.

not because he fears the punishment which certain legal norms attach to these crimes, the legal norms are — as far as this individual is concerned — completely superfluous; having no effect, they are, from a socio-psychological point of view, even not existent in relation to this individual. If we characterize human behavior from the point of view of its motives, the behavior of the individual in question is a religious, not a legal phenomenon, is a subject-matter of the sociology of religion, not of the sociology of law. If the legal order provides for punishment in case a man commits murder, theft, adultery, it is because the legislator supposes — rightly or wrongly — that the belief in God and His Ten Commandments, that other motives than fear of the legal punishment, do not suffice to induce men to refrain from murder, theft, and adultery. If there exists any legal order providing its specific sanctions, it is precisely because the men who create and execute this legal order suppose — rightly or wrongly — that other social orders providing no sanctions or other sanctions are not effective enough to bring about the behavior which the creators and executors of the legal order consider to be desirable.

What distinguishes the legal order from all other social orders is the fact that it regulates human behavior by means of a specific technique. If we ignore this specific element of the law, if we do not conceive of the law as a specific social technique, if we define law simply as order or organization, and not as a coercive order (or organization), then we lose the possibility of differentiating law from other social phenomena; then we identify law with society, and the sociology of law with general sociology.

This is a typical mistake of many legal sociologists, and especially of Eugen Ehrlich's sociology of law. His main thesis runs as follows: Law is a coercive order only if we identify the law with the rules according to which the courts have to decide the legal disputes that are brought before them. But the law is not, or is not only, the rule according to which the courts decide or have to decide, disputes; the law is the rule according to which men actually behave:

The rule of human conduct and the rule according to which the judges decide legal disputes may be two quite distinct things; for men do not always act according to the rules that will be applied in settling their disputes. No doubt the legal historian conceives of law as a rule of human conduct; he states the rules according to which, in antiquity or in the Middle Ages, marriages were entered into, husband and wife, parents and children lived together in the family; he tells whether property was held individually or in common, whether the soil was tilled by the owner or by a lessee paying rent or by a serf rendering services; how contracts were entered into, and how property descended. One would hear the same thing if one should ask a traveler re-turning from foreign lands to give an account of the law of the peoples he has become acquainted with. He will tell of marriage customs, of family life, of the manner of entering into contracts; but he will have little to say about the rules according to which law-suits are being decided.

This concept of law, which the jurist adopts quite instinctively when he is studying the law of a foreign nation or of remote times for a purely scientific purpose, he will give up at once when he turns to the positive law of his own country and of his own time. Without his becoming aware of it, secretly as it were, the rule according to which men act becomes the rule according to which their acts are being adjudged, by courts and other tribunals. The latter, indeed, is also a rule of conduct, but it is such but for a small part of the people, i.e. for the authorities, entrusted with the application of the law; but not like the former, for the generality of the people. The scientific view has given way to the practical view, adapted to the requirements of the judicial official, who, to be sure, is interested in knowing the rule according to which he must proceed. It is true, jurists look upon these rules as rules of conduct as well, but they arrive at this view by a jump in their thinking. They mean to say that the rules according to which courts decide are the rules according to which men ought to regulate their conduct. To this is added a vague notion that in the course of time men will actually regulate their conduct in accord-ance with the rules according to which the courts render their decisions. Now it is true that a rule of conduct is not only a rule according to which men customarily regulate their conduct, but also a rule according to which they ought to do so; but it is an altogether inadmissible assumption that this "ought" is determined either exclusively or even preponderantly by the courts. Daily experience teaches the contrary. Surely no one denies that judicial decisions influence the conduct of men, but we must first of all inquire to what extent this is true and upon what circumstances it depends.*

Ehrlich's answer to this question is that judicial decisions influence the conduct of men only to a very limited extent. The rules according to which the courts and other organs of the community decide disputes, and that means the rules providing for coercive acts as sanctions, are only a part, and not even an essential part, of the law which is the rule or the complex of rules according to which men — including the men who are not organs of the community — actually behave. But not every rule according to which men actually behave is a legal rule. What is the specific difference between legal rules and other rules of human be-havior? This means: what is the criterion of law, what is the specific object of a sociology of law in contradistinction to the object of general sociology? To this, Ehrlich has only the following answer:

Three elements, therefore, must under all circumstances be excluded from the concept of law as a compulsory order maintained by the state — a concept

* Ehrlich, Sociology of Law 10–11.

to which the traditional juristic science has clung tenaciously in substance, though not always in form. It is not an essential element of the concept of law that it be created by the state, nor that it constitute the basis for the decisions of the courts or other tribunals, nor that it be the basis of a legal compulsion consequent upon such a decision. A fourth element remains, and that will have to be the point of departure, i.e. the law is an ordering. . . . We may consider it established that, within the scope of the concept of the association, the law is an organization, that is to say, a rule which assigns to each and every member of the association his position in the association, whether it be of domination or of subjection (*Ueberordnung, Unterordnung*), and his duties; and that it is now quite impossible to assume that law exists within these associations chiefly for the purpose of deciding controversies that arise out of the communal relation. The legal norm according to which legal disputes are being decided, the norm for decision, is merely a species of legal norm with limited functions and purposes.*

The result of Ehrlich's attempt to emancipate the definition of law from the element of coercion is the definition: the law is an ordering of human behavior. But this is a definition of society, not of law. Every complex of rules regulating the mutual behavior of men is an order or organization which constitutes a community or association and which "assigns to each and every member of the association his position in the community and his duties." There are many such orders which have no legal character. Even if we limit the concept of order or organization to relatively centralized orders which institute special organs for the creation and application of the order, the law is not sufficiently determined by the concept of order. The law is an order which assigns to every member of the community his duties and thereby his position in the community by means of a specific technique, by providing for an act of coercion, a sanction directed against the member of the community who does not fulfill his duty. If we ignore this element, we are not able to differentiate the legal order from other social orders.

2. The Never-ending Series of Sanctions

Another argument against the doctrine that coercion is an essential element of law, or that sanctions form a necessary element within the legal structure, runs as follows: if it is necessary to guarantee the efficacy of a norm prescribing a certain behavior by another norm prescribing a sanction in the case the former is not obeyed, a never-ending series of sanctions, a *regressus ad infinitum*, is inevitable. For "in order to secure the efficacy of a rule of the nth degree, a rule of the $n + 1$ degree is necessary." † Since the legal order can be composed only by a definite

* EHRLICH, SOCIOLOGY OF LAW 23–24.
† N. S. TIMASHEFF, AN INTRODUCTION TO THE SOCIOLOGY OF LAW (1939) 264.

number of rules, the norms prescribing sanctions presuppose norms which prescribe no sanctions. Coercion is not a necessary but only a possible element of law.

The assertion that in order to secure the efficacy of a rule of the nth degree, a rule of the $n + 1$th degree is necessary, and that therefore it is impossible to secure the efficacy of all legal rules by rules providing for sanctions, is correct; but the rule of law is not a rule the efficacy of which is secured by another rule providing for a sanction, even if the efficacy of this rule is not secured by another rule. A rule is a legal rule not because its efficacy is secured by another rule providing for a sanction; a rule is a legal rule because it provides for a sanction. The problem of coercion (constraint, sanction) is not the problem of securing the efficacy of rules, but the problem of the content of the rules. The fact that it is impossible to secure the efficacy of all rules of a legal order by rules providing for sanctions does not exclude the possibility of considering only rules providing for sanctions as legal rules. All the norms of a legal order are coercive norms, i.e. norms providing for sanctions; but among these norms there are norms the efficacy of which is not secured by other coercive norms. Norm n, e.g., runs as follows: If an individual steals, another individual, an organ of the community, shall punish him. The efficacy of this norm is secured by the norm $n + 1$: If the organ does not punish a thief, another organ shall punish the organ who violates his duty of punishing the thief. There is no norm $n + 2$, securing the efficacy of the norm $n + 1$. The coercive norm $n + 1$: If the organ does not punish the thief, another organ shall punish the law-violating organ, is not guaranteed by a norm of the $n + 2$nd degree. But all the norms of this legal order are coercive norms.*

Finally, one objects to the doctrine that coercion is an essential element of law by alleging that among the norms of a legal order there are many rules which provide for no sanctions at all. The norms of the constitution are frequently pointed out as legal norms although they provide for no sanctions. We shall deal with this argument in a later chapter.†

C. Validity and Efficacy

The element of "coercion" which is essential to law thus consists, not in the so-called "psychic compulsion," but in the fact that specific acts

---

according to L. Petrazhitsky, Theory of Law and State (in Russian: 2d ed. 1909) 273–285.

* This does not mean that the execution of the sanction stipulated in a legal norm has always the character of a legal duty. Cf. *infra*, pp. 59 ff.

† Cf. *infra*, pp. 143 ff.

of coercion, as sanctions, are provided for in specific cases by the rules which form the legal order. The element of coercion is relevant only as part of the contents of the legal norm, only as an act stipulated by this norm, not as a process in the mind of the individual subject to the norm. The rules which constitute a system of morality do not have any such import. Whether or not men do actually behave in a manner to avoid the sanction threatened by the legal norm, and whether or not the sanction is actually carried out in case its conditions are fulfilled, are issues concerning the efficacy of the law. But it is not the efficacy, it is the validity of the law which is in question here.

a. The "Norm"

What is the nature of the validity, as distinguished from the efficacy of law? The difference may be illustrated by an example: A legal rule forbids theft, prescribing that every thief must be punished by the judge. This rule is "valid" for all people, to whom theft is thereby forbidden, the individuals who have to obey the rule, the "subjects." The legal rule is "valid" particularly for those who actually steal and in so doing "violate" the rule. That is to say, the legal rule is valid even in those cases where it lacks "efficacy." It is precisely in those cases that it has to be "applied" by the judge. The rule in question is valid not only for the subjects but also for the law-applying organs. But the rule retains its validity, even if the thief should succeed in escaping, and the judge, therefore, should be unable to punish him and thus apply the legal rule. Thus, in the particular case, the rule is valid for the judge even if it is without efficacy, in the sense that the conditions of the sanction prescribed by the rule are fulfilled and yet the judge finds himself unable to order the sanction. What is now the significance of the statement that the rule is valid even if, in a concrete case, it lacks efficacy, is not obeyed, or is not applied?

By "validity" we mean the specific existence of norms. To say that a norm is valid, is to say that we assume its existence or — what amounts to the same thing — we assume that it has "binding force" for those whose behavior it regulates. Rules of law, if valid, are norms. They are, to be more precise, norms stipulating sanctions. But what is a norm?

1. The Law as a Command, i.e., Expression of a Will

In our attempt to explain the nature of a norm, let us provisionally assume that a norm is a command. This is how Austin characterizes law. He says: "Every *law* or *rule* . . . is a *command*. Or, rather, laws or rules, properly so called, are a *species* of commands." * A command is the expression of an individual's will (or wish) the object of which is another individual's behavior. If I want (or wish) somebody else to conduct himself in a certain way and if I express this my will (or wish) to the other in a particular way, then this expression of my will (or wish) constitutes a command. A command differs from a request, from a mere "entreaty," by its form. A command is the expression in an imperative form of the will that somebody else shall behave in a certain manner. An individual is especially likely to give his will this form when he has, or believes himself to have, a certain power over the other individual, when he is, or thinks he is, in a position to enforce obedience. But not every command is a valid norm. A command is a norm only if it is binding upon the individual to whom it is directed, only if this individual ought to do what the command requires. When an adult directs a child to do something, this is not a case of a binding command, however great the superiority in power of the adult and however imperative the form of the command. But if the adult is the child's father or teacher, then the command is binding upon the child. Whether or not a command is binding depends upon whether or not the individual commanding is "authorized" to issue that command. Provided that he is, then the expression of his will is binding, even if, in fact, he should not have any superior power and the expression should lack imperative form. Austin, it is true, is of the opinion that "a command is distinguished from other significations of desire, not by the style in which the desire is signified, but by the power and the purpose of the party commanding to inflict an evil or pain in case the desire be disregarded." Further, he says: "A command is distinguished from other significations of desire by this peculiarity: that the party to whom it is directed is liable to evil from the other, in case he comply not with the desire. Being liable to evil from you if I comply not with a wish which you signify, I am *bound* or *obliged* by your command." † Thus he identifies the two concepts "command" and "binding command." But that is incorrect, since not every command issued by somebody superior in power is of a binding nature. The command of a bandit to deliver my cash is not binding, even if the bandit actually is able to enforce his will. To repeat: A command is binding, not because the individual commanding has an actual superiority in power, but because he is "authorized" or "empowered" to issue commands of a binding nature. And he is "authorized" or "empowered" only if a normative order, which is presupposed to be binding, confers on him this capacity, the competence

---

* 1 JOHN AUSTIN, LECTURES ON JURISPRUDENCE (5th ed. 1885) 88.
† 1 AUSTIN, JURISPRUDENCE 89.

to issue binding commands. Then, the expression of his will, directed to the behavior of another individual, *is* a binding command, even if the individual commanding has in fact no actual power over the individual to whom the command is addressed. The binding force of a command is not "derived" from the command itself but from the conditions under which the command is being issued. Supposing that the rules of law are binding commands, it is clear that binding force resides in those commands because they are issued by competent authorities.

2. The "Will" of the Parties in a Legal Transaction

On closer analysis, however, it is apparent that rules of law are "commands" only in a very vague sense. A command, in the proper sense of the word, exists only when a particular individual sets and expresses an act of will. In the proper sense of the word, the existence of a command presupposes two elements: an act of will, having somebody else's behavior as its object, and the expression thereof, by means of words or gestures or other signs. A command is in existence only as long as both these elements are present. If somebody gives me a command, and if, before executing it, I have satisfactory evidence that the underlying act of will no longer exists — the evidence might be the death of the individual commanding — then I am not really faced with any command, even if the expression of the command should still be there — as it may, for instance, if the command is in writing. The situation is totally different when the command is binding. Then, in common parlance, the command "subsists" even when the act of will no longer exists. A person's so-called "last will," his testament, is a command that assumes binding force first when the person himself is dead, thus when he is no longer capable of willing, and a command, in the proper sense of the word, could not possibly exist. That in which the binding force in this case resides must therefore be something else than the psychic act of will in the mind of the testator. If a real will on the side of the testator is at all necessary for the validity of a testament, then the binding force cannot belong to this will; it must belong to something which is "created" by the will of the testator, something the "existence" or "validity" of which outlasts the existence of that real will.

In order to establish a "binding contract," two individuals have to express their agreement, i.e. their agreeing intention or will concerning certain mutual conduct. The contract is the product of the will of the two contracting parties. However, the contract is supposed to remain in force even if later on one of the parties should change his mind and no longer want what he said he wanted when the contract was made. Thus the contract obliges this party even against his real will, and therefore it cannot be the "will" of the parties in which the binding force resides, and which continues, stays "valid," after the contract has been concluded. If we denote that which has the binding force by the term "contract," then the binding contract and the procedure by which it is created, i.e. the expression of the agreeing intentions of the parties, are two different phenomena. It is, furthermore, doubtful whether the procedure by which a binding contract is created necessarily involves that, in the mind of each party, there be a real intention, a "will," having as its object the contents of the contract.

3. The "Will" of the Legislator

If we designate a statute, decided upon by a parliament in the forms prescribed by the constitution, as a "command" or, what amounts to the same thing, as the "will" of the legislator, then a "command" in this sense has hardly anything in common with a command properly so called. A statute owing its existence to a parliamentary decision obviously first begins to exist at a moment when the decision has already been made and when — supposing the decision to be the expression of a will — no will is any longer there. Having passed the statute, the members of parliament turn to other questions and cease to will the contents of the law, if ever they entertained any such will. Since the statute first comes into existence upon completion of the legislative procedure, its "existence" cannot consist in the real will of the individuals belonging to the legislative body. A jurist who wishes to establish the "existence" of a law does not by any means try to prove the existence of psychological phenomena. The "existence" of a legal norm is no psychological phenomenon. A jurist considers a statute as "existing" even when those individuals who created it no longer will the content of the statute, nay even when nobody any longer wills its content, at least none of those who were competent to create the statute by their acts of will. It is indeed possible and often actually the case that a statute "exists" at a time when those who created it are long since dead and no longer able to have any sort of will. Thus, the binding statute cannot be the will in the mind of the individuals who make it, even if a real act of will were necessary for making the statute.

If we psychologically analyze the procedure by which a statute is constitutionally created, we shall further find that the act creating the binding rule need not necessarily be an act of "will" having the contents of the rule for its object. The statute is created by a decision of the parliament. The parliament — according to the constitution — is the authority competent to enact the statute. The procedure by which the parliament decides upon a statute consists essentially in the voting of a bill which has been submitted to its members. The statute is "decided" upon if a majority of the members has voted for the bill. Those members who vote against the bill do not "will" the contents of the statute. Despite the fact that they express a contrary will, the expression of their will is as essential for the creation of the statute as the expression of the will of those who vote for the bill. The statute is, it is true, the "decision" of the whole parliament, including the dissenting minority. But obviously this does not mean that the parliament "will" the statute in the psychological sense that every member of the parliament "wills" the contents of the statute. Let us consider only the majority that votes for the law. Even so, the statement that the members of this majority "will" the statute is clearly of a fictitious nature. To vote for a bill does not at all imply actually willing the contents of the statute. In a psychological sense, one may "will" only that of which one has an idea. It is impossible to "will" something of which one is ignorant. Now it is a fact that often, if not always, a considerable number of those who vote for a bill have at most a very superficial knowledge of its contents. All that is required of them by the constitution is that they vote for the bill by raising their hands or by saying "Yes." This they may do without knowing the contents of the bill and without having made its contents the object of their "will" — in the sense in which one individual "wills" that another individual shall conduct himself in a certain way when he commands the other to do so. We shall not here further pursue the psychological analysis of the fact that a member of parliament gives his constitutionally required "consent" to a bill. Suffice it to say that to consent to a bill is not necessarily to "will" the contents of the statute and that the statute is not the "will" of the legislator — if we understand by "will" a real will, a psychological phenomenon — and that therefore the statute is not a command in the proper sense of the term.

4. Customary Law as Command

The fictitious character of the common saying that a rule of law is a command is still more evident when we consider customary law. Suppose that, in a certain community, the following rule is considered valid: A debtor has to pay his creditor 5 per cent interest if there is no other agreement upon this point. Suppose further that this rule has been established through custom; that over a long period of time creditors have in fact demanded 5 per cent interest and debtors have in fact paid that amount. Suppose also that they have done this in the opinion that such interest "ought" to be paid, *opinione necessitatis*, as the Roman jurists formulated it.

Whatever may be our theory about the law-creating facts with respect to customary law, we shall never be able to contend that it is the "will" or "command" of those people whose actual conduct constitutes the custom, that every debtor shall pay 5 per cent interest, in case he has accepted a loan without agreeing upon another rate of interest. In each particular case, neither the creditor nor the debtor has any will whatsoever concerning the conduct of other people. An individual creditor wants an individual debtor to pay him 5 per cent interest, and this individual debtor actually pays the demanded interest to that individual creditor. Such is the nature of those particular facts which together constitute the existence of the "custom," creating the general rule that under certain circumstances the loan-debtor has to pay 5 per cent interest to the loan-creditor. The existence of the custom does not involve any will having this rule for its contents. When, in a particular case, a court of the community condemns the debtor to pay 5 per cent interest, the court bases its judgment on the presumption that in matters of loan one has to act as the members of the community have always acted. This presumption does not reflect the actual "will" of any legislator.

5. The "Ought"

When laws are described as "commands" or expressions of the "will" of the legislator, and when the legal order as such is said to be the "command" or the "will" of the State, this must be understood as a figurative mode of speech. As usual, an analogy is responsible for the figurative statement. The situation when a rule of law "stipulates," "provides for," or "prescribes" a certain human conduct is in fact quite similar to the situation when one individual wants another individual to behave in such-and-such a way and expresses this will in the form of a command. The only difference is that when we say that a certain human conduct is "stipulated," "provided for," or "prescribed" by a rule of law, we are employing an abstraction which eliminates the psychological act of will which is expressed by a command. If the rule of law is a command, it is, so to speak, a de-psychologized command, a command which does not imply a "will" in a psychological sense of the term. The conduct prescribed by the rule of law is "demanded" without any human being having to "will" it in a psychological sense. This is expressed by the statement that one "shall," one "ought" to observe the conduct prescribed by the law. A "norm" is a rule expressing the fact that somebody ought to act in a certain way, without implying that anybody really "wants" the person to act that way.

The comparison between the "ought" of a norm and a command is justified only in a very limited sense. According to Austin, it is the binding force of a law that makes it a "command." That is to say, when

calling a law a command we only express the fact of its being a "norm."
On this point, there is no difference between a law enacted by a parliament, a contract concluded by two parties, or a testament made by an individual. The contract, too, is binding, it is a norm, binding the contracting parties. The testament, too, is binding. It is a norm binding the executor and the heirs. If it is dubious whether a testament may, even by way of comparison, be described as a "command," it is absolutely impossible so to describe a contract. In the latter case, the same individuals would otherwise both issue the command and be bound by it. This is impossible, for nobody can, properly speaking, command himself. But it is possible that a norm be created by the same individuals who are bound by this norm.

Here the objection might be raised: The contract itself does not bind the parties, it is the law of the State that binds the parties to conduct themselves according to the contract. However, a law may sometimes come very close to a contract. It is of the essence of a democracy that the laws are created by the same individuals who are bound by these laws. Insofar as identity of the commanding and the commanded is incompatible with the nature of a command, laws created in a democratic way cannot be recognized as commands. If we compare them to commands, we must by abstraction eliminate the fact that these "commands" are issued by those at whom they are directed. One can characterize democratic laws as "commands" only if one ignores the relationship between the individuals issuing the command and the individuals at whom the command is directed, if one assumes only a relationship between the latter and the "command" considered as impersonal, anonymous authority. That is the authority of the law, above the individual persons who are commanded and who command. This idea that the binding force emanates, not from any commanding human being, but from the impersonal anonymous "command" as such, is expressed in the famous words *non sub homine, sed sub lege.* If a relation of superiority and inferiority is included in the concept of command, then the rules of law are commands only if we consider the individual bound by them as subject to the rule. An impersonal and anonymous "command" — that is the norm.

The statement that an individual "ought to" behave in a certain way implies neither that some other individual "wills" or "commands" so, nor that the individual who ought to behave in a certain way actually behaves in this way. The norm is the expression of the idea that something ought to occur, especially that an individual ought to behave in a certain way. By the norm, nothing is said about the actual behavior of the individual concerned. The statement that an individual "ought to" behave in a certain way means that this behavior is prescribed by a norm — it may be a moral or a legal norm or some other norm. The "ought" simply expresses the specific sense in which human behavior is determined by a norm. All we can do to describe this sense is to state that it is different from the sense in which we say that an individual actually behaves in a certain way, that something actually occurs or exists. A statement to the effect that something ought to occur is a statement about the existence and the contents of a norm, not a statement about natural reality, i.e. actual events in nature.

A norm expressing the idea that something ought to occur — although, possibly, it does not actually occur — is "valid." And if the occurrence referred to is the behavior of a certain individual, if the norm says that a certain individual ought to behave in a certain way, then the norm is "binding" upon that individual. Only by the help of the concept of a norm and the correlated concept of "ought" can we grasp the specific meaning of rules of law. Only thus can we understand their relevance to those for whose behavior they "provide," for whom they "prescribe" a certain course of conduct. Any attempt to represent the meaning of legal norms by rules describing the actual behavior of men — and thus to render the meaning of legal norms without having recourse to the concept of "ought" — must fail. Neither a statement about the actual behavior of those creating the norm, nor a statement about the actual behavior of those subject to the norm, can reproduce the specific meaning of the norm itself.

In summary: To say that a norm is "valid" for certain individuals is not to say that a certain individual or certain individuals "want" other individuals to behave in a certain way; for the norm is valid also if no such will exists. To say that a norm is valid for certain individuals is not to say that individuals actually behave in a certain way; for the norm is valid for these individuals even if they do not behave in that way. The distinction between the "ought" and the "is" is fundamental for the description of law.

b. General and Individual Norms

If law is characterized as "rules," it must be stressed that legal rules essentially differ from other rules and in particular from those which are presented as laws of nature (in the sense of physics). Whereas laws of nature are statements about the actual course of events, legal rules are prescriptions for the behavior of men. Laws of nature are rules which describe how natural events actually occur and why these events occur; that is to say what are their causes. Rules of law refer only to human behavior; they state how men ought to behave, and say nothing about the actual behavior of men and of the causes thereof. In order to prevent misunderstandings (as to the nature of law), it is therefore better in this context not to use the term "rule," but to characterize law as norms.

Another reason why the designation of law as "rule" is misleading is that the word "rule" carries the connotation of something "general." A "rule" does not refer to a single non-recurring event but to a whole class of similar events. The import of a rule is that a phenomenon of a certain kind occurs — or ought to occur — always or almost always when conditions of a certain kind are fulfilled. In fact, law is often explained as "general rules." Austin * draws an explicit distinction between "laws" and "particular commands": where a command, he says, "obliges *generally* to acts or forbearances of a *class*, a command is a law or rule. But where it obliges to a *specific* act or forbearance . . . a command is occasional or particular." Having identified "law" and "rule," we can of course recognize as law only general norms. But there is no doubt that law does not consist of general norms only. Law includes individual norms, i.e. norms which determine the behavior of one individual in one non-recurring situation and which therefore are valid only for one particular case and may be obeyed or applied only once. Such norms are "law" because they are parts of the legal order as a whole in exactly the same sense as those general norms on the basis of which they have been created. Examples of such particular norms are the decisions of courts as far as their binding force is limited to the particular case at hand. Suppose that a judge orders a debtor A to return $1000 to his creditor B. By expressly or tacitly threatening A with a civil sanction in case of non-payment, the judge here "commands" A to pay $1000 to B. The decision of the judge is a legal norm in the same sense and for the same reasons as the general principle that if somebody does not return a loan then a civil sanction ought to be inflicted upon him on the motion of the creditor. The "binding force" or "validity" of law is intrinsically related, not to its possibly general character, but only to its character as a norm. Since, by its nature, law is norm, there is no reason why only general norms should be considered law. If, in other respects, individual norms present the essential characteristics of law, they, too, must be recognized as law.

c. Conditional and Unconditional Norms

General legal norms always have the form of hypothetical statements. The sanction stipulated by the norm is stipulated under certain conditions. Also an individual legal norm may have this hypothetical form. The court decision just mentioned provides an example. The civil sanc-

---

* 1 AUSTIN, JURISPRUDENCE 92f.

tion is stipulated on the condition that the defendant does not observe the conduct prescribed by the court. There are, however, individual legal norms which have no hypothetical character. For instance, when a criminal court first establishes that a certain individual is guilty of a certain delict and then inflicts upon him a certain penalty, e.g., two years in jail, it is on the basis of a hypothetical general norm that the court creates the individual norm that the accused shall be deprived of personal freedom for two years. This norm is unconditional.

d. Norm and Act

The execution of this court decision — the process implying that the condemned is actually put in jail and kept there for two years — is not itself a legal norm. If we designate this process as a "legal act," thereby expressing that this act also belongs to law, then the definition of law as a system of norms would seem too narrow. Not only the execution of a legal norm, the enactment of the sanction which it stipulates, but also all acts by which legal norms are created, are such legal acts. That it regulates its own creation is a peculiarity of law which is of the utmost theoretical importance and which will later be discussed. The act through which a legal norm, general or individual, is created is therefore an act determined by the legal order, as much as the act which is the execution of a norm. An act is a legal act precisely because it is determined by a legal norm. The legal quality of an act is identical with its relation to a legal norm. An act is a "legal" act only because and only insofar as it is determined by a legal norm. It is therefore incorrect to say that law consists of norms and acts. It would be more nearly correct to say that law is made up of legal norms and legal acts as determined by these norms. If we adopt a static point of view, that is, if we consider the legal order only in its completed form or in a state of rest, then we notice only the norms by which the legal acts are determined. If, on the other hand, we adopt a dynamic outlook, if we consider the process through which the legal order is created and executed, then we see only the law-creating and law-executing acts. To this important distinction between statics and dynamics of law we shall return later.

e. Efficacy as Conformity of the Behavior to the Norm

In the foregoing, we have tried to clarify the difference between the validity and the efficacy of the law. Validity of law means that the legal norms are binding, that men ought to behave as the legal norms prescribe, that men ought to obey and apply the legal norms. Efficacy of law means that men actually behave as, according to the legal norms, they ought to behave, that the norms are actually applied and obeyed. The validity is a quality of law; the so-called efficacy is a quality of the actual behavior of men and not, as linguistic usage seems to suggest, of law itself. The statement that law is effective means only that the actual behavior of men conforms with the legal norms. Thus, validity and efficacy refer to quite different phenomena. The common parlance, implying that validity and efficacy are both attributes of law, is misleading, even if by the efficacy of law is meant that the idea of law furnishes a motive for lawful conduct. Law as valid norm finds its expression in the statement that men ought to behave in a certain manner, thus in a statement which does not tell us anything about actual events. The efficacy of law, understood in the last-mentioned way, consists in the fact that men are led to observe the conduct required by a norm by their idea of this norm. A statement concerning the efficacy of law so understood is a statement about actual behavior. To designate both the valid norm and the idea of the norm, which is a psychological fact, by the same word "norm" is to commit an equivocation which may give rise to grave fallacies. However, as I have already pointed out, we are not in a position to say anything with exactitude about the motivating power which men's idea of law may possess. Objectively, we can ascertain only that the behavior of men conforms or does not conform with the legal norms. The only connotation attached to the term "efficacy" of law in this study is therefore that the actual behavior of men conforms to the legal norms.

f. Behavior "Opposed" to the Norm

The judgment that actual behavior "conforms" to a norm or that somebody's conduct is such as, according to the norm, it ought to be, may be characterized as a judgment of value. It is a statement asserting a relation between an object, especially human behavior, and a norm which the individual making this statement presupposes to be valid. Such a judgment of value must be carefully distinguished from the statement asserting a relation between the object and an interest of the individual making the statement, or of other individuals. In judging that something is "good," we can mean that we (by which is meant the judging subject or other individuals) desire it or that we find it pleasant. Then, our judgment asserts an actual state of affairs: It is our own or other individuals' emotional attitude toward the thing called "good" that we ascertain. The same holds for the judgment that something is "bad," if thereby we express our attitude toward it, that is, that we do not desire it or that we find it unpleasant. If we designate such judgments as judgments of value, then these judgments of value are assertions about actual facts; they are not different — in, principle — from other judgments about reality.

The judgment that something — in particular human conduct — is "good" or "bad" can also mean something else than the assertion that I who make the judgment, or other individuals, desire or do not desire the conduct; that I who make the judgment, or other individuals, find the conduct pleasant or unpleasant. Such a judgment can also express the idea that the conduct is, or is not, in conformity with a norm the validity of which I presuppose. The norm is here used as a standard of valuation.* It could also be said that actual events are being "interpreted" according to a norm. The norm, the validity of which is taken for granted, serves as a "scheme of interpretation." That an action or forbearance conforms to a valid norm or is "good" (in the most general sense of the word) means that the individual concerned has actually observed the conduct which, according to the norm, he ought to observe. If the norm stipulates the behavior A, and the individual's actual behavior is A too, then his behavior "conforms" to the norm. It is a realization of the behavior stipulated in the norm. That an individual's conduct is "bad" (in the most general sense of the word) means that his conduct is at variance with the valid norm; that the individual has not observed the conduct which, according to the norm, he ought to have observed. His conduct is not a realization of the conduct stipulated in the norm. The norm stipulates the behavior A; but the actual behavior of the individual is non-A. In such a case we say: The behavior of the individual "contradicts" the norm. This "contradiction" is, however, not a logical contradiction. Although there is a logical contradiction between A and non-A, there is no logical contradiction between the statement expressing the meaning of the norm: "The individual ought to behave A," and the statement describing the individual's actual behavior: "The individual behaves non-A." Such statements are perfectly compatible with each other. A logical contradiction may take place only between two statements which both assert an "ought," between two norms; for instance: "X ought to tell the truth," and: "X ought not to tell the truth"; or between two statements which both assert an "is," for instance: "X tells the truth," and: "X does not tell the truth." The relations of "conformity" or "nonconformity" are relations between a norm which stipulates a certain behavior and is considered as valid, on the one hand, and the actual behavior of men on the other hand.

g. Efficacy as Condition of Validity

The statement that a norm is valid and the statement that it is efficacious are, it is true, two different statements. But although validity and

* Cf. *infra* pp. 47 ff.

efficacy are two entirely different concepts, there is nevertheless a very important relationship between the two. A norm is considered to be valid only on the condition that it belongs to a system of norms, to an order which, on the whole, is efficacious. Thus, efficacy is a condition of validity; a condition, not the reason of validity. A norm is not valid *because* it is efficacious; it is valid *if* the order to which it belongs is, on the whole, efficacious. This relationship between validity and efficacy is cognizable, however, only from the point of view of a dynamic theory of law dealing with the problem of the reason of validity and the concept of the legal order.* From the point of view of a static theory, only the validity of law is in question.

h. Sphere of Validity of the Norms

Since norms regulate human behavior, and human behavior takes place in time and space, norms are valid for a certain time and for a certain space. The validity of a norm may begin at one moment and end at another. The norms of Czechoslovakian law began to be valid on a certain day of 1918, the norms of Austrian law ceased to be valid on the day when the Austrian Republic had been incorporated into the German Reich in 1938. The validity of a norm has also a relation to space. In order to be valid at all, it must be valid, not only for a certain time, but also for a certain territory. The norms of French law are valid only in France, the norms of Mexican law only in Mexico. We may therefore speak of the temporal and the territorial sphere of validity of a norm. To determine how men have to behave, one must determine when and where they have to behave in the prescribed manner. How they shall behave, what acts they shall do or forbear from doing, that is the material sphere of the validity of a norm. Norms regulating the religious life of men refer to another material sphere than norms regulating their economic life. With reference to a certain norm, one can, however, raise not only the question of what shall be done or avoided, but also the question who shall perform or avoid it. The latter question concerns the personal sphere of validity of the norm. Just as there are norms valid only for a certain territory, for a certain time, and with respect to certain matters, so there are norms valid only for certain individuals, for instance for Catholics or for Swiss. The human behavior which forms the contents of the norms and which occurs in time and space consists of a personal and a material element: the individual who somewhere and at some time does or refrains from doing something, and the thing, the act, which he does or refrains from doing. Therefore, the norms have to regulate human behavior in all these respects.

* Cf. *infra* pp. 118 ff.

Among the four spheres of validity of a norm, the personal and the material spheres are prior to the territorial and the temporal spheres. The latter two are only the territory within which, and the time during which, the individual shall observe certain conduct. A norm can determine time and space only in relation to human behavior. To say that a norm is valid for a given territory is to say that it concerns human behavior that occurs within that territory. To say that a norm is valid for a certain time is to say that it refers to human behavior that occurs during that time. Any territory in which and any time during which human behavior occurs may form the territorial and temporal spheres of validity of norms.

Occasionally it is asserted that norms can have validity not for the past but only for the future. That is not so, and the assertion appears to be due to a failure to distinguish between the validity of a norm and the efficacy of the idea of a norm. The idea of a norm as a psychic fact can become efficacious only in the future, in the sense that this idea must temporally precede the behavior conforming to the norm, since the cause must temporally precede the effect. But the norm may refer also to past behavior. Past and future are relative to a certain moment in time. The moment which those who argue that a norm is valid only for the future have in mind is evidently the moment when the norm was created. What they mean is that norms cannot refer to events which had taken place before that moment. But this does not hold if we are considering the validity of a norm as distinguished from the efficacy of its idea. Nothing prevents us from applying a norm as a scheme of interpretation, a standard of evaluation, to facts which occurred before the moment when the norm came into existence. What someone did in the past we may evaluate according to a norm which assumed validity only after it had been done. In the remote past it was a religious duty to sacrifice human beings to the gods, and slavery was a legal institution. Today we say that these human sacrifices were crimes and that slavery, as a legal institution, was immoral. We apply moral norms valid in our time to these facts, though the norms which forbid human sacrifices and slavery came into existence long after the facts occurred that we judge now, according to these new norms, as crimes and immoral. Subsequent legitimation is possible and frequent, especially within the field of law. A special example is the German law by which certain murders, committed by order of the head of the State June 30, 1934, were retroactively divested of their character of delicts. It would also have been possible retroactively to give the character of sanctions to these acts of murder. A legal norm, e.g. a statute, can attach a sanction to facts accomplished before the creation of the norm. This norm is valid for the subject which shall refrain from the delict as well as for the organ which shall execute the sanction. Such a norm is, with respect to the subject, valid for the past.

i. *Retroactive Laws and* Ignorantia Juris

The moral and political value of retroactive laws may be disputed, but their possibility cannot be doubted. The constitution of the United States, for instance, says in Article I, section 9, clause 3: "No . . . *ex post facto* law shall be passed." The term "*ex post facto* law" is interpreted as penal law with retroactive force. Retroactive laws are considered to be objectionable and undesirable because it hurts our feeling of justice to inflict a sanction, especially a punishment, upon an individual because of an action or omission of which this individual could not know that it would entail this sanction. However, on the other hand, we recognize the principle — a fundamental principle of all positive legal orders — *ignorantia juris neminem excusat*, ignorance of the law excuses no one. The fact that an individual does not know that the law attaches a sanction to his action or omission is no reason for not inflicting the sanction upon him. Sometimes the principle in question is interpreted restrictively: ignorance of the law is no excuse if the individual did not know the law although it was possible to know the law. Then this principle seems not incompatible with the rejection of retroactive laws. For in case of a retroactive law it is indeed impossible to know the law at the moment when the act is performed to which the retroactive law attaches a sanction. The distinction, however, between a case in which the individual can know the law valid at the moment he commits the delict and a case in which the individual cannot know the law is more than problematical. In fact, it is generally presupposed that a law which is valid can be known by the individuals whose behavior is regulated by the law. In fact, it is a *presumptio juris et de jure,* i.e. an "irrebuttable presumption," a legal presumption against which no evidence is permitted, a legal hypothesis the incorrectness of which must not be proved, that all the norms of a positive legal order can be known by the individuals subject to this order. This is obviously not true; the presumption in question is a typical legal fiction. Hence, with respect to the possibility or impossibility of knowing the law, there is no essential difference between a retroactive law and many cases in which a non-retroactive law is not, and cannot, be known by the individual to whom this law has to be applied.

D. THE LEGAL NORM

a. *Legal Norm and Rule of Law in a Descriptive Sense*

If "coercion" in the sense here defined is an essential element of law, then the norms which form a legal order must be norms stipulating a coercive act, i.e. a sanction. In particular, the general norms must be norms in which a certain sanction is made dependent upon certain conditions, this dependence being expressed by the concept of "ought." This does not mean that the law-making organs necessarily have to give the norms the form of such hypothetical "ought" statements. The different elements of a norm may be contained in very different products of the law-making procedure, and they may be linguistically expressed in very different ways. When the legislator forbids theft, he may, for instance, first define the concept of theft in a number of sentences which form an article of a statute, and then stipulate the sanction in another sentence, which may be part of another article of the same statute or even part of an entirely different statute. Often the latter sentence does not have the linguistic form of an imperative or an "ought" sentence but the form of a prediction of a future event. The legislator frequently makes use of the future tense, saying that a thief "will be" punished in such and such a way. He then presupposes that the question as to who is a thief has been answered somewhere else, in the same or in some other statute. The phrase "will be punished" does not imply the prediction of a future event — the legislator is no prophet — but an "imperative" or a "command," these terms taken in a figurative sense. What the norm-creating authority means is that the sanction "ought" to be executed against the thief, when the conditions of the sanction are fulfilled.

It is the task of the science of law to represent the law of a community, i.e. the material produced by the legal authority in the law-making procedure, in the form of statements to the effect that "if such and such conditions are fulfilled, then such and such a sanction shall follow." These statements, by means of which the science of law represents law, must not be confused with the norms created by the law-making authorities. It is preferable not to call these statements norms, but legal rules. The legal norms enacted by the law creating authorities are prescriptive; the rules of law formulated by the science of law are descriptive. It is of importance that the term "legal rule" or "rule of law" be employed here in a descriptive sense.

b. *Rule of Law and Law of Nature*

The rule of law, the term used in a descriptive sense, is a hypothetical judgment attaching certain consequences to certain conditions. This is the logical form of the law of nature, too. Just as the science of law, the science of nature describes its object in sentences which have the character of hypothetical judgments. And like the rule of law, the law of nature, too, connects two facts with one another as condition and consequence. The condition is here the "cause," the consequence the "effect." The fundamental form of the law of nature is the law of causality. The difference between the rule of law and the law of nature seems to be that the former refers to human beings and their behavior, whilst the latter refers to things and their reactions. Human behavior, however, may also be the subject-matter of natural laws, insofar as human behavior, too, belongs to nature. The rule of law and the law of nature differ not so much by the elements they connect as by the manner of their connection. The law of nature establishes that if A is, B is (or will be). The rule of law says: If A is, B ought to be. The rule of law is a norm (in the descriptive sense of that term). The meaning of the connection established by the law of nature between two elements is the "is," whereas the meaning of the connection between two elements established by the rule of law is the "ought." The principle according to which natural science describes its object is causality; the principle according to which the science of law describes its object is normativity.

Usually, the difference between law of nature and norm is characterized by the statement that the law of nature can have no exceptions, whereas a norm can. This is, however, not correct. The normative rule "If someone steals, he ought to be punished," remains valid even if in a given case a thief is not punished. This fact involves no exception to the ought statement expressing the norm; it is an exception only to an "is" statement expressing the rule that if someone steals, he actually will be punished. The validity of a norm remains unaffected if, in a concrete instance, a fact does not correspond to the norm. A fact has the character of an "exception" to a rule if the statement establishing the fact is in a logical contradiction to the rule. Since a norm is no statement of reality, no statement of a real fact can be in contradiction to a norm. Hence, there can be no exceptions to a norm. The norm is, by its very nature, inviolable. To say that the norm is "violated" by certain behavior is a figurative expression; and the figure used in this statement is not correct. For the statement says nothing about the norm; it merely characterizes the actual behavior as contrary to the behavior prescribed by the norm.

The law of nature, however, is not inviolable.* True exceptions to a law of nature are not excluded. The connection between cause and effect

* WILLIAM A. ROBSON, CIVILISATION AND THE GROWTH OF LAW (1935) 340, says: "Men of science no longer claim for natural laws the inexorable, immutable, and objective validity they were formerly deemed to possess."

established in a law of nature describing physical reality has the character of probability only, not of absolute necessity, as assumed by the older philosophy of nature. If, as a result of empirical research, two phenomena are considered to be in a relation of cause and effect, and if this result is formulated in a law of nature, it is not absolutely excluded that a fact may occur which is in contradiction to this law, and which therefore represents a real exception to the law. Should such a fact be established, then the formulation of the law has to be altered in a way to make the new fact correspond to the new formula. But the connection of cause and effect established by the new formula has also only the character of probability, not that of absolute necessity. Exceptions to the law are not excluded.

If we examine the way in which the idea of causality has developed in the human mind, we find that the law of causality has its origin in a norm. The interpretation of nature had originally a social character. Primitive man considers nature to be an intrinsic part of his society. He interprets physical reality according to the same principles that determine his social relations. His social order, to him, is at the same time the order of nature. Just as men obey the norms of the social order, things obey the norms emanating from superhuman personal beings. The fundamental social law is the norm according to which the good has to be rewarded, the evil punished. It is the principle of retribution which completely dominates primitive consciousness. The legal norm is the prototype of this principle. According to this principle of retribution, primitive man interprets nature. His interpretation has a normative-juristic character. It is in the norm of retribution that the law of causality originates and, in the way of a gradual change of meaning, develops. Even during the nineteenth century, the law of causality was conceived of as a norm, the expression of the divine will. The last step in this emancipation of the law of causality from the norm of retribution consists in the fact that the former gets rid of the character of a norm and thereby ceases to be conceived of as inviolable.*

c. The Legal Norm as a Standard of Valuation †

The legal norm may be applied not only in the sense that it is executed by the organ or obeyed by the subject, but also in the sense that it forms the basis of a specific judgment of value qualifying the behavior of the organ, or the subject, as lawful (legal, right) or unlawful (illegal, wrong). These are the specifically juristic value judgments. Other value judg-

* Cf. my SOCIETY AND NATURE, pp. 233ff.

† Cf. my article *Value Judgments in the Science of Law* (1942) 7 J. OF SOCIAL PHILOSOPHY AND JURISPRUDENCE 312–333.

ments are concerned with the law itself, or with the activity of the individuals who create the law. These judgments assert that the legislator's activity or the product thereof, the law, is just or unjust. The activity of the judge is also, it is true, considered as just or unjust, but only insofar as he functions in a law-creating capacity. Insofar as he merely applies law, his behavior is regarded as lawful or unlawful just like the behavior of those who are subject to law. The value predicates involved in judgments to the effect that certain behavior is lawful or unlawful will here be designated as "values of law," while those involved in judgments to the effect that a legal order is just or unjust will be called "values of justice." Statements asserting values of law are objective, statements asserting values of justice are subjective judgments of value. The juristic value judgment that certain behavior is lawful or unlawful is an assertion of a positive or negative relation between the behavior and a legal norm whose existence is presumed by the person making the judgment. The existence of a legal norm is its validity; and the validity of legal norms, although not identical with certain facts, is conditioned by them. These facts are — as we shall show in a subsequent section * — the efficacy of the total legal order to which the norm belongs, the presence of a fact creating the norm, and the absence of any fact annulling the norm. A juristic value judgment that asserts a positive or negative relation between definite human behavior and a legal norm implies the assertion of the existence of a legal norm. This assertion, and therefore the juristic value judgment itself, can be verified by means of the facts which condition the existence of the norm. In this sense, the juristic value judgment has an objective character. The existence of the value of law is objectively verifiable. The value of justice, however, is not of the same nature as the value of law. When we judge a legal order or a legal institution as just or unjust, we intend to say something more than when we call a dish of food good or bad, meaning to say that we find or do not find it pleasing to the palate. The statement that a legal institution, e.g. slavery or private property, is just or unjust does not mean that somebody has an interest in this institution or its opposite. Its significance is that the institution in question corresponds or does not correspond to a norm whose validity is presumed by the person making the statement. But this norm is not a norm of positive law. Nevertheless, a judgment of justice claims to state an objective value.

The norms which are actually used as standards of justice vary, as we have pointed out, from individual to individual, and are often mutually irreconcilable. Something is just or unjust only for an individual for

---

* Cf. *infra* pp. 118ff.

whom the appropriate norm of justice exists, and this norm exists only for those who, for some reason or other, wish what the norm prescribes. It is impossible to determine the norm of justice in a unique way. It is ultimately an expression of the interest of the individual who pronounces a social institution to be just or unjust. But that is something of which he is unconscious. His judgment claims to assert the existence of a justice independent of human will. This claim to objectivity is particularly evident when the idea of justice appears under the form of "natural law." According to the doctrine of "natural law," the norm of justice is immanent in nature — the nature of men or the nature of things — and man can only apprehend but not create or influence this norm. The doctrine is a typical illusion, due to an objectivization of subjective interests.

The values of justice do not, it is true, consist in a relation to an interest but in a relation to a norm. This norm, however, is not, as the judging person believes, objective, but dependent upon a subjective interest of his. There are, therefore, not one standard of justice only but many different and mutually inconsistent standards of this kind.

There is, however, only one positive law. Or — if we wish to account for the existence of the various national legal orders — there is for each territory only one positive law. Its contents can be uniquely ascertained by an objective method. The existence of the values of law is conditioned by objectively verifiable facts. To the norms of positive law there corresponds a certain social reality, but not so to the norms of justice. In this sense the value of law is objective while the value of justice is subjective. From this point of view it makes no difference that sometimes a great number of people have the same ideal of justice. Juristic value judgments are judgments that can be tested objectively by the help of facts. Therefore they are admissible within a science of law. Judgments of justice cannot be tested objectively. Therefore, a science of law has no room for them.

Moral and political judgments are of the same nature as judgments of justice. They intend to express an objective value. According to their meaning, the object to which they refer is valuable for everybody. They presuppose an objectively valid norm. But the existence and contents of this norm cannot be verified by facts. It is determined only by a subjective wish of the subject making the judgment. Moral and political judgments of value and, in particular, judgments of justice, are based on ideologies which are not, as juristic judgments of value are, parallel to a definite social reality.

II. THE SANCTION

The concept of the legal rule in both its aspects — the legal rule as norm created by the legal authority to regulate human behavior, and as an instrument used by legal science to describe the positive law — is the central concept of jurisprudence. Other fundamental concepts are the sanction, the delict, the legal duty, the legal right, the legal person, and the legal order.

Sanctions are provided by the legal order to bring about certain human behavior which the legislator considers to be desirable. The sanctions of law have the character of coercive acts in the sense developed above. Originally, there was only one sort of sanction: criminal sanction, i.e. punishment in the narrow sense of the word, punishment involving life, health, freedom, or property. The most ancient law was criminal law only. Later, a differentiation was made in the sanction: there appeared, in addition to punishment, a specific civil sanction, civil execution, a forcible deprivation of property with the purpose of providing reparation, i.e. compensation for illegally caused damage. Thus there developed civil law besides criminal law. But civil law, the law regulating economic life, guarantees the desired conduct of men in its field in a manner not essentially different from that in which the criminal law accomplishes this in its domain, namely, by establishing for the case of contrary conduct a coercive measure, its own specific coercive measure, civil sanction. The difference between civil law and criminal law is a difference in the character of their respective sanctions. If we consider only the outward nature of the sanctions, we cannot, however, find any generally distinguishing characteristics. An instance: though the civil sanction always consists in the deprivation of some economic possession, the fine, which is a criminal sanction, is also of this nature. More fundamental is the difference in purpose: whereas criminal law aims at retribution or, according to the modern view, deterrence, i.e. prevention, civil law aims at reparation. This difference finds its expression in the content of the legal order. There are provisions concerning the use of the deprived possessions. These possessions, or the money obtained by their sale, have to be transferred — in the case of civil sanction — to the subject illegally prejudiced; in the case of criminal sanction, to the legal community (the fisc). Nevertheless, the difference between civil and criminal sanction — and, consequently, between civil and criminal law — has only a relative character. It can hardly be disputed that civil sanctions also, at least secondarily, serve the purpose of prevention by deterrence. A further difference may be seen in the procedure by which the two kinds of sanctions are effected, as the procedure has actually been established in the various legal orders. The procedure aiming at civil execution, i.e. the civil procedure of the courts, is initiated only by an action of a certain subject interested in the execution, the subject of the violated "right." The procedure aiming at the criminal sanction, i.e. the criminal procedure of the courts, is initiated *ex officio*, that is, by the act of an organ, the public prosecutor. However, this difference in procedure, of which more will be said later, is of minor importance. Thus, in spite of the differences which exist between the criminal and the civil sanction, the social technique is in both cases fundamentally the same. It is this very relative difference between civil and criminal sanction which is the basis of the differentiation between civil and criminal law.

III. THE DELICT

A. "MALA IN SE" AND "MALA PROHIBITA"

The sanction is made a consequence of the behavior which is considered detrimental to society and which, according to the intentions of the legal order, has to be avoided. This behavior is designated by the term "delict," the term understood in its broadest sense. If we are to define the concept of delict in conformity with the principles of a pure theory of law, then the "intentions of the legal order" or the "purpose of the legislator" may enter into the definition only to the extent that they are expressed in the material produced in the law-creating procedure, that they are manifested in the contents of the legal order. Otherwise, the concept of delict would not be a legal concept.

Considered from this standpoint, the delict is the condition to which the sanction is attached by the legal norm. Certain human conduct is a delict because the legal order attaches to this conduct, as a condition, a sanction as consequence. It is a criminal delict if it has a criminal sanction, and it is a civil delict if it has a civil sanction as its consequence. The usual assumption according to which a certain kind of human behavior entails a legal sanction because it is a delict is not correct. It is a delict because it entails a sanction. From the view-point of a theory the only object of which is the positive law, there is no other criterion of the delict than the fact that the behavior is the condition of a sanction. There is no delict in itself. In the traditional theory of criminal law a distinction is made between *mala in se* and *mala prohibita*,* that is conduct which is evil in itself, and conduct which is evil

* Cf. Jerome Hall, *Prolegomena to a Science of Criminal Law* (1941) 89 U. OF PA. L. REV. 549–580. The distinction between *mala in se* and *mala prohibita*, i.e., conduct which is evil in itself and conduct which is evil only because it is pro-

only because it is prohibited by a positive social order. This distinction cannot be maintained in a theory of positive law. The distinction is the typical element of a natural law doctrine.* It proceeds from an assumption — which cannot be proved scientifically — that certain patterns of human behavior are, by their very nature, delicts. The question, however, as to whether certain human conduct is a delict cannot be answered by an analysis of this conduct; it can be answered only on the basis of a certain legal order. The same behavior may be a delict according to the law of community A, and no delict at all according to the law of community B. Different legal orders of different peoples have stigmatized very different patterns of behavior as delicts at different times. It is true that different legal orders of the same cultural status agree, to a certain extent, in stigmatizing certain patterns of behavior as delicts; and that certain types of conduct are disapproved not only by positive law but also by the system of morals connected with this positive law. These facts, however, do not justify the assumption of *mala in se*. Furthermore, it is necessary to separate the juristic question, how shall the concept of delict be defined within a theory of positive law? from the moral-political question, what conduct should the legislator purposefully or justly connect with a sanction? Certainly, the legislator must first consider a certain kind of behavior harmful, a *malum*, in order to attach to it a sanction. Before the sanction is provided, however, the behavior is no *malum* in a legal sense, no delict. There are no *mala in se*, there are only *mala prohibita*, for a behavior is a *malum* only if it is *prohibitum*. This is nothing but the consequence of the principles generally accepted in the theory of criminal law: *nulla poena sine lege, nullum crimen sine lege* † — no sanction without a legal norm providing this sanction, no delict without a legal norm determining that delict. These principles are the expression of legal positivism in the field of

---

hibited by a positive social order, is almost identical with the distinction which Aristotle made in his *Ethica Nichomachea* (1134b) between the "natural" and the "legal." "The natural: that which everywhere has the same force and does not exist by people's thinking this or that; the legal: that which is originally indifferent, but when it has been laid down, is not indifferent."

* BLACKSTONE, COMMENTARIES, Introduction, § 65, distinguishes between natural and positive duties. "In regard to *natural duties*, and such offenses as are *mala in se:* here we are bound in conscience, because we are bound by superior laws, before those human laws were in being, to perform the one and abstain from the other. But in relation to those laws which enjoin only *positive duties* and forbid only such things as are not *mala in se* but *mala prohibita* merely, without any intermixture of moral guilt, annexing a penalty to non-compliance, here I comprehend conscience is not further concerned, than by directing a submission to the penalty, in case of our breach of those laws."

† Cf. Jerome Hall, *Nulla Poena sine Lege* (1937) 47 YALE L. J. 165–193.

criminal law, but they prevail also in the field of civil law as far as the civil delict and the civil sanction are concerned. They mean that human behavior can be considered a delict only if a positive legal norm attaches a sanction as a consequence to this behavior as a condition.

B. THE DELICT AS A CONDITION OF THE SANCTION

From a purely juristic point of view, the delict is characterized as a condition of the sanction. But the delict is not the only condition. In the case of a criminal delict, this is perhaps not quite as obvious as in the case of the civil delict, i.e., the delict which entails a civil, not a criminal sanction. Let us take as an example the non-fulfillment of a contract. The pertinent legal rule is: If two parties make a contract, and if one party does not fulfill the contract, and if the other party brings an action against the first party in the competent court, then the court shall order a sanction against the first party. But this formulation is by no means complete. It does not enumerate all possible conditions but only the conditions characteristic of the sanction in this special case. These conditions are the following three: (1) that a contract has been made; (2) that one of the two parties does not keep it, and (3) that the other party brings an action, i.e., demands that the judicial procedure be conducted which ultimately leads to the execution of the sanction. The delict, i.e., the fact that one party has not fulfilled the contract, is not sufficiently characterized by saying that it is "a condition of the sanction." The making of the contract and the suit of the other party are also such conditions. What then is the distinctive characteristic of that condition which is called the "delict"? Could no other criterion be found than the supposed fact that the legislator desires conduct contrary to that which is characterized as "delict," then the concept of delict would be incapable of a juristic definition. The concept of delict defined simply as socially undesired behavior is a moral or a political, in short, no juristic but a metajuristic, concept. Definitions characterizing the delict as a "violation of law," as an act which is contrary to law, "illegal" or "unlawful," as a "negation of law" — in German, "un-law" (Unrecht) — all are of this kind. All such explanations only amount to saying that the delict is against the purpose of law. But that is irrelevant to the legal concept of delict. From a merely juristic point of view, the delict is no "violation of law" — the specific mode of existence of the legal norm, its validity, is in no way endangered by the delict. Nor is the delict, from a juristic point of view, "contrary to law" or a "negation" of law; for the jurist, the delict is a condition determined by law as much as, in our example above, are the making of the contract and the action.

C. The Delict as Behavior of the Individual Against whom the Sanction is Directed

A juristic definition of delict must be based entirely upon the legal norm. And such a definition can in fact be given. Normally, the delict is the behavior of that individual against whom the sanction as a consequence of his behavior is directed. That is the juristic definition of delict. The criterion of the concept of "delict" is an element which constitutes the content of the legal norm. It is not a supposed intention of the legislator. It is an element of the norm by which the legislator expresses his intention in an objectively cognizable way; it is an element which can be found by an analysis of the content of the legal norm. From a political point of view, the reason why, and the purpose for which, the legislator stipulates the sanction and directs it against a certain individual is of course of the greatest interest. But from a juristic point of view the reason and purpose of the legislator come into consideration only insofar as they are expressed in the content of the norm; and the legislator expresses his intention normally by directing a sanction against the individual whose behavior is the contrary of the behavior desired by the legislator. Very often, the delict, especially the criminal delict, is an object of moral and religious disapproval, it is regarded as "sin," and such a connotation is attached to the words by which one usually designates the delict as "wrong," "illegal," "unlawful," "violation of law." But the legal concept of delict must be kept completely free from such elements. They are of no relevance to an analytical theory of positive law.

The definition of delict as the behavior of the individual against whom the sanction, as consequence of this behavior, is directed, presupposes — although it does not refer to the fact — that the sanction is directed against the individual whose behavior the legislator considers to be detrimental to society and, therefore, intends to prevent by the sanction. This holds true in principle for the laws of civilized peoples.

In this connection, it should be noticed that the fact of the delict may consist, not only in a certain kind of behavior, but also in the effects of that behavior. The legal order annexes a sanction to the conduct of an individual because of the effect which this conduct has on other individuals. The delict called "murder" consists in the behavior of an individual which is intended to bring about the death of another individual and actually does so. The behavior is not necessarily an action, it may also be an omission, the non-performance of an action. In such a case it might sometimes seem as if the sanction were directed against another individual than the perpetrator of the delict, the "delinquent," for instance, when a child causes somebody's death and when, according to positive law, the father is "therefore" punished. However, the delict is not here the child's action but the conduct of the father who has failed to prevent the child from committing its socially undesirable action; it is "because" of this omission that the father is punished. The father, not the child, is the "delinquent."

According to the criminal law of civilized peoples, the sanction is usually stipulated only for those cases where the socially undesirable effect was intentionally or negligently brought about by the delinquent. If intent is essential to the commission of the crime, a definite mental attitude on the part of the delinquent is a material ingredient of the delict; in this case the delict is psychologically qualified. If the socially undesirable effect was brought about neither intentionally nor negligently,* then no sanction has to be executed against the individual whose behavior led to the result. This presupposes the principle that the sanction must be directed only against the delinquent, that is, the individual who, by his own action or omission, directly or indirectly, brings about the socially detrimental effect. The principle that the sanction is directed against the individual whose behavior is considered to be detrimental to society, and that we may therefore juristically define the delict as the behavior of the individual against whom the sanction as the consequence of this behavior is directed, results from the purpose of the sanction, whether it be retribution or prevention (by deterrence). Only if the evil of the sanction is inflicted upon the evil-doer are the demands of retribution fulfilled and can the fear of the sanction prevent people from committing the delict.

In case the sanction is directed against somebody other than the individual whose behavior is considered to be socially detrimental, then the purpose of retribution or prevention (deterrence) can be attained only if this individual and the individual against whom the sanction is directed are, for some reason or other, identified; if the evil which the sanction intends for its immediate victim is also experienced as an evil by the other individual. Then, the sanction ultimately hits the individual whose behavior is considered to be detrimental to society; and then the delict can — from a juristic point of view — even in this case be defined as the behavior of the individual against whom the sanction, as a consequence of this behavior, is — indirectly — directed. By killing a child, one may punish the father, and that much more severely than by any evil which one may inflict upon him personally. On the fact that we more or less identify ourselves with the individuals belonging to our own group, be it family, village, political or religious com-

---

* Negligence is not a psychological qualification of the delict. Cf. *infra* pp. 66 ff.

munity, the cruel but efficacious practice of taking hostages is based. A hostage is an individual held as a pledge for the performance of some stipulation. If the stipulation is not obeyed, the hostage is executed. Since his death is felt as an evil by his relatives or fellow citizens the threat to kill him works as an indirect sanction against the potential violators of the stipulations.

The purpose of the civil sanction is, at least primarily, reparation of a damage by means of forcible deprivation of property. Almost without exceptions, the legal order here employs the technique of laying down as conditions of the sanction not only that the damage has been done, but also that the individual from whose property the reparation is to be taken does not voluntarily make good the damage. The sanction is always enacted against the individual who shall repair the damage but has not done so. The civil delict consists in not repairing the damage. Thus, the subject of the civil delict and the object of the civil sanction are always identical here, irrespective of whether or not the damage to be repaired was caused by the individual who has to repair it, or by another individual. The legal concept of delict presupposes in principle that the individual whose behavior has from a political point of view a socially detrimental character, and the individual against whom the sanction is directly or indirectly executed, coincide. Only on this condition is the juristic definition of the delict, as the behavior of the individual against whom the sanction as a consequence of this behavior is directed, correct.

D. Identification of the Delinquent with the Members of his Group

It might seem as if the principle according to which the sanction is directed against the delinquent had only a restricted validity. Primitive law at least appears to present exceptions. The transcendental sanction emanating from some superhuman power is, in the belief of primitive man, often directed, not only against the delinquent, but also against other people who neither took part in the delict nor were in any way able to prevent it. If somebody violates a taboo rule, and if later his wife or his child is struck by a disease, this is interpreted as a punishment. The same holds for the socially organized sanction in primitive law. The revenge for homicide is directed not only against the murderer, but also against his family, the whole social group of which he is a member. This legal technique is a consequence of the collective character of primitive thinking and feeling.* Primitive man does not

* Cf. my SOCIETY AND NATURE, pp. 6ff.

consider himself as an individual independent of the social group to which he belongs, but as an integral part of that group. He identifies himself with his group and identifies every other individual with the group to which this individual belongs. In the eyes of primitive man, there is no such thing as an independent individual. In various primitive tribes, the fact has been observed that if a man falls sick the supposed remedy is taken not only by the man himself but also by his wife and children. Every socially relevant action or forbearance of an individual is regarded as an action or forbearance of his social group. Naturally, therefore, the sanction is enacted against the whole group to which the delinquent belongs. According to primitive view, it is the whole group that has committed the delict. The group, not the individual, is the social unit. From the point of view of modern civilized man, the sanction of primitive law is directed against the delinquent and against all other members of his social group, who are united with the delinquent and therefore identified with him. In this case, too, the subject of the delict and the object of the sanction coincide. And in this case, too, the delict is the behavior of the being against whom the sanction as a consequence of this behavior is directed. But this being is not an individual, it is a collectivity. The juristic concept of delict therefore holds good also for primitive law. Its ideology is not yet prevention, it is retribution; and the demands of retribution are fulfilled even in case the sanction is directed against someone else than the delinquent, if, for some reason or other, the former is identified with the latter.

E. DELICT OF JURISTIC PERSONS

A similar situation is met within the laws of civilized peoples. A juristic person, a corporation, is in certain cases considered as a perpetrator of a delict which was committed directly by a single individual only who is an organ of the corporation. The sanction is then directed, not only against this responsible individual, but, in principle, against all the members of the corporation. Such is, for instance, the case in international law. If an international delict, a "violation" of international law occurs, a certain State is considered as the subject of this delict, despite the fact that the delict consists in the behavior of a definite individual, e.g., the chief of State or the foreign minister. Because this individual is an organ of the State, his behavior is considered as a delict committed by the State. Also the sanction of international law, reprisals or war, is directed against the State, and that means against all its members, not solely against the immediate delinquent. Insofar as the State is conceived of as a juristic person, the subject of the delict and the object of the sanction are identical. The delict is, in this case, too, the behavior of the subject against whom the sanction as a consequence of this behavior is directed.

The concept of the corporation as a juristic person stands, in a certain sense, for an identification of the individual and his social group, similar to the identification which occurs in primitive thought. If we wish to abstain from the use of this concept and the identification it implies, we must be content with the statement that the sanction is directed against individuals who stand in a certain legally determined relation to the delinquent. In order to include this case in our definition, we should have to define the delict as the behavior of the individual against whom the sanction is directed or who has a certain legally determined relation to those individuals against whom the sanction is directed.

It follows that the relationship between delict and sanction may be of two different types. In both cases, it is true, the subject of the delict and the object of the sanction are identical. But in the one case this identity is a real physical identity, in the other case it is only a fictitious legal one. In the one case, the sanction is undertaken against the individual who was the immediate perpetrator of the delict, the delinquent; in the other case against an individual who has, or individuals who have, a certain legally determined relationship to the delinquent.

IV. THE LEGAL DUTY

A. DUTY AND NORM

Intimately related to the concept of delict is the concept of legal duty. The concept of duty is originally a specific concept of morals and denotes the moral norm in its relation to the individual to whom certain conduct is prescribed or forbidden by the norm. The statement: "An individual has the (moral) duty, or is (morally) obligated, to observe such-and-such behavior" means that there is a valid (moral) norm enjoining this behavior, or that the individual ought to behave in that way.

The concept of legal duty is also nothing but a counterpart to the concept of legal norm. But the relationship is here more complex, since the legal norm has a more complicated structure than the moral norm. The legal norm does not, like the moral norm, refer to the behavior of one individual only, but to the behavior of two individuals at least: the individual who commits or may commit the delict, the delinquent, and the individual who ought to execute the sanction. If the sanction is directed against another individual than the immediate delinquent, the legal norm refers to three individuals. The concept of legal duty, as actually used in jurisprudence and as defined especially by Austin, refers only to the individual against whom the sanction is directed in case he commits the delict. He is legally obligated to refrain from the delict: if the delict is a certain positive action, he is obligated not to undertake that action; if the delict is an omission of a certain action, he is obligated to undertake that action. An individual is legally obligated to the behavior the opposite of which is the condition of a sanction directed against him (or against individuals having a certain legally determined relation to him). He "violates" his duty (or obligation), or, what amounts to the same, he commits a delict, when he behaves in such a way that his behavior is the condition of a sanction; he fulfills his duty (obligation), or, what amounts to the same, he abstains from committing a delict, when his behavior is the opposite to the former. Thus, to be legally obligated to a certain behavior means that the contrary behavior is a delict and as such is the condition of a sanction stipulated by a legal norm; thus, to be legally obligated means to be the potential subject of a delict, a potential delinquent. However, only in case the sanction is directed against the immediate delinquent is the subject of the duty he who is liable to a sanction stipulated by a legal norm, the potential object of the sanction. When the sanction is directed against an individual other than the immediate delinquent, the subject of the duty (that is to say, the potential delinquent) and the potential object of the sanction do not coincide, at least not in reality, but only according to a legal fiction. The existence of a legal duty is nothing but the validity of a legal norm which makes a sanction dependent upon the opposite of the behavior forming the legal duty. The legal duty is nothing apart from the legal norm. The legal duty is simply the legal norm in its relation to the individual to whose behavior the sanction is attached in the norm. The behavior opposite (contrary) to the behavior which as a delict is the condition of the sanction is the content of the legal duty. Legal duty is duty to refrain from the delict. It is the duty of the subject to "obey" the legal norm.

B. The Duty and the "Ought"

Under this definition of legal duty, the legal norm which obligates the subject to refrain from the delict by attaching a sanction thereto does not stipulate any legal duty of executing the sanction, of "applying" the norm itself. The judge — or, to use a more general expression, the law-applying organ — can be legally obligated to execute the sanction — in the sense in which the subject is obligated to refrain from the delict, to "obey" the legal norm — only if there is a further norm which attaches a further sanction to the non-execution of the first sanction. Thus there must be two distinct norms: one stipulating that an organ shall execute a sanction against a subject, and one stipulating that another organ shall execute a sanction against the first organ, in case the first sanction is not executed. Relative to the second norm, the organ of the first norm is not a law-"applying" "organ" but a "subject" obeying or disobeying the law. The second norm makes it the legal duty of the organ of the first norm to execute the sanction stipulated by the first norm. The organ of the second norm may in turn be obligated by a third norm to execute the sanction stipulated by the second norm, and so on and so forth.

However, this series of legal norms cannot be extended indefinitely. There must be a last norm of the series such that the sanction which it stipulates is not a legal duty in the sense defined. If the meaning of this last norm is also expressed by saying that under certain conditions a sanction "ought to" be enacted, then the concept of "ought" does not coincide with the concept of legal duty. An organ which "ought" to enact a sanction may, or may not, be legally obligated to do so. In primitive legal orders and in international law there is no legal duty for the organ to execute the legal sanction. If the legal norm is expressed by saying that when certain conditions are fulfilled the organ ought to order and execute the sanction, then the word "ought" only denotes the specific sense in which the sanction is "stipulated," "provided," "determined," in the norm. Nothing is thereby said on the question of whether the organ is "obligated" to enact the sanction. Within the field of morals, the concept of duty coincides with that of "ought." The behavior which is the moral duty of somebody is simply the behavior which he ought to observe according to a moral norm.

The concept of legal duty also implies an "ought." That somebody is legally obligated to certain conduct means that an organ "ought" to apply a sanction to him in case of contrary conduct. But the concept of legal duty differs from that of moral duty by the fact that the legal duty is not the behavior which the norm "demands," which "ought" to be observed. The legal duty, instead, is the behavior by the observance of which the delict is avoided, thus the opposite of the behavior which forms a condition for the sanction. Only the sanction "ought" to be executed.

C. THE SECONDARY NORM

If it is also said that the legal duty "ought" to be performed, then this "ought" is, so to speak, an epiphenomenon of the "ought" of the sanction. Such a presentation presupposes that the legal norm is split into two separate norms, two "ought" statements: one to the effect that a certain individual "ought" to observe certain conduct, and one to the effect that another individual ought to execute a sanction in case the first norm is violated. An example: One shall not steal; if somebody steals, he shall be punished. If it is assumed that the first norm which forbids theft is valid only'if the second norm attaches a sanction to theft, then the first norm is certainly superfluous in an exact exposition of law. If at all existent, the first norm is contained in the second, which is the only genuine legal norm. However, the representation of law is greatly facilitated if we allow ourselves to assume also the existence of the first norm. To do so is legitimate only if one is aware of the fact that the first norm, which demands the omission of the delict, is dependent upon the second norm, which stipulates the sanction. We may express this dependence by designating the second norm as the primary norm, and the first norm as the secondary norm. The secondary norm stipulates the behavior which the legal order endeavors to bring about by stipulating the sanction. If one makes use of the auxiliary concept of secondary norms, then the opposite of the delict appears as "lawful behavior," or behavior conforming with the secondary norm, and the delict as "unlawful behavior," or behavior contradicting the secondary norm. When the delict is defined simply as unlawful behavior, law is regarded as a system of secondary norms. But this is not tenable if we have realized law's character of a coercive order which stipulates sanctions. Law is the primary norm, which stipulates the sanction, and this norm is not contradicted by the delict of the subject, which, on the contrary, is the specific condition of the sanction. Only the organ can counteract law itself, the primary norm, by not executing the sanction in spite of its conditions being fulfilled. But when speaking of the delict of the subject as unlawful, one does not have in mind the unlawful behavior of the organ.

D. Obeying and Applying the Legal Norm

If by "validity" is meant the legal "ought," then law, i.e., the primary norm, is "valid" directly only for the organ which ought to execute the sanction. It is only if one makes use of the concept of secondary norms in the presentation of law that the subject "ought" to avoid the delict and perform the legal duty, and thus, indirectly, law acquires validity for the subject, too. Only the organ can, strictly speaking, "obey" or "disobey" the legal norm, by executing or not executing the stipulated sanction. As ordinarily used, however, the expressions "obeying the norm" and "disobeying the norm" refer to the behavior of the subject. The subject can "obey" or "disobey" only the secondary norm. If we countenance the common mode of expression according to which the subject obeys or disobeys law, it commends itself to say that the organ "applies" or "does not apply" law. Only by adopting some such terminological distinction shall we be able to see clearly the difference between law's relation to the subject, the potential delinquent, and its relation to the organ. As far as by law we understand the genuine, primary legal norm, law is efficacious if it is applied by the organ — if the organ executes the sanction. And the organ has to apply law precisely in the case where the subject "disobeys" law: this is the case for which the sanction is stipulated. There is, however, a certain connection between factual obedience and the factual application of law. If a legal norm is permanently disobeyed by the subjects, it is probably no longer applied by the organs either. Therefore, though the efficacy of law is primarily its being applied by the proper organ, secondarily its efficacy means its being obeyed by the subjects.

E. Austin's Distinction between Primary and Secondary Duties

One of the main shortcomings of Austin's theory is the lack of clear insight into the secondary character of the norm, which stipulates the behavior of the subjects intended by the legal order. He says: "A law is a command which obliges a person or persons." * The characteristic function of a legal command he sees in its creating a legal duty (an obligation): "Command and duty are, therefore, correlative terms." " 'To be obliged to do or forbear,' or 'to lie under a *duty* or *obligation* to do or forbear,' is to be liable or obnoxious to a sanction, in the event of disobeying a command." † If, as Austin presumes, the legal duty is a consequence of the sanction, then the behavior which it is our legal duty to observe cannot be identical with the behavior which the legal norm commands. What is commanded can only be the sanction. The legal norm does not stipulate the behavior which forms the legal duty. Only the opposite thereof, the behavior which is designated as "wrong," "unlawful," "injury," occurs in the legal norm as condition of the sanction, which is what the legal norm stipulates. It is because the legal norm attaches a certain sanction to a certain behavior that the opposite behavior becomes a legal duty. Austin, however, presents the matter as if the legal norm, by him called "command," prescribed the behavior which forms the legal duty. Thereby, he contradicts his own definition of legal duty. In Austin's command there is no room for the sanction. And yet it is only by means of the sanction that the command is obligating. Austin's "command" is that auxiliary concept which above has been designated as "secondary norm." Having realized that the sanction is an essential element of law, he ought to have defined the

* 1 Austin, Jurisprudence 96.
† 1 Austin, Jurisprudence 89, 444.

genuine rule of law as a "command" stipulating a sanction. His failure to do so involved him in contradictions.

It seems as if Austin himself was conscious of this fact, but nevertheless he did not succeed in arriving at a clear notion. In the chapter on "Law of Things" * — long after having defined the concepts of "command" and "duty" — he feels a need for distinguishing between "primary" and "secondary" rights and duties. An analysis shows that this distinction is really concerned with a difference between primary and secondary commands. Primary duties and rights — better: commands — are those whose substance is the behavior desired by the legislator. Secondary duties and rights — better: commands — are those whose substance is formed by the sanction to be executed in case the primary commands are not obeyed. Thus, Austin designates the secondary duties (and rights) as "sanctioning," "because their proper purpose is to prevent delicts or offences." They are the sanction-stipulating norms, or, in Austin's terminology, the sanction-stipulating commands. He identifies law and primary commands (duties, rights) when he says: "If the obedience to the law were absolutely perfect, primary rights and duties are the only ones which would exist." The law which creates these primary duties consists of commands which prescribe the lawful behavior of the subjects intended by the legislator, and they are commands which do not stipulate any sanction. Austin thus directly contradicts his own definitions of "command" and "duty" quoted above: "To be obliged is to be liable to a sanction." Were there no commands stipulating sanctions, there would not be any legal duties either. But in the command, which prescribes the lawful behavior, there is no room for the sanction. That is the reason why Austin is forced to introduce secondary or sanctioning commands, disguised as "rights and duties." However, the distinction between primary and secondary (or sanctioning) rights and duties is incompatible with his original position.

If it is assumed that, by attaching a sanction to the delict, the legal norm creates a duty to avoid the delict, this duty may also be presented in the form of a separate norm forbidding the delict. As already mentioned, the formulation of such a norm undoubtedly facilitates the exposition of law. But such a procedure is justifiable only if it is kept in mind that the only genuine legal norm is the sanctioning norm. For reasons already given, this is the primary norm, and if we want to make use of a norm forbidding the delict, such a norm will have the status of a secondary norm only. Austin finally realizes this when he points out that the sanctioning law alone is indispensable. First, it is true, he says

* 2 AUSTIN, JURISPRUDENCE 760ff.

only: "in some cases, the law which confers or imposes the primary right or duty, and which defines the nature of the injury, is contained by implication in the law which gives the remedy, or which determines the punishment." * Here the law, not rights and duties, is said to be sanctioning. But in what follows he no longer restricts the statement that the primary law is contained by implication in the secondary law to "some cases." He says only: "It is perfectly clear that the law which gives the remedy, or which determines the punishment, is the only one that is absolutely necessary. For the remedy or punishment implies a foregone injury, and a foregone injury implies that a primary right or duty has been violated. And, further, the primary right or duty owes its existence as such to the injunction or prohibition of certain acts, and to the remedy or punishment to be applied in the event of disobedience. The essential part of every imperative law is the imperative part of it: *i.e.*, the injunction or prohibition of some given act, and the menace of an evil in case of non-compliance." † Commenting on Bentham, who distinguishes between "imperative" and "punitory" law, he declares: "The two branches (imperative and punitory) of the law, *correlate*. If the imperative branch of the law did not import the sanctioning, it would not be *imperative*, and *e converso*." ‡ The whole distinction between primary and secondary law only serves the purpose of facilitating the presentation of law and says nothing about its nature. "The reason for describing the primary right and duty apart; for describing the injury apart; and for describing the remedy or punishment apart, is the clearness and compactness which results from the separation." § Finally we read: "In strictness, my own terms, 'primary and secondary rights and duties,' do not represent a logical distinction. For a primary right or duty is not of itself a right or duty, without the secondary right or duty by which it is sustained; and *e converso*." ‖ If the primary duty owes its existence entirely to the secondary or sanctioning duty, it seems more correct to call the former "secondary," the latter "primary," and to speak of primary and secondary commands instead of primary and secondary duties.

* 2 Austin, Jurisprudence 767.
† 2 Austin, Jurisprudence 767.
‡ 2 Austin, Jurisprudence 767.
§ 2 Austin, Jurisprudence 767.
‖ 2 Austin, Jurisprudence 768.

V. THE LEGAL RESPONSIBILITY

A. CULPABILITY AND ABSOLUTE LIABILITY

A concept related to that of legal duty is the concept of legal responsibility (liability). That a person is legally responsible for a certain behavior or that he bears the legal responsibility therefor means that he is liable to a sanction in case of contrary behavior. Normally, that is, in case the sanction is directed against the immediate delinquent, it is his own behavior for which an individual is responsible. In this case the subject of the legal responsibility and the subject of the legal duty coincide.

In traditional theory two kinds of responsibility (or liability) are distinguished: responsibility based on fault, and absolute responsibility (liability). As pointed out elsewhere, the legal order annexes a sanction to the conduct of an individual because of the effect of this conduct on other individuals. The technique of primitive law is characterized by the fact that the relation between the conduct and its effect has no psychological qualification. Whether the acting individual has anticipated or intended the effect of his conduct is irrelevant. It is sufficient that his conduct has brought about the effect considered by the legislator to be harmful, that an external connection exists between his conduct and the effect. No relationship between the state of mind of the delinquent and the effect of his conduct is necessary. This kind of responsibility is called absolute responsibility (liability).

A refined legal technique requires a distinction between the case when the acting individual has anticipated and intended the effect of his conduct and the case when an individual's conduct has brought about a harmful effect which has not been anticipated or intended by the acting individual. An individualistic ideal of justice requires that a sanction should be attached to the conduct of an individual only if the harmful effect of the conduct has been anticipated or intended by the acting individual and if the latter has intended to harm another individual by his conduct; his intention having the character of malice. An effect which the legislator considers to be harmful may be intentionally brought about by an individual but not with the intention of harming another individual. Thus, for instance, a son may kill his incurably sick father in order to terminate the latter's suffering. The son's intention to bring about the death of his father is not malicious.

The principle of annexing a sanction to the conduct of an individual only if the effect has been anticipated and maliciously intended by the acting individual is not completely accepted in modern law. Individuals are legally held responsible not only if the objectively harmful effect has maliciously been brought about by their conduct, but also if the effect has been intended without malice, or if the effect, without being intended, has been, at least actually, anticipated by the individual and nevertheless brought about by his action. But the sanctions may be different in these different cases. They are characterized by the fact that the conduct which constitutes the delict is psychologically conditioned. A certain state of mind of the delinquent, namely that he anticipates or intends the harmful effect (so-called *mens rea*) is an element of the delict. This element is designated by the term "fault" (*dolus* or *culpa* in a wider sense of the term). When the sanction is attached to a psychologically qualified delict only, one speaks of responsibility based on fault or culpability in contradistinction to absolute responsibility (liability).

Modern law, however, annexes sanctions also to a conduct by which a harmful effect has been brought about without having been intended or actually anticipated, especially if the individual has not taken the measures by which the harmful effect normally can be avoided. For modern law obliges the individuals to take such measures in order to avoid harmful effects of their conduct on others. Failure to exercise the care prescribed by the law is called negligence; and negligence is usually considered to be another kind of "fault" (*culpa*), although less grave than the fault which consists in anticipating and intending — with or without malice — the harmful effect. There is, however, an essential difference between the two cases. Only the latter is a psychological qualification of the delict; only in this case does a certain state of mind of the delinquent become an essential condition of the sanction. Negligence is characterized by a complete lack of anticipation and intention. It is not the specific qualification of a delict, it is a delict itself, the omission of certain measures of precaution, and that means the non-exercise of the degree of care that ought to be exercised according to the law. Negligence is a delict of omission, and responsibility for negligence is rather a kind of absolute responsibility than a type of culpability.

This becomes manifest when one compares a delict of omission which has the character of negligence with a delict of omission which constitutes culpability. A child playing on the shore of a lake falls into the water and is drowned. The mother who was with the child did not exercise the necessary care because she wished to get rid of the child. She foresaw clearly the possibility of the event and intended it maliciously. This is a case of "fault" or culpability. In another case the same thing happens, but the mother omits the necessary care not because she wishes the death of the child; on the contrary, she loves the child; but in the critical moment she is reading an exciting passage of a mystery story and forgets the external circumstances. This is a case of negligence. The mother did not anticipate the accident because her consciousness was completely filled up by the imaginary events of the mystery story; and she certainly did not intend the accident. But she should have anticipated the possibility of the accident and therefore should not have read an exciting story and forgotten the external circumstance that her child was playing on the shore of a lake. Her delict consists exactly in not anticipating the possibility of the accident and in not doing what was necessary to prevent it. But this is the legal or moral, not the psychological, aspect of the situation. From a psychological point of view, there is no relation between the death of the child and the conduct of the mother. Her state of mind with respect to the death of the child can be characterized only in a negative way. If absolute responsibility consists in the fact that a sanction is annexed to a conduct without regard to whether the harmful effect of the conduct has been anticipated or intended by the acting individual, if the delinquent is subjected to a sanction even if there is no psychological relation between his state of mind and the harmful effect of his conduct: then annexing a sanction to a delict negligently committed constitutes a kind of absolute responsibility.

Nevertheless there is a difference between this type of absolute responsibility and the absolute responsibility prevailing in primitive law. The latter does not oblige the individuals to take the necessary measures by which harmful effects of their conduct on other individuals can be avoided, and primitive law does not restrict sanctions to those cases where the harmful effect has been anticipated and intended by the delinquent, or where the obligation to exercise the necessary care has not been fulfilled. According to primitive law, a sanction is attached to a conduct even if its harmful effect has been brought about in spite of the exercise of necessary care. Modern law — although not completely rejecting the principle of absolute responsibility — has the tendency to restrict it to the non-fulfillment of the obligation to take the measures by which, normally, harmful effects of human conduct can be avoided. When an individual by his conduct has brought about a harmful effect on another he can, in principle, go free from criminal or civil sanction by proving that he has not anticipated or intended the harmful effect of his conduct and that he has fulfilled the legal duty to take the measures by which, under normal circumstances, the harmful effect could have been avoided.

B. Duty and Responsibility; Individual and Collective Responsibility

The terminological distinction between legal duty and legal responsibility or liability is necessary when the sanction is not, or not only, directed against the immediate delinquent but against individuals legally connected with him, this relation being determined by the legal order. The responsibility of a corporation for a delict committed by one of its organs affords an example. Suppose that a corporation fails to fulfill a contract and to repair the damage caused thereby. On suit being brought by the other party to the contract, a civil sanction is executed against the property of the corporation, which is the common property of the members. Or — to take another example — on command from the chief of State A, a regiment of soldiers of A occupy an island belonging to State B. In consequence of this violation of its rights, B goes to war against A; this means that the army of B attempts to kill or capture as many individuals belonging to A as possible, and to destroy as much of economic value of individuals belonging to A as possible. In both examples, the sanction is executed against individuals who have not themselves committed the delict but who stand in a certain legal relation to those who have committed the delict. Those whom the sanction hits belong to the corporation or the State whose organ or organs committed the delict. In juristic language the corporation and the State are personified: they are considered to be "juristic persons" in contradistinction to "natural persons," i.e., human beings, as subjects of duties and rights. As long as the situation is described in terms of the juristic person, the subject of the legal duty and the object of the sanction are identical. It is, in our first example, the corporation that has committed the delict and against which the sanction is directed. And it is, in our second example, the State A that has violated international law and against which the sanction of international law, war, is directed. It is, in both cases, a juristic person who is obligated to avoid the delict and who is responsible for it; duty and responsibility seem to coincide. But if one dissolves the personification and describes the legal relations between the individuals involved without the concept of juristic person, then the difference between the immediate subject of the delict and the immediate object of the sanction becomes apparent. The delict has been committed by a certain individual — the organ of the corporation or the organ of the State; the sanction is directed against all the members of the corporation and against all the subjects of the State.

And then, there are certain difficulties in answering the question: who is legally obligated to avoid the delict? It cannot be the individuals against whom the sanction is executed, because they are not in a position to fulfill the obligation and by no conduct of theirs can they avert the sanction. Only the competent organs of the corporation or the State can fulfill or violate the duty. The individuals against whom the sanction is directed cannot very well be under an "obligation" that certain other individuals, the organs, shall behave in a certain way. One can be obligated only to a line of conduct of one's own. Obligated to the behavior the opposite of which is the condition of the sanction is the individual who can fulfill or violate the duty, who by his own behavior can release or avert the sanction. The obligation is incumbent upon those individuals who, as competent organs, have to fulfill the duty of the juristic person. It is their behavior that forms the contents of this duty. But the sanction is not directed against them. Those against whom the sanction is directed are responsible (liable) for the non-fulfillment of the duty. One's responsibility (liability) may include also the behavior of others. The same legal relation, that between delict and sanction, is expressed in the concepts of obligation (duty) and responsibility (liability). But the two concepts refer to two different cases of the same relation. It is — to put it in other words — the same legal norm which is represented both as obligation (duty) and as responsibility (liability). The legal norm implies a duty in relation to the potential subject of the delict; it implies a responsibility for the potential object of the sanction. It is therefore advisable to distinguish between duty and responsibility in those cases where the sanction is not, or not only, directed against the delinquent, but against other individuals having a certain legally determined relation to the delinquent. The delinquent, the perpetrator or subject of the delict, is the individual whose behavior, determined by the legal order, is the condition of a sanction directed against him or against another individual (or rather individuals) who has (or who have) a legally determined relation to him. The subject of the legal duty, legally obligated, is he who is capable of obeying or disobeying the legal norm, that is, he whose behavior in its quality of delict is the condition of the sanction. Responsible (liable) for the delict is the individual, or are those individuals, against whom the sanction is directed, even if it is not his or their behavior, but his or their legally determined relation to the delinquent, which is the condition of the sanction being directed against him or them.

In the law of civilized peoples, the individual who is obligated to certain behavior is normally also the one who is responsible (liable) for this behavior. Usually, one is responsible (liable) only for one's own behavior, for the delict committed by oneself. But there are exceptional cases in which an individual is made responsible (liable) for behavior which forms the duty of somebody else, for a delict committed by another. Responsibility (liability) as well as duty (obligation) refers to the delict, but duty always to one's own delict, responsibility, possibly, to a delict committed by another.

It is not a case of responsibility for someone else's delict when, within the field of civil law, an individual — as one says — is liable for the damage caused by somebody else. Presupposing that no sanction is directed against him who caused the damage, the delict — as previously pointed out — consists in the fact that the duty of repairing the damage has not been fulfilled. But this duty is incumbent upon him against whom the sanction is executed. He who is liable to the sanction is here capable of averting the sanction by appropriate behavior, i.e., by repairing the damage somebody else has caused. It is his own behavior, his non-repairing the damage, and not his relation to the individual who caused the damage, which is the condition of the sanction. We must in this case assume a duty to that behavior, and the subject of the duty is therefore here simultaneously the subject of the responsibility (liability). When members of a corporation are responsible for a delict committed by an organ of that corporation, those responsible are not able to avert the sanction by any behavior of theirs. It is not their behavior, it is their specific relation to the individuals who committed the delict which is the condition of the sanction being directed against them. Thus, they cannot be considered as subjects of any legal duty.

When the sanction is directed against the individuals belonging to the same legal community as the individual who, as an organ of that community, committed the delict, when the relation between the delinquent and the individuals liable (responsible) for the delict is constituted by the fact that the delinquent and those liable (responsible) for the delict belong to the same legal community, one speaks of a collective responsibility (liability). Individual responsibility (liability) occurs when the sanction is directed only against the delinquent.

When the sanction is not directed against the delinquent, that is the individual who by his own behavior has committed the delict, but against other individuals who stand in a certain legal relationship to the delinquent — as in the case of collective responsibility — the responsibility of the individual, or the individuals, against whom the sanction is directed always has the character of absolute responsibility. Responsibility for a delict committed by an individual other than the responsible one can never be based on the responsible individual's fault, that is on the fact that he has anticipated or intended the harmful effect. Collective responsibility is always absolute responsibility (liability).

It is, however, possible that according to positive law collective responsibility takes place only when the delict has intentionally been committed by the immediate delinquent; so that no responsibility takes place if the harmful effect has been brought about by the immediate perpetrator without his intention. Then, the responsibility has the character of absolute responsibility with respect to the individuals responsible for the delict, but the character of a responsibility based on fault with respect to the delinquent, that is the individual who by his own behavior has committed the delict. It is a responsibility based on the fault of the delinquent; but since the delinquent is not, or not alone, the responsible one, it is, with respect to the latter, an absolute responsibility because it is not based on the latter's fault.

C. Austin's Concept of Duty

a. No Distinction between Duty (Obligation) and Responsibility

The concept of duty developed here is the concept which Austin's analytical theory aimed at but never quite succeeded in reaching. Austin argues on the assumption that the sanction is always directed against the delinquent. Unaware of the cases where the sanction is instead directed against individuals in a certain legal relation to the delinquent, he not realize the difference between being "obligated" to certain behavior and being "liable" (responsible) therefor. His definition of legal duty, as quoted above runs: " 'To be obliged to do or forbear,' or 'to lie under a *duty* or *obligation* to do or forbear,' is to be liable or obnoxious to a sanction, in the event of disobeying a command." * But what about the case where somebody other than he who disobeys the legal norm — the command, as Austin calls it — is liable to the sanction? According to Austin's definition, the legal norm would not stipulate any duty whatsoever in such cases. In Austin's theory it is, however, of the essence of a legal norm, a legal command, to stipulate a duty. It is the command which obligates the individuals.

b. The Legal Duty no Psychological Bond

The contradictions in Austin's theory are ultimately due to his adherence to the notion of a command and his failure to reach the concept of an impersonal norm. This shortcoming has a further and much more serious consequence for his doctrine of legal duty. The concept of legal duty is, from the standpoint of analytical jurisprudence, a purely normative concept, i.e., it expresses a certain relation belonging to the contents of a legal norm. The statement that an individual is legally obligated to certain behavior is an assertion about the contents of a legal norm and

* 1 Austin, Jurisprudence 444.

not about any actual events, especially not about the mental state of the obligated individual. In stipulating duties, in attaching sanctions to the violation of duties, to the delict, the legal order may intend to make individuals fulfill their duties out of fear of the sanctions. But the question whether anybody actually fears a sanction and, out of such fear, performs his duty, is irrelevant to legal theory. If the legal obligation is expressed by saying that an individual is "bound" by the legal order, this mode of expression must not be understood in the psychological sense that his idea of the legal order motivates his behavior. It means only that in a valid legal norm certain behavior of the individual is connected with a sanction. The juristic statement that an individual is legally obligated to certain conduct holds even if the individual is wholly ignorant of the fact that he is obligated. That ignorance of law does not exempt from obligation is a principle which prevails in all legal orders and which must prevail, since, otherwise, it would be almost impossible to apply the legal order. There are, in positive law, cases where the individual obligated by a legal norm could not possibly know about the norm. Those are the cases when legal norms, in particular statutes, are given retroactive force. A retroactive legal norm attaches a sanction to behavior which occurred before the promulgation of the norm, so that the norm was not yet valid at the moment when the delict could have been committed or omitted. It should be noticed that the legal duty becomes relevant precisely in the event that the legal order does not achieve the intended psychic effect, and the individual violates his duty because the idea of the legal order was not a sufficient motive to avoid the delict.

c. Duty as Fear of Sanction

Austin's definition is therefore entirely to the point: "The party is *bound* or *obliged* to do or forbear, because he is obnoxious to the evil." But Austin goes on to say: "and because he fears the evil. To borrow the current, though not very accurate expressions, he is *compelled* by his fear of the evil to do the act which is enjoined, or is *restrained* by his fear of the evil from doing the act which is forbidden." * This contradicts the other definition: "To be obliged . . . is to be liable to a sanction in the event of disobeying a command." Whether one is "liable to a sanction" or not is in no way dependent upon whether he fears the sanction or not. If it were true that "the party is bound or obliged because . . . he fears the evil," then the definition ought to run: "to be obliged is to fear the sanction." But such a definition is incompatible with the principles of analytical jurisprudence as conceived by Austin. Law is, in Austin's opinion, a system of commands, and no analysis of the contents

* 1 AUSTIN, JURISPRUDENCE 444.

of commands can establish the psychological fact of fear. Austin explicitly says: "In order that an obligation may be effectual (or, in other words, in order that the sanction may operate as a motive to fulfilment), two conditions must concur. 1st. It is necessary that the party should know the law, by which the *Obligation* is imposed, and to which the *Sanction* is annexed. 2ndly. It is necessary that he should actually know (or, by due attention or advertence, *might* actually know), that the given act, or the given forbearance or omission, would *violate* the law, or amount to a *breach* of the obligation. Unless these conditions concur, it is impossible that the sanction should operate upon his desires." * However, Austin does not deny that it is a principle of positive law that "ignorance of the law excuseth none." He gives an excellent reason for this principle: "The only *sufficient* reason for the rule in question, seems to be this: that if ignorance of law were admitted as a ground of exemption, the Courts would be involved in questions which it were scarcely possible to solve, and which would render the administration of justice next to impracticable. If ignorance of law were admitted as a ground of exemption, ignorance of law would always be alleged by the party, and the Court, in every case, would be bound to decide the point." † Of English law he says in particular: "I am not aware of a single instance in which ignorance of law (considered *per se*) exempts or discharges the party, civilly or criminally." ‡ Austin further admits the possibility of retroactive legal norms and thus the possibility of cases where the person obligated by a norm could not know it. Austin does not maintain that such norms — so called "*ex post facto* laws" — are invalid. He only raises certain legal-political objections against them: "that the objection to laws *ex post facto*, is deducible from the general principle already explained, namely, that intention or inadvertence is necessary to constitute an injury. The law was not in existence at the time of the given act, forbearance, or omission: consequently the party did not, and could not know that he was violating a law. The sanction could not operate as a motive to obedience, inasmuch as there was nothing to obey." § He even says: "It must be observed that a judicial decision *primae impressionis*, or a judgment by which a new point of law is for the first time decided, is always an *ex post facto* law with respect to the particular case on which the point first arose, and on which the decision was given." ‖

* 1 Austin, Jurisprudence 480–481.
† 1 Austin, Jurisprudence 482.
‡ 1 Austin, Jurisprudence 485–486.
§ 1 Austin, Jurisprudence 485–486.
‖ 1 Austin, Jurisprudence 487.

d. The Psychological Concept of Duty and Analytical Jurisprudence

Austin's acute logic makes him realize the contradiction which obtains between his psychological concept of duty and an analytical exposition of law. "With respect to ignorance or error regarding the state of the law, I put a difficulty which naturally suggests itself; it is this. In order that the obligation may be effectual, or in order that the sanction may determine the party from the wrong, it is necessary, 1st, that the party should know or surmise the law which imposes the obligation and to which the sanction is annexed; and 2ndly, that he should know, or might know by due attention or advertence, that the specific act, forbearance, or omission, would conflict with the ends of the law and of the duty. Unless both these conditions concur, the sanction cannot operate as a motive, and the act, forbearance, or omission, is not imputable to unlawful intention, or to negligence, heedlessness, or rashness. But although to render the sanction efficacious, it is necessary that the party should know the law, it is assumed generally or universally, in every system of law, that ignorance or error as to the state of the law shall not exempt the party from liability. This inflexible or nearly inflexible maxim would seem to conflict with the necessary principle, which I have so often stated, respecting the constituents of injury or wrong. For ignorance of the law is often inevitable, and where the injury or wrong is the consequence of that inevitable ignorance, it is not even remotely the effect of unlawful intention or of unlawful inadvertence." * But Austin never solves the difficulty: "The solution of this difficulty is to be found in the principles of judicial evidence. The admission of ignorance of law as a specific ground of exemption, would lead to interminable investigation of insoluble questions of fact, and would, in effect, nullify the law by hindering the administration of justice. This rule, therefore, is one which it is necessary to maintain, although it occasionally wounds the important principle, that unlawful intention or inadvertence is a necessary ingredient of injury." † But that is no "solution" of this difficulty. It is only a legal-political justification of the principle *ignorantia juris nocet*. The difficulty cannot be solved within Austin's theory, since it is a consequence of his definition of law as "command."

* 1 AUSTIN, JURISPRUDENCE 489.
† 1 AUSTIN, JURISPRUDENCE 489.

VI. THE LEGAL RIGHT

A. Right and Duty

The concept of duty is usually contrasted with the concept of right. The term "right" carries the most different meanings. Here we are concerned only with what is understood by "a legal right." This concept has to be defined from the standpoint of a pure theory of law.

Colloquial language seems to suggest a distinction between two kinds of "rights." One says: "I have a right to do or to omit doing such and such." One also says: "I have a right to demand that somebody else shall do or refrain from doing such and such." Linguistic usage thus makes a distinction between a right concerning one's own behavior and a right to somebody else's behavior. In colloquial language we make still another distinction. We say not only that one has a right to a certain behavior — to his own behavior or to somebody else's behavior; we say also that one has a right to a certain thing. Property is the typical example of a right to a certain thing. That I own a certain thing means that I have a right to this thing. Hence a distinction is made between *jus in rem*, that is a right to a thing, and *jus in personam*, that is a right to demand that somebody else shall behave in a certain way, the right to somebody else's behavior; for instance, the creditor has a right to demand that the debtor shall pay a certain sum of money. But the right to a thing (*jus in rem*) seems to be only a special case of the right concerning one's own behavior. That I own a thing means that I have the right to use or to destroy it, in short that I may dispose of it at will.

If the right is a legal right, it is necessarily a right to somebody else's behavior, to behavior to which the other is legally obligated. A legal right presupposes somebody else's legal duty. This is self-evident in case we speak of a right to somebody else's behavior. The creditor has a legal right to demand that the debtor shall pay a certain sum of money, if the debtor is legally obligated, has the legal duty to pay that sum of money. But we can also speak of a legal right concerning one's own behavior only if a corresponding duty is incumbent upon somebody else. The statement: I have the legal right to use a road running over someone else's estate, means: the owner of this estate is legally obligated not to prevent me from using this road. The statement that I have a right to behave in a certain way may have — it is true — only a negative meaning, namely, that I am not obliged to behave otherwise. By saying: I have the right to do something, I possibly intend to say only: I am not obligated to forbear from doing it; and by saying: I have the right to forbear from doing something, I possibly intend to say only: I am not obligated to do it. In this sense the statement: I have a right, has only the negative meaning: I am — with respect to certain behavior — free, there is no norm obligating me to this or an opposite behavior.

But in order to be legally free, with respect to certain behavior, another individual or all other individuals must be obligated to a corresponding line of conduct. I am not legally free to do what I wish to do if the others are not legally obligated to let me do what I wish to. My legal freedom is always another's legal subjection, my legal right is always another's legal duty. I have a legal right to do something, or to forbear from doing something, only because and insofar as another has the legal duty not to hinder me from doing or not doing it. If I have a right to use a road running over somebody else's property, this legally implies that the owner of that property and, for that reason, everybody else, is obligated not to prevent me from using the road. If they prevent me, they violate a duty imposed upon them by the legal order, and expose themselves to a sanction. That I own a thing means, from a legal point of view, that everybody else is obligated not to interfere with my disposal of that thing. If somebody interferes, he commits a delict which makes him liable to a sanction. And that I have a legal right to stay in my apartment, again means that if somebody should try to force me out of it, he would be guilty of a delict. There is no legal right for someone without a legal duty for someone else. The contents of a right is ultimately the fulfillment of someone else's duty.

On the other hand, the obligation of an individual to a certain line of conduct is always an obligation concerning behavior of this individual toward another individual. One is obliged to pay back a loan to one's creditor; one is obliged not to kill someone else; and so on. To the behavior a, to which an individual A is obliged, toward another individual B, there corresponds a behavior b of B, in the sense that B has a right to b, just because B has a right to a from A. To the paying back of a loan by the debtor corresponds the receiving back of the sum to be returned by the creditor. The debtor cannot pay back the loan to the creditor if the creditor refuses to receive back the sum to be returned. A is obliged to pay back a loan to B (A is obliged concerning behavior of his own toward B), B has the right to receive back this loan from A (B has a right concerning behavior of his own), because B has a right that A shall pay back the loan to him (because B has a right to someone else's behavior). That an individual "exercises," "makes use of," his "right," "enjoys" his right (*Rechts-Genuss*), means that he manifests the behavior which corresponds to the behavior to which some other individual is obliged. An individual is free to make use of his right or not.

B. Permission

The right to behave in a certain way is often interpreted as a permission. That I have a right to do or to omit doing something, is also expressed by saying that the law allows me to do or omit doing it. Accordingly, a distinction is drawn between legal norms which command or forbid, on the one hand, and legal norms which permit, on the other: "Law is imperative or permissive." But the distinction does not hold. The legal order gives somebody a permission, confers on somebody a right, only by imposing a duty upon somebody else. And law imposes a duty by stipulating a sanction. Therefore, if the stipulation of a sanction is called "imperative," it is incorrect to say that law is "imperative or permissive." Law is imperative for the one, and thereby permissive for the other. In that the legal norm obligates one individual to a certain behavior toward another individual, it guarantees the latter individual the behavior corresponding to the former's behavior. That is the fact which the rather unfortunate distinction between "imperative" and "permissive" law is intended to describe.

C. The Legal Right in a Narrow Sense

a. Right more than the Correlative of a Duty

If the legal order determines a course of conduct to which a certain individual is obligated, it determines at the same time a corresponding behavior of another individual to which — as it is usually termed — this other individual has a right. In this sense, to every obligation there corresponds a right. A "right" in this sense is nothing but the correlative of a duty. The right of one individual to conduct himself in a certain way is the duty of another individual to conduct himself in a certain way toward the former. Austin speaks of a "relative duty." He says: "The term 'right' and the term *relative* duty' are correlating expressions. They signify the same notions, considered from different aspects." * Austin's theory seems to recognize no concept of right different from that of duty. Such a concept, however, exists, and plays an important, even the decisive, part in jurisprudence. For when one speaks of the legal right of an individual one has in mind a narrower concept than that which coincides with the duty of another individual. Every obligation for one person does not entail a legal right for somebody else, the term taken in its narrower technical sense. What now is the criterion of the existence of a legal right in this narrower sense? Under what conditions

* 1 Austin, Jurisprudence 395.

does somebody have such a right? The contents of the legal norm itself must provide the answer to this question as well as to the earlier question, under what conditions somebody has a legal duty. The legal right is, like the legal duty, the legal norm in relation to a certain individual, designated by the norm itself. The fact that the legal norm obligates somebody to behave in a certain way toward somebody else does not in itself imply that the latter has a right to this behavior of the former, a legal right to demand that the former fulfill his obligation. The legal norm must have a quite specific content in order to constitute a legal right in the technical sense. The legal duty has been defined as the legal norm in its relation to the individual whose behavior represents the delict. This is the individual against whom the sanction is directed or the individual who has a definite relation to the former individual. Now, we must define the legal right in an analogous way.

b. Law and Right

The usual definition of a legal right does not satisfy the methodical demands of pure theory of law or analytical jurisprudence. It more or less consciously presupposes that law and right are two different phenomena which are not to be subsumed under a common general term. The English language countenances this dualism by the very fact that it has two entirely different words: "law" and "right," whereas the German and French languages have only one corresponding word, "Recht" and "droit," and law is distinguished from right by using the phrases "objektives Recht" and "subjektives Recht," "droit objectif" and "droit subjectif." Nevertheless, a dualistic view prevails also in German and French theory. "Objektives Recht," "droit objectif," and "subjektives Recht," "droit subjectif," are regarded as entities of a completely different nature. "Objektives Recht," "droit objectif," ("law") alone is recognized as rule or norm, while "subjektives Recht," "droit subjectif," ("right") is defined as "interest" or "will." The legal right, is not, it is true, interpreted as an unqualified interest or will, but as an interest protected by the legal order, or a will recognized and made effective by the legal order. In this way, right and law are brought in a certain relation to one another. But the dualism is still maintained, inasmuch as the legal right is considered as logically and temporally prior to law. In the beginning, there were rights only — in particular the prototype of all rights, the right of property (acquired by occupation) — and only at a later stage law as the order of the State was superinduced with the purpose of sanctioning and protecting rights which, independently from this order, had come into existence. This idea is most clearly developed in the theory of the Historic School, which has decisively influenced not only the legal positivism of the last century, but also the modern jurisprudence of the English-speaking countries. In Dernburg, for instance, we read: "Rights existed historically long before the State with a deliberate legal order had appeared. They had their basis in the personality of the individual and in the respect which he was able to obtain and to enforce. The concept of a legal order could be won from the perception of existing rights only by a gradual process of abstraction. It is therefore both historically and logically incorrect to assume that rights are nothing but emanations from law. The legal order guarantees and fashions legal rights but does not create them." *

c. The Right as Recognized Will or Protected Interest

It is easily seen that this theory of the priority of rights is untenable from a logical point of view as well as from a psychological one. The legal character of a phenomenon is not perceptible by the senses. The fact that an individual has a right or has no right to possess a thing cannot be seen or heard or touched. The statement that an individual has or has no right to possess a thing is a value-judgment which is logically as well as psychologically possible only if the individual who makes this statement presupposes the existence, and that means the validity, of a general norm regarding possession. This norm is neither logically nor psychologically the result of an abstraction based on a sum of similar perceptions of rights as, e.g., the general concept of tree is the result of an abstraction based on a sum of similar perceptions; for rights are not perceptible by the senses, as are trees. How the idea of a general rule comes into existence is a question which we do not have to answer here. We need only establish that, without presupposing a general norm regulating human behavior, no statement about the existence or non-existence of rights is possible. If there is a question of legal right, a legal rule must be presupposed. There can be no legal rights before there is law. The definition of a legal right as an interest protected by law, or a will recognized by law, vaguely expresses an insight into this

---

* Heinrich Dernburg, System des römischen Rechts (Der Pandekten achte, umgearbeitete Auflage) Erster Teil (1911) 65. Blackstone, Commentaries, Book I, § 167: "For the principal aim of society is to protect individuals in the enjoyment of those absolute rights, which were vested in them by the immutable laws of nature; but which could not be preserved in peace without that mutual assistance and intercourse, which is gained by the institution of friendly and social communities. Hence it follows, that the first and primary end of human laws is to maintain and regulate these *absolute* rights of individuals. Such rights as are social and *relative* result from, and are posterior to, the formation of states and societies. . . ." The so-called absolute rights are previous to the formation of the State.

fact. As long as a right has not been "guaranteed" by the legal order —
to use Dernburg's phrase — it is not yet a legal right. It is made into a
legal right first by the guarantee from the legal order. This means that
law precedes, or is concomitant with, rights.

Though logically untenable, the theory of the priority of rights is of
the utmost political significance. Its purpose is obviously to influence
the formation of law, rather than to analyze the nature of positive law.
If the legal order cannot create but merely guarantee rights, it cannot
abolish existing rights either. It is then legally impossible to abolish the
institution of private property, nay, legislation is then incapable of
depriving any particular individual of any particular proprietary right
of his. All these consequences of the doctrine of the priority of rights
are in contradiction to legal reality. The doctrine of the priority of
rights is not a scientific description of positive law but a political
ideology.

To define a legal right as an interest protected by law or a will recognized by law is likewise incorrect. Let us first critically analyze the
interest theory in which the basic mistake common to both theories is
perhaps most apparent. That somebody is interested in a certain course
of behavior by somebody else means that he desires this behavior because he thinks it useful to himself. The word "interest" signifies a certain mental attitude. Now, it is obviously not true that one has a legal
right to demand a certain course of behavior from somebody else only
so long as one has an actual interest in this behavior. Even if it is indifferent to you whether your debtor pays back a loan to you or if, for
some reason, you should wish him not to pay, you still have the legal right
to get your money back. When the legislator obligates one individual to
behave in a certain way towards another individual, so as to safeguard
an interest of the latter, this interest finds its specific expression in the
behavior by which the latter uses or exercises his right. But one may at
will use or not use one's own rights. One has a right even if one does not
use it. It is even possible to have a legal right without knowing it. In such
a case, there cannot exist any interest. On the other hand, one may be
intensely interested in another individual's fulfilling his legal duty, without having a legal right (in the narrower, technical sense of the term)
against the latter. Thus, one may have a right to a certain behavior on
the part of another individual without being interested in this behavior,
and one may also have the interest without having the right.

Undoubtedly, the legislator gives the creditor a right to get back his
money and the proprietor a right to dispose of his property, just because
he assumes that a creditor, as a rule, is interested in getting back his
money and that, as a rule, it is the interest of the proprietor that others

shall not interfere with his disposal of his property. The legislator assumes that people have certain interests under certain conditions, and he intends to protect some of these interests. But a right exists even in those cases where — contrary to the legislator's assumption — no actual interest exists. The right, therefore, must consist, not in the presumed interest, but in the legal protection. The protection the legislator gives a type of interest consists in the establishment of legal rules of a certain import. The right of the creditor, therefore, is the legal norm by which the debtor is obligated to return the loan; the right of the owner is the legal norm by which other individuals are obligated not to interfere with the former's disposition of his property. The legal right is, in short, the law.

d. The Right as Legal Possibility to Put in Motion the Sanction

As already mentioned, not every legal norm which obligates one individual to behave in a certain way towards another individual confers on the latter a legal right against the former. By obligating the individual not to kill another individual, criminal law does not confer on everyone who is protected by this norm a legal right not to be killed, a legal right in the technical sense in which the creditor has a right to get back his money from the debtor, and the owner has a right to the exclusive use of his property. Why is it not only "right" that the debtor pay back the money to the creditor, why is it "the right of the creditor," my right as creditor, that the debtor shall pay back the money? "Right" in its original sense is the same as "law"; thus for instance, in the statement "Right is might." What is the reason for saying that the law — in a given situation — is my law, that is: my right? What is the specific relation in which the creditor and the proprietor stand to the legal norms protecting their interests? What is the relation by virtue of which these norms are "their" law, and that means, "right"? What is the reason for considering the objective law, the system of norms regulating human behavior, or one norm of this system — under certain circumstances — as the right of one subject, a subjective law?

The doctrine that a legal right is a will recognized by the law, or a power granted by law, is closer to the solution of our problem than the doctrine that a right is an interest protected by law. The power which, according to this view, is the essence of an individual's right consists in the fact that the legal order attaches to the expression of the individual's will that effect at which the will is directed. The legal order really gives men such a "power," for instance the power to regulate their economic relations by legal transactions, especially by contracts. A contract is an agreement between two or more individuals concerning a certain mutual course of conduct. "Agreement" means that the wills which the contracting parties express with respect to their mutual behavior agree. A contract has the legal effect that the contracting parties are obligated to behave in accordance with the contract. Every contracting party has the "right" that the other shall behave according to the contract; his right is, however, not his will, the will which he expressed by making the contract. It is not his will or its expression, it is the agreement, the agreeing expression of the wills of all the contracting parties which — according to the legal order — creates the obligations of the contracting parties. The single individual does not have the legal power to obligate — by the expression of his will — the other individual. If the "right" which one of the contracting parties has against the other is a "will," it must be another will than the will expressed in the act by which the contract was made.

A contracting party has a right against the other contracting party only if the latter has a legal duty to behave in a certain way toward the former; and the latter has a legal duty to behave in a certain way toward the former only if the legal order provides a sanction in case of contrary behavior. But this does not suffice to constitute a legal right of the other party. One contracting party has a legal right against the other party because the legal order makes the execution of the sanction dependent, not only upon the fact that a contract has been made and that one party has failed to fulfill it, but also upon the other party's expressing a will that the sanction be executed against the delinquent. A party expresses such a will by bringing a suit against the other party before a court. In so doing the plaintiff puts in motion the coercive machinery of law. It is only by such a suit that the procedure may be initiated by which the delict, i.e., the breach of contract, is ascertained and the sanction issued by the court. This is part of the specific technique of civil law. The sanction is made dependent upon, among other conditions, the fact that one party has brought a suit, which means that one party has declared his will that the procedure mentioned be initiated. There is open to the party the legal possibility of bringing about the application of the pertinent legal norm providing the sanction. In this sense, therefore, this norm is "his" law, and that means, his "right." Only if an individual stands in such a relation to the legal norm, only if the application of the legal norm, the execution of the sanction, depends upon the expression of the will of an individual directed towards this aim, only if the law is at the disposal of an individual, can it be considered to be "his" law, a subjective law, and that means, a "right." Only then is the subjectivization of law which is implied in the concept of right, the presentation of an objective legal norm as a subjective right of an individual, justified.

Only if defined in this way does the concept of legal "right" not coincide with that of legal duty, is the right of A to certain behavior by B not identical with the duty of B to behave in this way towards A. In case there is open to an individual the legal possibility of "enforcing" by his suit the legal duty of another individual, the legal situation is not completely described by presenting only the duty of B to behave in a certain way towards A. If the concept of legal right is to be a concept different from that of legal duty, the former must be restricted to this case.

A right is, thus, a legal norm in its relation to the individual who, in order that the sanction shall be executed, must express a will to that effect. The subject of a right is the individual whose manifestation of will directed to the sanction, i.e., whose suit is a condition of the sanction. If we denote the individual on whom the legal order confers the possibility of bringing a suit, a potential plaintiff, then it is always a potential plaintiff who is the subject of a right. The legal order usually confers that possibility on the individual in whom the legislator presumes a certain interest in the sanction. But if the legal order confers that possibility upon an individual, this individual has a right even if, in a concrete case, he should lack such an interest and thus also a "will" that the sanction be executed. A right is no more the interest or the will of the individual to whom it belongs than a duty is the fear of the sanction or the compulsion in the mind of the obligated individual. The legal right is, like the legal duty, the legal norm in its relation to an individual designated by the norm, viz., the potential plaintiff.

e. Right and Representation

The statement that the subject of the right is the potential plaintiff does not seem to hold in all cases. Through a certain legal transaction an individual may bring it about that certain declarations by another individual, his "agent," have the same effect as similar declarations by himself, the principal. If somebody avails himself of this legal institute, so-called "consensual representation," he may also bring a suit through the intervention of his agent. There are even certain individuals who, according to modern law, must have a representative — for instance minors and mentally deficient individuals. In case of such a "nonconsensual representation" the representative, called "guardian," is instituted not by a legal transaction between him and the individual he represents, his "ward," but either directly by the legal order without an act of appointment, as e.g., in the case of the father who is the legal representative of his child, or by an act of a public authority, especially a court, as e.g., the guardian of an insane individual. Also, the guardian may bring a suit on behalf of his ward in the same way as the agent may on behalf of his principal. That the agent or guardian expresses a will "on behalf of" the principal or ward means that his declaration of will has the same legal effect as if it had been made by the principal or ward — provided, in the latter case, that the ward had been of mature age or in mental health. This complicated state of affairs is described in a very simplified way by the fictitious formula that the declarations of will by the agent or guardian are to be considered as declarations by the principal or ward. If it is the right of the principal or ward that the agent or guardian pursues by bringing a suit, then the subject of the right is not the potential plaintiff, but an individual who stands in a specific, legally determined relation to the potential plaintiff, in the relationship of consensual or non-consensual representation. The subject of the legal right is therefore the potential plaintiff or the individual legally represented by the former.

D. The Right as a Specific Legal Technique

To make the execution of the sanction dependent upon a suit by a certain individual (the plaintiff), to grant "rights" in the technical sense of the term, is — as pointed out — typical of the technique of civil law. The actual application of the legal norm is then in each particular case dependent upon whether the subject of the right (or his representative) is actually sufficiently interested in the application of the legal norm to initiate by his "suit" the procedure leading to the execution of the sanction. In making the application of the legal norm dependent upon the declaration of will of a definite individual, the legislator has considered the interest of this individual as decisive. Frequently, however, the application of a legal norm is of interest to all the other or to most other members of the legal community, and not only to one particular individual. That the sanction provided by the legal order is executed against a debtor who fails to fulfill his obligations is of interest to everybody who may ever become a creditor, nay, to everybody who wants the legal order to be maintained. It is — as one usually says — in the interest of the legal community that all the norms of the legal order be obeyed and applied. In a legal order based on the principles of private capitalism, the technique of civil law is determined by the fact that the legislator disregards the collective interest in the application of the norms and attributes real importance only to the interest of particular individuals. This is why the process leading up to the execution of the sanction is initiated and carried out only in consequence of a declaration of will to that effect by a particular individual, the plaintiff.

In this respect, criminal law presents an opposite technique. A criminal process can not, as a rule, be initiated by the person whose interests were most directly injured by the delict. It is in general some public authority, an organ of the community, who is competent to bring the necessary action and who is usually also obligated to do so. Since the criminal sanction is not dependent upon a suit by any private individual, no private individual has a "right" not to be robbed or killed — in general, not to be made the victim of a criminal delict. But since the execution of the sanction is dependent upon an action by a competent organ of the State, one may speak of a "right" of the State that the members of the community shall refrain from crimes. In this field, where especially vital interests of the community have to be protected, the legislator puts the collective interest above the private interest. Nevertheless, the criminal process has the same form, at least the same outside appearance, as the civil process; it shows a dispute between two parties: the criminal process a dispute between the legal community, the State represented by a public organ, and a private individual, the accused; the civil process a dispute between two private individuals, the plaintiff and the defendant.

The technique of modern law, civil and criminal, according to which the process leading to the sanction can be initiated only upon a suit by a designated individual, the legal technique according to which the procedure of the law-applying organs, the courts, has the character of a dispute between two parties, is not the only conceivable technique. The sanction could well be applied by a public organ without any previous action by another public organ, as in criminal law, or by the private party, as is the case in civil law. If the legal order were of this nature, it would still create a legal duty to refrain from the delict but it would no longer give anybody a legal right that the duty be performed. No legal right is conceivable without a corresponding duty, but there could well exist a legal duty without any corresponding legal right (in this narrower sense of the word).

E. Absolute and Relative Rights

Inasmuch as the right of one individual is possible only in relation to the duty of another, all rights are relative rights. All duties are relative, however, only insofar as one is obligated to behave in a certain way relative to another individual, who may, but need not necessarily be, the subject of a corresponding right (in the narrower, technical sense of the term).

The terms "absolute" and "relative" are, however, understood in another sense when one distinguishes between absolute and relative duties and rights. Relative duties are such as one has relative to a designated individual, whereas absolute duties are such as one has relative to an undetermined number of individuals or to all other individuals. Not to kill, not to steal, not to interfere with other individuals' disposition of their property, are absolute duties. The duty of a debtor to return a loan to his creditor is a relative duty. A relative right in this narrower sense is a right to which corresponds a duty of some designated individual only, whereas an absolute right entails duties for an undetermined number of individuals. A typical relative right is the creditor's right against the debtor; it is only from the debtor that he has a right to demand the loan back. Property is a typical absolute right: the proprietor has a right to demand from everybody to be left in undisturbed possession of his property. To an absolute right there corresponds an absolute duty, to a relative right a relative duty. The distinction between *jus in personam* and *jus in rem* goes back to the distinction between relative and absolute rights. But the term *jus in rem* is misleading. The *jus in rem* is, strictly speaking, a *jus in personam*, a right against persons and not a right over things, as the term would suggest. The well-known definition of property as an individual's exclusive dominion over a thing ignores the essential fact that everybody but the owner is excluded from the disposition of the object. The right of property is an individual's right against all other individuals that they shall behave in a certain way relative to the former, namely, that all the other individuals shall refrain from any interference with the former's disposition of a certain thing. All the individuals except the proprietor are legally excluded from any disposition of the object of the property; and they are obliged to refrain from any interference with the disposition of the thing relative to any possible owner of it. Like the right, the corresponding duty, too, is directed against an undetermined number of individuals. The right of A as the proprietor of the estate *a* to use a road, running across the estate *b* of B, has the character of a servitude, a *jus in rem*, provided that not only B but everybody and especially any possible proprietor of the estate *b* is legally obligated not to prevent A or any proprietor of the estate *a* from using the road. Any proprietor of the estate *a* has the right, any proprietor of the estate *b* has the corresponding duty. Estate *a* is called the "dominant," *b* the "servient" estate, as if the right were attached or rooted like a tree in the one, the duty in the other estate. That is a figurative and very demonstrative but also very misleading description of the legal situation. The right, or the duty, is not a thing that may be linked to another thing. Right and duty are specific relations of one individual to other individuals. A *jus in rem* is not a right over a thing but a right against an undetermined number of individuals that they shall behave in a certain way with respect to a certain object; it is an absolute right to which corresponds an absolute duty.

F. The Right as Participation in the Creation of Law

The legal order — as pointed out — confers a "right" upon an individual in that it gives him, or his representative, the possibility of releasing the process which ultimately leads to the execution of the sanction. The court decision — which is the typical act determining the sanction in a concrete case — creates an individual norm which, conditionally or unconditionally, stipulates the sanction. The judicial decision of a criminal court, for instance, orders that a certain individual who — according to the statement of the court — has committed theft shall be imprisoned for two years. This individual norm is to be executed by other public organs.

The decision of a civil court orders that a certain individual, the defendant, who — according to the statement of the court — has not paid in due time the rent for his home, shall pay a certain sum of money to his landlord, the plaintiff, within ten days; and that — if the sum of money should not be paid within this time — a civil execution shall be directed against the defendant. This is an individual norm; but whereas the individual norm, the ordering of the sanction in this case, has a conditional character — if the defendant does not pay within ten days a civil execution shall be directed against him — the ordering of the sanction, the individual norm, in the criminal case is unconditional: the delinquent shall be imprisoned. The creation of the individual norm by the decision of the civil court is the immediate purpose of the judicial procedure which is initiated by the plaintiff's suit. From this dynamic point of view, the plaintiff thus plays an essential part in the creation of the individual norm, which the sentence of the court represents. To have a right is to have the legal capacity of participating in the creation of an individual norm, of that individual norm by which a sanction is ordered against the individual who — according to the statement of the court — has committed the delict, has violated his duty. If a legal right is a phenomenon of law, then this individual norm must also have the character of law. Law cannot consist only of general norms or rules.

G. Civil and Political Rights

If, from a dynamic point of view, the nature of a right is the capacity of participating in the creation of law, then the difference between the rights of "private law," the so-called "private rights," and the rights of public law, the so-called "political rights," cannot be as fundamental as is usually assumed. By political rights we understand the possibilities open to the citizen of taking part in the government, in the formation of the "will" of the State. Freed from metaphor, this means that the citizen may participate in the creation of the legal order. One thereby has in mind especially the creation of general norms, or "legislation," in the most general sense of the term. Participation in legislation by the individuals subjected to the legal order is characteristic of democracy, distinguishing it from autocracy where the subjects are excluded from legislation, have no political rights. In a democracy, the legislative power may be exercised either directly by the people in primary assembly, or by an elected parliament alone, or in coöperation with an elected chief of State. Democracy may be either a direct or an indirect (representative) democracy. In a direct democracy the decisive political right is the right of the citizen to participate in the deliberations and decisions of the popular assembly. In an indirect democracy, the formation of the will of the State, as far as it is a creation of general norms, takes place in two stages: first, the election of parliament and the chief of State, and then the creation of the general norm, the statute; either by the parliament alone, or in collaboration with the chief of State. Correspondingly, the decisive political right in an indirect (representative) democracy is the right of voting, i.e., the citizen's right to participate in the election of the parliament, the chief of State, and other law-creating (and law-applying) organs.

It might seem as if the concept of legal right, which we have previously reached by a consideration of civil law, were entirely different from the concept of political right. The problem of political rights will be given a more complete treatment in the theory of the State and public law. Here, I shall try to show only how it is possible to subsume the so-called "political" right together with the "private" right under the same general term of "right"; what the plaintiff has in common with the voter, what there is in common between bringing an action and giving one's vote.

If the political right is "right" in the same sense as the private right, there must be a duty corresponding to the political right. What is the duty corresponding to the right of voting? It is the duty of those public organs that are entrusted with the election to accept the ballot of the voter and to treat it according to the prescripts of law, in particular to declare that individual elected who has received the prescribed number of votes. The right of a subject to vote is the right to have his vote received and counted, according to the laws concerned, by the proper election officers. To the citizen's right of vote corresponds the duty of the election officers. This duty is guaranteed by certain sanctions; and in the event that the duty should be violated, the voter may exercise an influence upon the application of these sanctions analogous to the influence which may be exercised by the subject of a private right upon the application of the sanction directed against the individual responsible for the violation of the corresponding duty. In various legal orders there are special organs, for instance, electoral courts, whose task it is to protect the interest which the voter has in the public organ's fulfilling its corresponding duty. Where the voter may appeal to such an electoral court in case his right has been violated, the right of voting is a legal right in exactly the same technical sense as is a private right.

Even if the function of the voter is not guaranteed in this way, namely, by conferring upon the voter such a "right" in the technical sense, his function has an essential element in common with the exercise of a private right. It is the participation in the law-creating process. The difference consists in the fact that the function called "voting" is an indirect participation in the law-creating process. The voter takes part only in the creation of an organ — parliament, chief of State — whose function it is to create the will of the State, legal norms; and the legal norms which this organ has to create are general norms, statutes. The subject of a private right participates directly in the creation of a legal norm, and this legal norm — the judicial decision — is an individual norm. The exercise of a private right, too, signifies participation by the subject in the creation of the "will of the State," for the will of the State manifests itself also in the judicial decision; the court, too, is an organ of the State.

Elected organs, such as a parliament and a chief of State, are, by and large, organs for the creation of general norms. However, organs for the creation of individual norms may also sometimes be elected — for example, judges elected by popular vote. In such a case, the difference between the function called the political right of voting and a private right is reduced to the fact that the right of voting means only an indirect participation in the creation of legal norms.

From the point of view of the function within the whole law-creating process, there is no essential difference between a private and a political right. Both allow their holder to take part in the creation of the legal order, "the will of the State." A private right is also ultimately a political right. The political character of private rights becomes still more obvious as soon as one realizes that the conferring of private rights upon individuals is the specific legal technique of civil law, and that civil law is the specific legal technique of private capitalism, which is at the same time a political system.

If the legal right is seen as a particular function within the law-creating process, then the dualism of law and right vanishes. Then, too, the legal priority of duty over right becomes clear. Whereas the legal obligation is the essential function of every legal norm within every legal order, the legal right is merely a specific element of particular legal systems — the private right the institution of a capitalistic, the political right the institution of a democratic legal order.

VII. COMPETENCE (LEGAL CAPACITY)

A legal norm may determine human behavior not only as content of a duty or a right, but also in other ways. An example is the sanction which by a legal norm is made the consequence of certain conditions. To order or execute the sanction is obviously not a "right" of the law-applying organ; the organ may, however, be obligated to order or execute the sanction; but this is not necessarily so. It is obligated only if another legal norm stipulates this obligation by providing for a sanction against the organ which does not order or execute the sanction stipulated by the first norm. Human behavior which is qualified neither as a duty nor as a right occurs also among the conditions of a sanction. Let us consider as an example the legal norm which obligates a debtor to return a loan to his creditor. Schematically, this norm may be formulated thus: If two individuals make a loan contract, if the debtor does not return the loan in due time, and if the creditor brings a suit against the debtor, then the court has to order a certain sanction against the debtor. The making of the contract is an act which does not form the content either of a duty or a right of the two parties. They are not legally obliged, nor have they a legal right, to make the contract; they get legal rights and duties through the contract, after the contract is made. But they are legally capable of making a contract. Nor does there exist either a duty or a right to commit a delict. But there is a legal capacity to commit delicts. The organ has no legal right to order the sanction and it may not even be obliged to do so. But it is legally capable of ordering the sanction. When a norm qualifies the act of a certain individual as a legal condition or a legal consequence, this means that only that individual is "capable" of performing or omitting to perform that act; only he is "competent" (the term used in its broadest sense). Only if this capable or competent individual performs or omits performing the act does that act or omission occur which according to the norm is a legal condition or a legal consequence.

It has already been pointed out that human behavior as regulated by a legal norm consists of two elements: a material and a personal one, the thing which has to be done or omitted, and the individual who has to do or omit it. In determining human behavior as a legal condition or legal consequence, the legal norm determines both these elements. The relation constituted by the legal norm between the personal and the material element is what in German and French terminology is denoted by "competence," the term taken in its most general sense. That an individual is "competent" of a certain action means that the action is accorded the quality of legal condition or legal consequence only if performed by that individual. Even a delict presupposes the "competence," in this most general sense, of the delinquent. Not every being can commit a delict. In the legal orders of civilized peoples, only human beings are capable of committing delicts. It is otherwise in primitive law, where animals, plants, and even inanimate objects are considered capable of committing delicts. And not even all human beings are punishable according to modern civilized law; children and lunatics are as a rule not liable to any sanctions and they are thus incapable of committing delicts.

The term "competence" is ordinarily taken in a narrower sense, it is true. One usually speaks only of a competence to actions, not of a competence of omissions. Further, the term is used to designate only the legal capacity of undertaking actions, other than delicts, actions by which legal norms are created. The parliament is said to be "competent" to enact a statute. But this mode of expression really implies nothing but the fact that it is a certain behavior of the individuals forming the parliament which the legal order determines as legislative function; and that therefore these individuals are capable of making laws. The judge is said to be competent to make a decision. This means that it is a certain behavior of a certain individual which the legal order determines as judicial function, and that, therefore, this individual is capable of making decisions. The concept of jurisdiction as used in English legal terminology is nothing but the general concept of competence as applied to a special case. Jurisdiction properly so called is the competence of courts. However, administrative authorities also have their "jurisdiction," nay, any organ of the State has its "jurisdiction," the capacity of performing an act, which the legal order determines as an act of just that and no other organ. And as soon as this fact has been realized, one must recognize a certain "jurisdiction" in any human individual, viz., his capacity to perform or omit an act which the legal order has determined as an act or omission of that individual. This is the essence of the concept of "competence," and that concept is used when it is said that only certain individuals are "capable" of committing delicts.

VIII. IMPUTATION (IMPUTABILITY)

This capacity of committing delicts is often expressed by the concept of imputation (German: *Zurechnung*). Sanctions, especially criminal ones, are, as already mentioned, attached only to the behavior of individuals having certain qualities, a certain minimum age and a certain mental capacity. Now it is usually said that a delict is not "imputable" to a child or a lunatic. In German, a child or lunatic is characterized as *unzurechnungsfähig* (irresponsible). The statement that a delict is not imputable to a child or a lunatic is, however, misleading. Their behavior does not constitute any delict at all. It would have been a delict only if they had reached the requisite age or been mentally sound. Whether a certain type of action, e.g., murder, is or is not a delict depends upon whether the acting individual has certain qualities determined by the legal order as general conditions of the sanction. But the action is, of course, under all circumstances "his" action, and that means that the action is imputed to him, even if this action is — as in this case — no delict. A lunatic can commit murder, that is to say, he can by his action intentionally cause another man's death. There is no question whether the murder is his action; this, at least, is no juristic question. The only question is whether this murder is a delict. And the murder is no delict because the legal order does not attach any sanction to the murder committed by a lunatic. It is therefore not the murder which is not "imputable," i.e., which cannot be imputed to the lunatic, it is the sanction. That an individual is *unzurechnungsfähig*, irresponsible, means that no sanction can be directed against him because he does not fulfill certain personal requirements, conditions for a sanction. When an individual's irresponsibility is identified with the fact that he has not reached the requisite age and is not in mental health and so on — in short, that he does not fulfill the personal conditions under which the legal order makes people liable to sanctions — then one lets the word "responsibility" denote what is only the prerequisite for responsibility. An individual's legal irresponsibility is simply his non-liability to sanctions. The English term "irresponsible" is equivalent to the German *unzurechnungsfähig*, which literally means incapable of being a subject to whom something can be imputed. The word "imputation" conveys, it is true, the idea that some event or other is attributed to or brought into a connection with a certain individual. But the imputation which is in question here is not the relation between an individual and an action of his, but the relation between the legal sanction and the action, and thus indirectly the acting individual himself. What cannot be brought into connection with a legally irresponsible individual is the sanction and not the fact which would have been a delict if committed by somebody else. The concept of imputation refers to the specific relation between delict and sanction.

IX. THE LEGAL PERSON

A. Substance and Quality

The concept of a legal person is another general concept used in the presentation of positive law and closely related to the concepts of legal duty and legal right. The concept of the legal person — who, by definition, is the subject of legal duties and legal rights — answers the need of imagining a bearer of the rights and duties. Juristic thinking is not satisfied with the insight that a certain human action or omission forms the contents of a duty or a right. There must exist something that "has" the duty or the right. In this idea, a general trend of human thought is manifested. Empirically observable qualities, too, are interpreted as qualities of an object or a substance, and grammatically they are represented as predicates of a subject. This substance is not an additional entity. The grammatical subject denoting it is only a symbol of the fact that the qualities form a unity. The leaf is not a new entity in addition to all the qualities — green, smooth, round and so on — but only their comprehensive unity. In ordinary thinking, determined by the forms of language, the substance is made into a separate entity supposed to have an independent existence besides "its" qualities. The grammatical subject, the substance, appears, so to say, as a new member of the series, formed by the predicates, the qualities inherent in the substance.

This duplication of the object of knowledge is characteristic of the primitive mythological thinking which is called animism. According to the animistic interpretation of nature, every object of the perceptual world is believed to be the abode of an invisible spirit who is the master of the object, who "has" the object in the same way as the substance has its qualities, the grammatical subject its predicates. Thus, the legal person, as ordinarily understood, also "has" its legal duties and rights in this same sense. The legal person is the legal substance to which duties and rights belong as legal qualities. The idea that "the person has" duties and rights involves the relation of substance and quality.

In reality, however, the legal person is not a separate entity besides "its" duties and rights, but only their personified unity or — since duties and rights are legal norms — the personified unity of a set of legal norms.

B. The Physical Person

a. Physical Person and Human Being

What constitutes this kind of unity? When does a set of duties and rights, a set of legal norms, have this kind of unity? There are two different criteria which emerge from an analysis of the two types of legal persons that are usually distinguished: physical (natural) and juristic persons.

The common way of defining the physical (natural) person and, at the same time, distinguishing him from the juristic person is to say: the physical person is a human being, whereas the juristic person is not. Austin for instance gives the definition: "a human being considered as *invested with rights*, or considered as *subject to duties*." * A person is, in other words, a human being considered as subject of duties and rights. To say that a human being A is the subject of a certain duty, or has a certain duty, means only that certain conduct of the individual A is the contents of a legal duty. To say that a human being A is the subject of a certain right or has a certain right, means only that certain conduct of the individual A is the object of a legal right. The meaning of both statements is that certain conduct of the individual A is, in a specific way, the contents of a legal norm. This legal norm determines only a particular action or forbearance of the individual A, not his whole existence. Even the total legal order never determines the whole existence of a human being subject to the order, or affects all his mental and bodily functions. Man is subject to the legal order only with respect to certain specified actions and forbearances; with respect to all others, he is in no relation to the legal order. In juristic considerations we are concerned with man only insofar as his conduct enters into the contents of the legal order. Only those actions and forbearances of a human being which are qualified as duties or rights in the legal order are thus relevant to the concept of the legal person. The person exists only insofar as he "has" duties and rights; apart from them the person has no existence whatsoever. To define the physical (natural) person as a human being is incorrect, because man and person are not only two different concepts but also the results of two entirely different kinds of consideration. Man is a concept of biology and physiology, in short, of the natural sciences. Person is a concept of jurisprudence, of the analysis of legal norms.

That man and person are two entirely different concepts may be regarded as a generally accepted result of analytical jurisprudence. Only, one does not always draw therefrom the last consequence. This consequence is that the physical (natural) person as the subject of duties and rights is not the human being whose conduct is the contents of these duties or the object of these rights, but that the physical (natural) person is only the personification of these duties and rights. Formulated more exactly: the physical (natural) person is the personification of a

* 1 John Austin, Lectures on Jurisprudence (5th ed. 1885) 350.

set of legal norms which by constituting duties and rights containing the conduct of one and the same human being regulate the conduct of this being. A *jus in rem* is, as we have seen, not a right attached to a certain thing, but a right to demand that other individuals shall behave in a certain way with respect to a certain thing. The thing is not the object of a *jus in rem* but — as Austin aptly puts it — "the *compass* of the right." * Thus, the human being is not the physical (natural) person but, so to speak, only "the compass" of a physical (natural) person. The relation between a so-called physical (natural) person and the human being with whom the former is often erroneously identified consists in the fact that those duties and rights which are comprehended in the concept of the person all refer to the behavior of that human being. That a slave is legally no person, or has no legal personality, means that there are no legal norms qualifying any behavior of this individual as a duty or a right. That a man A is a legal person or has a legal personality, means contrariwise that there are such norms. The "person A" is the comprehension of all the legal norms qualifying acts of A as duties or rights. We arrive at the "personality of A" when we conceive of these norms as forming a single unity, which we personify.

b. Physical Person: a Juristic Person

The concept of physical (natural) person means nothing but the personification of a complex of legal norms. Man, an individually determined man, is only the element which constitutes the unity in the plurality of these norms.

That the statement "the physical (natural) person is a human being" is incorrect is obvious also from the fact that what is true of the human being who is said to be a "person" is by no means always true of the person. The statement that a human being has duties and rights means that legal norms regulate the behavior of that human being in a specific way. The statement that a person has duties and rights, on the other hand, is meaningless or is an empty tautology. It means that a set of duties and rights, the unity of which is personified, "has" duties and rights. To avoid this nonsense, we have to interpret the "has" as "is": a set of duties and rights "is" duties and rights. It makes good sense to say that law imposes duties and confers rights upon human beings. But it is nonsense to say that law imposes duties and confers rights upon persons. Such a statement means that law imposes duties upon duties and confers rights upon rights. Only upon human beings — and not upon persons — can duties be imposed and rights conferred, since only

* 1 AUSTIN, JURISPRUDENCE 369.

the behavior of human beings can be the contents of legal norms. The identification of man and physical (natural) person has the dangerous effect of obscuring this principle which is fundamental to a jurisprudence free of fictions.

The physical (natural) person is, thus, no natural reality but a construction of juristic thinking. It is an auxiliary concept that may but need not necessarily be used in representing certain — not all — phenomena of law. Any representation of law will always ultimately refer to the actions and forbearances of the human beings whose behavior is regulated by the legal norms.

C. The Juristic Person

Since the concept of the so-called physical (natural) "person" is only a juristic construction and, as such, totally different from the concept of "man," the so-called "physical" (natural) person is, indeed, a "juristic" person. If the so-called physical (natural) person is a juristic person, there can be no essential difference between the physical (natural) person and what is usually exclusively considered as a "juristic" person. Traditional jurisprudence is inclined, it is true, to concede that the so-called physical person is also in truth a "juristic" person. But in defining the physical (natural) person as man, the juristic person as non-man, traditional jurisprudence again blurs their essential similarity. The relation between man and physical person is no more intimate than the relation between man and juristic person in the technical sense. That every legal person is, at bottom, a juristic person, that only juristic persons exist within the realm of law, is after all only a tautology.

a. The Corporation

The typical case of a "juristic" person (in the narrower technical sense) is a corporation. The usual definition of a corporation is: a group of individuals treated by the law as a unity, namely as a person having rights and duties distinct from those of the individuals composing it. A corporation is regarded as a person because there the legal order stipulates certain legal rights and duties which concern the interests of the members of the corporation but which do not seem to be rights and duties of the members and are, therefore, interpreted as rights and duties of the corporation itself. Such rights and duties are, in particular, created by acts of the organs of the corporation. A building is, for instance, rented by an organ on behalf of the corporation. The right to use the building is then, according to the usual interpretation, a right of the corporation and not one of its members. The obligation to pay the rent is incumbent upon the corporation itself and not upon its members. Or — to mention another example — an organ of a corporation buys real estate. This real estate is then the property of the corporation and not of its members. In case somebody infringes upon the right of the corporation, it is again the corporation itself and not any one member that has to bring a lawsuit. The indemnity which is secured by the civil sanction is added to the property of the corporation itself. If an obligation of the corporation remains unfulfilled — if for instance the rent is not paid in due order — a suit is likewise brought against the corporation itself, not against its members, and the civil sanction is eventually directed against the corporation itself, not against its members; this means that the civil sanction is directed against the property of the corporation itself, not against the property of its members. Those cases where the sanction is directed also against the property of the members — this may, e.g., occur if the property of the corporation does not suffice to repair the damage — may here be disregarded. The decisive reason why a corporation is considered as a legal person seems to be the fact that liability for civil delicts of the corporation is, in principle, limited to the property of the corporation itself.

b. Duties and Rights of a Juristic Person as Duties and Rights of Men

When one describes the situation by saying that the corporation as a juristic person enters into legal transactions, makes contracts, brings lawsuits, and so on, that the corporation as a juristic person has duties and rights, because the legal order imposes upon the corporation, as a juristic person, duties and confers rights upon it, all these statements are obviously only figures of speech. It cannot be seriously denied that actions and forbearances can only be actions and forbearances of a human being. When one speaks of actions and forbearances of a juristic person, it must be actions and forbearances of human beings which are involved. The only problem is to establish the specific character of those actions and forbearances of human beings, to explain why those actions and forbearances of human beings are interpreted as actions or forbearances of the corporation as a juristic person. And indeed acts of a juristic person are always acts of human beings designated as acts of a juristic person. They are the acts of those individuals who act as organs of the juristic person. Jurisprudence is thus faced with the task of determining when an individual is to be considered as acting as an organ of a juristic person. This is the problem of the corporation as an acting person. Quite analogous is the problem of the corporation as subject of duties and rights.

Since the legal order can impose duties and confer rights only upon human beings, because only the behavior of human beings can be regulated by the legal order, the duties and rights of a corporation as a juristic person must also be duties and rights of individual human beings. Again the problem arises of determining when duties and rights of individuals are considered as duties and rights of a juristic person. It is *a priori* excluded that the so-called duties and rights of a juristic person are not — at least at the same time — duties and rights of human beings.

c. The By-laws of the Corporation (Order and Community)

An individual acts as an organ of a corporation if his behavior corresponds in a certain way to the special order which constitutes the corporation. Several individuals form a group, an association, only when they are organized, if every individual has a specific function in relation to the others. They are organized when their mutual conduct is regulated by an order, a system of norms. It is this order — or, what amounts to the same thing, this organization — which constitutes the association, which makes the several individuals form an association. That this association has organs means just the same as that the individuals forming the association are organized by a normative order. The order or organization which constitutes the corporation is its statute, the so-called "by-laws" of the corporation, a complex of norms regulating the behavior of its members. It should be noticed here that the corporation is legally existent only through its statute. If one distinguishes the corporation from its statute, considering the former as an "association" or a "community," the latter as an order constituting this association or community, one is guilty of a duplication of the kind that was characterized at the beginning of this chapter. The corporation and "its" statute, the normative order regulating the behavior of some individuals and the association (community) "constituted" by the order, are not two different entities, they are identical. To say that the corporation is an association or a community is only another way of expressing the unity of the order. Individuals "belong" to an association or form an association only insofar as their behavior is regulated by the order "of" the association. Insofar as their behavior is not regulated by the order, the individuals do not "belong" to the association. The individuals are associated only through the order. If we use the term "community" instead of "association," we express the idea that the individuals "forming" an association have something in common. What they have in common is the normative order regulating their mutual behavior. It is therefore misleading to say that an association or a community is "formed" by or composed of individuals, as if the community or association were just a mass of individuals. The association or community is made up only of those acts of individuals which are determined by the order; and these acts "belong" to the association or community only insofar as they form the contents of the norms of the order. The association or community is nothing but "its" order.

d. The Organ of the Community

The corporation as a community manifests its existence only in the acts of individual human beings, of those individuals who are its organs. An individual is, as was said before, acting as an organ of a community only when his act is determined by the order in a specific way. An act performed by an individual in his capacity as organ of the community is distinguishable from other acts of this individual which are not interpreted as acts of the community only by the fact that the former act corresponds, in a specific sense, to the order. An individual's quality of being an organ lies entirely in his relation to the order. That the action or forbearance of an individual is interpreted as the act of a community means that the action or forbearance of the individual is referred to the order which determines the individual's behavior in a specific way. The act of the individual is referred to the order represented as a unit, and that means, to the community as a personification of the order. To refer the act of an individual to the community as personified order is to impute the act to the community.

e. The Imputation to the Order

However, this is then another kind of imputation than the one we spoke of when treating the problem of imputability as the legal capacity of committing a delict. This is a specific connection between two facts determined by the legal order. The imputation of the action or forbearance of an individual to the community concerns the relation of a fact to the legal order determining this fact in a specific way, the legal order taken as a unit.

This imputation allows us to speak of the community as of an acting person. The imputation to the community involves the personification of the order taken as a unit.

f. The Juristic Person as Personified Order

The juristic person, in the narrower sense of the term, is nothing but the personification of an order regulating the behavior of several individuals, so to speak — the common point of imputation for all those human acts which are determined by the order. The so-called physical person is the personification of a complex of norms regulating the behavior of one and the same individual. The substratum of the personification is thus in principle the same in both cases. A difference obtains only between the elements which give unity to the personified complex of norms.

What it is that makes one order out of a number of different norms is a question of which more will be said later. Suffice it here to stress the fact that corporations are partial legal orders within the total legal order constituting the State. The legal order constituting the State thus stands in quite another relation to a juristic person subject thereto than to human individuals upon whom it imposes duties and confers rights. The relation between the total legal order constituting the State, the so-called law of the State or national legal order, and the juristic person of a corporation is the relation between two legal orders, a total and a partial legal order, between the law of the State and the by-laws of the corporation. To be more specific, it is a case of delegation.

g. Obligating and Empowering of Juristic Persons

In imposing duties and conferring rights upon a juristic person, the "law of the State," the national legal order, regulates the behavior of individuals, makes actions and forbearances of human beings the contents of legal duties and the object of legal rights. But it does so only indirectly. The total legal order constituting the State determines only the material element of the behavior, leaving the task of determining the personal element to the partial legal order constituting the corporation, i.e., to its statute. This order determines the individual who as an organ has to perform the acts by which rights and duties of the corporation are created, and by which the rights of the corporation are exercised and its duties fulfilled. When the "law of the State," the total legal order, imposes duties and confers rights upon the juristic person of a corporation, it is human individuals who as "organs" of the corporation are thus obligated and authorized; but the function of imposing duties and conferring rights is divided between two orders, a total and a partial order, one of which, the latter, completes the former. That the "law of the State" gives a juristic person rights and duties does not mean that a being other than a human individual is obligated or authorized; it only means that duties and rights are indirectly given to individuals. To serve as an intermediary in this process is the characteristic function of the partial legal order of which the juristic person of the corporation is a personification.

h. The Concept of the Juristic Person as Auxiliary Concept

Any order regulating the behavior of several individuals could be regarded as a "person," — that means, could be personified. A juristic person, in the narrow and technical sense of the term, is, however, assumed only when the organs of the community regarded as a person are capable of representing legally the corporation, i.e., the individuals belonging to it, and that means, to enter legal transactions, appear before courts, and make binding declarations, all that on behalf of the community, i.e., of the individuals belonging to it, and when the liability of the community (i.e., of the individuals belonging to it) is limited in a specific way. It is limited to the extent of the property of the juristic person which is the collective property of its members; so that the members of the juristic person (corporation) are liable only with their collective property, the property which they have as members of the corporation — not with their individual property. This is possible only if the "law of the State" gives such an effect to the fact that a statute constituting a corporation has been established. This is intended by the expression that the "law of the State" grants a corporation legal personality. The jurist may at will use or dispense with the concept of a juristic person. But this auxiliary concept is especially useful when the "law of the State" gives to the establishment of a corporation the effects just mentioned; namely: that organs of the corporation are capable of entering legal transactions and of appearing before courts on behalf of the corporation, i.e., its members, and that the civil liability of the members is limited to the property of the corporation, i.e., the collective property of the members. In such a case, there may arise rights and duties which belong to the members of a corporation in quite another way than those rights and duties which they have independently of their membership. And by presenting those rights and duties as belonging to the corporation itself we bring out this difference. Such a difference exists; but it does not consist in that the duties and rights presented as duties and rights of the corporation are not duties and rights of the individuals belonging to it; this is impossible, since duties and rights can be only duties and rights of human beings. The difference consists in that the duties and rights presented as duties and rights of the corporation are duties and rights which the individuals belonging to the corporation possess in a specific way, in a way different from the way in which they possess duties and rights without being members of a corporation.

i. Duties and Rights of a Juristic Person: Collective Duties and Rights of Men

That the corporation which is conceived of as a juristic person has the obligation to observe a certain behavior, means, first, that the law of the State makes certain behavior the contents of a duty, but that the individual whose behavior is the contents of the duty, who in his capacity as an organ of the corporation, has to perform the duty, is determined by the statute of the corporation, by the partial legal order which constitutes the corporation. The duty is incumbent upon a definite individual. But since this individual is determined by the partial order constituting the corporation, and since this individual has to perform the duty as an organ of the corporation, it is possible to impute his duty to the corporation, to speak of a "duty of the corporation."

Let us consider the example of the corporation which has bought a building and is obligated by the contract to pay the price. The payment of the price is a duty stipulated by the "law of the State." Normally, the individual who as a buyer contracted the purchase has to pay. But if a contract of purchase has been made by a corporation through a competent organ, i.e., through the individual determined by the statute of the corporation, then it is again an organ of the corporation that has to pay the price from the corporation's property.

This property is of importance also in another respect. For the fact that the corporation has the obligation to observe a certain behavior also means that if the obligation is not fulfilled, a sanction can be directed against the property which is considered to be the corporation's property. This presupposes that the juristic person possesses rights, because the property means only the sum of those rights which represent a monetary value. In order to understand the meaning of a juristic person's having a legal duty one must first understand the meaning of its having a legal right.

That a corporation as a juristic person has a relative or absolute right means that a definite individual or an indefinite number of individuals are obligated by the "law of the State" to a certain behavior towards the corporation and that in case the obligation is not fulfilled a sanction shall be executed upon a suit brought "by the corporation," i.e., upon a suit brought by an individual designated by the statute of the corporation. To have an obligation towards the corporation is to have an obligation towards its members. But there is a difference between having an obligation towards an individual, simply, and having an obligation towards several individuals in their quality of being members of a corporation. The difference lies in the way in which obligations corresponding to the rights are pursued in case of their violation. In the case of a corporation's right, the sanction constituting the corresponding obligation cannot be put in motion by every individual towards whom, as a member of the corporation, one is obligated, but only by that individual who is authorized by the statute of the corporation to bring a suit on behalf of the corporation. The indemnity enforced by the sanction goes to the property of the corporation.

Another difference which exists between the right of a definite individual and the right of a corporation concerns the way in which the right is "exercised" in the sense that the individual "makes use" of his right, "enjoys" his right. It is always by individuals that the rights of a corporation are exercised in this sense. For human beings only can exercise a right, can consume a thing, spend money, inhabit a house, make use of a telephone, and so on. In this sense, only the individuals belonging to the corporation have the right which is interpreted as the right of the corporation. Thus, if a club owns a golf course, it is the club members, not the club itself, the juristic person, that play on the course, and thus exercise the right of property. The right of a corporation is exercised by individuals in their capacity as members and that means as organs (using the term in a wider sense) of the corporation. Whereas, however, normally a right may be exercised at will by the individual who has it, the statute of a corporation regulates how a right which is regarded as belonging to the corporation is to be exercised by its members.

In a more general formulation, the right of a juristic person is the right of those individuals whose behavior is regulated by the partial legal order constituting the community presented as person. The right, however, is not exercised by those individuals at their will. The partial legal order constituting the community determines the way in which those individuals may exercise the right. They have the right, not in the usual, i.e., in an individual, but in a collective fashion. A juristic person's right is a collective right of the individuals whose behavior is regulated by the partial legal order constituting the community presented as juristic person.

j. The Civil Delict of a Juristic Person

That a juristic person has a legal duty means, as already stated, that in case this duty is not fulfilled a sanction has to be executed against the property of the person upon a suit by the party who has the corresponding right. Does this also imply that the delict consisting in the nonfulfillment of the duty may be imputed to the corporation, and may be considered to be a delict of a juristic person? Every delict consists in a human being's doing or omitting to do something. What an individual does or omits to do, can, however, be imputed to a juristic person only if this conduct of the individual is determined by the partial legal order constituting the juristic person. This is the only criterion of imputability as far as juristic persons are concerned. Since the validity of the partial legal order constituting the juristic person, especially the by-laws of a corporation, is ultimately dependent upon the law of the State, by-laws according to which the organs of the corporation have to commit delicts cannot — in general — be considered as valid, especially not when the by-laws are established under the control of State authorities. When an organ of a juristic person commits a delict, it usually does not act in its capacity as an organ. The delict is not imputed to the juristic person. A corporation may, however, be responsible for a delict committed by one of its members if the delict is in a certain connection with the function which the member has to perform as organ of the corporation. In such a case, the sanction, conditioned by the delict, may be directed against the property of the corporation. That means that the members of the corporation are collectively responsible for a delict committed by one of them. If, for instance, a corporation is obligated to pay the rent for a building it has rented, but the proper organ fails to do so, the members of the corporation are collectively responsible with the property of the corporation for the failure to pay. It is possible, though, that a delict committed by an organ may be imputable to the corporation itself. Suppose, for instance, that, in our previous example, in failing to pay the rent the organ executed a decision of a general meeting of stockholders and that the by-laws give the stockholders assembled in meeting competence to make decisions of that kind. The meeting might have been erroneously advised by the corporation's attorney that the rent was not legally due. A decision of the stockholders creates a norm belonging to the partial legal order constituting the corporation in precisely the same way as a decision of the parliament creates a norm belonging to the total legal order of the State. The failure to pay would therefore, in such a case, be imputable to the corporation. And the corporation would be responsible for a delict of its own.

k. The Criminal Delict of a Juristic Person

We have so far considered only civil sanctions and civil delicts. Can a criminal delict be imputed to a juristic person? And can a juristic person be liable to a criminal sanction? Neither question can be unconditionally answered in the negative.

Sometimes the doctrine *societas non potest delinquere* (an association cannot commit a crime) is based on the fact that a juristic person cannot have a guilty mind, meaning that specific state of mind which constitutes culpability, since a juristic person, not being a real person, cannot have a state of mind at all. This argument is not conclusive. The rule of *mens rea* is not without exceptions. Absolute liability is not excluded, even in modern criminal law.* Besides, if it is possible to impute a physical act performed by a human being to the juristic person although the latter has no body, it must be possible to impute psychic acts to the juristic person although the latter has no soul. If the law provides a

---

* Cf. *supra*, pp. 65ff.

criminal sanction against a juristic person under the condition only that its organ has acted intentionally and maliciously, then it is quite possible to say that the juristic person must have a guilty mind in order to be punished. Imputation to a juristic person is a juristic construction, not the description of a natural reality. It is therefore not necessary to make the hopeless attempt to demonstrate that the juristic person is a real being, not a legal fiction, in order to prove that delicts and especially crimes can be imputed to a juristic person. More delicate is the question whether a criminal sanction can be directed against a juristic person.

Juristic persons are often fined because of tax frauds imputed to the juristic person as such. But, from our point of view, fines do not essentially differ from civil sanctions; they are both directed against the juristic person's property. To inflict upon a corporation a fine is certainly not more problematic than to direct a civil sanction against its property. It seems, however, impossible to inflict upon a corporation corporal punishment such as death penalty or imprisonment. Only human beings can be deprived of life or freedom. But although only human beings can act, nevertheless we conceive of the corporation as an acting person since we impute human actions to it. Whether corporal punishment can be inflicted upon a corporation, implies the same problem of imputation as the question whether a corporation can act. It is the question, whether the suffering of a corporal punishment by certain individuals can be imputed to the corporation whose members the individuals are. That such an imputation is possible cannot be denied. Other questions are under what circumstances such imputation is possible and whether it is practical.

To impute the suffering of death or imprisonment, inflicted upon individuals as punishment, to the corporation whose members these individuals are, to interpret these facts as punishment of the corporation, comes into consideration only if a delict to which capital punishment or imprisonment is attached is to be imputed to the corporation. Such imputation presupposes that the legally valid by-laws of the corporation contain a norm obligating or authorizing an organ to commit such a criminal delict. The question is of less importance as long as we are concerned only with juristic persons existing within the legal order of the State. Here, such a partial legal order or its special norm obligating or authorizing the organ to commit a criminal delict has, as a rule, to be considered as void. But the same question becomes very important — as we shall realize later — for the juristic persons which the States themselves form within the frame of international law. The legal order constituting the State can legally oblige an individual in his capacity as an organ of the State to behavior which — from the standpoint of international law — is a delict, i.e., the condition of a sanction provided by international law. The State as a juristic person is the possible subject of international delicts, of violations of international law. The international delict is imputed to the State as a juristic person. The sanctions of international law, especially war, it is true, are usually not interpreted as punishments; but they have, nevertheless, in principle, the same character as the sanctions of criminal law — forcible deprivation of life and freedom of individuals; the international sanctions are considered to be directed against the State as such. It is therefore not superfluous to examine the question: under what conditions may the forcible deprivation of life or liberty, capital punishment or imprisonment of individuals, be considered as sanctions directed against a juristic person? The answer is: when the sanction is directed in principle against all the members of the community which is presented as a juristic person, although the delict has been committed only by one of them, though in his capacity as organ of the community. The sanction is not directed against a definite human being determined individually, but against a group of individuals determined collectively by the legal order. That is the meaning of the statement that a sanction is directed against a juristic person. The sanction is applied to individuals, because human beings only can be the objects of a sanction, the victims of forcible deprivation of life and freedom. But the sanction is applied to them not individually, but collectively. That a sanction is directed against a juristic person means that collective responsibility is established of the individuals who are subject to the total or partial legal order personified in the concept of juristic person.

The specific sanctions of international law, war and reprisals, have this character. Insofar as they imply forcible deprivation of life and freedom of individuals, they are directed against human beings, not because these individuals have committed an international delict, but because they are subjects of the State whose organ has violated international law. In modern criminal law, however, the principle of individual responsibility prevails. It is not very likely that the criminal code of a civilized country would establish capital punishment or imprisonment to be executed against individuals who have not committed a crime but who are members of a corporation to which a crime is imputed because an individual in his capacity as organ of the corporation has committed a crime punishable by death or imprisonment.

Responsibility of a corporation for its own delicts, i.e., delicts imputed to the corporation, must not be confused with responsibility of a corporation for delicts committed by its members and not imputed to the corporation. It is quite possible to make a corporation responsible, by inflicting upon it a fine or executing a civil sanction against its property, for a delict which one of its members has committed, even when he was not acting in his capacity as an organ of the corporation. This is a kind of indirect or vicarious responsibility.*

l. Juristic Person and Representation

The true nature of the juristic person is usually misunderstood because one has an incorrect idea of what a physical person is. An individual, it is assumed, must have a will in order to be a person. That, by definition, a person has duties and rights is falsely interpreted to mean that a person has a will by which he may create and pursue duties and rights. Consequently, one finds that a corporation must have a will in order to be a juristic person. Most jurists, now, realize that a juristic person cannot have any will in the sense in which a human being has a will. They therefore explain that human beings, the organs of the juristic person, will "in its name," that they manifest a will, "instead" of the juristic person, and that the legal order attaches to these declarations of will the effect of creating duties and rights of the juristic person. This explanation is supported by pointing to the supposedly similar relation between an infant, or a lunatic, and his guardian. Just as the juristic person has himself no will but has, nevertheless, thanks to the will of its organ, duties and rights, the infant and the lunatic have no (legally recognized) will and have, nevertheless, thanks to the will of their guardian, duties and rights. The organ of the corporation is looked upon as a kind of guardian for the corporation, which is in turn thought of as a kind of infant or lunatic. The will of an organ is "attributed" to the corporation in the same way as the guardian's will is attributed to his ward. Gray says: "Now it is to be observed, that thus far there is nothing peculiar to juristic persons. The attribution of another's will is of exactly the same nature as that which takes place when the will, for instance of a guardian is attributed to an infant." † There is, however, the essential difference that the relation between guardian and ward is a relation between two individuals which the relation between organ and juristic person is not. The organ is, it is true, a representative. But it represents the beings who are members of the corporation and not the corporation itself. The relation between the organ and the corporation is the relation between an individual and a special legal order. Representation, however, is always, as in the case of a guardian and his ward or an agent and his principal, a relation between human beings. The organ creates

* Cf. *infra* pp. 358ff.
† JOHN CHIPMAN GRAY, THE NATURE AND SOURCES OF THE LAW (2d. ed. 1938) 51.

through its transactions collective rights and duties for the members of the corporation. The comparison with the relation between guardian and ward is further unfortunate, since that is a case of non-consensual representation. The relation between an organ of a corporation and its members is, at least within a democratically organized corporation, a consensual representation like the relation between agent and principal. The organ is made the representative of the members of the corporation by appointment, especially by election on behalf of the members. No analogies of this kind can, however, elucidate the organ's relation to the corporation, since the organ is not a representative of the corporation but of its members.

m. Juristic Person as Real Being (Organism)

The basic error of the theory that the juristic person is represented by its organs in the way a ward is represented by its guardian or a principal by his agent is that the juristic person is thought of as a kind of human being. If the physical person is a man, then the juristic person must be, it is thought, a superman. The theory that the juristic person, though only a fiction, has a will, viz., the will of the organ which is "attributed" to it, is therefore not so different from the theory that the juristic person, especially the corporation, is a real entity, an organism, a superman which has a will of its own which is not the will of its members, that the will of the juristic person is a real will which the law of the State recognizes and — as some writers contend — has to recognize. The theory that the juristic person is a real entity and has a real will has sometimes the conscious or unconscious tendency to induce the legislator to a definite regulation with reference to corporations, to justify this regulation as the only "possible" and hence the only right one.

The idea that corporations are real beings with a real will is on a level with the animistic beliefs which led primitive man to endow things in nature with a "soul." Like animism, this juristic theory duplicates its object. An order regulating the behavior of individuals is personified and then the personification is regarded as a new entity, distinct from the individuals but still in some mysterious fashion "formed" by them. The duties and rights of the individuals stipulated by this order are then attributed to the superhuman being, the superman consisting of men. And so the order is hypostatized — that is to say: the order is made into a substance, and this substance is regarded as a separate thing, a being distinct from the order and the human beings whose behavior is regulated by this order.

n. Corporation as "Body of Men"

Even our common language and especially legal parlance has a tendency to such an hypostatization. We call a corporation a "body" and are naturally inclined also to think of it as a body. If the corporation is a body, this body must be assumed to be composed of the bodies of those individuals whose behavior is regulated by the organization of the corporation, i.e., by its by-laws. One thereby loses sight of the fact that the statement "individuals form a community," or "belong to a community," is nothing but a very figurative expression of the fact that their behavior is regulated by the legal order constituting the community. Besides that legal order, there is no community, no corporation, as little as there is a body of the corporation besides the bodies of its members.

A typical definition of a corporation is this one given by Gray: * "A corporation is an organized body of men to which the State has given powers to protect its interests, and the wills which put these powers in motion are the wills of certain men determined according to the organization of the corporation." A merit of Gray's is his clear attempt to avoid the usual hypostatization. But he comes precariously close to it when he defines the corporation as a "body of men." The corporation is not an organized body of men but an organization of men, that is to say, an order regulating the behavior of men. Gray's statement that the State gives powers to the corporation contains the same inaccuracy twice. It is not the State but the national legal order which is called State that gives powers, and it gives them not to the corporation but to those men whose behavior is determined by the corporative organization. The phrase "the organization of the corporation" in Gray's definition is a pleonasm. It expresses the same duplication as the saying "a community has an organization" or "a community is established through an organization." The community is nothing but its organization.

* GRAY, NATURE AND SOURCES OF THE LAW 51.

NOMODYNAMICS

X. THE LEGAL ORDER

A. THE UNITY OF A NORMATIVE ORDER

a. The Reason of Validity: the Basic Norm

THE legal order is a system of norms. The question then arises: What is it that makes a system out of a multitude of norms? When does a norm belong to a certain system of norms, an order? This question is in close connection with the question as to the reason of validity of a norm.

In order to answer this question, we must first clarify the grounds on which we assign validity to a norm. When we assume the truth of a statement about reality, it is because the statement corresponds to reality, because our experience confirms it. The statement "A physical body expands when heated" is true, because we have repeatedly and without exception observed that physical bodies expand when they are heated. A norm is not a statement about reality and is therefore incapable of being "true" or "false," in the sense determined above. A norm is either valid or non-valid. Of the two statements: "You shall assist a fellowman in need," and "You shall lie whenever you find it useful," only the first, not the second, is considered to express a valid norm. What is the reason?

The reason for the validity of a norm is not, like the test of the truth of an "is" statement, its conformity to reality. As we have already stated, a norm is not valid because it is efficacious. The question why something ought to occur can never be answered by an assertion to the effect that something occurs, but only by an assertion that something ought to occur. In the language of daily life, it is true, we frequently justify a norm by referring to a fact. We say, for instance: "You shall not kill because God has forbidden it in one of the Ten Commandments"; or a mother says to her child: "You ought to go to school because your father has ordered it." However, in these statements the fact that God has issued a command or the fact that the father has ordered the child to do something is only apparently the reason for the validity of the norms in question. The true reason is norms tacitly presupposed because taken for granted. The reason for the validity of the norm, You shall not kill, is the general norm, You shall obey the commands of God. The reason for the validity of the norm, You ought to go to school, is the general norm,

Children ought to obey their father. If these norms are not presupposed, the references to the facts concerned are not answers to the questions why we shall not kill, why the child ought to go to school. The fact that somebody commands something is, in itself, no reason for the statement that one ought to behave in conformity with the command, no reason for considering the command as a valid norm, no reason for the validity of the norm the contents of which corresponds to the command. The reason for the validity of a norm is always a norm, not a fact. The quest for the reason of validity of a norm leads back, not to reality, but to another norm from which the first norm is derivable in a sense that will be investigated later. Let us, for the present, discuss a concrete example. We accept the statement "You shall assist a fellowman in need," as a valid norm because it follows from the statement "You shall love your neighbor." This statement we accept as a valid norm, either because it appears to us as an ultimate norm whose validity is self-evident, or — for instance — Christ has bidden that you shall love your neighbor, and we postulate as an ultimate valid norm the statement "You shall obey the commandments of Christ." The statement "You shall lie whenever you find it useful," we do not accept as a valid norm, because it is neither derivable from another valid norm nor is it in itself an ultimate, self-evidently valid norm.

A norm the validity of which cannot be derived from a superior norm we call a "basic" norm. All norms whose validity may be traced back to one and the same basic norm form a system of norms, or an order. This basic norm constitutes, as a common source, the bond between all the different norms of which an order consists. That a norm belongs to a certain system of norms, to a certain normative order, can be tested only by ascertaining that it derives its validity from the basic norm constituting the order. Whereas an "is" statement is true because it agrees with the reality of sensuous experience, an "ought" statement is a valid norm only if it belongs to such a valid system of norms, if it can be derived from a basic norm presupposed as valid. The ground of truth of an "is" statement is its conformity to the reality of our experience; the reason for the validity of a norm is a presupposition, a norm presupposed to be an ultimately valid, that is, a basic norm. The quest for the reason of validity of a norm is not — like the quest for the cause of an effect — a *regressus ad infinitum*; it is terminated by a highest norm which is the last reason of validity within the normative system, whereas a last or first cause has no place within a system of natural reality.

b. The Static System of Norms

According to the nature of the basic norm, we may distinguish between two different types of orders or normative systems: static and dynamic systems. Within an order of the first kind the norms are "valid" and that means, we assume that the individuals whose behavior is regulated by the norms "ought" to behave as the norms prescribe, by virtue of their contents: Their contents has an immediately evident quality that guarantees their validity, or, in other terms: the norms are valid because of their inherent appeal. This quality the norms have because they are derivable from a specific basic norm as the particular is derivable from the general. The binding force of the basic norm is itself self-evident, or at least presumed to be so. Such norms as "You must not lie," "You must not deceive," "You shall keep your promise," follow from a general norm prescribing truthfulness. From the norm "You shall love your neighbor" one may deduce such norms as "You must not hurt your neighbor," "You shall help him in need," and so on. If one asks why one has to love one's neighbor, perhaps the answer will be found in some still more general norm, let us say the postulate that one has to live "in harmony with the universe." If that is the most general norm of whose validity we are convinced, we will consider it as the ultimate norm. Its obligatory nature may appear so obvious that one does not feel any need to ask for the reason of its validity. Perhaps one may also succeed in deducing the principle of truthfulness and its consequences from this "harmony" postulate. One would then have reached a norm on which a whole system of morality could be based. However, we are not interested here in the question of what specific norm lies at the basis of such and such a system of morality. It is essential only that the various norms of any such system are implicated by the basic norm as the particular is implied by the general, and that, therefore, all the particular norms of such a system are obtainable by means of an intellectual operation, viz., by the inference from the general to the particular. Such a system is of a static nature.

c. The Dynamic System of Norms

The derivation of a particular norm may, however, be carried out also in another way. A child, asking why it must not lie, might be given the answer that its father has forbidden it to lie. If the child should further ask why it has to obey its father, the reply would perhaps be that God has commanded that it obey its parents. Should the child put the question why one has to obey the commands of God, the only answer would be that this is a norm beyond which one cannot look for a more ultimate norm. That norm is the basic norm providing the foundation for a system of dynamic character. Its various norms cannot be obtained from the basic norm by any intellectual operation. The basic norm merely establishes a certain authority, which may well in turn vest norm-creating power in some other authorities. The norms of a dynamic system have to be created through acts of will by those individuals who have been authorized to create norms by some higher norm. This authorization is a delegation. Norm creating power is delegated from one authority to another authority; the former is the higher, the latter the lower authority. The basic norm of a dynamic system is the fundamental rule according to which the norms of the system are to be created. A norm forms part of a dynamic system if it has been created in a way that is — in the last analysis — determined by the basic norm. A norm thus belongs to the religious system just given by way of example if it is created by God or originates in an authority having its power from God, "delegated" by God.

B. THE LAW AS A DYNAMIC SYSTEM OF NORMS

a. The Positivity of Law

The system of norms we call a legal order is a system of the dynamic kind. Legal norms are not valid because they themselves or the basic norm have a content the binding force of which is self-evident. They are not valid because of their inherent appeal. Legal norms may have any kind of content. There is no kind of human behavior that, because of its nature, could not be made into a legal duty corresponding to a legal right. The validity of a legal norm cannot be questioned on the ground that its contents are incompatible with some moral or political value. A norm is a valid legal norm by virtue of the fact that it has been created according to a definite rule and by virtue thereof only. The basic norm of a legal order is the postulated ultimate rule according to which the norms of this order are established and annulled, receive and lose their validity. The statement "Any man who manufactures or sells alcoholic liquors as beverages shall be punished" is a valid legal norm if it belongs to a certain legal order. This it does if this norm has been created in a definite way ultimately determined by the basic norm of that legal order, and if it has not again been nullified in a definite way, ultimately determined by the same basic norm. The basic norm may, for instance, be such that a norm belongs to the system provided that it has been decreed by the parliament or created by custom or established by the courts, and has not been abolished by a decision of the parliament or through custom or a contrary court practice. The statement mentioned above is no valid legal norm if it does not belong to a valid legal order — it may be that no such norm has been created in the way ultimately determined by the basic norm, or it may be that, although a norm has been created in that way, it has been repealed in a way ultimately determined by the basic norm.

Law is always positive law, and its positivity lies in the fact that it is created and annulled by acts of human beings, thus being independent of morality and similar norm systems. This constitutes the difference between positive law and natural law, which, like morality, is deduced from a presumably self-evident basic norm which is considered to be the expression of the "will of nature" or of "pure reason." The basic norm of a positive legal order is nothing but the fundamental rule according to which the various norms of the order are to be created. It qualifies a certain event as the initial event in the creation of the various legal norms. It is the starting point of a norm-creating process and, thus, has an entirely dynamic character. The particular norms of the legal order cannot be logically deduced from this basic norm, as can the norm "Help your neighbor when he needs your help" from the norm "Love your neighbor." They are to be created by a special act of will, not concluded from a premise by an intellectual operation.

b. Customary and Statutory Law

Legal norms are created in many different ways: general norms through custom or legislation, individual norms through judicial and administrative acts or legal transactions. Law is always created by an act that deliberately aims at creating law, except in the case when law has its origin in custom, that is to say, in a generally observed course of conduct, during which the acting individuals do not consciously aim at creating law; but they must regard their acts as in conformity with a binding norm and not as a matter of arbitrary choice. This is the requirement of so-called *opinio juris sive necessitatis*. The usual interpretation of this requirement is that the individuals constituting by their conduct the law-creating custom must regard their acts as determined by a legal rule; they must believe that they perform a legal duty or exercise a legal right. This doctrine is not correct. It implies that the individuals concerned must act in error: since the legal rule which is created by their conduct cannot yet determine this conduct, at least not as a legal rule. They may erroneously believe themselves to be bound by a rule of law, but this error is not necessary to constitute a law-creating custom. It is sufficient that the acting individuals consider themselves bound by any norm whatever.

We shall distinguish between statutory and customary law as the two fundamental types of law. By statutory law we shall understand law created in a way other than by custom, namely, by legislative, judicial, or administrative acts or by legal transactions, especially by contracts and (international) treaties.

C. The Basic Norm of a Legal Order

a. *The Basic Norm and the Constitution*

The derivation of the norms of a legal order from the basic norm of that order is performed by showing that the particular norms have been created in accordance with the basic norm. To the question why a certain act of coercion — e.g., the fact that one individual deprives another individual of his freedom by putting him in jail — is a legal act, the answer is: because it has been prescribed by an individual norm, a judicial decision. To the question why this individual norm is valid as part of a definite legal order, the answer is: because it has been created in conformity with a criminal statute. This statute, finally, receives its validity from the constitution, since it has been established by the competent organ in the way the constitution prescribes.

If we ask why the constitution is valid, perhaps we come upon an older constitution. Ultimately we reach some constitution that is the first historically and that was laid down by an individual usurper or by some kind of assembly. The validity of this first constitution is the last presupposition, the final postulate, upon which the validity of all the norms of our legal order depends. It is postulated that one ought to behave as the individual, or the individuals, who laid down the first constitution have ordained. This is the basic norm of the legal order under consideration. The document which embodies the first constitution is a real constitution, a binding norm, only on the condition that the basic norm is presupposed to be valid. Only upon this presupposition are the declarations of those to whom the constitution confers norm-creating power binding norms. It is this presupposition that enables us to distinguish between individuals who are legal authorities and other individuals whom we do not regard as such, between acts of human beings which create legal norms and acts which have no such effect. All these legal norms belong to one and the same legal order because their validity can be traced back — directly or indirectly — to the first constitution. That the first constitution is a binding legal norm is presupposed, and the formulation of the presupposition is the basic norm of this legal order. The basic norm of a religious norm system says that one ought to behave as God and the authorities instituted by Him command. Similarly, the basic norm of a legal order prescribes that one ought to behave as the "fathers" of the constitution and the individuals — directly or indirectly — authorized (delegated) by the constitution command. Expressed in the form of a legal norm: coercive acts ought to be carried out only under the conditions and in the way determined by the "fathers" of the constitution or the organs delegated by them. This is, schematically formulated, the basic norm of the legal order of a single State, the basic norm of a national legal order. It is to the national legal order that we have here limited our attention. Later, we shall consider what bearing the assumption of an international law has upon the question of the basic norm of national law.

b. The Specific Function of the Basic Norm

That a norm of the kind just mentioned is the basic norm of the national legal order does not imply that it is impossible to go beyond that norm. Certainly one may ask why one has to respect the first constitution as a binding norm. The answer might be that the fathers of the first constitution were empowered by God. The characteristic of so-called legal positivism is, however, that it dispenses with any such religious justification of the legal order. The ultimate hypothesis of positivism is the norm authorizing the historically first legislator. The whole function of this basic norm is to confer law-creating power on the act of the first legislator and on all the other acts based on the first act. To interpret these acts of human beings as legal acts and their products as binding norms, and that means to interpret the empirical material which presents itself as law as such, is possible only on the condition that the basic norm is presupposed as a valid norm. The basic norm is only the necessary presupposition of any positivistic interpretation of the legal material.

The basic norm is not created in a legal procedure by a law-creating organ. It is not — as a positive legal norm is — valid because it is created in a certain way by a legal act, but it is valid because it is presupposed to be valid; and it is presupposed to be valid because without this presupposition no human act could be interpreted as a legal, especially as a norm-creating, act.

By formulating the basic norm, we do not introduce into the science of law any new method. We merely make explicit what all jurists, mostly unconsciously, assume when they consider positive law as a system of valid norms and not only as a complex of facts, and at the same time repudiate any natural law from which positive law would receive its validity. That the basic norm really exists in the juristic consciousness is the result of a simple analysis of actual juristic statements. The basic norm is the answer to the question: how — and that means under what condition — are all these juristic statements concerning legal norms, legal duties, legal rights, and so on, possible?

c. The Principle of Legitimacy

The validity of legal norms may be limited in time, and it is important to notice that the end as well as the beginning of this validity is determined only by the order to which they belong. They remain valid as long as they have not been invalidated in the way which the legal order itself determines. This is the principle of legitimacy.

This principle, however, holds only under certain conditions. It fails to hold in the case of a revolution, this word understood in the most general sense, so that it also covers the so-called *coup d'État*. A revolution, in this wide sense, occurs whenever the legal order of a community is nullified and replaced by a new order in an illegitimate way, that is in a way not prescribed by the first order itself. It is in this context irrelevant whether or not this replacement is effected through a violent uprising against those individuals who so far have been the "legitimate" organs competent to create and amend the legal order. It is equally irrelevant whether the replacement is effected through a movement emanating from the mass of the people, or through action from those in government positions. From a juristic point of view, the decisive criterion of a revolution is that the order in force is overthrown and replaced by a new order in a way which the former had not itself anticipated. Usually, the new men whom a revolution brings to power annul only the constitution and certain laws of paramount political significance, putting other norms in their place. A great part of the old legal order "remains" valid also within the frame of the new order. But the phrase "they remain valid," does not give an adequate description of the phenomenon. It is only the contents of these norms that remain the same, not the reason of their validity. They are no longer valid by virtue of having been created in the way the old constitution prescribed. That constitution is no longer in force; it is replaced by a new constitution which is not the result of a constitutional alteration of the former. If laws which were introduced under the old constitution "continue to be valid" under the new constitution, this is possible only because validity has expressly or tacitly been vested in them by the new constitution. The phenomenon is a case of reception (similar to the reception of Roman law). The new order "receives," i.e., adopts, norms from the old order; this means that the new order gives validity to (puts into force) norms which have the same content as norms of the old order. "Reception" is an abbreviated procedure of law-creation. The laws which, in the ordinary inaccurate parlance, continue to be valid are, from a juristic viewpoint, new laws whose import coincides with that of the old laws. They are not identical with the old laws, because the reason for their validity is different. The reason for their validity is the new, not the old, constitution, and between the two continuity holds neither from the point of view of the one nor from that of the other. Thus, it is never the constitution merely but always the entire legal order that is changed by a revolution.

This shows that all norms of the old order have been deprived of their validity by revolution and not according to the principle of legitimacy. And they have been so deprived not only *de facto* but also *de jure*. No jurist would maintain that even after a successful revolution the old constitution and the laws based thereupon remain in force, on the ground that they have not been nullified in a manner anticipated by the old order itself. Every jurist will presume that the old order — to which no political reality any longer corresponds — has ceased to be valid, and that all norms, which are valid within the new order, receive their validity exclusively from the new constitution. It follows that, from this juristic point of view, the norms of the old order can no longer be recognized as valid norms.

d. Change of the Basic Norm

It is just the phenomenon of revolution which clearly shows the significance of the basic norm. Suppose that a group of individuals attempt to seize power by force, in order to remove the legitimate government in a hitherto monarchic State, and to introduce a republican form of government. If they succeed, if the old order ceases, and the new order begins to be efficacious, because the individuals whose behavior the new order regulates actually behave, by and large, in conformity with the new order, then this order is considered as a valid order. It is now according to this new order that the actual behavior of individuals is interpreted as legal or illegal. But this means that a new basic norm is presupposed. It is no longer the norm according to which the old monarchical constitution is valid, but a norm according to which the new republican constitution is valid, a norm endowing the revolutionary government with legal authority. If the revolutionaries fail, if the order they have tried to establish remains inefficacious, then, on the other hand, their undertaking is interpreted, not as a legal, a law-creating act, as the establishment of a constitution, but as an illegal act, as the crime of treason, and this according to the old monarchic constitution and its specific basic norm.

e. The Principle of Effectiveness

If we attempt to make explicit the presupposition on which these juristic considerations rest, we find that the norms of the old order are regarded as devoid of validity because the old constitution and, therefore, the legal norms based on this constitution, the old legal order as a whole, has lost its efficacy; because the actual behavior of men does no longer conform to this old legal order. Every single norm loses its validity when the total legal order to which it belongs loses its efficacy as a whole. The efficacy of the entire legal order is a necessary condition for the validity of every single norm of the order. A *conditio sine qua non*, but not a *conditio per quam*. The efficacy of the total legal order is a condition, not the reason for the validity of its constituent norms. These norms are valid not because the total order is efficacious, but because they are created in a constitutional way. They are valid, however, only on the condition that the total order is efficacious; they cease to be valid, not only when they are annulled in a constitutional way, but also when the total order ceases to be efficacious. It cannot be maintained that, legally, men have to behave in conformity with a certain norm, if the total legal order, of which that norm is an integral part, has lost its efficacy. The principle of legitimacy is restricted by the principle of effectiveness.

f. Desuetudo

This must not be understood to mean that a single legal norm loses its validity, if that norm itself and only that norm is rendered ineffective. Within a legal order which as a whole is efficacious there may occur isolated norms which are valid and which yet are not efficacious, that is, are not obeyed and not applied even when the conditions which they themselves lay down for their application are fulfilled. But even in this case efficacy has some relevance to validity. If the norm remains permanently inefficacious, the norm is deprived of its validity by "desuetudo." "Desuetudo" is the negative legal effect of custom. A norm may be annulled by custom, viz., by a custom contrary to the norm, as well as it may be created by custom. Desuetudo annuls a norm by creating another norm, identical in character with a statute whose only function is to repeal a previously valid statute. The much-discussed question whether a statute may also be invalidated by desuetudo is ultimately the question whether custom as a source of law may be excluded by statute within a legal order. For reasons which will be given later, the question must be answered in the negative. It must be assumed that any legal norm, even a statutory norm, may lose validity by desuetudo.

However, even in this case it would be a mistake to identify the validity and the efficacy of the norm; they are still two different phenomena. The norm annulled by desuetudo was valid for a considerable time without being efficacious. It is only an enduring lack of efficacy that ends the validity.

The relation between validity and efficacy thus appears to be the following: A norm is a valid legal norm if (a) it has been created in a way provided for by the legal order to which it belongs, and (b) if it has not been annulled either in a way provided for by that legal order or by way of desuetudo or by the fact that the legal order as a whole has lost its efficacy.

g. The "Ought" and the "Is"

The basic norm of a national legal order is not the arbitrary product of juristic imagination. Its content is determined by facts. The function of the basic norm is to make possible the normative interpretation of certain facts, and that means, the interpretation of facts as the creation and application of valid norms. Legal norms, as we pointed out, are considered to be valid only if they belong to an order which is by and large efficacious. Therefore, the content of a basic norm is determined by the facts through which an order is created and applied, to which the behavior of the individuals regulated by this order, by and large, conforms. The basic norm of any positive legal order confers legal authority only upon facts by which an order is created and applied which is on the whole effective. It is not required that the actual behavior of individuals be in absolute conformity with the order. On the contrary, a certain antagonism between the normative order and the actual human behavior to which the norms of the order refer must be possible. Without such a possibility, a normative order would be completely meaningless. What necessarily happens under the laws of nature does not have to be prescribed by norms: The basic norm of a social order to which the actual behavior of the individuals always and without any exception conforms would run as follows: Men ought to behave as they actually behave, or: You ought to do what you actually do. Such an order would be as meaningless as an order with which human behavior would in no way conform, but always and in every respect contradict. Therefore, a normative order loses its validity when reality no longer corresponds to it, at least to a certain degree. The validity of a legal order is thus dependent upon its agreement with reality, upon its "efficacy." The relationship which exists between the validity and efficacy of a legal order — it is, so to speak, the tension between the "ought" and the "is" — can be determined only by an upper and a lower borderline. The agreement must neither exceed a certain maximum nor fall below a certain minimum.

h. Law and Power (Right and Might)

Seeing that the validity of a legal order is thus dependent upon its efficacy, one may be misled into identifying the two phenomena, by defining the validity of law as its efficacy, by describing the law by "is" and not by "ought" statements. Attempts of this kind have very often been made and they have always failed. For, if the validity of law is identified with any natural fact, it is impossible to comprehend the specific sense in which law is directed towards reality and thus stands over against reality. Only if law and natural reality, the system of legal norms and the actual behavior of men, the "ought" and the "is," are two different realms, may reality conform with or contradict law, can human behavior be characterized as legal or illegal.

The efficacy of law belongs to the realm of reality and is often called the power of law. If for efficacy we substitute power, then the problem of validity and efficacy is transformed into the more common problem of "right and might." And then the solution here presented is merely the precise statement of the old truth that though law cannot exist without power, still law and power, right and might, are not the same. Law is, according to the theory here presented, a specific order or organization of power.

i. The Principle of Effectiveness as Positive Legal Norm (International and National Law)

The principle that a legal order must be efficacious in order to be valid is, in itself, a positive norm. It is the principle of effectiveness belonging to international law. According to this principle of international law, an actually established authority is the legitimate government, the coercive order enacted by this government is the legal order, and the community constituted by this order is a State in the sense of international law, insofar as this order is, on the whole, efficacious. From the standpoint of international law, the constitution of a State is valid only if the legal order established on the basis of this constitution is, on the whole, efficacious. It is this general principle of effectiveness, a positive norm of international law, which, applied to the concrete circumstances of an individual national legal order, provides the individual basic norm of this national legal order. Thus, the basic norms of the different national legal orders are themselves based on a general norm of the international legal order. If we conceive of international law as a legal order to which all the States (and that means all the national legal orders) are subordinated, then the basic norm of a national legal order is not a mere presupposition of juristic thinking, but a positive legal norm, a norm of international law applied to the legal order of a concrete State. Assuming the primacy of international law over national law, the problem of the basic norm shifts from the national to the international legal order. Then the only true basic norm, a norm which is not created by a legal procedure but presupposed by juristic thinking, is the basic norm of international law.

j. Validity and Efficacy

That the validity of a legal order depends upon its efficacy does not imply, as pointed out, that the validity of a single norm depends upon its efficacy. The single legal norm remains valid as long as it is part of a valid order. The question whether an individual norm is valid is answered by recourse to the first constitution. If this is valid, then all norms which have been created in a constitutional way are valid, too. The principle of effectiveness embodied in international law refers immediately only to the first constitution of a national legal order, and therefore to this order only as a whole.

The principle of effectiveness may, however, be adopted to a certain extent also by national law, and thus within a national legal order the validity of a single norm may be made dependent upon its efficacy. Such is the case when a legal norm may lose its validity by desuetudo.

D. The Static and the Dynamic Concept of Law

If one looks upon the legal order from the dynamic point of view, as it has been expounded here, it seems possible to define the concept of law in a way quite different from that in which we have tried to define it in this theory. It seems especially possible to ignore the element of coercion in defining the concept of law.

It is a fact that the legislator can enact commandments without considering it necessary to attach a criminal or civil sanction to their violation. If such norms are also called legal norms, it is because they were created by an authority which, according to the constitution, is competent to create law. They are law because they issue from a law-creating authority. According to this concept, law is anything that has come about in the way the constitution prescribes for the creation of law. This dynamic concept differs from the concept of law defined as a coercive norm. According to the dynamic concept, law is something created by a certain process, and everything created in this way is law. This dynamic concept, however, is only apparently a concept of law. It contains no answer to the question of what is the essence of law, what is the criterion by which law can be distinguished from other social norms. This dynamic concept furnishes an answer only to the question whether or not and why a certain norm belongs to a system of valid legal norms, forms a part of a certain legal order. And the answer is, a norm belongs to a certain legal order if it is created in accordance with a procedure prescribed by the constitution fundamental to this legal order.

It must, however, be noted that not only a norm, i.e., a command regulating human behavior, can be created in the way prescribed by the constitution for the creation of law. An important stage in the law-creating process is the procedure by which general norms are created, that is, the procedure of legislation. The constitution may organize this procedure of legislation in the following way: two corresponding resolutions of both houses of parliament, the consent of the chief of State, and publication in an official journal. This means that a specific form of law-creation is established. It is then possible to clothe in this form any subject, for instance, a recognition of the merits of a statesman. The form of a law — a declaration voted by parliament, consented to by the chief of State, published in the official journal — is chosen in order to give to a certain subject, here to the expression of the nation's gratitude, the character of a solemn act. The solemn recognition of the merits of a statesman is by no means a norm, even if it appears as the content of a legislative act, even if it has the form of a law. The law as the product of the legislative procedure, a statute in the formal sense of the term, is a document containing words, sentences; and that which is expressed by these sentences need not necessarily be a norm. As a matter of fact, many a law — in this formal sense of the term — contains not only legal norms, but also certain elements which are of no specific legal, i.e. normative, character, such as, purely theoretical views concerning certain matters, the motives of the legislator, political ideologies contained in references such as "justice" or "the will of God," etc., etc. All these are legally irrelevant contents of the statute, or, more generally, legally irrelevant products of the law-creating process. The law-creating process includes not only the process of legislation, but also the procedure of the judicial and administrative authorities. Even judgments of the courts very often contain legally irrelevant elements. If by the term "law" is meant something pertaining to a certain legal order, then law is anything which has been created according to the procedure prescribed by the constitution fundamental to this order. This does not mean, however, that everything which has been created according to this procedure is law in the sense of a legal norm. It is a legal norm only if it purports to regulate human behavior, and if it regulates human behavior by providing an act of coercion as sanction.

XI. THE HIERARCHY OF THE NORMS

A. THE SUPERIOR AND THE INFERIOR NORM

The analysis of law, which reveals the dynamic character of this normative system and the function of the basic norm, also exposes a further peculiarity of law: Law regulates its own creation inasmuch as one legal norm determines the way in which another norm is created, and also, to some extent, the contents of that norm. Since a legal norm is valid because it is created in a way determined by another legal norm, the latter is the reason of validity of the former. The relation between the norm regulating the creation of another norm and this other norm may be presented as a relationship of super- and sub-ordination, which is a spatial figure of speech. The norm determining the creation of another norm is the superior, the norm created according to this regulation, the inferior norm. The legal order, especially the legal order the personification of which is the State, is therefore not a system of norms coördinated to each other, standing, so to speak, side by side on the same level, but a hierarchy of different levels of norms. The unity of these norms is constituted by the fact that the creation of one norm — the lower one — is determined by another — the higher — the creation of which is determined by a still higher norm, and that this *regressus* is terminated by a highest, the basic norm which, being the supreme reason of validity of the whole legal order, constitutes its unity.

B. The Different Stages of the Legal Order

a. The Constitution

1. Constitution in a Material and a Formal Sense; Determination of the Creation of General Norms

The hierarchical structure of the legal order of a State is roughly as follows: Presupposing the basic norm, the constitution is the highest level within national law. The constitution is here understood, not in a formal, but in a material sense. The constitution in the formal sense is a certain solemn document, a set of legal norms that may be changed only under the observation of special prescriptions, the purpose of which it is to render the change of these norms more difficult. The constitution in the material sense consists of those rules which regulate the creation of the general legal norms, in particular the creation of statutes. The formal constitution, the solemn document called "constitution," usually contains also other norms, norms which are no part of the material constitution. But it is in order to safeguard the norms determining the organs and the procedure of legislation that a special solemn document is drafted and that the changing of its rules is made especially difficult. It is because of the material constitution that there is a special form for constitutional laws or a constitutional form. If there is a constitutional form, then constitutional laws must be distinguished from ordinary laws.

The difference consists in that the creation, and that means enactment, amendment, annulment, of constitutional laws is more difficult than that of ordinary laws. There exists a special procedure, a special form for the creation of constitutional laws, different from the procedure for the creation of ordinary laws. Such a special form for constitutional laws, a constitutional form, or constitution in the formal sense of the term, is not indispensable, whereas the material constitution, that is to say norms regulating the creation of general norms and — in modern law — norms determining the organs and procedure of legislation, is an essential element of every legal order.

A constitution in the formal sense, especially provisions by which change of the constitution is made more difficult than the change of ordinary laws, is possible only if there is a written constitution, if the constitution has the character of statutory law. There are States, Great Britain for instance, which have no "written" and hence no formal constitution, no solemn document called "The Constitution." Here the (material) constitution has the character of customary law and therefore there exists no difference between constitutional and ordinary laws. The constitution in the material sense of the term may be a written or an unwritten law, may have the character of statutory or customary law. If, however, a specific form for constitutional law exists, any contents whatever may appear under this form. As a matter of fact, subject-matters which for some reason or other are considered especially important are often regulated by constitutional instead of by ordinary laws. An example is the Eighteenth Amendment to the Constitution of the United States, the prohibition amendment, now repealed.

2. Determination of the Content of General Norms by the Constitution

The material constitution may determine not only the organs and the procedure of legislation, but also, to some degree, the contents of future laws. The constitution can negatively determine that the laws must not have a certain content, e.g., that the parliament may not pass any statute which restricts religious freedom. In this negative way, not only the contents of statutes but of all the other norms of the legal order, judicial and administrative decisions likewise, may be determined by the constitution. The constitution, however, can also positively prescribe a certain content of future statutes; it can, as does, for instance the Constitution of the United States of America, stipulate "that in all criminal prosecutions the accused shall enjoy the right to a speedy and public trial, by an impartial jury of the State and district wherein the crime shall have been committed, which district shall have been previously ascertained by law, etc. . . ." This provision of the constitution determines the contents of future laws concerning criminal procedure. The importance of such stipulations from the point of view of legal technique will be discussed in another context.

3. Custom as Determined by the Constitution

If, within a legal order, there exists by the side of statutory also customary law, if the law-applying organs, especially the courts, have to apply not only the general norms created by the legislative organ, the statutes, but also the general norms created by custom, then custom is considered to be a law-creating fact just as is legislation. This is possible only if the constitution — in the material sense of the word — institutes custom, just as it institutes legislation, as a law-creating procedure. Custom has to be, like legislation, a constitutional institution. This might be stipulated expressly by the constitution; and the relation between statutory and customary law might be expressly regulated. But the constitution itself can, as a whole or in part, be unwritten, customary law. Thus it might be due to custom that custom is a law-creating fact. If a legal order has a written constitution which does not institute custom as a form of law-creation, and if nevertheless the legal order contains customary law besides statutory law, then, in addition to the norms of the written constitution, there must exist unwritten norms of constitution, a customarily created norm according to which the general norms binding the law-applying organs can be created by custom. Law regulates its own creation, and so does customary law.

Sometimes it is maintained that custom is not a constitutive, that is to say, a law-creating fact, but has only a declaratory character: it merely indicates the preëxistence of a rule of law. This rule of law is, according to the natural law doctrine, created by God or by nature; according to the German historic school (at the beginning of the 19th century), it is created by the "spirit of the people" (*Volksgeist*). The most important representative of this school, F. C. von Savigny,* advocated the view that the law cannot be "made" but exists within and is born with the People since begotten in a mysterious way by the *Volksgeist*. He consequently denied any competence to legislate, and characterized customary observance not as cause of law but as evidence of its existence. In modern French legal theory the doctrine of the

---

* 1 Friedrich Carl von Savigny, System des heutigen roemischen Rechts (1840) 35: "So ist also die Gewohnheit das Kennzeichen des positiven Rechts, nicht dessen Entstehungsgrund" ("Custom, therefore is an indication of the existence and not a ground of origin of positive law"). Cf. also Savigny, Vom Beruf unserer Zeit fuer Gesetzgebung und Rechtswissenschaft (1815).

Volksgeist is replaced by that of "social solidarity" (*solidarité sociale*). According to Léon Duguit * and his school, the true, i.e. the "objective," law (*droit objectif*) is implied by the social solidarity. Consequently, any act or fact the result of which is positive law — be it legislation or custom — is not true creation of law but a declaratory statement (*constatation*) or mere evidence of the rule of law previously created by social solidarity. This doctrine has influenced the formulation of Article 38 of the Statute of the Permanent Court of International Justice, by which the Court is authorized to apply customary international law: "The Court shall apply . . . international custom, as evidence of a general practice accepted as law."

Both the German doctrine of the *Volksgeist* and the French doctrine of *solidarité sociale* are typical variants of the natural-law doctrine with its characteristic dualism of a "true" law behind the positive law. What has been said against the latter can be maintained to refute the former. From the viewpoint of a positivistic theory of law the law-creating, and that means the constitutive, character of custom can be denied just as little as can that of legislation.

There is no difference between a rule of customary law and a rule of statutory law in their relationship to the law-applying organ. The statement that a customary rule becomes law only by recognition on the part of the court applying the rule † is neither more nor less correct than the

---

* LÉON DUGUIT, L'ÉTAT, LE DROIT OBJECTIF ET LA LOI POSITIVE (1901), 8off., 616.

† 1 AUSTIN, LECTURES ON JURISPRUDENCE (5th ed., 1885) 101f.: "The custom is transmuted into positive law, when it is adopted as such by the courts of justice, and when the judicial decisions fashioned upon it are enforced by the power of the state. But before it is adopted by the courts, and clothed with the legal sanction, it is merely a rule of positive morality: a rule generally observed by the citizens or subjects; but deriving the only force, which it can be said to possess, from the general disapprobation falling on those who transgress it." Austin overlooks the fact that the rule created by custom may be a rule providing sanctions — and must be such a rule in order to be a rule of law — so that "custom" is "clothed with the legal sanction" before it is "adopted by the courts." It is true that the court which has to apply customary law must ascertain that the rule to be applied to a concrete case has actually been created by custom, just as the court which has to apply statutory law must ascertain that the statute to be applied to the concrete case has been actually created by the legislative organ. That means, however, that the rule to be applied is actually a rule of law; and this ascertainment is certainly a constitutive act, whether it is a rule of customary or statutory law which is to be applied by the court. (Cf. *infra* pp. 143f.) Austin presupposes that only the State (the "sovereign") can make law. The courts and the legislative organ are organs of the State. Since custom is constituted by acts of "citizens or subjects," not by acts of State, the customary rule can become a rule of law only by adoption on the part of the courts. This is a fallacy. The assumption that the courts have to apply rules created by custom necessarily implies the assumption that the written or un-

same statement made with reference to a rule enacted by the legislative organ. Each was law "before it received the stamp of judicial authentication," * since custom is a law-creating procedure in the same sense as legislation. The real difference between customary and statutory law consists in the fact that the former is a decentralized whereas the latter is a centralized creation of law.† Customary law is created by the individuals subject to the law created by them, whereas statutory law is created by special organs instituted for that purpose. In this respect, customary law is similar to law made by contract or treaty, characterized by the fact that the legal norm is created by the same subjects upon whom it is binding. Whereas, however, conventional (contractual) law is, as a rule, binding only upon the contracting subjects, the individuals creating the norm being identical with those subject to the norm, a legal rule created by custom is binding not exclusively upon the individuals who by their conduct have constituted the law-creating custom. It is consequently not correct to characterize the law-creating custom as a tacit contract or treaty, as is sometimes done, especially in the theory of international law.

b. General Norms Enacted on the Basis of the Constitution; Statutes, Customary Law

The general norms established by way of legislation or custom form a level which comes next to the constitution in the hierarchy of law. These general norms are to be applied by the organs competent thereto, especially by the courts but also by the administrative authorities. The law-applying organs must be instituted according to the legal order, which likewise has to determine the procedure which those organs shall follow when applying law. Thus, the general norms of statutory or customary law have a two-fold function: (1) to determine the law-applying organs and the procedure to be observed by them and (2) to determine the judicial and administrative acts of these organs. The latter by their acts create individual norms, thereby applying the general norms to concrete cases.

---

written constitution institutes custom as a law-creating procedure; and this implies that the individuals who by their conduct constitute the custom are organs of the legal order or, what amounts to the same, of the legal community constituted by this order: the State, just as are the parliament and the courts. Since the State is nothing but the personification of "its" law, the law of the State, that is to say national law, is necessarily law made "by the State," meaning law created according to the legal order constituting the State.

* HOLLAND, ELEMENTS OF JURISPRUDENCE (13th ed. 1924) 60.
† Cf. *infra* pp. 308ff.

c. Substantive and Adjective Law

To these two functions correspond the two kinds of law, which are commonly distinguished: material or substantive and formal or adjective law. Beside the substantive criminal law there is an adjective crim· inal law of criminal procedure, and the same is true also of civil law and administrative law. Part of procedural law, of course, are also those norms which constitute the law-applying organs. Thus two kinds of general norms are always involved in the application of law by an organ: (1) the formal norms which determine the creation of this organ and the procedure it has to follow, and (2) the material norms which determine the contents of its judicial or administrative act. When speaking of the "application" of law by courts and administrative organs, one usually thinks only of the second kind of norms; it is only the substantive civil, criminal, and administrative law applied by the organs one has in mind. But no application of norms of the second kind is possible without the application of norms of the first kind. The substantive civil, criminal, or administrative law cannot be applied in a concrete case without the adjective law regulating the civil, criminal, or administrative procedure being applied at the same time. The two kinds of norm are really inseparable. Only in their organic union do they form the law. Every complete or primary rule of law, as we have called it, contains both the formal and the material element. The (very much simplified) form of a rule of criminal law is: If a subject has committed a certain delict, then a certain organ (the court), appointed in a certain way, shall, through a certain procedure, especially on the motion of another organ (the public prosecutor), direct against the delinquent a certain sanction. As we shall show later, a more explicit statement of such a norm is: If the competent organ, that is the organ appointed in the way prescribed by the law, has established through a certain procedure prescribed by the law, that a subject has committed a delict, determined by the law, then a sanction prescribed by the law shall be directed against the delinquent. This formulation clearly exhibits the systematic relation between substantive and adjective law, between the determination of the delict and the sanction, on the one hand, and the determination of the organs and their procedure, on the other.

d. Determination of the Law-applying Organs by General Norms

The general norms created by legislation or custom bear essentially the same relation to their application through courts and administrative authorities as the constitution bears to the creation of these same general norms through legislation and custom. Both functions — the judicial or

administrative application of general norms, and the statutory or customary creation of general norms — are determined by norms of a higher
level, formally and materially, with respect to the procedure and with
respect to the contents of the function. The proportion, however, in
which the formal and the material determination of both functions stand
to one another, is different. The material constitution chiefly determines
by what organs and through what procedure the general norms are to be
created. Usually, it leaves the contents of these norms undetermined or,
at least, it determines their contents in a negative way only. The general
norms created by legislation or custom according to the constitution,
especially the statutes, determine, however, not only the judicial and
administrative organs and the judicial and administrative procedure but
also the contents of the individual norms, the judicial decisions and
administrative acts which are to be issued by the law-applying organs.
In criminal law, for instance, usually a general norm very accurately
determines the delict to which the courts, in a concrete case, have to
attach a sanction, and accurately determines this sanction, too; so that
the content of the judicial decision — which has to be issued in a concrete case — is predetermined to a great extent by a general norm. The
degree of material determination may of course vary. The free discretion
of the law-applying organs is sometimes greater, sometimes less. The
courts are usually much more strictly bound by the substantive civil and
criminal laws they have to apply than are the administrative authorities
by the administrative statutes. This, however, is beside the point. Important is the fact that the constitution materially determines the general
norms created on its basis to a far less extent than these norms materially
determine the individual norms enacted by the judiciary and the administration. In the former case, the formal determination is predominant; in the latter case, formal and material determination balance one
another.

e. Ordinances (Regulations)

Sometimes the creation of general norms is divided into two or more
stages. Some constitutions give certain administrative authorities, for
instance, the chief of State or the cabinet ministers, the power to enact
general norms by which the provisions of a statute are elaborated. Such
general norms, which are not issued by the so-called legislative but by
another organ on the basis of general norms issued by the legislator, are
designated as regulations, or ordinances. According to some constitutions, certain administrative organs — especially the chief of State or the
cabinet ministers as chiefs of certain branches of administration — are
authorized, under extraordinary circumstances, to issue general norms to

regulate subject-matters which are ordinarily to be regulated by the legislative organ through statutes. The distinction between statutes and regulations (ordinances) is evidently of legal importance only when the creation of general norms is, in principle, reserved to a special legislative organ which is not identical with the chief of State or the cabinet ministers. The distinction is especially significant where there is a popularly elected parliament and the legislative power is in principle separated from the judicial and the executive powers. Disregarding customary law, general legal norms then must have a special form: they are to be the contents of parliamentary decisions, these decisions sometimes need the consent of the chief of State and require sometimes publication in an official journal in order to have legal force. These requirements constitute the form of a law. Since any contents whatsoever, and not only a legal norm regulating human behavior, may appear under this form, one then has to distinguish between laws in a material sense (general legal norms in the form of a law) and laws in a formal sense (anything which has the form of a law). It may happen that a declaration without any legal significance whatsoever is made in the form of a law. There exists, then, a legally indifferent content of the law-creating process, a phenomenon of which we have already spoken.*

f. The "Sources" of Law

The customary and the statutory creation of law are often regarded as the two "sources" of law. In this context, by "law" one usually understands only the general norms, ignoring the individual norms which, however, are just as much part of law as are the general ones.

"Source" of law is a figurative and highly ambiguous expression. It is used not only to designate the above-mentioned methods of creating law, custom and legislation (the latter term understood in its widest sense comprising also creation of law by judicial and administrative acts and legal transactions) but also to characterize the reason for the validity of law and especially the ultimate reason. The basic norm is then the "source" of law. But, in a wider sense, every legal norm is a "source" of that other norm, the creation of which it regulates, in determining the procedure of creation and the contents of the norm to be created. In this sense, any "superior" legal norm is the "source" of the "inferior" legal norm. Thus, the constitution is the "source" of statutes created on the basis of the constitution, a statute is the "source" of the judicial decision based thereon, the judicial decision is the "source" of the duty it imposes upon the party, and so on. The "source" of law is thus not, as the phrase

* Cf. *supra*, p. 123.

might suggest, an entity different from and somehow existing independently from law; the "source" of law is always itself law: a "superior" legal norm in relation to an "inferior" legal norm, or the method of creating an (inferior) norm determined by a (superior) norm, and that means a specific content of law.

The expression "source of law" is finally used also in an entirely non-juristic sense. One thereby denotes also all those ideas which actually influence the law-creating organs, for instance, moral norms, political principles, legal doctrines, the opinions of juristic experts, etc. In contradistinction to the previously mentioned "sources" of law, these "sources" do not as such have any binding force. They are not — as are the true "sources of law" — legal norms or a specific content of legal norms. It is, however, possible for the legal order, by obliging the law-creating organs to respect or apply certain moral norms or political principles or opinions of experts, to transform these norms, principles, or opinions into legal norms and thus into true sources of law.

The ambiguity of the term "source of law" seems to render the term rather useless. Instead of a misleading figurative phrase one ought to introduce an expression that clearly and directly describes the phenomenon one has in mind.

g. Creation of Law and Application of Law

1. Merely Relative Difference between Law-creating and Law-applying Function

The legal order is a system of general and individual norms connected with each other according to the principle that law regulates its own creation. Each norm of this order is created according to the provisions of another norm, and ultimately according to the provisions of the basic norm constituting the unity of this system of norms, the legal order. A norm belongs to this legal order only because it has been created in conformity with the stipulations of another norm of the order. This *regressus* finally leads to the first constitution, the creation of which is determined by the presupposed basic norm. One may also say that a norm belongs to a certain legal order if it has been created by an organ of the community constituted by the order. The individual who creates the legal norm is an organ of the legal community because and insofar as his function is determined by a legal norm of the order constituting the legal community. The imputation of this function to the community is based on the norm determining the function. This explanation, however, does not add anything to the previous one. The statement "A norm belongs to a certain legal order because it is created by an organ of the legal community constituted by this order" and the statement "A norm belongs to a legal order because it is created according to the basic norm of this legal order" assert one and the same thing.

A norm regulating the creation of another norm is "applied" in the creation of the other norm. Creation of law is always application of law. These two concepts are by no means, as the traditional theory presumes, absolute opposites. It is not quite correct to classify legal acts as law-creating and law-applying acts; for, setting aside two borderline cases of which we shall speak later, every act is, normally, at the same time a law-creating and a law-applying act. The creation of a legal norm is — normally — an application of the higher norm, regulating its creation, and the application of a higher norm is — normally — the creation of a lower norm determined by the higher norm. A judicial decision, e.g., is an act by which a general norm, a statute, is applied but at the same time an individual norm is created obligating one or both parties to the conflict. Legislation is creation of law, but taking into account the constitution, we find that it is also application of law. In any act of legislation, where the provisions of the constitution are observed, the constitution is applied. The making of the first constitution can likewise be considered as an application of the basic norm.

2. Determination of the Law-creating Function

As pointed out, the creation of a legal norm can be determined in two different directions: the higher norm may determine: (1) the organ and the procedure by which a lower norm is to be created, and (2) the contents of the lower norm. Even if the higher norm determines only the organ, and that means the individual by which the lower norm has to be created, and that again means authorizes this organ to determine at his own discretion the procedure of creating the lower norm and the contents of this norm, the higher norm is "applied" in the creation of the lower norm. The higher norm must at least determine the organ by which the lower norm has to be created. For a norm the creation of which is not determined at all by another norm cannot belong to any legal order. The individual creating a norm cannot be considered the organ of a legal community, his norm-creating function cannot be imputed to the community, unless in performing the function he applies a norm of the legal order constituting the community. Every law-creating act must be a law-applying act, i.e., it must apply a norm preceding the act in order to be an act of the legal order or the community constituted by it. Therefore, the norm-creating function has to be conceived of as a norm-applying function even if only its personal element, the individual who has to create the lower norm, is determined by the higher norm. It is this higher norm determining the organ which is applied by every act of this organ.

That creation of law is at the same time application of law, is an immediate consequence of the fact that every law-creating act must be determined by the legal order. This determination may be of different degrees. It can never be so weak that the act ceases to be an application of law. Nor can it be so strong that the act ceases to be a creation of law. As long as a norm is established through the act, it is a law-creating act, even if the function of the law-creating organ is in a high degree determined by the higher norm. This is the case when not only the organ and the law-creating procedure but also the contents of the norm to be created are determined by a higher norm. However, in this case, too, an act of law-creating exists. The question whether an act is creation or application of law is in fact quite independent of the question as to the degree to which the acting organ is bound by the legal order. Only acts by which no norm is established may be merely application of law. Of such a nature is the execution of a sanction in a concrete case. This is one of the two borderline cases mentioned above. The other is the basic norm. It determines the creation of the first constitution; but being presupposed by juristic thinking, its presupposition is not itself determined by any higher norm and is therefore no application of law.

h. Individual Norms Created on the Basis of General Norms

1. The Judicial Act as Creation of an Individual Norm

As an application of law, traditional doctrine considers above all the judicial decision, the function of courts. When settling a dispute between two parties or when sentencing an accused person to a punishment, a court applies, it is true, a general norm of statutory or customary law. But simultaneously the court creates an individual norm providing that a definite sanction shall be executed against a definite individual. This individual norm is related to the general norms as a statute is related to the constitution. The judicial function is thus, like legislation, both creation and application of law. The judicial function is ordinarily determined by the general norms both as to procedure and as to the contents of the norm to be created, whereas legislation is usually determined by the constitution only in the former respect. But that is a difference in degree only.

2. The Judicial Act as a Stage of the Law-creating Process

From a dynamic standpoint, the individual norm created by the judicial decision is a stage in a process beginning with the establishment of

the first constitution, continued by legislation and custom, and leading
to the judicial decisions. The process is completed by the execution of
the individual sanction. Statutes and customary laws are, so to speak,
only semi-manufactured products which are finished only through the
judicial decision and its execution. The process through which law constantly creates itself anew goes from the general and abstract to the
individual and concrete. It is a process of steadily increasing individualization and concretization.

The general norm which, to certain abstractly determined conditions,
attaches certain abstractly determined consequences, has to be individualized and concretized in order to come in contact with social life,
to be applied to reality. To this purpose, in a given case it has to be
ascertained whether the conditions, determined *in abstracto* in the general norm, are present *in concreto*, in order that the sanction, determined
in abstracto in the general norm, may be ordered and executed *in concreto*. These are the two essential elements of the judicial function.
This function has, by no means, as is sometimes assumed, a purely
declaratory character. Contrary to what is sometimes asserted, the
court does not merely formulate already existing law. It does not only
"seek" and "find" the law existing previous to its decision, it does not
merely pronounce the law which exists ready and finished prior to its
pronouncement. Both in establishing the presence of the conditions
and in stipulating the sanction, the judicial decision has a constitutive
character. The decision applies, it is true, a preëxisting general norm
in which a certain consequence is attached to certain conditions. But the
existence of the concrete conditions in connection with the concrete
consequence is, in the concrete case, first established by the court's decision. Conditions and consequences are connected by judicial decisions in
the realm of the concrete, as they are connected by statutes and rules of
customary law in the realm of the abstract. The individual norm of the
judicial decision is the necessary individualization and concretization of
the general and abstract norm. Only the prejudice, characteristic of
the jurisprudence of continental Europe, that law is, by definition, only
general norms, only the erroneous identification of law with the general
rules of statutory and customary law, could obscure the fact that the
judicial decision continues the law-creating process from the sphere of
the general and abstract into that of the individual and concrete.

3. The Ascertainment of the Conditioning Facts

The judicial decision is clearly constitutive as far as it orders a concrete sanction to be executed against an individual delinquent. But it
has a constitutive character also, as far as it ascertains the facts condi-

tioning the sanction. In the world of law, there is no fact "in itself," no "absolute" fact, there are only facts ascertained by a competent organ in a procedure prescribed by law. When attaching to certain facts certain consequences, the legal order must also designate an organ that has to ascertain the facts in the concrete case and prescribe the procedure which the organ, in so doing, has to observe. The legal order may authorize this organ to regulate its procedure at its own discretion; but organ and procedure by which the conditioning facts are to be ascertained must be — directly or indirectly — determined by the legal order, to make the latter applicable to social life. It is a typical layman's opinion that there are absolute, immediately evident facts. Only by being first ascertained through a legal procedure are facts brought into the sphere of law or do they, so to speak, come into existence within this sphere. Formulating this in a somewhat paradoxically pointed way, we could say that the competent organ ascertaining the conditioning facts legally "creates" these facts. Therefore, the function of ascertaining facts through a legal procedure has always a specifically constitutive character. If, according to a legal norm, a sanction has to be executed against a murderer, this does not mean that the fact of murder is "in itself" the condition of the sanction. There is no fact "in itself" that A has killed B, there is only my or somebody else's belief or knowledge that A has killed B. A himself may either acquiesce or deny. From the point of view of law, however, all these are no more than private opinions without relevance. Only the establishment by the competent organ has legal relevance. If the judicial decision has already obtained the force of law, if it has become impossible to replace this decision by another because there exists the status of *res judicata* — which means that the case has been definitely decided by a court of last resort — then the opinion that the condemned was innocent is without any legal significance. As already pointed out, the correct formulation of the rule of law is not "If a subject has committed a delict, an organ shall direct a sanction against the delinquent," but "If the competent organ has established in due order that a subject has committed a delict, then an organ shall direct a sanction against this subject."

C. The Legal Transaction (Juristic Act)

a. The Legal Transaction as Law-creating and Law-applying Act

1. Private Autonomy

The conditions of the sanction, the presence of which the court has to ascertain, are different depending upon whether criminal or civil law has to be applied by the court. We have already pointed out that the court has to order a concrete sanction in the procedure of criminal law on the motion of an organ of the community, the public prosecutor, in the procedure of civil law upon the suit of a private party, the plaintiff. It is especially characteristic of civil law that a legal transaction may appear among the conditions of the sanction. The delict consists in the fact that one party fails to fulfill an obligation imposed upon him by the legal transaction. The legal transaction is an act by which the individuals authorized by the legal order regulate certain relations legally. It is a law-creating act, for it produces legal duties and rights of the parties who enter the transaction. But at the same time it is an act of law-application, and thus it both creates and applies law. The parties make use of general norms which render legal transactions possible. By entering a legal transaction, they apply these general legal norms. By giving individuals the possibility of regulating their mutual relations through legal transactions, the legal order grants individuals a certain legal autonomy. It is in the law-creating function of the legal transaction that the so-called "private autonomy" of the parties manifests itself. By a legal transaction, individual and sometimes even general norms are created regulating the mutual behavior of the parties.

It is important clearly to distinguish between the legal transaction as the act by which the parties create a norm for themselves, and the norm created in this way. Both phenomena are usually designated by the same word. The term "contract" in particular has such a double use. "Contract" designates both the specific procedure by which the contractual duties and rights of the contracting parties are created and the contractual norm created by this procedure, an equivocation which is the source of typical errors in the theory of contract.

2. The Secondary Norm as Product of a Legal Transaction

If it is said that legal norms are created by legal transactions, it is secondary norms which are meant. For they give rise to legal duties and rights only in connection with those general primary norms which attach a sanction to the breach of a transaction. Here, the secondary norm, stipulating directly the lawful behavior of the parties, is not a mere auxiliary construction of juristic theory, of which we spoke in a foregoing chapter.* It is the content of a legal act provided for by the general primary norm as a condition of the sanction. An example may serve to illustrate this. By a lease, one party, A, assumes the obligation to let another party, B, live in a certain building, and the other party,

* Cf. *supra*, pp. 60f.

B, assumes the obligation to pay a certain rent to the first party, A. Both obligations are formulated in the text of the lease as secondary norms: A ought to let B live in the building X; B ought to pay a rent to A. But the legal duties of A and B are constituted only by the fact that, according to a general primary norm which the courts have to apply, A and B are liable to a sanction if they do not behave as the secondary norm, created by the contract, prescribes, and if the other party brings a suit against the party who has violated this secondary norm. In this point there exists a characteristic difference between the technique of civil and criminal law. The legal duty of the individual to forbear from stealing is directly stipulated by the general primary norm attaching a punishment to theft. The secondary norm, "Everybody and therefore I, too, ought to refrain from stealing," is here nothing but an auxiliary construction of juristic theory. It is not indispensable. The legal reality can be described without it. A statement reproducing the contents of the primary norm "If A steals, he ought to be punished," is sufficient to characterize A's legal duty. The legal duty of A, the landlord, to let B, the tenant, live in a certain building, and the legal duty of the tenant B to pay a certain rent to the landlord A, are not directly stipulated by the general primary norm regulating leases by attaching sanctions to the breach of lease-contracts. Here, a specific law-creating act must be added to the general norm, a legal transaction by which an individual secondary norm is created constituting the concrete duties and rights of the landlord A and the tenant B. The general primary norm empowers the parties to make such legal transactions, that means, to create, by a certain procedure, an individual norm. This individual norm which stipulates that A ought to let B live in a certain building, and that B ought to pay A a certain rent, is a secondary norm, for it constitutes only in connection with the general primary norm the legal duties of A and B.

That in the province of criminal law individual legal duties are stipulated directly by the general primary norm, whereas in the domain of civil law the general primary norm stipulates individual legal duties only indirectly, through the medium of legal transactions, is not a rule without exceptions. The typical exception concerns the duty to repair damage caused illegally.

3. Reparation

As we have explained in another context, the sanction provided by a general legal norm of civil law is not only conditioned by behavior of the individual contrary to the secondary norm created by the legal transaction, but also by the fact that the damage caused by this violation has not been repaired. In other terms, between the violation of the secondary norm created by the legal transaction, and the sanction, a duty to repair the illegally caused damage is usually inserted. The general norm on the basis of which, e.g., leases are agreed upon, runs: "If two parties make a lease, if one of them breaks it and does not repair the damage thereby caused, then a civil sanction shall be executed against him upon a suit by the other party." There exists, however, according to the civil law of all the legal orders, a legal duty to repair an illegally caused damage not merely in case the illegal behavior constituted a violation of the secondary norm created by a legal transaction. A general legal norm attaches a civil sanction directly to the fact that an individual does not repair an injury caused by his behavior, even without any previous legal transaction, just as a criminal sanction is attached to certain behavior of an individual. Then there is in this regard no difference between the technique of civil and that of criminal law. The individual duty to repair an injury is stipulated directly by the general primary norm attaching a civil sanction to non-repairing an injury caused by certain behavior. The legal duty of repairing an injury caused by behavior which is not a violation of a secondary norm created by a legal transaction is usually characterized by saying that it is not a duty *ex contractu* but a duty *ex delicto*.

The behavior may, but need not, have the character of a criminal delict. It may constitute only a civil delict. The behavior which has caused the damage constitutes a criminal delict if it is the condition of a criminal sanction, and the non-repairing of the damage caused by this behavior is the condition of a civil sanction. As a rule, there is a legal obligation to repair the damage caused by a criminal delict. The fact that a general legal norm attaches to the non-repairing of an injury caused by a certain act of an individual a civil sanction directed against this individual is usually described by a statement of two legal duties: the duty of an individual not to cause damage by his behavior, and his duty to repair the damage his behavior caused. In case the damage is caused by an act which constitutes the violation of a secondary norm created by a legal transaction, one usually distinguishes between the legal duty to observe the secondary norm, e.g., the duty of the landlord to let the tenant live in the building, and the duty to repair the damage caused by a violation of the first duty, i.e., the violation of the secondary norm. The relationship between these two duties is characterized by the fact that the second duty supplants the first. By fulfilling the second duty, i.e., by repairing the illegally caused damage, one avoids the sanction attached to the violation of the first duty, i.e., the duty not to cause damage or to observe the secondary norm created by the legal transaction, e.g., the duty of the landlord to let the tenant live in a certain building. The legal obligation to repair a loss caused by a civil delict is substituted for the original legal obligation; it is a substitute obligation. If, however, the behavior by which the damage is caused has the character of a criminal delict, it is not possible to avoid the criminal sanction by repairing the damage. If somebody breaks a contract, he avoids the civil sanction by compensating for the damage he has caused. But if somebody causes severe bodily injuries to somebody else, and does not repair the damage, he has to sustain the civil and the criminal sanction. In this case, the obligation to repair the damage is not substituted for the obligation to forbear from committing the delict. The obligation to repair the damage caused by a criminal delict is added to the original obligation; it is not a substitute, but an additional obligation.

4. Legal Transaction and Delict

Both the legal transaction and the delict are conditions of a sanction. They differ inasmuch as the legal consequences of the legal transaction — the validity of the secondary norm constituting duties and rights of the parties — are intended by the legal transaction, while — as a rule — no legal consequences are intended by the delict. The legal transaction is a law-creating fact, the delict is not.* According to the intention of the legal transaction, a certain secondary norm is to be created; if the norm is violated and the damage caused thereby is not repaired, a sanction shall be executed. The legal transaction is a condition of a civil delict and only as such an (indirect) condition of the civil sanction. The (civil or criminal) delict is a direct condition of the sanction; and the sanction is not intended by the delict, it is executed even against the will of the delinquent.

b. The Contract

1. The Will and its Expression

The typical legal transaction of civil law is the contract. It consists of the identical declarations of will of two or more individuals. The declarations of the contracting parties are directed towards a certain behavior of these parties. The legal order may, but does not need to, prescribe a special form for these declarations. But the parties must always in some way express their will. Otherwise, the fact that a contract is made could not be established in a legal procedure, especially by

---

* There are, however, exceptions to this rule. Thus, for instance, the act of revolution: it aims at the establishment of a new or the change of the old constitution by violating the latter. It is a delict with respect to the old, and a law creating act with respect to the new constitution. Cf. also *infra*, p. 368.

the courts; and only facts that can be established in a legal procedure are of juristic importance.

A discrepancy can exist between the actual will of a contracting party and its expression. Theoretical jurisprudence cannot decide what consequences such a discrepancy shall have. This question can be solved only by the legislator or the law-applying organ. They may attach more importance to the actual will of the party, or to the declaration. The contract may be considered to be void if one party is able to show that his actual will did not correspond to what is interpreted as a declaration of his will. Or the validity of the contract may be considered as independent thereof, and the contract be considered as valid if the external declarations are identical. Which of the two solutions is preferable depends on different politico-juristic value judgments.

2. Offer and Acceptance

That the parties make identical declarations usually does not suffice for the making of a contract. The declaration of the one party must be directed to, and accepted by, the other party. A contract is therefore said to consist in an offer and an acceptance. This distinction between offer and acceptance presupposes that the two declarations are not made simultaneously. The question then arises whether the offeror must maintain his actual will until the moment of acceptance. Must both parties have the actual will to make the contract at this moment, so that no contract is accomplished, and that means, no binding norm created, if the offeror demonstrates that he no longer had any will to contract at the moment the other party accepted the offer? Can the offeror withdraw the offer at any moment before it has been accepted? This question is again of the kind that only the legal order itself, no theory of law, can solve. If the legal order answers the question in the affirmative, it makes it very difficult for absent persons to make a contract. In order to remove this inconvenience, the legal order therefore sometimes stipulates that, under certain circumstances, the offeror is bound by his offer for a certain length of time. This means that the contract is valid if the offer is accepted within this period, even if the offeror has changed his mind. By the acceptance of the offer, a norm obligating the parties may then be created without or even against the will of the offeror.

3. The Norm Created by the Contract

The actual will of the parties and their declarations thereof are of importance in the act we call the making of a contract. Each of the contracting parties must will the same; the parties must, so to speak, have parallel wills, if not at the same moment, at least one after the other. The norm created by this act, the contract as a norm, is, however, no will. This norm remains valid, even when one or both of the parties have ceased to have any corresponding will. For its continued existence, for its validity, the norm is dependent upon the actual will of the parties only insofar as they may annul it through another contract, that is, through a contrary norm created by another contract.

The norm created by the contract may be individual or general. General contracts play a prominent rôle in labor law and international law. With respect to the contents of the contractual norm, we distinguish between contracts which impose duties only on one party and rights only on the other, and contracts which impose duties and confer rights upon both contracting parties. By contracts of the latter kind the parties may be obligated either to parallel or to intersecting lines of conduct. The first type of contract occurs, for instance, when two merchants agree to sell a certain kind of merchandise at a fixed identical price. A purchase is an example of a contract of the second kind; one party is obligated to deliver a certain ware and the other party is obligated to pay a sum of money. In all these cases, and especially in the case where the contracting parties are obligated by the contractual norm to different kinds of conduct, the will of all contracting parties in making the contract must have the same contents, must be directed toward the whole content of the contractual norm.

4. One-sided and Two-sided Legal Transactions

A contract is a two-sided legal act, insofar as the secondary norm obligating and authorizing the contracting parties is created by the collaboration of at least two individuals. But there also occur one-sided legal acts where the secondary norm is created by one individual only. It is characteristic of civil law that normally an individual can obligate only himself by such a one-sided legal act. In civil law, the principle of autonomy prevails, according to which nobody can be obligated against, or even without, his own consent. This is, as we shall see, the decisive difference between private and public law. An example of a one-sided legal act is the offer which is binding upon the offeror for a certain time before the acceptance, in the sense that it cannot during this time be withdrawn. Such an offer creates a norm by which the offeror is obligated to the behavior determined by the offer on the condition that the other party accepts the offer within a certain time.

D. Nature of Constitutional Law

Since it is the function of the courts in their capacity as law-applying organs to apply the general norms of statutory and customary law to concrete cases, the court has to decide what general norm is applicable to the case. The court must find out whether the legal order contains a norm attaching a sanction to the behavior which the public prosecutor claims to be a criminal delict, or the private plaintiff claims to be a civil delict, and what sanction is provided. The court has to answer not only the *quaestio facti* but also the *quaestio juris*. It has in particular to examine whether the general norm it intends to apply is really valid, and that means: whether it has been created in the way prescribed by the constitution. Only if legislation or custom has produced a general norm to the effect that theft shall be punished with imprisonment must the court put a prosecuted thief in jail. This function of the court is especially obvious when it is doubtful whether the behavior of the defendant or accused really is a civil or criminal delict, according to the legal order which the court has to apply. A man has, for instance, made a promise of marriage to a girl, which he does not keep. Some legal orders do not consider such a promise binding, but some do. Should the girl sue the man because of his broken promise, the court must ascertain whether there is within the legal order to be applied by this court a statute or a rule of customary law according to which a civil sanction has to be directed against a man who has broken his promise of marriage and has not repaired the damage caused thereby. The court has to ascertain the existence of this norm, just as it has to ascertain the existence of the delict. The function of ascertaining the existence of the general norm to be applied by the court implies the important function of interpreting this norm, of determining its meaning. The fact that the general norm to be applied by the court has been created in the way prescribed by the constitution is one of the conditions on which depends whether an individual sanction has to be ordered by the court in the concrete case.

If we assume a constitution according to which general legal norms may be created only through decisions of a parliament elected in a certain way, then the norm which makes theft punishable would have to be formulated thus: "If the parliament has decided that thieves shall be punished and if the competent court has ascertained that a certain individual has stolen, then. . . ." The norms of the constitution which regulate the creation of the general norms to be applied by the courts and other law-applying organs are thus not independent complete norms. They are intrinsic parts of all the legal norms which the courts and other organs have to apply. On this ground constitutional law cannot be cited as an example of legal norms which do not stipulate any sanctions. The norms of the material constitution are law only in their organic connection with those sanction-stipulating norms which are created on their basis. What, from a dynamic point of view, is the creation of a general norm determined by a higher norm, the constitution, becomes in a static presentation of law one of the conditions to which the sanction is attached as consequence in the general norm (which, from the dynamic point of view, is the lower norm in relation to the constitution). In a static presentation of law, the higher norms of the constitution are, as it were, projected as parts into the lower norms.

E. Relationship between the Judicial Act and the Preexistent Norm Applied by the Judicial Act

a. Determination of the Judicial Act only by Adjective Law

From the dynamic point of view, the decision of the court represents an individual norm, which is created on the basis of a general norm of statutory or customary law in the same way as this general norm is created on the basis of the constitution. The creation of the individual legal norm by the law-applying organ, especially by the court, must always be determined by one or more preëxistent general norms. This determination may have — as we have explained in a foregoing chapter * — different degrees. Normally, the courts are bound by general norms determining their procedure as well as the contents of their decisions. It is, however, possible that the legislator is content with instituting courts, and that these courts are authorized by the legal order to decide the concrete cases at their own discretion. This is the principle according to which in Plato's Ideal State the "royal judges" exercise their almost unlimited power. Even in this case, however, the courts are not only law-creating but also law-applying organs. In every judicial decision, the general norm of adjective law is applied by which this, and only this, individual is authorized to act as a judge and to decide the concrete case at his own discretion or according to a general norm of substantive law. It is this general norm of adjective law by which the judicial power is delegated to the courts. Without this norm, it would be impossible to recognize the individual who decides the concrete case as a "judge," as an organ of the legal community, and his decision as law, as a binding norm belonging to the legal order constituting the legal community.

* Cf. *supra*, pp. 129f.

b. Determination of the Judicial Act by Substantive Law

If the function of the court is regulated both by substantive and by adjective law — that means if both its procedure and the contents of its decisions are determined by preëxistent general norms — in this case, too, the court may be bound in different degrees. Here, the following facts must above all be taken into consideration:

When a judicial decision has to be made, it is normally the case that the public prosecutor or a private plaintiff claims before the court that a certain individual, the accused or the defendant, has, by certain behavior, violated a legal obligation (and that means a general legal norm of statutory or customary law), that he has committed a criminal or civil delict. The court has to ascertain whether or not the legal order really contains the asserted general norm and whether or not the accused or defendant has really behaved contrary to this general norm. If the court finds that the general norm is valid, and that the accused or defendant has committed the delict, it has to order the sanction which the legal order provides.

If there is no general norm stipulating the obligation, the competence of the court may be determined in two different ways. The court may have to acquit the accused or to reject the plaintiff's demand. In this case, too, the court applies substantive law, inasmuch as it declares that the positive legal order does not obligate the accused or defendant to behave in the way the prosecutor or plaintiff claims; it declares that, according to prevailing law, the accused or defendant was permitted to act as he did.

c. Discretion of the Court (Judge as Legislator)

The other way in which the competence of the court may be determined in case there is no general norm stipulating the obligation of the accused or defendant claimed by the prosecutor or plaintiff, is the following: The court is authorized by the legal order to decide the case at its own discretion, to condemn or to acquit the accused, to find for or against the plaintiff, to order or to refuse to order a sanction against the accused or defendant. The court is authorized to order a sanction against the accused or defendant in spite of the lack of a general norm violated by the latter, provided the court finds the lack of such a general norm stipulating the obligation of the accused or defendant claimed by the prosecutor or plaintiff to be unsatisfactory, unjust, or inequitable. That means that the court is authorized to create for the concrete case the norm of substantive law it considers satisfactory, just, or equitable. The court then functions as a legislator.

There is, however, only a difference of degree between this case and the case where the court applies preëxisting substantive law. In ordering a sanction, the court is always a legislator, since it creates law, just as the legislator is always a law-applying organ, since in legislation the constitution is applied. But the court is more legislator if it is not bound by substantive, but only by adjective law; if it is authorized to create the substantive law for the concrete case without its decision being determined by a preëxistent general norm of substantive law. It should, however, not be overlooked that if the court orders a sanction against the accused or defendant although the latter has not violated a preëxistent general rule of positive law, the individual norm created by the decision of the court has the effect of an *ex post facto* law. For this norm which first attaches the sanction to a certain act of the accused or defendant, and thus makes the act a delict, comes into existence after this act has been performed.

It should further be observed that the decision of the court can never be determined by a preëxistent general norm of substantive law to such a degree that this general norm which the court applies is, as it were, reproduced only by the individual norm of the decision. However detailed the general norm attempts to be, the individual norm created by the judicial decision will always add something new. Suppose a criminal law that says "If somebody steals something the value of which exceeds $1,000, he shall be imprisoned for two years." A court applying this law to a concrete case will have to decide, for instance, when the imprisonment shall begin and where it shall take place. The individualization of a general norm by a judicial decision is always a determination of elements which are not yet determined by the general norm and which cannot be completely determined by it. The judge is, therefore, always a legislator also in the sense that the contents of his decision never can be completely determined by the preëxisting norm of substantive law.

F. Gaps (Lacunae) of Law

a. The Idea of "Gaps": a Fiction

The previously mentioned authorization to order a sanction which has not been provided by a preëxisting general norm is often given to the courts indirectly, by way of a fiction. It is the fiction that the legal order has a gap, — meaning that prevailing law cannot be applied to a concrete case because there is no general norm which refers to this case. The idea is that it is logically impossible to apply the actually valid law to a concrete case because the necessary premise is missing.

Typical is the first paragraph of the Code Civil Suisse: "A défaut d'une disposition légale applicable, le juge prononce selon le droit coutumier, et à défaut d'une coutume, selon les règles qu'il établirait s'il avait à faire acte de législateur." Presumably, this provision does not refer to cases where statutory or customary law positively stipulates the obligation of the defendant which the plaintiff claims to be violated by the defendant in the concrete case. In such cases an applicable general norm exists, according to paragraph 1 of the Swiss Civil Code. Its provision, presumably, refers only to cases where the obligation which the plaintiff claims to be violated by the defendant is not stipulated by any general norm. In those cases the judge shall not be obliged to reject the claim of the plaintiff. He shall have the possibility of stipulating as legislator the asserted obligation for the concrete case. But he shall have the other possibility, too, of refusing the suit on the ground that prevailing law does not stipulate the asserted obligation.

If the judge makes use of this latter possibility, no "gap of law" is assumed. The judge indubitably applies valid law. He does not apply, it is true, an affirmative rule obligating individuals to certain conduct. Just because no norm exists which obligates the defendant to the behavior claimed by the plaintiff, the defendant is free according to positive law, and has not committed any delict by his behavior. If the judge dismisses the suit, he applies, as it were, the negative rule that nobody must be forced to observe conduct to which he is not obliged by law.

The legal order cannot have any gaps. If the judge is authorized to decide a given dispute as legislator in case the legal order does not contain any general norm obligating the defendant to the behavior claimed by the plaintiff, he does not fill a gap of actually valid law, but he adds to the actually valid law an individual norm to which no general norm corresponds. The actually valid law could be applied to the concrete case — by dismissing the suit. The judge, however, is authorized to change the law for a concrete case, he has the power to bind legally an individual who was legally free before.

But when shall the judge dismiss a suit, and when shall he create a new norm to meet it? The first paragraph of the Swiss Civil Code, and the theory of gaps which it expresses, give no clear answer. The intention obviously is that the judge has to assume the rôle of legislator if there is no general legal norm stipulating the obligation of the defendant asserted by the plaintiff and if the judge considers the lack of such a norm unsatisfactory, unjust, inequitable. The condition under which the judge is authorized to decide a given dispute as legislator is not — as the theory of gaps pretends — the fact that the application of the actually valid law is logically impossible, but the fact that the application of the actually valid law is — according to the opinion of the judge — legally-politically inadequate.

b. *The Purpose of the Fiction of Gaps*

The legislator, that is, the organ which is authorized by the constitution to create the general legal norms, realizes the possibility that the general norms he enacts may in some cases lead to unjust or inequitable results, because the legislator cannot foresee all the concrete cases which possibly may occur. He therefore authorizes the law-applying organ not to apply the general norms created by the legislator but to create a new norm in case the application of the general norms created by the legislator would have an unsatisfactory result. The difficulty is that it is impossible to determine beforehand the cases in which it will be desirable that the judge shall act as a legislator. If the legislator could know these cases, he would be able to formulate his general norms in a way making it superfluous to authorize the judge to act as a legislator. The formula, "The judge is authorized to act as a legislator if the application of existing general norms appears unjust or inequitable to him," gives too much play to the judge's discretion, since the latter might find the application of the norm created by the legislator inadequate in too many cases. Such a formula means the abdication of the legislator in favor of the judge. This is the (probably unconscious) reason why the legislator uses the fiction of "gaps of law," that is, the fiction that the valid law is logically inapplicable to a concrete case.

This fiction restricts the authorization of the judge in two directions. First, it limits the authorization to those cases where the obligation which the plaintiff claims the defendant has violated is not stipulated in any general norm. It excludes all those cases where the obligation of the defendant claimed by the plaintiff is positively stipulated by one of the existent general norms. This restriction is entirely arbitrary. To stipulate an obligation may be as "unjust" or "inequitable" as to omit doing so. The failure of the legislator to foresee all possible cases can of course make him omit to enact a norm as well as to formulate a general norm and thus stipulate obligations which he would not have stipulated had he foreseen all cases.

The other restriction involved in the formula using the fiction of "gaps of law" has a psychological rather than a juristic character. If the judge is authorized to act as a legislator only on the condition that there is a "gap" in the law, and that means, that the law is logically inapplicable to the concrete case, the true nature of the condition is concealed, which is that the application of the law — although it is logically possible — appears unjust or inequitable to the judge. This may have the effect that the judge makes use of the authorization only in those rather rare cases where it seems to him so evidently unjust to reject the plaintiff's claim that he feels himself compelled to believe such a decision incompatible with the intentions of the legislator. Then he reaches the conclusion: Had the legislator foreseen this case, he would have created a norm stipulating the obligation of the defendant. Since the legal order does not yet contain this norm, it is not applicable to the concrete case; and since he, the judge, is obliged to decide the case, it is this case for which he is authorized to act as a legislator. The theory of gaps in law — it is true — is a fiction; since it is always logically possible, although sometimes inadequate, to apply the legal order existing at the moment of the judicial decision. But the sanctioning of this fictitious theory by the legislator has the desired effect of restricting considerably the authorization of the judge to act as a legislator and that means, in the cases under consideration, to issue an individual norm with retroactive force.

G. GENERAL NORMS CREATED BY JUDICIAL ACTS

a. Precedents

The judicial decision may also create a general norm. The decision may have binding force not only for the case at hand but also for other similar cases which the courts may have to decide. A judicial decision may have the character of a precedent, i.e., of a decision binding upon the future decision of all similar cases. It can, however, have the character of a precedent only if it is not the application of a preëxisting general norm of substantive law, if the court acted as a legislator. The decision of a court in a concrete case assumes the character of a precedent binding upon the future decision of all similar cases by a generalization of the individual norm created by the first decision. It is the binding force of the general norm thus obtained which is the essence of a so-called precedent. Only on the basis of this general norm is it possible to establish that other cases are "similar" to the first case, the decision of which is considered to be the "precedent," and that, consequently, these other cases have to be decided in the same way. The general norm may be formulated by the court itself which created the precedent. Or it may be left to every court bound by the precedent to derive the general norm from it, whenever a pertinent case arises.

The law-creating function of the courts is especially manifest when the judicial decision has the character of a precedent, and that means when the judicial decision creates a general norm. Where the courts are entitled not only to apply preëxisting substantive law in their decisions, but also to create new law for concrete cases, there is a comprehensible inclination to give these judicial decisions the character of precedents. Within such a legal system, courts are legislative organs in exactly the same sense as the organ which is called the legislator in the narrower and ordinary sense of the term. Courts are creators of general legal norms.

We have spoken here of general norms which originate in a single decision of a court. This kind of law-creation must be clearly distinguished from the creation of general norms through permanent practice of the courts, i.e., through custom.

b. "All the Law is Judge-made Law"

1. The Doctrine of J. C. Gray

Our analysis of the judicial function shows that the view according to which the courts merely apply law is not borne out by the facts. The opposite view, however — that there is no law existing before the judicial decision and that all law is created by the courts — is equally false. This view is held by one of the most important American legal theorists, John Chipman Gray. "The Law of the State," he writes, "or of any organized body of men is composed of the rules which the courts, that is, the judicial organs of that body, lay down for the determination of legal rights and duties." * He says further: "the body of rules that they lay down is not the expression of preëxisting Law, but the Law itself"; † and he stresses: "that the fact that the courts apply rules is what makes them Law, that there is no mysterious entity 'the Law' apart from these rules, and that the judges are rather the creators than the discoverers of the Law." ‡ "It has been sometimes said that the Law is composed of two parts — legislative law and judge-made law, but, in truth, all the Law is judge-made Law." § To prove his theory, Gray cites this example: "Henry Pitt has built a reservoir on his land, and has filled it with water; and without any negligence on his part, either in the care or construction of his reservoir, it bursts, and the water, pouring forth, floods and damages the land of Pitt's neighbor, Thomas Underhill. Has Underhill a right to recover compensation from Pitt?" ‖ Gray presumes that "there is no statute, no decision, no custom

* Gray, The Nature and Sources of the Law (2d ed. 1927) 84.
† Gray, Nature and Sources of the Law 96.
‡ Gray, Nature and Sources of the Law 121.
§ Gray, Nature and Sources of the Law, 125.
‖ Gray, Nature and Sources of the Law 96.

on the subject" in the State by whose courts the case is to be settled (Nevada). Nevertheless, "the court has to decide the case somehow." And when the court decides the case, it cannot take guidance from any preëxisting norm: "To say that on this subject there was really Law existing in Nevada, seems only to show how strong a root legal fictions can strike into our mental processes." *

2. No Judicial Decision without Preëxisting Law

First of all, Gray overlooks the fact that the court may decide the case in two different ways. It may reject Underhill's suit, his claim to recover compensation from Pitt, on the ground that according to positive law Pitt is not legally obligated to repair the damage caused by the bursting of the reservoir, that Nevada's law does not contain any norm justifying Underhill's claim. In this case, the court undoubtedly applies the preëxisting substantive law of Nevada. The situation is the same as if Underhill had raised an absolutely unreasonable claim, for instance that Pitt shall pay $5,000 to Underhill because Pitt has married Underhill's daughter. Without doubt, the court would apply Nevada's law if it rejected such a claim as unfounded. The law is applied not only by a judicial decision by which the accused is condemned, or the court finds for the plaintiff according to the prevailing legal order, but also by a judicial decision by which the accused is acquitted, or the court finds against the plaintiff according to the prevailing legal order. Application of law can take place not only in a positive but also in a negative sense, not only by the law-applying organ's ordering and executing a sanction but also by this organ's refusing to order or execute a sanction.

But the court of Nevada may decide the case of Pitt's reservoir in a different way: It may find for the plaintiff. This presupposes, however, that the court is authorized by the law of Nevada, not only to apply preëxistent general norms of substantive law, but also to change this law under certain circumstances, namely, if the obligation of the defendant claimed by the plaintiff is not stipulated by a preëxistent general norm and the court considers the lack of such a norm unsatisfactory. Preëxisting law must authorize the court to go beyond the given substantive law. The court would therefore apply in this case, too, preexisting law. Gray is wrong when he assumes "that on this subject [the case under discussion] there was really no law existing in Nevada." There must be law existing in Nevada on this subject in order that the case can be decided by a court of Nevada. Only in applying the law of

---

* GRAY, NATURE AND SOURCES OF THE LAW 98.

Nevada does the court act as a court of Nevada. The court always applies preëxisting law, but the law it applies may not be substantive, but adjective law. The court may apply only those general norms which determine its own existence and procedure, the general norms which confer upon certain individuals the legal capacity to act as a court of a certain State. Only as far as the individuals whom Underhill asks to settle his dispute with Pitt apply such preëxisting norms of adjective law do they function as a "court" and has their decision the binding force of law.

Gray himself says: "Is the power of the judges then absolute? . . . Not so; the judges are but organs of the State; they have only such power as the organization of the State gives them." * "The organization of the State" can only mean the legal order, the constitution and the legal norms created on the basis of the constitution, the law existing at the moment the judge has to decide a concrete case. Gray thinks that "what the organization is, is determined by the wills of the real rulers of the State." But in another context he says: "To determine who are the real rulers of a political society is well-nigh an impossible task — for Jurisprudence a well-nigh insoluble problem." "The real rulers of a political society are undiscoverable." † If the organization of the State were actually the will of unknown and undiscoverable individuals, then the organization of the State itself would be unknown and undiscoverable. But the organization of the State is actually known. It is the "valid," and that means also the efficacious, constitution, it is the valid norms created on the basis of the constitution, and that means the system of norms which, on the whole, is efficacious. The "real" rulers are the organs by whose acts norms are created which, by and large, are efficacious. Since the efficacy of the legal order is a condition of the validity of its norms, there cannot be any essential difference between the "real" and the legal ruler of the State. What individuals influence those who create valid norms of the legal order constituting the State may be unknown and undiscoverable. But it is also without juristic interest.

3. Only Law can be "Source" of Law

The case of *Underhill* v. *Pitt* only shows that sometimes the courts may have to apply merely adjective law. But mostly there is some preëxisting substantive law, too. When Gray unconditionally states that there is "no law previous to the judicial decision," he can do so only because he does not regard the general norms of substantive or adjective

* Gray, Nature and Sources of the Law 121.
† Gray, Nature and Sources of the Law 79.

law which determine the judicial decisions as "law" but only as "sources of law." He asks: "From what *sources* does the State or other community direct its judges to obtain the Law?" * These sources of law are, according to Gray, statutes, judicial precedents, opinions of experts, customs, and principles of morality. He fails to distinguish between sources which have a legally binding force, and sources which do not. Of statutes, he says: "The State requires that the acts of its legislative organ shall bind the courts, and so far as they go, shall be paramount to all other sources." He stresses that "legislative acts, statutes, are to be dealt with as sources of Law, and not as part of the Law itself." And he applies the same distinction to all the other phenomena he designates as sources of law. By ignoring the difference between legislation, judicial precedents, and legal customs on one hand, and the opinions of experts and principles of morality on the other hand, by ignoring that the former are legally binding, the latter legally not binding, Gray does not see that these "sources of law" which are legally binding, are legal norms, are really law. He overlooks the fact that, if the law-applying organs are legally bound by these so-called "sources," what he denotes by the figurative expression "source of law" is only one stage in the process of law-creation, one of the manifestations of law. Gray is right in maintaining against traditional doctrine that the courts create law. But he errs in his belief that law is created only by the courts. Especially if one realizes the dynamic relationship between judicial decision and legislation, it becomes impossible to explain why only the one but not the other should represent law. Gray's thesis means the first step towards a deeper understanding of the structure of law. The next step must lead to the insight into the hierarchical structure of the legal order.

H. Conflicts between Norms of Different Stages

a. *Concordance or Discordance between the Judicial Decision and the General Norm to be Applied by the Decision*

Gray's contention that law consists only in the judicial decision is based also on the following consideration: "Rules of conduct laid down and applied by the courts of a country are coterminous with the Law of that country, and as the first change, so does the latter along with them. Bishop Hoadly has said: 'Whoever hath an *absolute authority* to *interpret* any written or spoken laws, it is he who is truly the Law-giver to all intents and purposes, and not the person who first wrote or spoke them'; *a fortiori*, whoever hath an absolute authority not only to inter-

---

* Gray, Nature and Sources of the Law 123f.

pret the Law, but to say what the Law is, is truly the Law-giver." * In accordance with Bishop Hoadly's view, Gray tries to show that even the statute applied by the court is really a judge-made law. "The shape in which a statute is imposed on the community as a guide for conduct is that statute as interpreted by the courts. The courts put life into the dead words of the statute." † It is difficult to understand why the words of a statute which, according to its meaning, is binding upon the courts should be dead, whereas the words of a judicial decision which, according to its meaning, is binding upon the parties should be living. The problem is not: why the statute is dead and the judicial decision is living; here we are in fact faced with a problem which, generally speaking, comes to this: The higher norm, the statute or a norm of customary law, determines, to a greater or lesser extent, the creation and the contents of the lower norm of the judicial decision. The lower norm belongs, together with the higher norm, to the same legal order only insofar as the former corresponds to the latter. But, who shall decide whether the lower norm corresponds to the higher, whether the individual norm of the judicial decision corresponds to the general norms of statutory and customary law? Only an organ that has to apply the higher norm can form such a decision. Just as the existence of a fact to which a legal norm attaches certain consequences can be ascertained only by an organ in a certain procedure (both determined by the legal order), the question whether a lower norm corresponds to a higher norm can be decided only by an organ in a certain procedure (both determined by the legal order) The opinion of any other individual is legally irrelevant. The decision of the question whether a lower norm corresponds to a higher implies the application of the higher norm. If plaintiff or defendant believes that the decision of the court does not correspond to the general norms of statutory or customary law, which the court has to apply in his case, he may appeal to another higher court. This court has the power to annul the lower court's decision or to replace it by another decision which — according to the opinion of the higher court — corresponds to the general norm which has to be applied in the given case. This is the typical process by which the legal order endeavors to guarantee the legality of judicial decisions. But this process cannot be continued indefinitely; there must be an end to it, because there must be an end of the dispute between the parties. There must exist a court of last resort, entitled to give a final decision of the dispute, an authority whose decision cannot be annulled or changed any more. With this decision, the case becomes *res judicata*.

* GRAY, NATURE AND SOURCES OF THE LAW 102.
† GRAY, NATURE AND SOURCES OF THE LAW 125.

There can, therefore, never exist any absolute guarantee that the lower norm corresponds to the higher norm. The possibility that the lower norm does not correspond to the higher norm which determines the former's creation and content, especially that the lower norm has another content than the one prescribed by the higher norm, is not at all excluded. But as soon as the case has become a *res judicata*, the opinion that the individual norm of the decision does not correspond to the general norm which has to be applied by it, is without juristic importance. The law-applying organ has either, authorized by the legal order, created new substantive law; or it has, according to its own assertion, applied preëxisting substantive law. In the latter case, the assertion of the court of last resort is decisive. For it is the court of last resort which alone is competent to interpret in a definitive and authentic manner the general norms to be applied to the concrete case. From a juristic point of view, there cannot occur any contradiction between a judicial decision with force of law and the statutory and customary law which shall be applied in the decision. The decision of a court of last resort cannot be considered to be illegal as long as it has to be considered as a court decision at all. It is a fact that the question whether there exists a general norm which has to be applied by the court and what the content of this norm is can legally be answered only by this court (if it is a court of last resort); but this fact does not justify the assumption that there exist no general legal norms determining the decisions of the courts, that law consists only of court decisions.

b. Concordance or Discordance between Statute and Constitution (The Unconstitutional Statute)

The problem of a possible conflict between higher and lower norm arises, not only with respect to the relation between statute (or customary law) and judicial decision, but also with respect to the relation between constitution and statute. It is the problem of the unconstitutional statute. The usual saying that an "unconstitutional statute" is invalid (void), is a meaningless statement, since an invalid statute is no statute at all. A non-valid norm is a non-existing norm, is legally a nonentity. The expression "unconstitutional statute," applied to a statute which is considered to be valid, is a contradiction in terms. For if the statute is valid it can be valid only because it corresponds to the constitution; it cannot be valid if it contradicts the constitution. The only reason for the validity of a statute is that it has been created in a way provided for by the constitution. What is meant by the expression is, however, that a statute, according to the constitution, may for a special reason be annulled in another than the ordinary way. Ordinarily, a statute is annulled by another statute, according to the principle *lex posterior derogat priori*; or a statute is annulled by a contrary rule of customary law, by so-called *desuetudo*. If the constitution prescribes a certain procedure to be observed in the enactment of statutes and if it also lays down certain provisions with regard to their contents, it must foresee the possibility that sometimes the legislator may not follow these prescriptions. The constitution may then designate the organ that has to decide whether or not the prescriptions regulating the legislative function were observed. If this organ is different from the legislative organ, it forms an authority above the legislator, a thing that might be politically undesirable, especially if this organ has the power to annul a statute which it considers to be unconstitutional. If no organ different from the legislative is called upon to inquire into the constitutionality of statutes, the question whether or not a statute is constitutional has to be decided only and exclusively by the legislative organ itself. Then, everything that is passed by the legislative organ as a statute has to be accepted as a statute in the sense of the constitution. In this case, no statute enacted by the legislative organ can be considered to be "unconstitutional."

This situation may also be described in the following terms: The provisions of the constitution concerning the procedure of legislation and the contents of future statutes do not mean that laws can be created only in the way decreed and only with the import prescribed by the constitution. The constitution entitles the legislator to create statutes also in another way and also with another content. The constitution authorizes the legislator, instead of the constitution, to determine the procedure of legislation and the contents of the laws, provided that the legislator deems it desirable not to apply the positive provisions of the constitution. Just as the courts may be authorized, under certain circumstances, not to apply the existing statutory or customary law but to act as legislator and to create new law, so the ordinary legislator may be authorized, under certain circumstances, to act as constitutional legislator. If a statute enacted by the legislative organ is considered to be valid although it has been created in another way or has another content than prescribed by the constitution, we must assume that the prescriptions of the constitution concerning legislation have an alternative character. The legislator is entitled by the constitution either to apply the norms laid down directly in the constitution or to apply other norms which he himself may decide upon. Otherwise, a statute whose creation or contents did not conform with the prescriptions directly laid down in the constitution could not be regarded as valid.

c. Guarantees of the Constitution

1. Abrogation of the "Unconstitutional" Statute

The application of the constitutional rules concerning legislation can be effectively guaranteed only if an organ other than the legislative body is entrusted with the task of testing whether a law is constitutional, and of annulling it if — according to the opinion of this organ — it is "unconstitutional." There may be a special organ established for this purpose, for instance, a special court, a so-called "constitutional court"; or the control of the constitutionality of statutes, the so-called "judicial review," may be conferred upon the ordinary courts, and especially upon the supreme court. The controlling organ may be able to abolish completely the "unconstitutional" statute so that it cannot be applied by any other organ. If an ordinary court is competent to test the constitutionality of a statute, it may be entitled only to refuse to apply it in the concrete case when it considers the statute to be unconstitutional, while other organs remain obliged to apply the statute. As long as a statute has not been annulled, it is "constitutional" and not "unconstitutional," in the sense that it contradicts the constitution. It is then the will of the constitution that this statute shall also be valid. But the constitution intends the statute to be valid only as long as it has not been annulled by the competent organ. The so-called "unconstitutional" law is not void *ab initio*, it is only voidable; it can be annulled for special reasons. These reasons are that the legislative organ has created the statute in another way, or has given it another content, than directly prescribed by the constitution. The legislator, it is true, is authorized to do so; he is entitled not to apply the direct prescriptions of the constitution in a concrete case. The constitution, however, gives the preference to the first of the two possibilities over the second one. This preference is manifested in the fact that a statute which comes into force in the second way can be annulled not only — as a so-called "constitutional" statute — by an act of the legislative organ, but also by an act of the organ different from the legislator, entrusted with the judicial review of the statute.*

2. Personal Responsibility of the Organ

The same preference may also find other expressions. If a statute — with respect to the procedure of its creation, or its contents — departs from what the constitution directly prescribes, the constitution may omit

---

* Cf. my article *Judicial Review of Legislation: A Comparative Study of the Austrian and the American Constitution* (1942) 4 J. OF POLITICS 183–200.

to authorize another organ than the legislator to annul this statute for this reason, but the constitution may provide that certain organs which have participated in the creation of the so-called "unconstitutional" statute, for instance, the chief of State who has promulgated the statute or the cabinet minister who has countersigned the promulgation, may be made responsible and punished for this. Personal responsibility of the norm-creating organ for the legality of the created norm is a very efficacious means of guaranteeing the legality of the norm-creating procedure. But one makes use of this means less frequently in the relationship between constitution and statute than in the relationship between statutes and the regulations (ordinances) which administrative organs have to issue on the basis of statutes. If the administrative organ enacts an illegal regulation (ordinance) it can be punished for this by a special organ competent to test the legality of regulations (ordinances). But the so-called "illegal" regulation (ordinance) can be abolished only in the normal way, not by the act of a special organ entrusted with the review of these norms. If the legal order provides only a personal responsibility of the norm-creating organ for the constitutionality or legality of the norm created by the responsible organ, and not the possibility of annulling the so-called unconstitutional or illegal norm, then the act of creating an "unconstitutional" statute or an illegal regulation (ordinance) is a delict, because it is the condition of a sanction; but this delict gives rise to a valid norm. Such a state of affairs is politically undesirable, it is true; and ordinarily the legal order makes it possible to annul a norm created by an illegal act. As a matter of fact, however, it sometimes occurs that the legal order fails to make such provisions. Apparently, then, the legal order authorizes the norm-creating organ to create lower norms, not only in the way directly determined by the higher norm, but also in another way which the organ competent to create norms may choose itself. The legal order, it is true, tries to prevent the creation of norms in this second way by attaching a sanction to it. If, however, the responsible organ chooses this way, it is liable to a sanction, but it creates law. *Ex injuria jus oritur.* The contrary thesis, *Ex injuria jus non oritur,* is a rule not without important exceptions. Theft may give rise to ownership, revolution may create a new constitution. A norm-creating act may — exceptionally — have the character of a delict.

d. Res Judicata (Force of Law)

The relation between the statute or a general norm of customary law and a judicial decision may be interpreted in the same manner. The judicial decision creates an individual norm which is to be considered as valid, and therefore legal, as long as it has not been annulled, in the manner prescribed by law, because of its "illegality" ascertained by the competent organ. The law not only decrees that the court shall observe a certain procedure in arriving at its decision and that the decision has to have a certain content; the law also prescribes that a judicial decision which does not conform to these direct stipulations shall remain in force until it has been abolished by the decision of another court in a certain procedure, because of its being "illegal." This is the ordinary way of annulling a judicial decision, whereas a statute because of its "unconstitutionality" is not annulled in the ordinary way, i.e., by another statute, but in an extra-ordinary way, namely in the way of judicial review. If this procedure is exhausted, or if no such procedure has been provided, then there is *res judicata*. In relation to the higher norm, the lower norm possesses the force of law. Thus, the determination of the lower norm by the higher norm has, in the relation between the individual norm of the judicial decision and the general norm of statutory or customary law determining this decision, the character of an alternative prescription. If the judicial decision which is the lower norm corresponds to the first one of the two alternatives which the higher norm presents, and that means: if the organ — namely a higher court — competent to test the conformity of the lower to the higher norm does not find the former illegal, or if no test of the legality of the lower norm is provided, the latter (the judicial decision) has — so to speak — full validity, and that means, that it cannot be annulled. If it corresponds to the second alternative it has — so to speak — only a restricted validity, and that means that it can, for this reason, be annulled by the special act of an organ normally different from the organ which created the lower norm and competent to test the conformity of the lower to the higher norm. There is no third possibility: a rule that cannot be annulled in this way must be either a fully valid norm or no norm at all.

e. Nullity and Annullability

The general principle which is at the basis of this view may be formulated in the following way: a legal norm is always valid, it cannot be nul, but it can be annulled. There are, however, different degrees of annullability. The legal order may authorize a special organ to declare a norm nul, that means, to annul the norm with retroactive force, so that the legal effects, previously produced by the norm, may be abolished. This is usually — but not correctly — characterized by the statement that the norm was void *ab initio* or has been declared "nul and void." The "declaration" in question has, however, not a declaratory but a constitutive character. Without this declaration of the competent organ the norm cannot be considered to be void. The legal order may authorize not only a special organ but every subject to declare a legal norm, that is to say, something that presents itself as a legal norm, as no legal norm at all; and that means: the legal order may authorize every subject to annul a legal norm even with retroactive force. What is usually called nullity is only the highest degree of annullability, the fact that every subject, and not only a special organ, is authorized to annul the norm.*

In modern national law, nullity, as the highest degree of annullability, is practically excluded. A status where everybody is authorized to declare every norm, that is to say, everything which presents itself as a norm, as nul, is almost a status of anarchy. It is characteristic of a primitive legal order which does not institute special organs competent to create and to apply the law. Such a primitive, and that means completely decentralized, legal order is the general international law. Here every subject, or more correctly, every State, is competent to decide whether in a given case a norm, that is to say something which presents itself as a norm, is valid or not. This is, of course, a very unsatisfactory situation. Modern national law which has the character of a relatively centralized order, or, what amounts to the same thing, is statal law, reserves the competence to declare a norm as nul, that is to annul a legal norm, for special organs. What is practically possible within a national legal order is, at most, that everybody is authorized to consider a legal norm as nul, but at the risk that his conduct, if contrary to the norm, might be considered by the competent organ to be a delict, provided the competent organ does not confirm the subject's opinion as to the invalidity of the norm.

That does not mean that everything which presents itself as a norm is legally a norm, though an annullable norm. There are, it is true, cases where something which presents itself as a norm is no norm at all, is nul *ab initio*, cases of absolute nullity characterized by the fact that no legal procedure is necessary to annul them. These cases, however, lie beyond the legal system.

What is the difference between an annullable norm and something which presents itself as a norm but which is no norm at all, nul *ab initio*? Under what conditions is something which presents itself as a norm nul

---

* The *void ab initio* theory is not generally accepted. Cf. for instance Chief Justice Hughes in *Chicot County Drainage District v. Baxter State Bank*, 308 U.S. 371 (1940). The best formulation of the problem is to be found in *Wellington et al. Petitioners*, 16 Pick. 87 (Mass., 1834), at 96: "Perhaps, however, it may be well doubted whether a formal act of legislation can ever with strict legal propriety be said to be void; it seems more consistent with the nature of the subject, and the principles applicable to analogous cases, to treat it as voidable."

ab initio and not a norm which has to be annulled in a legal procedure? Only the legal order itself could answer that question. A legal order may state, for instance, that something which presents itself as a norm is nul *ab initio* if this sham norm has not been issued by the competent organ, or has been issued by an individual who has no competence whatever to issue legal norms or has no quality of an organ at all. If the legal order should determine such conditions on which something which presents itself as a norm is nul *ab initio* so that it need not be annulled in a legal procedure, the legal order would still have to determine a procedure the purpose of which is to ascertain whether or not these conditions are fulfilled in a given case, whether or not the norm in question has really been issued by an incompetent organ or by an individual not competent to issue legal norms, etc. The decision made by the competent authority that something that presents itself as a norm is nul *ab initio* because it fulfills the conditions of nullity determined by the legal order, is a constitutive act; it has a definite legal effect; without and prior to this act the phenomenon in question cannot be considered to be "nul." Hence the decision is not "declaratory," that is to say, it is not, as it presents itself, a declaration of nullity; it is a true annulment, an annulment with retroactive force. There must be something legally existing to which this decision refers. Hence, the phenomenon in question cannot be something nul *ab initio*, that is to say, legally nothing. It has to be considered as a norm annulled with retroactive force by the decision declaring it nul *ab initio*. Just as everything King Midas touched turned into gold, everything to which the law refers becomes law, i.e., something legally existing. The case of absolute nullity lies beyond the law.

f. No Contradiction between an Inferior and a Superior Norm

The alternative character of the higher norm determining the lower norm precludes any real contradiction between the higher and the lower norm. A contradiction with the first of the two alternative prescriptions of the higher norm is no contradiction with the higher norm itself. Further, the contradiction between the lower norm and the first of the two alternatives presented by the higher norm is relevant only as established by the competent authority. Any other opinion concerning the existence of a contradiction than that of this authority is legally irrelevant. The competent authority establishes the legal existence of such a contradiction by annulling the lower norm.

The "unconstitutionality" or "illegality" of a norm which, for some reason or other, has to be presupposed as valid, thus means either the possibility of its being annulled (in the ordinary way if it is a judicial decision, in another than the ordinary way if it is a statute); or the possibility of its being nul. Its nullity means the negation of its existence by juristic cognition. There cannot occur any contradiction between two norms from different levels of the legal order. The unity of the legal order can never be endangered by any contradiction between a higher and a lower norm in the hierarchy of law.

XII. NORMATIVE AND SOCIOLOGICAL JURISPRUDENCE

A. SOCIOLOGICAL JURISPRUDENCE NOT THE ONLY SCIENCE OF LAW

The theory of law which has been presented here is a juristic theory, allowance being made for the tautology. It shows the law to be a system of valid norms. Its object is norms, general and individual. It considers facts only insofar as they are in some way or other determined by norms. The statements in which our theory describes its object are therefore not statements about what is but statements about what ought to be. In this sense, the theory may also be called a normative theory.

Since about the beginning of this century, the demand for another theory of law has been raised. A theory is asked for which describes what people actually do and not what they ought to do, just as physics describes natural phenomena. Through observation of actual social life, one can and should — it is argued — obtain a system of rules that describe the actual human behavior which presents the phenomenon of law. These rules are of the same kind as the laws of nature by means of which natural science describes its object. A sociology of law is required which describes law in terms of "real rules," not of ought-rules or "paper rules." This theory of law is also spoken of as "realistic jurisprudence." *

Whether such a sociological or realistic theory of law is possible or not will be investigated later. But if such a theory is possible, it would still not be the only possible "science" of law, as many of its advocates seem to believe. Such a belief can only arise if one identifies science with natural science and considers society in general and law in particular merely as parts of nature. This identification is all the easier since modern natural science no longer interprets the connection between cause and effect, established in the "laws" by which this science describes its object, as a relation of absolute necessity but only as a relation of probability. It seems that social life must also be subject to such laws of probability. However, even if it should be possible to describe the phenomenon of law in terms of such laws, a normative jurisprudence

* This is how one of the most distinguished exponents of this theory expresses it: Karl N. Llewellyn, *A Realistic Jurisprudence — The Next Step* (1930) 30 COL. L. REV. 447f.

aiming at a structural analysis of law as a system of valid norms is also both possible and indispensable. During two thousand years, this has been in fact the only intellectual approach to the phenomenon of law besides the purely historical approach; and there is no reasonable ground why we should deny the name of "science" to this continuous tradition of intellectual dealing with law.

B. NORMATIVE JURISPRUDENCE AS EMPIRICAL AND DESCRIPTIVE SCIENCE OF LAW

It is also false to characterize sociological jurisprudence as an "empirical" or "descriptive" discipline in contradistinction to normative jurisprudence as a "non-empirical" or "prescriptive" one. The connotation of the term "empirical" is tied up with the opposition between experience and metaphysics. An analytical description of positive law as a system of valid norms is, however, no less empirical than natural science restricted to a material given by experience. A theory of law loses its empirical character and becomes metaphysical only if it goes beyond positive law and makes statements about some presumed natural law. The theory of positive law is parallel to the empirical science of nature, natural-law doctrine to metaphysics.

Like any other empirical science, normative jurisprudence describes its particular object. But its object is norms and not patterns of actual behavior. The statements by means of which it describes the norms in their specific connection within a legal order are not themselves norms. Only the law-creating authorities can issue norms. The ought-statements in which the theorist of law represents the norms have a merely descriptive import; they, as it were, descriptively reproduce the "ought" of the norms. It is of the utmost importance to distinguish clearly between the legal norms, products of the law-creating process, which are the object of jurisprudence, and the statements of jurisprudence. Traditional terminology shows a dangerous inclination to confuse them, and to identify law and the science of law. One often speaks of "law" when referring only to a certain juristic doctrine. This feature of our terminology is not without a political background; it is connected with the claim of jurisprudence to be recognized as a source of law — a claim that is characteristic of the doctrine of natural law but irreconcilable with the principles of legal positivism.

The statements by which normative jurisprudence describes law are different from the statements by which a sociology of law describes its object. The former are ought-statements, the latter are is-statements of the same type as laws of nature. But there exists a certain analogy between the statements in which normative jurisprudence describes law and the laws of nature. The statements of jurisprudence are, like the laws of nature, general hypothetic statements. The difference lies in the sense in which the consequence is connected with the condition. A law of nature says that if an event A (the cause) occurs, then an event B (the effect) also occurs. A juristic statement, the legal rule used in a descriptive sense, says that if an individual A behaves in a certain way, then another individual B ought to behave in a certain other way. The difference between natural science and normative jurisprudence does not consist in the logical structure of the statements by which both sciences describe their respective objects, but in the specific sense of the description. In the statements of natural science, the laws of nature, the condition is connected with the consequence by an "is"; in the statements of normative jurisprudence, the rules of law, the term used in a descriptive sense, the condition is connected with the consequence by an "ought."

In an article which is one of the earliest contributions of American sociological jurisprudence * Joseph W. Bingham remarked: "If we are to view the law as a field of study analogous to that of any science, we must look at it from the position of the law teacher, the law student, the legal investigator, or the lawyer who is engaged in searching the authorities to determine what the law is. These men are not directly acting as part of the machinery of government. Their study is not part of the external phenomena which compose the field of law. They are studying that field from without and therefore from the position which will give a wholly objective and the least confusing view." This is exactly the standpoint of normative jurisprudence. Normative jurisprudence approaches the law "from without," too, and it tries to gain a "wholly objective" view of law. But juristic theory endeavors to grasp the specific meaning of the legal rules, which are created and applied by the organs of the legal community, the sense with which these rules are directed to the individuals whose behavior they regulate. This sense is expressed by means of the "ought." Bingham and other representatives of sociological jurisprudence believe that law can be described "from an external point of view" only by rules which have the same character as laws of nature. This is a mistake. Normative jurisprudence describes law from an external point of view although its statements are ought-statements.

* Joseph W. Bingham, *What is the Law?* (1912) 11 Mich. L. Rev. 10.

C. The Prediction of the Legal Function

a. T. H. Huxley's Distinction between "Law of Men" and Law of Nature

Assuming that it is of the essence of causal laws to make predictions possible, the advocates of a sociological jurisprudence maintain that it is the task of the jurist to predict the behavior of the members of society according to "real" rules, just as a physicist has to predict the future movements of a body according to a law of nature. T. H. Huxley * believed legal rules to be similar to laws of nature. "A law of men," he says, "tells us what we may expect society will do under certain circumstances; and a law of nature tells us what we may expect natural objects will do under certain circumstances. Each contains information addressed to our intelligence." It seems doubtful whether the laws of nature really imply predictions of future events, instead of being merely explanations of present events by past ones. Such predictions are possible only under the scientifically unfounded presupposition that the past will repeat itself in the future. By a law of nature, we make a statement about our experience, and our experience lies in the past, not in the future. This, however, is beside the point. As a matter of fact, we make use of the laws of nature which we believe we have discovered in such a way that we try to foresee the future, assuming that things will react in future just as they have reacted in the past. When characterizing the "laws of men" as statements about what society will do in the future, Huxley cannot have in mind the laws created by the legal authorities. They do not constitute information addressed to our intelligence but prescriptions addressed to our will. The statements by which normative jurisprudence describes law constitute, it is true, information addressed to our intelligence. But they tell us, not what the members of society will do, but what they ought to do — according to the legal norms.

Huxley points out "that the laws of nature are not the causes of the order of nature, but only our way of stating as much as we have made out of that order. Stones do not fall to the ground in consequence of the law (that anything heavy falls to the ground if it is unsupported) as people sometimes carelessly say; but this law is a way of asserting that such invariably happens when heavy bodies at the surface of the earth, stones among the rest, are free to move." This is correct; but Huxley is wrong in continuing: "The laws of nature are in fact, in this respect, similar to the laws which men make for the guidance of their conduct

* T. H. Huxley, Introductory (Science Primers, 1882), 12f.

towards one another. There are laws about payment of taxes, and there are laws against stealing and murder. But the law is not the cause of man's paying his taxes, nor is it the cause of his abstaining from theft and murder. The law is simply a statement of what will happen to a man if he does not pay his taxes, and if he commits theft or murder." Huxley confuses the law as legal norm and the rule of law using the term in a descriptive sense. If the legal norm, enacted by the legislator, provides sanctions, and if such a "law" becomes the content of man's consciousness, it can very well become a motive of his behavior and hence a cause of his paying his taxes or his abstaining from theft and murder. A legislator enacts norms only because he believes that these norms, as motives in the mind of men, are capable of inducing the latter to the behavior desired by the legislator.*

b. O. W. Holmes' and B. N. Cardozo's Concept of Jurisprudence as Prophecy

Justice Oliver Wendell Holmes, too, considers it as the task of jurisprudence to predict what the organs of society, especially the courts, will do. In the famous article, "The Path of the Law," he explains: "People want to know under what circumstances and how far they will run the risk of coming against what is so much stronger than themselves, and hence it becomes a business to find out when this danger is to be feared. The object of our study, then, is prediction, the prediction of the incidence of the public force through the instrumentality of the courts." † Accordingly, his definition of law, which is truly a definition of the science of law, is: "The prophecies of what the courts will do in fact, and nothing more pretentious, are what I mean by the law." ‡ In conformity with this view, he defines the concepts of duty and right in the following way: "The primary rights and duties with which jurisprudence busies itself again are nothing but prophecies." § "A legal duty so called is nothing but a prediction what if a man does or omits certain things he will be made to suffer in this or that way by judgment of the court; and so of a legal right." ‖ "The duty to keep a contract at common law means a prediction that you must pay damages if you do not keep it —

---

* W. A. ROBSON, CIVILISATION AND THE GROWTH OF LAW (1935) 339: "Juridical laws . . . presuppose a voluntary element in the activities to which they relate and are to some extent designed for the express purpose of producing in the real world relations which would not otherwise exist."

† O. W. HOLMES, COLLECTED LEGAL PAPERS (1920) 167.

‡ HOLMES, COLLECTED LEGAL PAPERS 173.

§ HOLMES, COLLECTED LEGAL PAPERS 168.

‖ HOLMES, COLLECTED LEGAL PAPERS 169.

and nothing else." * Justice B. N. Cardozo advocates the same view. He says: "What permits us to say that the principles are law is the force or persuasiveness of the prediction that they will or ought to be applied." † "We shall unite in viewing as law that body of principle and dogma which with a reasonable measure of probability may be predicted as the basis for judgment in pending or in future controversies. When the prediction reaches a high degree of certainty or assurance, we speak of the law as settled, though, no matter how great the apparent settlement, the possibility of error in the prediction is always present. When the prediction does not reach so high a standard, we speak of the law as doubtful or uncertain." † Cardozo agrees with Wu's statement: "Psychologically law is a science of prediction *par excellence*." § To the question: "Why do we declare that a certain rule is a rule of law?" Cardozo answers: "We do so because the observation of recorded instances . . . induces a belief which has the certainty of conviction that the rule will be acted on as law by the agencies of government." And he adds: "As in the process of nature, we give the name of law to uniformity of succession." ‖ Cardozo considers, like Huxley, the rule of law as a kind of law of nature.

D. The Specific Meaning of a Juristic Statement

It can easily be shown that the meaning jurists attach to the concepts of legal duty and legal right is not a prediction of the future behavior of the courts. The fact that a court orders a certain sanction against an individual accused of a certain delict depends upon various circumstances, but especially upon the ability of the court to establish that the individual has committed the delict. If at all, the decision of the court can be predicted only with a certain degree of probability. Now it may happen, for example, that somebody commits a murder in a way that makes it highly improbable that a court would be able to establish his guilt. If the accused person, according to Justice Holmes' definition of the law, consults a lawyer about "what the courts will do in fact," the lawyer would have to tell the murderer: "It is improbable that the court will condemn you; it is very probable that the court will acquit you."

---

* HOLMES, COLLECTED LEGAL PAPERS 175.

† BENJAMIN N. CARDOZO, THE GROWTH OF THE LAW (1924) 43. Only the statement that a principle "will" be applied, not the statement that it "ought" to be applied, is a prediction.

‡ CARDOZO, GROWTH OF THE LAW 44.

§ John C. H. Wu, *The Juristic Philosophy of Mr. Justice Holmes* (1923) 21 MICH. L. REV. 523 at 530.

‖ CARDOZO, GROWTH OF THE LAW 40.

But would this statement be equivalent to the statement: "There was no legal duty for you not to murder"? Certainly not. The significance of the statement: "A is legally obliged to certain behavior," is not "It is probable that a court will enact a sanction against A," but: "If a court establishes that A has behaved in the opposite way, then it ought to order a sanction against A." Only if the lawyer gives the murderer an answer of this kind does he give legal information. The existence of a duty is the legal necessity, not the factual probability, of a sanction. Likewise, right means the legal possibility of causing a sanction, not the probability that one will cause it.

E. No Prediction of the Legislative Function

Holmes' definition of law as "the prophecies of what the courts will do in fact" is scarcely adequate in those cases where a court acts as a legislator and creates substantive law for the case at hand without being bound by any preëxisting substantive law. To predict with a reasonable degree of probability what a court will do when acting as a legislator is as impossible as to predict with a reasonable degree of probability what laws a legislative body will pass. Cardozo tries to interpret this case as one where prediction reaches only a very low degree of probability. He says: "Farther down" — than the point where prediction does not even reach a standard to speak of doubtful law — "is the vanishing point where law does not exist, and must be brought into being, if at all, by an act of free creation." * However, law which came into being by an act of "free creation" is law too, although it is evidently an unpredictable law. This law, too, is an object of the science of law, and a very important, if not the most important one, since almost all the general rules of statutory and customary law, and a remarkable part of the judge-made law are products of "free creation" and hence unpredictable. Only if one restricts his view of law to the ordinary activity of the courts, and that means to their law-applying function, may one be led to define the science of law — not the "law" — as a "science of prediction."

F. The Law not a System of Doctrines (Theorems)

Clearly the preëxisting rules which the courts apply in their decisions are not "prophecies of what the courts will do in fact." The rule which a judge applies in a concrete case does not tell the judge how he actually will decide, but how he ought to decide. The judge does not turn to law for an answer to the question what he actually will do, but for an answer

---

* Cardozo, Growth of the Law 40.

to the question what he ought to do. The subjective meaning of a rule to which an individual wishes to conform his behavior, which he feels obliged to apply or to obey, can be only an "ought," cannot be an "is." A rule which states that something is, or will be, has nothing to say to an individual who wishes to know how he ought to behave. A rule expressing how the individuals subjected to the legal order customarily behave, or how the courts predominantly decide disputes, would not give the individual or the judge the information he is asking for. The opposite may seem to be the case only because consciously or unconsciously one presumes that one ought to behave as people customarily behave, that a court ought to decide as courts usually decide, because one presupposes a norm which institutes custom as a law-creating fact. It is this norm which the court applies or obeys when it wishes to know how people customarily behave or how courts usually decide. The law of nature: "If a body is heated, it expands," cannot be "applied" or "obeyed." Only the prescription can be "applied" or "obeyed" that if you wish to expand a body you must heat it. A technical prescription can be applied or obeyed, not a doctrine of natural science. The law which courts apply is no scientific treatise describing and explaining actual facts. It is not a system of theorems which are the product of scientific cognition, but a set of prescriptions regulating the behavior of the subjects and organs of the legal community, a system of norms which are products of acts of will. This is the sense with which law is directed to courts. It is this sense which normative jurisprudence represents.

G. The Difference Between the Statements of a Normative and of a Sociological Jurisprudence

In order to predict what the courts will do, a sociological jurisprudence would have to study the actual behavior of the courts in order to obtain the "real" rules which actually determine the behavior of the courts. *A priori* it seems to be quite possible that these general rules, abstracted by sociology from the actual behavior of the courts, may be very different from the general norms created by legislation and custom, represented by normative jurisprudence in ought-statements; different not only with respect to the sense of the statements but also with respect to their contents. It may be that, according to the "real" rules established by sociology, the courts show a behavior totally different from that one which they ought to show according to the "paper" rules represented by normative jurisprudence.

We cannot be assured *a priori* that those patterns of behavior which sociology shows to be actually prevailing among the courts will be identical with those that the legal norms prescribe. If one were to believe the advocates of sociological jurisprudence, one would even have to expect that in certain circumstances the courts would behave quite differently from what is prescribed by the norms which, according to normative jurisprudence, are binding upon the courts. Such is, however, not the case. The reason is that normative jurisprudence asserts the validity of a norm, and that means its "existence," only when that norm belongs to a legal order which as a whole is efficacious, i.e., when the norms of this order are, by and large, obeyed by the subjects of the order and, if not obeyed, are by and large applied by its organs. The norms which normative jurisprudence regards as valid are norms that are ordinarily obeyed or applied. The rules by which sociological jurisprudence describes the law, the is-statements predicting what the courts will actually do under certain circumstances, therefore differ from the ought-statements, the legal rules by which normative jurisprudence describes the law, only in the sense in which conditions and consequences are connected. Under the same conditions under which, according to sociological jurisprudence, the courts actually behave in a certain way and probably will behave in the future, the courts ought to behave in the same way according to normative jurisprudence. In the interpretation of normative jurisprudence, the statement "a subject A is legally obliged to behave in a certain way" means that in case A does not behave in that way an organ X of the community ought to execute a sanction against A. As interpreted by sociological jurisprudence, the statement "A is obliged to behave in a certain way" signifies that in case A does not behave in this way an organ X of the community will probably execute a sanction against A. However, normative jurisprudence assumes that an organ ought to execute a sanction only if the norm prescribing the sanction belongs to an efficacious legal order. The norm's belonging to an efficacious legal order in turn implies the probability of the organ's actually applying the sanction.

The statement "a subject A has a right to demand certain behavior from another subject B" by normative jurisprudence is interpreted to mean that, in case B fails to observe the behavior in question, and A brings a suit against B, an organ X of the community ought to execute a sanction against B (or, that the subject A has the legal possibility of putting into motion the legal procedure leading to a sanction against B). In the translation of sociological jurisprudence, the juristic statement "a subject A has a right to demand certain behavior from another subject B" means that there exists a certain probability that an organ X of the community will execute a sanction against B, upon a suit of A, in case B does not observe the behavior in question (or, that the subject A has a factual possibility of putting into motion the coercive machinery of the State against B). Again, however, normative jurisprudence maintains that A has the legal possibility of putting into motion a sanction against B, only if A has the factual possibility of so doing. This is the unavoidable consequence of the fact that a legal order is accepted as valid by normative jurisprudence only if the order is efficacious as a whole, i.e., only if there exists a certain degree of probability that the sanctions stipulated by the order will be actually carried out under the circumstances anticipated by the order.

H. Sociological Elements in Austin's Analytical Jurisprudence

So subtle is in fact the difference between the juristic and the sociological definitions of duty and right that we occasionally find Austin employing the sociological definitions without his being aware of having abandoned his specific juristic method. He defines the legal duty as the "chance" of incurring the evil of the sanction. He explains: "The greater the eventual evil, and the greater the chance of incurring it, the greater is the efficacy of the command, and the greater is the strength of the obligation: Or (substituting expressions exactly equivalent), the greater is the *chance* that the command will be obeyed, and that the duty will not be broken. But where there is the smallest chance of incurring the smallest evil, the expression of a wish amounts to a command, and, therefore, imposes a duty. The sanction, if you will, is feeble or insufficient; but still there *is* a sanction, and, therefore, a duty and a command." *
This definition of the legal duty is in complete accordance with the requirements of sociological jurisprudence. In what is perhaps the most important attempt at a foundation of the sociology of law, in Max Weber, we find in fact definitions which agree with those of Austin's up to the choice of words. Max Weber † says: "The sociological significance of the fact that somebody has, according to the legal order of the State, a legal right, is that he has a chance, actually guaranteed by a legal norm, of requesting the aid of a coercive machinery for the protection of certain (ideal or material) interests." Max Weber has not given any sociological definition of the legal duty. But there is no doubt as to how his sociological translation of this concept would run. Slightly adapting the above definition of legal right, we obtain the following definition of an individual's being legally obligated to certain behavior: "There is a chance, actually guaranteed by the legal order, that the coercive machinery of

* 1 Austin, Lectures on Jurisprudence (5th ed. 1885) 90.
† Max Weber, Wirtschaft und Gesellschaft (Grundriss der Sozialökonomik, III. Abt., 1922) 371.

the State will be put into motion against the individual in case of contrary behavior." Essentially, this amounts to the same as Austin's explanation that there is a "chance" of incurring the sanction threatened by the legal command.

I. Predictability of the Legal Function and Efficacy of the Legal Order

From the point of view of a consistently analytical jurisprudence, this formulation is incorrect and it departs from the other — correct — definition given by Austin: "Obligation is liability to a sanction." "Liability" signifies a legal possibility, whereas "chance" signifies a factual possibility. But the difference between the two definitions lies entirely in the sense in which the sanction is attached to the delict by the legal rule of normative jurisprudence and the "real" rule of sociological jurisprudence. The facts which are being connected by the two kinds of rules are exactly the same. What sociological jurisprudence predicts that the courts will decide, normative jurisprudence maintains that they ought to decide. If there is no preëxisting norm, in the sense of normative jurisprudence, inasmuch as the court is entitled to create new law, and if, therefore, normative jurisprudence cannot tell how the courts ought to decide a concrete case, then sociological jurisprudence can foretell how the court will decide no more than it can foretell what laws the legislator will enact. If there exists a general norm of customary law which, in the sense of normative jurisprudence, determines the decision of the court, the most probable prediction which sociological jurisprudence can make seems to be that the court will decide in conformity with this general norm of customary law. The concept of customary law is only the normative translation of a rule describing how the subjects, and especially the courts, actually behave. If the preëxisting general norm with which the decision of the court has to conform according to normative jurisprudence has the character of statutory law, two cases have to be considered: (a) During the period following immediately upon the enactment of the statute, the statute is always considered valid, that means that at this moment normative jurisprudence maintains that the courts ought to apply the statute and to decide concrete cases as the statute prescribes. At this moment, sociological jurisprudence can hardly make another prediction than that the courts probably will apply the statute and decide concrete cases as the statute prescribes. It would hardly be possible to foresee at the moment of its enactment that the statute will not be applied by the courts. As long as the legal order as a whole retains its efficacy, as long as the government is able generally to obtain obedience, of all possibilities the most likely seems to be that a regulation issued by the competent authorities will actually be carried out. Exceptions are, if not completely, almost precluded. Immediately after the enactment of a statute, there will thus be hardly any disagreement between the results of normative and those of sociological jurisprudence. (b) Sometimes the courts fail to apply a statute to which normative jurisprudence accords validity. As soon as a sociological consideration of the actual behavior of the judiciary has given us reason to believe that in the future the courts will also probably not apply the statute, normative jurisprudence is forced to acknowledge that *desuetudo* has deprived the statute of its validity and that, therefore, the courts ought not to apply the statute. Again, there is no discrepancy between sociological and normative jurisprudence.

What has here been said concerning the predictability of the judicial decisions holds for the function of all law-applying organs. The function of the legislator is, however, as already mentioned, unpredictable. It is unpredictable because the constitution determines the contents of future laws, if at all, chiefly in a negative fashion. The functions of a legal community are predictable only insofar as they are determined by the legal order, in the sense of normative jurisprudence. What sociological jurisprudence is able to predict is fundamentally only the efficacy or non-efficacy of the legal order; its efficacy, however, is an essential condition for its validity, its non-efficacy for its non-validity, in the sense of normative jurisprudence. This is the reason why any discrepancy between the results of sociological and normative jurisprudence is almost impossible, except as far as the sense of their statements is concerned. Were not the legal order, by and large, efficacious, it would not be valid either, in the sense of normative jurisprudence; and then, no predictions would be possible with respect to the functioning of the law-applying organs. The fact that the legal order is efficacious forms the only basis for possible predictions. Sociological jurisprudence cannot consider any other decision as probable than one normative jurisprudence declares lawful.

J. IRRELEVANCY OF INDIVIDUAL CIRCUMSTANCES

What a certain judge will decide in a certain concrete case depends in actual fact on a multitude of circumstances. To investigate them all is really out of the question. Disregarding the fact that today we still entirely lack the scientific methods for completing such an investigation, for other reasons also it would be impossible to submit the judge to such an investigation before he has announced his decision. No sociological jurist has ever thought of such a foolish enterprise. All the peculiarities of the concrete case — the character of the judge, his disposition, his philosophy of life, and his physical condition — are, it is true, facts which are essential to a real understanding of the causal chains. But they are of no importance for that estimation of the probabilities as to the future decision of the judge in which sociological jurisprudence is interested. The only relevant question is, whether the judge will apply the law — such as it is described by normative jurisprudence, that is as a system of valid norms — in a concrete case. And the only prediction possible on the basis of our knowledge of facts is that as long as the total legal order is efficacious on the whole, a certain probability exists that the judge in question will actually apply the valid law. If, for some reason or another, he fails to do so, this is no more relevant to sociological jurisprudence than is to physics the case where heat does not make the mercury in a thermometer rise because by accident the thermometer has been broken.

K. Sociology of Law and Sociology of Justice

To investigate the causes of the efficacy, by and large, of a certain legal order is certainly an important problem of sociology. But it can hardly be asserted that we are today in a position to solve it. At any rate, sociological jurisprudence has not so far made any attempt at answering the question with regard to any one of the existing legal orders. Nay, we do not even possess a description of a single legal order carried out according to the principles of sociological jurisprudence. What goes under the name of sociological jurisprudence is hardly more than methodological postulates.

It is possible, however, to deal successfully with special sociological problems connected with the phenomenon of law. If we examine, e.g., the motives of the men who create, apply, and obey the law we find in their minds certain ideologies, among which the idea of justice plays an essential part. It is an important task to analyze critically this ideology, to establish a sociology of justice. The problem of justice, by its very nature, lies beyond the borderlines of a normative jurisprudence confined to a theory of positive law; but the belief in justice is a proper subject for sociological jurisprudence; perhaps even its specific subject. For, as already pointed out, the results of a sociology of positive law cannot essentially differ from those of normative jurisprudence.

L. Sociological Jurisprudence Presupposes the Normative Concept of Law

a. Difference between the Legal and the Illegal Act

The value of a description of positive law in sociological terms is further diminished by the fact that sociology can define the phenomenon of law, the positive law of a particular community, only by having recourse to the concept of law as defined by normative jurisprudence. Sociological jurisprudence presupposes this concept. The object of sociological jurisprudence is not valid norms — which form the object of normative jurisprudence — but human behavior. What human behavior? Only such human behavior as is, somehow or other, related to "law." What distinguishes such behavior, sociologically, from behavior which falls outside the field of the sociology of law? An example may serve to illuminate the problem. Somebody receives a notice from the taxation authorities, requesting him to pay an income tax of $10,000, in default whereof a punishment is threatened. The same day, the same person receives a notice from the head of a notorious gang requesting him to deposit $10,000 in a designated place, failing which he will be killed, and a third letter in which a friend asks for a large contribution toward his support. In what respect does the taxation notice differ, sociologically, from the blackmail letter, and both from the letter of the friend? It is obvious that there exist three different phenomena, not only from a juristic, but also from a sociological point of view, and that at least the friend's letter with its effect on the receiver's behavior is not a phenomenon which falls within the field of a sociology of law.

b. Max Weber's Definition of Sociology of Law

The most successful attempt so far to define the object of a sociology of law has been made by Max Weber. He writes: "When we are concerned with 'law', 'legal order', 'rule of law', we must strictly observe the distinction between a juristic and a sociological point of view. Jurisprudence asks for the ideally valid legal norms. That is to say . . . what normative meaning shall be attached to a sentence pretending to represent a legal norm. Sociology investigates what is actually happening in a society because there is a certain chance that its members believe in the validity of an order and adapt [orientieren] their behavior to this order." * Hence, according to this definition, the object of a sociology of law is human behavior which the acting individual has adapted (orientiert) to an order because he considers that order to be "valid";

---

* WEBER, WIRTSCHAFT UND GESELLSCHAFT 368.

and that means, that the individual whose behavior forms the object of sociology of law considers the order in the same way as normative jurisprudence considers the law. In order to be the object of a sociology of law, the human behavior must be determined by the idea of a valid order.

c. Legal and De Facto Authority

From the point of view of normative jurisprudence, the order to pay taxes differs from the gangster's threat and the request made by the friend by the fact that only the tax order is issued by an individual who is authorized by a legal order assumed to be valid. From the standpoint of Max Weber's sociological jurisprudence, the difference is that the individual who receives the notice to pay his tax interprets this notice in such a way. He pays the tax considering the command to pay it as an act issued by an individual authorized by an order which the taxpayer considers to be valid. Outwardly, he may act in an identical manner with respect to the notice from the taxation authorities, the threat from the gangster band, and the letter from his friend. He may, for instance, pay the required amount in all three cases. From a juristic point of view, there is, however, still a difference. The one payment is fulfillment of a legal obligation, the others are not. From a sociological point of view, a difference between the three cases can be maintained only by considering the juristic concept of law as it is, in fact, present in the minds of the individuals involved. Sociologically, the decisive difference between the three cases is the fact that the behavior of the taxpayer is determined — or at least accompanied — by the idea of a valid order, of norm, duty, authority, whereas his behavior in the other cases is not determined or accompanied by such an idea. If the behavior in case of the gangster threat is at all the object of a sociology of law, it is because it represents a crime, legally determined as blackmail. The third case doubtless falls outside the field of a sociology of law, because the human behavior in question has no relation to the legal order as a system of norms.

Llewellyn * explains that, from the point of view of a sociology of law, "authority does not refer to any efflux of a 'normative system' but to the basic situation which exists when Jones says 'Go' and Smith goes, as distinct from that in which Smith does not go; and the drive of *de facto* authority of this sort to provide itself with felt rightness or rightfulness is regarded, again, as a behavior drive observable among men-in-groups." The "rightness or rightfulness" can be nothing but an idea which accompanies the behavior of Jones and Smith. This idea, too, is "observable."

* K. N. Llewellyn, *The Normative, the Legal, and the Law-Jobs; The Problem of Juristic Method* (1940) 49 YALE L. J. 1355f.

For observable is not only the external but also the internal behavior of individuals, their ideas and feelings which accompany their external behavior. The psychologist observes only the internal behavior, and sociology is, to a great extent, social psychology. Ideas are psychic acts which are distinguishable by their contents. They cannot be described without reference to their contents. The individuals living within the State have an idea of law in their minds, and this idea is — as a matter of fact — the idea of a body of valid norms, the idea of a normative system. Some of their actions are characterized by the fact that they are caused or accompanied by ideas the contents of which is the law as a normative system. Sociological jurisprudence cannot describe the difference existing between the behavior of Smith in case he considers Jones to be a gangster, without referring to the contents of certain ideas which accompany the behavior of Smith. The difference of his behavior in the two senses consists essentially in the difference which exists between the contents of the ideas accompanying Smith's behavior. In the one case, Smith interprets the command issued by Jones as the act of an authority authorized by the normative system of positive law, in the other case he interprets Jones' command according to the normative system of positive law as a crime. In the third case, he does not refer Jones' request to the legal order at all. It is exactly by these different interpretations — in the mind of Smith — that his behavior is sociologically different in the three cases. A sociology cannot describe the difference between the first two cases without referring to law as a body of valid norms, as a normative system. For law exists as such a body of valid norms in the minds of individuals, and the idea of law causes or accompanies their behavior, which is the object of a sociology of law. The sociology of law can eliminate the third case from its special field only because there is no relation between Smith's behavior and the law.

Sociology of law, as defined by Max Weber, is possible only by referring the human behavior which is its object to the law as it exists in the minds of men as contents of their ideas. In men's minds, law exists, as a matter of fact, as a body of valid norms, as a normative system. Only by referring the human behavior to law as a system of valid norms, to law as defined by normative jurisprudence, is sociological jurisprudence able to delimit its specific object from that of general sociology; only by this reference is it possible to distinguish sociologically between the phenomenon of legal and the phenomenon of illegal behavior, between the State and a gang of racketeers.

M. The Object of the Sociology of Law: Behavior Determined by the Legal Order

From the juristic point of view, the threat from the gang constitutes a delict, the crime of blackmailing; a valid legal norm makes it the condition of a certain sanction. From a sociological point of view, it can be considered as a delict only because there is a certain chance that the sanction provided for by the valid legal order will be executed.

Max Weber's definition of the object of sociological jurisprudence: human behavior adapted (*orientiert*) by the acting individual to an order which he considers to be valid, is not quite satisfactory. According to this definition, a delict which was committed without the delinquent's being in any way conscious of the legal order would fall outside the relevant phenomena. In this respect, his definition of the object of sociology is obviously too narrow. A sociology of law investigating the causes of criminality will also take into consideration delicts which are committed without the delinquent's adapting (*orientieren*) his behavior to the legal order. Every act which, from a juristic point of view, is a "delict," is also a phenomenon belonging to the domain of the sociology of law, insofar as there is a chance that the organs of society will react against it by executing the sanction provided by the legal order. It is an object of the sociology of law even if the delinquent has committed the delict without thinking of law. Human behavior pertains to the domain of the sociology of law not because it is "oriented" to the legal order, but because it is determined by a legal norm as condition or consequence. Only because it is determined by the legal order which we presuppose to be valid does human behavior constitute a legal phenomenon. Human behavior so qualified is an object of normative jurisprudence; but it is also an object of the sociology of law insofar as it actually occurs or probably will occur. This seems to be the only satisfactory way of drawing the line between the sociology of law and general sociology. This definition, as well as Max Weber's formulation, shows clearly that sociological jurisprudence presupposes the juristic concept of law, the concept of law defined by normative jurisprudence.

PART TWO

THE STATE

I. THE LAW AND THE STATE

A. The State a Real (Sociological) or Juristic Entity

a. The State as Personification of the National Legal Order

A DEFINITION of "the State" is made very difficult by the variety of objects which the term commonly denotes. The word is sometimes used in a very broad sense, to denote "society" as such, or some special form of society. But the word is also quite frequently used in a much narrower sense, to denote a particular organ of society — for instance, the government, or the subjects of the government, a "nation," or the territory that they inhabit. The unsatisfactory situation of political theory — which essentially is a theory of the State — is largely due precisely to the fact that different authors treat widely different problems under the same name and that even one and the same author unconsciously uses the same word with several meanings.

The situation appears simpler when the State is discussed from a purely juristic point of view. The State is then taken into consideration only as a legal phenomenon, as a juristic person, that is as a corporation. Its nature is thus in principle determined by our earlier definition of the corporation. The only remaining question is how the State differs from other corporations. The difference must lie in the normative order that constitutes the State corporation. The State is the community created by a national (as opposed to an international) legal order. The State as juristic person is a personification of this community or the national legal order constituting this community. From a juristic point of view, the problem of the State therefore appears as the problem of the national legal order.

Positive law appears empirically in the form of national legal orders connected with each other by an international legal order. There is no absolute law; there are only various systems of legal norms — English, French, American, Mexican law, and so on — whose spheres of validity are limited in characteristic ways; and in addition to these, a complex of norms that we speak of as international law. To define law, it is not sufficient to explain the difference between so-called legal norms and other norms regulating human behavior. We must indicate also what is the specific nature of those systems of norms which are the empirical manifestations of positive law, how they are delimited and how they are interrelated. This is the problem which the State as a legal phenomenon presents and which it is the task of the theory of the State to solve, as a branch of the theory of law.

b. The State as Order and as Community Constituted by the Order

According to the traditional view it is not possible to comprehend the essence of a national legal order, its *principium individuationis*, unless the State is presupposed as an underlying social reality. A system of norms, according to this view, possesses the unity and individuality by which it merits the name of a national legal order, just because it is in some way or other related to one State as an actual social fact; because it is created "by" one State or valid "for" one State. French law is supposed to be based on the existence of one French State as a social, not a juristic entity. The relation between law and State is regarded as analogous to that between law and the individual. Law — although created by the State — is assumed to regulate the behavior of the State, conceived of as a kind of man or superman, just as law regulates the behavior of men. And just as there is the juristic concept of person beside the biological-physical concept of man, a sociological concept of State is believed to exist beside its juristic concept and even to be logically and historically prior to the latter. The State as social reality falls under the category of society; it is a community. The law falls under the category of norms; it is a system of norms, a normative order. State and law, according to this view, are two different objects. The duality of State and law is in fact one of the cornerstones of modern political science and jurisprudence.

However, this dualism is theoretically indefensible. The State as a legal community is not something apart from its legal order, any more than the corporation is distinct from its constitutive order. A number of individuals form a community only because a normative order regulates their mutual behavior. The community — as pointed out in a foregoing chapter — consists in nothing but the normative order regulating the mutual behavior of the individuals. The term "community" designates only the fact that the mutual behavior of certain individuals is regulated by a normative order. The statement that individuals are members of a community is only a metaphorical expression, a figurative description of specific relations between the individuals, relations constituted by a normative order.

Since we have no reason to assume that there exist two different normative orders, the order of the State and its legal order, we must admit that the community we call "State" is "its" legal order. French law can be distinguished from Swiss or Mexican law without recourse to the hypothesis that there are a French, a Swiss, and a Mexican State as so many independently existing social realities. The State as community in its relation to law is not a natural reality, or a social reality analogous to a natural one, such as man is in relation to law. If there is a social reality related to the phenomenon we call "State," and therefore a sociological concept as distinguished from the juristic concept of State, then priority belongs to the latter, not the former. The sociological concept — whose claim to the term "State" will be further examined — presupposes the juristic concept; not *vice versa*.

c. The State as Sociological Unity

Social community means unity of a plurality of individuals or of actions of individuals. The assertion that the State is not merely a juristic but a sociological entity, a social reality existing independently of its legal order, can be substantiated only by showing that the individuals belonging to the same State form a unity and that this unity is not constituted by the legal order but by an element which has nothing to do with law. However, such an element constituting the "one in the many" cannot be found.

1. Social Unity (Body) Constituted by Interaction

The interaction that allegedly takes place between individuals belonging to the same State has been pronounced such a law-independent sociological element constituting the unity of the individuals belonging to one and the same State, and therefore constituting the State as a social reality. A number of people form a real unit — it is said — when one influences the other and is himself in his turn influenced by the other. It is obvious that all human beings, nay all phenomena whatsoever, so interact. Everywhere in nature we find interaction, and the bare concept of interaction, therefore, cannot be used to interpret the unity characteristic of any particular natural phenomenon. In order to apply the interaction theory to the State, we must assume that interaction allows of degrees and that the interaction between individuals belonging to the same State is more intense than the interaction between individuals belonging to different States. But such an assumption is unfounded. Whether it is economic, political, or cultural relations we have in mind when speaking of interaction, it can not seriously be questioned that people belonging to different States frequently have more intense contact than citizens of the same State. Think of the case where individuals of the same nationality, race, or religion are divided between two neighboring States whose populations lack homogeneity. Membership in the same language community, religion, class, or profession often creates far closer ties than common citizenship. Being of a psychological nature, social interaction is not limited to people living together within the same space. Thanks to present-day means of communication, the liveliest exchange of spiritual values is possible between people scattered over the whole earth. In normal times, State borders are no hindrance to close relationships between people. If, *per impossibile*, one could exactly measure the intensity of social interaction, one would probably find that mankind is divided into groups in no way coinciding with existing States.

The assertion that the interaction between individuals belonging to one and the same State is more intense than the interaction between individuals belonging to different States, is a fiction whose political tendency is patent. When the State is considered as a social unit, the criterion of unity is undoubtedly quite different from social interaction. The juristic nature of the criterion is evident from the fashion in which the sociological problem is stated. To say that the State is an actual social unit of interaction is to say that individuals who, in a juristic sense, belong to the same State also have a relation of mutual interaction; i.e., that the State is a real social unit besides being a juristic unit. The State is presupposed as a juristic unit when the problem as to its sociological unity is formulated. We have seen that the interaction theory does not offer any tenable answer to this problem, and it would seem that any attempted positive solution must involve the same type of political fiction.

2. Social Unity (Body) Constituted by Common Will or Interest

Another sociological approach to the problem of the State proceeds from the assumption that the individuals belonging to one and the same State are united by the fact that they have a common will or — what amounts to the same thing — a common interest. One speaks of a "collective will" or a "collective interest," and one assumes that this "collective will" or "collective interest" constitutes the unity and therefore the social reality of the State. One also speaks of a "collective sentiment," a "collective consciousness," a kind of collective soul, as the fact that constitutes the community of the State. If the theory of the State is not to transcend the data of experience and degenerate into metaphysical speculation, this "collective will" or "collective consciousness" can not be the will or consciousness of a being different from the human individuals belonging to the State; the term "collective will" or "collective consciousness" can signify only that several individuals will, feel or think the same way and are united by their awareness of this common willing, feeling, thinking. A real unity then exists only among those who actually are in an identical state of mind, and it exists only in those moments when this identity actually prevails. It is unlikely that such identity would ever exist except in relatively small groups whose extension or membership would also be constantly changing. To assert that all citizens of a State permanently will, feel, or think the same is an obvious political fiction, closely similar to that which the interaction theory was seen to embody.

Still more fictitious is the view that the State is or has a "collective will" over and above the wills of its subjects. Such an assertion in fact can only be considered as a figurative expression for the binding force that the national legal order has upon the individuals whose behavior it regulates. To pronounce the will of the State a psychological or sociological reality is to hypostatize an abstraction into a real agency, that is, to ascribe to a normative relation between individuals substantial or personal character. This is, as we pointed out, a typical tendency of primitive thinking; and political thinking has, to a great extent, a primitive character. The tendency to hypostatize the will of a super-individual, and that means, a superhuman being, has an ideological purpose which is unmistakable.

This ideological purpose is seen more clearly when the real unity of the State is described as a "collective interest." In reality, the population of a State is divided into various interest-groups which are more or less opposed to each other. The ideology of a collective State-interest is used to conceal this unavoidable conflict of interests. To call that interest which is expressed in the legal order the interest of all is a fiction even when the legal order represents a compromise between the interests of the most important groups. Were the legal order really the expression of interests common to all, and that means, were the legal order in complete harmony with the wishes of all individuals subject to the order, then this order could reckon with the voluntary obedience of all its subjects; then it would not need to be coercive; then, being completely "just," it would not even need to have the character of law.

3. The State as Organism

Another theory of the same type is the widespread doctrine that the State is a natural organism. Under this theory the sociology of the State assumes the form of social biology. Such biology could simply be rejected as absurd were it not for the political importance it possesses. The real aim of the organic theory, an aim of which many of its proponents seem unaware, is not at all scientifically to explain the phenomenon of the State, but to ensure the value of the State institution as such, or of some particular State; to confirm the authority of the State organs and to increase the obedience of the citizens. Otto Gierke, one of the most distinguished exponents of the organic theory, reveals its true purpose when he points to its ethical significance. The insight into the organic character of the State is "the only source for the idea that the community is something valuable in itself. And only from the superior value of the whole as compared to its parts can be derived the obligation of the citizen to live and, if necessary, to die for the whole. Were the people only the sum of its members, and the State only an institution for the welfare of born and unborn citizens, then the individual might, it is true, be forced to give his energy and life for the State. But he could not be under any moral obligation to do so. The glory of a high ethical ideal, that has always transfigured the death for the fatherland, then would fade. Why should the individual sacrifice himself for the welfare of others who are equal to him?" * The moral and legal obligation for the individual, under certain circumstances, to give his own life is indubitable. But it is in equal degree indubitably not the task of science to ensure the fulfillment of this or that obligation — least of all by fashioning a theory whose only justification would lie in the fact that people will better fulfill their duties to the State if they are induced to believe the theory.

4. The State as Domination

The most successful attempt at a sociological theory of the State is perhaps the interpretation of social reality in terms of "domination." The State is defined as a relationship where some command and rule and the others obey and are ruled. This theory has in mind the relation constituted by the fact that one individual expresses his will that another individual behave in a certain way, and this expression motivates the other individual to behave accordingly. In actual social life, there exists an infinity of such relations of motivation. There will hardly be any human relationship that does not sometimes and to some degree assume this character. Even the relationship we call love is not completely free from this element, for even here there is always someone who dominates and someone who is dominated. What is the criterion by which those relations of domination that constitute the State are distinguished from those which do not? Let us consider the relatively simple case of a State where one single individual rules in an autocratic or tyrannic way. Even in such a State, there are many "tyrants," many people who impose their will upon others. But only one is essential to the existence of the State. Who? The one who commands "in the name of the State." How then do we distinguish between commands "in the name of the State" and other commands? Hardly otherwise than by means of the legal order which constitutes the State. Commands "in the name of the State" are such as are issued in accordance with an order whose validity

---

* OTTO GIERKE, DAS WESEN DER MENSCHLICHEN VERBÄNDE (1902) 34f.

the sociologist must presuppose when he distinguishes between commands which are acts of State and commands which do not have this character.* The ruler of a State is that individual who exercises a function determined by this order. It is hardly possible to define the concept of a ruler functioning as "organ of the State" without presupposing the legal order constituting the community we call State. The concept of a "ruler of the State" thus implies the idea of a valid legal order.

Assume, however, that there were a purely sociological criterion by which one could distinguish the ruler of the State. A study of actual social behavior would perhaps reveal that this ruler himself is ruled by other people, by an adviser, his mistress, or his chamberlain, and that the commands he issues are the result of influences these other individuals exercise upon him. A sociology of the State, however, will ignore these relations of domination in which the ruler himself holds the place of the ruled. Why? Because these relations fall outside the legal order constituting the State; because they are irrelevant from the point of view of that order.

There is, as a matter of fact, no State where all commands "in the name of the State" originate in one single ruler. There are always more than one commanding authority, and always a large number of actual relations of domination, numerous acts of commanding and obeying, the sum of which represents the "sociological State." What brings unity to this multitude and justifies us in considering the State as one relation of domination? Only the unity of the legal order according to which all the different acts of commanding and obeying take place.

This legal order, considered as a system of valid norms, is essential also to the sociological concept of domination as applied to the State; for, even from a sociological point of view, only a domination considered to be "legitimate" can be conceived of as "State." The bare fact that an individual (or a group of individuals) is in a position to enforce a certain pattern of behavior is not a sufficient ground for speaking of a relation of domination such as constitutes a State. Even the sociologist recognizes the difference between a State and a robber gang.†

The sociological description of the State as a phenomenon of domination is not complete if only the fact is established that men force other men to a certain behavior. The domination that characterizes the State claims to be legitimate and must be actually regarded as such by rulers and ruled. The domination is legitimate only if it takes place in accordance with a legal order whose validity is presupposed by the acting

* Cf. *supra*, pp. 175ff.
† Cf. *infra*, pp. 191ff.

individuals; and this order is the legal order of the community the organ of which is the "ruler of the State." The domination which has, sociologically, the character of "State" presents itself as creation and execution of a legal order, that is, a domination which is interpreted as such by the rulers and the ruled. Sociology has to record the existence of this legal order as a fact in the minds of the individuals involved; and if sociology interprets the domination as a State organization, then sociology itself must assume the validity of this order. Even as an object of sociology, "State domination" is not a bare fact but a fact together with an interpretation. This interpretation is made both by the rulers and the ruled and by the sociologist himself who is studying their behavior.

d. Juristic Concept of State and Sociology of State

1. Human Behavior Oriented to the Legal Order

The task of sociology is, in Max Weber's words, "to understand social behavior by interpretation." * Social behavior is behavior that has a significance because the acting individuals attach significance to it, because they interpret it. Sociology is the interpretation of actions which have already been subjected to an interpretation by the acting individuals. While, to the jurist, the State is a complex of norms, an order, to the sociologist it appears, Max Weber thinks, as a complex of actions, "a process of actual social behavior." These actions have a certain significance because they are interpreted by the acting individuals according to a certain scheme. These actions are, in Max Weber's terminology, "oriented," and that means, adapted to a certain idea; this idea is a normative order, the legal order. The legal order furnishes that scheme according to which the individuals themselves, acting as subjects and organs of the State, interpret their behavior and according to which, therefore, a sociology that wishes to grasp the "State" has to interpret its object. It is rather misleading to say that this object is the State, the "sociological" State. The State is not identical with any of those actions which form the object of sociology, nor with the sum of them all. The State is not an action or a number of actions, any more than it is a human being or a number of human beings. The State is that order of human behavior that we call the legal order, the order to which certain human actions are oriented, the idea to which the individuals adapt their behavior. If human behavior oriented to this order forms the object of sociology, then its object is not the State. There is no sociological concept of the State besides the juristic concept. Such a double concept

---

* WEBER, WIRTSCHAFT UND GESELLSCHAFT 1.

of the State is logically impossible, if for no other reason because there cannot be more than one concept of the same object. There is only a juristic concept of the State: the State as — centralized — legal order. The sociological concept of an actual pattern of behavior, oriented to the legal order, is not a concept of the State, it presupposes the concept of the State, which is a juristic concept.

The demand for a sociological definition of the State arises from the impression that one formulates by saying: "After all, the State is a highly real fact." However, if by scientific analysis one is led to the result that there is no sociological concept of the State, that the concept of the State is juristic, one by no means denies or ignores those facts which pre-scientific terminology designates by the word "State." These facts do not lose any of their reality if it is asserted that their "State"-quality is nothing but the result of an interpretation. These facts are actions of human beings, and these actions are acts of State only insofar as they are interpreted according to a normative order the validity of which has to be presupposed.

2. Normative Character of the State

It is the juristic concept of the State that sociologists apply when they describe the relations of domination within the State. The properties they ascribe to the State are conceivable only as properties of a normative order or of a community constituted by such an order. Sociologists also consider an essential quality of the State to be an authority superior to the individuals, obligating the individuals. Only as a normative order can the State be an obligating authority, especially if that authority is considered to be sovereign. Sovereignty is — as we shall see later — conceivable only within the realm of the normative.

That the State must be a normative order is obvious also from the "conflict" between State and individual, which is a specific problem not only of social philosophy but also of sociology. If the State were an actual fact, just as the individual is, then there could not exist any such "conflict," since facts of nature never are in "conflict" with each other. But if the State is a system of norms, then the will and the behavior of the individual can conflict with these norms, and so can arise the antagonism between the "is" and the "ought" which is a fundamental problem of all social theory and practice.

e. The State as "Politically" Organized Society (The State as Power)

The identity of State and legal order is apparent from the fact that· even sociologists characterize the State as a "politically" organized society. Since society — as a unit — is constituted by organization, it is more correct to define the State as "political organization." An organization is an order. But in what does the "political" character of this order lie? In the fact that it is a coercive order. The State is a political organization because it is an order regulating the use of force, because it monopolizes the use of force. This, however, as we have seen, is one of the essential characters of law. The State is a politically organized society because it is a community constituted by a coercive order, and this coercive order is the law.

The State is sometimes said to be a political organization on the ground that it has, or is, "power." The State is described as the power that lies back of law, that enforces law. Insofar as such a power exists, it is nothing but the fact that law itself is effective, that the idea of legal norms providing for sanctions motivates the behavior of individuals, exercises psychic compulsion upon individuals. The fact that an individual has social power over another individual manifests itself in that the former is able to induce the latter to the behavior which the former desires. But power in a social sense is possible only within the framework of a normative order regulating human behavior. For the existence of such a power, it does not suffice that one individual is actually stronger than another and can force him to a certain behavior — as one forces an animal into submission or makes a tree fall. Power in a social or political sense implies authority and a relation of superior to inferior.

Such a relation is possible only on the basis of an order by which the one is empowered to command and the other is obligated to obey. Social power is essentially correlative to social obligation, and social obligation presupposes social order or, what amounts to the same, social organization. Social power is possible only within social organization. This is particularly evident when the power does not rest with a single individual but — as is usually the case in social life — with a group of individuals. Social power is always a power which in some way or other is organized. The power of the State is the power organized by positive law — is the power of law; that is, the efficacy of positive law.

Speaking of the power of the State, one usually thinks of prisons and electric chairs, machine guns and cannons. But one should not forget that these are all dead things which become instruments of power only when used by human beings, and that human beings are generally moved to use them for a given purpose only by commands they regard as norms. The phenomenon of political power manifests itself in the fact that the norms regulating the use of these instruments become efficacious. "Power" is not prisons and electric chairs, machine guns and cannons; "power" is not any kind of substance or entity hidden behind the social order. Political power is the efficacy of the coercive order recognized as law. To describe the State as "the power behind the law" is incorrect, since it suggests the existence of two separate entities where there is only one: the legal order. The dualism of law and State is a superfluous doubling or duplication of the object of our cognition; a result of our tendency to personify and then to hypostatize our personifications. A typical example of this tendency we found in the animistic interpretation of nature, that is, primitive man's idea that nature is animated, that behind everything there is a soul, a spirit, a god of this thing: behind a tree, a dryas, behind a river, a nymph, behind the moon, a moon-goddess, behind the sun, a sun-god. Thus, we imagine behind the law, its hypostatized personification, the State, the god of the law. The dualism of law and State is an animistic superstition. The only legitimate dualism here is that between the validity and the efficacy of the legal order. But this distinction — presented in the first part of this book — does not entitle us to speak of the State as a power apart from, or back of, the legal order.

f. The Problem of the State as a Problem of Imputation

The necessary unity of State and law can be seen also through the following considerations. Even exponents of the organic theory recognize that the State is not an object that can be apprehended by the senses. Even if, in some sense, the State were formed out of human beings, it could not be a body composed of individual human bodies as a natural organism is composed of cells. The State is not a visible or tangible body. But, then, how does the invisible and intangible State manifest itself in social life? Certain actions of individual human beings are considered as actions of the State. Under what conditions do we attribute a human action to the State? Not every individual is capable of performing actions which have the character of acts of the State; and not every action of an individual capable of performing acts of the State has this character. How can we distinguish human actions which are, from human actions which are not, acts of the State? The judgment by which we refer a human action to the State, as to an invisible person, means an imputation of a human action to the State. The problem of the State is a problem of imputation. The State is, so to speak, a common point into which various human actions are projected, a common point of imputation for different human actions. The individuals whose actions are considered to be acts of the State, whose actions are imputed to the State, are designated as "organs" of the State. Not every individual, however, is capable of performing an act of the State, and only some actions by those capable are acts of the State.

What is the criterion of this imputation? This is the decisive question leading to the essence of the State. An analysis shows that we impute a human action to the State only when the human action in question corresponds in a specific way to the presupposed legal order. The imputation of a human action to the State is possible only on the condition that this action is determined in a specific way by a normative order; and this order is the legal order. Though, in reality, it is always a definite individual who executes the punishment against a criminal, we say that the criminal is punished "by the State" because the punishment is stipulated in the legal order. The same State is said to exact a fine from a negligent tax-payer since it is the same legal order that stipulates the fine. An action is an act of the State insofar as it is an execution of the legal order. The actions by which the legal order is most directly executed are the coercive acts provided as sanctions by the legal order. But, in a wider sense, the legal order is executed by all those actions which serve as a preparation for a sanction, in particular actions by which sanction-stipulating norms are created. Acts of State are not only human actions by which the legal order is executed but also human actions by which the legal order is created, not only executive but also legislative acts. To impute a human action to the State, as to an invisible person, is to relate a human action as the action of a State organ to the unity of the order which stipulates this action. The State as a person is nothing but the personification of this unity. An "organ of the State" is tantamount to an "organ of the law."

The result of our analysis is that there is no sociological concept of the State different from the concept of the legal order; and that means, that we can describe the social reality without using the term "State."

B. THE ORGANS OF THE STATE

a. The Concept of the State-Organ

Whoever fulfills a function determined by the legal order is an organ. These functions, be they of a norm-creating or of a norm-applying character, are all ultimately aimed at the execution of a legal sanction. The parliament that enacts the penal code, and the citizens who elect the parliament, are organs of the State, as well as the judge who sentences the criminal and the individual who actually executes the punishment.

An organ, in this sense, is an individual fulfilling a specific function. The quality of an individual of being an organ is constituted by his function. He is an organ because and in so far as he performs a law-creating or law-applying function. Besides this concept there is, however, another, narrower, "material" concept, according to which an individual is an "organ" of the State only if he personally has a specific legal position. A legal transaction, e.g., a contract, is a law-creating act just as a judicial decision is. The contracting parties, as well as the judge, perform a law-creating function; but the judge is an organ of the State in the narrower sense of this term, whereas the contracting parties are not considered to be State-organs. The judge is an "organ" of the State in this narrower sense of the term because he is elected or appointed to his function, because he performs his function professionally and therefore receives a regular payment, a salary, from the treasury of State. The State as subject of property is the Fisc (*Fiscus*). The property of the State is created by the income of the State and the income of the State consists in the imposts and taxes paid by the citizens. These are the essential characteristics of a State-organ in the narrower sense of the term: The organ is appointed or elected for a specific function; the performance of this function has to be his main or even legally exclusive profession; he has the right to receive a salary from the treasury of State.

The organs of the State, in this narrower sense, are called officials. Not every individual who actually functions as an organ of the State in the wider sense holds the position of an official. The citizen who takes part in the election of the parliament by voting performs a very important function by participating in the creation of the legislative organ; but he is no State-organ in the narrower sense, no official. There are many intermediate cases between an organ who clearly has the character of an official and an organ who clearly lacks that character. Consider, for instance, the members of parliament whose function does not have the character of an exclusive profession; they are, in addition to their position as legislators, physicians, lawyers, merchants, etc., and are entitled to exercise these professions; sometimes they do not receive any or any regular salary. Another example is the members of a jury.

b. *The Formal and the Material Concept of the State*

This narrower, material, concept of organ has its counterpart in a narrower, material, concept of imputation to the State. In this narrower and material sense, a human action is imputed to the State, is considered to be an act of State, not because it presents itself as creation or execution of the legal order, but only because the action is performed by an individual who has the character of a State organ in the narrower and material sense of the term. Whereas an individual is an organ in the wider and formal sense of the term because he performs a function which is imputed to the State, a certain function is imputed to the State because it is performed by an individual in his capacity as organ of the State in the narrower, material sense of the term, in his capacity as an official. In the first case, the quality of an individual of being an organ is constituted by his function; in the second case, the quality of a function of being an act of the State is constituted by the quality of the individual who performs this act in his capacity as organ. When we speak not only of "courts of the State," but also of schools, hospitals, and railroads "of the State," this means that we impute to the State the activity of those individuals who erect and run such institutions. And the activity of these individuals is imputed to the State, is considered to be a function of the State, because the acting individuals are qualified as State-organs in the narrower, material sense, and in particular because, according to law, the necessary expenses of their activity are covered by the Fisc to which also go the resulting receipts. These functions, too, are, by their formal nature, legal functions; they represent the fulfillment of legal duties and the exercise of legal rights. By these functions, too, the legal order is executed; but it is not indifferently any of the norms of the legal order that they realize, but only norms of a certain materially characterized type.

The concept of the State that corresponds to this concept of imputation is different from that which identifies the State with the total legal order, or its personified unity. If the latter is a formal concept of the State, the former is a material concept. It designates the bureaucratic apparatus formed by the officials of the State. The phrase "the bureaucratic apparatus" is a figure of speech signifying the system of norms constituting the "Fisc" and determining the activities of the officials financed thereby. The State, in this sense, is not the total legal order but only a certain part thereof, a partial legal order distinguished by a material criterion.

This material concept of the State is a secondary concept, presupposing the formal concept. Whereas the former is restricted to the narrower community, comprising only the officials, the machinery of the State, so to speak, the latter represents the wider community, comprising also the individuals who, without being "organs" of the State, are subjected to the legal order.

The State as a subject of imputation, the State as acting person, is only the personification of the total or partial legal order, the criterion of which we have specified. The validity of the legal order has to be presupposed in order to interpret a human action as an act of State, in order to impute such an action to the State. The criterion of this imputation — be it formal, that is, an imputation to the State in the wider sense, or material, that is, an imputation to the State in the narrower sense — is always juristic. Imputation of a human action to the State is possible only on the basis of a total or partial legal order that we presuppose as valid.

c. The Creation of the State Organ

The State acts only through its organs. This often expressed and generally accepted truth means that the legal order can be created and applied only by individuals designated by the order itself. It does not suffice that the legal order declare in general terms which individuals are qualified to perform these functions. The order must also provide a procedure by which the particular individual is made an organ. The personal qualifications stipulated by the general norm may be so specified that they are filled by one definite individual only. An example is provided by the order of succession in an hereditary monarchy where the eldest son always succeeds his father to the throne, or by the republican constitution of a new State, prescribing that an individually mentioned person shall be the first head of State. Such organs are directly instituted by the law; no special act is needed by which the individual who fills the legal requirements is instituted as an organ. No special act is needed by which one organ is "created" by another organ.

An organ may be "created" by appointment, election or lot. The difference between appointment and election lies in the character and legal position of the creating organ. An organ is "appointed" by a superior individual organ. It is "elected" by a collegiate organ, composed of individuals who are legally subordinated to the elected organ. An organ is superior to another if the former is capable of creating norms obligating the latter. Appointment and election, as we defined them, are ideal types between which there are mixed types for which no special terminology exists. A collegiate organ may appoint a subordinate organ; for instance, a court may appoint its clerk; such an act may be characterized equally well as election and as appointment.

d. The Simple and the Composite Organ

According to whether the function is performed by an act of a single individual or by the convergent acts of several individuals, the organs may be divided into simple and composite. The individual whose act together with the acts of other individuals constitutes the total function is a partial organ. The total function is composed of partial functions. The partial functions may enter into the total function in two different ways. The acts of the partial organs have either the same or different contents. The so-called dyarchy is an example of a function which is composed of two acts which have the same contents. In a dyarchy, the politically decisive acts of State have to be performed in common by two organs — in Sparta, for instance, by the two kings, in Rome by the two consuls. A legislative function composed of two acts which have the same contents is the function of a parliament composed of two houses. The two partial actions out of which the total function is composed may have the same contents, even if they are named differently. Such is the case, for instance, when the constitution stipulates that a parliamentary "decision" becomes law only when "consented to" by the head of State. The "consent" of the head of State has the same contents as the "decision" of the parliament. The content of the law is the object of the "wills" of both organs. A special case of a function composed of two acts of identical contents is the case where the act of one organ has a legal effect only if it is not counteracted by another organ, i.e., if the other organ does not veto the act of the first.

A function may consist of more than two partial acts. The prototype is the so-called collegiate organ, characterized by the fact that the partial organs function simultaneously in mutual contact, and under the leadership of a chairman according to a definite order. Examples are: a parliament, a court. The act of a collegiate organ may be either an election or a decision — depending upon whether it creates an organ or a norm. The so-called electorate, the body of individuals entitled to vote in the election of parliament, is an example of a collegiate organ the function of which is to create other organs. The parliament is a collegiate organ the function of which is to create norms. The principle according to which the act of the collegiate organ takes place is either that of unanimity or majority.

A characteristic example of a function composed of acts which have different contents is the process of legislation in a constitutional monarchy. Its typical stages are the following: (1) Initiatory motion brought forward by the government or by members of parliament; (2) two coinciding decisions of the two houses; (3) consent of the monarch; (4) promulgation, which means that the head of State or the government ascertains that the decision of the parliament was made in accordance with the constitution; and, finally (5), publication of the decision, as approved by the monarch, in the way prescribed by the constitution.

e. Procedure

When a function is composed of several partial acts, it is necessary to regulate the merging of these acts into their resultant. One speaks, for instance, of the legislative "process" or "procedure." Process in a narrower sense — civil and criminal process — is only a special instance of this general concept of "process," for the judicial function has to be considered also as a sequence of partial acts. A chain of legal acts leads from the action brought by the plaintiff to the judgment pronounced by the first court, from this to the judgment of the court of last resort, and from there on to the execution of the sanction. From the point of view of the total judiciary-function, each one of these acts is only an incomplete partial act.

The highly relative character of the distinction between partial and total act and partial and total organ is here clearly exhibited. Any act of any organ can be regarded as merely partial, since it is only by virtue of its systematic connection with other acts that it contributes to that function which alone deserves the name of total function, namely: the total function of the State as the legal order. Thus we see that all organs are merely parts of one single organ which, in this sense, is an "organism": the State.

C. The State as Subject of Duties and Rights

a. The Auto-obligation of the State

The State, as a subject acting through its organs, the State as subject of imputation, the State as juristic person, is the personification of a legal order. By what properties those legal orders that have the character of States are distinguished from those that do not will be explained later. Here we shall only attempt to answer the much-discussed question, how the State — being merely the personification of the legal order by which obligations and rights are stipulated — can itself, as a juristic person, have obligations and rights.

Assuming the duality of State and law, traditional doctrine puts that question in this slightly different way: If the State is the authority from which the legal order emanates, how can the State be subject to this order and, like the individual, receive obligations and rights therefrom? In this form, it is the problem of the auto-obligation of the State that plays such a great role, especially in German jurisprudence. The problem is considered as one of paramount difficulty. And yet there is no difficulty at all, unless the person of the State, this personification of the national legal order, is hypostatized into a super-individual being, and one then speaks of obligations and rights of the State in the same sense as of obligations and rights of the individuals. In this sense there are, indeed, no obligations or rights of the State. Obligations and rights are always obligations and rights of individuals. That an individual has obligations and rights means that certain legal effects are attached to his behavior. Only individuals can "behave" in this sense. The legal order cannot, in this sense, impose obligations and confer rights upon the State, since to speak of the behavior of an order has no meaning. The statement: The legal order obligates and authorizes the legal order, is meaningless. But the statement that the State cannot be a subject of legal obligations or legal rights in the same sense as individuals are subjects of obligations and rights has not the meaning which some writers attribute to it, when they advocate the thesis that the State, by its very nature, cannot be subjected to law. It has not the meaning that the government, the men representing the State, are not bound by legal norms in their relation to the citizens. To deny the possibility of an auto-obligation of the State does not imply an argument for absolutism. The statement in question has no political, it has only a theoretical, significance.

The difficulty of conceiving of obligations and rights of the State does not consist — as the traditional theory assumes — in the fact that the State, being the law-creating power, cannot be subjected to law. Law, in reality, is created by human individuals, and individuals who create law can undoubtedly themselves be subject to law. Nay, only insofar as they act in accordance with the norms regulating their law-creating function are they organs of the State; and law is created by the State only insofar as it is created by a State organ, and that means, as law is created according to law. The statement that law is created by the State means only that law regulates its own creation. The difficulty which traditional theory finds in acknowledging the existence of obligations and rights of the State comes from the fact that one makes a superhuman being out of the State, considering it as a kind of man and simultaneously as an authority. According to this view, the idea of an auto-obligation of the State becomes nonsense, since the authority from which an obligation springs can be only a normative order, and it is impossible to impose duties or confer rights upon an order. To be legally obligated or to be legally authorized (entitled) means to be the object of legal regulation. Only human beings, or — more correctly — only human behavior, can be the object of legal regulation; but there is not the slightest reason to doubt that human beings, even in their capacity of State organs, can and must be subjected to law.

The problem of the so-called auto-obligation of the State is one of those pseudo-problems that result from the erroneous dualism of State and law. This dualism is, in turn, due to a fallacy of which we meet numerous examples in the history of all fields of human thought. Our desire for the intuitive representation of abstractions leads us to personify the unity of a system, and then to hypostasize the personification. What originally was only a way of representing the unity of a system of objects becomes a new object, existing in its own right. What, in fact, is only a tool for the understanding of an object becomes a separate object of knowledge, existing besides the original object. Then the pseudo-problem arises as to the relationship between these two objects. In the attempt to establish such a relationship, however, the tendency prevails to reduce the artificially created duality to the original unity. The search for unity is an inseparable part of all true scientific endeavor.

b. The Duties of the State (The Delict of the State)

Obligations and rights of the State do not mean that some being, existing apart from human individuals, "has" these obligations and rights. We speak of such obligations and rights when we impute to the State, to the personified unity of the legal order, those human acts which form the contents of these obligations and rights. The latter are obligations and rights of individuals who, in fulfilling these duties, in exercising these rights, have the capacity of State organs. Obligations and rights of the State are obligations and rights of State organs. The existence of obligations and rights for the State does not imply the problem of auto-obligation but that of imputation. Obligations and rights of the State are the obligations and rights of those individuals who, according to our criterion, are to be considered as State organs, that is to say, who perform a specific function determined by the legal order. This function can be the contents of either an obligation or a right.

The function is the contents of an obligation when an individual, if the function is not performed, is liable to a sanction. This sanction is not directed against the individual in his capacity as a State organ. The violation of the duty of a State organ, the delict constituted by the fact that a State organ has not performed his function in the way prescribed by the legal order, cannot be imputed to the State, since an individual is an organ (in particular, an official) of the State only insofar as his behavior conforms with the legal norms determining his function. Insofar as an individual violates a legal norm, he is not an organ of the State. The imputation to the State does not refer to actions or omissions which have the character of delicts. A delict which is a violation of the national legal order cannot be interpreted as a delict of the State, cannot be imputed to the State, since the sanction — which is the legal reaction to the delict — is interpreted as an act of the State. The State cannot — figuratively speaking — "will" both delict and sanction. The opposite view is at least guilty of a teleological inconsistency.

A delict which is a violation of international law, however, can be imputed to the State, just as a delict which is a violation of national law can be imputed to any other juristic person within the national legal order. The sanction is in both cases thought of as emanating from a person other than him to whom the delict is attributed. The sanction of international law is imputed to the international legal community, just as the sanction, in national law, is imputed to the State. Hence the

State can do no wrong in the sense of national law, but the State can do wrong in the sense of international law.

Though no delict in the sense of national law can be imputed to the State, the State can nevertheless be obliged to repair the wrong which consists in the non-fulfillment of its obligation. This means that an organ of the State is obliged to annul the illegal act committed by an individual who, as an organ of the State, was obliged to, but did not, fulfill the State's obligation, to punish this individual, and to repair out of the property of the State the illegally caused damage. A violation of this obligation again entails a sanction directed against the individual who as organ of the State has to fulfill this obligation of the State; the sanction is not directed against the State. The idea that the State executes sanctions against itself cannot be carried out. It is usual to characterize the obligation of the State to repair the wrong done by individuals who, as its organs, are obliged to fulfill its obligations as the State's responsibility for the wrong done by its organs, or by individuals in their capacity as State organs, or by individuals in the exercise of their official functions. These formulas, however, are not correct. First, because responsibility — as pointed out — is not an obligation but a condition whereby an individual is subjected to a sanction. If the sanction is not directed against the State, the State cannot be considered to be responsible. Second, the individual who performs an illegal act by not fulfilling the State's obligation (in the sense of national law) is not acting as organ of the State, or in the exercise of his official function. He is acting only in connection with his official function as State organ. Only if the illegal act committed by him is in connection with his function as State organ may the State be obliged to repair the wrong.

c. The Rights of the State

A right of the State exists when the execution of a sanction is dependent upon a law-suit brought by an individual in his capacity as organ of the State in the narrower sense of the term, as "official." Especially within the field of civil law, the State can possess rights in this sense to the same extent as private persons. The right of the State here has as its counterpart a duty of a private person. The relationship between the State and the subjects of the obligations created by criminal law allows of the same interpretation, insofar as the criminal sanction is applied only upon a suit by the public prosecutor. The act by which the judicial procedure leading to the sanction is put into motion is then to be considered an act of the State; and it is possible to speak of a legal right of the State to punish criminals, and to say that the criminal has violated a right of the State.

d. Rights against the State

To an obligation of the State there corresponds a right of a private person only if the private person whose legally protected interest is violated can be a party in the process issuing in case the obligation remains unfulfilled. The process need not necessarily lead to a sanction against that State organ which was immediately responsible for the fulfillment of the obligation. If the right is violated by an illegal act of the organ, the aim of the process can be to have the illegal act annulled; if the right is violated by the illegal omission of an act of the State prescribed by law, the aim of the process can be to bring about the legal act. In both cases, the aim of the process can be to obtain reparation for the illegally caused damage. Such rights of private persons against the State exist, not only in civil law, but also in constitutional and administrative law, so-called "public" law.

D. PRIVATE AND PUBLIC LAW

a. The Traditional Theory: State and Private Persons

The distinction between private and public law, in traditional jurisprudence, is made the basis of the systematization of law. Yet we look in vain for an unambiguous definition of the two concepts. Among the various theories on the subject perhaps the most common is that which derives the distinction from the difference between the subjects in the legal relationships. A typical statement of this view is found in Holland * who is followed by Willoughby.† The theory is based upon the fact that, within its own legal sphere, that is, within national law, the State as subject of duties and rights is always faced with private persons. If there is an obligation whose fulfillment is imputed to the State, then the individual's behavior that forms the contents of the corresponding right is not imputed to the State. If one of the two parties of a right-duty relationship is an organ of the State, then the other party is not an organ of the State. This is the consequence of the fact that there is — within a national legal order — only one person which has to be considered as the State. Hence, if one subject in a legal relationship is the State, the other subject cannot be the State; the other subject must be a "private" person.

The concept of a "private" person has the negative connotation of an individual whose behavior is not imputed to the State. Traditional

---

* HOLLAND, ELEMENTS OF JURISPRUDENCE 128f.
† W. W. WILLOUGHBY, THE FUNDAMENTAL CONCEPTS OF PUBLIC LAW (1924) 37.

theory designates as "private law" the norms stipulating duties and rights between private persons, and as "public" law the norms stipulating duties and rights between the State, on the one hand, and private persons, on the other. The notions of "State" and what is "public" are identified. Holland defines public law as ". . . the law which regulates rights where one of the persons concerned is 'public'; where the State is, directly or indirectly, one of the parties. Here the very power which defines and protects the right is itself a party interested in or affected by the right." * If neither of the two subjects concerned is the State, then there is private law.

This definition, however, is not intended to exclude the State from the legal relations between private persons. "In private law the State is indeed present, but it is present only as arbiter of the rights and duties which exist between one of its subjects and another. In public law the State is not only arbiter, but is also one of the parties interested. The rights and duties with which it deals concern itself on the one part and its subjects on the other part." † The characteristic feature of public law is "this union in one personality of the attributes judge and party."

b. The State as Subject of Private Law

This theory is obviously not satisfactory. In all modern legal orders, the State, as well as any other juristic person, may have rights *in rem* and rights *in personam*, nay any of the rights and duties stipulated by "private law." When there is a civil code, its norms apply equally to private persons and to the State. Disputes concerning such rights and obligations of the State are usually settled in the same way as similar disputes between private parties. The fact that a legal relationship has the State for one of its parties does not necessarily remove it from the domain of private law. The difficulty in distinguishing between public and private law resides precisely in the fact that the relation between the State and its subjects can have not only a "public" but also a "private" character.

When the State purchases or rents a house from a private person, according to many legal systems the legal relation between buyer and seller (or tenant and lessee) is exactly the same as if the buyer or tenant had been a private person. Since a "person" exists only in "his" duties and rights, the legal personality of the State is no different from the legal personality of a private individual, insofar as the duties and rights of the State have the same contents as the duties and rights of the private person. There is no juristic difference between the State as owner

* HOLLAND, ELEMENTS OF JURISPRUDENCE 128.
† HOLLAND, ELEMENTS OF JURISPRUDENCE 366.

or tenant of a house and a private owner or tenant if the "rights" of both are the same, which is possible and often is actually the case.

The fact that, in one case, the State is party as well as judge, while in the other it is judge only, does not furnish an effective criterion for distinguishing public and private law. This criterion refers only to the procedure by which a dispute is settled, which concerns the duties and rights in question; and the difference may consist only in the fact that in one case the function of the plaintiff or defendant is imputed to the State, whereas in the other case it is not. This imputation calls forth the idea that the two cases are different because only in the second but not in the first is the principle maintained according to which nobody shall be judge in his own case. In reality, however, the principle is maintained in both cases. For the so-called duties and rights of the State are duties and rights of organs of the State, that is, duties and rights of individuals whose actions are imputed to the State. The organ which represents the State as subject of a duty or a right is not the same as the organ that represents the State as a judge. These two organs are two totally different individuals, they are, in reality, no less different than the judge on the one hand and plaintiff or defendant on the other hand, in a case where both parties are private persons. The necessary impartiality in the conduct of the process is therefore not impaired by the fact that the acts of the plaintiff or defendant are imputable to the State; and only the lack of the necessary impartiality could constitute a real difference between the two cases. If we look, through the veil with which the imputation and personification conceals the legal reality, at the acting human individuals, we see that there is no "union of the attributes judge and party," even when the functions of different individuals who act as judge and party are interpreted to be acts of "one personality."

c. Superiority and Inferiority

The difference between private and public law, according to another theory, is a difference between legal relations where both parties are equal and legal relations where one is inferior to the other. Any private person is equal to any other and is inferior only to the State. There are, however, it is said, situations in which the State appears as an equal of private persons, and those where the State is superior to private persons. As owner, as creditor and debtor, the State is a subject of private law, since, here, it is equal to the subjects to whom it stands in legal relation. As court and as administrative authority the State is the subject of public law, since here it is superior to the subjects to whom it stands in legal relation.

In what, however, does this relation of legal superiority and inferiority consist? As a subject of rights and duties, the State, as well as other persons, is subjected to the legal order. As subjects of rights and duties the State and the individual are equal. The relation of legal superiority and inferiority can therefore not consist in the nature of the subjects and of their mutual rights and duties. The distinction which the theory under discussion has in mind — but usually fails to state clearly — refers to the way in which the legal relationship is brought about, to the method by which the individual duty is created to which corresponds the right of the subject who is considered to be equal or superior to the subject of the duty. The distinction between private and public law which the theory under discussion has in mind refers to the creation of the secondary norm determining for a concrete case the behavior the contrary of which is the delict. An example may serve to illustrate this.

The duty of paying back a loan arises from the contract between debtor and creditor. The legal order delegates to individuals the regulation by contracts of their economic relationships. That is to say, the legal order stipulates: "If two individuals make a contract, if one of them breaks it and if the other brings an action against the first, then the court shall execute a sanction against the first." On the basis of this general norm, the obligation of the individual is determined by the individual norm which the contract creates. This individual norm is of a secondary nature, and presupposes the above-mentioned general norm.

Another example is the following: A finance bill obligates individuals to pay taxes according to their incomes, by providing for sanctions in case the tax is not paid. But, according to some legal orders, a concrete individual comes under the actual obligation of paying such and such a tax only if a competent organ, a tax officer, after estimating his income, orders him to do so. The order issued by the taxation organ, an individual secondary norm, constitutes the concrete obligation of the individual.

d. Autonomy and Heteronomy (Private and Administrative Law)

These two examples illustrate two different methods of creating secondary norms by which concrete obligations may be imposed upon an individual. In our first example, the loan contract, the obligation of the debtor is determined by a secondary norm in the creation of which the individual to be obligated participates. This is an essential of all contractual obligations. These obligations do not come into existence against or without the will of the individual to be obligated. The contract — the contractual creation of obligations — corresponds to the principle of autonomy. In the second of our examples, the taxation order, the obligation of the taxpayer is determined by a secondary norm in the creation of which the subject to be obligated does not participate. The taxation order is a typical administrative act. It creates a secondary norm by which an individual is obligated without, even against his will. This way of creating norms corresponds to the principle of heteronomy.

It is this antagonism between autonomy and heteronomy which is the ground for the distinction between private and public law, insofar as this opposition is interpreted to mean that private law regulates the relations between equal subjects, while public law regulates those between an inferior and a superior subject. In the field of private law the subject of an obligation is faced with the subject of the corresponding right. Here, the two parties of a right-duty relationship may in fact be considered as equal insofar as the secondary norm, constituting this relationship, is created by their identical declarations of will, by a legal transaction. Private law is characterized by the fact that the secondary norm, the violation of which is a condition of the sanction, is created by a legal transaction, and that the legal transaction, the typical representation of which is the contract, corresponds to the principle of autonomy.* In the field of administrative law, the secondary norm constituting the concrete obligation of the individual is created by an administrative act which is analogous to the legal transaction. Here the subject of an obligation is faced with an organ of the State that appears as the subject of a competence rather than as that of a right. The State organ may be considered as superior to the private person, not because the organ represents the State, but because it is empowered to obligate the private person by one-sided declarations of will. But this interpretation is inaccurate. Strictly speaking, the subject of an obligation is subjected to the authority of the obligating norm only, not to the norm-creating individual, the organ. The difference between administrative law, as public law, and private law does not lie in the fact that the relationship between State and private person is different from the relationship between private persons but in the difference between a heteronomous and an autonomous creation of secondary norms.

The antagonism of heteronomy and autonomy, which, with reference to the creation of secondary norms, constitutes the difference between public and private law, is decisive also in the creation of the primary legal norms. Here it constitutes the difference between autocracy and democracy and thus furnishes the criterion for the classification of governments.

* Cf. *supra*, pp. 136f.

e. Family Law; International Law

Most, though not all, of the norms which are designated as public and private law may be distinguished by the criterion here given. There are norms, however, considered as a part of private law, which create obligations against the will of the persons obligated. In family law, for instance, a wife may be legally obligated to obey her husband, and children their father. There are likewise norms, traditionally counted as public law, but which permit of concrete legal relationships being created by contracts just as in private law. One speaks of a contract of public law without, however, being able to distinguish it clearly from a contract of private law. This holds in particular of the treaty of international law which is commonly referred to the domain of public law though it almost without exception conforms with the principle of autonomy.

f. Public or Private Interest (Private and Criminal Law)

On the other hand, one considers as public law legal norms which do not at all create any legal relationships whose parties could be regarded either as equal or as inferior and superior. The norms of criminal law, in particular, fall into this category. The concrete obligation of an individual is here not determined by a secondary norm created by a legal transaction or an administrative act.* The reason why the criminal law is classified as public law thus cannot be the same as the reason why administrative law is so classified. This difference between criminal as public law, and private law does not appear in the norms of substantive but of adjective law. Criminal law differs in fact from private law in the matter of the norms of procedure. As pointed out,† in the field of private law it is up to the private party whose interests have been violated to put in motion the procedure leading to the sanction, while, in the field of criminal law, a special organ of the State has this function. This difference in the technique of private (civil) and criminal law is explained by the fact that the legal order providing punishment as sanction does not recognize as decisive the interest of the private individual directly violated by the delict, but the interest of the legal community, the organ of which is the public prosecutor.

In view of this fact, it has often been thought possible to define the norms of private law as those which protect private interests, and the norms of public law as those which safeguard the interests of the State.

* Cf. *supra*, pp. 137f.
† Cf. *supra*, pp. 84f.

This definition, however, is invalidated by the fact that the State can be a party to a legal relation within the domain of private law. In this case, the norms of private law undoubtedly perform the function of protecting the interests of the State, the so-called "public" interest. Disregarding this special case, one cannot deny that the maintenance of private law, too, is in the public interest. If it were not, the application of private law would not be entrusted to organs of the State. The only distinction which is valid from the point of view of analytic jurisprudence is that based on the difference in technique of civil and criminal procedure. But that distinction cannot be used to segregate administrative law from private law.

The distinction between private and public law thus varies in meaning depending upon whether it is criminal law or administrative law that one wishes to separate from private law. The distinction is useless as a common foundation for a general systematization of law.

II. THE ELEMENTS OF THE STATE

A. THE TERRITORY OF THE STATE

a. The Territory of the State as the Territorial Sphere of Validity of the National Legal Order

If the State is a legal order, then all problems arising within a general theory of the State must be translatable into problems that make sense within the general theory of law. All properties of the State must be capable of being presented as properties of a legal order. What, then, are the characteristic properties of a State?

Traditional doctrine distinguishes three "elements" of the State: its territory, its people, and its power. It is assumed to be of the essence of a State that it occupies a certain limited territory. The existence of the State, Willoughby says,* "is dependent upon the claim upon the part of the State to a territory of its own." The State, conceived as an actual social unity, seems to imply a geographical unity as well: one State — one territory. A closer examination, however, shows that the unity of the State territory is in no way a natural geographic one. The territory of a State must not necessarily consist of one piece of land. Such territory is named "integrate" territory. The State territory may be "dismembered." Sometimes, to one and the same State territory belong parts of space which are not physically contiguous, but separated from each other by territories belonging to another State or to no State at all. To the territory of a State belong its colonies, from which it may be

* W. W. WILLOUGHBY, FUNDAMENTAL CONCEPTS OF PUBLIC LAW 64.

separated by the ocean, and also so-called "enclosures" that are completely surrounded by the territory of another State. These geographically disconnected areas form a unity only insofar as one and the same legal order is valid for all of them. The unity of the State territory, and therefore, the territorial unity of the State, is a juristic, not a geographical-natural unity. For the territory of a State is in reality nothing but the territorial sphere of validity * of the legal order called State.

Those normative orders that are designated as States are characterized precisely by the fact that their territorial spheres of validity are limited. This distinguishes them from other social orders, such as morality and international law, which claim to be valid wherever human beings live. Their territorial spheres of validity are — in principle — unlimited.

b. The Limitation of the Territorial Sphere of Validity of the National Legal Order by the International Legal Order

The limitation of the sphere of validity of the coercive order called State to a definite territory means that the coercive measures, the sanctions, provided by the order have to be established for this territory only, and have to be executed only within it. Actually, it is not impossible that a general or individual norm of the legal order of a certain State should prescribe that a coercive act shall be carried out within the territory of another State, and that an organ of the former State should execute this norm. But should such a norm be enacted or executed, the enactment of the norm and its execution, that is, the performance of the coercive act within the territory of the other State, would be illegal. The legal order violated by these acts is the international law. For it is positive international law that determines and thus delimits from each other the territorial spheres of validity of the various national legal orders. If their territorial spheres of validity were not legally delimited, if the States did not have any fixed boundaries, the various national legal orders, and that means the many States, could not possibly coexist without conflicts. This delimitation of the territorial spheres of validity of the national legal orders, the boundaries of the States, has a purely normative character. The territory of the State is not the area where the acts of the State, and especially the coercive acts, are actually carried out. By the fact that an act of the State is carried out in a certain territory the territory does not become the territory of the State whose organ has carried out the act. An act of the State may be carried out illegally on the territory of another State. "Illegally" means, as pointed out, contrary to international law. The territory of

* Cf. *supra*, pp. 42ff.

the State is the space within which the acts of the State and especially its coercive acts are allowed to be carried out, the space within which the State, and that means, its organs, are authorized by international law to execute the national legal order. The international legal order determines how the validity of the national legal orders is restricted to a certain space and what are the boundaries of this space.

That the validity of the national legal order is restricted by the international legal order to a certain space, the so-called territory of the State, does not mean that the national legal order is authorized to regulate only the behavior of individuals living within this space. The restriction refers in principle only to the coercive acts provided by the national legal order and the procedure leading to these acts. The restriction does not refer to all the conditioning facts to which the legal order attaches coercive acts as sanctions, especially not to the delict. A State can, without violating international law, attach sanctions to delicts committed within the territory of another State. International law is violated only when a norm is enacted which prescribes a coercive act to be carried out in the territory of another State or when a coercive act, or an act preparing such a coercive act, is actually carried out in the territory of another State. The penal code of a State may stipulate that the courts have to sentence delinquents irrespective of where the delicts are committed, without thereby violating international law. But international law is infringed if a State detains and punishes a criminal in the territory of another State. With certain exceptions, this principle holds also for the coercive acts provided by civil and administrative law.

The principle that international law delimits the territorial sphere of validity of the national legal order only with respect to the coercive act, the sanction, and its preparation, is disputed as far as criminal law is concerned. As to criminal law, the competence of a State to punish crimes committed in a foreign country is — according to some writers — restricted to the punishment of its own citizens. As far as foreigners are concerned, they argue "that at the time such criminal acts are committed the perpetrators are neither under the territorial nor under the personal supremacy of the States concerned; and that a State can only require respect for its laws from such aliens as are permanently or transiently within its territory." But, says Oppenheim,* this "is not a view which, consistently with the practice of States and with common sense, can be rigidly adopted in all cases." According to Oppenheim, a State has the right to jurisdiction over acts of foreigners committed in foreign countries if the acts are performed "in preparation of and participation in common crimes committed or attempted to be committed

* 1 L. OPPENHEIM, INTERNATIONAL LAW (5th ed. 1937) 268f.

in the country claiming jurisdiction"; or if by these acts subjects of the State claiming jurisdiction are injured, or if these acts are directed against its own safety. But does a State violate international law by exercising jurisdiction over other acts of foreigners committed in foreign countries?

In the *Lotus* Case the Permanent Court of International Justice * expressed the opinion, in 1927, that there is no rule of International Law which prohibits a State from exercising jurisdiction over a foreigner in respect of an offence committed outside its territory. "The territoriality of criminal law is . . . not an absolute principle of International Law, and by no means coincides with territorial sovereignty."

That the power of the State is limited to its own territory does not mean that no act of the State may legally be carried out outside this State's territory. The limitation refers in principle only to coercive acts in the wider sense of the term, including also the preparation of coercive acts. Only these acts may not be executed on the territory of another State without violating international law. During his stay in a foreign State, the head of a State can conclude international treaties, promulgate laws, or appoint officials by putting his signature on the documents concerned, all without infringing upon the international rights of the State he is visiting. But he would violate international law if he were to have his police arrest one of his subjects on the territory of the State where he is a guest. The facts that the limitation of the territorial validity of the national legal order by international law refers only to the coercive acts provided by this order, and that by restricting these coercive acts to a certain territory the legal existence of the State is restricted to this territory, show clearly that the ordering of coercive acts, which is an essential element of law, is at the same time the essential function of the State.

c. The Territory of the State in a Narrower and in a Wider Sense

Within the territorial sphere of validity of the national legal order, that is, within the space where a certain State is authorized to perform coercive acts, we have to distinguish the territory of the State in a narrower and in a wider sense. The territory of the State in a narrower sense is that space within which in principle one State, the State to which the territory belongs, is entitled to carry out coercive acts, a space from which all the other States are excluded. It is the space for which, according to general international law, only one definite national legal order is authorized to prescribe coercive acts, the space within

---

* Series A, No 10, and Series C, No 13–II.

which only the coercive acts stipulated by this order may be executed. It is the space within the so-called boundaries of the State.

But there are also areas where all States are permitted to carry out coercive acts, with certain restrictions: Such areas are the open sea (or high seas) and the territories which have the character of no State's land because they do not legally belong to any particular State. The open sea is that part of the sea which lies beyond the territorial waters. The territorial waters (the maritime belt) legally belong to the territory of the littoral States, but the latter are here, according to international law, subjected to certain restrictions. The most important restriction is this: The littoral State is obliged, in time of peace, to allow the merchantmen of every other State to pass inoffensively through its territorial waters. As far as foreign men-of-war are concerned it is assumed that the right of passage through such parts of the maritime belt as form part of the highways for international traffic cannot be denied. The open sea is an area where any State is entitled to undertake any action, and especially exercise its coercive power, on board its own ships, that is, on board the ships which legitimately sail under the flag of this State. The exercise of a State's coercive power on the open sea is restricted only insofar as the State is not entitled to exercise its coercive power against the vessels of other States except under certain circumstances. Thus, it has the right to punish all such foreign vessels as sail under its flag without being authorized to do so; and to punish piracy even if committed by foreigners.

Territories which are the land of no State have a legal status similar to that of the open sea. Here, every State may exercise its coercive power without violating international law. But there is a difference. The territory which is no State's land may be annexed by any State by way of actual occupation, without violating international law: but every attempt by a State to occupy a part of the open sea constitutes a violation of international law. No part of the open sea is allowed by international law to be subjected to the exclusive domination by one State, to become the exclusive sphere of validity of one national legal order, to become the territory of a State in the narrower sense. That is the legal principle of the "freedom of the open sea," one of the fundamental principles of general international law.* The open sea and the territories

* Oppenheim formulates this principle as follows (1 INTERNATIONAL LAW 468): "The term 'Freedom of the Open Sea' indicates the rule of the Law of Nations that the open sea is not, and never can be, under the sovereignty of any State whatever. Since, therefore, the open sea is not the territory of any State, no State has as a rule a right to exercise its legislation, administration, jurisdiction, or police over parts of the open sea." This formulation is not quite correct. For every State

which are no State's land are territory of all States, but they are not the exclusive territory of one State, not the exclusive territorial sphere of validity of one national legal order. They are a space where, so to speak, the territorial spheres of validity of the different national legal orders penetrate each other.

d. The "Impenetrability" of the State

The principle that the national legal order has exclusive validity for a certain territory, the territory of the State in the narrower sense, and that within this territory all individuals are subjected only and exclusively to this national legal order or to the coercive power of this State, is usually expressed by saying that only one State can exist on the same territory, or — borrowing a phrase from physics — that the State is "impenetrable." There are, however, certain exceptions to this principle. A State can by international treaty be accorded the right to undertake certain actions, especially to perform coercive acts, on the territory of another State, acts that would not be allowed according to general international law. In wartime, a State is, even by general international law, permitted to undertake coercive actions on foreign territory that it occupies militarily. Another exception is the so-called *condominium* or *co-imperium* exercised by two (or more) States over the same territory. The legal order valid for this territory is a common part of the legal orders of the States exercising the *condominium*. The norms of this legal order are established by an agreement between the States exercising the *condominium* and executed by common organs of these States. The territory of the *condominium* is a common territory of these States, a common territorial sphere of validity of their national legal orders.

The federal State is sometimes cited as a further exception; the territory of each member State, it is argued, is simultaneously part of the territory of the federal State. We are, however, faced with an actual exception only if we recognize the so-called member States of a federal State as genuine States. We shall return to this question later.

---

has a right to exercise its sovereignty on the open sea; only, no State has the right to exercise its sovereignty exclusively, i.e., excluding by force another State from exercising the same right on the open sea. Oppenheim continues: "Since, further, the open sea can never be under the sovereignty of any State, no State has a right to acquire parts of the open sea through occupation. . . ." It is more correct to say that no part of the open sea can be exclusively under the sovereignty of one State; that is the reason why no State has the right to acquire parts of the open sea through occupation.

e. The Boundaries of the State Territory (Changes in the Territorial Status)

The principle that the national legal order is valid exclusively for a certain territory means that from this territory the validity of any other national legal order is excluded. But the validity of the international legal order is not excluded from the territorial sphere of validity of the national legal order. The territorial sphere of validity of the international legal order comprises the spheres of validity of all national legal orders. For the spheres of the latter are determined by international law; they are determined according to the principle of effectiveness.

The exclusive validity of a national legal order extends, according to international law, just as far as this order is, on the whole, efficacious, that is, permanently applied, as far as the coercive acts provided for by this order are actually carried out. This is the legal principle according to which the boundaries of the States running on the surface of the earth are determined.

Traditional theory distinguishes between "natural" and "artificial," i.e., legal, boundaries; but the boundaries of a State have always a legal character, whether or not they coincide with such "natural" frontiers, as, for instance, a river or a mountain range.

The boundaries of a State may be determined by an international treaty. One State may, for example, cede a part of its territory to another State by treaty. Such a treaty gives the cessionary a legal title against the ceding State. The former acquires, by the treaty of cession, the right to occupy the ceded territory, that is to extend the validity and efficacy of its legal order to that area. The ceded territory, however, does not cease to be part of the territory of the ceding State and does not become part of the cessionary's territory until the latter's legal order becomes actually efficacious within the ceded territory, until the cessionary has actually taken possession of the ceded territory. The legal change in the territorial status takes place according to the principle of effectiveness. If there is a treaty of cession, then the change of territory in the relationship between two States does not imply any violation of international law. If there is no agreement between the States concerned, then the occupation, that is taking possession of the territory of one State by another State, constitutes a violation of international law, which obligates States to respect each other's territorial integrity. The violation of international law entails the consequences provided by this legal order: the State whose right is violated by the illegal occupation is entitled to resort to war or reprisals against the State responsible for the violation.*

Nevertheless, there occurs, according to international law, a territorial change, provided that the occupation, made with the intention of incorporating the occupied territory into the territory of the occupying State, assumes a permanent character, and that means that the legal order of the occupying State becomes efficacious for the territory in question. Usually one speaks of "occupation," as a title of acquisition, only when the territory previously did not belong to another State. When, on the contrary, the territory belonged to another State, one speaks of "annexation," having in mind the case of conquest, that is, the case of taking possession of enemy territory through military force in time of war. Traditional theory admits that annexation of conquered enemy territory, whether of the whole (subjugation) or of part, constitutes acquisition of the territory by the conquering State, if the conquest is firmly established.† Taking possession through military force of the territory of another State against the latter's will is possible, however, without any military resistance on the part of the victim. Provided that a unilateral act of force performed by one State against another is not considered to be war in itself (war being, according to traditional opinion, "a contention between two or more States through their armed forces" and hence at least a bilateral action ‡) annexation is not only possible in time of war, but also in time of peace. The decisive point is that annexation, that is, taking possession of another State's territory with the intention to acquire it, constitutes acquisition of this territory even without the consent of the State to which the territory previously belonged, if the possession is "firmly established." It makes no difference whether the annexation takes place after an *occupatio bellica* or not. (*Occupatio bellica*, the belligerent occupation of enemy territory, is a specific aim of warfare; it does not, in itself, imply a territorial change.)

If the extension of the efficacy of a national legal order to the territorial sphere of validity of another national legal order, the efficacious annexation of the territory of one State by another State implies a violation of international law, the guilty State, as pointed out, exposes itself to the sanctions provided by general or particular international law. The fact that the act of annexation is illegal does not prevent, however, the annexed territory from becoming part of the occupying State's territory, provided that the annexation is firmly established. *Ex injuria jus oritur.* This follows from the legal principle of effectiveness prevailing

* Cf. *infra*, pp. 328ff.
† Cf. 1 OPPENHEIM, INTERNATIONAL LAW 427f., 450.
‡ Cf. 2 OPPENHEIM, INTERNATIONAL LAW (6th ed. 1940) 166f.

in international law. It is the same principle according to which the territory of a State can be extended to a territory which previously was no State's land. The difference between the acquisition of territory which has the character of no State's land and the annexation of territory belonging to another State consists simply in the fact that in the first case the occupation of the territory constituting the change in the territorial status according to the principle of effectiveness is always legal, whereas in the second case it is legal only if it is the execution of a treaty of cession.

It is possible that a treaty of cession follows the occupation of the ceded territory by the acquiring State, as for instance in the case where the cession is the outcome of war and the ceded territory has been in the military occupation of the State to which it is now ceded. If the occupation preceding the treaty of cession had the character of a violation of international law, the following treaty has the function of legalizing the occupation.

Traditional theory also considers accretion, that is, the increase of land through new formations, such as the rise of an island within a river or within the maritime belt, as a mode of acquiring territory. It is assumed that according to general international law, "enlargement of territory, if any, created through new formations, takes place *ipso facto* by the accretion, without the State concerned taking any special step for the purpose of extending its sovereignty." * This rule, however, presupposes that the new territory lies within the sphere of effective control on the part of the acquiring State.

Under "prescription" in international law, which is likewise considered a mode of acquiring State territory, the rule is understood that an undisturbed continuous possession produces "a title for the possessor, if the possession has lasted for some length of time." † Since no rule exists as regards this length of time, it is scarcely possible to distinguish "prescription" from the general principle of effectiveness, according to which firmly established possession exercised by the possessing State with the intention to keep the territory as its own constitutes acquisition of this territory. According to the principle of effectiveness, too, possession must last for some length of time in order to be considered as "firmly established." Oppenheim states: "The basis of prescription in International Law is nothing else than general recognition of a fact, however unlawful in its origin, on the part of the members of the Family of Nations." ‡

* 1 OPPENHEIM, INTERNATIONAL LAW (5th ed.) 445.
† 1 OPPENHEIM, INTERNATIONAL LAW 455.
‡ 1 OPPENHEIM, INTERNATIONAL LAW 455.

He says further "that in the practice of the members of the Family of Nations, a State is considered to be the lawful owner even of those parts of its territory of which originally it took possession wrongfully and unlawfully, provided that the possessor had been in undisturbed possession for such a length of time as is necessary to create the general conviction that the present order of things is in conformity with international order." But he admits at the same time "that no general rule can be laid down as regards the length of time"; * and that annexation of conquered territory "confers a title only after a *firmly established* conquest," † without regard to the legal or illegal character of the conquest and to the length of time which expired after it.

Traditional theory distinguishes between derivative and original modes of acquisition, according "as the title they give is derived from the title of a prior owner-State, or not." ‡ Since the "ownership," that is, the fact that a certain territory legally belongs to a certain State, is based only and exclusively on the permanent efficacy of the coercive order of that State for the territory in question and not on the "ownership" of the prior State, there is no derivative acquisition at all. The characteristic of cession is not — as usually assumed — that this mode of acquisition is derivative, but that it makes possible the acquisition of the territory of another State without violation of international law.

The different modes of losing territory correspond to the modes of acquiring territory and are, like the latter, determined by the principle of effectiveness. This is especially true of so-called "dereliction," which corresponds to occupation. We speak of dereliction when a State abandons a part of its territory without intending or being able to retake it.

A mode of losing territory which does not correspond to a mode of acquiring is the establishment of a new State on a part of the territory of an old State by a part of its population. The coming into existence of a new State takes place, as we shall see later, according to the principle of effectiveness, whether the establishment of a new State is the outcome of a revolutionary secession of a part of the population, as for instance in the case of the United States, or of an international treaty, as for instance in the case of Danzig and the Vatican State. The constitutive fact is that a new national legal order becomes efficacious for a territory which previously was part of the territory of an existing State; and that consequently the previously valid national legal order ceases to be efficacious for this territory.

* 1 Oppenheim, International Law 456.
† 1 Oppenheim, International Law 450.
‡ 1 Oppenheim, International Law 429.

f. The Territory of the State a Space of Three Dimensions

The territory of a State is usually considered as a definite portion of the earth's surface. This idea is incorrect. The territory of the State, as the territorial sphere of validity of the national legal order, is not a plane, but a space of three dimensions. The validity as well as the efficacy of the national legal order extends not only in width and length but also in depth and height. Since the earth is a globe, the geometrical form of this space — the space of the State — is approximately an inverted cone. The vertex of this cone is in the center of the earth, where the conic spaces, the so-called territories of all the States, meet. What traditional theory defines as "territory of the State," that portion of the earth's surface delimited by the boundaries of the State, is only a visible plane formed by a transverse section of the State's conic space. The space above and below this plane belongs legally to the State as far as its coercive power, and that means juristically the efficacy of the national legal order, extends.

Many writers assume that the entire space above and below the State territory (as part of the surface of the earth) belongs to the territorial State without regard to the extent of its effective control. This view, however, is not compatible with the general principle of effectiveness. As far as the air space is concerned, Article 1 of the International Air Convention concluded in 1919 declares that every State has "complete and exclusive sovereignty" in the air space above its territory and territorial waters. According to Article 2 of the Convention the contracting parties agree "in time of peace to accord freedom of innocent passage" above their territory and territorial waters to the aircraft of the other contracting States who observe the conditions prescribed in the Convention. According to Article 3 any State has the right "for military reasons or in the interest of public safety" to map out "prohibited areas" provided this is published and notified to the other contracting States. It stands to reason that a State can enforce the provisions of this convention or of its own national legal order against the aircraft of another State only within that part of the air space over which it has effective control. The validity of any legal order cannot extend beyond this sphere. On the other hand, there is no rule of general international law constituting a free air space or a free subsoil analogous to the principle of "freedom of the open sea." From the lack of such a norm does not necessarily follow the consequence that the entire space above and below the surface belongs to the territory of the State concerned. It is quite possible that the air space as well as the subsoil which is beyond the effective control of the territorial State has the character of no State's land. It seems, however, that, according to general international law, the other States have no right to occupy this space even if they have the technical ability to do so. The only way to characterize these parts of the space in conformity with the principle of effectiveness is to assume an exclusive right of the territorial State to occupy, that is to say, to extend according to the progress of its technical means, the efficacy of its legal order to those parts of the air space and subsoil which before were beyond its effective control.

g. *Relationship between the State and its Territory*

In traditional doctrine, a certain prominence is given to the question of the relationship between the State as a juristic person and "its" territory. The problem arises from the anthropomorphic idea that the State is a kind of man or superman, and its territory a kind of estate that he owns. There are, it is true, certain similarities between the laws regulating the transfer of real estate and the rules of international law concerning territorial changes. But nevertheless the problem must be discarded as a pseudo problem. There is no relation at all between the State, considered as a person, and its territory, since the latter is only the territorial sphere of validity of the national legal order. It is therefore pointless to ask whether the State's relationship to its territory has the character of a *jus in rem* or a *jus in personam*. The determination of the sphere of validity of the national legal order by international law is something wholly different from the stipulations of the national legal order by which a *jus in rem* or a *jus in personam* is constituted.

B. TIME AS AN ELEMENT OF THE STATE

a. *The Temporal Sphere of Validity of the National Legal Order*

It is characteristic of traditional theory that it considers space — the territory — but not time as an "element" of the State. A State exists, however, not only in space but also in time, and if we regard territory as an element of the State, then we have to regard the period of its existence as an element of the State, too. When it is said that not more than one State can exist within a given space, it is obviously meant that not more than one State can exist within the same space at the same time. It is taken as self-evident that, as history shows, two different States can exist one after the other, at least partly, within the same space. Just as territory is an element of the State, not in the sense of a natural space which the State fills up like a physical body, but only in the sense that it is the territorial sphere of validity of the national legal order, so time, the period of existence, is an element only in the sense that it is the corresponding temporal sphere of validity. Both spheres are limited. Just as the State is spatially not infinite, it is temporally not eternal. It is the same order which regulates the spatial coexistence of the many States and their temporal sequence. It is international law which delimits the territorial as well as the temporal sphere of validity of the national legal order. The point of time when a State begins to exist, that is, the moment when a national legal order begins to be valid, as well as the moment in which a national legal order ceases to be valid, is determined by positive international law according to the principle of effectiveness. It is the same principle according to which the territorial sphere of validity of the national legal order is determined.

b. Birth and Death of the State

1. Limitation of the Temporal Sphere of Validity of the National Legal Order by the International Legal Order

The problem of the temporal sphere of validity of the national legal order is usually presented as the problem of the birth and death of the State. It is generally recognized that the question whether a new State has come into existence, or an old State has ceased to exist, is to be answered on the basis of international law. The relevant principles of international law are commonly stated as follows: A new State in the sense of international law has come into existence if an independent government has established itself by issuing a coercive order for a certain territory and if the government is effective, i.e., if the government is able to obtain permanent obedience to its order on the part of the individuals living in this territory. It is presupposed that the territory in which the coercive order has been put into force has not previously formed, together with the individuals living thereon, the territory and the population of one State. It must be a territory which, together with the individuals living thereon, has until now belonged to no State at all, or to two or more States, or has formed only part of the territory and the population of one State. If a government has established itself which is able to obtain permanent obedience to its order in a territory and over a population which were already the territory and the population of one State, if territory and population are identical, then ro new State in the sense of international law has come into existence; only a new government has been established. A new government in this sense is assumed only if it is established through revolution or *coup d'état*.

2. The Identity of the State

A State remains the same as long as the continuity of the national legal order is maintained, that is to say, as long as the changes of this order, even fundamental changes in the contents of the legal norms or of the territorial sphere of validity, are the result of acts performed in conformity with the constitution; provided that the change does not imply the termination of the validity of the national legal order as a whole. The latter is the case, for example, when a State, by an act of its own legislation, merges into another State. Thus the Austrian Republic, by a law voted by its National Assembly on November 12, 1918 (but not executed) and later on by a law enacted by its government on March 13, 1938, was declared a part of the German Reich.

Only from the point of view of the national legal order itself does the latter's continuity coincide with the identity of the State constituted by this legal order. If, however, the change is the result of a revolution or a *coup d'état*, the question of the identity of the State can be answered on the basis of the international legal order only. According to international law, the State remains the same as long as the territory remains essentially the same. The identity of the State in time is based directly upon the identity of the territory and only indirectly upon the identity of the population living in the territory. According to traditional theory, a State ceases to exist when the government is no longer able to obtain obedience to the coercive order which until now has been efficacious for this territory. In order to assume that a State ceases to exist it is necessary that no other government be able to obtain permanent obedience to the coercive order valid for the territory under discussion. The latter may become no State's land or part of the territory of another State, or part of the territories of two or more other States. If the territory in question remains in its entirety territory of one State it is not possible to assume that one State has ceased to exist and another State has come into existence in the same territory. It is the same State which continues to exist, but under a new government which came into power by revolution or *coup d'état*.

3. Birth and Death of the State as Legal Problems

The problem as to the beginning and ending of the existence of a State is a legal problem only if we assume that international law really embodies some such principles as indicated in the foregoing chapter. Even though some authors advocate the opposite view, the whole problem, as usually formulated, has a specifically juristic character. It amounts to the question: Under what circumstances does a national legal order begin or cease to be valid? The answer, given by international law, is that a national legal order begins to be valid as soon as it has become — on the whole — efficacious; and it ceases to be valid as soon as it loses this efficacy. The legal order remains the same as long as its territorial sphere of validity remains essentially the same, even if the order should be changed in another way than that prescribed by the constitution, in the way of revolution or *coup d'état*. A victorious revolution or a successful *coup d'état* does not destroy the identity of the legal order which it changes. The order established by revolution or *coup d'état* has to be considered as a modification of the old order, not as a new order, if this order is valid for the same territory. The government brought into permanent power by a revolution or *coup d'état* is, according to international law, the legitimate government of the State, whose identity is not affected by these events. Hence, according to international law, victorious revolutions or successful *coups d'état* are to be interpreted as procedures by which a national legal order can be changed. Both events are, viewed in the light of international law, law-creating facts. Again, *ex injuria jus oritur*; and it is again the principle of effectiveness that is applied.

c. Recognition

1. Recognition of a Community as a State

General international law determines the conditions on which a social order is a national legal order or, what amounts to the same thing, the conditions on which a community is a State and, as such, a subject of International Law. If States are subjects of international law, the latter must determine what a State is, just as national law has to determine who are the subjects of duties and rights stipulated by it; for instance, only human beings and not animals, or only free men and not slaves. If international law did not determine what a State is, then its norms would not be applicable.

According to international law, a social order is a national legal order if it is a relatively centralized coercive order regulating human behavior, if this order is inferior only to the international legal order, and if it is efficacious for a certain territory. The same rule, if expressed in the usual language of personification, runs as follows: A community is a State if the individuals belonging to this community are living in a certain territory under an independent and effective government. This is the fact "State in the sense of international law." It is a fact to which international law attaches various important consequences.

If a legal order in an abstract rule attaches certain consequences to a certain fact, it must, as pointed out in a previous chapter, determine a procedure through which the existence of the fact, in a concrete case, is ascertained by a competent authority. In the realm of law, there is no fact "in itself," no immediately evident fact, there are only facts ascertained by the competent authorities in a procedure determined by law.

Since general international law consists of general norms it can determine the legal fact "State" in abstract terms only. But how, according to general international law, is the question to be decided: Does the legal fact "State in the sense of international law" exist in a given case? Does a given community of men actually possess those qualities required of a subject of international law? In other words, is international law applicable to this community in its relations to other States? Which is the procedure by which the fact "State in the sense of international law" is to be ascertained; who is competent to ascertain the fact in question? The procedure provided by general international law to ascertain the fact "State in the sense of international law" in a concrete case, is called recognition; competent to ascertain the existence of this fact are the governments of the other States interested in the existence of the State in question.

In traditional theory some confusion prevails as to the problem of recognition. The reason for this confusion is that one does not distinguish clearly between two totally different acts, both called recognition: the one is a political, the other a legal act.* The political act of recognizing a State means that the recognizing State is willing to enter into political and other relations with the recognized State, relations of the kind which normally exist between members of the Family of Nations. Since a State according to general international law is not obliged to entertain such relations with other States, namely, to send or receive diplomatic envoys, to conclude treaties, etc., political recognition of a State is an act which lies within the arbitrary decision of the recognizing State. This recognition can be brought about either by a unilateral declaration of the recognizing State, or by a bilateral transaction, namely, by an exchange of notes between the government of the recognizing State, on the one hand, and the government of the recognized State on the other. Political recognition may be conditional or unconditional. However, these questions are unimportant from a legal point of view, as long as the declaration of willingness to enter into political and other relations with a State does not institute any concrete legal obligation.

Such an obligation can arise only by a treaty between the two States, and such a treaty contains more than a mere declaration of recognition. This declaration in itself has no legal consequences, although it may be of great importance politically, especially for the prestige of the State to be recognized. The political act of recognition, since it has no legal effect whatsoever, is not constitutive of the legal existence of the recognized

---

* Cf. my article *Recognition in International Law: Theoretical Observations* (1941) 35 AM. J. INTERNATIONAL LAW 605f.

State. Political recognition presupposes the legal existence of the State to be recognized. If one wishes to indicate the negative fact that an act has no legal consequences by saying that the act is only "declaratory," then the political act of recognition can be characterized as "declaratory."

Entirely different from the political is the legal act of recognition. The latter is the above-mentioned procedure provided by international law to ascertain the fact "State" in a concrete case. That a State recognizes a community as a State legally means that it declares that the community is a State in the sense of international law.

According to international law, such recognition is indeed necessary. General international law determines under what conditions a community has to be considered a State; and consequently provides a procedure to decide whether or not in a concrete case a community fulfills these conditions and therefore is, or is not, a State in the sense of international law. To decide this question international law authorizes the governments of the States which — according to general international law — have duties and rights in relation to the community under discussion, provided this community is a State. The government of a State interested in the existence or non-existence of another State is, it is true, not an objective and impartial authority to decide that question. But since general international law does not institute special organs to create and apply the law, there is no other way to ascertain the existence of facts but the ascertainment of these facts, and that means their "recognition," by the interested governments. Recognition of a community as a State in the sense of international law is only a particular case of the general principle of recognition, that is, the principle according to which the existence of facts to which international law attaches legal consequences has to be ascertained by the governments which are interested in these facts in a concrete case. This is a consequence of the far-reaching decentralization of international law.

In deciding the question whether a community which claims to be a State is actually a State in the sense of international law, the governments of the other States are by no means free. They are, it is true, not obliged to recognize a community as a State; but if a State recognizes another community as a State, it is bound by international law which determines in a general way the essential elements of a State. By the mere act of not recognizing a community as a State, a State can never violate international law.

But a State violates international law and thus also infringes upon the rights of other States if it recognizes as a State a community which does not fulfill the requirements of international law. As soon as a State, through its government, has certified that a community is a State in the sense of international law — that is to say, that a State has recognized the community as a State — the recognizing State has towards the recognized community all the obligations and all the rights that are stipulated by general international law; and, vice versa, international law becomes applicable to the relationship of the recognizing to the recognized State. But recognition has to be reciprocal in order that international law may become applicable also to the relationship of the recognized to the recognizing State.

Recognition or the *actus contrarius*, non-recognition, as the ascertainment that the fact "State" in the sense of international law exists or does not exist in a concrete case, is of importance not only for the coming into being of a new State, but also for the extinction of an old State. When a State through its government certifies that a community hitherto recognized as a State no longer corresponds to the requirements of international law, that is to say, when a State withdraws recognition from a community, the latter ceases to exist legally as a State in relation to the former. The legal existence of States has a thoroughly relative character. States exist legally as subjects of international law only in relationship to other States on the basis of reciprocal recognition.

Just as international law is not violated if the competence to recognize a community as a State is not exercised, neither can it be violated if the competence to withdraw recognition is not exercised. There is no duty to perform this act. But just as international law can be violated by an act of recognition, it can also be violated by the act of withdrawing recognition. Recognition as well as the *actus contrarius* can be performed in contradiction to international law. A State may declare that a community which has been a State ceases to be a State although the community in fact still fulfills all conditions laid down by international law. Thus the right of the community concerned is violated. The question of its legal existence is disputed between the community and the State which denies its existence. In this case the same rules become applicable which, according to general international law, are to be applied in case the question is disputed whether a State has violated the right of another State.

A State may declare "not to recognize" the annexation of another State by a third State because the annexation involves a violation of international law. If, however, the annexation is effective, that is to say, firmly established, the government of the non-recognizing State cannot maintain that the incorporated community still exhibits all the elements essential to a State in the sense of international law. Then, the "non-recognition" cannot imply the opinion of the non-recognizing government that the illegally incorporated community continues to exist as an independent State. The "non-recognition" may have a political significance. It may express a certain disapproval on the part of the non-recognizing government and its wish to see the illegally annexed community restored as an independent State. To impute to such a non-recognition the meaning that the community concerned has not ceased to exist as a State implies a fiction, in contradiction to legal reality determined by the principle of effectiveness.

Since the recognition of a State is, as a legal act, the establishment of a fact determined by international law, it cannot be conditional. The question whether a given community is a State in the sense of international law can only be answered "Yes" or "No." The content of the declaration of recognition excludes any possibility of a condition. Recognition of a State can only be unconditional. In the case of a conditional recognition, e.g., the declaration of State A to recognize the new State B on condition that the new State grant specific rights to a certain minority of its population, the condition cannot refer to the establishment of the fact that community B is a State in the sense of international law, contained implicitly in the act of recognition. The condition can only refer to the political act of recognition, which is in this case connected with the legal act. If community B, recognized as a State, has accepted the declaration of State A, i.e., if B is under obligation to A to grant to a certain minority of its population specific rights and does not fulfill this obligation, then B violates a right of A with all the consequences of a violation of law according to general international law. For the legal existence of State B in relation to State A, based on the legal act of recognition, this violation of law has no importance.

2. *De jure* and *De facto* Recognition

In theory and in practice one is accustomed to distinguish between *de jure* and *de facto* recognition. The significance of this distinction is not quite clear. In general it is believed that *de jure* recognition is final, whereas *de facto* recognition is only provisional and thus may be withdrawn. If such a distinction is made with reference to the political act of recognition, it must be observed that the declaration of willingness to enter into normal political and economic relations with the new State does not constitute any legal obligation. Even if this political recognition has no provisional character, it is not a legal act, and thus, in this sense, not *de jure*. In order that political recognition may not be withdrawn unilaterally, it has to have the form of a treaty between the recognizing and the recognized State, a treaty constituting legal obligations. Then the contents of the declaration of both States must comprise more than a mere recognition.

The distinction in question can be applied to the legal act of recognition only with the restriction that the so-called *de facto* recognition is also a *de jure* recognition because it represents a legal act. But perhaps this legal act of a so-called *de facto* recognition differs somehow from the act of a *de jure* recognition, using the term in a narrower sense. In this connection it must be observed that it is sometimes difficult to answer the question whether a given community fulfills all the conditions prescribed by international law in order to be a State. Immediately after a new community which claims to be a State has come into existence, it is in some cases doubtful whether the given fact corresponds completely to the requirements of international law, especially whether the new order is permanently effective and independent. If the legal act of recognition is made in this stage, the recognizing State may wish to refer to the situation in its act by declaring its recognition to be merely *de facto*. The expression is, as indicated, not quite exact, for even such a recognition is a legal act and has in the relations between the recognizing and the recognized State the same effects as a *de jure* recognition. If it turns out later that the recognized community does not in fact fulfill all the conditions prescribed by international law, the recognizing State may at any time establish this, but such establishment is also possible if the recognition was announced not as a *de facto*, but as a *de jure*, recognition. We have only to recall that any State is entitled, according to general international law, at any time to establish the fact that a community which has been a State in an international law sense, has ceased to be such, because it no longer fulfills the conditions prescribed by general international law.

From a juristic point of view, the distinction between *de jure* and *de facto* recognition has no importance.

3. Recognition with Retroactive Force

Since States, according to general international law, are not obliged, but only empowered, to determine whether a community is or has ceased to be a State, this can be established at any time regardless of the date when, in the opinion of the State so determining, the community in question began to fulfill the prescribed conditions. The State competent to establish this can fix the date in its declaration. The recognizing State may perform its recognition or the *actus contrarius* with retroactive force by declaring that the community in question began or ceased to fulfill the conditions prescribed by international law before the date of the recognition or the *actus contrarius*. Legal acts with retroactive force are possible according to general international law. There is no reason to suppose that the act of recognition or its *actus contrarius* forms an exception to this rule. Whether these acts have retroactive force or not is to be decided according to the intention of the acting State. This intention must be expressed in some way. No special form is prescribed by general international law; in fact, neither is there one for the act of recognition nor for its *actus contrarius*.

With regard to the organ of the State which is competent to perform the act of recognition or its opposite, general international law has no special ruling. Here the general rule applies according to which international law delegates the national legal order to determine the organs which represent the State in its relations with other States. In this connection it has to be observed that, according to the principle of effectiveness prevailing in international law, only the effective constitution of a State is to be regarded as delegated by international law. The actually effective constitution of a State does not necessarily correspond to its written one.

4. Recognition by Admission into the League of Nations

A State can transfer its competence to recognize the existence of another State by means of an international treaty to another State, to a union of States, or to its organs. It is in this sense that we must interpret Article I, Section 2 of the Covenant of the League of Nations which runs as follows: "Any fully self-governing State, Dominion or Colony not named in the Annex may become a Member of the League of Nations if its admission is agreed to by two-thirds of the Assembly. . . ." This provision does not imply that only the States recognized by all members of the League can by majority vote of the Assembly be admitted to the League. Thus it is possible that a community may become a member of the League, even if this community has not yet been recognized by one or another member voting against its admission. By admission into the League the community in question becomes a subject of the rights and duties stipulated by the Covenant in relation to all the other members, even those who have voted against the admission of the new member; and the other members of the League, even those who voted against its admission, obtain, according to the rules laid down in the Covenant, certain rights and incur certain obligations in relation to the newly admitted member. This is only possible under the supposition that the new member, by admission to the League, is recognized as a State in relation to those members which have not yet recognized it. The resolution of the Assembly by which the new member is admitted implies the act of recognition for those members which have themselves not yet recognized the new member. A State, by subjecting itself to the Covenant of the League of Nations, transfers to the Assembly the competence to recognize as a State a community which it has not yet recognized. However, this transfer of competence is limited to the case that the community in question should be admitted to the League. There is an analogous situation if States conclude a treaty by which a court is instituted, that is, if the treaty has a clause of unlimited accession. If a community which has not been recognized by one or another of the treaty-members as a State becomes a treaty party and pleads in the court against a State which has not yet recognized it, then the court has to decide, over the objection of the defendant, that the plaintiff is no "State in the sense of international law," on the status of the plaintiff in a manner binding the defendant. In such a case a right to be recognized exists.

5. Recognition of Governments

The recognition of an individual or a body of individuals as the government of a State offers essentially the same problem as the recognition of a community as a State. The legal act of recognition of a government must in principle be distinguished from the political act of recognition. The first act, as has been pointed out, is the establishment of the fact that an individual or a body of individuals is actually the government of a State. The second act is the declaration of willingness to enter into mutual relations with this government. A government, according to the norms of international law, is the individual or body of individuals which, by virtue of the effective constitution of a State, represents the State in its relations with other States, *i.e.*, is competent to act on behalf of the State in its relations to the community of States. Since, however, a State must in this sense have a government, and a community which has no government in the sense of international law is no State, the recognition of a community as a State implies that the community recognized has a government. The legal act of the recognition of a government cannot be separated from the legal act of the recognition of a State. So long as a State admits that another community is a State in the sense of international law, and so long as it does not declare that this community has ceased to be a State, it cannot declare that this State has no government. A State is, however, free to enter or refuse to enter into political and other relations with a government; that is, it may grant or refuse to the government political, but never legal, recognition.

The refusal of political recognition is, however, possible only to a limited degree. It is commonly held that a State, the government of which is not politically recognized by another State, nevertheless remains a subject of international law in relation to the latter State, that all rights and duties stipulated by general and particular international law remain in force in the mutual relations of both States. It is, however, the government which fulfills international obligations and puts in motion international rights. Let us suppose that State A refuses to recognize the government of State B, not State B as such, and requests from State B the fulfillment of its duties in relation to State A. Then State A must accept the fact that the obligations of State B are fulfilled by its government not recognized by State A; neither can State A refuse to fulfill a duty towards B simply because the fulfillment was requested by a government not recognized by A. That the recognition or non-recognition of an individual or a body of individuals as the government of a State can only have a political, not a legal, significance, follows from the rule of international law according to which a State is free to institute for itself any government it wishes, provided thereby that no rights of other States are violated and that the government is effective. The freedom of a State to recognize or not to recognize the government of another State rests upon the fact that no State is required to have political or other relations with another State, to conclude treaties with it, etc., and that any State may break off these normal relations with another State if the government of that other State is politically not acceptable. This rupture of relations must, however, not affect existing legal obligations.

6. Recognition of Insurgents as a Belligerent Power

Besides the recognition of States and governments, the recognition of insurgents as a belligerent power is also of importance in international law. It presupposes a civil war. Under certain conditions determined by international law this civil war may assume the character of an international war.

These are the conditions:

(1) The insurgents must have a government and a military organization of their own.

(2) The insurrection must be conducted in the usual technical forms of war, *i.e.*, the conflict must be more than a mere petty revolt and must assume the true characteristics of a war as that term is generally understood.

(3) The government of the insurgents must in fact control a certain part of the territory of the State in which the civil war takes place, *i.e.*, the order established by the insurgents must be effective for a certain part of the territory of this State.

The legal act of recognition of insurgents as a belligerent power implies that the above-mentioned facts, determined generally by international law, exist in a given case. This recognition may be made by the legitimate government against which the insurrection is directed as well as by the governments of other States. As to the effect of the recognition of insurgents as a belligerent power, opinions differ. The only point commonly accepted is that by recognition the international norms concerning war and neutrality become applicable to the relations between the recognizing State and the community recognized as a belligerent power. For the legitimate government against which the insurrection is directed, the recognition of the insurgents as a belligerent power implies the release from any responsibility for events which may happen in the territory occupied by the insurgents.

The two most significant functions of this act of recognition are the transformation of civil war into international war, with all its legal consequences, and the regulation of international responsibility corresponding to the change of political power within the State involved in civil war, not only with respect to the legitimate but also to the insurgent government. Clearly to determine the responsibility of both would be a highly important task for a codification which on this point could bring into existence rules of international law which are now only in *statu nascendi.*

The recognition of insurgents as a belligerent power resembles more the recognition of a community as a State than the recognition of an individual or a body of individuals as a government. By the effective control of the insurgent government over part of the territory and people of the State involved in civil war, an entity is formed which indeed resembles a State in the sense of international law. This is of great importance as far as the extent of responsibility of the insurgent government is concerned.

d. Succession of States

The territory of one State may become part of the territory of another State or of several other States when a State merges voluntarily into another or into several other States by international treaty; or when the whole territory of one State is — against its own will — annexed by another or by several other States; or when several States establish a Federal State by an international treaty, provided that the so-called Member States have no international personality at all. Part of the territory of one State may become the territory of another State by international treaty, as, for instance, Danzig, or the State of the Vatican City; or by revolution when a part of the population of a State breaks away and establishes, in the territory where it lives, a new State. Part of the territory of one State may become part of the territory of another State by a treaty of cession or, against the will of the government concerned, by annexation on the part of another State.

When the territory of one State becomes, totally or partially, part of the territory of another State or of several other States, or when part of the territory of one State becomes the territory of one other State, the question arises whether and to what extent, according to general international law, the duties and rights of the predecessor devolve upon the successor. This is the problem of so-called succession of States. That the whole territory of one State becomes the territory of one other State is impossible since, if the territory is identical, the identity of the State is maintained. Hence no succession of States can take place.

Succession does not concern the duties imposed and the rights conferred upon a State by general international law. These duties and rights are duties and rights of the successor with respect to the territory in question by virtue of general international law directly, not by virtue of succession. Succession refers only to duties and rights established by particular international law, especially by international treaties, and by national law as, for instance, the public debts of States. It is assumed that, according to general international law, succession takes place with regard to such international duties and rights of the predecessor as are locally connected with the territory which became territory of the successor. The latter is considered to be bound by treaties concluded by its predecessor with other States if these treaties establish duties of the predecessor inherent in its territory as, for instance, duties concerning boundary lines, navigation of rivers, and the like. But also the rights arising from such treaties devolve on the successor of the State which has concluded the treaty. Succession takes place also with regard to the fiscal property of the predecessor found on the territory which becomes territory of the successor. As far as the debts of the predecessor are concerned, succession takes place only when the whole territory of a State becomes territory of another State or of several other States, and with regard to debts only the creditors of which are nationals of another than the succeeding State. Then their home State is entitled to claim that the successor takes over these debts. When the territory becomes territory of more than one State and hence there are several successors to the fiscal property of the predecessor, the rule is that proportionate parts of the debts must be taken over by the different successors.

e. State Servitudes

When by an international treaty duties of one State are created which, in the interest of the other State, are perpetually connected with the territory of the obligated State so that succession to these duties and the corresponding rights takes place in case the territory of one or the other contracting State becomes territory of another State, one speaks of State servitudes. Such duties perpetually connected with the territory of a

State or a part thereof in favor of another State include, besides the duties mentioned in the foregoing paragraph, the duty not to fortify a certain place, to allow passage of troops, to allow fishing or the laying of cables within the territorial waters, and the like. The term "servitude" is taken from civil law. According to the usual definition, a servitude is a charge laid on an estate for the use of another estate belonging to another proprietor; for instance, the right of passage over an estate in order to make better use of another estate. Hence one speaks of a "serving" and a "dominant" estate. Analogously, one defines State servitudes as those "restrictions made by treaty on the territorial supremacy of a State by which a part or the whole of its territory is in a limited way made perpetually to serve a certain purpose or interest of another State." * One speaks of a "serving territory" and a "dominant territory" (*territorium serviens* and *territorium dominans*), of international rights inherent in the object with which they are connected as rights *in rem*, in contradistinction to international personal rights as rights *in personam*, and the like. However, the analogy between servitudes of civil law and so-called servitudes of States, international servitudes, is problematical, since the relationship of the State to its territory is not ownership. The decisive element of the phenomenon in question is that succession to the duties and rights takes place by virtue of their connection with a certain territory. This is not correctly expressed by saying that State servitudes are "rights" which "remain valid and may be exercised however the ownership of the territory to which they apply may change." † State servitudes are, primarily, duties because they are restrictions of a State, and secondarily only rights of the other State in whose favor the duties are established. Servitudes in the true sense of the term presuppose ownership, and there is no ownership with respect to the territory in question.

State servitudes may be established not only by treaty but also by a particular custom, that is to say, by the mutual conduct of two States fulfilling all the conditions on which customary law is created. If a State servitude is created by an international treaty concluded by two States, this treaty evidently presents an exception to the general principle that treaties impose duties and confer rights upon the contracting States only. A treaty establishing a State servitude imposes duties on every State to which the territory belongs with which the duty is connected. Such a treaty confers a right upon every State that is the successor of the contracting State in whose favor the right has been established. A treaty establishing a State servitude is an international treaty *à la*

---

* 1 Oppenheim, International Law 419.
† 1 Oppenheim, International Law 424.

charge and *en faveur* of a third State. General international law recognizes the intention of the contracting States to establish "perpetual" duties and rights and thus authorizes the contracting parties, by the conclusion of a treaty, to obligate and empower third States.

C. The People of the State

a. The People of the State as the Personal Sphere of Validity of the National Legal Order

A second "element" of the State, according to traditional theory, is the people, that is, the human beings residing within the territory of the State. They are regarded as a unity. As the State has one territory only, so it has only one people; and as the unity of the territory is a juristic, not a natural one, so is the unity of the people. It is constituted by the unity of the legal order valid for the individuals regarded as the people of the State. The people of the State are the individuals whose behavior is regulated by the national legal order; that is, the personal sphere of validity of this order. Just as the territorial sphere of validity of the national legal order is limited so also is the personal sphere. An individual belongs to the people of a given State if he is included in the personal sphere of validity of its legal order. As every contemporary State comprises only a part of space, so it also comprises only a part of mankind. And as the territorial sphere of validity of the national legal order is determined by international law, so also is its personal sphere.

b. Limitation of the Personal Sphere of Validity of the National Legal Order by the International Legal Order

How does international law determine the personal sphere of validity of the national legal order? Whose behavior is the national legal order authorized by international law to regulate? Or, in other terms, what individuals can the State subject to its power without violating international law and consequently the rights of other States?

The legal order regulates the behavior of an individual by attaching a coercive sanction to the opposite behavior, as condition. But, according to international law, the coercive act provided by the national legal order may be directed only against individuals who are within the territory of the State, that is, within the space which international law determines as the territorial sphere of validity of the national legal order. This does not mean that the national legal order can attach coercive acts only to acts performed within the territory of the State. As pointed out in a foregoing chapter, the behavior constituting the condition of the sanction can — at least in principle — be the behavior of individuals outside the territory of the State. But these sanctions can be actually executed only against individuals who are within the territory. In this way, the personal sphere of validity of the national legal order is determined by international law. It is an indirect determination. It results from the determination of the territorial sphere of validity.

c. Exterritoriality; Protection of Aliens

A State can, in principle, direct coercive acts against anybody within its territory. But this rule of international law is subject to exceptions. It is the international institution of so-called exterritoriality by which the above-mentioned rule is restricted. According to international law, certain individuals, such as heads of State or diplomatic envoys or armed forces of other States, e.g., enjoy exemption from the operation of the ordinary laws of the State. No coercive act, not even a legal procedure aiming at a coercive act, is allowed to be directed against these individuals. This privilege constitutes a direct restriction of the personal sphere of validity of the national legal order.

Another restriction results from the fact that international law obligates the State to treat individuals who stay within its territory but are organs or citizens of another State in a certain way. The head of a foreign State and diplomatic envoys must be granted special protection as regards their personal safety and unrestrained intercourse with their governments. As far as citizens of a foreign State are concerned, the legal order of the State on whose territory they are staying has to grant these individuals a minimum of rights, and must not impose upon them certain duties, otherwise a right of the State to which they legally belong is considered to be violated.

This right accorded to the State by international law presupposes the legal institution of citizenship. What is the essence of this institution? What is legally the difference between a citizen and an alien, that is, an individual who is living within the territory of a State and is a citizen of another — a foreign — State, or of no State?

d. Citizenship (Nationality)

1. Military Service

Citizenship or nationality is a personal status the acquisition and loss of which are regulated by national and international law. The national legal order makes this status the condition of certain duties and rights. The most prominent among those duties that are usually imposed only upon citizens is the duty to do military service. According to international law, a State is not allowed to obligate citizens of another State to do military service against their will. If it does so, it violates the right of the State to which the individual belongs, unless the latter is at the same time a citizen of the obligating State also. A State does not violate the right of another State by accepting citizens of the latter as volunteers in its army. The creation of foreign legions is not forbidden by international law. But a State is forbidden to compel citizens of another State to take part in the operations of war directed against their own country, even if they have been in the service of the former State before the commencement of war.

2. Allegiance

Allegiance is usually cited as one of the specific duties of citizens. When a person is granted citizenship, he has sometimes to swear allegiance to his new State. It is defined as "the duty which the subject owes to the sovereign, correlative with the protection received." * This concept does not have any definite legal significance but is rather of a moral and political nature. There is no special legal obligation covered by the term allegiance. Legally, allegiance means no more than the general obligation of obeying the legal order, an obligation that aliens also have and that is not created by the oath of allegiance.

3. Political Rights

The so-called political rights are among those which the legal order usually reserves for citizens. They are commonly defined as those rights which give their possessor an influence on the formation of the will of the State. The main political right is the right to vote, that is, the right to participate in the election of the members of the legislative body and other State officials, such as the head of State and the judges. In a direct democracy, the paramount political right is that of participating in the popular assembly. Since the will of the State expresses itself only in the creation and execution of legal norms, the essential characteristic of a political right is that it affords the individual the legal possibility of participating in the creation or execution of the legal norms. As already mentioned, political rights, so defined, are not essentially different from the rights of civil law. It is only that those rights which are classified as political are of greater importance for the formation of the legal order than the rights of civil law. This is the reason why citizenship is normally the condition of political, not of civil rights. In democracies only do all the citizens have political rights; in more or less autocratic States political rights are reserved to more or less extensive classes of citizens. According to the German law of September 15, 1935, only persons of

* 1 BOUVIER'S LAW DICTIONARY (3rd revision, 1914) 179.

"German or cognate blood" enjoy full political rights. These persons only are called "citizens" (*Staatsbuerger*), the others are designated as "nationals" (*Staatsangehoerige*). From the point of view of international law such distinction has no importance.

Political rights need not necessarily be reserved for citizens only. The national legal order may grant political rights to non-citizens, especially to citizens of another State, without violating the right of this State.

As political rights one usually considers also certain liberties guaranteed by the constitution, such as religious freedom, the freedom of speech and press, the right to keep and bear arms, the right of the people to be secure in their persons, houses, papers and effects, the right against unreasonable searches and seizures, the right not to be deprived of life, liberty, or property without due process of law, not to be expropriated without just compensation, etc. The legal nature of this so-called Bill of Rights, which is a typical part of modern constitutions, will be discussed later. The liberties it states are rights in a juristic sense only if the subjects have an opportunity to appeal against acts of State by which the provisions of the constitution are violated in order to get them annulled. All these rights are not necessarily limited to citizens; they may also be granted to non-citizens.

As a political right one considers usually also the capacity — normally reserved to citizens — of being elected or appointed to a public office. An individual has a right in the technical sense to be elected or appointed to a certain public office only if there is open to him the legal possibility of enforcing his election or appointment.

4. Expulsion

Only citizens have, as a rule, a right to reside within the territory of the State, that is the right not to be expelled therefrom. There exists a right of residence in a technical sense only if the citizen has a legal remedy against an illegal act of expulsion, if there is open to him the possibility of having this act annulled through a legal procedure. The government usually reserves to itself the power to expel aliens at any time and for any reason. This power may be limited by special international treaties. In earlier periods some legal orders provided for expulsion of their own citizens as a punishment, which was called "banishment." Even now, international law does not forbid it as such, but its practical applicability is limited. For the banished individual is a foreigner in any other State; and every State has the right at any time to expel any foreigner. The expelled foreigner's own State would violate this right by refusing to permit him to return.

5. Extradition

Extradition is to be distinguished from expulsion. A State may ask another State for the extradition of an individual, especially in order to be able to prosecute him legally because of a delict he has committed on the territory of the State which asks for extradition. A State is obliged to grant the request on the basis of special treaty. There are in fact numerous treaties of extradition. Some governments do not extradite individuals who are their own citizens. Normally, the individuals who are the object of extradition have no personal right to be or not to be extradited. Extradition treaties establish duties and rights of the contracting States only.

6. Protection of Citizens

One sometimes speaks of a citizen's right to be "protected" by his State as the counterpart of his allegiance. The citizen, so one argues, owes his State allegiance and is entitled to its protection. Allegiance and protection are considered reciprocal obligations. But just as allegiance signifies nothing beyond the duties which the legal order imposes upon the citizens subject thereto, so the citizen's right to protection has no contents besides the duties that the legal order imposes upon the organs of the State toward the citizens. Legally, allegiance and protection mean no more than that the organs and the subjects of the State have to fulfill the legal obligations imposed upon them by the legal order. It is, in particular, wrong to maintain that the individual has a natural claim to protection for certain interests such as life, freedom, property. Even if it is the typical function of the legal order to protect certain interests of individuals in a certain way, both the circle of interests and the circle of individuals that enjoy such protection vary greatly from one national legal order to the other. There are instances of States which treat a large number of their subjects as slaves. That means that these individuals are not protected by the legal order at all, or not to the same extent, as are the so-called free men. And there are States whose legal orders do not recognize any personal freedom or any private property.

A more concrete right is the citizen's claim to diplomatic protection by the organs of his own State against foreign States. According to international law, every State is entitled to safeguard the interests of its citizens against violations by the organs of other States, and if the laws of the State expressly provide for such protection, the right becomes an obligation of the government towards the citizens.

7. Jurisdiction over Citizens Abroad

It is often asserted that the difference between citizen and foreigner consists in the fact that the former but not the latter is subject to the power of the State, even if he does not stay within its territory. To be subject to the power of the State means to be legally subject to the national legal order. An individual is subject to a legal order when his behavior is actually, or can be virtually, regulated by the legal order. Legally, the problem runs as follows: Can the legal order of a State regulate the behavior of a citizen of this State, who is within the territory of another State, to a larger extent than it can regulate that of a foreigner under the same conditions? At least insofar as coercive measures are concerned, there is no difference. As pointed out in another context, such coercive measures may be ordered and executed against foreigners as well as against citizens only insofar as they are within the territorial sphere of validity of the national legal order which provides for such coercive measures. If there is any difference, it could lie only in the fact that the legal order of a State might be authorized to attach sanctions to the behavior of its citizens residing within the territory of another State, but might not be authorized to attach sanctions to the same behavior of a foreigner under the same circumstances. An example will illustrate this: The legal order of a State obligates the citizens of this State living abroad to pay a certain tax, by providing for sanctions in case the tax is not paid. The sanction, of course, can be executed only if the citizen has property within the territory of his State, or if he returns to his country. Is such a law admissible from the point of view of international law, and is it inadmissible if the law applies to individuals who are not citizens of the State enacting the law? Is the above-mentioned principle that the legal order of a State may attach sanctions to any action or omission irrespective of where it takes place limited to actions and omissions of this State's citizens? Such a limitation could only be derived from international law. There are in fact certain tendencies toward such a limitation, but they have not as yet brought results in the form of any definite norms.

8. Acquisition and Loss of Citizenship

Acquisition and loss of citizenship is — in principle, and without regard to an exception of which we shall speak later — regulated by the national legal orders. The various legal orders contain quite different stipulations concerning the acquisition and loss of citizenship. Usually the wife shares her husband's citizenship, legitimate children their father's, and illegitimate children their mother's. Citizenship is often acquired through birth within the territory of the State, or through residence of a certain length. Other grounds of acquisition are legitimation (of children born out of wedlock), adoption, legislative or administrative act. "Naturalization" is an act of the State granting citizenship to an alien who has applied for it. When a territory is transferred from one State to another, the inhabitants who are nationals of the State which has lost the territory and remain in this territory become *ipso facto* nationals of the State which acquires the territory. At the same time they lose their former nationality. In this case, acquisition and loss of nationality are regulated directly by general international law. Treaties of cession often confer upon the inhabitants of the ceded territory the right to decide, by a declaration called "option," whether they will become nationals of the acquiring State or keep their former nationality. In the latter case, they can be compelled to leave the territory.

The loss of citizenship takes place in ways corresponding to those in which it is acquired. It may be lost also through emigration or long residence abroad, by entering into foreign military or civil service without permission of one's own State, and also by so-called denaturalization or release, analogous to naturalization. The release is granted on the application of the individual concerned. Forcible expatriation, that is deprivation of citizenship without or against the will of the individuals concerned, may be effected by legislative or administrative acts of the home State. Thus the German law of July 14, 1933, authorizes the Government to expatriate German citizens for political reasons.

Since the acquisition of a new citizenship is normally not dependent upon, and often does not cause, the loss of the previously existent citizenship, cases of individuals having two or more citizenships, as well as individuals having no citizenship at all, are not uncommon. If an individual is a citizen of two or more States, neither of them is able to give him diplomatic protection against the other, and if he is without any citizenship, no State protects him against any other. The situation becomes especially difficult when — as sometimes occurs — an individual is a citizen of two States that are at war with one another. International treaties have been concluded with a view to preventing multiple citizenship and complete lack of citizenship (statelessness). The Convention on Certain Questions Relating to the Conflict of Nationality Laws, adopted by the Hague Codification Conference of 1930, establishes the principle of so-called effective nationality. Article 5 stipulates: "Within a third State, a person having more than one nationality shall be treated as if he had only one. Without prejudice to the application of its law in matters of personal status and of any conventions in force, a third State shall, of the nationalities which any such person possesses, recognize exclusively in its territory either the nationality of the country in which he is habitually and principally resident, or the nationality of the country with which in the circumstances he appears to be in fact most closely connected."

9. Nationality of Juristic Persons

If certain laws of a State are applicable only to its citizens, not to aliens, and if at the same time they claim validity for juristic persons, the question arises which juristic persons are subject to them. It is usually presupposed that in order to answer that question one has to decide whether juristic persons may have citizenship, and what is the criterion according to which their citizenship is determined. But this is to interpret the question erroneously. Only human beings can be citizens of a State, just as only human beings can possess duties and rights. The duties and rights of a juristic person are the duties and rights of human beings as members or organs of the community presented as juristic person. When all the individuals who — as one says — form a juristic person, e.g., a corporation, are citizens of the same State whose law, applicable only to its citizens, is in question, the problem is easily solved. The juristic person, however, may be subject to this law not because the juristic person is a citizen of this State, but because all the individuals whose behavior is regulated by the by-laws, presented as a juristic person, are citizens of this State. Analogous is the case where all the individuals forming the juristic person are citizens of one and the same foreign State; then the juristic person cannot be subject to the laws applicable only to citizens. The problem becomes intricate first when the individuals concerned are partly citizens of the State under discussion and partly citizens of foreign States. Then, different solutions are possible. The juristic person may be subject to the laws applicable only to citizens of the State if the majority of the individuals forming the juristic person are citizens of this State, or — in case of a joint-stock company — if the majority of the shares is in the hands of citizens of this State, or if the managing committee has its seat within the territory of this State, and so on. The different possible solutions do not interest us here. This problem is a legislative, not a theoretical one. Each legislator has to solve the question for his own legal order by positive norms. Only the correct formulation of the problem is theoretically interesting. The question is not whether and when a certain juristic person is the citizen of a certain State, but whether and when it is advisable to subject juristic persons to the laws of a State which, according to their provisions, are applicable only to citizens of this State.

10. Is Citizenship a Necessary Institution?

Citizenship is an institution common to all modern national legal orders. But is it also necessary, because essential, to the State? Is it an indispensable requisite of the national legal order to distinguish among the individuals subject to it those who are citizens from those who are not? The existence of a State is dependent upon the existence of individuals that are subject to its legal order, but not upon the existence of "citizens." If the nature of citizenship consists in the fact that it is the condition of certain obligations and rights, then it must be stressed that none of them is essential to a legal order of the kind that we designate as State. There are historic examples of States in which none of these obligations and rights exist. It is, for instance, in democracy only that the citizens have political rights. In an autocracy the individuals subject to the legal order do not participate in its creation; the great mass of the people are politically without any rights. They are, to use Rousseau's distinction, *sujets* but not *citoyens*.* Since the individuals are here "subjects" only, the difference between those who are citizens and therefore possess political rights, and those who are not citizens and therefore do not possess political rights, is almost without importance. In a radical democracy, on the other hand, the tendency to enlarge, as far as possible, the circle of those who possess political rights may have the result of granting these rights — under certain circumstances — to aliens, too, for instance, if they have their permanent residence within the territory of the State. Then, here, too, the difference between citizens and non-citizens, and hence the importance of citizenship, is diminished.

A State whose legal order did not establish a special citizenship, and therefore did not contain any norms concerning acquisition and loss of this status, would not be able to grant its diplomatic protection to any of its subjects against violation of their interests by other States. The legal institution of citizenship is of greater importance in the relations between the States than it is within a State. The most important of the obligations which presuppose citizenship is the obligation to render military service. But this obligation is not essential to a national legal order. In many States, compulsory military service does not — or at least did not — exist even in wartime. When a national legal order does not contain any norms which, according to international law, are applicable to citizens only — and the norms concerning military service are practically the only ones — then citizenship is a legal institution lacking import.

* Rousseau, *The Social Contract*, Book I, chap. VI.

D. The Competence of the State as the Material Sphere of Validity of the National Legal Order

Besides the questions as to the space, the time, and the individuals for which the national legal order is valid, the question arises as to the subject matters which this order may regulate. It is the question of the material sphere of validity of the national legal order, presented usually as the problem of how far the competence of the State reaches in relation to its subjects.

The national legal order can regulate human behavior in very different respects and to very different degrees. It can regulate different subject matters and can, by doing so, limit more or less the personal freedom of individuals. The more subject matters are regulated by the legal order, the wider its material sphere of validity; the more the competence of the State is expanded, the more limited is the personal freedom of its subjects. The question as to the proper extent of this limitation (and this is the question as to the subject matters which the national legal order may, or may not, regulate) is answered in a different way by different political systems. Liberalism stands for the utmost restriction of the material sphere of validity of the national legal order, especially in matters of economy and religion. Other political systems, such as socialism, maintain the opposite view.

Again and again the attempt is made to derive from the very nature of the State and the human individual a limit beyond which the competence of the State must not be expanded, the freedom of the individual must not be limited. This attempt is typical of the theory of natural law. A scientific theory of the State is not in a position to establish a natural limit to the competence of the State in relation to its subjects. Nothing in the nature of the State or the individuals prevents the national legal order from regulating any subject matter in any field of social life, from restricting the freedom of the individual to any degree. The competence of the State is not limited by its nature; and in historical reality the actual competence of the different States is very different. Between the liberal State of the nineteenth century and the totalitarian State of our days there are many intermediate stages.

The fact that the competence of the State is not limited "by nature" does not prevent the material sphere of validity of the national legal order from being limited legally. The question arises whether international law, which limits the territorial, temporal, and personal sphere of validity of the national legal order, does not limit also its material sphere. The discussion of this question, however, must be postponed until the systematic investigation of the relation between national law and international law has been presented.

E. Conflict of Laws

In close connection with the sphere of validity of the different national legal orders is the problem of so-called "Conflict of Laws" or "Private International Law" (in contradistinction to "Public International Law"). This concept is usually defined as that body of legal rules which are to be applied to a conflict between two systems of law in the decision of cases having contact with more than one territory.* The principal topic of these rules is considered to be the decision as to which law in such cases is to have superiority, or the choice of the law to be applied to these cases. This, however, is not a correct characterization of the legal norms in question.

As a rule, the law-applying organs of a State, especially the courts (but not only the courts), are legally bound to apply norms of the national legal order only, that is to say, the law of the State whose organs they are. This law is the legal norms created according to the written or unwritten constitution of the State by the legislative organs of the State, by its courts (including so-called customary law), or by other agents competent to create law. As an exception to this rule, the law-applying organs of a State, especially its courts, are bound to apply norms of another legal order, that is to say, the law of another State, to certain cases determined by their own law. These cases are characterized by the fact that they stand in a certain relationship to the territorial or personal sphere of validity of a foreign legal order. Typical cases of so-called conflicts of laws or private international law are the validity of a marriage contracted within the territory of a foreign State, rights and duties concerning real estate located within the territory of a foreign State, a crime committed on foreign territory, the acquisition or the loss of foreign citizenship of a person who has his residence in the State claiming jurisdiction. The latter case does not have contact with more than one territory; but it has relationship to the territorial sphere of validity of one and the personal sphere of validity of another national legal order.

The norms of the foreign law which are to be applied by the organ of a State may be norms of the private or the public law of the other State, and in the latter case, norms of criminal or administrative law. If the

* Cf., e.g., A. S. Hershey, The Essentials of International Public Law and Organization (1939) 5; 1 Bouvier's Law Dictionary 596; Arthur Nussbaum, Principles of Private International Law (1943) 13.

rules prescribing the application of foreign law are called private international law, then there exist also a criminal and an administrative international law. The legal problem is exactly the same in all these cases.

The essential point of the problem seems to be the application of the law of one State by the organs of another State. But, if the organ of a State, bound by the law of this State, applies the norm of a foreign law to a certain case, the norm applied by the organ becomes a norm of the legal order of the State whose organ applies it. As pointed out in the first part of this book,* a legal norm belongs to a certain legal system, for instance, to the law of the United States or of Switzerland, it is a norm of the law of a certain State if it is valid for the sphere of validity of the law of that State according to the latter's constitution. The organ of a State, especially a court, is in a position to apply the norm of the law of another State only if bound to do so by the law of its own State — in the last resort by its written or unwritten constitution. The norm applied by the organ of the State is valid for the sphere of validity of the State's law only if its application is prescribed by that law. With reference to its reason of validity it is a norm of the legal system of that State. The rule obliging the courts of a State to apply norms of a foreign law to certain cases has the effect of incorporating the norms of the foreign law into the law of this State. Such a rule has the same character as the provision of a new, revolution-established constitution stating that some statutes valid under the old, revolution-abolished constitution should continue to be in force under the new constitution. The contents of these statutes remains the same, but the reason for their validity is changed. Instead of reproducing the contents of the old statutes (in order to put them in force under the new constitution) the latter simply refers to the contents of the old statutes as norms of another legal system, based on the old, revolution-abolished constitution. The making of such "reference" is but an abridged legislation.

Likewise the norms of so-called private international law prescribing the application of norms of a foreign law to certain cases "refer" to norms of another legal system instead of reproducing the contents of these norms. The norm of a foreign law applied by the organ of a State is "foreign" only with respect to its contents. With respect to the reason for its validity it is a norm of the State whose organ is bound to apply it. Strictly speaking, the organ of a State can apply only norms of the legal order of its own State. Consequently, the statement that a rule of the legal order of a certain State obliges an organ of this State to apply — in certain cases — a norm of the legal order of another State, is not a correct

* Cf. *supra*, pp. 110ff., 117.

description of the legal facts involved. The true meaning of the rules of so-called private international law is: that the law of a State directs its organs to apply to certain cases norms which are norms of the State's own law, but which have the same contents as corresponding norms of another State's law. Only if we constantly keep in mind its true meaning, may we use the expression that one State applies the law of another State.

With respect to the application of the law of one State by the organs of another State two different possibilities may be distinguished: (a) the State is legally free to apply or not to apply the law of another State to certain cases; (b) the State is legally bound by general or particular international law to apply the law of another State to certain cases. Some writers deny that there are rules of general international law obliging the State to apply the law of another State to certain cases. But if a court or another law-applying organ has to decide the question whether a foreigner has legally acquired some private right in his own country, it will always apply the law of this country; if, however, the court should decide that the right in question is not legally acquired because not acquired according to the law of the deciding court, the government of the State whose citizen the foreigner is could probably consider the decision a violation of international law.* However, it is true that general international law imposes the obligation of applying foreign law to a very limited extent. If there is no international treaty obliging the State to apply foreign law to certain cases, the State is — as a rule — legally free in this respect. It may regulate by its own law the application of foreign law to certain cases according to principles which it considers to be adequate, just, and the like. Consequently, private (criminal, administrative) international law is, in so far as there is no rule of general or particular international law obliging the State to apply foreign law to certain cases, not international but national law. As a rule, only so-called "public" international law is international law. If a norm of general or particular international law obliges a State to apply the law of another State to certain cases, this norm is neither "private" nor "public" law, since the distinction between private and public law is not applicable to international law. It is a distinction between two kinds of norms of the same national legal order. The terms "private" and "public" international law are misleading since they seem to indicate an opposition within the international legal order, although public international law is simply international law, the adjective "public" being completely superfluous, while private international law is, at least normally,

---

* This is, e.g., the opinion of A. von VERDROSS, VÖLKERRECHT (1937) 143.

a set of norms of national law characterized by the subject matter of legal regulation.

The norms of the different national legal orders regulating the application of foreign law may differ much from each other. The same is true of the theory justifying the enactment of norms prescribing the application of foreign law to certain cases. Different States may, for very different reasons and to different ends, apply foreign law. As far as the "theory" of private international law aims at a justification of the rules in question, there is no "theory" that is correct for all the different legal systems. Thus, for instance, the theory of "vested rights" prevailing in the United States is the principle that rights wherever acquired must be protected. This is a political principle which may, or may not, influence the legislator. It is a legal rule, a norm of positive law, only if it is incorporated into a legal system by a law-creating act. Presented as a "theory" it is correct only for this legal system.

Although the State as such, that is to say, its law-creating organs, is, as a rule, free to enact norms prescribing the application of foreign law to certain cases, when such norms are once enacted, the law-applying organs, especially the courts, are not free but are legally bound to apply the norms of foreign law determined by the norms of so-called private (criminal, administrative) international law to certain cases likewise determined by these norms. This is true whether the general norms called private international law are statutory, customary, or judge-made law. The organ of the State, especially the court, which, determined by the general norms of so-called private international law, applies foreign law to a certain case has no "choice" between the law of its own State and a foreign law. The organ is obliged to apply the law of a definite foreign State; the norms to be applied are pre-determined by the organ's own legal order. They are norms which, on behalf of this pre-determination, have become norms of the organ's own law. The norms of so-called private international law do not place the law-applying organ in a position to make a choice between different legal systems. It is within one and the same legal system, the legal order of the law-applying organ, that the procedure takes place regulated by so-called private international law. By this procedure legal norms are incorporated (and that means, created) which are norms of the law of the law-applying organ, just as norms are created in the ordinary way by the legislative body of the State. The fact that these norms have the same contents as corresponding norms of a foreign law cannot alter their character as norms of the law of the applying organ. The term "choice-of-law" rules is misleading since it produces the appearance of a choice where no such choice exists.

The term "choice-of-law" probably results from the idea of a "conflict" between a State's own law and foreign law. But there is no conflict, since the foreign law does not claim to be applied by the organs of the State whose private international law is in question; and the latter does not refuse the application of the former. On the contrary. Expressed in the usual terminology, the law of one State prescribes the application of the law of another State; and the latter does not object or demand it. It has no right to do so since it is not really its own law which is applied by the other State. The latter applies norms of its own law. The fact that these norms have the same contents as corresponding norms of another State does not concern the latter. The only excuse for the terms "conflict of laws," or "choice-of-law" rules is that they are shorter and more manageable than an expression which would characterize correctly so-called private (criminal, administrative) international law. Since the specific technique of these norms consists in "referring" to the norms of another system and by so doing incorporating norms of identical contents into their own legal system, it would be more justifiable to call them "reference rules" or "incorporation rules."

The reference rule, that is — expressed in the usual terminology — the norm regulating the application of foreign law, may be distinguished from the norm to be applied, that is, the norm referred to. Only the former, the reference rule, is a norm of private international law. But from a functional point of view, the one is essentially connected with the other. Only if taken together do they form a complete rule of law. It would be quite possible to describe the relationship between the reference or choice-of-law rule and the norm referred to, the norm of foreign law to be applied, by saying that the latter is virtually contained in the former. The reference rule, as mentioned above, is only an abridged formula whose purpose is to replace norms reproducing the contents of the norms of foreign law referred to. It is by applying the reference or choice-of-law rule that the court arrives at the application of the norm of foreign law (which, in truth, is a norm of its own law). It is, therefore, correct to call the former the "preliminary," the latter the "final" rule.*

The close connection between the reference or choice-of-law rule and the rule of foreign law referred to manifests itself in the fact that the former, if it is a rule of national law, is of the same kind as the latter. If the norm referred to is a norm of private law, the reference rule is of private law too; if the norm referred to is a norm of criminal or administrative law, criminal or administrative law is involved. If, however, the norm obliging the State to apply the norm of another State to cer-

---

* As Nussbaum, *Principles of Private International Law* 69, suggests.

tain cases is a norm of international law, the international obligation of the State, as such, is an obligation neither of private nor of criminal nor of administrative law, but simply of international law. But if the norm of international law prescribing the application of foreign private, criminal, or administrative law is considered together with the norm to be applied, then, and then only, is it to a certain extent justifiable to speak of international private (criminal, administrative) law. This term seems to be more exact than the term "private (criminal, administrative) international law."

F. The So-called Fundamental Rights and Duties of the States

a. Natural-Law Doctrine applied to the relationship between States

According to a view prevailing in the eighteenth and nineteenth centuries and maintained even today by some writers, every State has — in its capacity as a member of the Family of Nations — some fundamental rights and duties. These rights and duties are, according to this doctrine, not stipulated by general customary international law or by international treaties as are the other rights and duties of the States, but originate in the nature of the State or the international community. These fundamental rights and duties — it is said — have "a broader and deeper significance than the ordinary positive rules of the Law of Nations of which they are in large measure the ultimate basis or source and have a greater obligatory force . . . they are in the nature of controlling or fundamental principles based upon conditions essential to State existence and international life in our time." *

The idea that the States have fundamental rights and duties is the application of the doctrine of natural law to the relationship between States. It is only another version of this natural law doctrine if one tries to maintain the theory of fundamental rights of the States by arguing in the following way: In any legal order it is necessary to distinguish the rights stipulated by this order from the legal principles presupposed by this legal order. The so-called fundamental rights of the States are, according to Verdross, the legal principles which are the conditions on which international law is possible at all, the legal principles on which positive international law is built up. We can find out these principles by an analysis of the nature of international law.† In other terms: the fundamental rights of the States can be deduced from the nature of international law. This is the same doctrine as the one according to which

* Hershey, Essentials of International Public Law and Organization 230f.
† Verdross, Völkerrecht 199.

the fundamental rights of the States are "the ultimate basis or source" of positive international law and have therefore "a greater obligatory force" than the other rules of international law.

This version of the natural-law doctrine is logically impossible just as the classical version of this doctrine is. Legal principles can never be presupposed by a legal order; they can only be created by this order. For they are "legal" only and exclusively because and in so far as they are established by a positive legal order. Certainly the creation of positive law is not a creation out of nothing. The legislator as well as custom is directed by some general principles. But these principles are moral or political principles and not legal principles, and, consequently, cannot impose legal duties or confer legal rights upon men or States as long as these principles are not stipulated by legislation or custom. As legal principles they are not the source or basis of the legal order by which they are stipulated; on the contrary, the positive legal order is their basis or source. Hence they have no greater obligatory force than the other rules stipulated by the positive legal order unless the positive legal order itself grants them a greater obligatory force by making their abolition more difficult. This is impossible if the legal order, as general international law, has the character of customary law, and if, consequently, the rules of this order acquire as well as lose their validity by custom.

The so-called fundamental rights and duties of the States are rights and duties of the States only in so far as they are stipulated by general international law, which has the character of customary law. Such rights have been chiefly enumerated as the right of existence, the right of self-preservation, the right of equality, the right of independence, the right of territorial and personal supremacy, the right of intercourse, the right of good name and reputation, and the right of jurisdiction. L. Oppenheim correctly states that the so-called fundamental rights and duties are rights and duties "which the States customarily enjoy." * Nevertheless he tries to deduce these rights and duties from the nature of the State as an international personality. He writes: "International Personality is the term which characterizes fitly the position of the States within the Family of Nations, since a State acquires international personality through its recognition as a member. What it really means can be ascertained by going back to the basis of the Law of Nations. Such basis is the common consent of the States that a body of legal rules shall regulate their intercourse with one another." † However, "international person-

* 1 OPPENHEIM, INTERNATIONAL LAW 217f.
† 1 OPPENHEIM, INTERNATIONAL LAW 219.

ality of the State" means only that general international law imposes duties and confers rights upon States (and that means upon individuals as organs of the States). The State is an international personality because it is a subject of international duties and rights. This statement says nothing about the contents of these rights and duties. The concept of legal personality is a thoroughly formal concept. Hence it is impossible to deduce from the fact that the State is an international personality any definite rights and duties of the State, such as the right of independence or the right of self-preservation, the duty of non-intervention, and so forth.

The statement that the basis of international law is "the common consent of the States that a body of legal rules shall regulate their intercourse with one another" has a fictitious character, since it is impossible to prove the existence of such "common consent." The theory that the basis of international law is a common consent of the States, a kind of contract tacitly concluded by the States, has exactly the same character as the natural-law doctrine concerning the basis of the State or the national legal order, that is the doctrine of the social contract. According to this theory, men are in their state of nature free and equal. The State, the national legal order, comes into existence owing to the fact that free and equal individuals assent to an agreement concerning a social order regulating their mutual behavior. Every individual voluntarily restricts his freedom in the interest of all the other individuals on the condition that the others restrict their freedom in the same way. Since such an event has never taken place, the doctrine of social contract is a fiction, the function of which is not to explain the origin of the State but to justify the existence of the fact that the individuals are bound by a legal order imposing duties and conferring rights upon them. The theory of a common consent of the States as the basis of international law or the international community constituted by international law rests on the same fiction. It is an indubitable fact that the States are considered to be bound by general international law without and even against their will.* Oppenheim says further: "Now a legally regulated intercourse between sovereign States is only possible under the condition that a certain liberty of action is granted to every State, and that, on the other hand, every State consents to a certain restriction of action in the interest of the liberty of action granted to every other State. A State that enters into the Family of Nations retains the natural liberty of action due to it in consequence of its sovereignty, but at the same time takes over the obligation to exercise self-restraint and to restrict its liberty of action in

* Cf. *infra*, pp. 380ff.

the interest of that of other States." * The State, however, does not voluntarily enter into the international legal community. By coming into legal existence, the State is subjected to preëxisting international law. It is not the State which, by its own free will, consents to a certain restriction of its liberty; it is general international law which restricts the liberty of the States without regard to whether they consent to this restriction or not. Finally, the State as international personality must not be considered to be sovereign, in the sense that the term sovereign denotes absolute liberty; Oppenheim, however, when speaking of the State as a personality voluntarily entering into the international community, takes the term sovereignty in this sense. In its capacity as an international personality the State is subjected to international law and, hence, is not "sovereign," just as the human individual in his capacity as a legal personality, and that means as subject of duties and rights, is subjected to the national legal order and consequently is not and cannot be "sovereign." Hence it is inadmissible to deduce from the sovereignty of the State any rights or duties.

Oppenheim continues: "In entering into the Family of Nations a State comes as an equal to equals; it demands that certain consideration be paid to its dignity, the retention of its independence, of its territorial and its personal supremacy." † Equality with other States is not a property with which a State is endowed when it enters into the international community. The States are equal because and in so far as international law treats them in this way. Whether the States are legally equal or not can be ascertained only by an analysis of positive international law, and cannot be deduced from the nature or the sovereignty of the State. Only by an analysis of positive international law — and not by supposing that the State by entering into the Family of Nations demands respect for its dignity, independence, and supremacy — can we answer the question whether consideration has to be paid to the dignity of the State, whether its independence has to be respected, its territorial and personal supremacy to be maintained, and so forth. Oppenheim says: "Recognition of a State as a member of the Family of Nations involves recognition of such State's equality, dignity, independence, and territorial and personal supremacy. But the recognized State recognizes in turn the same qualities in other members of that family, and thereby it undertakes responsibility for violations committed by it." ‡ Recognition of a community as a State by another State means only that the

---

* 1 OPPENHEIM, INTERNATIONAL LAW 219.
† 1 OPPENHEIM, INTERNATIONAL LAW 219.
‡ 1 OPPENHEIM, INTERNATIONAL LAW 219.

latter ascertains that the community in question fulfills all the requirements of a State in the sense of international law, which is a condition of
the application of international law to the relationship between the recognizing and the recognized State.* The recognition of a community as
a State is not and cannot be a recognition of international law, since the
recognition of a community as a State is an act provided for by international law, an act which is based on international law and which, consequently, presupposes the existence and validity of international law.†
It is therefore not the State which — by recognizing another State —
undertakes responsibility for violations committed by it. It is general
international law, valid independently of the recognition on the part
of the States, which imposes upon the States responsibility for their
violations of international law. "International personality," says Oppenheim, "may be said to be the fact . .'. that equality, dignity, independence, territorial and personal supremacy, and the responsibility of
every State are recognized by every other State." International personality is not the fact that the so-called fundamental rights of the State
are recognized by other States. International personality is simply the
fact that international law imposes duties and confers rights — and not
only the so-called fundamental duties and rights — upon the States.

b. The Equality of the States

Among the fundamental rights of the States the right of equality plays
an important role. Equality before international law is considered an
essential characteristic of the States.

The term "equality" seems at first glance to signify that all States
have the same duties and the same rights. This statement, however, is
obviously not correct, for the duties and rights established by international treaties constitute a great diversity among States. Consequently,
the statement must be restricted to general customary international law.
But even according to general customary law, all the States have not
the same duties and rights. A littoral State, for example, has other
duties and rights than an inland State. The statement must be modified
as follows: according to general international law all the States have
the same capacity of being charged with duties and of acquiring rights;
equality does not mean equality of duties and rights, but rather equality
of capacity for duties and rights. Equality is the principle that under
the same conditions States have the same duties and the same rights.
This is, however, an empty and insignificant formula because it is ap-

* Cf. *supra*, pp. 221ff.
† Cf. *infra*, pp. 380ff.

plicable even in case of radical inequalities. Thus, a rule of general international law conferring privileges on Great Powers could be interpreted as in conformity with the principle of equality, if formulated as follows: any State, on the condition that it is a Great Power, enjoys the privileges concerned. The principle of equality so formulated is but a tautological expression of the principle of legality, that is the principle that the rules of law ought to be applied in all cases in which, according to their contents, they ought to be applied. Thus the principle of legal equality, if nothing but the principle of legality, is compatible with any actual inequality. The States are "equal" before international law since they are equally subjected to international law and international law is equally applicable to the States. This statement has exactly the same meaning as the statement that the States are subjects of international law or that the States have duties and rights under international law; but it does not mean that these duties and rights are equal.

It is, therefore, understandable that most of the writers on international law try to attribute a more substantial import to the concept of equality. When characterizing the States as equal, they mean that according to general international law no State can be legally bound without or against its will. Consequently, they reason that international treaties are binding merely upon the contracting States, and that the decision of an international agency is not binding upon a State which is not represented in the agency or whose representative has voted against the decision, thus excluding the majority vote principle from the realm of international law. Other applications of the principle of equality are the rules that no State has jurisdiction over another State (and that means over the acts of another State) without the latter's consent, and that the courts of one State are not competent to question the validity of the acts of another State in so far as those acts purport to take effect within the sphere of validity of the latter State's national legal order. Understood this way, the principle of equality is the principle of autonomy of the States as subjects of international law.

There are, however, important restrictions to the rules of international law by which the autonomy of the States is established. There are, as we shall see later, international treaties which, according to general international law, impose duties and confer rights upon third States. There are cases where a State has jurisdiction over the acts of another State without the latter's consent. By a treaty an international agency may be established in which only a part of the contracting States are represented and which is authorized by the treaty to adopt by majority vote norms binding upon all the contracting States. Such a treaty is not incompatible with the concept of international law or with the concept of the State as a subject of international law; and such a treaty is a true exception to the rule that no State can be legally bound without or against its own will. The fact that the competence of the international agency is based on the consent of all the States concerned because the competence of the agency is the result of a treaty concluded by all the States which may be bound by the majority decisions of the agency, does not permit the conclusion that all the decisions of the agency are adopted with the consent of all the States which are contracting parties to the treaty and that, consequently, no decision is adopted without or against the will of one of the States bound by the decision. This is a fiction, which is in open contradiction to the fact that a State which is not represented in the agency has in no way expressed its will with reference to the decision, and that a State whose representative has voted against the decision has expressly declared its opposite will.

The fact that a State has, by concluding the treaty, given its consent to the competence of the agency established by the treaty is quite compatible with the fact that the State can change its will, expressed at the conclusion of the treaty. This change of will is legally irrelevant, however, since the contracting State remains legally bound by the treaty, even if it ceases to will what it declared to will at the moment it concluded the treaty. Only at that moment is concordance of the wills of the contracting States necessary in order to create the duties and rights established by the treaty. The fact that the contracting State remains legally bound by the treaty without regard to a unilateral change of will clearly proves that a State can be bound even against its will. The will whose expression is an essential element of the conclusion of the treaty is not at all the will which the State has, or has not, with respect to the decision adopted by the agency established by the treaty.

Since it is undoubtedly possible that such a treaty can be concluded by "equal" States on the basis of general international law, it is a misuse of the concept of equality to maintain that it is incompatible with the equality of the States to establish an agency endowed with the competence to bind by a majority vote States represented, or not represented, in the law-making body. The equality of the States does not exclude the majority vote principle from the realm of international law.

If the equality of the States means their autonomy, it is not an absolute and unlimitable, but a relative and limitable, autonomy which international law confers upon the States.

G. The Power of the State

a. The Power of the State as the Validity and Efficacy
of the National Legal Order

The power of the State is usually listed as its third so-called element. The State is thought of as an aggregate of individuals, a people, living within a certain limited part of the earth's surface and subject to a certain power: One State, one territory, one people, and one power. Sovereignty is said to be the defining characteristic of this power. Though the unity of the power is held to be as essential as the unity of the territory and the people, it is nevertheless thought possible to distinguish between three different component powers, the legislative, the executive, and the judicial power of the State.

The word "power" has different meanings in these different usages. The power of the State to which the people is subject is nothing but the validity and efficacy of the legal order, from the unity of which is derived that of the territory and of the people. The "power" of the State must be the validity and efficacy of the national legal order, if sovereignty is to be considered as a quality of this power. For sovereignty can only be the quality of a normative order as an authority that is the source of obligations and rights. When, on the other hand, one speaks of the three powers of the State, power is understood as a function of the State, and three different functions of the State are distinguished. We shall first turn our attention to these three functions.

b. The Powers or Functions of the State: Legislation and Execution

A dichotomy is in reality the basis for the usual trichotomy. The legislative function is opposed to both the executive and the judicial functions, which latter are obviously more closely related to each other than to the first. Legislation (*legis latio* of Roman law) is the creation of laws (*leges*). If we speak of "execution," we must ask what is executed. There is no other answer but the statement that it is the general norms, the constitution and the laws created by the legislative power, which are executed. Execution of laws, however, is also the function of so-called judicial power. This power is not distinguishable from the so-called "executive" power by the fact that only the organs of the latter "execute" norms. In this respect, the function of both is really the same. By the executive as well as by the judicial power, general legal norms are executed; the difference is merely that, in the one case, it is courts, in the other, so-called "executive" or administrative organs, to which the execution of general norms is entrusted. The common trichotomy is thus at bottom a dichotomy, the fundamental distinction of *legis latio* and *legis executio*. The latter function is subdivided into the judicial and the executive functions in the narrower sense.

The executive power in turn is often differentiated into two separate functions, the so-called political and the so-called administrative function. (The former is in French and German terminology labeled "the government" in a narrower sense.) To the former are usually referred certain acts which are aimed at the direction of administration and are therefore politically important. They are performed by the highest administrative organs, such as the head of State and the chiefs of various administrative departments. These acts, too, are acts of execution; by these acts, too, general legal norms are executed. Many of these acts are left largely to the discretion of the executive organs. But no amount of discretion can divest an act of the executive power from its character of a law-executing act. Accordingly, the acts of the highest executive organs too are acts which execute general legal norms. The differentiation of the executive power into a governmental (political) and an administrative function has, therefore, a political rather than a juristic character. From a legal point of view, one might designate the whole domain of the executive power as administration.

The functions of the State thus prove to be identical with the essential functions of law. It is the difference between creation and application of law that expresses itself in the distinction between the three powers of the State.

c. The Legislative Power

By legislative power or legislation one does not understand the entire function of creating law, but a special aspect of this function, the creation of general norms. "A law" — a product of the legislative process — is essentially a general norm, or a complex of such norms. ("The law" is used as a designation for the totality of legal norms only because we are apt to identify "the law" with the general form of law and erroneously ignore the existence of individual legal norms.)

By legislation, further, is understood not the creation of all general norms, but only the creation of general norms by special organs, namely by the so-called legislative bodies. This terminology has historical and political origins. Where all the functions of the State are centered in the person of an absolute monarch, there is little ground for the formation of a concept of legislation as a function distinct from other functions of the State, especially if general norms are created by way of custom. The modern concept of legislation could not arise until the deliberate creation of general norms by special central organs began to take its place beside or instead of customary creation and this function was entrusted to an organ which was characterized as the representative of the people or a class of the people. The theoretical distinction between the three powers of the State must be seen against the background of the political doctrine of the separation of powers, which is incorporated in the constitutions of most modern democracies and constitutional monarchies. According to this principle, the creation of general norms — in principle of all the general norms, the "laws" — belongs to the legislative body, either alone or together with the head of State. This principle is, however, subject to certain exceptions.

The creation of general norms by an organ other than the legislative body, namely, by organs of the executive or judicial power, is usually conceived of as an executive or a judicial function.

From a functional point of view, there is no essential difference between these norms and "laws" or statutes (general norms) created by the legislative body. The general norms created by the legislative body are called "statutes" in contradistinction to those general norms which, exceptionally, an organ other than the legislative body — the head of State or other executive or judicial organs — may create. The general norms issued by organs of the executive power are usually not called "statutes" but "ordinances" or "regulations." Regulations or ordinances not issued on the basis of a statute which they put into effect but issued instead of statutes are called *"décrets-lois"* in French, *Verordnungen mit Gesetzeskraft* in German terminology.

From a systematic point of view, it is particularly unsound to refer to the executive function the creation of general norms where, under exceptional circumstances, such norms are created by the head of State instead of the legislative body. The function is here exactly the same as that which is ordinarily performed by the legislative body. A similar impropriety is involved when general norms created by a court are classified as decisions and referred to the judicial function.

A law-creating function not taken into account at all by the usual trichotomy is the creation of general norms by way of custom. The general norms of customary law, although not created by the legislative power, are executed by the organs of the so-called "executive" as well as by the organs of the judicial power. Custom is a law-creating process completely equivalent to the legislative procedure. The customary creation of general legal norms is a *legis latio* just as much as what is ordinarily designated as legislation. The general norms of customary law are applied by the executive power just as are the statutes.

d. The Executive and Judicial Power

It is only as an exception that the organs of the executive and judicial powers create general norms. Their typical task is to create individual norms on the basis of the general norms which are created by legislation and custom, and to put into effect the sanctions stipulated by these general and individual norms. The putting into effect of the sanction is "execution" in the narrowest sense of this term. The administration has — as we shall see later — also other functions to perform than that of enacting individual norms and effectuating (administrative) sanctions.

Insofar as the so-called executive and judicial function consists in the creation of individual norms on the basis of general norms and in the final execution of the individual norms, the legislative power, on the one hand, and the executive and judicial power, on the other, represent only different stages of the process by which the national legal order — according to its own provisions — is created and applied. This is the process by which the law or, what amounts to the same thing, the State, regenerates itself permanently.

The doctrine of the three powers of the State is — juristically — the doctrine of the different stages of the creation and application of the national legal order. Since the law regulates its own creation, the creation of general norms, too, must take place in accordance with other general norms. The legislative process, that is, the creation of general legal norms, is divided into at least two stages: the creation of general norms which is usually called legislation (but comprises also the creation of customary law) and the creation of the general norms regulating this process of legislation. The latter norms form the essential contents of that normative system which is designated as the "constitution."

e. The Constitution

1. The Political Concept of the Constitution

Since the State is here understood as a legal order, the problem of the constitution — which is traditionally treated from the point of view of political theory — finds its natural place in the general theory of law. It has already been treated in the first part of this book from the point of view of the hierarchy of the legal order.

The constitution of the State, usually characterized as its "fundamental law," is the basis of the national legal order. The concept of the constitution, as understood in the theory of law, is, it is true, not quite the same as the corresponding concept of political theory. The former is what we have previously called the constitution in a material sense of the term, covering the norms which regulate the process of legislation.

As used in political theory, the concept is made to embrace also those norms which regulate the creation and the competence of the highest executive and judicial organs.

2. Rigid and Flexible Constitutions

Since the constitution is the basis of the national legal order, it sometimes appears desirable to give it a more stable character than ordinary laws. Hence, a change in the constitution is made more difficult than the enactment or amendment of ordinary laws. Such a constitution is called a rigid, stationary, or inelastic constitution, in contradistinction to a flexible, movable, or elastic one, which may be altered in the same way as ordinary laws. The original constitution of a State is the work of the founders of the State. If the State is created in a democratic way, the first constitution originates in a constituent assembly, what the French call *une constituante*. Sometimes any change in the constitution is outside the competence of the regular legislative organ instituted by the constitution, and reserved for such a *constituante*, a special organ competent only for constitutional amendments. In this case it is customary to distinguish between a constituent power and a legislative power, each being exercised according to different procedures. The device most frequently resorted to in order to render constitutional amendments more difficult is to require a qualified majority (two-thirds or three-fourths) and a higher quorum (the number of the members of the legislative body competent to transact business) than usual. Sometimes, the change has to be decided upon several times before it acquires the force of law. In a federal State, any change of the federal constitution may have to be approved by the legislatures of a certain number of member States. And still other methods exist, too. It is even possible that any amendment of the constitution may be prohibited; and as a matter of fact some historical constitutions declare certain of their provisions, or the entire constitution within a certain space of time, as unamendable. Thus, for instance, Art. 8, Par. 4, of the French Constitution of February 25, 1875 (Article 2 of the Amendment of August 14, 1884) declares: "The Republican form of Government shall not be made the subject of a proposed revision." In these cases it is not possible legally to amend the entire constitution by a legislative act within the fixed time or to amend the specific provision. If the norm of the constitution which renders an amendment more difficult is considered to be binding upon the legislative organ, the norm excluding any amendment has to be considered valid, too. There is no juristic reason to interpret the two norms in different ways, and to declare — as some writers do — a provision forbidding any amendment invalid by its very nature.

Every provision, however, whose purpose it is to render more difficult or even impossible an amendment of the constitution, is efficacious only against amendments carried out by an act of the legislative organ. Even the most rigid constitution is "rigid" only with respect to statutory, not with respect to customary law. There is no legal possibility of preventing a constitution from being modified by way of custom,* even if the constitution has the character of statutory law, if it is a so-called "written" constitution.

The distinction made by traditional theory between "written" and "unwritten" constitutions is, from a juristic point of view, the difference between constitutions the norms of which are created by legislative acts and constitutions whose norms are created by custom. Very often the constitution is composed of norms which have partly the character of statutory and partly the character of customary law.

If there exists a specific procedure for constitutional amendment different from the procedure of ordinary legislation, then general norms whose contents have nothing in common with the constitution (in a material sense) can be created through this special procedure. Such laws can be altered or abolished only in this way. They enjoy the same stability as the rigid constitution. If these laws are considered to be part of the "constitution," this concept of constitution is understood in a purely formal sense. "Constitution" in this sense does not mean norms regulating certain subject matters; it means nothing but a specific procedure of legislation; a certain legal form which may be filled with any legal content.†

3. The Content of the Constitution

As a matter of fact, the constitution, in the formal sense of the word, contains the most diverse elements besides the norms that are constitutional in a material sense. At the same time, there are constitutional norms (in a material sense) which do not appear in the specific form of the constitution, even when there is one.

a. The preamble. A traditional part of the instruments called "constitutions" is a solemn introduction, a so-called "preamble," expressing the political, moral, and religious ideas which the constitution is intended to promote. This preamble usually does not stipulate any definite norms for human behavior and thus lacks legally relevant contents. It has an ideological rather than a juristic character. If it were dropped, the real import of the constitution would ordinarily not be changed in

* Cf. *supra,* p. 119.
† Cf. *supra,* pp. 124f.

the least. The preamble serves to give the constitution a greater dignity and thus a heightened efficacy. Invocation of God and declarations that justice, freedom, equality, and public weal shall be safeguarded are typical of the preamble. Depending upon whether the constitution has a more democratic or a more autocratic tenor, it presents itself in the preamble either as the will of the people or as the will of a ruler installed by the grace of God. Thus the Constitution of the United States of America says: "We, the people of the United States, in order to form [etc.] do ordain and establish this Constitution for the United States of America." However, the people — from whom the constitution claims its origin — comes to legal existence first through the constitution. It can therefore be only in a political, not in a juristic sense that the people is the source of the constitution. It is further obvious that those individuals who actually created the constitution represented only a minute part of the whole people — this even if one takes into consideration those who elected them.

β. *Determination of the contents of future statutes.* The constitution contains certain stipulations not only concerning the organs and the procedure by which future laws are to be enacted, but also concerning the contents of these laws. These stipulations may be either negative or positive. An example of a negative stipulation is the First Amendment to the Constitution of the United States: "Congress shall make no law respecting an establishment of religion, or prohibiting the free exercise thereof, or abridging the freedom of speech or of the press; or the right of the people peaceably to assemble and to petition the government for a redress of grievances." Other examples are the stipulations of Article I, Section 9: "No bill of attainder or *ex post facto* law shall be passed," and "No tax or duty shall be laid on articles exported from any State." The constitution can also determine that laws are to have certain positive contents: thus it may require that if certain matters are regulated by law they must be regulated in the way prescribed by the constitution (which leaves it to the discretion of the legislative organ whether or not these matters shall be regulated) or the constitution, without leaving the legislative organ any discretion, may prescribe that certain matters are to be regulated by the legislative organ and are to be regulated in the way determined by the constitution.

The constitution of the German Reich of 1919 (Weimar Constitution) contains many provisions concerning the contents of future laws. Thus, for instance, Article 121 runs as follows: "By means of legislation, opportunity shall be provided for the physical, mental, and social nurture of illegitimate children, equal to that enjoyed by legitimate children."

Or Article 151: "The organization of economic life must correspond to the principles of justice, and be designed to ensure for all a life worthy of a human being. . . ."

There is a remarkable technical difference between provisions of the constitution forbidding and provisions prescribing a certain content for future laws. The former have, as a rule, legal effects, the latter have not. If the legislative organ issues a law the contents of which are forbidden by the constitution, all the consequences take place which an unconstitutional law entails according to the constitution. If the legislative organ, however, simply omits issuing the law prescribed by the constitution, it is hardly possible to attach legal consequences to such an omission.

γ. *Determination of the administrative and judicial function.* Norms of the constitution need not necessarily be provisions for the legislative organ only. They may be immediately applicable, being direct prescriptions for the administrative and judicial organs, especially the courts. This is the case with the Sixth Amendment to the Constitution of the United States, already mentioned and also with the Seventh Amendment: "In suits at common law, where the value in controversy shall exceed twenty dollars, the right of trial by jury shall be preserved, and no fact tried by a jury shall be otherwise reëxamined in any court of the United States, than according to the rules of the common law." Prescriptions of this kind may be applied by the judicial and administrative organs without any legislative act being interposed between the constitution and the administrative or judicial act executing the constitution directly. They are no part of the constitution in a material sense but of civil, criminal, administrative or procedural law, general norms which in the form of a constitutional provision directly determine the acts of the administrative and judicial organs. They belong to the constitution in the material sense only insofar as they also determine legislation, prescribing a certain content for future statutes.

Negative and positive stipulations concerning future legislation may be combined, as in the Fifth Amendment to the American Constitution: "No person shall . . . be deprived of life, liberty, or property, without due process of law; nor shall private property be taken for public use without just compensation."

δ. *The "unconstitutional" law.* To regulate the contents of future legislation by the constitution is a meaningful legal technique only if changes in the constitution have to take place according to a special procedure different from the ordinary routine of legislation. Only then is a statute that fails to conform with the constitution "unconstitutional," and only then can its "unconstitutionality" have any legal consequences.*

* Cf. *supra*, pp. 155ff.

If the constitution can be changed in the same way as an ordinary stat-ute, then any "unconstitutional" statute really means a change in the constitution, at least for the sphere of validity of this statute. Then a conflict between a statute and the constitution has the same character as a conflict between a new and an old statute. It is a conflict which has to be solved according to the principle *lex posterior derogat priori.*

If there is no special procedure prescribed for constitutional legisla-tion, there can not exist any "unconstitutional" law, just as there can not exist an "unlawful" law. Suppose that a constitution that may be changed as an ordinary statute prescribes that "no soldier shall in time of peace be quartered in any house without the consent of the owner" (a stipulation in the Third Amendment to the Constitution of the United States). If now a statute were enacted that ignored this pre-scription, the statute would by no means be "contrary to the consti-tution," because the statute would itself change the constitution. A prescription like the one just mentioned would bind only the executive and judicial organs, not the legislative organ.

ε. *Constitutional prohibitions.* In order to see clearly the legal sig-nificance of prohibitions directed by the constitution against the organs of the legislative, executive, and judicial powers, provisions of the con-stitution forbidding these organs to encroach upon certain interests of the subjects (such as the Fifth Amendment to the Constitution of the United States: "No private property shall be taken for public use without just compensation," or the Eighth Amendment: "Excessive bail shall not be required, nor excessive fines imposed, nor cruel and unusual punishments inflicted,") one must notice the following fact: the organs of the legisla-tive, executive, and judicial powers are incapable of functioning without being authorized by a general legal norm, whether it be a customary or statutory law. It may be a norm that in quite general terms merely authorizes the organ to act on its own discretion. But at any rate, every action on the part of the organ must be based upon some general norm stipulating at least that the organ has to act, even if it does not tell how the organ has to act, leaving to the organ's discretion the determination of its own actions. In this way the constitution, as a rule, determines the function of the legislative organ. It authorizes a certain organ to legis-late, without determining the contents of this function; but exception-ally the contents of the statute to be enacted may, also, be prescribed by the constitution. The legislative organ, too, is thus in reality an executive organ. Every legislative act is an act of executing the constitu-tion. Otherwise, legislation could not be recognized as a function and the legislator as an organ of the State.

It is therefore self-evident that there can be an "executive" power in the usual sense only if there is some general norm — some statute or rule of customary law — to be executed. Also the judicial power is executive in this sense, for the court, too, is an organ of the State and it functions as an organ of the State only if it executes a norm of the legal order. An individual acts as a State organ only insofar as he acts upon authorization by some valid norm. This is the difference between the individual and the State as acting persons; and that means, between the individual acting not as State organ and the individual acting as State organ. An individual who does not function as a State organ is allowed to do whatever he is not forbidden to do by the legal order, whereas the State, that is, an individual who functions as a State organ, can do only what the legal order authorizes him to do. It is, therefore, from the point of view of legal technique, superfluous to forbid a State organ anything. It suffices not to authorize it. If an individual acts without authorization from the legal order, he no longer acts as an organ of the State. His act is illegal for this reason alone that it is not backed up by any legal authorization. It is not required that the act be forbidden by a legal norm. It is necessary to forbid an organ to perform certain acts only when one wishes to restrict a previous authorization. Thus, the constitution normally gives the legislative organ an unlimited authority to create general norms. In order to prevent norms of a certain kind from being created by the legislative organ, the constitution therefore has explicitly to prohibit their creation. The organs of the executive and judicial powers, on the other hand, do not normally have any unlimited competence of creating individual norms. They are merely authorized to execute statutes and norms of customary law. Even if the constitution did not forbid the executive and judicial organs to require excessive bail, to impose unreasonable fines, or to inflict cruel and unusual punishments, these organs could not legally do any of these things unless they were explicitly authorized to do so by some statute or rule of customary law.

The stipulation in the Fifth Amendment, quoted above, is, however, not a pure prohibition. It implies that private property may be taken for public use on just compensation. As such a positive authorization the stipulation is not at all superfluous, and it has significance also relative to the executive and judicial organs.

That no State organ can act without positive authorization from the legal order does not, as one might think, hold only for democratic States. It is true also of an autocratic State, for instance, an absolute monarchy. The constitution — the absolute monarchy, too, has a constitution, because every State has a constitution — here gives the monarch an almost unlimited authority to issue, not only general, but also individual norms and to perform coercive acts, so that every act of the monarch or of an organ authorized by him appears as an act of the State if it presents itself as such. The constitution of the absolute monarchy is chiefly characterized by this extensive competence of the executive power vested in the person of the monarch. If there exists such a wide competence of the executive power, the subjects can be protected against certain encroachments on the part of the organs of this power by means of constitutional prohibitions directed to these organs. In the historical process, in which democracies have developed out of absolute monarchies, constitutional prohibitions directed to the organs of the executive power have played an important role. This explains why this legal technique has been preserved even under circumstances which rendered it superfluous to direct constitutional prohibitions to organs of the executive power, since these organs no longer have an unlimited competence.

In a modern democracy, where the organs of the executive and judicial power can act only on the basis of a positive legal authorization, constitutional prohibitions directed toward these organs are justified not only if they have the effect of restricting a competence previously conferred upon them, but also if they are intended to render more difficult the extension of their competence with respect to certain acts. The constitutional prohibitions have the desired effect only if they are directed also to the legislative organ, and if the constitution is a rigid, not a flexible, one.

The prohibitions are sometimes stated in the form that interference with certain interests of the individual are forbidden except when they are provided for "by law." Thus, the Third Amendment to the Constitution of the United States says: "No soldier shall, in time of peace, be quartered in any house without the consent of the owner, nor in time of war, but in a manner to be prescribed by law." Such a stipulation is superfluous since the organs of the executive power can never act without authorization by "law," this term comprising statutory and customary law. Constitutions often establish freedom of speech by saying that freedom of speech is granted "within the limits of the law," or that this freedom can "be restricted only by law." Even if the constitution does not expressly state such a restriction, many jurists are inclined to interpret the constitution in this way. However, if the "freedom" or the "right" granted by the constitution can be restricted or even abolished by a simple law, the constitutional norm granting the "freedom" or the "right" is in reality without value. The purpose of a constitutional norm granting a particular freedom or right is precisely that of preventing the organs of the executive power from being authorized by simple law to encroach upon the sphere of interest determined by the "freedom" or the "right." Without authorization by law, they cannot act at all.

When the constitution delegates to ordinary legislation the power to restrict or to abolish a prohibition established by the constitution, it takes
back with one hand what it pretended to give with the other. A typical
example of such a provision is Article 112 of the Weimar Constitution,
which runs as follows: "Every German is entitled to emigrate to countries outside the Reich. Emigration may be restricted only by law of the
Reich." The expression "only" by law of the Reich is misleading, for
without such a law emigration cannot legally be restricted.* By such
provisions the illusion of a constitutional guarantee is created where in
reality there is none.

ζ. *Bill of rights.* A catalogue of freedoms or rights of the citizens is
a typical part of modern constitutions. The so-called "Bill of Rights"
contained in the first ten Amendments to the Constitution of the United
States is an example. These amendments mostly have the character
of prohibitions and commands addressed to the organs of the legislative,
executive, and judicial powers. They give the individual a right in the
technical sense of the word only if he has a possibility of going to law
against the unconstitutional act of the organ, especially if he can put into
motion a procedure leading to the annulment of the unconstitutional act.
This possibility can be given him only by positive law, and consequently
the rights themselves can only be such as are founded in positive law.

This, however, was not the view of the Fathers of the American Constitution. They believed in certain natural inborn rights, which exist independent of the positive legal order and which this order has only to
protect — rights of individuals which the State has to respect under any
circumstances, since these rights correspond to the nature of man and
their protection to the nature of any true community. This theory —
the theory of natural law — was current in the eighteenth century. It
is clearly expressed in the Ninth Amendment: "The enumeration in the
Constitution of certain rights shall not be construed to deny or disparage
others retained by the people." By this, the authors of the Constitution
meant to say that there are certain rights which may neither be expressed in the constitution nor in the positive legal order founded thereupon. Nevertheless, the effect of this stipulation, from the point of view
of positive law, is to authorize the State organs who have to execute
the constitution, especially the courts, to stipulate other rights than those
established by the text of the constitution. A right so stipulated is
also granted by the constitution, not directly, but indirectly, since it

* Article 112 cannot be considered as necessary because it excludes restriction of
emigration by laws of the member-States. According to Article 6 the Reich has exclusive legislation as regards emigration, so that legislation of the member-States in
this matter has already been excluded by this Article and need not be excluded by
Article 112.

is stipulated by a law-creating act of an organ authorized by the constitution. Such a right is thus no more "natural" than any other right countenanced by the positive legal order. All natural law is turned into positive law as soon as it is recognized and applied by the organs of the State on the basis of constitutional authorization. Only as positive law is it relevant in juristic considerations.

η. *Guarantees of the constitution.* The essential function of the constitution in the material sense of the term is to determine the creation of general legal norms, that is, to determine the organs and the procedure of legislation and also — to some degree — the contents of future laws. Thus the problem arises how to assure observance of these provisions of the constitution, how to guarantee the constitutionality of laws. This is a special case of the more general problem of guaranteeing that a lower norm shall conform with the higher norm which determines its creation or contents. We have already discussed this problem in the chapter on the hierarchy of the legal order. As the result of our examination, we have established that positive law knows two methods for securing concordance between the lower and the higher norm. The legal order may provide for a procedure by which the lower norm can be tested as to its conformity with the higher norm, and abolished if it is found to be lacking in such conformity. The legal order can also make the organ that creates an illegal norm liable to personal sanction. Either method may be used in isolation, or they can both be applied simultaneously. In the case of unconstitutional laws, the former method is almost exclusively employed; the members of the legislative body are seldom made personally responsible for the violation of the constitution by adopting an unconstitutional law.

Examination and abolition of a law because of its unconstitutionality may take place according to several methods.* There are two important types of procedure in which an unconstitutional law can be tried and abolished. The organ that has to apply the law in a concrete case can be authorized to examine it as to its constitutionality and to refuse to apply it in the concrete case if it is found unconstitutional. If the power to examine the constitutionality of laws is conferred upon courts, we speak of judicial review of legislation. The examination of the law can be undertaken by the competent organ, especially by the court, either *ex officio* or upon a petition of a party in a lawsuit in which the law is to be applied. By refusing to apply the law to the concrete case, the organ invalidates it, not generally, that is, not for all possible cases to which the law is to be applied according to its own contents, but in-

* Cf. my article *Judicial Review of Legislation: A Comparative Study of the Austrian and the American Constitution* (1942) 4 J. OF POLITICS 183f.

dividually only, that is, for the one case at hand. The law as such remains valid and applicable to other cases, if not again declared unconstitutional and abolished for the concrete case. If the legal order does not contain any explicit rule to the contrary, there is a presumption that every law-applying organ has this power of refusing to apply unconstitutional laws. Since the organs are entrusted with the task of applying "laws," they naturally have to investigate whether a rule proposed for application really has the nature of a law. Only a restriction of this power is in need of explicit provision. Although the power of a law-applying organ to examine the constitutionality of laws to be applied to concrete cases, and to refuse the application of a law recognized by it as unconstitutional, can never be completely eliminated, it can be restricted in different degrees. The law-applying organ can, for instance, be entitled to investigate only whether the norm which has to be applied to a concrete case was actually passed by the legislative organ; or whether the norm has been created by a legislative or executive organ competent to issue general legal norms. If that is found to be the case, the law-applying organ may have no further right to dispute the constitutionality of the norm.

If the unlimited power of testing laws as to their constitutionality is reserved for one organ alone, for instance for the supreme court, this organ may be authorized to abolish an unconstitutional law, not only individually, that is, for the concrete case, but generally, for all possible cases. The unconstitutional law may be generally abolished by an express decision pronouncing its annulment; or in the way that the court refuses to apply the law in the concrete case on the professed ground of its unconstitutionality, and that this decision is then given the status of a precedent, so that all other law-applying organs, especially all the courts, are bound to refuse the application of the law. The annulment of a law is a legislative function, an act — so to speak — of negative legislation. A court which is competent to abolish laws — individually or generally — functions as a negative legislator.

The power to examine the laws as to their constitutionality and to invalidate unconstitutional laws may be conferred, as a more or less exclusive function, on a special constitutional court, while the other courts have only the right to make applications to the constitutional court for examination and annulment of laws which they have to apply, but which they consider to be unconstitutional. This solution of the problem means a centralization of the judicial review of legislation.

The possibility of a law issued by the legislative organ being annulled by another organ constitutes a remarkable restriction of the former's power. Such a possibility means that there is, besides the positive, a negative legislator, an organ which may be composed according to a totally different principle from that of the parliament elected by the people. Then an antagonism between the two legislators, the positive and the negative, is almost inevitable. This antagonism may be lessened by providing that the members of the constitutional court shall be elected by parliament.*

III. THE SEPARATION OF POWERS

A. The Concept of "Separation of Powers"

The judicial review of legislation is an obvious encroachment upon the principle of separation of powers. This principle lies at the basis of the American Constitution and is considered to be a specific element of democracy. It has been formulated as follows by the Supreme Court of the United States: "that all the powers intrusted to government, whether State or national, are divided into the three grand departments, the executive, the legislative and the judicial. That the functions appropriate to each of these branches of government shall be vested in a separate body of public servants, and that the perfection of the system requires that the lines which separate and divide these departments shall be broadly and clearly defined. It is also essential to the successful working of this system that the persons intrusted with power in any one of these branches shall not be permitted to encroach upon the powers confided to the others, but that each shall by the law of its creation be limited to the exercise of the powers appropriate to its own department and no other." †

The concept of "separation of powers" designates a principle of political organization. It presupposes that the three so-called powers can be determined as three distinct coördinated functions of the State, and that it is possible to define boundary lines separating each of these three functions from the others. But this presupposition is not borne out by the facts. As we have seen, there are not three but two basic functions of the State: creation and application (execution) of law, and these functions are not coördinated but sub- and supra-ordinated. Further, it is not possible to define boundary lines separating these functions from each other, since the distinction between creation and application of law — underlying the dualism of legislative and executive power (in the broadest sense) — has only a relative character, most acts of State being at the same time law-creating and law-applying acts. It is impossible to assign

---

* Cf. my article *Judicial Review of Legislation* 187f.
† Kilbourn v. Thompson, 103 U.S. 168, 190f. (1880).

the creation of law to one organ and the application (execution) of law to another so exclusively that no organ would fulfill both functions simultaneously. It is hardly possible, and at any rate not desirable, to reserve even legislation — which is only a certain kind of law-creation — to a "separate body of public servants," and to exclude all the other organs from this function.

B. Separation of the Legislative from the Executive Power

a. Priority of the So-called Legislative Organ

By "legislation" as a function we can hardly understand anything other than the creation of general legal norms. An organ is a legislative organ insofar as it is authorized to create general legal norms. It never occurs in political reality that all the general norms of a national legal order have to be created exclusively by one organ designated as legislator. There is no legal order of a modern State according to which the courts and administrative authorities are excluded from creating general legal norms, that is, from legislating, and legislating not only on the basis of statutes and customary law, but also directly on the basis of the constitution. What counts practically is only an organization of the legislative function according to which all the general norms have to be created either by the organ called "legislative" or on the basis of an authorization on the part of this organ by other organs which are classified as organs of the executive or judicial power. The general norms created by these organs are called ordinances or regulations or have specific designation; but functionally they have the same character as statutes enacted by an organ called legislator. The habit of characterizing only one organ as "legislative" organ, of calling the general norms created by this organ "laws" or "statutes," is justified, however, to a certain extent if this organ has a certain prerogative in creating general norms. This is the case if all the other organs may enact general norms only on the basis of an authorization emanating from the so-called legislative organ. Then the so-called legislative organ is the source of all general norms, in part directly and in part indirectly through organs to which it delegates legislative competence.

b. Legislative Function of the Chief of the Executive Department

Most constitutions that are supposed to embody the principle of the separation of powers authorize the head of the executive department to enact general norms in place of the legislative organ, without a special authorization emanating from this organ in the form of an "authorizing statute" (*Ermächtigungsgesetz*), when special circumstances are present, such as war, rebellion, or economic crisis. Besides the ordinary legislative organ, these constitutions thus countenance an extraordinary legislative organ, from which only the designation "legislative" is withheld.

The legislative competence vested in the head of the executive department is sometimes very extensive. He can be capable of regulating matters that, as one says, have not before been regulated either by statutes or by customary law. This formula determining the legislative competence of the chief of State is, however, not quite correct. If there is any legal order at all, consisting of statutory or customary law, there are no matters that are not legally regulated. Such a thing as a legal *vacuum* is impossible. If the legal order does not obligate the individuals to a certain behavior, the individuals are legally free; they cannot legally be forced to behave in that way. Whoever attempts to force them thereto commits a delict himself, and that means that he violates existing law. Insofar as the legal order is silent it constitutes a sphere of individual liberty. This sphere is protected and hence regulated by the legal order obligating the State organs not to encroach upon this sphere. Only on the authority of a norm are the State organs allowed to interfere with the freedom of the individual; but every such norm means that the individual is obligated to observe a certain behavior, that his sphere of liberty is restricted. If the chief of State is authorized by the constitution to regulate by an ordinance subject matters which have not before been regulated by the legal order, the subject matters intended are those which have not before been regulated positively, that is to say, by norms imposing legal duties upon the subjects, but which have been regulated negatively because they fall within a legally protected sphere of liberty of the individuals. What the inadequate description aims at is the fact that the head of the executive department can be competent to regulate matters that before have not in any way been subject to positive regulation.

The vesting of such a competence in the head of the executive department usually does not mean that the ordinary legislative body is deprived of the possibility of regulating those same matters positively. Usually the head of the executive department is competent to regulate them only as long as the legislative organ fails to do so. He loses his competence as soon as the legislative organ submits the matter to a regulation of its own.

The head of the executive department exercises a legislative function when he has a right to prevent by veto norms decided upon by the legislative organ from becoming laws, or when such norms cannot become laws without first receiving his approval. His veto can be either absolute or suspensive. In the latter case, a new decision by the legislative organ is necessary to give a bill the force of law. The head of the executive department, in fact, fulfills a legislative function even from the mere fact that he may have a right to take the initiative in the legislative procedure, to submit a bill to the legislative organ. This right appertains sometimes to the cabinet and to every cabinet minister within his own sphere of competence. Such participation in legislation by the head of the executive department or by the cabinet is provided even by constitutions which are based upon the principle of the separation of powers.

c. Legislative Function of the Judiciary

We have already seen that courts fulfill a legislative function when authorized to annul unconstitutional laws. They do so also when they are competent to annul a regulation on the ground that it appears to be contrary to a law, or — as is sometimes the case — that it seems "unreasonable." In the latter case, the legislative function of courts is especially obvious.

Courts further exercise a legislative function when their decision in a concrete case becomes a precedent for the decision of other similar cases. A court with this competence creates by its decision a general norm which is on a level with statutes originating with the so-called legislative organ.

Where customary law is valid, the creation of general norms is not reserved for the so-called legislative organ even in the sense that other organs can create such norms only upon authorization from the former. Custom is a method of creating general norms that is a genuine alternative to legislation. As to the effect of their legal function, custom and legislation are in no way different. Customary and statutory law are equally obligating for the individual.

C. Not Separation but Distribution of Powers

Thus one can hardly speak of any separation of legislation from the other functions of the State in the sense that the so-called "legislative" organ — to the exclusion of the so-called "executive" and "judicial" organs — would alone be competent to exercise this function. The appearance of such a separation exists because only those general norms that are created by the "legislative" organ are designated as "laws" (leges). Even when the constitution expressly maintains the principle of the separation of powers, the legislative function — one and the same function, and not two different functions — is distributed among several organs, but only one of them is given the name of "legislative" organ. This organ never has a monopoly on the creation of general norms, but at most a certain favored position such as was previously characterized. Its designation as legislative organ is the more justified the greater the part it has in the creation of general norms.

D. Separation of the Judicial from the Executive (Administrative) Power

a. *Nature of the Judicial Function*

A separation of the judicial from the so-called executive power is also possible only in a comparatively limited measure. A strict separation of the two powers is impossible, since the two types of activity usually designated by these terms are not essentially distinct functions. The judicial function is in fact executive in exactly the same sense as the function which is ordinarily described by this word; the judicial function, too, consists in the execution of general norms. What particular kind of execution of general norms is called "judicial"? The question can be answered only by a description of the typical activities of the civil and criminal courts.

The judicial function consists, essentially, of two acts. In each concrete case (1) the court establishes the presence of a fact that is qualified as a civil or criminal delict by a general norm to be applied to the given case; and (2) the court orders a concrete civil or criminal sanction stipulated generally in the norm to be applied. The judicial procedure usually has the form of a controversy between two parties. One party claims that the law has been violated by the other party, or that the other party is responsible for a violation of law committed by another individual, and the other party denies that this is the case. The judicial decision is the decision of a controversy. From the point of view of the general norm which has to be executed by the judicial function, the controversial character of the judicial procedure is of secondary importance. Especially in the procedure of criminal courts, the controversial character is obviously a mere formality. It would also be a mistake to characterize the judicial function as a procedure by which obligations and rights of the contesting parties are determined. The decisive point is that obligations and rights of the parties are determined by establishing that a delict has been committed and by ordering a sanction. The court primarily establishes that a (civil or criminal) delict has been committed and decides upon a sanction. Only secondarily are obligations and rights of the parties determined thereby.

b. Judicial Function of the Organs of the Executive Power
(Administration)

The organs of the "executive" power frequently serve the same function as the courts. Public administration is based upon administrative law, as the jurisdiction of courts is based upon civil and criminal law. As a matter of fact, administrative law, which developed later than civil and criminal law, has more the character of statutory than of customary law. The legal basis of public administration is furnished by administrative statutes. Like civil and criminal law, administrative law tries to bring about a certain behavior by attaching a coercive act, administrative sanction, to the opposite behavior, the administrative delict. As in civil and criminal law, the sanction provided by administrative law is forcible deprivation of property or freedom. Taxation laws, for instance, stipulate that every individual with a given income must pay a certain tax and that, in case of his failure to do so, a coercive measure must be taken against his property. Sanitary laws, again, determine that, in case of certain contagious diseases, certain individuals must give notice to certain sanitary authorities, and are to be punished in case they do not. The production and sale of alcoholic beverages is, according to some trade regulations, permitted only upon special license, granted by administrative authorities, and whoever produces or sells such beverages without the required license is to be punished. The execution of these administrative laws is, according to many legal orders, conferred upon so-called administrative authorities, that is, organs which are not designated as courts because they do not belong to the body of officials conventionally called the judiciary. The administrative authorities alone are competent to enforce these laws, they alone have to establish whether an administrative delict has been committed, and they alone have to inflict the administrative sanction. This function of the administrative organs is exactly the same as the function of the courts, although the latter is called "judicial," and the former "executive" or "administrative." The cases settled by the administrative organs have the same character as those settled by the civil or criminal courts. They may even be conceived of as controversies. That in this respect there exists no essential difference between the so-called judicial and the so-called administrative functions may be shown by the fact that the excessive use made in the United States of the courts for the settlement of controversies has led here to a program of removing whole categories of cases from the courts and vesting their handling in administrative authorities.* Such a

---

* Cf. W. F. WILLOUGHBY, PRINCIPLES OF JUDICIAL ADMINISTRATION (1929) 18.

transfer of competence from courts to administrative organs is possible only insofar as the functions of both are identical.

c. Independence of Judges

Even where the administrative function has the same character as the judicial function, the legal position and procedure of the courts may differ from those of the administrative organs. The judges are, for instance, ordinarily "independent," that is, they are subject only to the laws and not to the orders (instructions) of superior judicial or administrative organs. Administrative authorities, however, are mostly not independent. If the administration is organized hierarchically, the administrative organs are bound by commands from higher organs. But this differentiation does not always exist. Where the administration is not hierarchic, its organs are independent too. And even when the administration is hierarchic, not only the highest administrative organs but also others are quite often independent. Nevertheless, they are not considered to be "courts."

Where the function of the administrative organ is the same as the function of the courts, the administrative procedure is as a matter of fact more, or less similar to the judicial procedure. At any rate, there is a clear tendency to render the administrative procedure similar to the judicial one.

Thus there does not exist any clear-cut separation of the judicial and executive powers as an organic separation of two different functions. One identical function is distributed among different bureaucratic machines, the existence and different denominations of which can be explained only on historical grounds. Differences in the respective position of the organs and in their procedures likewise are not derived from any difference of function but permit only of an historical explanation.

d. The Specific Administrative Function: the Administrative Act

The administrative organs, however, have to undertake certain actions that are not usually performed by the courts. The taxation authority, for instance, has to establish that an individual has a certain income and then order him to pay the corresponding tax. Only in case the individual does not comply with this administrative order is the procedure initiated in which the taxation authority exercises the same function as a court. In order to execute the administrative law concerning the production and sale of alcoholic beverages, the competent administrative authority has to grant or refuse to grant the license provided by the law. If an individual attempts to produce or sell such beverages without the necessary license, the administrative authority may order him to cease his illegal enterprise before the authority initiates the procedure of penal admin-istrative law in which it exercises the same function as a criminal court.

Such orders enacted by administrative organs, such licenses granted or refused by them, are acts entirely distinct from the acts constituting the specific judicial function. They correspond to the legal transactions of civil law. The specific administrative acts, such as the administrative order or the license, differ from legal transactions in that the former can only be acts of State organs, whereas the latter may be, and normally are, acts of private individuals, and the prototype of the former is a unilateral declaration of will, whereas the prototype of the latter is the contract. But there exist in administrative law also contracts, so-called administrative contracts which are concluded between an administrative authority and a private individual and the non-fulfillment of which is prosecuted in administrative procedure before an administrative author-ity. Contracts of appointment fall within this category. (Since the ap-pointment of a public servant usually requires his explicit acceptance, appointments as a rule take the form of contracts.) The differences that might exist between the contracts of administrative law and those of civil law are not important in this connection. Noteworthy is only the fact that controversies arising from an administrative contract may be settled by administrative authorities, rather than by courts.

e. *Administration under the Control of the Judiciary*

The principle of the separation of powers would be satisfied if the administrative organs were limited to the specific administrative acts described in the foregoing paragraph, and if the specific judicial function — establishing the delict and ordering the sanction — were reserved for the courts. (By the "courts" we here understand the organs belonging to that historically developed bureaucratic machinery which has to apply "civil" and "criminal" law and which is usually designated as the "judi-ciary.") Within such an organization, the relationship between the ad-ministrative organs and the courts would have the following character: A taxation authority, for instance, would issue tax orders in accordance with the law. But in case an individual failed to comply with the order, the administrative authority — like a private creditor — would have to prosecute him before a court. It would be for the court to establish that the taxation law had been violated by the defendant, and to inflict the sanction provided by the law. Again, an administrative organ would have to grant licenses for the production and sale of alcoholic beverages; and if an individual were to enter upon such production and sale without the requisite license, the same administrative authority could request him to cease his illegal activity. But in order to have the occurrence of the delict ascertained and a punishment inflicted the administrative organ would have to turn to a court for assistance. Likewise, only a court would be competent to settle disputes arising out of a contract between an administrative organ and a private party. Public administration would be only a very subordinate agency in the whole process of government.* The State, represented through its administrative organs, would be in the same position as a private individual before the courts.

This ideal, which is part of the liberal conception of the State, has prevailed within English and American law longer than within the law of the European continent (especially French and German law). But the ideal has never been completely realized. In every legal order, there are cases where other organs than the courts have to exercise judicial functions, have to establish the occurrence of a delict and order the sanction stipulated by the law. Taxation and police authorities especially are almost everywhere called upon to fulfill judicial or quasi-judicial functions. As soon as the legal order authorizes the public administration to interfere more extensively by its specific acts with economic and cultural life, the tendency arises to refer to the administrative organs also the judicial function that is organically connected with the specific administrative function.

f. Close Connection between the Administrative and the Judicial Function

The specific acts of administration are, it is true, distinct from those of the judiciary. But, like private legal transactions, the administrative acts are part of the conditions to which general legal norms attach sanctions. Simplified, the general norm of civil law says: If two parties conclude a contract, and if one party breaks it and if the other party brings a suit against him, then the court must ascertain the breach of contract by the defendant and, if the breach is ascertained, must inflict upon him a civil sanction. The general norm of administrative law, likewise simplified, runs as follows: If an administrative organ issues an order to an individual and the individual fails to comply therewith, then an administrative organ (the same or another) shall establish this administrative delict and inflict the administrative sanction upon the delinquent. Or: If an individual exercises a certain trade without having received a license from the competent administrative organ, this (or another) administrative organ shall inflict an administrative punishment upon the delinquent. Or: If an administrative organ concludes an administrative contract with a private party and one of the contracting

* Cf. Roscoe Pound, *Organization of Courts* (1927) 11 J. OF THE AM. JUDICATURE SOCIETY 69–70.

parties breaks the contract, and the other party files suit against the former, an administrative organ different from that which is a party to the contract shall ascertain the breach of the contract and order the sanction provided.

The specific administrative function can fulfill its purpose only in co-operation with the specific judicial function. It is therefore quite natural to entrust the judicial function, insofar as the latter is in organic connection with a specific administrative function, to administrative organs. When, for instance, the legal order authorizes the administrative organs to issue commands, and obligates individuals to obey these administrative commands, or when the legal order obligates the individuals not to exercise certain trades without licenses, then it is only consistent not to lessen the authority of the administrative organs by conferring the enforcement of the administrative obligations of the individuals affected upon other than administrative organs, that is, upon courts.

g. Administrative Procedure

The actual organization and procedure of the courts give a stronger guarantee of legality than do those of the administrative organs. This is no doubt the reason why it is thought necessary to refer to the courts the judicial function connected with the administrative function. But there is nothing to prevent us from giving the public administration, insofar as it exercises a judicial function, the same organization and procedure as have the courts. Sanctions are coercive acts, and sanctions inflicted upon individuals by administrative organs are certainly encroachments upon the property, freedom, and even life of the citizens. If the constitution prescribes that no interference with the property, freedom, or life of the individual may take place except by "due process of law," this does not necessarily entail a monopoly of the courts on the judicial function. The administrative procedure in which a judicial function is exercised can be formed in such a way that it corresponds to the ideal of "due process of law."

E. COERCIVE ACTS OF THE ADMINISTRATIVE ORGANS

According to most legal orders, and especially according to legal orders recognizing the principle of the separation of powers, administrative organs are authorized to interfere with the property or freedom of the individual in a summary procedure, when such interference is the only way of quickly averting dangers to public safety. In all civilized States, administrative organs are thus authorized to evacuate forcibly inhabitants of houses that threaten to collapse, to demolish buildings in order to stop the spread of fires, to slaughter cattle stricken with certain diseases, to intern individuals whose physical or mental condition is a danger to the health or life of their fellow citizens. It is especially the police that are empowered to carry out such coercive acts. These acts are often no less important to the individuals concerned than sanctions executed in a judicial procedure or coercive acts preparatory to such sanctions as, e.g., the imprisonment of individuals accused or suspected of a crime.

These coercive acts — to which administrative organs, especially organs of the police, are authorized — differ from sanctions, and coercive acts preparatory to sanctions, in that they are not conditioned by a certain human conduct against which the coercive act, as a sanction, is directed. They are conditioned by other circumstances. The fact that a building is on the verge of collapsing, not the conduct of its owner or its inhabitants, is the condition of the forcible removal of the latter; the fact that an individual is afflicted with a contagious disease or insanity, not a particular action or omission of his, is the condition of his forcible internment in a hospital or asylum. Since sanctions are conditioned by a certain human behavior, they can be avoided by the contrary behavior. Since the coercive acts in question are not conditioned by human behavior, they cannot be avoided by the individuals concerned nor are they supposed to be. These encroachments upon the property or freedom of the individuals are not sanctions, but they would be delicts if they were not stipulated by law. By authorizing administrative organs to perform such coercive acts which are not sanctions the legal order makes an exception to the rule that coercive measures are allowed only as sanctions.

F. Direct and Indirect Administration

These coercive acts of administration which do not have the character of sanctions in fact represent an executive function that is clearly distinct from the judicial. Their peculiarity consists in the fact that the desired behavior is brought about by obligating organs of the State (in the material sense of the word), not private individuals. This kind of administration can be called direct as opposed to indirect administration. Acts of direct administration need not necessarily be coercive acts. Any activity whatsoever can occur as direct administration by the State. The following example may serve to illustrate the general distinction between direct and indirect administration: When citizens of a district are obliged by an administrative statute to build and maintain a public road, and administrative agencies are authorized to punish citizens who do not fulfill this obligation, this is indirect administration. But when the road has to be built and maintained by organs of the State, that is to say, when the actions desirable from the point of view of public administration are duties of State officials, the administration is direct.

While the function of indirect administration has the same character as the judicial function, direct administration is of an essentially different nature. Even the latter, however, remains within the boundaries of the specific technique of law, insofar as it attains its aim by obligating individuals. The difference between the two kinds of administration lies only in the legal quality of the individuals obligated.

It is worth mentioning that the coercive measures decided upon by the courts are actually carried out by administrative organs, such as the inspectors of a prison, executioners, and others. These are not considered as "judges" in spite of the fact that their function certainly is an organic part of the judicial function.

G. Legal Control of Administration by Ordinary or by Administrative Courts

When administrative organs have to turn to an ordinary court for the enforcement of the administrative law, it may be within the competence of the court to examine not only the constitutionality of the law but also the legality or even the usefulness of the administrative act. The court has this competence even when the administrative organ itself has a judicial function, since although the administrative organ has to establish the occurrence of the delict and to decide upon the sanction the individual against whom the decision is directed may appeal to a court. The legal control of the administration need not be in the hands of the ordinary courts; it may be exercised by special administrative courts.

The fact that control of administration by courts is considered to be necessary throws a clear light on the shortcomings of the theory of the separation of powers. This principle would seem to require that none of the three powers should be controlled by any of the other two. It is nevertheless the principle of the separation of powers which is invoked to justify the strictest control of administration by courts, a state which is reached where the administrative organs have to turn to the courts for enforcement of the administrative laws.

H. Control of Legislation by Courts

When courts are competent to examine not only individual administrative measures but also administrative regulations and administrative laws, then these legislative functions are actually under the control of courts. As pointed out, such a control is not compatible with the principle of the separation of powers. Yet the judicial review of legislation as a prerogative of the courts is instituted by those very constitutions which especially stress this principle. By this type of organization, a certain distrust of the legislative and executive organs is expressed. It is characteristic of the constitutional monarchy, which arose by restricting the power of the absolute monarch. In the field of the judiciary, this tendency was most successful. As a result, the courts gained independence, which was originally independence from the monarch. Within the legislative domain, he retained a stronger influence. He remained the legislator, although he could no longer function without the concurrence of parliament. Even in this field, however, the influence of parliament steadily increased and finally surpassed that of the erstwhile all-powerful monarch. Within the field of the so-called executive power, the monarch maintained more of his original position than he did in the other fields. This historical development explains the privileged position of the courts within the political system, their prerogative to control legislation and administration, the deep-rooted belief that the rights of the individuals can be protected only by the judicial branch of the government, the view — characteristic especially of the English law — that the concurrence of a court, as an authority independent of the legislator, must be obtained before the expression of the latter's will can become a rule of conduct.*

The control of legislation and administration by courts has a clear political meaning within a constitutional monarchy. Here it effectuates the tendency to have two branches of government, where the influence of the monarch still prevails, controlled by organs which are independent of him. The so-called judicial power works as a kind of counterweight to the legislative and executive power. The wish to establish such a balance was one of the prime movers in the evolution of the constitutional monarchy out of the absolute monarchy.

I. The Historical Role of the "Separation of Powers"

It was, therefore, a mistake to describe the fundamental principle of the constitutional monarchy as the "separation of powers." The functions that were originally combined in the monarch's person have not been "separated" but rather each one of them has been divided between monarch, parliament, and courts. The legislative, executive, and judicial "powers," which those formulating the principle of separation had in mind, are not three logically distinct functions of the State but the competences which parliament, monarch, and courts have historically ob-

* F. J. Goodnow, *The Principles of the Administrative Law of the United States* (1905) pp. 11–12.

tained in the so-called constitutional monarchy. The historical significance of the principle called "separation of powers" lies precisely in the
fact that it works against a concentration rather than for a separation
of powers. The control of the legislative and executive functions by the
courts means that legislative, executive, and judicial functions are combined in the competence of the courts. Thus, this control implies that
the legislative and executive powers are divided between the so-called
legislative and executive organs on the one hand, and the courts, on the
other. Likewise, the participation of the monarch in legislation means
that his competence includes both legislative and executive functions,
and thus that the legislative power is divided between monarch and parliament. The fact that, in a constitutional monarchy, the head of the
executive department is not responsible to the parliament, is a remainder
of the absolute monarchy and not — as one might be inclined to assume
— an application of the principle of separation, which in reality is a
principle of division of powers. A concession to this principle is the provision that the acts of the monarch have to be countersigned by his cabinet
ministers who are responsible to the parliament. Thus, parliament, although an organ of legislation, has control over the administration.

J. Separation of Powers and Democracy

The principle of a separation of powers understood literally or interpreted as a principle of division of powers is not essentially democratic.
Corresponding to the idea of democracy, on the contrary, is the notion
that all power should be concentrated in the people; and where not
direct but only indirect democracy is possible, that all power should be
exercised by one collegiate organ the members of which are elected by
the people and which should be legally responsible to the people. If this
organ has only legislative functions, the other organs that have to execute the norms issued by the legislative organ should be responsible to
the latter, even if they themselves are elected by the people, too. It is
the legislative organ which is most interested in a strict execution of the
general norms it has issued. Control of the organs of the executive and
judicial functions by the organs of the legislative function corresponds
to the natural relationship existing between these functions. Hence
democracy requires that the legislative organ should be given control over
the administrative and judicial organs. If separation of the legislative
function from the law-applying functions, or a control of the legislative
organ by the law-applying organs, and especially if control of the legislative and administrative functions by courts is provided for by the constitution of a democracy, this can be explained only by historical reasons,
not justified as specifically democratic elements.

IV. FORMS OF GOVERNMENT: DEMOCRACY AND AUTOCRACY

A. Classification of Constitutions

The central problem of political theory is the classification of governments. From a juristic point of view, it is the distinction between different archetypes of constitutions. Hence, the problem may be presented also as the distinction between different forms of State.

a. Monarchy and Republic

The political theory of Antiquity distinguished three forms of State: monarchy, aristocracy, and democracy, and modern theory has not gone beyond this trichotomy. The organization of the sovereign power is cited as the criterion of this classification. When the sovereign power of a community belongs to one individual, the government or the constitution is said to be monarchic. When the power belongs to several individuals, the constitution is called republican. A republic is an aristocracy or a democracy, depending upon whether the sovereign power belongs to a minority or a majority of the people.

The number of individuals with whom the sovereign power rests is, however, a very superficial criterion of classification. The power of the State is, as we have seen, the validity and efficacy of the legal order. Aristotle had already described the State as τάξις, that is, as order.* The criterion by which a monarchical constitution is distinguished from a republican one, and an aristocratic constitution from a democratic one, is the way in which the constitution regulates the creation of the legal order. Essentially, a constitution (in the material sense) regulates only the creation of general legal norms by determining the organs and the procedure of legislation. If the constitution (in the formal sense) contains also stipulations concerning the highest organs of the administration and judiciary, it is because these, too, create legal norms. The classification of governments is, in reality, a classification of constitutions, the term being used in its material sense. For the distinction between monarchy, aristocracy, and democracy refers essentially to the organization of legislation. A State is regarded as a democracy or aristocracy if its legislation is democratic or aristocratic in nature, although its administration and judiciary may have a different character. Likewise, a State is classified as a monarchy because the monarch appears legally as the legislator, even if his power in the field of the executive is

---

* Aristotle, Politics, Book III, 1274b, 1278b.

rigorously restricted and in the field of the judiciary practically non-existent.

b. Democracy and Autocracy

It is not only the criterion of the traditional classification, it is also the traditional trichotomy which is insufficient. If the criterion of the classification is the way in which, according to the constitution, the legal order is created, then it is more correct to distinguish, instead of three, two types of constitutions: democracy and autocracy. This distinction is based on the idea of political freedom.

Politically free is he who is subject to a legal order in the creation of which he participates. An individual is free if what he "ought to" do according to the social order coincides with what he "wills to" do. Democracy means that the "will" which is represented in the legal order of the State is identical with the wills of the subjects. Its opposite is the bondage of autocracy. There the subjects are excluded from the creation of the legal order, and harmony between the order and their wills is in no way guaranteed.

Democracy and autocracy as so defined are not actually descriptive of historically given constitutions, but rather represent ideal types. In political reality, there is no State conforming completely with one or the other ideal type. Every State represents a mixture of elements of both types, so that some communities are closer to the one, some closer to the other pole. Between the two extremes, there is a multitude of intermediate stages, most of which have no specific designation. According to the usual terminology, a State is called a democracy if the democratic principle prevails in its organization; and a State is called an autocracy if the autocratic principle prevails.

B. DEMOCRACY

a. The Idea of Freedom

1. The Metamorphosis of the Idea of Freedom

The idea of freedom has originally a purely negative significance. It means the absence of any bond, any obligating authority. But society means order, and order means bonds. The State is a social order by which individuals are bound to a certain behavior. In the original sense of freedom, therefore, he only is free who lives outside society and State. Freedom, in the original sense, is to be found only in that "state of nature" which the theory of natural law in the eighteenth century contrasted with the "social state." Such freedom is anarchy. Hence, in order to furnish the criterion according to which different types of States are distinguished, the idea of freedom must assume another than its originally negative connotation. Natural freedom becomes political liberty. This metamorphosis of the idea of freedom is of the greatest importance for all our political thinking.

2. The Principle of Self-determination

The freedom that is possible within society, and especially within the State, cannot be the freedom from any bond, it can only be from a particular kind of bond. The problem of political freedom is: How is it possible to be subject to a social order and still be free? Thus, Rousseau * has formulated the question to which democracy is the answer. A subject is politically free insofar as his individual will is in harmony with the "collective" (or "general") will expressed in the social order. Such harmony of the "collective" and the individual will is guaranteed only if the social order is created by the individuals whose behavior it regulates. Social order means determination of the will of the individual. Political freedom, that is, freedom under social order, is self-determination of the individual by participating in the creation of the social order. Political freedom is liberty, and liberty is autonomy.

b. The Principle of Majority

1. Self-determination and Anarchy

The ideal of self-determination requires that the social order shall be created by the unanimous decision of all its subjects and that it shall remain in force only as long as it enjoys the approval of all. The collective will (the *volonté générale*) must constantly agree with the will of the subjects (the *volonté de tous*). The social order can be changed only with the approval of all subjects; and each subject is bound by the order only as long as he consents thereto. By withdrawing his consent, each individual can at any moment put himself outside the social order. Where self-determination in its pure and unmitigated form prevails, there can be no contradiction between the social order and the will of any subject. Such an order could not be "violated" by any of its subjects. The difference between a state of anarchy where no social order is valid and a

---

* Rousseau, THE SOCIAL CONTRACT, Book I, chap. vi: "To find a form of association which may defend and protect with the whole force of the community the person and property of every associate, and by means of which each, coalescing with all, may nevertheless obey only himself, and remain free as before. Such is the fundamental problem of which the social contract furnishes the solution." Through the social contract, the "state of nature" is replaced by a state of social order.

social order whose validity is based on the permanent consent of all its subjects exists only in the sphere of ideas. In social reality, the highest degree of political self-determination, that is, a state where no conflict is possible between the social order and the individual, is hardly distinguishable from a state of anarchy. A normative order regulating the mutual behavior of individuals is completely superfluous if every conflict between the order and its subjects is excluded *a priori*. Only if such a conflict is possible, if the order remains valid even in relation to an individual who by his behavior "violates" the order, can the individual be considered to be "subject" to the order. A genuine social order is incompatible with the highest degree of self-determination.

If the principle of self-determination is to be made the basis of a social organization, it must be somewhat restricted. The problem then arises how to limit the self-determination of the individual just as far as is necessary to make society in general, and the State in particular, possible.

2. Necessary Restriction of Liberty by the Principle of Majority

The original creation of social order is a problem beyond practical considerations. Usually, an individual is born into a community constituted by a pre-existing social order. The problem thus can be narrowed down to the question how an existing order can be changed. The greatest possible degree of individual liberty, and that means, the greatest possible approximation to the ideal of self-determination compatible with the existence of a social order, is guaranteed by the principle that a change of the social order requires the consent of the simple majority of those subject thereto. According to this principle, among the subjects of the social order the number of those approving thereof will always be larger than the number of those who — entirely or in part — disapprove, but remain bound by the order. At the moment when the number of those who disapprove the order, or one of its norms, becomes greater than the number of those who approve, a change is possible by which a situation is reëstablished in which the order is in concordance with a number of subjects which is greater than the number of subjects with whom it is in discordance. The idea underlying the principle of majority is that the social order shall be in concordance with as many subjects as possible, and in discordance with as few as possible. Since political freedom means agreement between the individual will and the collective will expressed in the social order, it is the principle of simple majority which secures the highest degree of political freedom that is possible within society. If an order could not be changed by the will of a simple majority of the subjects but only by the will of all (that means, unanimously), or by the will of a qualified majority (for instance, by a two-thirds or a three-fourths majority vote), then one single individual, or a minority of individuals, could prevent a change of the order. And then the order could be in discordance with a number of subjects which would be greater than the number of those with whose will it is in concordance.

The transformation of the principle of self-determination into that of majority rule is a further important stage in the metamorphosis of the idea of freedom.

3. The Idea of Equality

The view that the degree of freedom in society is proportionate to the number of free individuals implies that all individuals are of equal political value and that everybody has the same claim to freedom, and that means, the same claim that the collective will be in concordance with his individual will. Only if it is irrelevant whether the one or the other is free in this sense (because the one is politically equal to the other), is the postulate justified that as many as possible shall be free, that the mere number of free individuals is decisive. Thus, the principle of majority, and hence the idea of democracy, is a synthesis of the ideas of freedom and equality.

c. *The Right of the Minority*

The principle of majority is by no means identical with absolute dominion of the majority, the dictatorship of majority over minority. The majority presupposes by its very definition the existence of a minority; and the right of the majority thus implies the right of existence of the minority. The principle of majority in a democracy is observed only if all citizens are permitted to participate in the creation of the legal order, although its contents are determined by the will of the majority. It is not democratic, because against the principle of majority, to exclude any minority from the creation of the legal order, even if the exclusion should be decided upon by a majority.

If the minority is not eliminated from the procedure in which the social order is created, there is always a possibility for the minority of influencing the will of the majority. Thus it is possible to prevent, to a certain extent, the contents of the social order determined by the majority from coming into absolute opposition to the interests of the minority. This is a characteristic element of democracy.

d. *Democracy and Liberalism*

The will of the community, in a democracy, is always created through a running discussion between majority and minority, through free consideration of arguments for and against a certain regulation of a subject matter. This discussion takes place not only in parliament, but also, and foremost, at political meetings, in newspapers, books, and other vehicles of public opinion. A democracy without public opinion is a contradiction in terms. Insofar as public opinion can arise only where intellectual freedom, freedom of speech and press and religion, are guaranteed, democracy coincides with political — though not necessarily economic — liberalism.

e. Democracy and Compromise

Free discussion between majority and minority is essential to democracy because this is the way to create an atmosphere favorable to a compromise between majority and minority; and compromise is part of democracy's very nature. Compromise means the solution of a conflict by a norm that neither entirely conforms with the interests of one party, nor entirely contradicts the interests of the other. Insofar as in a democracy the contents of the legal order, too, are not determined exclusively by the interest of the majority but are the result of a compromise between the two groups, voluntary subjection of all individuals to the legal order is more easily possible than in any other political organization. It is precisely because of this tendency towards compromise that democracy is an approximation to the ideal of complete self-determination.

f. Direct and Indirect (Representative) Democracy

The ideal type of democracy is realized by the different constitutions in different degrees. So-called direct democracy represents the comparatively highest degree. A direct democracy is characterized by the fact that legislation, as well as the main executive and judicial function, is exercised by the citizens in mass meeting or primary assembly. Such an organization is possible only within small communities and under simple social conditions. Even in the direct democracies that we find among the Germanic tribes and in ancient Greece the democratic principle is considerably restricted. By no means all the members of the community have a right to take part in the deliberations and decisions of the popular assembly. Children, women, and slaves — where slavery exists — are excluded. In wartime, the democratic principle has to yield to a strictly autocratic one: everybody must pay unconditional obedience to the leader. When the leader is chosen by the assembly, he at least comes into office in a democratic way. But, especially among the more warlike tribes, the office of the leader is frequently hereditary.

Today, only the constitutions of some small Swiss cantons have the character of direct democracies. The popular assembly is called *Landsgemeinde*. Since these cantons are very small communities and only member States of a federal State, the form of direct democracy does not play any important role in modern political life.

g. *The Fiction of Representation*

Differentiation of social conditions leads to a division of labor not only in economic production but within the domain of the creation of law as well. The function of government is transferred from the citizens organized in a popular assembly to special organs. The democratic principle of self-determination is limited to the procedure by which these organs are nominated. The democratic form of nomination is election. The organ authorized to create or execute the legal norms is elected by the subjects whose behavior is regulated by these norms.

This is a considerable weakening of the principle of political self-determination. It is characteristic of so-called indirect or representative democracy. This is a democracy in which the legislative function is exercised by a popularly elected parliament, and the administrative and judicial functions by officials who are likewise chosen by an electorate. According to the traditional definition, a government is "representative" because and insofar as its officials during their tenure of power reflect the will of the electorate and are responsible to the electorate. According to this definition, "a government by functionaries, whether legislative, executive, or judicial who are appointed or selected by other processes than popular election, or who, if chosen by a democratically constituted electorate, do not in fact reflect the will of the majority of the electors, or whose responsibility to the electorate is incapable of enforcement, is not truly representative." *

There can be no doubt that, judged by this test, none of the existing democracies called "representative" are really representative. In most of them, the administrative and judicial organs are selected by other methods than popular election; and in almost all democracies called "representative" the elected members of parliament and other popularly elected officials, especially the head of State, are not legally responsible to the electorate.

In order to establish a true relationship of representation, it is not sufficient that the representative be appointed or elected by the represented. It is necessary that the representative be legally obliged to execute the will of the represented, and that the fulfillment of this obligation be legally guaranteed. The typical guarantee is the power of the

---

* J. W. GARNER, POLITICAL SCIENCE AND GOVERNMENT (1928) 317.

represented to recall the representative in case the latter's activity does not conform with the former's wishes. The constitutions of modern democracies, however, only exceptionally confer upon the electorate the power to recall elected officials. Such exceptions are the constitutions of some member States of the United States of America, for instance the constitution of California, which in Article XXIII, section 1, stipulates: "Every elective public officer of the State of California may be removed from office at any time by the electors entitled to vote for a successor of such incumbent, through the procedure and in the manner herein provided for, which procedure shall be known as the recall. . . ." Another exception is the Weimar constitution of the German Reich, which stipulates in its Article 43: "The President of the Reich may, upon the motion of the Reichstag, be removed from office before the expiration of his term by the vote of the people. The resolution of the Reichstag must be carried by a two-thirds majority. Upon the adoption of such a resolution, the President of the Reich is prevented from the further exercise of his office. Refusal to remove him from office, expressed by the vote of the people, is equivalent to reëlection and entails the dissolution of the Reichstag."

Normally, the elected head of State or other elected organs can be removed from their office before expiration of their term only by decision of courts, and only because of a violation of the constitution or other laws. The members of parliament in modern democracies, especially, are, as a rule, not legally responsible to their constituencies; they cannot be recalled by their electorate. The elected members of a modern parliament are not legally bound by any instructions from their constituencies. Their legislative mandate does not have the character of a *mandat impératif*, as the French term the function of an elected deputy if he is legally obliged to execute his electors' will. Many democratic constitutions expressly stipulate the independence of the deputies vis-à-vis their electors. This independence of the parliament from the electorate is a characteristic feature of modern parliamentarism. It is exactly by this independence from the electorate that a modern parliament is distinguished from elected legislative bodies in the period prior to the French Revolution. The members of these bodies were true representatives, — real agents of the class or professional group which chose them, for they were subject to instructions and could be recalled by it at any time. It was the French constitution of 1791 which solemnly proclaimed the principle that no instructions should be given the deputies, for the deputy should not be the representative of any particular district but of the entire nation.

The formula that the member of parliament is not the representative of his electors but of the whole people, or, as some writers say, of the whole State, and that therefore he is not bound by any instructions of his electors and cannot be recalled by them, is a political fiction. Legal independence of the elected from the electors is incompatible with legal representation. The statement that the people is represented by the parliament means that, while the people cannot exercise the legislative power directly and immediately, they exercise it by proxy.* But if there is no legal guarantee that the will of the electors is executed by the elected, if the elected are legally independent from the electors, no legal relationship of proxy or representation exists. The fact that an elected organ has no chance or only a lessened chance of being reëlected if his activity is not considered by his electors to be satisfactory, constitutes, it is true, a kind of political responsibility; but this political responsibility is quite different from a legal responsibility and does not justify the assumption that the elected organ is a legal representative of his electorate, and much less the assumption that an organ elected only by a part of the people is the legal representative of the whole State. Such an organ "represents" the State in no other way than a hereditary monarch or an official appointed by the latter.

If political writers insist on characterizing the parliament of modern democracy, in spite of its legal independence from the electorate, as a "representative" organ, if some writers even declare that the *mandat impératif* is contrary to the principle of representative government,† they do not present a scientific theory but advocate a political ideology. The function of this ideology is to conceal the real situation, to maintain the illusion that the legislator is the people, in spite of the fact that, in reality, the function of the people — or, more correctly formulated, of the electorate — is limited to the creation of the legislative organ.‡

* H. J. FORD, REPRESENTATIVE GOVERNMENT (1924) 3, says that representative democracy is based on the idea that while the people cannot be actually present in person at the seat of government, they are considered to be present by proxy.

† For instance, A. ESMEIN, ÉLÉMENTS DE DROIT CONSTITUTIONNEL (5th ed. 1909) 83, 263, 386.

‡ Lord Brougham, *The British Constitution* in 11 WORKS (1861) 94, says: "The deputy chosen represents the people of the whole community, exercises his own judgment upon all measures, receives freely the communications of his constituents, is not bound by their instructions, though liable to be dismissed by not being reëlected in case the difference of opinion between him and them is irreconcilable and important. The people's power being transferred to the representative body for a limited time, the people are bound not to exercise their influence so as to control the conduct of their representatives, as a body, on the several measures that come before them." This statement is very characteristic. The parliament "represents" the people, but "the people are bound not to exercise their influence so as to control the conduct of their representatives, as a body." For: "the people's power has been transferred to

The answer to the question of whether, *de lege ferenda*, the elected member of a legislative body should be legally bound to execute the will of his electors and therefore be responsible to the electorate depends upon the opinion to what extent it is desirable to realize the idea of democracy. If it is democratic that legislation be exercised by the people, and if, for technical reasons, it is impossible to establish a direct democracy and necessary to confer the legislative function upon a parliament elected by the people, then it is democratic to guarantee as far as possible that the activity of every member of parliament reflect the will of his electors. The so-called *mandat impératif* and the recall of elected officers are democratic institutions, provided the electorate is democratically organized. The legal independence of parliament from the electorate can be justified only by the opinion that the legislative power is better organized when the democratic principle, according to which the people should be the legislator, is not carried to extremes. Legal independence of parliament from the people means that the principle of democracy is, to a certain extent, replaced by that of the division of labor. In order to conceal this shifting from one principle to another, the fiction is used that parliament "represents" the people.

A similar fiction is used to conceal the loss of power which the monarch suffered through the achievement of independence on the part of the courts. The ideology of constitutional monarchy embodies the doctrine that a judge, although any influence on his function by the monarch is constitutionally eliminated, "represents" the monarch: his decisions are given "in the name of the king." In English law, one even goes so far as to assume that the king is present in spirit at the moment the court's decision is pronounced.

h. The Electoral Systems

1. The Electoral Body

In a so-called representative democracy where the democratic principle is reduced to the election of the law-creating organs, the electoral system is decisive for the degree to which the idea of democracy is realized. Voting is a procedure of creating organs. Certain individuals, the voters or electors, nominate one or more individuals to some function. The number of voters is always considerably larger than the number of in-

---

the representative body." The last words alone describe the political reality, and even this description is not completely free from ideological elements. It presupposes that the legislative power belongs — historically or by its very nature — to the people and has been transferred from the people to parliament, which, obviously, is not true.

dividuals to be elected. The act by which an individual is elected, the election, is composed of the partial acts of the voters, the acts of voting.

The instrumentality through which the function of voting is exercised is the ballot. The voters, entitled to elect one or several individuals, form the electoral body or electorate. The election is the function of this electorate, the single voter is a partial organ of this body, and the latter is an organ of the whole legal community, an organ whose function is the creation of other organs, so-called representative organs. The electoral body must be organized; it must itself have certain organs to collect and count the votes and establish the result.

If a composite central organ of the whole State, e.g., a parliament, is to be elected, the total electoral area may be divided into as many districts as there are delegates to be elected, and each district may elect just one delegate. The voters belonging to one such district form an electoral body on a territorial basis.

2. The Right of Suffrage

The right of suffrage is the individual's right to participate in the electoral procedure by casting his vote. We have examined in another connection the question under what circumstances the right of voting is a right in the technical sense of the term.* The fact that suffrage is a public function by which essential organs of the State are created is not incompatible with its organization as a right in the technical sense of the term; but the question may arise whether it is advisable to leave the exercise of this vital function to the citizen's free discretion, which is the case if suffrage is a right. If the electoral function is considered to be an essential condition in the life of the State, it is only consistent to make suffrage a duty of the citizen, a legal, and not merely a moral duty, and that means, to provide a sanction to be executed against the citizen who does not exercise the function of voting as prescribed by the law. Although many writers and statesmen advocate compulsory voting, arguing that all those who have been invested with the electoral franchise should participate in the choice of public officers or in referendal elections on legislative projects or questions of public policy submitted to them, since otherwise the results of the election may not accurately represent the real will of the electorate,† this principle has rarely been adopted by States.

It is in the nature of democracy that the right of suffrage should be universal. As few individuals as possible should be excluded from the

* Cf. *supra*, pp. 87ff.
† Cf. GARNER, POLITICAL SCIENCE AND GOVERNMENT 548.

right, and the minimum age at which the right is obtained should be as low as possible. It is especially incompatible with the democratic idea of universal suffrage to exclude women or individuals belonging to a certain profession, as for instance soldiers or clergymen.

Democracy requires that the right of suffrage should be not only as nearly universal but also as nearly equal as possible. That means that the influence which each voter exercises on the result of the election should be the same, in other terms, the weight of vote of every voter should be equal to that of every other voter. Mathematically formulated, the weight of vote is a fraction whose denominator is the number of voters of one electoral body, and whose numerator is the number of delegates to be elected by this body.

The equality of the right of suffrage is directly infringed if individuals who satisfy special requirements — who are literate or who pay a certain amount of tax — are given more votes than others. This is called "plural voting." Indirectly, the equality is impaired if the proportion between the number of voters and the number of delegates to be elected changes from one electoral body to the other. If, for instance, two electoral bodies — one with 10,000 voters and the other with 20,000 voters — elect the same number of delegates, the weight of vote of a voter belonging to the first body is twice as great as that of a voter belonging to the second.

3. Majority and Proportional Representation

Who is to be considered as elected? If an electoral body elects just one delegate, the principle of majority will, of course, decide. From a democratic viewpoint, an absolute majority must be required here. If a nominee who had obtained only the relatively largest number of votes would be elected, this would be equivalent to a dominion by a minority over a majority. The formation of an absolute majority is, however, endangered if the voters are allowed an unlimited freedom in the choice of their candidates. A majority is the result of a certain integration. Integration of individuals is the function of political parties.

a. The political party. In a parliamentary democracy, the isolated individual has little influence upon the creation of the legislative and executive organs. To gain influence he has to associate with others who share his political opinions. Thus arise political parties. In a parliamentary democracy, the political party is an essential vehicle for the formation of the public will. The majority principle essential to democracy can work only if the political integration results in a group that comprises more than half of the voters. If no political party achieves an absolute majority, two or several of them have to coöperate.

The constitution can subject the formation and the activity of political parties to the control of the government. The idea of democracy implies a far-reaching freedom in the formation of political parties; but the democratic character of a constitution would in no way be impaired if it contained stipulations designed to guarantee a democratic organization of political parties.* In view of the decisive role that political parties play in the election of legislative and executive organs, it would even be justifiable to make them into organs of the State by regulating their constitutions. It is essential for a democracy only that the formation of new parties should not be excluded, and that no party should be given a privileged position or a monopoly.

β. *Electorate and representative body.* If the voters are divided into a number of electoral districts, the outcome of the election may fail to reflect the political structure of the total electorate. Let us assume, for instance, that 1000 voters are divided into 10 districts with 100 voters in each, and that each district is to elect one delegate. Assume further that there are two opposing political parties, A and B. In four districts, A has 90 members and B only 10. But in the remaining 6 districts, B

---

* Cf. the decision of the Supreme Court of the United States of April 3, 1944, concerning the legal rights of Negroes to vote in primaries (meetings of voters belonging to the same political party). Smith *v.* Allwright, 321 U. S.; 88 L. ed. Adv. Op. 701, 64 S. Ct. 751. In the decision it is said: "We think that this statutory system [of Texas] for the selection of party nominees for inclusion on the general election ballot makes the party which is required to follow these legislative directions an agency of the state in so far as it determines the participants in a primary election. The party takes its character as a state agency from the duties imposed upon it by state statutes; the duties do not become matters of private law because they are performed by a political party." "When primaries become a part of the machinery for choosing officials, state and national, as they have here, the same tests to determine the character of discrimination or abridgment should be applied to the primary as are applied to the general election. If the state requires a certain electoral procedure, prescribes a general election ballot made up of party nominees so chosen and limits the choice of the electorate in general elections for state offices, practically speaking, to those whose names appear on such a ballot, it endorses, adopts and enforces the discrimination against Negroes, practiced by a party entrusted by Texas law with the determination of the qualifications of participants in the primary. This is state action within the meaning of the Fifteenth Amendment." "The United States is a constitutional democracy. Its organic law grants to all citizens a right to participate in the choice of elected officials without restriction by any state because of race. This grant to the people of the opportunity for choice is not to be nullified by a state through casting its electoral process in a form which permits a private organization to practice racial discrimination in the election. Constitutional rights would be of little value if they could be thus indirectly denied." "The privilege of membership in a party may be . . . no concern of a state. But when, as here, that privilege is also the essential qualification for voting in a primary to select nominees for a general election, the state makes the action of the party the action of the state."

has 60 members while A has 40. In the total electorate, A thus carries the majority with 600 voters, while B musters only a minority of 400 voters. Nevertheless, party A gets only 4 candidates elected, while B gets 6. The party that is in a majority among the voters returns a minority among the delegates, and *vice versa*. The division into electoral districts can thus seriously endanger, even completely eliminate, the majority vote principle and lead to its opposite, a minority rule.

γ. *The idea of proportional representation.* The possibility of such a result is excluded by a system of proportional representation. This system can be applied only when more than one delegate is to be elected by one electoral body. In the example given above this system would have given as a result six delegates from party A, and four from party B. Proportional election insures that the relative strength of the parties in the representative body is the same as in the electoral body. The political structure of the former reflects the political structure of the latter.

The system of proportional representation is applicable only to the election of a representative body but not to the decisions of that body itself. These decisions have to be made according to the majority principle. The system of proportional representation, however, is characterized by the fact that in the procedure of the election the majority–minority relation has no importance. In order to be represented, a political group does not need to comprise the majority of the voters; for every group is represented, even if it is not a majority group, according to its numerical strength. In order to be represented, a political group must have only a minimum number of members. The smaller this minimum number, the more members the representative body has. In the mathematical borderline case where the minimum is one, the number of delegates is equal to the number of voters — the representative body coincides with the electorate. This is the case of direct democracy. The system of proportional representation shows a tendency in this direction.

Proportional representation must be distinguished from so-called minority representation, an electoral system whose purpose it is to guarantee adequate representation only to one, namely, the comparatively strongest minority group, and thus to prevent the majority from being alone represented. The latter would be the result of the election should the principle of majority be carried out without any restriction. This is not the case, as shown by the above mentioned example, if the whole electorate is divided into electoral bodies organized on a territorial basis. The division of the electorate into territorial electoral bodies offers a minority the possibility of being represented, provided that the political structure of the electoral districts is not the same as the political structure of the whole electorate, so that a group which has the minority in the whole electorate will have a majority in one or several districts. But the division into territorial electoral bodies may have the result that a minority group will obtain a much stronger representation than corresponds to its numerical strength, even a stronger representation than the majority group. According to the system of majority representation combined with a territorial division of the electorate, it is more or less accidental whether and to what extent a minority is represented.

This shows clearly why the territorial division of the electorate is incompatible with the idea of proportional representation. If all political groups, and not only the majority and one minority, are to be represented in proportion to their strength, the electorate must form one single electoral body. The groups into which the voters are divided must not be constituted by the voters living in one of the districts into which the whole electoral territory is divided. These groups must coincide with the political parties themselves, whose members may be spread over the whole electoral territory. If the system of proportional representation is consistently carried out, it is irrelevant in which part of the electoral territory a voter lives. For he forms, together with his party comrades, one electoral group. Insofar as this group comes into being by the fact alone that individuals agree upon certain candidates, each group chooses its candidates unanimously. It is, however, possible to separate the act by which the group is integrated from the act by which it elects its delegates. The first act consists in the declaration of the voter that he belongs to a certain political group. After the numerical strength of the different groups is established and the number of delegates due to every group according to its strength is determined, the second act takes place: the nomination of delegates by the different groups. In this case, the candidates are elected on the basis of a competition within the group.

One of the advantages of the system of proportional representation is that no competition of candidates of different political parties is necessary. According to the system of majority representation, every delegate is elected with the votes of one — the majority — group, against the votes of another — the minority — group. According to the system of proportional representation, every delegate is elected only with the votes of his own group without being elected against the votes of another group. The system of proportional representation is the greatest possible approximation to the ideal of self-determination within a representative democracy, and hence the most democratic electoral system.

i. Functional Representation

According to the democratic idea of equality of all citizens, the single voter counts only as a member of the whole people or, where proportional representation exists, as a member of a political party. Hence purely democratic electoral systems do not attach significance to the social class or profession of the voter. The democratic forms of representation therefore have been called merely mechanical, and they have been contrasted with organic or functional representation, where economic or occupational groups form the electoral bodies. Such an electoral system implicitly denies the equality of all citizens, and the mandates are consequently distributed between the various groups, not according to their numerical strength, but according to their alleged social importance. Since it is impossible to find an objective criterion for determining the social importance of the different groups, this system is in reality very often nothing but an ideology, whose function it is to conceal the domination of one group over the other.

j. Democracy of Legislation

The will of the State, that is, the legal order, is created in a procedure that runs, as we have pointed out, through several stages. The question as to the method of creation, that is, the question whether the creation of law is democratic or autocratic, must, therefore, be formulated for each stage separately. That the creation of norms is democratic at one stage by no means implies that it is so at every other stage too. Very often, the legal order is created on the different stages according to different methods, so that, from the standpoint of the antagonism between democracy and autocracy, the total process is not uniform.

1. Unicameral and Bicameral System

Democracy at the stage of legislation means — disregarding direct democracies — that, in principle, all the general norms are created by a parliament elected by the people. The unicameral system would seem to correspond most closely to the idea of democracy. The bicameral system that is typical of the constitutional monarchy and the federal State is always an attenuation of the democratic principle. The two chambers must be formed according to different principles, if the one is not to be a useless duplicate of the other. If the one is perfectly democratic, the other must be somewhat lacking in democratic character.

2. Popular Initiative and Referendum

At the stage of legislation it is possible to combine, to a certain extent, the principle of indirect and that of direct democracy. Such a combination is the institution of "popular initiative," which means that parliament must decide upon proposals for legislation signed by a certain number of citizens. Another way of combining direct and indirect democracy is the "referendum," meaning that certain bills decided upon by parliament must be submitted to popular vote before obtaining the force of law. Popular initiative and referendum can be combined with one another in several ways. The constitution may stipulate that when a certain number of citizens so require a bill decided upon by parliament has to be submitted to a referendum; or it may provide that popular initiative can at once propose a bill and require that it shall be submitted to referendum., The more these two institutions are made use of, the closer the ideal of direct democracy is approached.

k. Democracy of Execution

The creation of general norms by other organs than the parliament is democratic or autocratic depending upon whether or not these organs are elected by the people. Appointment by an organ elected by the people is in itself a weakening of the democratic principle since appointment is an autocratic method. The ideal of democracy can be realized to a higher degree when the elected organ is collegiate than when it consists of a single individual. An individual organ can be elected by a majority vote only, while minorities can be represented in a collegiate organ and influence its decisions. A parliament elected by the whole people is more democratic than a president likewise so elected.

l. Democracy and Legality of Execution

It might seem that the ideal of democracy is most perfectly realized when not only legislation but also execution (administration and judiciary) are completely democratized. A closer examination, however, shows that this is not necessarily the case. Since execution, by its very definition, is execution of laws, the organization of the executive power has to guarantee the legality of execution. The administrative and judicial function has to conform as well as possible with the laws enacted by the legislative organ. If the legislation is democratic, and that means, if it expresses the will of the people, then the execution is the more democratic the more it corresponds to the postulate of legality. Legality or loyalty of execution, however, is not necessarily best guaranteed by a democratic organization.

The following example may serve to illustrate this assertion. Let us assume that the territory of a State is divided into districts, and the administration of each district is entrusted to a local body elected by the citizens of the district. If the administration is left entirely to the discretion of these bodies, such an organization would be perfectly democratic. But if the administrative bodies are bound by laws enacted by a central parliament, the legality of the administration would be somewhat endangered under such an organization. The party that has a majority in parliament can very well be in the minority in one of the local bodies, and *vice versa*. A local body where the parliamentary minority is in the majority would be inclined to disregard, or to apply less conscientiously, laws enacted by parliament against the votes of the minority.

One of the most effective guarantees for the legality of a function is the personal responsibility of the organ. Experience shows that such responsibility is much easier to enforce in the case of individual organs than in the case of collegiate organs. To safeguard the legality of administration it may therefore be advisable to put it in the hands of individual organs, appointed by the elected head of State and personally responsible to him. Legality is sometimes better ensured under a comparatively autocratic organization of administration than under a radically democratic one. And when legislation is democratic, the best method of guaranteeing legality of execution is democratic, too.

C. AUTOCRACY

a. The Absolute Monarchy

The most pronounced historical form of autocracy is the absolute monarchy, such as it existed in Europe in the eighteenth century and in the Orient during the most diverse periods and among the most diverse peoples. Under this form of government, also known as despotism, the legal order is in all its stages created and applied either directly by the monarch, or by organs which he has appointed. The monarch is personally irresponsible; he is not under the law, since he is not liable to any legal sanctions. The position of monarch is hereditary, or each monarch nominates his own successor.

b. The Constitutional Monarchy

In the constitutional monarchy, the power of the monarch is restricted, in the field of legislation by the participation of a parliament which is normally composed of two chambers, in the field of adjudication by the independence of the courts, and in the field of administration by the coöperation of cabinet ministers. The latter are normally the chiefs of the different branches of administration. They are appointed by the monarch but are responsible to the parliament. Their responsibility is a legal and a political one. The legal responsibility consists in their being subject to impeachment for violation of the constitution and other laws committed by acts performed in connection with their office as cabinet ministers. One of the two houses of parliament functions as accuser, the other as court; or both houses have the right to bring an action against a cabinet minister before a special court. The political responsibility of the ministers consists in their being obligated to resign when they lose the confidence of one of the houses of parliament. The monarch is not responsible at all. But no act of the monarch is valid without the countersignature of a responsible minister. Judges and administrative officials are generally appointed by the monarch. He is the commander-in-chief of the military forces and represents the State vis-à-vis other States; he is in particular empowered to conclude international treaties, even if certain such treaties require approval by parliament.

c. The Presidential Republic, and the Republic with Cabinet Government

The presidential republic, in which the chief executive is elected by the people, is modeled upon the constitutional monarchy. The power of the president is the same or greater than that of a constitutional monarch. It is only within the domain of legislation that the president is less powerful than the former. The president has a veto, while the consent of the monarch is necessary before a bill decided upon by parliament acquires the force of law. There are, however, constitutional monarchies in which the monarch has only a veto or where he has lost the possibility of refusing his consent to a parliamentary decision. A characteristic element of the presidential system is that neither the president nor the members of cabinet appointed by him are responsible to parliament; the members of cabinet are subordinated to the president and hold their office at his pleasure.

A different type is the democratic republic with cabinet government. The chief executive is elected by the legislature to which the members of the cabinet, appointed by the president, are responsible. Another type is characterized by the fact that the government is a collegiate organ, a kind of executive council, elected by the legislature. The head of State is not a chief executive but the chairman of the executive council.

The constitutional monarchy and the presidential republic are democracies in which the autocratic element is relatively strong. In the republic with cabinet government and the republic with collegiate government, the democratic element is comparatively stronger.

d. The Party Dictatorship

1. The One-party State (Bolshevism and Fascism)

In recent times, a new form of autocracy has arisen in the party dictatorship of Bolshevism and Fascism. In Russia, the new form is a product of the socialist revolution that followed the first World War. Its intellectual basis is the Marxist theory of the class struggle and the dictatorship of the proletariat. In reality, this dictatorship has become that of a party, representing the interests of the proletarians, and opposed to all other parties, even if they be proletarian. The word "Bolshevism" was originally applied only to the party exercising the dictatorship in Russia, but it has come to designate a type of government.

In Italy, the Fascist party was a middle-class party that rose to dictatorship in struggle against proletarian parties. The word "Fascism" — like "Bolshevism" — has come to be used as the name for a type of government, viz., the dictatorship of a middle-class party. The National Socialist State in Germany belongs to this type.

The ruling party in a party dictatorship has itself an autocratic character. Its members are under the absolute rule of the party leader who at the same time is the head of State. Since Bolshevism originally maintained the fiction of a separation of party and State and, further, did not have an ideology of "leadership," the leader was for a long time officially only the general secretary of the party. But in reality there is in this point no difference between the two forms of party dictatorship.

From the outside, it is hard to judge how far the autocratic principle has actually been carried out within the party. In all three dictatorships, however, there exists or existed a well-developed leader cult — even in Russia, where it is difficult to reconcile with the Marxist-colored ideology.

2. Complete Suppression of Individual Freedom

In the party dictatorship, the freedom of speech and press and every other political liberty is completely suppressed. Not only the official State organs but also the party organs can arbitrarily interfere with the freedom of the citizen. Even the independence of the courts is abolished insofar as the interests of the ruling party are concerned.

3. Irrelevancy of Constitutional Institutions

Since both the creation and application of law are entirely in the hands of the ruling party, it is without significance that the Italian constitution countenances hereditary monarchy, or that, according to the constitutions of all the three party dictatorships, there are popularly elected central parliaments and even certain other democratic institutions such as plebiscites.

Alleged expressions of the popular will are entirely worthless since nobody can voice another opinion than that accepted by the party without endangering his property, freedom, and life. Within the party dictatorships, elections and plebiscites have as their sole purpose concealing the fact of dictatorship. Even the Bolshevist "Soviets" (councils of peasants and soldiers) and the Fascist "corporations" (authorized to represent various groups of workers and employers) — organizations aiming at a kind of functional representation — have an ideological rather than a legal importance. To describe the Fascist State as "corporative" is to ignore its inner nature for the façade.

4. The Totalitarian State

In the proletarian as well as the two middle-class dictatorships, economy is to a large extent regulated in an authoritarian way. Bolshevism is State communism, Fascism and National Socialism show a tendency toward State capitalism. In all the three dictatorial States, the legal order penetrates not only into the economic sphere but also into other interests of the private individual to a much higher degree than in any other present-day State. In view of this fact, the party dictatorships have also been called "totalitarian" States. A totalitarian State, abolishing all individual liberties, is not possible without an ideology systematically propagated by the government. The State ideology of the proletarian dictatorship is Socialism, the State ideology of the bourgeois dictatorships is Nationalism.

V. FORMS OF ORGANIZATION: CENTRALIZATION AND DECENTRALIZATION

A. CENTRALIZATION AND DECENTRALIZATION AS LEGAL CONCEPTS

The State is, as we have found, a legal order. Its "elements," territory and people, are the territorial and personal spheres of validity of that legal order. The "power" of the State is the validity and efficacy of the legal order, while the three "powers" or functions are different stages in the creation thereof. The two basic forms of government, democracy and autocracy, are different modes of creating the legal order. In view of these results to which our previous considerations have led, it is evident that centralization and decentralization, generally considered as forms of State organization with reference to territorial division, must be understood as two types of legal orders. The difference between a centralized and a decentralized State must be a difference in their legal orders. All the problems of centralization and decentralization are in fact, as we shall see, problems concerning the spheres of validity of legal norms and the organs creating and applying them. Only a juristic theory can provide the answer to the question as to the nature of centralization and decentralization.*

B. The Static Concept of Centralization and Decentralization

a. The Juristic Concept of Territorial Division

The conception of a centralized legal order implies that all its norms are valid throughout the whole territory over which it extends; this means that all its norms have the same territorial sphere of validity. A decentralized legal order, on the other hand, consists of norms that have different territorial spheres of validity. Some of the norms will be valid for the entire territory — otherwise this would not be the territory of a single order — while others will be valid only for different parts thereof. The norms valid for the whole territory we suggest be called central norms, the norms valid only for some part of the territory, decentral or local norms.

The local norms valid for one and the same part of the total territory form a partial or local legal order. They constitute a partial or local legal community. The statement that the State is decentralized or that the territory of the State is divided into territorial subdivisions means that the national legal order contains not only central but also local norms. The different territorial spheres of validity of the local orders are the territorial subdivisions.

The central norms of the total, or national legal order, form also a partial order, that is, the central legal order. They also constitute a partial, that is, the central legal community. The central legal order constituting the central legal community forms, together with the local legal orders constituting the local legal communities, the total or national legal order constituting the total legal community, the State. The central community as well as the local communities are members of the total community.

Two norms that are valid for different regions but relate to the same subject matter, that is, norms having a different territorial but the same material sphere of validity, may regulate the same subject matter (trade, for instance) differently for their respective regions. One of the main reasons for decentralization is precisely that it provides this possibility of the same matter's being regulated differently for different regions. The considerations which render such differentiation of the national

* Cf. my essay *Centralization and Decentralization*, a paper delivered at the Harvard Tercentenary Conference of Arts and Sciences, in AUTHORITY AND THE INDIVIDUAL (Harvard Tercentenary Publications, 1937) 210–239.

legal order advisable may be geographical, national, or religious. The larger the territory of the State, and the more varied the social conditions, the more imperative will decentralization by territorial division be.

b. Principles of Organization Based on Territorial or on Personal Status

The legal community may be divided on a basis other than territorial. The partial communities of which the total community consists need not be established on a territorial basis. The norms of a legal order, while all have the same territorial sphere, may differ as to their personal spheres of validity. The same subject matter, for instance marriage, may be regulated for the whole territory but in different ways for different groups distinguished on the basis of religion, so that the matrimonial law of one and the same national legal order may be different for Roman Catholics, Protestants, and Mohammedans. Or the norms regulating the duties and rights of the citizens in the field of public education may be different for the English-speaking and the French-speaking part of the population. The legal order may further contain laws valid only for individuals of a certain race, conferring upon them certain privileges or placing them under various disabilities.

A set of norms whose validity has the same personal sphere constitutes a partial community within the total community, just as the local or central norms of a legal order constitute partial communities. But these partial communities are organized in one case on a personal, in the other case on a territorial basis. The criterion of the latter is the territory within which an individual lives, the criterion of the former, his religion, language, race, or other personal qualities.

Differentiation of the personal sphere of validity of the legal order, or organization based on personal status, may be necessary if the individuals belonging to different religions, languages, races, etc., are not settled in distinct parts of the territory but are spread over the whole territory of the State. In this case, decentralization by territorial subdivision would not permit the desired differentiation of the legal order. The system of proportional representation where the whole electorate is not divided into territorial electoral bodies on the basis of a division of the territory into electoral districts, but into political parties, is an example already mentioned of organization based on the principle of personal status.

However, we speak of decentralization only if the organization is carried out according to the territorial principle, if the norms of a legal order are differentiated with respect to their territorial sphere of validity, although the differentiation with respect to their personal sphere of validity has a similar effect. These territorial spheres of validity of the local norms are often called provinces, and decentralization thus implies the existence of provinces.

c. Total and Partial Centralization and Decentralization

The centralization or decentralization of a legal order may be quantitatively of varying degree. The degree of centralization or decentralization is determined by the relative proportion of the number and importance of central and local norms of the order. One can, accordingly, distinguish between total and partial decentralization and centralization. Centralization is total if all the norms are valid for the whole territory. Decentralization is total if all the norms are valid only for different parts of the territory, for territorial subdivisions. In the former case, decentralization is of degree zero, while in the latter the same holds for centralization. When neither centralization nor decentralization is total, we speak of partial decentralization and partial centralization, which thus are the same. Total centralization and decentralization are only ideal poles. There is a certain minimum below which centralization cannot sink, a certain maximum which decentralization cannot surpass without dissolution of the legal community; at least one norm, namely the basic norm, must be a central norm, must be valid for the whole territory, otherwise this would not be the territory of a single legal order, and we could not speak of decentralization as the territorial division of one and the same legal community. Positive law knows only partial centralization and decentralization.

d. Criteria of the Degrees of Centralization and Decentralization

The quantitative degree of centralization and decentralization depends, in the first place, on the number of stages in the hierarchy of the legal order to which centralization or decentralization extends; in the second place, on the number and importance of subject matters regulated by central or local norms. Only one stage, or several stages, in the hierarchy of the legal order may be centralized or decentralized; and centralization or decentralization may refer only to one, to several, or to all the subject matters of legal regulation. The constitution alone, for instance, may be central, that is to say, only the norms regulating legislation may be central norms, valid for the whole territory, while all the other stages (legislation, administration and adjudication) are decentralized in regard to all matters. In this case, all the general norms, the statutes created by the legislative organs in conformity with the central constitution, and all the individual norms issued by administrative authorities and courts on the basis of the statutes (or customary law), regardless of their subject matter, are local norms; they are valid only for partial territories (territorial subdivisions). It is further possible that legislation and execution be only partially centralized or decentralized; this is the case when only the general norms (statutes or rules of customary law) regulating specific subject matters, and the individual norms issued on the basis of these general norms, have a local character. Decentralization may, for instance, apply only to agriculture or industry, while other subject matters of legal regulation are centralized; or criminal law only and its application by criminal courts may be decentralized, while civil law and its application by civil courts is centralized.

If legislation and execution are partially centralized and partially decentralized, the material sphere of validity of the legal order, the competence of the total community is divided between the central order (or the central legal community constituted by this order) and the local orders (or the local legal communities constituted by these local orders). As an alternative, not only the stage of constitution but also that of legislation may be centralized in regard to all subject matters of legal regulation, whereas only the stage of execution (administration and adjudication) may be decentralized. In other words: all general norms, the constitution as well as all the statutes (and rules of customary law), are central norms; only the individual norms (created by administrative acts and judicial decisions) are local norms. Finally, the execution itself may be totally or partially centralized or decentralized, depending on whether all the individual norms issued by administrative authorities or courts, or only those pertaining to particular subject matters, have a central or a local character.

e. *Method of Restricting the Territorial Sphere of Validity*

In order fully to understand the restriction of the territorial sphere of validity, and with it the nature of local as opposed to central norms, we must keep in mind the structure of the legal norm as it has been outlined in an earlier chapter.* The legal norm attaches a coercive act, a sanction, as consequence to certain facts as condition. Among the conditioning facts, the delict is a common element of all legal norms. In the norms of civil law the legal transaction appears among the conditioning facts; in the norms of administrative law, the administrative act. The territorial sphere of validity of a legal norm may be restricted to a certain part-territory with respect to the conditioning facts or with respect to the consequence provided for by the legal norms, or with respect to both. In other words, the norm can attribute legal consequences only to (conditioning) facts, to delicts, legal transactions, administrative acts, occur-

---

* Cf. *supra*, pp. 45ff.

ring within the part-territory, and simultaneously stipulate that the legal consequence — the sanction and its procedural preparation — shall take place within the same part-territory. But the restriction of the territorial sphere of validity may concern only one of the two parts of the legal norm. If the international legal order delimits the territories of the States, that is to say, the sphere of validity of the national legal orders, this delimitation is accomplished — as we have seen — in principle by restricting to its own territory only the coercive acts provided in the norms of that particular State's legal order. In other words, the legal order of each individual State, according to international law, must direct the coercive acts it prescribes to be carried out only within its own territory, which, therefore, is a partial territory of the universal international legal order. However, the legal order of the individual State may attach the coercive act as a consequence to conditioning facts which have occurred even outside its territory.

In an above-mentioned case of partial decentralization of the national legal order, decentralization refers only to the stage of individual norms; constitution and legislation remain centralized, and only administration and judiciary are partially decentralized: the territorial sphere of validity of certain individual norms issued by administrative authorities or courts is restricted. These norms are local norms. That means that the territorial competence of the administrative authorities and the courts is restricted. They are local authorities, local courts. The territory of the State is divided into several administrative or judicial districts. This can mean: (1) that the local administrative authority or the local civil or criminal court is authorized to order a concrete sanction only if the administrative act or the legal transaction conditioning the (administrative or civil) delict has taken place within the district, or if the (administrative, civil or criminal) delict has been committed within the district; (2) that the local administrative authority or the local court is authorized to order a concrete sanction which can be executed only within its district. The restriction of the territorial sphere of validity of an individual norm issued by an administrative or judicial organ is the restriction of the territorial jurisdiction (competence) of these organs.

C. The Dynamic Concept of Centralization and Decentralization

a. Centralized and Decentralized Creation of Norms

The problem of centralization and decentralization has a dynamic as well as a static aspect. It is concerned not only with the territorial sphere of validity of legal norms, but also with the methods of creating and executing such norms. Whether the central or local norms are created and executed by one and the same organ or by several organs, and how these organs themselves are created, become important questions.

Decentralization, in the static sense, is independent of whether or not there is one single organ creating all the central norms; and likewise decentralization, in the static sense, is independent of whether or not the local norms are created by corresponding local organs. The idea of centralization, however, finds its most significant expression when all central norms are created and executed by a single individual, who resides in the geographical center of the State, and so to speak forms its legal center. The idea of decentralization is commonly connected with the idea of a number of organs each located in the district to which its competence extends. There is an inclination to speak of decentralization whenever there is a plurality of norm-creating organs, regardless of the territorial spheres of validity of the norms created by these organs. When we do so, the term "decentralization" acquires a dynamic meaning, totally distinct from its static meaning.

If, for instance, central norms regulating different matters are created by different organs — as is the case where a cabinet government is established, the public administration is divided into different branches, and every branch of administration is placed under the direction of a cabinet minister — there is decentralization in this dynamic sense alone. In theory, it is possible for all norms, local as well as central, to be created by one individual organ. This would amount to the coincidence of a partial static decentralization and a total dynamic centralization. The fact that the same individual functions here as the organ creating the central and the local norms means that a personal union exists between the organs of the different orders constituted by the central and by the local norms. The same individual is not the same organ in his capacity as creator of central norms and in his capacity as creator of local norms; and not the same organ in his capacity as creator of local norms of different territorial spheres of validity. In spite of the personal union that would then exist between the organs of the different partial legal orders, it should be borne in mind that there still would exist one central and several local legal orders. Decentralization is usually resorted to just because it allows the same subject matter to be regulated differently for different regions. It will therefore generally be preferable not to allow the same individual to create the norms of the central order as well as those of the different local orders. It will be preferable to have different individuals act as law-creating organs of the different partial orders and thus to avoid a personal union of the organs of the different orders.

For the dynamic concept of centralization and decentralization, not only the number of norm-creating organs, but also the manner of their institution is important. The contrast between a centralized and a decentralized creation of organs is clearly brought out by an hereditary monarch, on the one hand, and a president elected by the whole nation, on the other. Such a president elected by the whole nation, in his turn, is instituted in a much more centralized manner than, for instance, the senate in a federal State, composed of representatives of the member States elected by the legislatures or the peoples of the member States. As far as the creation of organs is concerned, the senate has a much more decentralized character than the president, regardless of the respective territorial spheres of validity of the norms created by those two organs.

The decentralization is both static and dynamic if the legal order valid only for a partial community is created by organs elected simply by the members of this partial community. An instance is a federal State where statutes that are valid for the territory of a member State only must have been passed by the local legislature elected by the citizens of this member State. Static decentralization is combined with dynamic centralization, for instance, when an hereditary monarch enacts different statutes on religion for different provinces of his realm.

Once more it must be emphasized that the dynamic and static concepts of centralization and decentralization are entirely different. Whether or not the terms should be reserved for the static concept is a terminological question. But it is essential to observe the distinction that traditional theory has blurred.

b. Form of Government and Form of Organization

Since centralization and decentralization are forms of organization, the question arises whether there is any internal connection between these two forms of organization and the forms of government: autocracy and democracy.

Assuming the dynamic concept of centralization and decentralization, democracy can be described as a decentralized method of creating norms, since in a democracy the legal norms are created by the plurality of the individuals whose behavior they regulate, and these law-creating organs are dispersed over the whole territory for which the legal order is valid. In an autocracy, the legal order is created by a single individual different and independent of the plurality of individuals subject to the order. Since the law-creating function is here concentrated in the person of the autocrat, autocracy can be characterized as a centralized method of creating norms.

The dynamic distinction between centralization and decentralization also puts the difference between statutory and customary law in a new light. The creation of customary law by the uniform and continuous behavior of the same individuals who are to be subject to the law has a decentralized character for the same reason as the democratic procedure; it is in fact a form of democratic law-making since it is based on a real though unconscious autonomy. Statutory law, on the other hand, is characterized by the fact that it is created by an organ intentionally instituted for this purpose. In direct democracy, the difference between customary and statutory law is not yet conspicuous. The difference becomes important only if legislation is enacted by a special organ according to the principle of division of labor, as in an indirect democracy. The fact that in the absolute monarchy of the eighteenth century a part of the legal order — especially civil law — had the character of customary law and thus was practically withdrawn from the legislative power of the monarch, implied a political counterpoise. The technical development from customary to statutory law created by special organs according to the principle of division of labor signifies dynamic centralization and simultaneously attenuation of the democratic method of law-creation.

Like law-creation by custom, law-creation by contract and treaty has a decentralized character, and insofar as in this case, too, the legal norm is created by the same individuals who are subject to it, the contractual creation of law is a democratic procedure.

If we assume the static concept of centralization and decentralization, no direct connection exists between these forms of organization and the two forms of government. Autocracies and democracies may be centralized as well as decentralized in a static sense. A legal order created in an autocratic way as well as a legal order created in a democratic way may be composed only of central norms, norms valid for the whole territory, or may be composed of central and local norms, norms valid for the whole territory and norms valid only for partial territories. Autocracy and democracy are both possible with, as well as without, territorial subdivision of the State.

There is, however, an indirect connection between autocracy and democracy on the one hand, and centralization and decentralization in a static sense on the other hand. Autocracy is not only a method of law-creating whose character is centralistic in a dynamic sense; it has also an immanent tendency towards centralization in a static sense. And democracy is not only a method of law-creating whose character is decentralistic in a dynamic sense; it has also an immanent tendency towards decentralization in a static sense.

c. Democracy and Decentralization

Autocracy — as we have pointed out — is possible with a centralized as well as with a decentralized organization (in a static sense), that is to say, with or without subdivision into provinces. If, however, the State is to be territorially divided into provinces, it is practically inevitable that the autocrat will appoint for every province a governor who, as his representative, is competent to create the norms valid only for that territory. Static decentralization entails dynamic decentralization, and dynamic decentralization involves a transfer of power from the autocrat to his representative, and hence a weakening of the autocratic principle. The autocrat is always opposed to such a transfer of power to other organs and is inclined to concentrate the greatest possible number of functions in his own person. In order to avoid dynamic decentralization, he has to avoid as far as possible static decentralization, and to try to regulate the greatest possible number of subject matters by central norms. As a matter of fact, autocracies show a natural preference for static centralization.

Democracy, too, may be centralized as well as decentralized in a static sense; but decentralization allows a closer approach to the idea of democracy than centralization. This idea is the principle of self-determination. Democracy demands the utmost conformity between the general will as expressed in the legal order and the will of the individuals subject to the order; this is why the legal order is created by the very individuals who are bound by it according to the principle of majority. Conformity of the order with the will of the majority is the aim of democratic organization. But the central norms of the order, valid for the whole territory, may easily come into contradiction with the majority will of a group living on a partial territory. The fact that the majority of the total community belongs to a certain political party, nationality, race, language, or religion, does not exclude the possibility that within certain partial territories the majority of the individuals belong to another party, nationality, race, language, or religion. The majority of the entire nation may be socialistic or Catholic, the majority of one or more provinces may be liberal or Protestant. In order to diminish the possible contradiction between the contents of the legal order and the will of the individuals subject to it, in order to approximate as far as possible the ideal of democracy, it may be necessary, under certain circumstances, that certain norms of the legal order be valid only for certain partial territories and be created only by majority vote of the individuals living in these territories. Under the condition that the population of the State has no uniform social structure, territorial division of the State territory into more or less autonomous provinces (and this means decentralization in a static sense) may be a democratic postulate. Circumstances of settlement may render it impossible to adjust the organization of the State by territorial subdivision to the social structure of the population.

In such a case, division on the basis of personal status instead of territorial division may be attempted, as far as this is technically possible.

d. Perfect and Imperfect Centralization and Decentralization

Besides the quantitative distinction between total and partial decentralization, it is necessary to make a qualitative distinction between perfect and imperfect decentralization. We speak of perfect decentralization when the creation of local norms is final and independent. It is final when there is no possibility that the local norm may be abolished and replaced by a central norm. The division of the legislative power in the federal State between a central and several local organs furnishes an example of decentralization that is not final. Certain subject matters are here reserved for local legislation, that is, legislation of member States; but in some instances a local (member State) statute may be abolished or replaced by a contrary central (federal) statute, on the principle that federal law overrides member State law. The creation of local norms is independent if their contents are in no way determined by central norms. Decentralization is accordingly imperfect when a central law contains the general principles to which local legislation has only to give a more detailed application.

e. Administrative Decentralization

Administrative decentralization is imperfect decentralization in the domain of the executive power. It applies not only to public administration in the narrower sense but also to the administration of justice (judicial administration). Under this system, the State is usually divided into administrative and judicial provinces, the provinces into counties. For each region, an administrative authority and a court are instituted, authorized to create individual norms (by administrative acts and judicial decisions) for that particular region. These organs stand in a hierarchical order. In the field of public administration: The chief executive or a cabinet minister competent for the whole territory of the State; a governor for each province; and an administrator for each county. In the field of the judiciary: the supreme court for the whole territory; under the supreme court, the courts of the provinces; under each provincial court, the county courts. The execution of a general norm (statute or rule of customary law) is carried out by the administrative or judicial organs in three successive stages beginning with an act of the lowest administrative or judicial authority, with an administrative act of the administrator of a county or with the decision of a county court. But the norm created by these acts is not final. The party concerned may appeal from the lower to the higher authority, from the administrator of the county to the governor of the province, from the county court to the province court. The higher authority has the power to abolish the norm created by the lower authority, with the effect that the latter has to enact a new norm; or the higher authority has the power to replace the norm created by the lower authority by another individual norm. But this norm, too, is not final, if there is a possibility of appeal to the highest authority, the chief executive or cabinet minister, or the supreme court.

Under the system of administrative decentralization, the norms created by the administrative authorities are not independent, whereas the norms created by the courts are independent. The higher administrative authority has the power to determine the contents of the norm to be created by the lower authority. The latter is obliged to obey the former's instructions. This is not the case in the relationship between the higher and the lower courts. The courts are independent; that means that, as a rule, their decisions cannot be determined by a higher judicial or administrative authority, but only by the legislative organ, by a statute or a general rule of customary law. If decisions of a higher court have the character of precedents the lower courts are less independent and the administration of justice is less decentralized (more centralized). On the whole, the "independence of the courts" implies a higher degree of decentralization within the system of so-called administrative decentralization. The decentralization of the judicial procedure is more perfect than that of the administrative procedure. Since the highest administrative organs are central organs, and since at this stage there is no decentralization, there is no difference between the highest administrative and the judicial organs, as far as independence is concerned. The highest administrative authorities are, by their very nature, independent just as are the courts.

f. Decentralization by Local Autonomy

So-called local autonomy is a direct and deliberate combination of the ideas of decentralization and democracy. The organs creating local norms are here elected by those for whom these norms are valid. An example of an autonomous local unit is the municipality and the mayor. It is a local, decentralized self-government. The decentralization refers only to certain subject matters of special local interest; and the scope of municipal authority is restricted to the stage of individual norms. But sometimes the elected administrative body, the municipal council, is competent to issue general norms, so-called autonomous statutes; but these statutes have to stay within the framework of central statutes, issued by the legislative organ of the State.

Local autonomy represents normally a type of a comparatively perfect decentralization. The norms issued by the autonomous organs are final and independent, at least with respect to the central administrative organs of the State, especially if these organs have a more or less autocratic character, that means, if they are not themselves collegiate organs elected by the people, but individual organs appointed by the chief executive, especially by a monarch. It is in the monarchy that local autonomy is of the greatest importance. Sometimes the central administrative authorities are competent to supervise the activity of the autonomous bodies; they may annul norms issued by autonomous organs which violate central statutes issued by the legislative organ of the State, but they may not replace such norms by norms created by themselves.

Several autonomous units may be combined into a higher autonomous unit, so that the administration is democratic, not only at the lowest, but also at the higher stage. In this case, the territorially larger autonomous community under an elected council and mayor (or governor) is subdivided into smaller autonomous communities. Since the superior as well as the inferior administrative organ has a democratic character, the degree of decentralization in the relationship between the two may be diminished. Decentralization may be less perfect than in the case where the superior administrative authority has a more or less autocratic character. The parties may have the right to appeal from a decision of the organs of the smaller community to the organs of the larger community; and the latter may have the power to annul the norms issued by the former, or to replace them by a norm created by themselves.

The comparatively high degree of decentralization which the autonomous bodies, especially municipalities, enjoy within the modern State can, in the main, be traced back to the historical fact that they originated at a time when the States, and especially their central organs, had a more or less autocratic character, whereas the local government, especially the administration of the cities, was more or less democratic. Decentralization by democratically organized local governments meant the elimination of the influence of autocratic central organs. The struggle for local autonomy originally was a struggle for democracy within an autocratic State. But when the State already has an essentially democratic organization, the grant of local autonomy to a territorially defined group means only decentralization.

The local autonomy of self-governing bodies is not — as is often asserted — a right of these bodies against the State; that is only a political postulate presented by a natural-law doctrine as a natural right. There is no antagonism between State administration and administration by local autonomy. The latter is only a certain stage of State administration. If this stage has a democratic, the other stages an autocratic character, then the appearance of an antagonism may arise. But if the whole State is democratically organized, there is no longer any reason to oppose State administration to administration by local autonomy.

g. Decentralization by Autonomous Provinces

In the case of local autonomy, the decentralization is in principle restricted to administration, that is, to individual norms created by administrative organs. But decentralization may be extended to legislation, the creation of general norms. This is normally connected with a comparatively larger territorial sphere of validity of the norms concerned. This is the type of decentralization by autonomous provinces. The organs of the autonomous provinces are a local legislative body, elected by the citizens of the province, and possibly also a local administrative body, elected by the local legislature or directly by the people of the province. It is often the case that the chief of the autonomous administration of the province is a governor elected by the citizens or by the legislative body of the province. If the governor is appointed by the head of State, the degree of decentralization and, therefore, of autonomy, is smaller. The governor may function together with the elected administrative body, or may be independent of it. There are usually no judicial organs of the autonomous province. The courts are considered as State courts, not as courts of the autonomous province. That means that the judiciary is no more decentralized than corresponds to the type of administrative decentralization. Only legislation and administration, not the judiciary, have an autonomous character; only legislation and administration are divided between a central and a local legal community.

D. FEDERAL STATE AND CONFEDERACY OF STATES

a. Centralization of Legislation

1. Federal State

Only the degree of decentralization distinguishes a unitary State divided into autonomous provinces from a federal State. And as the federal State is distinguished from a unitary State, so is an international confederacy of States distinguished from a federal State by a higher degree of decentralization only. On the scale of decentralization, the federal State stands between the unitary State and an international union of States. It presents a degree of decentralization that is still compatible with a legal community constituted by national law, that is, with a State, and a degree of centralization that is no longer compatible with an international legal community, a community constituted by international law.

The legal order of a federal State is composed of central norms valid for its entire territory and local norms valid only for portions of this territory, for the territories of the "component (or member) States." The general central norms, the "federal laws," are created by a central legislative organ, the legislature of the "federation," while the general local norms are created by local legislative organs, the legislatures of the component States. This presupposes that in the federal State the material sphere of validity of the legal order, or, in other words, the legislative competence of the State, is divided between one central and several local authorities. On this point there exists a great similarity between the structure of a federal State and that of a unitary State subdivided into autonomous provinces. The broader the competence of the central organs, the competence of the federation, the narrower is the competence of the local organs, the competence of the component States, and the higher the degree of centralization. On this point, a federal State differs from a unitary State with autonomous provinces only by the fact that the matters subject to the legislation of the component States are more numerous and important than those subject to the legislation of the autonomous provinces.

The central norms form a central legal order by which a partial legal community is constituted comprising all the individuals residing within the whole territory of the federal State. This partial community constituted by the central legal order is the "federation." It is part of the total federal State, just as the central legal order is part of the total legal order of the federal State. The local norms, valid only for definite parts of the whole territory, form local legal orders by which partial legal communities are constituted. Each partial legal community comprises the individuals residing within one of these partial territories. These partial legal communities are the "component States." Every individual thus belongs simultaneously to a component State and to the federation. The federal State, the total legal community, thus consists of the federation, a central legal community, and the component States, several local legal communities. Traditional theory erroneously identifies the federation with the total federal State.

Each of the partial communities, the federation and the component States, rests upon its own constitution, the constitution of the federation and the constitution of the component State. The constitution of the federation, the "federal constitution," however, is simultaneously the constitution of the whole federal State.

The federal State is characterized by the fact that the component

States possess a certain measure of constitutional autonomy, that is to say, that the legislative organ of each component State is competent in matters concerning the constitution of this community, so that changes in the constitutions of the component States can be accomplished by statutes of the component States themselves. This constitutional autonomy of the component States is limited. The component States are bound by certain constitutional principles of the federal constitution; for instance, according to the federal constitution, the component States may be obliged to have democratic-republican constitutions. By this constitutional autonomy of the component States — even if limited — the federal State is distinguished from a relatively decentralized unitary State, organized in autonomous provinces. If these are regarded merely as autonomous provinces and not as component States, it is not only because their competence, especially the competence of the provincial legislation, is relatively restricted, but also because these provinces have no constitutional autonomy, because their constitutions are prescribed for them by the constitution of the State as a whole and can be changed only by a change in this constitution. The legislation in matters of the constitution is here completely centralized, whereas in the federal State it is only incompletely centralized; that is to say, up to a certain point it is decentralized.

The centralization in the federal State, that is, the fact that a considerable portion of the norms of the total legal order are valid throughout the entire extent of the federation, is limited by the fact that the central law-creating organ is composed in the following manner, especially typical of the federal State: it consists of two Houses; the members of one are elected directly by all the people of the federal State; this is the so-called House of Representatives, or Chamber of Deputies, also called the Popular House. The second chamber is composed of individuals chosen either by the people or by the legislative organ of each component State. They are looked upon as representatives of these component States. This second chamber bears the name of House of States, or Senate. It corresponds to the ideal type of the federal State that the component States should be equally represented in the House of States, the Senate, that each component State, without regard to its size, that is, without regard to the extent of its territory or the number of its inhabitants, should send the same number of representatives to the House of States, the Senate.

Normally, a federal State comes into existence through an international treaty concluded by independent States. The fact that each component State is represented in the Senate by the same number of delegates shows that the component States were originally independent

States, and are still to be dealt with according to the principle of international law known as equality of States. This composition of the House of States, or the Senate, guarantees that the component States, the local communities, "as such," take part in the central procedure of legislation, which amounts to an element of decentralization. But this element of decentralization based on the idea of the equality of the component States is almost completely neutralized by the fact that the House of States passes its resolutions according to the principle of majority. It is by virtue of this fact that this legislative organ is divested of its international character.

2. Confederacy of States

A purely international union of States, amounting to an organized community, a so-called confederacy of States, as, for instance, the League of Nations, can resemble a federal State in many respects. The constitution of this community is the content of an international treaty, as is normally the case with a federal State as well. The constitution of a confederacy of States is a legal order valid throughout the territory of all the States of this international community. It has the character of a central order and constitutes a partial community, the "confederation." The separate States, the so-called "member States," are, like the component States of the federal State, partial communities, too, constituted by local, namely, by their national, legal orders. The confederation together with the member States form the total community, the confederacy. The constitution of the central community which is at the same time the constitution of the total community, the confederacy, can set up a central organ competent to enact norms valid for all the States of the community, that is, throughout the entire extent of the union. This organ can be compared to the central legislative organ of a federal State. It is ordinarily a board composed of representatives of the member States; these representatives are appointed by their governments. The central organ normally votes its resolutions binding on the members of the union unanimously, each member State represented in the central organ having the same number of votes. Binding majority resolutions are not excluded, but they are the exception. The Assembly of the League of Nations is such an organ, for instance.

The constitution of the confederacy ordinarily contains no provision in regard to the constitutions of the member States. Yet it is possible for the constitutional autonomy of the members even of a purely international union to be restricted to a certain extent. For instance, the Covenant of the League of Nations requires that each member of the League must be a "fully self-governing" State. There would be nothing to prevent the agreement comprising the constitution of a confederacy from obliging the member States to have democratic-republican constitutions.

b. Centralization of Execution

1. Federal State

In the federal State it is not only the legislative competence that is divided between the federation and the component States, but also the judicial and the administrative competence. Besides federal courts, there are the courts of the component States; besides the administrative organs of the federation, there are those of the component States. The supreme federal court is competent not only for the settlement of certain conflicts and for the punishment of certain crimes of private individuals, but also for the decision of conflicts between the component States. At the head of the federal administration there is a federal government vested with executive power that can be employed not only in the form of execution of sanctions against individuals but also — as so-called federal execution — against the component States as such, whenever they, that is, their organs, violate the constitution of the federation, which is — as has been pointed out — at the same time the constitution of the whole federal State.

At the head of the administration of each component State there is a government of that State. The form of the government — of the federation or of the component States — can be monarchical or republican, and, in the latter case, corresponds more or less to democratic principles. The government may be an individual or a collegiate organ, that is to say, it may consist of a single individual or of several, and these may — but need not — constitute a board, passing its resolutions by majority vote. The government, especially the head of a republican federal State, is chosen, either directly by the people or by the legislative organ.

2. Confederacy of States

The constitution of an international confederacy, a union or a league of States, can also set up a central court and central government. But the court is, normally, competent only for the settlement of conflicts between the member States; only exceptionally may private persons be admitted as plaintiffs and defendants. The central governing organ has the character of a board. If it is to be an organ different from the central legislative organ already mentioned, then not all the members can be represented on it, or not all in the same way. An example is the

Council of the League of Nations, upon which only the great powers are permanently represented, and for periods of time, a portion of the other member States. For the decisions of this organ, too, the rule of unanimity prevails.

c. Distribution of Competence in a Federal State and a Confederacy of States

Among the subject matters that in a federal State usually fall within the competence of the federation, are all foreign affairs, hence, specifically the conclusion of international treaties, declaration of war, conclusion of peace, and control of the armed forces. This is to say that the army, navy and air force are organs of the federation, not organs of the component States which as such have nothing to do with international affairs. The armed forces usually are under the command of the head of the federal State. It may happen that the component States retain certain jurisdiction concerning the armed forces. But this can only be very unimportant, as the armed forces are most closely connected with the foreign policy, and this appertains exclusively to the federation. Just in those fields where the so-called power of the State is most evident, a federal constitution leads to a very considerable restriction of the competence of the component States, or of their sovereignty as one usually calls their competence in this connection.

The competence of an international confederacy is usually limited to the settlement of disputes between the member States and defense against external aggression. The competence of the member States in the field of external politics and military affairs remains practically unrestricted. There is no centralization of the executive power. The confederacy has no police, army, navy, or air force of its own. The member States remain in unrestricted possession of all their instruments of power, especially of their armed forces. If it becomes necessary to wage war against States outside the confederacy, the member States must place at the disposal of the central organ of the confederacy the necessary armed forces. If a military sanction is to be executed against a member State guilty of violating the constitution of the confederacy, this, too, is possible only with the armed forces of the other member States contributing to this end. As the State against which the sanction is directed has an army, navy, and air force of its own, the execution of the sanction means war within the community. And the violation of the constitution of the confederacy may consist in one member State's resorting to war against another. All this is precluded in a federal State if the executive power is so centralized that the component States have no military armed forces at their disposal, which is usually the case.

d. Citizenship

It is a characteristic element of a federal State that there is federal citizenship even if each component State also has its State citizenship. If this is so, then each individual is a citizen of a certain component State as well as a citizen of the federation; and stipulations must be provided to regulate the relations between the two institutions. In the international confederacy, there is no citizenship of the confederation. The individuals are citizens of the member States only. They belong legally to the international community only indirectly, through their States.

e. Direct and Indirect Obligating and Authorizing

The jurisdiction of the central organ of the federal State in other matters is not so important as in the field of foreign affairs, military matters and State citizenship. Ordinarily, the federation has considerable rights in the economic field, too, especially in relation to monetary matters, and in the field of customs (in connection with foreign relations). Usually the federal State constitutes a single customs and currency unit. It is important, however, that the federation have the right to levy and collect taxes to cover the expenses of its activity in the field of legislation, the judiciary and the administration. By the tax laws and by the military laws of the federation, individuals are directly obligated to the performance of certain duties. In the confederacy of States, the member States have to contribute contingents of troops and fixed sums of money to the confederacy; and, hence, have on their own part first to enact the required laws by which the individuals are obligated to military service and to the payment of taxes. In the federal State, however, the requirements from individuals are the subject matter of legal duties which are stipulated directly by the federal statutes. And the fact that the central norms, the federal laws, obligate and authorize individuals directly, without any mediation of local norms, of laws of the component States, is a characteristic of the federal State.

In this it is distinguished especially strikingly from the international confederacy of States. The central norms of the legal order constituting the confederation obligate and authorize directly only States; individuals are affected only indirectly by the medium of the legal orders of the States to which they belong. The mere indirect obligating and authorizing of individuals is, as shall be shown later,* a typical element of the technique of international law. The very fact that the central norms

---

* Cf. *infra*, pp. 341ff.

of the legal order of a federal State set up direct obligation and authorization of individuals, proves that this order is a national, not an international, legal order. And in this connection, in consideration of the relation of the central to the local norms of the legal order of a federal State, it becomes apparent that the difference between direct and indirect obligating and authorizing of individuals can also be conceived of from the point of view of centralization and decentralization. It is obvious that it implies a certain decentralization, or a lesser degree of centralization, if central norms can obligate and authorize individuals only through the medium of local norms; and, *vice versa*, it implies a certain centralization if the central norms have no need for this mediation of local norms to obligate and authorize individuals. In this respect, too, the federal State in comparison with a purely international confederacy of States, presents a higher degree of centralization, and is just on this account a State and not merely a union of States.

This difference is also apparent in the fact that the member States of an international community, especially of a confederacy of States, can normally leave the community, withdrawing from the union, whereas for the component States of a federal State, no such possibility legally exists. The component States of a federal State normally are not subjects of international law. Only the federal State has international rights and duties. If it is considered to be an essential element of the State to be a subject of international law, the so-called component States of a federal State are not States in the real sense of the term, at least not States in the sense of international law.

f. Internationalization and Centralization

If the entire foreign policy is entrusted to the central organs of a federal State, especially if all international treaties are concluded by the competent organ of the federation, then it must be possible for the federation to execute these treaties. As international treaties may relate to any conceivable subject matter, even to subject matters which are reserved for the legislation and execution of the component States, it must be possible for the federation to interfere in this competence of the component States. Hence, with extensive internationalization of the cultural or economic life, the competence of the component States must be correspondingly limited. This tendency toward centralization, the gradual transition of the federal State to a unitary State, is favored by other circumstances, also, that tend to State control of economic life, to the development of State capitalism. It is almost unavoidable that such centralization in the economic field should lead to a political centralization and, hence, to a certain leveling of the cultural field as well, if the component States that are united in a federal State represented originally different cultures.

g. Transformation of a Unitary State into a Federal State or into a Confederacy of States

Only if the essence of the federal State is conceived of as a particular degree and a specific form of decentralization is it possible to recognize a concrete positive constitution by its mere contents as a federal State. From this point of view, the mode of its creation becomes irrelevant: whether it has come into existence by an international treaty (establishing the federal constitution) between hitherto "sovereign" States, i.e., States subordinated only to the international legal order; or by the legislative act of a unitary State transforming itself into a federal State by increasing the degree of its decentralization. In this way, the Austrian republic, a unitary State with autonomous provinces, was transformed in 1920 into a federal State by an amendment to the constitution.

The same is true of the confederacy of States. Normally, a confederacy of States is established by an international treaty; but it is not excluded that a State, especially a federal State, should be transformed by an act of its legislative organ modifying its constitution into a confederacy of States. That, e.g., is the way in which the British Empire became a mere union of States through the so-called Statute of Westminster, 1931 (an Act of the British Parliament).

It is a way of decentralization. If the new constitution presents such a degree of decentralization as is characteristic of a confederacy of States, the component States of the federal State become full States in the sense of international law. The federal State disappears. A development in the opposite direction is possible too. Several independent States may, by an international treaty, unite not only into a federal, but also into a unitary State if the constitution established by the treaty presents the appropriate degree of centralization.

If the constitution of a federal or a unitary State is the content of an international treaty, it has the character of international law and, as constitution of a State, and that means as basis of a national legal order, at the same time that of national law. If the constitution of a federal State is transformed by a legislative act of this State into the constitution of a confederacy of States, it assumes the character of international law although it is, as the content of a statute enacted by the organ of a State, at the same time national law.

E. The International Legal Community

a. No Absolute Borderline between National and International Law

The indubitable fact that States (mostly federal States) have been established by international treaty, and a confederacy of States by a legislative act, shows clearly that the traditional view according to which national (municipal) law cannot be created by international law, and international law cannot owe its origin to national law,* is incorrect. There is no absolute borderline between national and international law. Norms which have, with respect to their creation, the character of international law, because established by an international treaty, may have, with respect to their contents, the character of national law because they establish a relatively centralized organization. And *vice versa*, norms which have, with respect to their creation, the character of national law, because enacted by the act of one State, may, with respect to their contents, have the character of international law because they constitute a relatively decentralized organization.

b. National Law as a Relatively Centralized Legal Order

The difference between national and international law is only a relative one; it consists, in the first place, in the degree of centralization or decentralization. National law is a relatively centralized legal order. It is especially the centralization of the application of law, the institution of central judicial organs competent to establish the delict and to order and execute the sanction, which is characteristic of a legal order constituting a State. By the centralization of the judiciary, the State can be distinguished from the pre-statal legal community. It is likewise the degree of centralization by which the State is distinguished from the inter- or super-statal legal community, constituted by the international legal order. International law, compared with national law, is a more decentralized legal order. It presents the highest degree of decentralization occurring in positive law.

c. The Decentralization of International Law

In order to realize this, one has to consider all positive law, the international legal order as well as all the national legal orders, as one universal legal system. Within this system, the norms of so-called general international law are the central norms, valid for a territory comprising the territories of all actually existing States, and the territory where States can potentially exist. The legal orders of the States are local norms

* Cf. W. W. Willoughby, Fundamental Concepts of Public Law 284.

of this system. While the territory of a State, the territorial sphere of validity of a national legal order, is limited by provisions of international law, the territorial sphere of validity of the international legal order itself is legally not limited. International law is valid wherever its norms must be applied.

This, however, is no absolute difference between international and national law. It is only the actually valid legal orders which have such a limited territorial sphere of validity. It is not *a priori* excluded that the evolution of international law will lead to the establishment of a world State. This means, that the actually valid international legal order would be transformed by way of centralization into a national legal order whose territorial sphere of validity would coincide with that of actually valid international law.

1. Static Decentralization

The high degree of decentralization of international law, or the international legal community called the "Family of States," manifests itself, in the first place, by the fact that the central norms of this legal order, the norms of so-called general international law, are far surpassed, in number and importance, by the local norms, the norms of the national legal orders. They are partial legal orders within the universal legal order; and the legal communities constituted by these partial legal orders, the States, are partial legal communities within the universal legal community. Within this universal legal order, general international law, too, forms only a partial legal order which, together with the national legal orders, forms the universal legal order.

The national legal orders, however, are not the only local norms of the universal order. Local norms are also the norms of so-called particular international law, which as a rule is created by international treaties. The territorial spheres of these norms usually comprise the territories of the States that concluded the treaty to which the norms owe their existence. The norms of general international law are inferior in number and importance also to these norms of particular international law. Thus, within the universal legal order, the local norms clearly outweigh the central ones. The universal legal order strikingly shows the high degree of its decentralization if compared with the type of legal orders to which it is most closely related: a federal State or a confederacy of States.

Another aspect of the decentralization of international law is that its norms, as a rule, obligate and authorize only juristic persons, namely States, which means that international law, as we shall see later, regulates the behavior of individuals only indirectly, through the medium of the national legal orders. The fact that indirect obligating and authorizing has a decentralizing effect has already been pointed out in the chapter dealing with the difference between federal States and confederacies of States.*

2. Dynamic Decentralization

The dynamic decentralization of the universal legal order is still greater than its static. General international law does not establish any special organs working according to the principle of the division of labor. As far as general international law goes, both the creation and the application of law is entirely up to the subjects of international law, the States. Custom and treaty — both decentralized methods of creating law — are the only sources of law known by general international law. It is especially worthy of note that the application of law, too, is completely decentralized. General international law leaves it to the parties to a controversy to ascertain whether one of them is responsible for a delict, as the other claims, and to decide upon, and execute, the sanction. General international law is, in this respect, too, a primitive law. It has the technique of self-help. It is the State, violated in its right, which is authorized to react against the violator by resorting to war or reprisals. These are the specific sanctions provided by general international law.

3. Relative Centralization by Particular International Law

A higher degree of centralization can be achieved by particular international law. Courts, administrative organs, and even legislative organs can be established by international treaties. Such treaties constitute international communities the centralization of which far surpasses that of the international community constituted by general international law. Such a relatively centralized international community is the confederacy of States. If the centralization goes still further, the community becomes a federal State or even a unitary State, and the legal order created by international treaty assumes the character of national law.

Such then is the structure of the assumed universal legal community. But is there really such a universal legal community? Is it admissible to interpret the actually existing international order in such a way? Is it possible to conceive of positive international law together with the positive law of the different States as one universal legal order? That is the question with which the last part of this treatise has to deal.

* Cf. *supra*, p. 323.

VI. NATIONAL AND INTERNATIONAL LAW

A. The Legal Character of International Law

a. Delict and Sanction in International Law

Before considering whether the international legal order and the various national legal orders are all part of one legal system, we must first answer the question whether the norms designated as "international law" are really "law" in the same sense as national law, that is to say, law in the sense of the definition established in the first part of this treatise. Scientifically stated, this is the question whether so-called international law can be described in terms of "rules of law."

A rule of law, as stated in the first part of this book,* is a hypothetical judgment making a coercive act, forcible interference in the sphere of interests of a subject, the consequence of a certain act of the same or another subject. The coercive act which the rule of law provides as the consequence is the sanction; the conduct of the subject set forth as the condition is characterized as "illegal," it is the delict. The sanction is interpreted as a reaction of the legal community against the delict. The delict is undesirable behavior, especially forcible interference in the sphere of interests of another subject, a coercive act. The coercive act is therefore either a delict, a condition of the sanction, and hence forbidden, or a sanction, the consequence of a delict, and hence permitted. This alternative is an essential characteristic of the coercive order called law.

International law is law in this sense if the coercive act of a State, the forcible interference of a State in the sphere of interests of another, is permitted only as a reaction against a delict, and the employment of force to any other end is forbidden, if the coercive act undertaken as a reaction against a delict can be interpreted as a reaction of the international legal community. If it is possible to describe the material which presents itself as international law in such a way that the employment of force directed by one State against another can be interpreted only as either delict or sanction, then international law is law in the same sense as national law.

In speaking of international law, reference is made only to general international law, not to particular international law. The problem must therefore be formulated as follows: First, is there according to general international law such a thing as a delict, conduct of a State usually characterized as illegal? Second, is there according to general international law such a thing as a sanction, a coercive act provided as the con-

* Cf. *supra*, pp. 45ff.

sequence of a delict and directed against a State which conducts itself illegally; a deprivation of possessions by the employment of force, if necessary; a forcible interference in the normally protected sphere of interests of the State responsible for the delict? From what has been said in the first part, it follows that, juristically, specific conduct of a State can be considered a delict only if international law attaches to this conduct a sanction.

It is a commonly accepted view that there exists in international law such a thing as a delict, that is, conduct of a State which is considered illegal, contrary to international law, and, therefore, a violation of international law. This follows from the fact that international law is regarded as a system of norms which prescribe a certain conduct for States, i.e., establish this conduct as a pattern which ought to be followed. If a State without a specific reason recognized by international law invades territory which, according to international law, belongs to another State, or if a State fails to observe a treaty concluded with another State according to international law, its conduct is considered contrary to the order in the same sense as is the conduct of an individual who tells a lie, from the standpoint of morality. In this sense, there is without doubt a delict in international law. But is there in international law such a thing as a delict in the specifically juristic sense, that is, is there also a sanction prescribed by international law, a sanction directed against the State responsible for the delict?

By "sanction" in international law many theorists mean the obligation to repair the wrong, especially the illegally caused damage. That is, so to speak, a substitute obligation, a duty which arises when a State has failed to fulfill its main or original obligation. The duty to make a reparation replaces the obligation violated.* It is, however, doubtful whether the obligation to make reparation is provided by general international law as an automatic consequence of the delict, or is only the result of a treaty concluded between the State affected by the delict and the State responsible for it. The author inclines to the latter view.† But even if the obligation to make reparation is provided by general international law as an automatic consequence of the delict, this substitute obligation cannot be considered a sanction. Only the consequence of not fulfilling this substitute obligation, the last consequence stated by the rule of law, constitutes a true sanction. The specific sanction of a legal order can only be a coercive act, a coercive act provided by the legal order for the case where an obligation is violated, and, if a substitute obligation is also established, for the case where this substitute obligation

* Cf. *supra*, pp. 138ff.
† Cf. *infra*, pp. 357f.

is also violated. Are there coercive acts provided by general international law as the consequence of international delicts; are there forcible interferences in the normally protected spheres of interests of the States responsible for the delict? These are the questions.

b. Reprisals and War

If all the material known under the name of international law be investigated, there appear two different kinds of forcible interference in the sphere of interests of a State, normally protected by international law. The distinction rests upon the degree of interference; whether this interference is in principle limited or unlimited; whether the action undertaken against a State is aimed solely at the violation of certain interests of this State, or is directed toward its complete submission or total annihilation.

As to the characterization of limited interference in the sphere of interests of one State by another, a generally accepted opinion prevails: Such an interference is considered either as a delict, in the sense of international law, or as a reprisal. It is permitted as a reprisal, however, only insofar as it takes place as a reaction against a delict. The idea that a reprisal, a limited interference in the normally protected sphere of interests of another State, is only admissible as a reaction against a wrong committed by this State, has been universally accepted and forms an undisputed part of positive international law. It is not essential that interference in the sphere of interests of a State, undertaken as a reprisal, be accompanied by the use of force, but the use of force in a resort to reprisal is permissible, especially if resistance makes it necessary. Similarly, the sanctions of national law, punishment and civil sanction, are executed by force only in the case of resistance.*

There is nothing to prevent our calling a reprisal a sanction of international law. Whether this is true also as to unlimited interference in the sphere of interests of another State remains to be seen. Such an interference is usually called war because it is an action executed by armed forces, the army, the navy, the air force. Our problem leads, therefore, to the question: what is the meaning of war according to international law? Is it possible to interpret war, like the limited interference in the sphere of interests of another State, as either a delict or a reaction against a delict, a sanction? In other words, is it possible to say that according to international law war is permitted only as a sanction, and any war which does not have the character of a sanction is forbidden by international law, is a delict?

* Cf. *supra*, pp. 18f.

c. The Two Interpretations of War

Two diametrically opposed views exist as to the interpretation of war. According to one opinion, war is neither a delict nor a sanction. Any State that is not expressly bound by special treaty to refrain from warring upon another State, or is bound to resort to war only under certain definite conditions, may proceed to war against any other State on any ground without violating international law. According to this opinion, therefore, war can never constitute a delict. For the behavior of a State which is called war is not forbidden by general international law; hence, to this extent, it is permitted. But war cannot constitute a sanction either. For according to this opinion there is in international law no special provision which authorizes the State to resort to war. War is not set up by general international law as a sanction against illegal conduct of a State.

The opposite opinion, however, holds that according to general international law war is forbidden in principle. It is permitted only as a reaction against an illegal act, a delict, and only when directed against the State responsible for this delict. As with reprisals, war has to be a sanction if it is not to be characterized as a delict. This is the theory of *bellum justum*.

It would be naïve to ask which of these two opinions is the correct one. For each is sponsored by outstanding authorities and defended with weighty arguments. This fact in itself makes any clear decision, any definite choice between the two theories extremely difficult.

By what arguments can the thesis be attacked or defended that according to general international law no war is permissible save as a reaction against a wrong suffered, against a delict? The mere statement of the problem in this form suggests that the position of those who represent the theory of *bellum justum* is more difficult to maintain; for the burden of proof is theirs, while the opposite view limits itself to a denial of this thesis, and, as is well known, *negantis major potestas*.

d. The Doctrine of Bellum Justum

1. International Public Opinion

If it be asked how it is possible to prove the thesis of the *bellum justum* theory, that general international law forbids war in principle, the first difficulty is encountered. According to strict juristic thinking, an act is prohibited within a certain legal system when a specific sanction is attached to this act. The only possible reaction that can be provided by general international law against an unpermitted war is war itself, a kind of "counter war" against the State which resorted to war in disregard of international law. No other sanction is possible according to the present technical condition of general international law. But this implies that war, or, to be more exact, counter war, must be presupposed as a sanction, in order to interpret war as a delict. Such a view, however, obviously begs the question, and is, therefore, logically inadmissible as proof of the thesis of the *bellum justum* theory.

There is, however, another way to go about this: by examining the historical manifestations of the will of the States, diplomatic documents, especially declarations of war and treaties between States; all these show quite clearly that the different States, i.e., the statesmen representing them, consider war as an illegal act, in principle forbidden by general international law, permitted only as a reaction against a wrong suffered. That proves the existence of a legal conviction that corresponds to the thesis of the *bellum justum* theory. This conviction manifests itself in the fact that the governments of States resorting to war always try to justify this to their own people as well as to the world at large. There is hardly an instance on record in which a State has not tried to proclaim its own cause just and righteous. If such proclamations do not appear in the official declaration of war, they can be found in other documents, or perhaps in the State-controlled press. Never yet has a government declared that it was resorting to war only because it felt at liberty to do so, or because such a step seemed advantageous. An examination of the various justifications for resorting to war reveals that it is usually contended that the other State has done wrong, or is on the verge of doing so, by committing an unwarranted act of aggression, or at least is preparing such an act, or has the intention of so doing. There can be little doubt that, on the whole, national public opinion, like international public opinion, disapproves of war and permits it only exceptionally as a means of realizing a good and just cause. The most radical exponents of war, the most extreme philosophers of imperialism, in their attempts to glorify war and to vilify pacifism, justify war only as a means to a good end.

2. The Idea of *Bellum Justum* in Positive International Law

It is generally admitted that intervention is, as a rule, forbidden by international law. Intervention is the dictatorial interference by a State in the affairs of another State. Dictatorial interference means interference implying the use or threat of force. The duty of non-intervention in the external and internal affairs of another State is considered to be the consequence of the fact that international law protects the internal and external independence of the States. This principle is incompatible with the doctrine that the State, by virtue of its sovereignty, can resort to war for any reason against any other State, without violating general international law. War is an unlimited interference in the affairs of another State implying the use of force; it is an intervention which possibly leads to the complete destruction of another State's external and internal independence. The generally accepted principle of non-intervention presupposes the *bellum justum* doctrine. An analysis of the circumstances under which — according to the traditional opinion * — a State, exceptionally, has the right of intervention shows that dictatorial interference in the affairs of another State is allowed only as a reaction against a violation of international law on the part of the State against which the intervention takes place. The violation may consist in the fact that this State does not comply with a treaty restricting its external or internal independence, such as intervention on the basis of a treaty of protectorate, or on the basis of a treaty guaranteeing the form of government of another State, or intervention in a State's external affair which, by an international treaty, is at the same time an affair of the intervening State. The violation may consist in noncompliance with a rule of general international law, such as the principle of the freedom of the open sea, or the rule obliging the State to treat foreigners in a certain way. Some writers maintain that intervention is not illegal if performed in the interest of self-preservation; but self-preservation is only a moral-political excuse for a violation of international law, not a right of the State. Some writers maintain also that intervention in the interest of the balance of power is admissible. But this, too, is a political rather than a legal principle. Intervention is legally allowed only if exercised as a reaction against a violation of international law; a rule which confirms the *bellum justum* doctrine.

It is easy to prove that the theory of *bellum justum* forms the basis of a number of highly important documents in positive international law, namely, the Peace Treaty of Versailles, the Covenant of the League of Nations, and the Kellogg Pact.

Article 231 of the Treaty of Versailles which establishes the war guilt of Germany justifies the reparation imposed on Germany by maintaining that she and her allies are responsible for an act of aggression. This means that Article 231 characterizes this aggression as an illegal act, as a delict, which would have been impossible if the authors of the Peace Treaty had shared the opinion that every State had a right to resort to war for any reason against any other State. If the aggression which Germany was forced to admit had not been considered "illegal," then it could not have been relied on to justify Germany's obligation to make

---

* Cf. 1 OPPENHEIM, INTERNATIONAL LAW 251f.

reparation for the loss and damage caused by the aggression. The Treaty of Versailles did not impose upon Germany a "war-indemnity" but the duty to make "reparation" for illegally caused damages. The aggression of Germany and her allies was considered illegal because the war to which they resorted in 1914 was considered to have been a war "imposed" upon the Allied and Associated Governments. This can mean only that Germany and her allies resorted to war without sufficient reason, that is, without having been wronged by the Allied and Associated Powers, or by any one of them. Only on the basis of the *bellum justum* doctrine is the idea of "war guilt" possible.

Article 15, paragraph 6, of the Covenant of the League of Nations permits members of the League, under certain conditions, to proceed to war against other League members, but only "for the maintenance of right and justice." Only a just war is permitted.

The Kellogg Pact forbids war, but only as an instrument of national policy. This is a very important qualification of the prohibition. A reasonable interpretation of the Kellogg Pact, one not attempting to make of it a useless and futile instrument, is that war is not forbidden as a means of international policy, especially not as a reaction against a violation of international law, as an instrument for the maintenance and realization of international law. This is exactly the idea of the *bellum justum* theory. Since, however, the Peace Treaty of Versailles, the Covenant of the League of Nations and the Kellogg Pact are instances of particular international law valid only for the contracting parties, these statements dealing with the "illegality" of war may be considered merely indications of the actual existence of a commonly accepted international legal conviction.

3. The Idea of *Bellum Justum* in Primitive Society

The legal conviction just mentioned is by no means an achievement of modern civilization. It is to be found under the most primitive conditions. It is unequivocally expressed even in the relationship of wild tribes. Normally, war between primitive tribes or groups is essentially a vendetta, an act of revenge; as such it is a reaction against a violation of certain interests, a reaction against what is considered a wrong. The vendetta is probably the original form of socially organized reaction against a suffered wrong, the first socially organized sanction. If law is the social organization of sanction, the original form of law must have been inter-tribal law, and, as such, a kind of international law.

The original inter-tribal law is, in its very essence, the principle of "just war." The well known ethnologist A. R. Radcliffe-Brown describes the wars between the very primitive Australians as follows: "The waging of war is in some communities, as among the Australian hordes, normally an act of retaliation, carried out by one group against another that is held responsible for an injury suffered, and the procedure is regulated by a recognized body of customs which is equivalent to the international law of modern nations." * In general, this is typical of all wars among primitive peoples. If international law is a primitive law, then it is quite natural that the principle of *bellum justum* should have been observed in this legal order.

4. The *Bellum Justum* Theory in Antiquity, the Middle Ages, and Modern Times

It is therefore hardly surprising that one should encounter the idea of just war in the inter-State law of the ancient Greeks. In his book on the international law of the early Greeks and Romans, Coleman Phillipson has this to say: "No war was undertaken without the belligerents' alleging a definite cause considered by them as a valid and sufficient justification therefor." † Even Roman imperialism believed it could not get along without an ideology by which its wars could be justified as legal actions. The law of war was closely connected with the so-called *jus fetiale*. Only such wars were considered "just wars" as were undertaken in observance of the rules of the *jus fetiale*. These rules had, it is true, essentially only a formal character; but Cicero, who may be regarded as the representative legal philosopher of ancient Rome, and who on this point, too, probably only expresses the generally prevailing public opinion, states that only such wars could be considered legal actions as were undertaken either for reasons of defense or for reasons of vengeance: *Illa injusta bella sunt quae sunt sine causa suscepta, nam extra ulciscendi aut propulsandorum hostium causam bellum geri justum nullum potest.* ("Wars undertaken without reasons are unjust wars. For except for the purpose of avenging or repulsing an enemy, no just war can be waged.") ‡ Saint Augustine and Isidoro de Sevilla are influenced in their theory of "just war" by Cicero.§ From the writings of these Christian authors the theory of "just war" is taken over by the *Decretum Gratiani*, to be ultimately incorporated in the *Summa Theologica* of St. Thomas Aquinas. It became the dominating doctrine of the Middle Ages, only to be absorbed by the natural-law theories of the sixteenth, seventeenth, and

---

* A. R. Radcliffe-Brown, *Primitive Law* (1933) 9 ENCYC. OF THE SOCIAL SCIENCES 203.

† 2 COLEMAN PHILLIPSON, THE INTERNATIONAL LAW AND CUSTOM OF ANCIENT GREECE AND ROME (1911) 179.

‡ CICERO, DE REPUBLICA, III, xxiii.

§ Cf. WILLIAM BALLIS, THE LEGAL POSITION OF WAR (1937) 27f.

eighteenth centuries. Grotius in particular expounds the view that according to natural law every war must have a just cause, and that, in the last analysis, this "just cause" can only be a wrong suffered. This idea, which remains predominant until the end of the eighteenth century, disappeared almost entirely from the theories of positive international law during the nineteenth century, although it still formed the basis of public opinion and of political ideologies of the different governments. Only after the close of the first World War was this doctrine of "just war" again taken up by certain authors.*

e. Arguments against the Bellum Justum Theory

The different arguments against the theory that according to general international law war is in principle forbidden, being permissible only as a reaction against a violation of international law, are of varying importance. Certainly the weakest of them, current during the nineteenth century, is that which was most frequently and most successfully relied upon during that period, namely, that it would be inconsistent with the sovereignty of a State to limit its right to resort to war. According to this view, it is especially in war that the sovereignty of a State manifests itself, and sovereignty is the true essence of the State.

Undoubtedly, any norm which forbids a State to resort to war against another State save as a reaction against a wrong suffered by it is contrary to the idea of the sovereignty of the State. This argument is directed not so much against the theory of *bellum justum*, however, as against international law in general, against every normative legal ordering of the conduct of States. For any legal order obligating States to behave in a certain manner can be conceived only as an authority above the State, and is, therefore, incompatible with the idea of their sovereignty. For to attribute sovereignty to a State means that it is itself the highest authority, above and beyond which there can be no higher authority regulating and determining its conduct. This particular argument does not really constitute a conception of international law opposed to the theory of "just war." It does not afford a different answer to the question of the content of positive international law. It rather denies international law *in toto* as a legal order obligating and authorizing States. Any discussion of the legal importance of war, however, presupposes the existence of a legal order obligating and authorizing States.

A more serious argument is that everything which can be said in favor of the *bellum justum* theory proves only that war is morally forbidden. It does not prove that international law forbids war in principle,

---

* Cf. Leo Strisower, Der Krieg und das Völkerrecht (1919).

and that it permits it only as a reaction against a wrong suffered. To this it might be replied that should it be possible to prove that States, or the individuals representing them, actually base their reciprocal behavior on the idea that any war which is not a reaction against a wrong itself constitutes a wrong, that only a war waged to right a wrong is a justifiable war, there would seem to be no good reason why this kind of war should not be regarded as a sanction. And if this is so, the judgment regarding the nature of war is definitely a "juristic judgment." Under these circumstances, it is possible to describe the phenomenon "war" in its relation to other phenomena in the form of a legal rule, using the term in a purely descriptive sense. Thus any war that is not merely a sanction can be characterized legally as a "delict."

Particularly serious is the objection that war of one State against another could never be set up as a sanction because for technical reasons no war can function as a sanction. War never guarantees that the wrongdoer alone will be hit by the evil which a sanction is supposed to mete out. In war not he who is in the "right" is victorious, but he who is the strongest. For this reason, war cannot be a reaction against a wrong, if the party which suffered this wrong is the weaker of the two. There can be no question of a sanction unless there exists an organization to carry out the act of coercion with powers so superior to the power of the wrongdoer that no serious resistance is possible.

The weightiest objection to the theory of just war, however, is the one which claims that according to general international law war cannot be interpreted either as a sanction or as a delict. Who is to decide the disputed issue as to whether one State actually has violated a right of another State? General international law has no tribunal to decide this question. It can only be decided, therefore, through mutual agreement between the parties. But this would be the exception, inasmuch as a State would hardly admit having violated the rights of another State. If no agreement can be reached between the parties to the conflict, the questions of whether or not international law has actually been violated and who is responsible for the violation cannot be uniformly decided, and certainly not — as is now and then believed — by the science of law. Not the science of law, not jurists, but only and exclusively the governments of the States in conflict are authorized to decide this question; and they may decide the question in different ways. If there is no uniform answer to the question whether in a given case there has or has not been a delict, then there is no uniform answer to the question whether the war waged as a reaction is or is not actually a "just war"; whether the character of this war is that of a sanction or of a delict. Thus the distinction between war as a sanction and war as a delict would become highly problematic. Moreover, there would seem to be no difference between the theory which holds that the State has a right to resort to war whenever and against whomever it pleases, and the theory according to which war is permitted only as a reaction against a delict, any other war being itself a delict, but which has to admit that within general international law it is almost impossible to apply these principles satisfactorily in any concrete instance.

f. The Primitive Legal Order

The attempt to meet all these objections is by no means intended to veil the theoretical difficulties of the enterprise. The objections raised against the theory of "just war" (and therefore against the legal character of international law in general) are grounded primarily in the technical insufficiency of general international law.

In its technical aspects, general international law is a primitive law, as is evidenced among other ways by its complete lack of a particular organ charged with the application of legal norms to a concrete instance. In primitive law,* the individual whose legally protected interests have been violated is himself authorized by the legal order to proceed against the wrongdoer with all the coercive means provided by the legal order. This is called self-help. Every individual takes the law into his own hands. Blood revenge is the most characteristic form of this primitive legal technique. Neither the establishment of the delict nor the execution of the sanction is conferred upon an authority distinct from the parties involved or interested. In both these aspects the legal order is entirely decentralized. There is neither a court nor a centralized executive power. The relatives of the murdered person, the bereaved, must themselves decide whether an avenging action should be undertaken, and if so, against whom they should proceed.

Nevertheless, in a primitive community the man avenging the murder of his father upon one whom he considers to be the murderer is himself regarded not as a murderer but as an organ of the community. For by this very act he executes a legal duty, a norm of the social order constituting the community. It is this norm which empowers him, and him only, under certain circumstances, and under these circumstances only, to kill the suspected murderer. This same man would not be acting as an organ or instrument of his community but merely as a murderer himself should this same action on his part be prompted by circumstances other than those provided by the legal order of his community, should he not be acting merely as an avenger. The distinction between murder, as a

* Cf. *supra*, pp. 17, 327.

delict, and homicide, as a fulfillment of a duty to avenge, is of the greatest importance for primitive society. It means that killing is only permitted if the killer acts as an organ of his community, if his action is undertaken in execution of the legal order. The coercive act is reserved to the community, and is, in consequence, a monopoly of this community. The decentralization of the application of the law does not prevent the coercive act as such from being strictly monopolized. This is the way such events are interpreted in primitive society; and this interpretation is one of the most important ideological foundations of primitive society, although it may well be doubted in a concrete instance whether the killing constitutes merely an avenging, a sanction, or should itself be regarded as a delict, and despite the fact that blood revenge is hardly a suitable means for protecting the weak against the strong.

A social order which has not progressed beyond the principle of self-help may produce a state of affairs leaving much to be desired. Nevertheless it is possible to consider this state a legal state, and this decentralized order a legal order. For this order can be interpreted as an order according to which the coercive act is a monopoly of the community, and it is permissible to interpret the primitive social order in this way because the individuals subjected to this order themselves interpret it in this way. History teaches that evolution everywhere proceeds from blood revenge toward the institution of courts and the development of a centralized executive power, that is, toward steadily increasing centralization of the coercive social order. We are entirely justified in calling the still decentralized coercive social order of primitive society "law," in spite of its rather crude techniques such as self-help; for this decentralized order constitutes the first step in an evolution which ultimately leads to the law of the State, to a centralized coercive order. As the embryo in the mother's womb is from the beginning a human being, so the decentralized coercive order of primitive self-help is already law, law *in statu nascendi*.

g. *International Law as Primitive Law*

From what has been said so far it may be inferred that general international law, characterized by the legal technique of self-help, can be interpreted in the same manner as a primitive legal order characterized by the institution of blood revenge (*vendetta*). This primitive law can be understood only if we distinguish — as does primitive man — between killing as a delict, and killing as a sanction. In order to understand international law, a differentiation must also be made between war as a delict and war as a sanction, despite the fact that the practical application of this distinction in a concrete case may be difficult, in some cases even impossible, and although war — like *vendetta* — is technically insufficient as a sanction.

Everything that has been said against interpreting war as a sanction can also be said against reprisals. Yet the opponents of the theory of "just war," which recognizes war only as a sanction, do not find it necessary to use their arguments against interpreting reprisals as sanctions.

Should we, however, contrary to the theory of "just war," refuse to regard war as in principle forbidden and permitted only as a reaction against a delict, we would no longer be in a position to conceive of general international law as an order turning the employment of force into a monopoly of the community. Under these circumstances, general international law could no longer be considered as a legal order. If the unlimited interference in the sphere of another's interests called "war" is not in principle forbidden by international law, and if any State is at liberty to resort to war against any other State, then international law fails to protect the sphere of interests of the State subjected to its order; the States have no protected sphere of interests at all, and the condition of affairs created by so-called international law cannot be a legal state.

Whether or not international law can be considered as true law depends upon whether it is possible to interpret international law in the sense of the theory of *bellum justum*, whether, in other words, it is possible to assume that, according to general international law, war is in principle forbidden, being permitted only as a sanction, i.e., as a reaction against a delict.

The opponents of the theory of the just war, or at least the majority of them, do not intend to question the legal character of international law. On the contrary, they insist upon calling international law true law. For this very reason, they do not deny that a reprisal, that is, a limited interference in the sphere of interests of a State, is permitted only as a reaction against a wrong, as a sanction. This is in truth an interpretation of international law which entails results that are more than paradoxical. No State would be entitled to a limited interference in the sphere of interests of another State, but every State would be fully justified in committing an unlimited interference in such a sphere. According to this interpretation, a State violates international law if it causes limited damage to another State, and in this case its enemy is authorized to react against it with reprisals. But the State does not violate international law, and does not render itself liable to a sanction, if its interference in the sphere of interests of the other State is adequate to afflict the whole population and the whole country of its enemy with death and destruction. This is similar to a social order according to which petty thievery is punished while armed robbery goes free.

Such an order is logically not impossible, but it is politically very improbable that a positive social order, especially international law, should have such a content, even if the intention of the order to reserve the employment of force to the community, to establish a monopoly of force in the community, be imperfectly realized.

The technical inadequacies of general international law do indeed to a certain extent justify the interpretation of the opponents of the *bellum justum* theory. But whoever attempts this interpretation must be consistent; he must not regard international law as true law. The opposite interpretation, however — that based on the *bellum justum* theory — is also possible, as has been shown. The situation is characterized by the possibility of a double interpretation. It is one of the peculiarities of the material which forms the object of the social sciences to be sometimes liable to a double interpretation. Hence, objective science is not able to decide for or against one or the other. It is not a scientific but a political decision which gives preference to the *bellum justum* theory. This preference is justified by the fact that only this interpretation conceives of the international order as law, although admittedly primitive law, the first step in an evolution which within the national community, the State, has led to a system of norms which is generally accepted as law. There can be little doubt that the international law of the present contains all the potentialities of such an evolution; it has even shown a definite tendency in this direction. Only if such an evolution could be recognized as inevitable would it be scientifically justified to declare the *bellum justum* theory the only correct interpretation of international law. Such a supposition, however, reflects political wishes rather than scientific thinking. From a strictly scientific point of view a diametrically opposite evolution of international relations is not absolutely excluded. That war is in principle a delict and is permitted only as a sanction is a possible interpretation of international relations, but not the only one.

Having shown that so-called international law can be regarded as "law" in the same sense as national law, we shall now turn to an examination of the relationship between the international legal order and the various national legal orders.

B. International Law and State

a. The Subjects of International Law: Indirect Obligating and Authorizing of Individuals by International Law

The relation between international and national law is by traditional doctrine considered under the aspect of the relation between international law and State. We have already seen that the State bears an intrinsic relation to international law: all the "elements" of the State are determined by international law. The same relationship is now approached from the side of international law. We shall see that international law presupposes the national legal orders just as they presuppose international law. International law regulates the mutual behavior of States; but this does not mean that international law imposes duties and confers rights only upon States, not upon individuals. The traditional opinion that subjects of international law are only States, not individuals, that international law is by its very nature incapable of obligating and authorizing individuals, is erroneous.

All law is regulation of human behavior. The only social reality to which legal norms can refer are the relations between human beings. Hence, a legal obligation as well as a legal right cannot have for its contents anything but the behavior of human individuals. If, then, international law should not obligate and authorize individuals, the obligations and rights stipulated by international law would have no contents at all and international law would not obligate or authorize anybody to do anything.

The present problem is similar to a problem discussed in the first part of this treatise:* the question how the national legal order can impose duties and confer rights upon juristic persons. The State, as a subject of international law, is in fact simply a juristic person. The State, as an acting person, is manifested solely in actions of human beings considered as its organs. That a person acts as an organ of the State signifies that his action is imputed to the personified unity of the national legal order. Thus when international law obligates and authorizes States this does not mean that it does not obligate and authorize human individuals; it means that international law obligates and authorizes those human individuals who are State organs. But international law regulates the behavior of these individuals indirectly, through the medium of the national legal order. This is, indeed, a technical particularity of international law. It is evidently this particularity which the traditional theory has in mind, but interprets incorrectly, when it states that only States, not individuals, are subjects of international law. When international law imposes upon a State the obligation to behave in a certain way *vis-à-vis* another State, and thus confers a right on the latter to claim the fulfillment of the former's obligation, it is determined only what ought to be done in the name of one State and what may be done in the name of the other; but it is not determined who, that is to say, which individual as organ of the State, has to fulfill the obligation stipulated by international

* Cf. *supra*, pp. 96ff.

law, and who, that is to say, which individual as organ of the State, has to exercise the right stipulated by international law. The determination of the individuals whose behavior forms the contents of international obligations and rights is left to the legal order of the States obligated and authorized by international law. This is the way in which international law obligates and authorizes individuals indirectly.

b. The Norms of International Law Incomplete Norms

In the first part of this treatise, it has been shown that the human behavior regulated by a legal norm consists of two elements: the material element, i.e., what has to be done or forborne, and the personal element, i.e., he by whom it has to be done or forborne. A norm is complete only if it determines both elements. The norms of international law usually determine only the material element, and are, in this sense, incomplete. They await supplementation by the norms of national law.

The following example may illustrate the above statement. There is a time-honored rule of common international law to the effect that war must not be begun without a previous formal declaration of war. The Third Hague Convention of 1907 codified this rule in the stipulation (Article I) that hostilities "must not commence without a previous and unequivocal warning, which shall take the form either of a declaration of war giving reasons, or of an ultimatum with a conditional declaration of war."

This norm states only that a declaration of war has to be delivered, not by whom — that is to say, by which individual as organ of the State — it has to be done. Most constitutions empower the head of the State to declare war. The Constitution of the United States (Article I, Section 8) says that "the Congress shall have power to declare war." By thus determining the personal element, the American constitution completes the norm of international law just mentioned.

The characteristic of international law that it "obligates States only" consists merely in the fact that its norms generally determine only the material element, leaving the determination of the personal element to national law.

c. Direct Obligating and Authorizing of Individuals by International Law

1. Individuals as Direct Subjects of International Duties

There are, however, important norms of international law which impose obligations or confer rights directly upon individuals. The norm prohibiting piracy is of this kind. Piracy is every act of illegal violence committed on the open sea by the crew of a private vessel against another vessel. All maritime States are authorized by general international law to capture on the open sea individuals who are guilty of piratical acts in order to punish them. This norm of international law attaches to the fact of "piracy" which this norm itself defines, a sanction directed against individuals practicing piracy. It prohibits piracy by obligating individuals, not by obligating States, to refrain from this delict. The individuals are obligated by international law to refrain from piracy in the same direct manner in which they are obligated by national law.

That the capture and punishment of a pirate is the execution of a sanction provided by a norm of international law can be seen from the fact that in the absence of this norm it would be contrary to international law to perform acts of coercion against pirates on the open sea. It is the principle of the freedom of the open sea, a very important principle of international law, which forbids every act of coercion against foreign ships on the open sea. The rule authorizing the States to capture and punish pirates is a restriction of the rule concerning the freedom of the sea; and as the latter is a rule of general international law, the former must likewise be a rule of general international law.

International law authorizes the States to resort to sanctions against pirates, but it does not directly determine these sanctions; it leaves the determination to the discretion of the States, that means, to the national legal orders. Nevertheless, this sanction, like war and reprisals, must be considered as a reaction of international law. The sanction provided — indirectly — by international law against piracy has, however, a character totally different from that of the ordinary sanctions provided directly by international law. War and reprisals are directed against the State as such; that means that they are executed according to the principle of collective responsibility. For this reason, they constitute legal obligations of the State as a juristic person.* The sanction provided against piracy is not directed against a State and, in particular, not against the State of which the pirate is a citizen. The sanction is directed against the pirate as against an individual who has violated his obligation under international law. This sanction of international law is executed according to the principle of individual responsibility. For that reason, it constitutes the international legal obligation of an individual without constituting the legal obligation of a State. In these exceptional cases where general international law directly obligates individuals, exceptional sanctions appear which are directed against individuals directly determined by international law. The sanction itself, however,

* Cf. *supra*, pp. 103ff.

need not be determined directly by the international legal order; it may be specified by the national legal order which international law delegates to this end.

Whatever may be the act of coercion prescribed by the legal order of the State with regard to the pirate, the State punishing him acts as an organ of the international legal community. For it is international law which the State applies against the pirate. That it may at the same time apply norms of its own national law, provisions of its own penal code concerning the crime of piracy, is incidental. One might even ask if such provisions are really necessary for the application of these norms of international law. The principle *nulla poena sine lege* is really respected even in the absence of any norm of national law, since a norm of international law exists authorizing the State to punish the pirate.

Other obligations of individuals directly stipulated by international law result from the rules concerning blockade and contraband of war. Breach of blockade, that is, the unallowed ingress or egress of a vessel in spite of a declared and effective blockade, is a delict or, as some writers declare, a "criminal act," directly determined by general international law. The sanction directly provided for by general international law is confiscation of the vessel and the cargo. The sanction is not directed against the State and, in particular, not against the State to which the vessel or its owner or the owner of the cargo belongs. The sanction is directed against the property of private individuals. It has not the character of a punishment in the specific sense of the term. Subjects of the obligation to refrain from breach of blockade are the commanders of the vessels of all nations. Legally responsible for the delict are the owners of the vessels and the cargo. In former times, when imprisonment and even capital punishment of the crew were legal sanctions authorized by general international law, the members of the crew were also subjects of the legal obligation to refrain from the delict, or legally responsible for the delict. Hence individuals are, as subjects of legal obligations and legal responsibilities, direct subjects of international law. An analysis of the norms relative to contraband of war has analogous results. Carriage of contraband is a delict determined directly by general international law; and its sanction, likewise determined directly by general international law, is the confiscation not only of the contraband cargo itself but also of all other parts of the cargo together with the vessel. In this case, too, the sanction is not directed against the State, but against private individuals.

According to the rules of general international law concerning the conduct of war, hostile acts on the part of individuals who do not belong to the armed forces of the enemy, are acts of illegitimate warfare. The authorities of the offended State are authorized to treat the offenders as war criminals and consequently punish them. By conferring upon the States the right to treat private individuals who, during war, take up arms against their armed forces as criminals, general international law determines directly this particular delict of illegitimate warfare, and indirectly the sanction leaving its specification and execution to the offended State. Thus international law imposes a legal obligation to abstain from the delict directly upon individuals.*

The difference between the norms of international law concerning piracy and the above-mentioned act of illegitimate warfare, on the one hand, and the norms concerning blockade and contraband of war, on the other hand, consists in that the latter determine the sanction directly whereas the former determine it only indirectly. The delict, however, is determined in all these cases directly by general international law with respect to the personal as well as to the material element of the illegal act.

Individuals may be subjects of international obligations not only according to general but also according to particular international law. Article 2 of the International Convention for the Protection of Submarine Telegraph Cables, signed at Paris on March 14, 1884, stipulates: "The breaking or injury of a submarine cable, done wilfully or through culpable negligence, and resulting in the total or partial interruption or embarrassment of telegraphic communication, shall be a punishable offense, but the punishment inflicted shall be no bar to a civil action for damages." A norm of conventional international law directly defines a delict and attaches criminal as well as civil sanctions to an act committed by an individual determined by this norm. The Convention obliges the States to specify by their national laws the sanctions (punishment and civil execution) provided by Article 2, and obliges the State

---

* 2 OPPENHEIM, INTERNATIONAL LAW 170 maintains that according to a generally recognised customary rule of International Law, hostile acts on the part of private individuals are not acts of legitimate warfare, and the offenders may be treated and punished as war criminals. But Oppenheim says also: "Although International Law by no means forbids, and, as a law between States, is not competent to forbid, private individuals to take up arms against an enemy, it does give a right to the enemy to treat hostilities committed by them as acts of illegitimate warfare." By giving a right to the State to punish an individual who has performed an act determined by international law, the latter forbids this act as a delict, and proves to be competent to impose legal duties upon private individuals. International law is a "law between States" because it is a law between individuals belonging to different States. The erroneous opinion that international law, by its very nature (as law between "States"), is not competent to impose duties upon individuals, is due to the fact that Oppenheim does not dissolve the personification "State" and takes the State as a being different from the individuals who "form" the State.

to which the vessel belongs and on board which the delict defined in Article 2 was committed, to execute the sanction. The national courts, by punishing an individual for the breaking or injury of a submarine cable or by ordering reparation of the damage caused by the delict, execute international law even if they apply their national law at the same time. The individuals concerned are obliged by international law to abstain from a delict determined by international law even if their national law also requires the same conduct.

Another example of direct obligation of individuals is the abortive treaty relating to the use of submarines, signed at Washington on February 6, 1922. Article 3 of this treaty states that any person in the service of any State who shall violate any rule of this treaty relative to the attack, capture, or destruction of commercial ships, whether or not he is under order of a governmental superior, "shall be deemed to have violated the laws of war and shall be liable to trial and punishment as if for an act of piracy and may be brought to trial before the civil or military authorities of any Power within the jurisdiction of which he may be found." In this case, too, a norm of particular international law directly determines the personal as well as the material element of a delict and attaches to it a sanction by authorizing the States to punish the individual delinquent.

2. Individuals as Direct Subjects of International Rights

Individuals can have international rights only if there is an international court before which they can appear as plaintiffs. International treaties may establish such courts. According to Article 2 of the abortive Convention relative to the creation of an International Prize Court, signed at the Hague, October 18, 1907, jurisdiction in matters of prize is exercised in the first instance by the prize courts of the belligerent captor. According to Article 3, the judgments of national prize courts may be brought before the International Prize Court; according to Article 4, an appeal may be brought not only by a neutral Power but also, under certain circumstances, "by a neutral individual" and "by an individual subject or citizen of an enemy Power." Thus the treaty confers upon individuals international rights. Other examples are offered by the Treaty of Versailles and the other peace treaties that terminated the first World War. These treaties authorize nationals of the Allied and Associated Powers to claim compensation in respect of damages caused by extraordinary war measures on Germany's part (Article 297, e); and they provide for the institution of mixed arbitral tribunals before which such nationals may bring actions against Germany.

These arbitral tribunals are also (by Article 304, b) given jurisdiction to settle all disputes arising out of contracts concluded previous to the Versailles Treaty between German nationals and citizens of the Allied and Associated Powers. The competence of German tribunals is here brushed aside in favor of an international court. Both the plaintiff and defendant are in these cases private individuals; and, since the court is functioning according to international law, these private individuals are subjects of rights and duties of international law. The text of the Treaty does not stipulate anything concerning what law the tribunals shall apply in settling disputes of this kind. If they should apply the national law of one of the parties, this law would become international law by reception. But, aside from this, the procedural law is in any event international; and it is procedural law which constitutes a right in the technical sense, and hence the quality of a subject of right. (The decision of the tribunal — by Article 304, g —has to be executed by the State to which the condemned belongs.)

The German-Polish Convention of May 15, 1922 regarding Upper Silesia furnishes another example of rights of individuals under international law. This agreement, in its Article 5, authorizes private individuals to bring a suit before an international court against the State which has violated certain interests of these individuals protected by the convention.

It is, however, only in exceptional cases that international law directly obligates or authorizes individuals. If this should become the rule, the borderline between international and national law would disappear.

d. National Law "Delegated" by International Law

On the whole, present international law obligates and authorizes individuals indirectly, through the medium of the various national legal orders. The norms of international law are mostly incomplete norms; they require completion by norms of national law. The international legal order presupposes the existence of the national legal orders. Without the latter, the former would be an inapplicable fragment of a legal order. Hence, a reference to national law is inherent in the meaning of the norms of international law. In this sense, the international legal order "delegates" to the national legal orders the completion of its own norms.

The relation between international and national law is here similar to that between national law and morality, when, for instance, the civil law of a State obligates people to behave in a certain situation according to prevailing moral norms. The civil law then presupposes the existence of these norms; it does not regulate a certain relationship between individuals directly by its own norms; it "delegates" the regulation of these matters to the norms of morality. Thus, international law too, "delegates" to national law the determination of the personal element of its norms. The relationship between the international legal order and the national legal orders is even more similar to that existing between the national legal order and a corporation. In the first part of this treatise * it has been shown that a national legal order imposes duties and confers rights upon a corporation by imposing duties and conferring rights upon individuals determined by the by-laws constituting the corporation. The by-laws of a corporation are a partial legal order within the national legal order which makes possible the organization of corporations by determining the condition under which by-laws can be established.

e. The Essential Function of International Law

If we examine the norms of present international law with respect to the subject matter they regulate, we can distinguish two different groups. The first consists of norms referring to matters that can be regulated only by international law and do not allow of regulation through national law. In these norms, the essential function of international law is manifest. The second includes norms referring to subject matters that can be regulated also by national law, and that actually are regulated only by national law insofar as customary or contractual international law does not regulate them, as, for instance, norms concerning the acquisition and loss of citizenship. The latter are norms that are possibly norms of international law; the former are norms that are necessarily norms of international law.

When norms are classified as being necessarily norms of international law because they refer to subject matters that, by their very nature, cannot be regulated by national law, one presupposes a certain conception of the relationship of States. It is a concept accepted by almost all internationalists, whatever may be their opinion on the nature of international law. According to this concept, all States are equal, each of them existing within its own sphere delimited by a normative order from that of the others. In examining the so-called elements of the State, we have already established that this sphere of existence is delimited at least in a territorial and a personal respect. Each State can claim as "its territory" only a part of space, and as "its people" only a part of mankind. Interference by one State with the sphere of another State is considered as forbidden, as a "violation" of the "right" of the other State. Such a normative delimitation of the spheres of existence of the States is acknowledged even by those who deny the legal character of the interna-

* Cf. *supra*, pp. 96ff.

tional order. The further question whether this normative delimitation has also a legal character is unimportant in this connection. But it is necessary to bear in mind that it is only this normative delimitation which renders it possible for the States to coexist peacefully side by side as equal subjects.

The delimitation could not be achieved by norms belonging to the legal order of one State, since every such order is limited in its validity to the territory and the people of that State. The delimitation must originate in a normative order whose territorial and personal sphere of validity comprises the territorial and personal spheres of validity of all the national legal orders. The only normative order we know of that fulfills this requirement is international law. It is in fact by international law that the territorial and personal, as well as the temporal, spheres of validity of the national legal orders are determined. This determination is the essential function of international law. The norms regulating this subject matter are essentially and necessarily norms of international law.

f. The Determination by the International Legal Order of the Sphere of Validity of the National Legal Order

The result of our analysis of the so-called elements of the State * is that the territorial and personal spheres of validity of the national legal order, the territorial and personal existence of the State, is determined and delimited in relation to other States by international law, according to the principle of effectiveness. A coercive order of human behavior is valid law, and the community constituted by it, a State in the sense of international law, for that territory and that population with regard to which the coercive order is permanently efficacious. By means of this principle international law determines also the temporal sphere of validity of the national legal order, the birth and the death of the State; for a coercive order remains valid, and the community constituted by it remains a State, only as long as the coercive order is efficacious.

International law is relevant to the material sphere of validity of the national legal order, too. Since its norms, especially the norms created by international treaties, can regulate any subject matter whatever and therefore also those subject matters which can be regulated by national law, it limits the latter's material sphere of validity. The States, it is true, remain competent, even under international law, to regulate in principle all matters which can be regulated by an order limited in its territorial sphere; but they retain this competence only insofar as international law does not regulate a particular subject matter. The fact that

* Cf. *supra*, pp. 207ff.

a subject matter is regulated by international law has the effect that it can no longer be regulated arbitrarily by national law. An international treaty concerning certain matters is legally binding upon the contracting States with respect to the regulation of these matters by their own legislation. If, for instance, two States have concluded a treaty by which each of them is obligated to naturalize citizens of the other under certain conditions only, the enactment of a statute regulating naturalization in another way is a violation of international law. This means that the material competence of the State, its power to regulate any subject matter it chooses, is limited by international law; but it is legally limited only by international law.

The national legal order, that is, an order which constitutes a State, can thus be defined as a relatively centralized coercive order whose territorial, personal, and temporal spheres of validity are determined by international law and whose material sphere of validity is limited by international law only. This is the juristic definition of the State. It is obviously possible only on the assumption that international law is a valid order.

g. The State as Organ of the International Legal Order
(The Creation of International Law)

Since the international legal order not only requires the national legal orders as a necessary complementation, but also determines their spheres of validity in all respects, international and national law form one inseparable whole.

An aspect of this unity is the fact that the States as acting persons are organs of international law, or of the community constituted by it. The creation and execution of an order are the functions of its organs and the international legal order is created and executed by States.

It is especially the creation of international law by treaties that clearly reveals the States as organs of the international community. International treaties are, in the opinion of many authors, the only method by which international law can be created. The creation of international law by custom, the other source of international law, is, accordingly, interpreted by these authors as "tacit" treaty. This is an obvious fiction motivated by the desire to trace back all international law to the "free will" of the State and thereby to maintain the idea that the State is "sovereign," which means that it is not subject to a superior legal order restricting its liberty.

The theory that international custom is a "tacit" treaty, and that hence treaties are the only source of international law, does not serve the purpose for which it was devised. International custom is characterized as a treaty because it is assumed that the norm created by an international treaty obligates only the contracting parties. If treaties were the only source of international law, no State could be legally obligated without or against its will. Custom, however, cannot be interpreted as a treaty, because a legal rule created by international custom also obligates States which obviously have not participated in the creation of the customary rule. General international law, obligating all the members of the international community, is customary law; but it is generally accepted that a State cannot escape from the validity of a norm of general international law by proving that it did not participate in the creation of this norm. Otherwise, it would be impossible to consider a new State as subject to general international law, or a State which hitherto was an inland State after acquiring access to the sea, as subject to general maritime law.

The fiction that international custom is a "tacit" treaty is useless also for the reason that the principle according to which an international treaty obligates only the contracting parties is not without important exceptions. Positive international law recognizes treaties which have effect upon third States, even treaties conferring duties upon States which are not contracting parties. Third States are obligated, for instance, by treaties establishing State servitudes as pointed out in a previous chapter.*

Another category of international treaties which possibly stipulate obligations of third States are treaties by which a new State is created. Thus, for instance, the Peace Treaty of Versailles created the State of Danzig and imposed upon this State certain obligations in relation to Poland. Since the State of Danzig was not, and could not be, a contracting party to the Treaty of Versailles, this treaty was, with respect to Danzig, an international treaty obligating a third State.† Another example is the so-called Lateran Treaty of February 11, 1929, concluded between the Pope, as the head of the Roman Catholic Church, and the Italian government. By this treaty the State of the Vatican City was established. The treaty imposed upon the newly created State the duty not to take part in temporal rivalries between other States and in international conferences concerned with such matters save and except in the event of such parties making a mutual appeal to the pacific mission of the Holy See, the latter reserving in any event the right of exercising its moral and spiritual power.

International treaties conferring rights upon third States are possible,

* Cf. *supra*, pp. 207ff.

† Cf. my article *Contribution à la théorie du traité international* (1936) 10 REVUE INTERNATIONALE DE LA THÉORIE DU DROIT 253–292.

too. Such a treaty is, for instance, the convention between Poland and the Principal Allied and Associated Powers, signed June 28, 1919, concerning the protection of minorities. In this treaty, Poland undertook to assume certain obligations in respect to persons belonging to racial, religious, or linguistic minorities. Article 12, paragraph 2, runs as follows: "Poland agrees that any Member of the Council of the League of Nations" — and there were States which were members of the Council without being contracting parties to this treaty — "shall have the right to' bring to the attention of the Council any infraction, or any danger of infraction, of any of these obligations, and that the Council may thereupon take such action and give such direction as it may deem proper and effective in the circumstances." Even more important is paragraph 3: "Poland further agrees that any difference of opinion as to the questions of law or fact arising out of these Articles between the Polish Government and any one of the Principal Allied and Associated Powers or any other Power, a Member of the Council of the League of Nations, shall be held to be a dispute of an international character under Article 14 of the Covenant of the League of Nations. The Polish Government hereby consents that any such dispute shall, if the other party thereto demands, be referred to the Permanent Court of International Justice. The decision of the Permanent Court shall be final and shall have the same force and effect as an award under Article 13 of the Covenant." That means that this treaty confers rights upon States which are members of the Council, although not contracting parties to the treaty. These States have, according to this treaty, real rights, for they are entitled to invoke not only the Council of the League of Nations but also the Permanent Court of International Justice against Poland's violation of its obligations stipulated by this treaty.

Even if all international law had the character of contractual law, it would not be possible to maintain the idea that the States are sovereign because they are not subject to a superior legal order restricting their free will. For the rule *pacta sunt servanda*, the legal basis of all international treaties, as a rule of positive international law, corresponds only in a limited way to the principle of autonomy.

Moreover, this rule can have validity only as part of a legal order to which the States are subject, because this order obligates the States and thus restricts their liberty. A treaty concluded by two States can have a legal effect, that is to say, can give rise to obligations and rights of the contracting parties or third States — in other terms, an international treaty can create an individual norm obligating and authorizing the contracting parties (or third States) — only if there is a general norm by which the treaty is qualified as a norm-creating fact. This general norm cannot belong to the legal order of any one individual State. A norm of the legal order of one State cannot impose duties or confer rights upon another State, since the competence of each State, the scope of validity of a national legal order, is limited to its own sphere. Nor can two States together, by means of their own legal orders only, establish a norm valid for the spheres of both, as a norm created by an international treaty. The competence of two States cannot be added together like mathematical magnitudes. To be capable of creating a norm valid for more than one State, the States must be empowered by a legal order superior to their own legal orders, a legal order whose territorial and personal sphere of validity comprises the spheres of the States for which the norm shall be valid. The requisite norm must therefore be part of that legal order which delimits the spheres of the individual States.

It is international law, as a legal order superior to the States, that makes possible the creation of norms valid for the sphere of two or more States, that is, international norms. It is general international law, especially by its rule *pacta sunt servanda*, which establishes the norm which obligates the States to respect treaties, to behave as treaties concluded by them prescribe.

Law regulates its own creation. So does international law. Its creation is its own function. When two States conclude a treaty they function as organs of international law. The representatives of the two contracting parties together form the composite organ that creates the contractual norm. It is an organ of the international community constituted by general international law. Of this composite organ, the representatives of the contracting States are part organs. It is the international legal order which leaves it to each national legal order to determine the individual who, as a representative of the State, is competent to conclude treaties with the representative of another State. Hence the representative of a contracting State is primarily a (partial) organ of the international community, and only secondarily an organ of his own State. Under the influence of the dogma of sovereignty, it is commonly said that the individual States create international law by treaty. In reality, it is the international community that, using the individual States as its organs, creates international law, just as it is the national community, the State, which by its organs creates national law.

"The State as an organ of international law" — this is only a metaphorical expression of the fact that the legal order of each State, each national legal order, is organically connected with the international legal order and through this order with every other national legal order, so that all legal orders merge into one integrated legal system.

h. The International Responsibility of the State

1. Collective Responsibility of the State and Individual Responsibility of Individuals as Subjects of International Law

The fact that international law imposes obligations upon the States is essentially connected with the fact that the State is legally responsible for the violation of these obligations. If the legal duty of the State is not fulfilled because the competent organ does not behave in the way prescribed by international law, or, what amounts to the same thing, if international law is violated by the State, the sanction provided by international law is not directed against the individual who, in his capacity as organ of the State, was obliged to behave in a certain way but has not behaved in this way. According to a rule of general international law no State can claim jurisdiction over another State, and that means, over the acts of another State. If a violation of international law has the character of an act of State, the individual who in his capacity as organ of the State has performed the act must not be held responsible by the courts of the injured State. The latter may resort to reprisals or war against the State responsible for the violation of law; but the courts of the injured State have no criminal or civil jurisdiction in regard to the acts of the guilty State, they are not competent to prosecute an individual for an act done by him in his capacity as organ of the State concerned. It is the State, not its organ, that is legally responsible for violations of international law committed by acts of State.* That means that the sanctions of international law — reprisals or war — are directed against the State as such. This is usually expressed by the statement that the State whose right has been violated by another State is authorized by general international law to resort to reprisals or war against the violator of its right.

It seems that after the Pact of Paris — the so-called Kellogg Pact — came into force, the States which ratified this treaty lost the legal possibility of resorting to war except against a State which violated the Pact. This is, at least, the usual interpretation of the Pact. But the Pact forbids war only as an instrument of national policy, and war as a reaction against a violator of international law is an instrument of international, not of national, policy. According to such a restrictive interpretation, war may be considered — even by the contracting parties to the Pact of Paris — in addition to reprisals, a sanction of international law.

* Cf. my article, *Collective and Individual Responsibility in International Law with Particular Regard to the Punishment of War Criminals* (1943) 31 California Law Review, 538ff.

Reprisals are a limited, war is an unlimited, violation of interests of the State against which they are directed. But reprisals as well as war consist in forcible deprivation of life, liberty, or property of human beings belonging to the State against which these sanctions are directed. These individuals neither committed the delict nor were in a position to prevent it. Hence the individuals forming the population of the State are responsible for the delict committed by the latter. The so-called responsibility of the State for its violation of international law is the collective responsibility of its subjects for the non-fulfillment of the State's international duties by its organs. That the international responsibility of the State is a collective and not an individual responsibility becomes manifest when we dissolve the personification implied in the concept of the State, if we try to look through the veil of this personification at the legal reality, that is to say, at the legal relations between individuals. If, however, the State is considered as a real being, a kind of superman, the illusion is created that the sanctions provided by international law are directed against the same individual who has violated the law; in other words, we have the illusion of the individual responsibility of the State as an international person.

As pointed out, international law imposes obligations not only upon States, but, as an exception, also upon individuals. In these cases the sanctions provided by international law are — by their very nature — not directed against the States as such, as are reprisals and war. The latter constitute collective responsibility. In the cases in which international law directly imposes duties upon individuals, the principle of individual responsibility prevails, since the sanctions are directed against a person individually determined by international law, and not against the State to which this individual belongs as a subject. The sanctions are either directly determined by international law, as in the case of breach of blockade and carriage of contraband of war: here the sanction consists in the capture and confiscation of the vessel and its cargo. Or the sanction is indirectly determined by international law, as in the case of piracy and acts of illegitimate warfare: here international law authorizes the States to punish the individuals who have violated the rules of international law concerned and leaves it to these States to determine the punishment as well as the procedure by which the punishment is to be inflicted upon the criminals. Violations of international duties imposed directly upon the individuals by international law are called "international crimes," in contradistinction to violations of international duties imposed upon States, which are called "international delinquencies." So-called "crimes against the Law of Nations" are violations of national law, namely, the criminal law of a State by which certain acts against foreign States are rendered criminal.

2. Duty of Reparation

According to a generally accepted opinion, any international delict committed by a State entails the latter's obligation to repair the injury, and that means, to restore the situation exactly to its former state, or, if this is impossible, to repair the moral as well as the material damage caused by the delict. Reparation may be made by expiatory acts such as a formal apology, salute to the flag or the coat of arms of the wronged State, and the like; by the annulment of the act violating international law; by the punishment of the guilty individual, by pecuniary compensation in case of material damage. General international law does not determine the contents of reparations with respect to the different delicts. In order to establish a concrete duty of reparation a treaty concluded between the delinquent State and the State injured by the delict is necessary in order to determine the contents of the reparation. If such a treaty cannot come about because the delinquent State refuses to provide the reparation demanded by the wronged State, the latter is authorized to resort to reprisals or war against the former.

It may be doubted whether general international law really stipulates a duty of reparation, since such a duty exists only if its contents are determined, and general international law does not provide a procedure by which the contents of this duty can be determined under any circumstances. In this respect general international law differs from national law. The latter, in contradistinction to the former, institutes courts with compulsory jurisdiction, so that in any case of an illegally caused damage a definite reparation can be determined by an impartial authority. To establish an international tribunal, an international treaty concluded voluntarily by the States concerned is necessary; and the will to conclude a treaty of arbitration authorizing the tribunal to determine the reparation is frequently wanting.

It is even doubtful whether the wronged State is obliged by general international law to try to bring about an agreement with the delinquent State concerning the latter's reparation, before resorting to reprisals or war. On the other hand, the delinquent State is not obliged to accept whatever the wronged State demands as reparation. If the demand is exaggerated, the delinquent State is justified in rejecting it, and then no concrete obligation to repair the injury comes into force.

Be that as it may, the obligation to repair the wrong inflicted upon another State, whether directly stipulated by general international law or established by agreement between the two States concerned, is not a sanction — as it is sometimes characterized — but a substitute obligation which replaces the original obligation violated by the international delict. The non-fulfillment of the obligation to repair the moral and material damage caused by a delict is the condition to which international law annexes its specific sanctions, reprisals or war.

To be legally responsible for a delict means — according to our definition — to be subjected to the sanctions annexed to this delict. As pointed out, the individual who is legally obliged to abstain from the delict need not necessarily be responsible for the delict. The concept of legal responsibility is not identical with the concept of legal obligation. Hence it is not correct to identify legal responsibility with any legal obligation, in particular with the obligation to repair the moral or material damage caused by the delict. The State is legally responsible for an international delict not because it is legally obliged to repair the damage caused by the delict, but because and in so far as the sanction attached to the delict, reprisals or war, is directed against the State, and that means, because and in so far as the collective responsibility takes place which is constituted by this kind of sanction. Since these sanctions are attached only and exclusively to delicts committed by the State, the State is always responsible for its own delicts. But the State may be legally obliged to repair the moral and material damage caused by a violation of international law that has not been committed by the State itself. Only for the non-fulfillment of this obligation to repair the wrong is the State legally responsible; this again is responsibility for its own delict, and not responsibility for a delict committed by another person.

3. So-called "Indirect" or "Vicarious" Responsibility

Some writers distinguish between "direct" and "indirect" responsibility of the State. According to this distinction, the State is directly responsible for its own acts, and is indirectly responsible for the acts of individuals by which international law has been violated.* Oppenheim †
distinguishes between "original" and "vicarious" responsibility. " 'Original' responsibility is borne by a State for its own — that is, for its Government's — actions, and such actions of the lower agents or private individuals as are performed at the Government's command or with its authorisation. But States have to bear another responsibility besides that just mentioned. For States are, according to the Law of Nations, in a sense responsible for certain acts other than their own — namely, certain unauthorised injurious acts of their agents, of their subjects, and even of such aliens as are for the time living within their territory. The responsibility of States for acts other than their own is 'vicarious' responsibility."

The State's "indirect" or "vicarious" responsibility, however, consists

---

* Hershey, Essentials of International Public Law 253.

† 1 Oppenheim, International Law (5th ed.) 274.

in nothing else but the State's obligation to repair the moral and material damage caused by internationally illegal actions which, for some reason or another, are not considered to be acts of the State; and in some cases, to prevent such actions and to punish the delinquents.

The whole problem is focused on the concept of "act of State." Who performs an act of State? The answer to this question is different according to whether it is given on the basis of national or of international law. According to national law, an act of State is an act performed by an organ of the State. It is an act performed by an individual but imputed to the State, that is to the personified unity of the national legal order. Such imputation is possible only if the act is performed in conformity with the legal order. Conformity with the legal order is an essential condition for the imputation of an act to the State as the personification of the national legal order. Within national law, only legal acts can be imputed to the State; but this does not exclude the fact that individuals who by performing legal acts have the character of State organs sometimes perform illegal acts, and that the State is legally obliged to annul these acts, to punish the guilty individuals, to repair the damage caused by these illegal acts.

It is usual to speak of illegal acts performed by an individual "in the exercise of his official function as a State organ." As pointed out, this formula is not correct, since the individual, in performing an illegal act, cannot be considered to be an organ of the State. It is more correct to speak of illegal acts performed by an individual in connection with his official function as a State organ.*

Whereas, according to national law, the act of any organ of the State is an act of State, according to international law acts of State are only acts performed by an organ competent to represent the State in relation to other States. This organ is the Government, the term taken in a sense including also the Head of the State. The Government may act through lower organs commanded or authorized by it. According to the constitution of modern States, not all the organs of the State are subjected to the Government, and that means: not all the organs can legally be commanded or authorized by the Government. The parliament and the courts are independent of the Government. Only the administrative organs (including the diplomatic agents and the armed forces of the State) are at the disposal of the Government. Hence acts of the parliament or of the courts are not considered as acts of State in the sense of international law. But this does not exclude international law being violated by such acts, just as international law can be violated by acts of adminis-

* Cf. *supra*, p. 200.

trative organs which are not authorized or commanded by the Government and consequently are no acts of State in the sense of international law, or by acts of private individuals.

The previously mentioned distinction between acts of State organs performed in conformity with the national legal order and illegal acts performed by individuals in connection with their official function as State organs is irrelevant from the point of view of international law. Any act performed by a member of the Government directly or through a lower organ commanded or authorized by it, whether in conformity with the national legal order or not, but performed in connection with the official function of the acting individual as a State organ, has to be considered, from the viewpoint of international law, as an act of State. And if this act constitutes a violation of international law, it has to be considered as a delict of the State, or, in the usual phraseology, an international delinquency of the State; for these acts the State is responsible.

Violations of international law which are not delicts of the State or international delinquencies are: acts committed by administrative organs of the State without being commanded or authorized by the Government; acts committed by parliaments or courts; acts committed by private individuals.

The State is legally obliged to make full reparation for the moral and material damage caused by acts committed by administrative organs without being commanded or authorized by the Government; the State is obliged to annul, disown, and disapprove of such acts by expressing its regret, or even apologizing to the Government of the injured State; to punish the guilty individuals, and to pay pecuniary compensation. Acts of parliament or courts, too, may give rise to the State's duty of reparation. In these cases, however, it is most frequently very difficult, if not impossible, to fulfill the obligation to repair the injury. Acts of parliament or judicial decisions cannot normally be annulled, they cannot be disowned or disapproved by the Government, since the Government has normally no legal authority over these organs. If an international obligation of the State can be fulfilled according to its constitution only by an act of parliament, by a statute, and if the parliament does not enact this statute, the Government has no legal power to fulfill the international obligation of the State or to make an adequate reparation. An analogous situation occurs if international law is violated by a positive act of legislation and if the Government has not the legal power to prevent the execution of the statute. The same is true with respect to decisions of independent courts. Reparation in such cases is practically possible only in the form of pecuniary compensation. But this kind of reparation might be considered inadequate in many cases.

With respect to violations of international law committed by private individuals, we must distinguish two different groups of cases: first, delicts such as piracy, hostilities committed by private individuals against the enemy, breach of blockade, carriage of contraband, and the like; in these cases the home State of the delinquent has no obligation at all to repair the wrong. Any State, as in the case of piracy, or the State injured by the illegal act, as in the cases of hostilities committed by private individuals against the enemy, breach of blockade, carriage of contraband, is authorized by international law to direct a definite sanction against the delinquent.

The second group comprises some acts of private individuals injurious to a foreign State, to its organs or to its citizens, as, for instance, acts by which the dignity of a foreign State is violated, the lives or property of its citizens is attacked, an armed expedition is prepared on the territory of a State against another State, and the like. According to general international law, every State is obliged to take the necessary measures to prevent the individuals living within its territory — citizens as well as foreigners — from committing such acts. If the State does not fulfill this obligation, it has to pay full reparation to the wronged State (including punishment of the offenders and payment of damages). If the State has taken all the necessary measures and if, nevertheless, the delict has been committed, the State is obliged to punish the offenders and to compel them to pay damages. In this case the State itself is not obliged to pay damages. This principle is also applicable to acts of insurgents and rioters.*

4. Absolute Responsibility (Liability) of the State

The question as to whether the international responsibility of the State has the character of absolute responsibility (liability), or responsibility based upon fault (culpability), is much discussed. The answer to this question depends on whether it refers to the individuals collectively responsible for the violation of international law committed by the conduct of a State organ, or to the individual who in his capacity as organ of the State has, by his conduct, violated international law. As pointed out,† collective responsibility is always absolute responsibility, since it cannot be based on the fault of the responsible individuals, that is, the individuals against whom the sanctions are directed. But these individuals may be made responsible only if the delict has been committed intentionally by the immediate delinquent. Then, their responsibility is based, not on their own, but on the delinquent's fault.

* Cf. 1 OPPENHEIM, INTERNATIONAL LAW 294ff.
† Cf. *supra*, pp. 70f.

A delict of the State is always the conduct of an individual acting as an organ of the State. Hence, the question whether the international responsibility of the State is absolute responsibility, or culpability, may also be formulated as the question whether the fault of the individual whose conduct is imputed to the State is an essential condition of the sanction provided by international law against the State. Some writers maintain that an act of State injurious to another State, which objectively constitutes a violation of international law, is nevertheless not an international delinquency (and that means, is not the condition of a sanction) if committed neither intentionally and maliciously nor negligently. Other writers maintain, on the contrary, that within general international law absolute responsibility — at least in principle — prevails with respect to the individuals whose conduct constitutes the delict. It is hardly possible to answer the question in a general way. There is no doubt that the State is responsible for negligence of its organs. As a rule, no sanction against the State is justified when it can be proved that the competent organs of the State have taken the necessary measures to avoid the violation of the other State. But the State cannot escape responsibility by proving only that its organs did not intentionally and maliciously violate international law. If by "responsibility based on fault (culpability)" is understood not only the case where the violation has been committed intentionally and maliciously, but also the case where the violation has been committed negligently, the international responsibility of the State has, with respect to the individuals collectively responsible, the character of absolute responsibility; but with respect to the individuals whose conduct constitutes the international delict, in principle, the character of culpability. If, however, negligence is not conceived of as a kind of fault (*culpa*) — and this is, as pointed out,* the correct opinion — the international responsibility of the State has the character of absolute responsibility, in every respect. There are cases where the State is responsible even though no negligence on the part of its organ has taken place. Thus, for instance, according to Article 3 of the Hague Convention of 1907 respecting the Laws and Customs of War on Land, the State is responsible for all acts violating the rules of warfare if committed by members of its armed forces, without regard to whether the acts have been committed intentionally and maliciously or with negligence. That the State is responsible only if the violation has been committed intentionally and maliciously and that it can escape responsibility by proving that only negligence has occurred, is out of the question. Even within national law negligence is, normally, not without sanction; only a less

* Cf. *supra*, pp. 66f.

severe sanction is provided in this case. But such differentiation of the sanction is unknown to general international law.

C. The Unity of National and International Law
(Monism and Pluralism)

a. The Monistic and the Pluralistic Theory

The analysis of international law has shown that most of its norms are incomplete norms which receive their completion from the norms of national law. Thus, the international legal order is significant only as part of a universal legal order which comprises also all the national legal orders. The analysis has further led to the conclusion that the international legal order determines the territorial, personal, and temporal spheres of validity of the national legal orders, thus making possible the coexistence of a multitude of States. We have finally seen that the international legal order restricts the material sphere of validity of the national legal orders by subjecting them to a certain regulation of their own matters that could otherwise have been arbitrarily regulated by the State.

This monistic view is the result of an analysis of the norms of positive international law referring to the States, and that means, to the national legal orders. It is from the standpoint of international law that its connection with national law and hence with a universal legal order is seen. But — however strange it may seem — most theorists of international law do not share this monistic view. International law and national law are, in their opinion, two separate, mutually independent, legal orders that regulate quite different matters and have quite different sources.

This dualism or — taking into account the existence of numerous national legal orders — this pluralism contradicts, as we have seen, the contents of international law, since international law itself establishes a relation between its norms and the norms of the different national legal orders. The pluralistic theory is in contradiction to positive law, provided international law is considered to be a valid legal order. And yet the representatives of this theory accept international law as positive law.

But the pluralistic view is untenable also on logical grounds. International law and national law cannot be different and mutually independent systems of norms if the norms of both systems are considered to be valid for the same space, and at the same time. It is logically not possible to assume that simultaneously valid norms belong to different, mutually independent systems.

The pluralists do not deny that the norms of international law and national law are simultaneously valid. On the contrary, assuming both to be valid simultaneously, they assert that a certain relation holds between the two, namely, the relation of mutual independence; which means that no relation exists between the two systems of valid norms. This is, as we shall see, a real contradiction.

b. The Subject-matter of National and International Law

The mutual independence of international and national law is often substantiated by the alleged fact that the two systems regulate different subject matters. National law — it is said — regulates the behavior of individuals, international the behavior of States. We have already shown that the behavior of a State is reducible to the behavior of individuals representing the State. Thus, the alleged difference in subject matter between international and national law cannot be a difference between the kinds of subjects whose behavior they regulate.

The pluralistic interpretation is also supported by the assertion that, while national law regulates relations that have their seat within one State, international law regulates relations which transcend the sphere of one State. Or — as it is also put — while national law is concerned with the "internal" relations, the so-called "domestic affairs" of the State, international law is concerned with the "external" relations of the State, its "foreign affairs." One visualizes the State as a solid, space-filling body, with an interior structure and exterior relations to other objects. When we try to find the thought behind the metaphor, and to formulate it without employing a metaphor, we arrive at the conclusion that the thought is wrong.

For it is impossible to distinguish the so-called "domestic affairs" from the "foreign affairs" of the State as two different subject matters of legal regulation. Every so-called domestic affair of a State can be made the subject of an international treaty and so be transformed into a foreign affair. The relation between employers and employees, for instance, is certainly an "internal" relationship within the State, and its legal regulation a typical "domestic" affair. But as soon as a State concludes a treaty with other States concerning the regulation of this relationship, it becomes a foreign affair. If we discard the spatial metaphor, we thus find that the attempted distinction between the subject matters of national and international law is a mere tautology. The so-called "domestic affairs" of a State are, by definition, those which are regulated by the national law; the "foreign affairs" are, by definition, those which are regulated by international law. The assertion that national law regulates domestic affairs, international law foreign affairs, boils down to the truism that national law regulates what is regulated by national law, international law what is regulated by international law.

Still there remains a certain truth in the statement that international law is "inter-State" law, whereas national law is, so to speak, one-State law. But this differentiation does not concern the subject matter, it concerns the creation of international and national law. While national law is created by one State alone, international law is usually created by the coöperation of two or several States. This holds of customary international law as well as of contractual international law. There are, it is true, certain matters specific to international law, matters which can be regulated only by norms created by the collaboration of two or several States. These matters are — as we know — the determination of the spheres of validity of the national legal orders, and — as we may now add — the procedures of creating international law itself. But there is no subject matter which can be regulated only by national law, and not by international law. Every matter that is, or can be, regulated by national law is open to regulation by international law as well. It is therefore impossible to substantiate the pluralistic view by a difference in subject matter between international and national law.

c. The "Source" of National and International Law

In support of the pluralistic theory, it has been argued that the different systems of norms come from different sources. The phrase "source of law" is another metaphorical expression which — as we have seen — carries at least two different connotations. A "source of law" is, on one hand, a procedure in which norms are created; on the other hand, the reason why norms are valid. Let us, to begin with, see how the argument fares if the phrase is understood in the former sense.

One distinguishes between two "sources of law" in this sense: custom and legislation (in the widest meaning of any statutory creation of law).* When one regards custom as a source of law, one presupposes that people ought to behave as they customarily behave. When one considers legislation as a source of law, one assumes that people ought to behave as special organs authorized to create law by their acts (the "legislator" in the widest sense) ordain. Legislation, in the usual narrower sense, is only a special case of statutory creation, viz., the creation of a general norm by a special organ. But an individual norm, too, may have the character of statutory — in contradistinction to customary — law, as, for instance, a judicial decision or a norm created by contract or treaty.

Both methods of creating law, the customary and the statutory one,

* Cf. *supra*, pp. 114f.

occur in international as well as in national law. General international law, it is true, does not recognize legislation and lawmaking by the judiciary, the two most important methods of norm-creation in the modern State. But courts and legislative organs can be created by international treaty, which is itself a method of creating statutory law. The decisions of an international court are norms of international law, and so are also certain decisions of the Assembly of the League of Nations, which bind all members of the League and thus are analogous to statutes of national law. Nothing prevents the creation by treaty of a collegiate organ that is competent to pass majority resolutions binding for the signatories of the treaty. If the centralization effected by the treaty does not go too far, such decisions would still be norms of international law (without having at the same time the character of national law).

Since international legislation and judicial lawmaking are possible only on the basis of a treaty, and the binding force of treaties is based on a rule of customary international law, it may be said that the primary source (in the sense of method of lawmaking) of international law is treaty and custom, whereas the primary source of national law may be custom or legislation. Further, it is true that custom and treaty, creating international law, involve the coöperation of two or several States, while custom and legislation creating national law are functions of the organs of one State only. The methods of lawmaking are thus, in this respect, different in national and international law; but this is not a difference in principle. And even if national law were created in a totally different way from that in which international law is created — which is not the case — such a difference in the sources would not mean that the norms created in different ways belong to different and mutually independent legal systems. The difference between custom and legislation is far greater than that between a treaty of international law and a contract of national law. Yet, one and the same national legal order contains both customary and statutory law.

d. The Reason of Validity of National and International Law

1. The Reason of Validity of the National Legal Order Determined by International Law

In order to answer the question whether international and national law are different and mutually independent legal orders, or form one universal normative system, in order to reach a decision between pluralism and monism, we have to consider the general problem of what makes a norm belong to a definite legal order, what is the reason that several norms form one and the same normative system. In the first part of this treatise,* it was shown that several norms belong to the same legal order if all derive their validity from the same basic norm. The question why a norm is valid necessarily leads back to an ultimate norm whose validity we do not question. If several norms all receive their validity from the same basic norm, then — by definition — they all form part of the same system. The question why a norm is a norm of American law or of international law is thus a question of the basic norm of the American and of the international law. To determine the relationship between national and international law, we have to examine whether the norms of both derive their validity from different norms or from the same basic norm.

The expression "source of law" is, as we have seen, sometimes understood to mean simply the reason why a norm is valid. If we adhere to this meaning of the term, the argument that international and national law are separate systems because they have separate "sources" is not incorrect. Thus, we have to inquire what is the ultimate reason of validity of national law, and what is that of international law.

In this way, the problem as to the relation between national and international law has already been formulated, especially in German literature.† But the answer usually offered — that the validity of national law has its reason in the "will" of one State, while the validity of international law is based on the "combined wills" of several States — is only an anthropomorphic metaphor. A logical analysis would disclose that the metaphor hides an empty tautology.

The answer to the question as to the basic norm of the national legal order has been given in the first part of this treatise.‡ If the national legal order is considered without reference to international law, then its ultimate reason of validity is the hypothetical norm qualifying the "Fathers of the Constitution" as a law-creating authority. If, however, we take into account international law, we find that this hypothetical norm can be derived from a positive norm of this legal order: the principle of effectiveness. It is according to this principle that international law empowers the "Fathers of the Constitution" to function as the first legislators of a State. The historically first constitution is valid because the coercive order erected on its basis is efficacious as a whole. Thus, the international legal order, by means of the principle of effectiveness, determines not only the sphere of validity, but also the reason of validity of the national legal orders. Since the basic norms of the national legal orders are determined by a norm of international law, they are

---

* Cf. *supra*, pp. 110ff.

† Cf. my treatise, DAS PROBLEM DER SOUVERÄNITÄT UND DIE THEORIE DES VÖLKERRECHTS (2d ed. 1923).

‡ Cf. *supra*, pp. 115ff.

basic norms only in a relative sense. It is the basic norm of the international legal order which is the ultimate reason of validity of the national legal orders, too.

A higher norm can either determine in detail the procedure in which lower norms are to be created, or empower an authority to create lower norms at its own discretion. It is in the latter manner that international law forms the basis of the national legal order. By stipulating that an individual or a group of individuals who are able to obtain permanent obedience for the coercive order they establish are to be considered as a legal and legitimate authority, international law "delegates" the national legal orders whose spheres of validity it thereby determines.

2. Revolution and *Coup d'État* as Law-creating Facts according to International Law

In determining the reason of validity of the national legal orders, international law regulates the creation of national law. This is clearly illustrated in the case, repeatedly mentioned here, where the constitution of a State is changed not in the way prescribed by the constitution itself, but violently, that means, by a violation of the constitution. If a monarchy is transformed into a republic by a revolution of the people, or a republic into a monarchy by a *coup d'état* of the president, and if the new government is able to maintain the new constitution in an efficacious manner, then this government and this constitution are, according to international law, the legitimate government and the valid constitution of the State. This is the reason why we have stated, in another connection,* that victorious revolution and successful *coup d'état* are, according to international law, law-creating facts. To assume that the continuity of national law, or — what amounts to the same — the identity of the State, is not affected by revolution or *coup d'état*, as long as the territory and the population remain by and large the same, is possible only if a norm of international law is presupposed recognizing victorious revolution and successful *coup d'état* as legal methods of changing the constitution. No jurist doubts, for instance, that it is legally the same Russian State that existed under the tsarist constitution and that now exists under the bolshevist constitution and under the new name of U. S. S. R. But this interpretation is not possible if we, ignoring international law, do not go beyond the Russian constitution as it exists at a given moment. Then the continuity of the legal order and the identity of the Russian State become incomprehensible. If the situation is judged from this point of view, the State and its legal order remain the same

* Cf. *supra*, pp. 220f.

only as long as the constitution is intact or changed according to its own provisions. That is the reason why Aristotle taught "that when the constitution (πολιτεία) changes its character and becomes different, the State too remains no longer the same." *

This view is inevitable if one tries, as Aristotle did, to comprehend the nature of the State without regard to international law. Only because modern jurists — consciously or unconsciously — presuppose international law as a legal order determining the existence of the State in every respect, according to the principle of effectiveness, do they believe in the continuity of national law and the legal identity of the State in spite of a violent change of constitution.

In regulating, by its principle of effectiveness, the creation of the constitution of the State, international law also determines the reason of validity of all national legal orders.

3. The Basic Norm of International Law

Since national law has the reason of its validity, and hence its "source" in this sense, in international law, the ultimate source of the former must be the same as that of the latter. Then the pluralistic view cannot be defended by the assumption that national and international law have different and mutually independent "sources." It is the "source" of national law by which that law is united with international law, whatever may be the "source" of this legal order. Which is the source, then, that is, the basic norm of international law?

To find the source of the international legal order, we have to follow a course similar to that which led us to the basic norm of the national legal order. We have to start from the lowest norm within international law, that is, from the decision of an international court. If we ask why the norm created by such a decision is valid, the answer is furnished by the international treaty in accordance with which the court was instituted. If, again, we ask why this treaty is valid, we are led back to the general norm which obligates the States to behave in conformity with the treaties they have concluded, a norm commonly expressed by the phrase *pacta sunt servanda*. This is a norm of general international law, and general international law is created by custom constituted by acts of States. The basic norm of international law, therefore, must be a norm which countenances custom as a norm-creating fact, and might be formulated as follows: "The States ought to behave as they have customarily behaved." Customary international law, developed on the basis of this norm, is the first stage within the international legal order. The

* Aristotle, Politics, Book III, 1276b.

next stage is formed by the norms created by international treaties. The validity of these norms is dependent upon the norm *pacta sunt servanda*, which itself is a norm belonging to the first stage of general international law, which is law created by custom constituted by acts of States. The third stage is formed by norms created by organs which are themselves created by international treaties, as for instance decisions of the Council of the League of Nations, or of the Permanent Court of International Justice.

4. The Historical and the Logico-juristic View

The custom by which international law is created consists in acts of States. Thus, one might object, there must have been States before there could be any international law. But how can national law derive its validity from international law, if the rise of the latter presupposes the existence of the former? The fact that customary international law exists does not necessarily imply that the existence of States preceded the existence of international law. It would be quite possible that primitive social groups developed into States simultaneously with the development of international law. The fact that tribal law is, at least, not a later product than inter-tribal law * allows such a conjecture. But even if the existence of States really preceded the existence of international law, the historical relation between national and international legal orders does not preclude the logical relation which, it is maintained, exists between their grounds of validity.

As long as there was no international law, the reason of validity of national law was not determined by international law. If international law does not exist, or is not presupposed to exist as a legal order obligating and authorizing the States, the principle of effectiveness is not a norm of positive law but only a hypothesis of juristic thinking.

When, however, an international law arose and the principle of effectiveness became a part thereof, the national legal orders were brought into that relationship to international law which is asserted by the monistic theory. The States are sovereign as long as no international law exists or is assumed to exist. But if international law exists or is presupposed to exist, a legal order superior to those of the States is valid. Thus, under international law, the States are not sovereign, or, what amounts to the same thing, the international legal order, by determining the sphere and the reason of validity of the national legal orders, forms, together with the latter, one universal legal order.

* Cf. *supra*, p. 334.

e. Conflicts between National and International Law

International law and national law are not, so it is said, parts of one normative system, because they can, and in fact do, contradict each other. When a State enacts a statute which is contrary to some norm of international law, this statute nevertheless obtains the force of law. Simultaneously, the norm of international law remains valid. According to the critics of the monistic theory, this situation involves a logical contradiction. If it were a logical contradiction, they would undoubtedly be right in their conclusion that national and international law do not form one normative system. But the contradiction is only apparent.

In case of a conflict between an established norm of international law and a more recent statute of national law, the organs of the State do not necessarily have to consider the statute as a valid norm. It is quite possible that the courts could be empowered to refuse to apply such a statute, just as they are sometimes competent to refuse to apply an unconstitutional statute. In existing positive law, this is, however, an exception. We shall therefore here assume that the State organs have to consider statutes as valid, even if they are contrary to international law.

The conflict between an established norm of international law and one of national law is a conflict between a higher and a lower norm. Such conflicts occur within the national legal order without the unity of this order thereby being endangered. When we studied this problem,* we arrived at the conclusion that a "norm-violating" norm — an "unconstitutional" statute or an "unlawful" or "illegal" decision of a court — is a highly misleading expression. That a lower norm, as one says, "does not correspond" to a higher norm, in reality means that the lower norm is created in such a way, or has such contents, that, according to the higher norm, it may be abrogated in another than the normal way; but, as long as the lower norm is not abrogated, it remains a valid norm, and that, according to the higher norm. The meaning of the latter is to render possible this abrogation.

The fact that a higher norm determines the creation or the contents of a lower norm, however, may signify only that the organ which created the lower norm "not corresponding" to the higher norm is liable to a personal sanction. Then, the norm created by the responsible organ will not be abrogated. In both cases, there is no logical contradiction between the higher norm and the lower norm which does "not correspond" to the former. Illegality of a norm means possibility of abrogating the norm or punishing the norm-creating organ.

* Cf. *supra*, pp. 153ff.

The framing of a "norm-violating" norm may be a delict to which the legal order attaches a sanction. From our earlier considerations, it is clear that the occurrence of a fact does not logically contradict the norm which makes it a delict. The delict is not in contradiction to law, it is not a negation of law, it is a condition determined by law. Thus, there is no logical difficulty in acknowledging that valid legal norms may arise out of a delict. The principle *Ex injuria jus non oritur* may belong to a given positive legal order, but does not necessarily do so. In its general form, it is not a logical but a political postulate. The creation of a valid constitution by revolution or *coup d'état* is a clear proof of this. The making of a certain norm may — according to a higher norm — be a delict and expose its author to a sanction, but the norm itself may — again according to the higher norm — be valid; valid not only in the sense that it may remain valid as long as it is not annulled, but also in the sense that it may not be voidable merely because of its origin in a delict.

This is exactly the case in the relationship between international and national law. International law usually obligates a State to give its norms certain contents in the sense that if the State enacts norms with other contents, then the State is liable to an international sanction. A norm that, as one says, is enacted in "violation" of general international law, remains valid even according to general international law. General international law does not provide any procedure in which norms of national law which are "illegal" (from the standpoint of international law) can be abolished. Such a procedure exists only in particular international law and in national law.

If the contents of norms of a national legal order are determined by international law, it is in an alternative sense only. The possibility of norms with contents other than those prescribed is not excluded. Such norms are discriminated against only insofar as the act of making them is made an international delict. But neither the international delict, consisting in the making of the norm, nor the norm itself, is in logical contradiction to international law, any more than the so-called unconstitutional law is in logical contradiction to the constitution. And just as the possibility of "unconstitutional laws" does not, therefore, affect the unity of the national legal order, so the possibility of a national law "violating" international law does not affect the unity of the legal system comprising both. The exponents of the pluralistic theory thus are mistaken when they think it possible to disprove the unity of national and international law by pointing at possible contradictions between the two.

f. The Unity of National and International Law
as a Postulate of Legal Theory

1. The Possible Relationship between Two Systems of Norms

The unity of national and international law is an epistemological postulate. A jurist who accepts both as sets of valid norms must try to comprehend them as parts of one harmonious system. This is *a priori* possible in either of two different ways. Two sets of norms can be parts of one normative system because one, being an inferior order, derives its validity from the other, a superior order. The inferior order has its relative basic norm, and that means, the basic determination of its creation, in the superior order. Or two sets of norms form one normative system because they both, being two coördinate orders, derive their validity from one and the same third order which, as a superior order, determines not only the spheres but also the reason of their validity, and that means, the creation of the two inferior orders.

The procedure of creation and, hence, the reason of validity of an inferior order, can be determined by a superior order, as pointed out, directly or indirectly. The superior order can either itself state the procedure in which the norms of the inferior order are to be created, or merely empower an authority to create norms for a certain sphere at its own discretion. The higher order is said to "delegate" the lower order. Since the relative basic norm of the inferior orders is part of the superior order, the inferior orders themselves can be conceived of as partial orders within the superior as a total order. The basic norm of the superior order is the ultimate reason of validity of all the norms, including those of the inferior orders.

The relationship of international and national law must correspond to one of these two types. International law can be superior to national law or *vice versa*; or international law can be coördinated to national law. Coördinaton presupposes a third order superior to both. Since there is no third order superior to both, they themselves must be in a relationship of superiority and inferiority. Entirely excluded is the possibility that they should exist side by side, one independent of the other, without being coördinated by a superior order.

The pluralistic theory, which asserts this to be the case, invokes the relationship between law and morality in support of its assertion. These two normative systems are, it is true, independent of one another, insofar as each has its own basic norm. But the relationship between law and morality itself shows that two normative systems cannot be simultaneously considered as valid unless they are thought of as parts of a single system.

2. The Relationship between Positive Law and Morality

Let us consider the case of a conflict between a norm of positive law and a norm of morality. Positive law can, for instance, stipulate an obligation to render military service, which implies the duty to kill in war, while morality, or a certain moral order, unconditionally forbids killing. Under such circumstances, the jurist would say that "morally, it may be forbidden to kill, but that is irrelevant legally." From the point of view of positive law as a system of valid norms, morality does not exist as such; or, in other words, morality does not count at all as a system of valid norms if positive law is considered as such a system. From this point of view, there exists a duty to perform military service, no contrary duty. In the same way, the moralist would say that "legally, one may be under the obligation to render military service and kill in war, but that is morally irrelevant." That is to say, law does not appear at all as a system of valid norms if we base our normative considerations on morality. From this point of view, there exists a duty to refuse military service, no contrary duty. Neither the jurist nor the moralist asserts that both normative systems are valid. The jurist ignores morality as a system of valid norms, just as the moralist ignores positive law as such a system. Neither from the one nor from the other point of view do there exist two duties simultaneously which contradict one another. And there is no third point of view.

To consider law and morality from one and the same point of view as simultaneously valid orders is possible only if one order is thought of as "delegating" the other. Positive law frequently refers to a certain system of morality, at least to regulate certain particular human relations; and many systems of morality acknowledge — with more or less extensive reservations — existing positive law. The delegated part of morality is part of positive law, and the delegated part of law has the same relation to morality. To consider law and morality from one and the same point of view as valid orders, or, what amounts to the same thing, to accept law and morality as simultaneously valid systems, means to assume the existence of a single system comprehending both.

All quest for scientific knowledge is motivated by an endeavor to find unity in the apparent multiplicity of phenomena. Thus, it becomes the task of science to describe its object in a system of consistent statements, that is, statements not contradicting each other. That is true also for the sciences of law and morality, sciences whose objects are norms. Contradictions are also banned within the sphere of these sciences. Just as it is logically impossible to assert both "A is," and "A is not," so it is logically impossible to assert both "A ought to be" and "A ought not to be." What is valid, can be described only in phrases like "You ought to. . . ." It is in such terms that the jurist describes the system of supposedly valid legal norms and the moralist describes the system of supposedly valid moral norms. Two norms which by their significance contradict and hence logically exclude one another, cannot be simultaneously assumed to be valid. It is one of the main tasks of the jurist to give a consistent presentation of the material with which he deals. Since the material is presented in linguistic expressions, it is *a priori* possible that it may contain contradictions. The specific function of juristic interpretation is to eliminate these contradictions by showing that they are merely sham contradictions. It is by juristic interpretation that the legal material is transformed into a legal system.

3. Collision of Duties

Against our thesis that two contradictory norms cannot both be valid, one might argue that, after all, there are such things as collisions of duties. Our answer is that terms like "norm" and "duty" are equivocal. On the one hand, they have a significance that can be expressed only by means of an ought-statement (the primary sense). On the other hand, they also are used to designate a fact which can be described by an is-statement (the secondary sense), the psychological fact that an individual has the idea of a norm, that he believes himself to be bound by a duty (in the primary sense) and that this idea or this belief (norm or duty in the secondary sense) disposes him to follow a certain line of conduct. It is possible that the same individual at the same time has the idea of two norms, that he believes himself bound by two duties which contradict and hence logically exclude one another; for instance, the idea of a norm of positive law which obligates him to render military service, and the idea of a norm of morality which obligates him to refuse to render military service. The statement describing this psychological fact, however, is no more contradictory than, for instance, the statement that two opposite forces work at the same point. A logical contradiction is always a relation between the meaning of judgments or statements, never a relation between facts. The concept of a so-called conflict of norms or duties means the psychological fact of an individual's being under the influence of two ideas which push him in opposite directions; it does not mean the simultaneous validity of two norms which contradict one another.

4. Normativity and Factuality

The failure to distinguish between the two senses of words like "norm" and "duty" is the main cause why one does not realize that two sets of valid norms must always be parts of one single system. When the word "norm" is used (in its secondary sense) to express the fact that individuals have the idea of norms, that individuals believe themselves bound by norms and are motivated by such ideas, if the term "norm" means an "is," not an "ought," then it is possible to assert that there exist norms which contradict each other; and it is then possible to assert that there "exist" side by side complexes of norms which are not parts of one and the same system of norms. But the norms of which these statements speak are an object of psychology and sociology, not of juristic theory. The latter is not concerned with what ideas and beliefs people actually have, for instance, with regard to military service, but with the question whether or not people legally ought to perform, are obliged to perform, military service, that is, with norms or duties in the primary sense. A sociologist or psychologist may observe that some people believe themselves to be obliged, that others believe the opposite, and that some oscillate between the two views. A sociologist or psychologist sees only the factual, not the normative aspect of law and morality. He conceives of law and morality as a complex of facts, not as a system of valid norms. He cannot, therefore, furnish any answer to the question whether one ought to render military service. That question can be answered only by the jurist or the moralist who considers law or morality as a system of valid norms, that is to say, of propositions about what men ought to do, and not of statements about what men actually do, or actually believe they ought to do. It is the point of view of normativity, not that of factuality.

g. Primacy of National Law, or Primacy of International Law

1. National and International Personality of the State

It is the law as a system of valid norms, not the law as a complex of facts, to which must be referred all that has been said here about the necessity of comprehending national and international law as elements of one universal system. This tendency toward establishing unity in the plurality of legal norms is immanent in all juristic thinking. And this tendency prevails even in the theory of those who advocate the pluralistic construction. Usually, they do not deny that the State is a subject of international law as well as the support of a national legal order. If, then, there were no unifying relation between international and national law, the State, in its former capacity, would have to be an entity totally separate from the State in its latter capacity. From the juristic point of view, there would then exist two different States under the same name, two Frances, two United States, and so on, a France of national law, and a France of international law, etc. This absurd consequence is not accepted by the pluralists.

Sometimes, it is true, the pluralists assert that the international and the national personality of the State are distinct.* But they mean only that the same identical State has both an international and a national personality, just as a human being has both a moral and a juristic one. It has never been disputed that it is the same Mexico that concludes an international treaty with another State in the sphere of international law, and that executes this treaty in the sphere of national law. Take for instance a treaty by which one State is obliged to naturalize citizens of another State only on the condition that they be released from their nationality by the other State. Then it is obviously the same State that, as a subject of international law, has concluded ·the treaty and, as a subject of national law, enacts a statute by which acquisition and loss of nationality are regulated according to the treaty. It is possible to say that a human being has both a legal and a moral personality, and that these personalities, as two different qualities of the same human being, are not identical. For the human being is a biologico-physiological unit, and as such the *substratum* of these two different personalities. That the same human being "has both a legal and a moral personality" is a metaphorical way of expressing the fact that the behavior of the same human being — as a certain biologico-physiological unit — is subject both to legal and to moral norms.

But the State is no biologico-physiological unit, not even a sociological one.† The relation between State and law is radically different from that between individual and law. The statement that law regulates the behavior of the State means that law regulates the behavior of human individuals in "State" fashion. The State is not, like human individuals, an object of legal regulation but is the legal regulation itself, a specific legal order. The State is believed to be an object of regulation only because the anthropomorphic personification of this order leads us first to liken it to a human individual and then to mistake it for a superhuman individual.

This inadmissible hypostatization is the source of the belief that the State, as well as an individual, can have two personalities. If the State is not — as a human being — the object of legal regulation but this

---

* DIONISIO ANZILOTTI, COURS DE DROIT INTERNATIONAL (1929) 54, 405. This author is a consistent advocate of the pluralistic theory. Therefore he says, speaking of the term "State": "The term 'State' signifying . . . the subject of a national legal order, determines a subject entirely different from the State as the subject of international law."

† Cf. *supra*, pp. 181ff.

regulation itself, a legal order, then the identity of the State is the identity of a legal order. The pluralists do not deny the identity of the State as the common *substratum* of its personality of international as well as national law. ' They cannot deny that it is the same State that, for instance, according to international law, is obliged to declare war before the commencement of hostilities against another State, and that, according to its constitution, actually issues a declaration of war. But if they have to describe the legal reality without the aid of an anthropomorphic personification, they have to admit that the identity of the State is not the identity of a *substratum* different from the order regulating it, but is, instead, the identity of the order regulating the behavior of individuals in their capacity as organs of this order. The identity of the State as subject of international law and as subject of national law means that, finally, the international legal order obligating and authorizing the State and the national legal order determining the individuals who, as organs of the State, execute its international duties and exercise its international rights, form one and the same universal legal order.

2. Transformation of International into National Law

If one assumes that national and international law are disconnected systems of norms, then one must also assume that norms of international law cannot be directly applied by the organs of a State, and that the latter, especially the courts, can apply directly only norms of national law. If a norm of international law, for instance, an international treaty, is to be applied by the courts of a State, the norm, according to this view, first has to be transformed into national law by a legislative act creating a statute or an ordinance having the same contents as the treaty. This consequence of the pluralistic theory does not tally with the actual contents of positive law. International law needs transformation into national law only when the necessity thereof is stated by the constitution of the State. If the constitution is silent on this point — as it sometimes is — the State courts are competent to apply international law directly, especially treaties concluded according to the constitution by their own government with the governments of other States. This is possible only if the norm created by the treaty according to its own meaning is to be applied directly by the State courts, which, for instance, is not the case if the international treaty obligates the State only to issue a statute whose contents are determined by the treaty.

Certainly there are norms of international law which are not intended for direct application by the judicial and administrative organs of the State. An international treaty to the effect that the State has to treat a minority in a particular manner can, for instance, have the meaning only that the State has to enact, through its legislative organ, an adequate statute which is to be applied by its courts and administrative organs. But the treaty may be formulated in such a way that it can be applied directly by the courts and administrative organs. Then, transformation of international into national law — by a legislative act of the State — is superfluous, unless it is necessary because for instance, the constitution of the State stipulates that the courts and administrative authorities are to apply only and exclusively statutes (or norms of customary national law) and ordinances.

If the State organs are authorized to apply international law directly (as they will be if national law does not prevent them from so applying it), the question arises what norm they have to apply if national and international law "contradict" one another. The question can be answered only by positive law. The constitution may state, either that national law shall always be applied, even if it is in conflict with international law, or that the conflict shall be solved according to the principle *lex posterior derogat priori*. In the latter case, the courts have to apply a statute which "contradicts" a preceding treaty although the latter has not been abolished by the statute according to international law. The application of the statute constitutes an international delict. Finally, the constitution may state that international law shall always have precedence over national law. The courts may be authorized to refuse application of statutes or even to annul statutes because of their being in conflict with an international treaty or a norm of common international law. Then, statutes violating international law are treated in the same way as, according to some constitutions, statutes violating the constitution are treated.

Which of these three possibilities obtains in a given case, can be decided only by an interpretation of the positive legal order in question. Likewise, the question whether a transformation of international law into national law is necessary can be answered only by positive law, not by a doctrine of the nature of international or national law or of their mutual relation. By deducing the general necessity of transformation from the alleged independence of national from international law, the pluralistic theory comes into conflict with positive law and thus proves its inadequacy. The inadequacy of the pluralistic theory is sufficiently patent from the fact alone that it assumes such transformation to be generally necessary.

3. Only One National Legal Order as a System of Valid Norms

If the pluralists were consistent, if they really considered national and international law, like law and morality, as two different and mutually independent orders, they would have to desist from considering both international and national law as systems of simultaneously valid norms. Just as the jurist ignores morality, the moralist law, so the international jurist would have to ignore national law, and the national jurist international law. A theorist of international law would have to accept national law, a theorist of national law, conversely, international law, only as a fact, not as a system of valid norms. The exponents of the pluralistic theory, however, regard national and international law as two systems of norms which are valid simultaneously, and they have to do so, since the international legal order is meaningless without the national legal order, and the legal existence of the State cannot be understood without taking into consideration the international law determining this existence.

Should one decide to consider national law as alone valid, one would have to choose one national order as the only system of valid norms. What has been said of the relationship between international and national law holds also of the relationship between the various national legal orders. Validity can be simultaneously predicated of two national legal orders only if they are thought of as forming one single system. International law is the only legal order that could establish such a connection between them. If national and international law are disconnected, the various national legal orders, therefore, must also be disconnected. A theorist adhering to the pluralistic view thus would have to pronounce one national legal order — for instance that of his own State — as the only valid legal order.

To recognize the social order of one's own group as being the only true "law" is a typically primitive view, comparable to the view that only the members of one's own group are true human beings. In the language of some primitive tribes, the term designating "human being" is the same as that by which the members of the tribe designate themselves, in contradistinction to members of other tribes. Originally, the ancient Greeks considered only their own "polis" as a legal community, dismissing all foreigners as outlawed barbarians. Even today, one is inclined not to accept the social order of another community as "law" in the full sense of the word, especially when the order embodies political principles different from one's own.

4. The Recognition of International Law

Since, on the one hand, the validity of national law is considered to be a matter of course, and, on the other hand, it is hardly possible to deny outright the validity of international law, the pluralists have recourse to a hypothesis by which they — unintentionally — nullify the mutual independence of national and international law that they wish to uphold.

By this hypothesis, they establish also a normative relationship between the various national legal orders and thus reopen the possibility of considering both the international and all the national legal orders as systems of valid norms. We refer to the well-known statement that international law is valid for a State only if it is "recognized" by the State.

This is by no means a rule of positive international law. Positive international law does not make its validity for a State dependent upon recognition by this State. When a new State comes into existence, this State, according to international law, immediately receives all obligations imposed and all rights conferred upon a State by this legal order, independently of whether or not the State recognizes international law. According to international law itself, it is not necessary to prove that a State has consented to a norm of general international law in order to be able to assert that, in a concrete case, this State has violated an obligation or another State has infringed upon its right stipulated by the norm in question. A norm of international law which makes its own validity for the State dependent upon its recognition by the State is logically impossible, because the validity of such a norm presupposes a validity of the international law independent of its recognition.

A different question is whether the legal existence of a State is dependent upon recognition by other States. This question has been answered in the affirmative in a previous chapter.* Some authors assume that recognition of international law by the State to be recognized is an essential condition of its recognition as a State. However, as pointed out, international law itself does not, and cannot, prescribe its recognition on the part of the States as a condition for its validity for the States. International law only makes its application to the relation between two communities dependent on the fact that they mutually recognize one another as States. It is positive international law itself that gives the recognition of one State by another its characteristic legal effects. Thus, mutual recognition of communities as States presupposes the validity of international law.

The recognition of a community as a State is an act provided by positive international law. The recognition of international law by a State — as a recognition of its validity for that State — cannot possibly be an act anticipated by international law, for such an act would — as pointed out — presuppose the validity of international law. The thesis that international law becomes valid for a State only if it is recognized by the State, is a hypothesis made by the theoretical jurist in his attempt to comprehend the world of law. It by no means concerns the contents of

* Cf. *supra*, pp. 221ff.

positive law; but it does concern the hypothetical reason of validity of international law. The opposite thesis, that international law is valid for the States without any recognition on their part, is also a juristic hypothesis only, not a positive norm of international law. The latter is, and has to be, silent on this point.

5. The Primacy of National Law

The thesis that international law becomes valid for a State only if recognized by that State amounts to saying that the reason why international law is valid for a State, is the "will" of this State. This means that international law, according to this view, is valid for a State only if the legal order of the State contains a norm stipulating that the relations of this State to other States are subject to international law. The relation between national and international law is thus regarded as analogous to that between national law and a given system of morality, when the former refers to the latter in order to regulate certain human relations, or — to use the term here suggested — when the legal order "delegates" the moral order to a certain extent. International law is considered as a part of national law.

Usually, the national legal order does not explicitly "delegate" international law, in other terms: normally, the State does not recognize international law by a legislative or executive act. One therefore speaks of a tacit recognition of international law by the State, evidenced by conclusive actions such as the sending of diplomatic agents to other States and the receiving of such agents from them, or the making of international treaties. It sometimes happens, it is true, that a norm of the national legal order expressly refers to international law. Thus, the Weimar constitution of Germany (Article 4) states: "The universally recognized rules of international law are valid as binding constituent parts of German Federal law." The interpretation of such a norm depends on our theory of the relationship between national and international law. If it is assumed that international law is valid for a State without any recognition on the part of this State, then the norm in question is but a general transformation of international into national law prescribed by this particular constitution. If, however, it is assumed that international law is valid for a State only if "recognized" by this State, the norm in question is considered to be a "recognition" of international by national law.

According to the first theory, international law is a legal order superior to all the national legal orders which, as inferior legal orders, are "delegated" by the international legal order, and form, together with the latter, one universal legal order. According to the second theory, the national legal order is superior to the international legal order which receives its validity from the former. Hence, international law forms a part of national law, and the unity of both is established also by this theory. To guarantee this unity is, in fact, the real purpose of the "recognition" theory which presupposes the primacy of national over international law, whereas the other theory presupposes the primacy of international law over national law.

h. Sovereignty

1. Sovereignty as a Quality of a Normative Order

The most important consequence of the theory which proceeds from the primacy of national law is that the State whose legal order is the starting point of the whole construction can be considered to be sovereign. For the legal order of this State is presupposed to be the supreme order, above which no other legal order exists. This is also a consequence of the pluralistic theory. This theory, too, refuses to consider international law as a legal order above the States and their legal orders. However, the pluralistic theory regularly embodies the recognition theory. By so doing, it abandons the dualism of national and international law, and hence juristic pluralism. We may, therefore, conjecture that its real purpose is not so much to assert the mutual independence of national and international law, but rather to maintain the idea of the sovereignty of the State.

The statement that sovereignty is an essential quality of the State means that the State is a supreme authority. "Authority" is usually defined as the right or power to issue obligating commands. The actual power of forcing others to a certain behavior does not suffice to constitute an authority. The individual who is, or has, authority must have received the right to issue obligating commands, so that other individuals are obliged to obey. Such a right or power can be conferred upon an individual only by a normative order. Authority is thus originally the characteristic of a normative order. Only a normative order can be "sovereign," that is to say, a supreme authority, the ultimate reason for the validity of norms which one individual is authorized to issue as "commands" and other individuals are obliged to obey. Physical power, a mere natural phenomenon, can never be "sovereign" in the proper sense of the word. As attributed to physical power, "sovereignty" could only mean, it seems, something like the property of being a first cause, a *prima causa*. But the idea of a *prima causa* is a contradiction in terms, if, according to the principle of causality, every phenomenon has to be considered as the effect of a cause, every phenomenon which is considered to be the cause of an effect must be considered to be at the same time the effect of another cause. In the infinite chain of causes and effects, that is to say, within natural reality, there cannot be a first cause, and, therefore, no sovereignty.

The State in its capacity as legal authority must be identical with the national legal order. That the State is sovereign means that the national legal order is an order above which there is no higher order. The only order that could be assumed to be superior to that of the national legal order is the international legal order. The question whether the State is sovereign or not thus coincides with the question whether or not international law is an order superior to national law.

That an order is "superior" to another order is — as we have pointed out — * a figurative expression. It means that one order, the inferior one, derives its reason of validity, its relative basic norm, from another, the superior order. The problem of the sovereignty of the State is not the problem whether a natural object does or does not have a given property. It cannot be answered in the same way as, for instance, the question of what is the specific weight of a metal; that is to say, by observation of natural reality or — in an analogous way — by an analysis of the contents of positive (national and international) law. The result of our analysis was that international law, through its principle of effectiveness, determines the sphere and reason of validity of national law, and thus the superiority of international to national law seems to be imposed by the contents of law itself. But from the point of view of the recognition theory, international law determines the sphere and reason of validity of national law only if international law has some validity; and it is valid only if recognized by the State. After the State has recognized international law, this order, by its very contents, determines the sphere and even the reason of validity of the national legal order. But since this effect is brought about only by recognition of international law on the part of the State, international law determines the sphere and the reason of validity of national law only in a relative sense. Finally, national law is the supreme order, and international law has its reason of validity in national law. According to the recognition theory, the basic norm of the national legal order is the absolute supreme source of the validity of all law and hence the State can be conceived of as sovereign.

The thesis of the recognition theory: the primacy of national over international law, is — as pointed out — only a juristic hypothesis, just like the opposite thesis: the primacy of international law. Hence, "sover-

* Cf. *supra*, pp. 123ff., 373ff.

eignty of the State" is not a fact which can, or cannot, be observed. The State neither "is" or "is not" sovereign; it can only be presupposed to be or not to be sovereign; and this presupposition depends upon the hypothesis with which we approach the sphere of legal phenomena. If we accept the hypothesis of the primacy of international law, then the State "is not" sovereign. Under this hypothesis, the State could be pronounced sovereign only in the relative sense that no other order but the international legal order is superior to the national legal order, so that the State is subjected directly to international law only. If, on the other hand, we accept the hypothesis of the primacy of national law, then the State "is" sovereign in the original absolute sense of the term, being superior to any other order, including international law.

2. Sovereignty as Exclusive Quality of Only One Order

If the phenomena of law are interpreted according to the hypothesis of the primacy of national law, one national legal order only, and therefore one State only, can be conceived as sovereign. This hypothesis is possible only from the point of view of one national legal order. Only that State can be presupposed to be sovereign whose legal order is the starting point for the whole structure. The necessary relationship between this State and the other States can be established only by international law, and only if it is admitted that international law determines the spheres of validity of the legal orders of these States. International law is, however, according to the basic hypothesis, valid only because it is recognized by the first-mentioned State, which "is" sovereign because the international legal order is considered as part of, and hence as inferior to, its legal order. Since the other national legal orders derive their validity from international law, they have to be considered as inferior to the legal order of the State which first is, and which, therefore, alone can be presupposed to be, sovereign. This national legal order, through the medium of international law which is part of it, comprises all the other national legal orders "delegated" by the international legal order. These other national legal orders are, according to international law, valid exclusively for their specific territorial and personal spheres, and can be created and modified only according to their own constitutions. But international law, which guarantees the other States this relative sovereignty, has — from the point of view of this interpretation — its reason of validity in the national legal order from which the interpretation proceeds. Only this national legal order which, with respect to the reason of validity, not with respect to the contents of other national legal orders, presents itself as the universal legal order, is absolute sovereign, and this means that only this State is sovereign in the original sense of the term.

The sovereignty of one State excludes the sovereignty of every other State.

This is an inevitable consequence of the recognition theory based on the hypothesis of the primacy of national law. Most exponents of these views, however, do not think them out to their last consequences. They conceive the world of law as a number of isolated national legal orders, each of which is sovereign and each of which contains international law as a part. For reasons that have already been explained, this legal pluralism is logically impossible. There would, incidentally, on this view, exist as many numerically different international legal orders as there are States or national legal orders. It is, however, logically possible that different theorists interpret the world of law by proceeding from the sovereignty of different States. Each theorist may presuppose the sovereignty of his own State, that is to say, he may accept the hypothesis of the primacy of his own national legal order. Then he has to consider the international law which establishes the relations to the legal orders of the other States and these national legal orders as parts of the legal order of his own State, conceived of as a universal legal order. This means that the picture of the world of law would vary according to what State is made the basis of the interpretation. Within each of these systems, erected on the hypothesis of the primacy of national law, one State only is sovereign, but in no two of them would this be the same State.

i. The Philosophical and Juristic Significance of the Two Monistic Hypotheses

1. Subjectivism and Objectivism

The hypothesis of the primacy of national law is a parallel to the subjectivistic philosophy which, in order to comprehend the world, proceeds from the philosopher's own *ego* and, hence, interprets the world as the will and idea of the subject. This philosophy, proclaiming the sovereignty of the *ego*, is incapable of comprehending another subject, the *non-ego*, the *tu* claiming to be also an *ego*, as an equal being. The sovereignty of the *ego* is incompatible with the sovereignty of the *tu*. The ultimate consequence of such a subjectivistic philosophy is solipsism.

The theory of the primacy of national law is State subjectivism. It makes the State which is the starting point of its construction, the theorist's own State, the sovereign center of the world of law. But this philosophy of law is incapable of comprehending other States as equal to the philosopher's own State, and that means, as legal beings which are sovereign, too. The sovereignty of the State-*ego* is incompatible with the sovereignty of the State-*tu*. The ultimate consequence of the primacy of national law is State solipsism.

The *ego* and the *tu* can be conceived of as equal beings only if our philosophy proceeds from the objective world within which both exist as parts, and neither of them as sovereign centers of the whole. Similarly, the idea of the equality of all States can be maintained only if we base our interpretation of legal phenomena on the primacy of international law. The States can be considered as equal only if they are not presupposed to be sovereign.

Neither the hypothesis of the primacy of international law, nor that of the primacy of national law is in any way concerned with the material contents of positive law. The international obligations and rights of the States are exactly the same whether the one or the other of the two hypotheses is assumed. The fact that the positive law of a certain State declares the international legal order a part of its national legal order cannot prevent legal theory from assuming that the validity of international law does not depend upon a recognition on the part of the State, that is, from accepting the hypothesis of the primacy of international law. Nor does the fact that positive international law determines the spheres and the reason of the validity of the national legal orders prohibit the assumption that international law is valid for a State only if recognized by this State, which is the hypothesis of the primacy of national law.

2. Wrong Uses of the Two Hypotheses

The two hypotheses — which are merely two different ways of comprehending all legal phenomena as parts of a single system — are, it is true, sometimes misused as the basis for assertions about the contents of positive law. From the assumed primacy of national or international law one attempts to draw conclusions which oppose the actual contents of the positive law. Thus, according to those who presuppose the primacy of national law, the sovereignty of the State implies that the State is not always bound by treaties which it has concluded with other States; or that the State cannot be subjected to the compulsory jurisdiction of an international court; or that it cannot be obligated against its will by majority resolutions of collegiate international organs; or that national law cannot have its origin in a procedure of international law; especially, that the sovereignty of the State is incompatible with the idea that its constitution is created by an international treaty; and so on. These are all questions which cannot be answered by deductions from the concept of sovereignty but only by an analysis of positive law; and positive law shows that all the assertions quoted here are inaccurate. Those who accept the hypothesis of the primacy of international law, however, are just as mistaken when they maintain that international law overrides national law, that a norm of national law is null if it contradicts a norm of international law. This would be the case only if there existed a positive norm providing a means of annulling a norm of national law because of its contradiction to a norm of international law. General international law, at any rate, does not contain any such norm.

The two monistic theories may be accepted or rejected in the face of any empirically given stipulations of positive national or international law — just because they are epistemological hypotheses that do not carry any implications in that respect.

3. The Choice between the Two Hypotheses

In our choice between them, we are as free as in our choice between a subjectivistic and an objectivistic philosophy. As the choice between the latter cannot be dictated by natural science, so the choice between the former cannot be made for us by the science of law. In our choice, we are obviously guided by ethical and political preferences. A person whose political attitude is one of nationalism and imperialism will naturally be inclined to accept the hypothesis of the primacy of national law. A person whose sympathies are for internationalism and pacifism will be inclined to accept the hypothesis of the primacy of international law. From the point of view of the science of law, it is irrelevant which hypothesis one chooses. But from the point of view of political ideology, the choice is important since tied up with the idea of sovereignty.

Even if the decision between the two hypotheses is beyond science, science still has the task of showing the relations between them and certain value systems of an ethical or political character. Science can make the jurist aware of the reasons for his choice and the nature of the hypothesis he has chosen, and so prevent him from drawing conclusions which positive law, as given in experience, does not warrant.

APPENDIX

NATURAL LAW DOCTRINE AND LEGAL POSITIVISM

BY

HANS KELSEN

TRANSLATED BY

WOLFGANG HERBERT KRAUS

*Assistant Professor of Political Science
in the University of Michigan*

I. THE IDEA OF NATURAL LAW AND THE ESSENCE OF POSITIVE LAW

A. Social Theory and the Problem of Justice

THE PROBLEM of society as an object of scientific knowledge was originally the problem of determining a just order of human relationships. Sociology made its appearance as ethics, politics, jurisprudence, whether independently or as a systematic part of theology. In each case it was a normative science, a doctrine of values. Only with the beginning of the nineteenth century does the tendency emerge to employ a causal method in the treatment of problems of social theory. It no longer promotes an inquiry into justice, but into the causal necessity in the actual conduct of men; it is not a study which seeks to determine how men ought to act, but how they actually do act and must act according to the laws of cause and effect.

The whole turn of social theory from a normative to a causal inquiry signified a denaturation of its object of knowledge. That the natural sciences should thus push the social sciences into something not unlike an act of self-destruction, cannot be explained entirely by the fact that the successes of natural science in the nineteenth and twentieth centuries commended its method as a model. This transformation of the science of social relationships from an ethical science into a causal sociology, explaining the reality of actual conduct and therefore indifferent to values, is largely accomplished today. It is, fundamentally, a withdrawal of social theory before an object which it has lost all hope of mastering, an involuntary admission on the part of a thousand-year-old science that, at least temporarily, it abandons its essential problem as insoluble.

It is particularly the juridical science of the nineteenth and twentieth centuries which expressly declares itself incapable of drawing the problem of justice into the scope of its inquiries. On principle. at least, positivism confines itself to a theory of positive law and to its interpretation. Accordingly, it is anxious to maintain the difference, even the contrast between "just" and "legal," an antithesis which manifests itself in the sharp separation of legal philosophy from legal science. This was not the case until the beginning of the nineteenth century. Before the victorious rise of the historical school of law, the question of justice was considered its fundamental problem by juridical science. This and nothing else is the meaning of the fact that until then the science of law was the science of the law of nature. It did not imply that the science of law was unconcerned with positive law, but merely that it believed in the necessity of treating positive law only in close connection with natural law, that is, with justice.

B. The Principle of Validity in Natural and Positive Law; the Factor of Coercion; Law and State

It was characteristic of the natural-law doctrine, whether as a part of ethics or theology or as an autonomous discipline, that it used to operate on the assumption of a "natural order." Unlike the rules of positive law, those prevailing in this "natural order" which govern human conduct are not in force because they have been "artificially" made by a specified human authority, but because they stem from God, nature or reason and thus are good, right and just. This is where the "positivity" of a legal system comes in, as compared with the law of nature: it is made by human will — a ground of validity thoroughly alien to natural law because, as a "natural" order, it is not created by man and by its own assumption cannot be created by a human act. In this lies the contrast between a material and a formal principle of validity. This formal principle is the main cause of the much emphasized and frequently misunderstood "formalism" of positive law.

Since the idea of a natural law is one of a "natural" order, it follows that its rules, directly as they flow from nature, God or reason, are as immediately evident as the rules of logic and thus require no force for their realization. This is the second point by which natural law is distinguished from positive law. Positive law is essentially an order of coercion. Unlike the rules of natural law, its rules are derived from the arbitrary will of human authority and, for this reason, simply because of the nature of their source, they cannot have the quality of immediate self-evidence. The content of the rules of positive law lacks the inner "necessity" which is peculiar to those of natural law by virtue of their origin. Rules of positive law do not lay down a final determination of social relations. They allow for the possibility that these relations could also be otherwise determined by other rules of positive law, be it subsequently by rules of the same, be it simultaneously by rules of another legal authority. Those whose conduct is regulated in this fashion cannot be assumed to acquire, with these rules, the conviction also of their rightness and justice. It is obviously possible that their actual conduct may differ from what is prescribed by the rules of positive law. For this reason, coercion becomes an integral part of positive law. The doctrine which declares coercion to be an essential characteristic of law is a positivistic doctrine and is solely concerned with positive law.

Since positive law is an order of coercion in the sense that it prescribes coercive acts, its development necessarily leads to the establishment of special agencies for the realization of appropriate acts of coercion. It is no longer, as in primitive law, the individual whose interests have been injured, who executes the law against the wrongdoer; it is a specialized "agency" or "organ" in the narrower meaning of the word (a "judge" or "officer") established on the basis of the division of labor. We can consider the creation of such organs as the true beginnings of "organization" in the strict, technical sense of the term. Positive law as a human, arbitrary order whose rules lack self-evident rightness necessarily requires an agency for the realization of acts of coercion and displays the inherent tendency to evolve from a coercive order into a specific coercive "organization." This coercive order, especially when it becomes an organization, is identical with the State. Thus it can be said that the State is the perfect form of positive law. Natural law is, on principle, a non-coercive, anarchic order. Every natural-law theory, as long as it retains the idea of a pure law of nature, must be ideal anarchism; every anarchism, from primitive Christianity down to modern Marxism, is, fundamentally, a natural-law theory.

C. The "Ought": Absolute and Relative Validity

Although positive law is a coercive and natural law a non-coercive order, both are, simply as orders, systems of norms whose rules can only be expressed by an "ought." The system of natural law, like that of positive law, does not conform to the rule of necessity in the causal sense but to the essentially different rule of the "ought," of normativity.

This rule of normativity must be understood in a thoroughly relative and formal sense, if it is to be taken as the form of both positive and natural law. First of all, the contrast of reality and norm ("is" and "ought") must be recognized as relative. For, in relation to the law of nature, positive law appears as something artificial, i.e., as something made by an empirical human act of will which occurs in the realm of being, that is, in the sphere of actual events. It appears, thus, as a reality which is confronted by natural law as a value. The possibility of a good or bad positive law arises from this relationship. Only by measuring it with the yardstick of a natural law whose validity is taken for granted does a specific positive law, the law of a certain historical community, appear to be good or bad, "just" or "unjust." On the other hand, positive law, as a norm, is from its own immanent point of view an "ought" and therefore a value, and confronts, in this guise, the reality of actual human conduct which it evaluates as lawful or unlawful. This, indeed, is the problem of the positivity of law: The law appears as "ought" and "is" at the same time, while logically these two categories are mutually exclusive.

Further, we must avoid the oft-repeated mistake of identifying the category of the "ought" with the idea of the "good," "right," or "just" in a material sense, if we wish to comprehend natural and positive law as normative and yet to maintain the distinction between them. Only the normative element in the rules of natural law carries that sense of the absolute which one ordinarily associates with the conception of the "just." We unavoidably find an "ought" expressed in positive law if we take it inherently to convey a norm or rule. It is an "ought," however, which can have only a relative meaning. It follows that the category of "ought" (normativity) has a formal meaning only, unless it is related to a determinate content which alone is qualified as "good" or "just." Of course, even if something is declared to be lawful only in the sense of positive law, that declaration means to express that it is somehow "right" or "just." Since the possibility still remains that something only positively lawful may, from some other point of view, be wrong or unjust, the "rightness" and "justice" embodied in the idea of positive law can only be a relative term. To be "relative" means here that a course of conduct prescribed by a positive legal norm is considered to be the content of this "ought" and consequently "right" and "just" only on an assumption whose "rightness" and "justice" have not been ascertained. In this sense, every material legal content, if it is positive law, must be taken to be "right" and "just." The "ought" of positive law can only be hypothetical. This necessarily follows from the nature of the ground of validity which distinguishes positive law from natural law. The norms of positive law are "valid," that is, they ought to be obeyed, not because they are, like the laws of natural law, derived from nature, God or reason, from a principle of the absolutely good, right or just, from an absolutely supreme value or fundamental norm which itself is clothed with the claim of absolute validity, but merely because they have been created in a certain way or made by a certain person. This implies no categorical statement as to the value of the method of law-making or of the person functioning as the positive legal authority; this value is a hypothetical assumption. If it be assumed that one ought to observe the commands of a certain monarch or that one should act according to the resolutions of a certain parliament, this monarch's orders and this parliament's resolutions are law. They are "valid" norms, and human conduct "ought" to conform to their contents. As the absolute validity of its norms corresponds to the idea of natural law, the merely hypothetical-relative validity of its norms corresponds to that of positive law. Accordingly, positive norms are valid only on one assumption: that there is a basic norm which establishes the supreme, law-creating authority. The validity of this basic norm is unproved and must remain so within the sphere of positive law itself.

D. The Basic Norm of Positive Law

This basic norm establishes the validity of positive law and expresses the hypothetical-relative character of a system of norms clothed only with the validity of positive law. It is not just the hypothesis of a special theory of law. It is merely the formulation of the assumption necessary for any positivistic grasp of legal materials. It merely raises to the level of consciousness what all jurists are, even unconsciously, doing when, in the comprehension of their subject, they reject natural law (i.e., limit themselves to positive law) and yet consider the data of their cognition not as mere facts of power, but as laws, as norms. They ordinarily understand the legal relationships with which they are concerned not as the natural relation of cause and effect, but as the normative relations of obligations and rights. But why is a human act, occurring in time and space and perceptible by the senses, interpreted as a legal act (a legal transaction or a judicial decision) within the meaning of any positive (German, French, or English) law? Why should such an act be considered a norm and not simply a mere event in reality? Why should the subjective meaning of this act also be given an objective meaning? Why, in other words, does one not simply say that a certain human individual demands that another act in a specified way, but actually contends that the one is entitled to prescribe and the other obligated to act in accordance with the prescription? Why do we assume that what the act in question subjectively conveys must be done, objectively, by law? The answer of the positivist jurist is: because this individual act is based upon a norm, a general rule, a statute, because the statute prescribes that one is to act as the parties have agreed in their legal transaction, or as the judge has ordered in his decision. One may still inquire, why this "statute" represents a norm, why it is objectively valid. Prima facie, the "statute" is a mere factual matter, namely, the event of several people having expressed their will that other people should henceforth act in a certain way. But why should the will expressed by these people under these particular circumstances signify a "statute," while, if it were done by others under other circumstances, it would by no means have the same significance? Here the answer will be: The event which we interpret as the making of a statute is in accordance with a still higher norm, the constitution, because these persons have been entrusted by the constitution with the power of making laws. This "constitution" is, in turn, nothing else but a prima-facie factual event whose normative meaning can only be found by recourse to the prior constitution according to whose rules it has been created. This recourse must ultimately end in the original constitution which can no longer be derived from a still earlier one. The positivistic jurist, who cannot go beyond the fundamental facts, assumes that this original historical fact has the meaning of "constitution," that the resolution of an assembly of men or the order of a usurper has the normative significance of a fundamental law. Only by making this assumption can he demonstrate the normative meaning of all other acts which he comprehends as legal acts simply because he ultimately traces them all back to the original constitution. The hypothetical basic norm which establishes the original legislator expresses this assumption; it consciously formulates it, nothing more. This means that legal positivism does not go beyond this original constitution to produce a material and absolute justification of the legal order. It stops at that point. The basic norm is an indispensable assumption because, without it, the normative character of the basic historical event could not be established. This ultimate act, to which the positivistic jurist takes recourse and beyond which he does not proceed, is interpreted as an act of law-making as it is expressed in the basic norm, which in turn is not justified by a higher norm and therefore itself transmits only hypothetical validity.

The essential characteristic of positivism, as contrasted with natural-law theory, may be found precisely in the difficult renunciation of an absolute, material justification, in this self-denying and self-imposed restriction to a merely hypothetical, formal foundation in the basic norm. Positivism and (epistemological) relativism belong together just as much as do the natural-law doctrine and (metaphysical) absolutism. Any attempt to push beyond the relative-hypothetical foundations of positive law, that is, to move from a hypothetical to an absolutely valid fundamental norm justifying the validity of positive law (an attempt which for obvious political reasons recurs often enough), means the abandonment of the distinction between positive and natural law. It means the invasion of natural-law theory into the scientific treatment of positive law, and, if an analogy with the natural sciences is permissible, an intrusion of metaphysics into the realm of science.

E. The Immutability of Natural Law

On the strength of its origin from an absolute value, natural law claims absolute validity and, therefore, in harmony with its pure idea, it presents itself as a permanent, unchangeable order. Positive law, on the other hand, with its merely hypothetical-relative validity is, inherently, an infinitely changeable order which can adjust itself to conditions as they change in space and time. An analysis of its specific methods shows that, again and again, natural-law theory has been inclined, directly or indirectly, to abandon or weaken the postulate of immutability. In place of, or in addition to, the absolute natural law, it contends there is a merely hypothetical-relative natural law which is variable and adjustable to special circumstances. In this fashion attempts are made to bridge the gap between pure natural law and positive law. By thus obscuring the boundary line between the two systems, one strives, consciously or not, to legitimize a variable positive law with a mere hypothetical-relative validity as natural law or, at least, as a kind of natural law: that is, one strives to demonstrate its justice.

F. THE LIMITATION OF THE NATURAL-LAW IDEA

The comparison of natural law with positive law, which clarifies the nature of both normative orders, ultimately takes us to a point where, in lieu of an essential difference, a fundamental affinity of the two comes to light — an affinity, moreover, which exposes the problematic character of natural law. The problem mainly consists in the necessity, inherent in any normative order (whether it be a system of natural or positive law) of individualizing (concretizing) the general (abstract) norms. Whenever natural law has to be realized, whenever its norms, like positive law, are immediately brought to bear upon the real conditions of social life which they are meant to determine, i.e., whenever they are to be applied to concrete cases, the question arises whether natural law can maintain its existence disassociated from positivity, whether its very idea permits the existence of a system of norms distinct from, and independent of, positive law. The question is whether natural law as such is at all possible.

A further examination of this question shows that the order of natural law, provided it exists, must necessarily be rendered positive in its application to the concrete conditions of social life, since the general abstract norms of natural law can only become concrete, individual norms by means of human acts. Assume that A asks B to pay back a loan with interest. B refuses to comply, asserting that he either did not receive the sum in question or that he did not receive it as a loan and used it only in the interest of A. If this controversy is to be decided according to a rule of natural law, it becomes necessary that the person who has to apply the norm in question be enabled to determine with perfect certainty whether the controversial sum was ever given as a loan, whether it was ever actually used in the interest of the lender, even if that occurred without the lender's mandate. He must know, in other words, whether the determinant facts requisite for the application of the rule of natural law in question are actually to be found in the present case. Moreover, he has to know what consequences natural law attributes to these determinant facts, and what it considers "right" or "just" in such a case: the return of the sum, with or without interest, or non-payment by reason of its use, etc. Finally, he must not only know all this, he must also be animated by the good will to decide in accordance with the rule of natural law, that is, to create an individual norm which corresponds to the general norm of natural law. This individual norm, even when it fully complies with the general norm can, at least formally, be only a positive norm, because it has been produced by a human act. It would be superfluous to establish special organs above the litigating parties for the settlement of controversies by individual norms, if the parties themselves directly had the requisite knowledge and will and would thus avoid any controversy. This is a plainly utopian assumption. If one drops such an assumption, one has to expect that inadequate knowledge (whether with regard to the conditioning facts or to the consequences) and ill will prevent the realization of natural law. Plainly, the norms of natural law, which are ideally independent of human action and volition, ultimately do require the mediation of human acts in order to fulfill their purpose. This purpose is the determination of the relations between men. Thus the realization of natural law becomes dependent upon the knowledge and will of men by whose doing alone abstract natural law is transmuted into a concrete legal relationship. To what a degree such a realization of natural law (always assuming its existence) is at all possible, in view of the inadequacy of human knowledge and will, is another question. In any case, it must be recognized that here we encounter the limitation of the natural-law idea.*

II. NATURAL AND POSITIVE LAW AS SYSTEMS OF NORMS

A. The Unity of Systems of Norms

Natural law and positive law have been described above as systems of norms.

Are they really two distinct systems of norms? It might appear doubt-

* This discussion is carried further in my essay *Die Idee des Naturrechts* (1928) 7 Zeitschrift für Öffentliches Recht 221f.

ful since both orders are obviously related to the same object, namely, human conduct. The methods, however, employed by the two in regulating human conduct are essentially different. One order proceeds by prescribing the socially desired conduct as content of an "ought," the other by providing a coercive act which ought to be applied to the person whose action constitutes the direct opposite of what is desired. The second manifests itself as a coercive order. Perhaps this difference would not in itself be important enough to establish two distinct systems, unless it is remembered that it goes back to the difference in their sources, that is, to their two respective reasons of validity. It is the unity and specific nature of the ultimate reason of validity which constitute the unity and specific nature of a normative system.

Different norms constitute one order and belong to one system of norms if ultimately they must all be traced back to the same reason of validity, if they flow from the same "source" — to use the common expression — or, to use the familiar anthropomorphic phrase, if the same "will" is the reason of their validity. This last formula has already a strongly positivistic tinge. It works on the assumption that norms are made by human will. Consequently, it is to be applied with caution and in the full knowledge of its merely analogical character to a system of natural law which, for instance, attributes the creation of its rules to the will of God. Otherwise one is prepared to accept a falsification or weakening of the pure natural-law idea. It has been stated that the ground of validity of any norm can only be another norm; an "ought" can only be derived from an "ought" and not from an "is," and the norm which is taken to be the supreme and ultimately valid one is the basic norm. Whenever inquiry into the reason of validity of two different norms leads us back to two distinct, mutually independent and exclusive basic norms, it means that they do not belong to the same system, but to two different orders which are individualized by the specific characteristics of their two fundamental norms.

B. The Static Principle of Natural Law and the Dynamic Principle of Positive Law

The essential relation of unity which prevails among the norms of one system with regard to their basic norm may be of different types. Static and dynamic systems may be distinguished by the method of "derivation" prevailing in them. The norms of an order may be directly or indirectly "derived" from its basic norm and thus obtain their validity. In the former case, the basic norm unfolds itself into norms of varying content, just as a general concept issues special concepts which are subsumed under it. The basic norm of truth or truthfulness yields the norms: "you shall not defraud," "you shall keep your promise," etc.; the basic norm of love: "you shall not injure anyone," "you shall help the needy," etc. From these particular norms more special ones follow, for instance: that the merchant must not conceal defects of his goods which are known to him, that the buyer shall pay the promised purchase price at the agreed time, that one must not injure anyone's reputation or inflict physical injury on anyone, etc. All these norms follow from the basic norm without requiring a special act of norm-making, an act of human will. They are all contained in the basic norm from the outset and are derivable from it by a mere intellectual operation. A dynamic system is different. Its basic norm merely empowers a specific human will to create norms. "Obey your parents" is such a basic norm. No mere intellectual operation can derive a single special norm from it. A parental order with a specific content is needed (for instance: "go to school"), that is, a special act of norm-creation or law-making. This particular norm does not have "validity" simply because its content is consistent with the basic norm, as a special thing is related to a general one, but only because the act of its creation is in keeping with the rule enunciated by the basic norm, because it was made as the basic norm prescribed. The authority which has received its power from the basic norm can, in turn, delegate its jurisdiction either for the whole or for a part of its sphere. Thus parents may delegate a teacher for the education of their children, and this delegation may continue further down the line. The unity of the dynamic system is the unity of a system of delegation.

It follows that natural law ideally tends to be a static system of norms, even though the question remains, whether that is possible in view of man's inadequate qualities of will and intellect. It is also evident from the preceding discussion that positive law, whose basic norm consists in the delegation of a law-making authority, constitutes a dynamic system. "Positivity" actually consists in this dynamic principle. The whole contrast between natural and positive law may, in a certain sense, be presented as the contrast between a static and a dynamic system of norms. To the extent that natural law theory ceases to develop its natural order according to a static principle and substitutes a dynamic one, that is, as it is impelled to introduce the principle of delegation because it has to realize itself in application to actual human conditions, it imperceptibly changes into positive law.

C. The Limitation of Positivism

The static principle, on the other hand, in turn gains access to the system of positive law. This is not because the authority constituted by the basic norm cannot itself create other than pure norms of delegation. The constitutional legislator does not determine merely organs for legislation, but also a legislative procedure; and, at times, his norms, that is the constitution, determine in the so-called fundamental rights and bills of liberty the content of the laws, when they prescribe a minimum of what they should and should not contain. The ordinary legislator in particular is by no means content with the establishment of agencies for adjudication and administration. He issues norms to regulate the procedure of these agencies and others by which he largely determines the content of those individual norms which law-applying agencies are called upon to create. The application of a general norm of positive law to a concrete case involves the same intellectual operation as the deduction of an individual from a general norm of natural law. Yet no individual norm, as a positive norm, simply emanates from a general legal norm (such as: "a thief should be punished") as the particular from the general, but only in so far as such an individual norm has been created by the law-applying organs. Within the system of positive law no norm, not even the material one, is valid, unless it has been created in a manner ultimately prescribed by the basic norm. The existence of other than purely delegating norms does not signify a limitation of the dynamic principle in positive law. Such a limitation comes from another direction.

Above all, even the validity of the basic norm of a given positive legal order does not rest on the dynamic principle. This principle makes its first appearance in and through the basic norm. The basic norm is not itself a made, but a hypothetical, presupposed norm; it is not positive law, but only its condition. Even this clearly shows the limitation of the idea of legal "positivity." The basic norm is not valid because it has been created in a certain way, but its validity is assumed by virtue of its content. It is valid, then, like a norm of natural law, apart from its merely hypothetical validity. The idea of a pure positive law, like that of natural law, has its limitation.

D. Positive Law as a Meaningful Order

This limitation further reveals itself in another aspect. The meaning of the basic norm in a positive order of law cannot be determined, as the idea of "positivity" would require it, as one of delegation pure and simple. The basic norm cannot merely mean the establishment of a law-making organ. True, it must not contain anything which would determine the norms of its positive legal order in the sense of a material, absolute "justice." The basic norm of a positive legal order cannot have the function of guaranteeing the "justice" of this system. That would be irreconcilable with the principle of "positivity." Yet, if the system of positive legal norms, reared upon the basic norm, is to be a meaningful whole, a comprehensible pattern, a possible object of cognition in any sense (an inevitable assumption for a juridical science which for the purpose of understanding uses the hypothesis of the basic norm), then the basic norm must make provision for it. It has to establish not a just, but a meaningful order. With the aid of the basic norm the legal materials which have been produced as positive law must be comprehensible as a meaningful whole, that is, they must lend themselves to a rational interpretation.

The pure principle of delegation cannot guarantee this. For it bestows validity upon any content, even the most meaningless, provided it has been created in a certain way. It justifies any norm, regardless of its content, on condition that it has been created by a certain procedure, even a norm with a self-contradictory content or two norms whose contents are logically incompatible. The principle of non-contradiction, as we shall see later on, applies equally to the normative ("ought") and to the factual ("is") sphere. In both, the judgments "A ought" and "A ought not" are just as mutually exclusive as "A is" and "A is not." If cognition encounters such sense-destroying contradiction in legal materials, if legal acts appear with these subjective meanings, such contradiction in one and the same system must be resolved. A self-contradictory subjective meaning cannot become an objective meaning.

Actually, juridical cognition starts, in the interpretation of its object, with the self-evident assumption that such contradictions are solvable. When the norms whose contents contradict one another are separated by the time of their origin, when one norm precedes the other in time, the principle *lex posterior derogat priori* applies. This principle, while it is not ordinarily stated as a positive rule of law, is taken for granted wherever a constitution provides for the possibility of legislative change. Generally speaking, it applies wherever the positive legal order presents itself as a system of variable norms. Insofar as such a principle has not been expressly stated it can only be established by way of interpretation, that is, through an interpretation of the legal materials. It merely means that it is very appropriately presupposed as a principle for the interpretation of the given materials, because a changeable legal order cannot be meaningfully interpreted without such a presupposition.

Besides, the principle of *lex posterior* is, as a rule, invoked when both norms belong to the same level. When the relation of a higher and a lower norm is involved, as, for instance, in the relation between a constitution and a simple statute or between a statute and a judicial decision, another principle may be applied: in case of conflict the lower norm gives way to the higher norm, i.e., it is voided. When the lower norm is later in time, the principle *lex prior derogat posteriori* may apply.

Possibly, one norm may be so interpreted that the conflict is only apparent and disappears with this interpretation. A statute, for instance, has been enacted in violation of the constitution. In such a case the constitutional rules governing the law-making process are interpreted merely to say that a statute should be enacted in a certain way, for instance, by the two-thirds majority resolution of a certain popularly elected parliament and with the approval of the head of the State. Yet, a statute which has been differently enacted by a simple majority is not void, but it may be declared to be void by a certain agency, such as a supreme court. It may even be provided that the making of such an "unconstitutional" statute is only the condition for the punishment of an organ which is held responsible for its constitutionality.

Again, a judicial decision may contradict the law. The contradiction is eliminated if the law is found to mean that the judge ought to decide according to the law, but that he can also make a valid judgment contrary to the law, if this judgment has acquired the force of law, that is, whenever the legal order makes it impossible to nullify or change the judge's decision (*res judicata*). This principle that the judicial decision is valid once it has legal force, even if it is not in accordance with the law, is generally recognized and accepted in all positive legal orders. All positive legal orders limit the possibility of voiding or changing a judicial decision because it violates the law. Generally it appears more important that a legal controversy be closed, once it is decided by a judgment, than that the judgment conform to the law under all circumstances. This simply means that even a judicial decision which is contrary to law may become valid law itself.

All these interpretations are not necessarily made in application of any positive legal rules of interpretation, but most often even in contravention of the wording of positive rules of law, which prescribe that the legislative process has to maintain certain forms and do not expressly allow acts which have been passed in violation of such rules to become valid statutes. Similarly, no criminal statute contains the express provision that not the "real" thief is to be punished, but only the individual upon whom, while he may not "really" have committed larceny, such a sentence has been passed with legal force by a court with the proper jurisdiction. This is the only acceptable interpretation of a criminal statute which provides that a sentence, after a certain lapse of time and under certain conditions, may no longer be voided or changed. Whoever is under a sentence which has attained the force of law has been lawfully sentenced. In the sphere of juridical thinking there is no "innocently" sentenced person. There are only sentences which may be voided or changed and other sentences which can no longer be voided or changed. The same law orders the punishment of the thief and provides that whoever has been legally declared to have committed larceny by the court of proper jurisdiction must be considered a thief. The statutory wording must be reinterpreted in this sense, in order to avoid the logical contradiction which would otherwise occur between statute and judicial sentence.

If a given statute contains logically contradictory, mutually exclusive provisions, two possibilities offer themselves. The statute may be so interpreted that it enables the organ charged with its application to use discretion and to decide one way or another, to apply one or the other provision. Or, it may be claimed that the provisions destroy each other, that the legal material furnishes no applicable meaning, and that, therefore, this content of the statute is legally irrelevant. These interpretations, too, are reinterpretations without foundation in positive law. They conflict with the wording and the intended, that is, the subjective, meaning of the legal material.

E. The Subjective and Objective Meaning of Legal Material

There are still other instances in which it is necessary for juridical cognition to disqualify legal materials, which have been created in accordance with the basic norm (the constitution), to consider them as non-law and legally irrelevant. This is true for all material which does not conform to the basic form of the positive rule of law, by which a definite coercive act is associated with definite conditions. All those materials belong here which are designated as *lex imperfecta*, rules which, though they appear in legal form as statute, ordinance, etc., cannot be directly or indirectly related to an act of coercion. This does not only apply to provisions without coercive sanction, but also to statements of a theoretical character, references to the legislator's motives, and similar matters, which are not infrequently found in the text of statutes, ordinances, treaties, and other legal instruments. If, for the sake of argument, one should disregard the existence of these materials, nothing would be changed in the real legal content.

Generally, it must be emphasized that the legal materials brought forth by the law-making process become meaningful only by means of an interpretation, which ultimately hinges upon the presupposed basic norm. This meaning is objective and arises from legal cognition. It may differ from the subjective meaning presented by the materials when submitted to objective interpretation. If, for instance, a constitution contains the provision: "The president of the republic appoints the officials of the State," a scientific interpretation will find that the meaning of this provision is not what it purports to be. It merely means that the president coöperates in the appointment of public officials as a partial organ, whenever the constitution contains another provision to the effect that each presidential act requires, for its validity, the coöperation of a cabinet minister. Even though another provision of positive law is here invoked, the reinterpretation of the former provision is made in open conflict with its positive legal formulation. This is done solely in an effort to overcome the logical contradiction which would occur, if the subjective meaning of the provision were accepted as its objective meaning. It is, of course, a contradiction that the president (a simple organ) should appoint the public officials, and that an entirely different organ (a composite one, made up of the president and a minister) should do the same thing.

While positivism means that only that is law which has been created by constitutional procedure, it does not mean that everything which has been thus created is acceptable as law, or that it is acceptable as law in the sense which it attributes to itself.

The assumption of a basic norm which establishes a supreme authority for the purpose of law-making is the ultimate presupposition which enables us to consider as "law" only those materials which have been fashioned by a certain method. The above-described interpretation of legal material has actually long been in use by legal science. If it is correct and if this imputation of an objective meaning is possible (without which there can be no legal science), then it must be the basic norm itself which gives the significance of law to material produced by a certain procedure. It must, moreover, be possible to ascertain from this basic norm which part of the material is valid "law," and also the objective meaning of the legal material, which actually may conflict with its own subjective meaning. The hypothesis of the basic norm simply expresses the assumptions necessary for legal cognition. The basic norm merely states the conditions under which the empirical material can be more closely defined as positive law by juridical science.

Its function is, therefore, in the first place, to establish a supreme law-making authority; it is above all a function of delegation. In this, however, it does not exhaust itself. The basic norm does not merely proclaim that whatever this authority has created shall be law because it has been created by this authority, and that therefore nothing else can be law. It also contains the guarantee that whatever has thus been created can be understood as meaningful. It states that one should act in obedience to the commands of the supreme authority and of the authorities delegated by it, and that these commands must be interpreted as a meaningful whole.

F. The Methodological Importance of the Basic Norm in Positive Law

If one considers the actual character of the material which is comprehensible as law by virtue of the basic norm, it becomes clear that the basic norm itself must already express the coercive character of positive law. Its formula, therefore, is not as it has just been stated in a somewhat abbreviated form: Whatever the supreme authority commands shall be done. More exactly it reads: Under certain conditions laid down by the supreme authority, coercion is to be applied in a fashion determined by that authority. The basic norm has the basic form and pattern of the legal rule. For this reason the interpretation may ignore as legally irrelevant whatever legal material has not assumed this form. Since this hypothesis of every positive legal order has the form of a legal rule, the idea of legality, i.e., conformity to law, is inherent in it. This is the idea that a certain consequence is linked to a certain factual condition, that, if this consequence is linked to this condition, only this consequence and none other (or no consequence) may follow. The basic norm states that under certain conditions X a certain consequence A ought to take place. It thereby states that, under like conditions X, non-A ought not to take place at the same time. For the principle of non-contradiction must be posited in the idea of law, since without it the notion of legality would be destroyed.

This presupposition alone, which is contained in the basic norm, allows legal cognition to supply a meaningful interpretation of the legal material. This does not inaugurate any new method of scientific jurisprudence. It merely reveals the logical assumptions of a long-used method through an analysis of the procedure actually followed. The principles of interpretation which have been discussed above, the principle of *lex posterior derogat priori*, the principle that the lower norm must give way to the higher, the reinterpretation of constitutional clauses concerning the enactment of statutes, the rule concerning two contradictory clauses of the same statute, the declaration that part of the content of a statute may be legally irrelevant, etc. — all of these have no other purpose than to give a meaningful interpretation to the material of positive law. They all do this by applying the principle of contradiction in the normative sphere. For the most part, they are not rules of positive law, not established norms, but presuppositions of legal cognition. This means that they are part of the sense of the basic norm, which thus guarantees the unity of the norms of positive law as the unity of a system which, if it is not necessarily just, is at least meaningful. It is ultimately the basic norm which guarantees this complex of norms as an order.*

III. THE RELATION OF NATURAL TO POSITIVE LAW. THE POLITICAL SIGNIFICANCE OF NATURAL-LAW THEORY

A. THE EXCLUSIVE VALIDITY OF A SYSTEM OF NORMS: THE LOGICAL PRINCIPLE OF CONTRADICTION IN THE SPHERE OF NORMATIVE VALIDITY

Two systems of norms may be reducible to two different basic norms, whose difference need not be as general or essential as that between a static and a dynamic type. Two different basic norms of the same character may be involved, for instance, the norm of love and the norm of the public good, or one which delegates the Pope as the deputy of God, and another which institutes the emperor or some other secular authority as supreme. If two different systems of norms are given, only one of them can be assumed to be valid from the point of view of a cognition which is concerned with the validity of norms.

For the sake of simplicity it may here be assumed that the norms of both systems relate to the same object, to human conduct, which occurs in time and space; that is, that they have the same temporal, spatial, personal, and material sphere of validity. This is true, of course, for natural and positive law, with whose relationship alone we are here concerned. It requires, therefore, no proof that a limitation of the object of the norms (that is, of the legal order's temporal, spatial, personal, and material sphere of validity) and, with it, the possibility of the coexistence of two normative systems with different objects, hinges upon a certain limitation of the basic norms which constitute the two systems. The basic norm, which establishes the system with a limited object, must be

---

* To simplify the problem, we take positive law in its manifestation as the legal order of a single State whose relation to international law is disregarded. If we were to consider the totality of a legal system which comprises international law and its subordinate national legal orders, the problem of the hypothetical basic norm would be shifted. In that case the norm which establishes the constitutional legislator in the national order appears as a mere positive legal rule of international law, with whose basic norm alone we would be concerned.

subordinated to a higher norm, which imposes such a limitation and, accordingly, to a higher system of norms. It follows that the two supposed basic norms are no genuine basic norms, that the systems of norms relatively established by them and limited in object (namely, in their sphere of validity) can only be partial orders. Clearly, two such orders, which are limited to different objects or spheres of validity, are possible only within the same total system. Hence the assumption of two truly different systems is revealed as false. If there should be two actually different systems of norms, mutually independent in their validity, because of the difference of the basic norms, both of which are related to the same object (in having the same sphere of validity), insoluble logical contradiction between them could not be excluded. The norm of one system may prescribe conduct A for a certain person, under a certain condition, at a certain time and place. The norm of the other system may prescribe, under the same conditions and for the same person, conduct non-A. This situation is impossible for the cognition of norms. The judgments "A ought to be" and "A ought not to be" (for example, "you ought to speak the truth" and "you ought not to speak the truth") are just as incompatible with one another as "A is" and "A is not." For the principle of contradiction is quite as valid for cognition in the sphere of normative validity as it is in that of empirical reality. The only reason why this should not be accepted as a matter of course is that "is" and "ought" are not sufficiently distinguished. Between the two judgments "A ought to be" and "A is not" (for example, "X ought to tell the truth" and "X lies here and now") there is no logical contradiction. They are both possible at the same time (X lies although he ought not to lie). They merely designate the situation of an actual conflict between what is and what ought to be, of, so to speak, a teleological but not a logical conflict. Only if the contents A and non-A both occur in the form of the "ought," or both in the form of the "is," do they logically exclude each other.

B. THE NORM AS AN "OUGHT" AND AS A PSYCHOLOGICAL FACT: COLLISION OF DUTIES AND CONTRADICTION OF NORMS

Disregard of this circumstance leads to the frequently reiterated objection: Does not "reality" show that two contradictory norms and that, therefore, two different systems of norms, which are mutually independent as to validity and content, can coexist and produce the "fact" of a "collision of duties," as, for instance, in the case of morals and positive law, or in that of the legal orders of two States? The apparent justification for this objection disappears, as soon as the equivocation of the terms "norm," "legal norm," "legal order" is shown, from which this argument derives its deceptive strength. These words do not mean only the "ought," the norm, the law, the order, in their specific validity, which is a normative validity. They are also used to designate the fact of imagining or willing a norm, a psychological act which occurs in the sphere of being. Only by shifting the use of the term "norm" in the course of the same argument, sometimes to this, sometimes to the other meaning, can the logical contradiction be concealed. It is contradictory to contend that norm A (as a moral norm) and norm non-A (as a legal norm) are valid at the same time, that is, that A and non-A ought to prevail at the same time. That one is a legal and the other a moral norm does not preclude a logical contradiction, if the two have been established as norms, that is, in the same sphere of the "ought" and, consequently, in the same system of cognition. No contradiction is involved, if one contends that legal norm A is valid, even though the empirical ("is") fact persists that men believe, imagine, or will that non-A ought to be. The normative validity of the legal norm prescribing behavior A is unaffected even by the fact that the individual who should act in obedience to this legal norm actually displays behavior non-A, and even less by his corresponding belief, imagination, or volition (because he is so motivated by a moral conception). The statement that an individual has the positive legal duty to obey the mobilization order of the head of State (that is, that the corresponding legal norm has "ought" validity), does not logically contradict the statement that the same individual, for moral reasons, considers himself bound to do the contrary, that is, the statement that the empirical fact of a conception or volition with this content exists. It is not the validity of a moral norm contradicting the legal norm which is here asserted. The judgment which establishes A as content of a positive legal norm (an "ought") is not confronted by one which establishes non-A as content of an "ought" of morality. That would be nonsense. Rather, the first normative judgment is confronted, or really placed side by side, with a factual ("is") judgment. What is ordinarily called a "collision of duties" is an event which does not occur in the normative sphere and does not involve a contradiction between two normative judgments, but rather a competition of two different motives, of two psychological impulses, pushing in different directions. It is a situation, then, which completely belongs to the sphere of empirical reality. A person becomes conscious that A and non-A are demanded of him at the same time from two different directions. The judgment stating this situation contains as little logical contradiction as that which states the effect of two opposed forces acting upon one body. They are essentially different from two judgments which state something about the "ought" of two conflicting contents, A and non-A. These latter are in no wise concerned with a psychological or bodily process, that is, with the sphere of being or empirical reality.

C. LAW AND MORALS: THE POSTULATE OF THE UNITY OF SYSTEM

Actually, such a contradiction is avoided. Whenever the conflict between law and morals is stated, closer scrutiny shows that it does not really suggest the simultaneous validity of the two orders. It rather signifies that something is commanded from the legal point of view, although it is forbidden from the moral one, and vice versa. One supposes, perhaps not quite consciously, that the circumstances may be judged either from the legal or the moral point of view, but that judging from one point of view excludes the other. This is the meaning of the stereotyped argument that a certain behavior may be morally objectionable, but legally only this and no other behavior is correct. It is evident to any jurist that, as a jurist — that is, when the cognition of legal norms is involved — he must disregard the moral aspect. No moralist would think of letting considerations of positive law interfere with the validity of norms which he has recognized from his point of view. Similarly, a judge can only apply, e.g., either German or French law in the decision of a case, for in this act of application which is specifically directed to the "ought," to the "validity" of the law, only French or German law can be recognized as valid, that is, as binding upon the organ that applies the law. In this connection, we must of course disregard cases in which the positive law expressly refers to moral norms, morality to rules of positive law, or German law to the application of French law (or vice versa). In the first of these cases the delegated morality becomes law; in the second, delegated law becomes morality; in the third, French law becomes German law (or vice versa). The delegated order is subordinated to the delegating order. Such a subordination, however, is only possible within the same total order, which comprises both the supraordinate and the subordinate orders. To know an object and to recognize it as a unity means the same thing.

A system of norms can only be valid if the validity of all other systems of norms with the same sphere of validity has been excluded. The unity of a system of norms signifies its uniqueness. This is simply a consequence of the principle of unity, a principle basic for all cognition, including the cognition of norms whose negative criterion is found in the impossibility of logical contradiction.

D. The Logical Impossibility of the Coexistence of Positive and Natural Law

Once positive law and natural law have been recognized as two systems of norms which differ from one another in their ultimate reason of validity, their relationship cannot be further discussed in the sense of two different and simultaneously valid systems. For a "relationship" is only possible between elements of the same system. Either natural or positive law may be claimed as systems of valid norms. In this sense, the relation of positive law to natural law is the same as that of positive law to morals, or as that of a national (domestic) legal order to international law.* Any attempt to establish a relationship between the two systems of norms in terms of simultaneously valid orders ultimately leads to their merging in terms of sub- and supraordination, that is, to the recognition of positive as natural law or of natural as positive law. There is a wealth of such attempts which express, usually without full awareness on the part of the theorists, the irrepressible tendency of knowledge toward the unity of its object. The insight that there is a logical necessity about the exclusive validity of a system of norms leads to a consequence which is of the utmost significance for the theory of natural law. If one assumes the validity of a natural legal order, one cannot, at the same time, assume the existence of a simultaneously valid positive legal order with the same sphere of validity. From the point of view of a consistent positivism, which regards the positive legal order as supreme, non-derivative, and therefore non-justifiable by reference to a superior system of norms, the validity of a natural law cannot be admitted. Likewise, from the point of view of natural law, in so far as it conforms to its pure idea, there is no room for the validity of a positive law. The coexistence of a natural and a positive law as two different systems of norms is logically excluded; for a contradiction between the two is possible. If the norms of positive law contradict the norms of natural law, the former must be considered unjust. It is this possibility which impels the differentiation of positive from natural law. There is, finally, not only a possible but also a necessary contradiction between positive and natural law, because the one is a coercive order, while the other, ideally, is not only non-coercive, but actually has to forbid any coercion among men. A positive law, then, beside natural law is not only impossible from the point of view of formal logic, it is also superfluous from a material-teleological point of view,

---

* Cf. my study *Les Rapports de système entre le droit interne et le droit international public* (1927) Académie de Droit International, Extrait du Recueil des cours.

if the assumptions hold which alone permit one to maintain the validity of a "natural" order. For, why should a human-arbitrary order be needed for the regulation of human conduct, if a just regulation can already be found in an order "natural," evident to all and in harmony with what all men of good will would propose? To provide any coercive acts for the realization of such a natural order would not only be superfluous, but could be considered positively harmful and apt to produce precisely those evils whose prevention and elimination are the sole justification of coercion.

E. The Impossibility of a Relationship of Delegation between Natural and Positive Law

From the point of view of the pure natural-law idea, any relationship of delegation between natural and positive law must be considered as impossible. It has been suggested above that, by means of such a delegation, one system would have to be merged with the other, so that any such construction would necessarily result in eliminating the specific character of one of the two systems. Take in particular the attempt, repeated often and in all possible variations, to found positive law upon a natural law delegation (for instance, public authority has been instituted by God). Closer scrutiny reveals that the order of natural law cannot provide such a delegation without contradicting the fundamental principle of its own validity, without actually dissolving itself and giving way to the order of positive law. This is a cardinal point of the historical doctrine of natural law; a theoretically sound grasp of it is a basic assumption for understanding the entire doctrine, as it has been represented for over two thousand years. Here it may suffice to state that a delegation of positive law by natural law can only mean one thing: the latter system must contain a norm whereby a supreme authority is empowered to make positive law, and whose norms are to have validity, not because of the justice of their content, but because they have been issued by this natural-law-made authority. The norms of natural law, on the other hand, in keeping with their basic idea, derive their validity from the objective "justice" of their content. That the norm of delegation is not in harmony with this idea is evident. To assume it, nevertheless, represents the logically impossible attempt to establish the positive-law principle of validity with the aid of the natural-law principle of validity, although the two principles are incompatible. In view of the fact that positive law is not, on principle, subject to limitations of at least its material and temporal validity (limitations upon the validity of the national by the international legal order may be disregarded here), the norm of natural law, which delegates the creation of positive law, cannot be allowed to have such a restriction either. If it be assumed that there are, beside this delegating norm, other material norms of natural law, the delegation of positive by natural law must mean that natural law empowers positive law to replace it. This actually is the consciously or unconsciously desired result of the theory of delegation, much as it may seek to conceal it by assurances to the contrary. Of all the norms of natural law, only the one remains which delegates positive law (and which in reality is no natural-law norm at all). A thus denatured natural law has no other function than that of legitimizing positive law. The idea of natural law has been transformed into an ideology of positive law. The attempt to comprehend positive law as "delegated" by natural law need not concern us any further in this connection, as it represents the obvious and admitted renunciation of the assumed validity of an autonomous natural-law order.

F. Positive Law as a Mere Fact in its Relation to Natural Law as a Norm

It may, nevertheless, be objected that the existence of positive law is a "fact" which manifests itself in the "life" of States and perhaps even of the community of States. If, in addition, one feels driven to assume also the existence of a "natural" order of law, the "relationship" between the two, which we have thus far denied, is obviously given, and the determination of its nature becomes an unavoidable task of legal science. But this objection, also, rests on the demonstrated equivocation of the term "norm" and its corollaries. We speak of the "existence" of law in the double sense of a normative validity of legal rules and of an effectiveness of human conceptions and volitions which embrace legal rules, that is, of a function with a cause-and-effect quality. If the validity of a natural-law order is assumed, the "factual" existence of positive law simply means that positive law is not to be taken as a system of norms with "ought" validity, but literally as a mere empirical fact. For this reason, an anarchist, for instance, who denied the validity of the hypothetical basic norm of positive law (theoretical anarchism always somehow shares the position of natural law, the theory of pure natural law that of anarchism), will view its positive regulation of human relationships (such as property, the hiring contract) as mere power relations and their description as "ought" norms a mere "fiction," as an attempt to supply a justifying ideology. Natural law and the fact of positive law (the latter as a factual phenomenon and not in its normative validity) are not related to one another as two valid normative systems, but only in the same sense as a norm and the factual event, which is materially coordinated to it: that is, they are in the relation of possible conformity or non-conformity. The conduct of an individual may conform to the governing norm, if the content of the actual conduct (an "is" content) agrees with that of the norm (an "ought" content). It may not conform to the norm, contradict or "violate" it, if its content logically contradicts that of the norm. It must always be kept in mind that the logical contradiction between the content of the norm (of the "ought") and the content of actual human conduct (of the "is") does not imply a logical contradiction between the norm itself (the "ought") and actual human conduct (the "is").

It is only in this sense that one can speak of a relation of natural to positive law, always taking natural law as a system of rules with normative validity: does the actual, external or internal, conduct of human beings who create or execute, issue or obey, rules of positive law, do the mental and physical acts involved in this conduct, conform to or violate the norms of a natural order? Whenever positive law, taken in its merely factual aspect, conforms to natural law, it is "just" in the same sense as actual conduct, such as the execution of a murderer after the imposition of a valid sentence by a competent court is "legal," inasmuch as it conforms to positive law, now taken in its normative aspect. As it is a "just" positive law because it corresponds to natural law, so it is "unjust" when it contradicts it. Because positive in relation to natural law has here no "validity" at all (being a mere fact and not a valid set of norms in the light of natural law), the question of the validity or invalidity of a positive norm by reason of its harmony or conflict with natural law cannot arise from the position of the pure and consistently developed idea of natural law.*

G. The Relation of Natural to Positive Law in the Historical Natural-Law Doctrine

In spite of this, the historical doctrine of the law of nature does not adhere to this pure natural-law idea. Natural law in actual reality, that is, as it has been represented by the natural-law doctrine for more than two thousand years, shows quite essential variations from the original picture as it has just been outlined. This is mainly due to the tendency

---

* The tendency which constantly recurs, even in a theory with positivistic pretensions, to identify the "validity" of positive law with its efficacy and to deny to positive law any specific validity apart from this efficacy, ultimately originates in natural-law speculation. It has a certain affinity to the "sociological" trend in legal science whose natural-law character is only ill-concealed by the terminology of causality.

of natural-law doctrine to view positive law not as a mere fact, but as a system of valid norms, as a legal order with normative validity, which exists side by side with a similarly understood natural law. Generally, the natural-law doctrine seeks to maintain that both natural and positive law are given as simultaneously valid orders. To this end, it constructs, directly or indirectly, consciously or unconsciously, a relationship between the two, which presupposes the unity of a system of norms comprising both. Owing to the preponderance of positive law once its validity has been accepted, natural law has to adjust itself to this positive law, in order somehow to gain access to the unified system which comprises positive law. It follows that natural law, at least in the particular guise of an idea which wholly excludes positive law, can no longer be maintained. It is this fundamental position of natural-law theory with respect to positive law which brings about all the various modifications that the natural-law idea itself undergoes at the hands of its various teachers; these modifications virtually lead to a more or less unnoticed elimination of natural law. It is a position which the doctrine holds and has to hold for reasons which lie outside the field of theory.

The natural-law doctrine of all nations and all times has emphatically denied the view that positive law coexisting with natural law is superfluous or harmful. This theory can even less afford to accept the idea that positive law coexisting with natural law is logically impossible.* One might, as a characteristic example, cite the following passage from a work by Melanchthon, who may be taken as a typical representative of natural-law doctrine. He is essentially rooted in the medieval Catholic theory of Thomas Aquinas and at the same time he laid the foundation of the almost exclusively Protestant natural-law doctrine of the seventeenth and eighteenth centuries. In his work on ethics he writes: *Etsi autem multi imperiti homines stolide vociferantur, non opus esse scriptis legibus, sed ex naturali judicio eorum, qui praesunt, res judicandas esse. Tamen sciendum est, hanc barbaricam opinionem detestandam esse, et homines docendos esse, melius esse habere scriptas leges, et has reverenter tuendas et amandas esse.†* The absolute necessity of positive law, as a system of valid normative rules beside natural law, is taken for granted by natural-law doctrine. It is evident that this position is not possible without a considerable modification of the pure natural-law idea. Once this dualism of natural and positive law is definitely established, the

---

* Cf. my article *Naturrecht und positives Recht: Eine Untersuchung ihres gegenseitigen Verhältnisses* (1928) 2 INTERNATIONALE ZEITSCHRIFT FÜR RECHTSTHEORIE (Brünn) 81ff.

† ETHICAE DOCTRINAE ELEMENTORUM LIBRI DUO. CORPUS REFORMATORUM, vol. XVI (Halis Saxonum, 1850) p. 234f.

problem of a possible conflict between the two becomes progressively more difficult.

H. Natural Law as a Justification of Positive Law

What is the attitude of the historical natural-law theory on this point, which is decisive for its appraisal? First of all, it avoids a clear and unequivocal presentation of the problem. The majority, even of the most important of the natural-law teachers, did not ask the question at all, or answered it only incidentally, as if it did not involve a fundamental theoretical problem. Besides, there has been little serious criticism of positive-law materials on the basis of the natural-law norms, as the theory developed them. The natural-law teachers scrutinize only the most important institutions of positive law, of any positive law of their time, with a view to their rightness in the light of the natural order, such as the magistracy, private property, slavery, marriage. The result is, almost without exception, the justification of these institutions on a natural-law basis, and, thereby, a legitimization of the positive order of law (which, after all, is only an unfolding of these basic institutions) through the higher order of natural law. In addition, the theory develops a host of methods with the aim either of making any conflict between positive and natural law appear impossible or, if conflict should be possible, of making it appear unlikely or without danger for natural law. Such methods, the specific methods of natural-law doctrine, are evidently indications of a further denaturing of the pure natural-law idea. For, in the process, its content has to be increasingly assimilated to positive law or reduced to empty formulas, such as "Equal things shall receive equal treatment"; "*Suum cuique*"; "Injure no one without a just cause"; "Do good and avoid evil," etc. Without presupposing the existence of a positive legal order all these formulas are devoid of sense; but if related to any positive legal order they can justify it. Furthermore, the natural-law teachers contend, in a version which has remained a stereotype from the church fathers down to Kant, that positive law derives its entire validity from natural law; it is essentially a mere emanation of natural law; the making of statutes or of decisions does not freely create, it merely reproduces the true law which is already somehow in existence, and positive law (the copy), whenever it contradicts natural law (the model or archetype), cannot have any validity.

A more detailed study of the sources will reveal that these theses were absolutely irrelevant to the validity of positive law: the character of natural-law doctrine in general, and of its main current, was strictly conservative. Natural law as posited by the theory was essentially an ideology which served to support, justify, and make an absolute of positive law, or, what is the same thing, of the authority of the State. The contention that natural law derogates positive law was rendered practically innocuous by an elaborate doctrine and had only to be maintained for the sake of appearance, in order to preserve for natural law its function of justifying a positive law. This is the typical picture which natural-law doctrine draws of the legal world — its legal-world picture so to speak: In the foreground is positive law, essentially in uncontested validity; behind positive law, duplicating it in a peculiar manner, is a natural law, representing a higher order, the source of all validity and social value, whose function in the main is the justification of positive law.

There were, of course, currents of opposition at all times, which in the face of the dominant trend advanced a more or less revolutionary theory and in the face of a natural law denatured by official science again expounded its pure idea. But little has been handed down to us of these intellectual movements. All the natural-law teachers to whom there is still attributed any eminence belong to the conservative trend. How could it have been otherwise? Were they not all either faithful and obedient servants of the State, or ministers of a State church, professors, envoys, privy councillors, etc.? After all, the climax of natural-law doctrine, its classical period, coincides with the time of the most unmitigated political absolutism, under whose pressure a revolutionary theory had no chance to develop as a literary movement, let alone to be officially taught in the universities.

I. The Supposedly Revolutionary Character of Natural-Law Doctrine

Why is it that the opinion concerning natural-law theory, which today prevails among scholars, presents exactly the opposite picture? It contends that its individualistic doctrine of the social contract had an emphatically revolutionary or, at least, a radically reformist character. We cannot here enter into a detailed discussion of the errors inherent in this view, especially its misunderstanding of the significance of the natural-law contract theory. Suffice it to say that the contention of the revolutionary-destructive character of natural law, initiated by Friedrich Julius Stahl * and later adopted by Bergbohm,† was caused by the fact that a particular phase in this millennial trend, namely Rousseau's mid-eighteenth-century legal and political theory, was simply identified

---

* 2 F. J. Stahl, Philosophie des Rechts (4th ed.) 175ff. and 289.

† C. Bergbohm, Jurisprudenz und Rechtsphilosophie (1892) 116, 200, 217 and *passim*.

with the natural-law doctrine in general. We can here ignore the question of the revolutionary character of Rousseau's teachings. It is, by the way, not at all as self-evident as is ordinarily assumed. Yet the French Revolution did furnish a thoroughly revolutionary interpretation of Rousseau's natural-law doctrine. Nothing can be more significant than the fact that this was the reason that official legal science, as taught in the universities, dropped the doctrine of natural law. Although for generations it had proved its conservative worth in support of throne and altar, it manifestly could also be used for diametrically opposed purposes. No wonder we find a new ideology emerging in place of the old natural-law doctrine, which no longer reliably served its function as a defender of the positive law, of the established order of the State: the historical school of law. We may disregard here the fact that it had no less of a natural-law character than official legal science had had before. It merely substituted the *Volksgeist* for reason or nature as the source of a natural order which was the opposite of an artificial one. This much only may be said: the historical school, to make its fight against the revolutionary version of the natural-law doctrine the more effective, used a device typical of any new theory. Any new theory makes it appear that the struggle against a part is a struggle against the whole, that its struggle against an error within the system is a struggle against the whole system, and that it represents a fundamental change in science. This is why the theory of the revolutionary character of natural-law doctrine found such wide acceptance in the nineteenth and twentieth centuries. It is an error in the history of ideas which was further strengthened by the fact that the idea of natural law may actually have a revolutionary character, while, in its historical reality, natural-law doctrine, with the exception mentioned above, has manifested just the opposite.

Natural-law doctrine does not owe its conservative character to these political motives alone as they have been sketched here, which, understandably enough, play an important role in any political and legal theory. This conservatism is fundamentally rooted in the epistemological situation of a science which seeks to understand the nature of the State and of law. Out of this arises an extraordinary difficulty, a handicap to the critical analysis of any political and legal theory: it is the more difficult to uncover a political motivation, whose effectiveness varies with the historical situation, the more the political motivation is paralleled by an epistemological tendency which may obscure and conceal it to a certain degree.

IV. THE EPISTEMOLOGICAL (METAPHYSICAL) AND PSYCHOLOGICAL FOUNDATIONS

A. The Metaphysical Dualism

a. The Duplication of the Object of Cognition in the Sphere of Natural Reality; the Image Theory

It is a peculiar and often discussed fact that human cognition, whenever it follows its original impulses naively and uncritically, has the tendency to duplicate its object. The reason is that man is not at all satisfied with what his own senses present and his own reason comprehends. His first passionate urge for knowledge remains unsatisfied, if he is to stop within the boundaries of what is given in his own being, with nature as he can sense and comprehend it through the energies of his own soul. The desire to penetrate into the essence of things moves him to inquire what is "behind" things. And because he cannot find an answer to this question within his experience, that is, in the sphere of the world of his senses as it is controlled and ordered by his reason, he boldly assumes a sphere beyond his experience. This is the sphere which is said to hide the grounds and causes he seeks, the ideas or archetypes of all earthly things experienced, the things as they are, the "things in themselves" as they exist independently of senses and reason, a sphere which, because it is inaccessible to his senses, is at the same time said to be eternally concealed from him. This strange hypothesis, by which man produces the illusion of growing beyond himself, this curious attempt of the eternal Munchausen to climb on his own shoulders, forms the elementary kernel of all metaphysics and religion. Although this truly tragi-comic undertaking has of old been the pride of the human spirit, it is ultimately rooted in a curious distrust which this human spirit has of itself. Only because man evidently lacks full confidence in his own senses and his own reason is he restless in his self-created and self-arranged world of knowledge. Only this undervaluation of his own self induces him to consider the world this self recognizes as a mere fragment, an inferior seedling of another world which is beyond its knowledge just because and as far as it is the "real," "final," "perfect," and "true" world.

The metaphysical dualism of the "here and now" and the "beyond," of this world and another world, of experience and transcendence, necessarily leads to the widely accepted epistemological doctrine known as the image theory. It states that, essentially, human cognition merely furnishes, mirrorwise, an image of things as they "really" are, as they are "in themselves." Because of the inadequacy of the material used in the mirror (the merely human senses, the merely human reason), it is an inadequate, shadowy image of that reality or truth which is never within the reach of man. The decisive importance of this comparison of human cognition with a mirror lies in the fact that the true and real world is beyond the mirror, that is, beyond human cognition, and that, whatever is comprehended in its frame — the world as man experiences it with his senses and reason — is only appearance, only the dim reflection of a higher, transcendent world. The metaphysical dualism is so deep-rooted in our ordinary thinking that this conception of the relation of our knowing to its object, as determined by the specifically dualistic image theory, is more understandable than any other despite its obviously paradoxical nature. It even appears self-evident and is therefore almost ineradicable. Yet nothing is more contradictory and, therefore, incomprehensible, than the assumption that our cognition reflects a world which is inaccessible to our cognition. Nothing is more problematic than the attempt to explain that which is given by that which is not, the comprehensible by the incomprehensible. And no less paradoxical is the psychological background of this epistemological situation: a diminished sense of self allows the function of the human spirit to degenerate into a merely dependent, and not at all creative, copying; at the same time it permits this spirit which, in the process of knowing, is only capable of inadequate reproduction, to construct, with its own means, a whole transcendent world. It is as if the human spirit, while holding its reason and senses in contempt, were compensating itself with its wish-fulfilling imagination.

b. The Duplication of the Object of Cognition in the Realm of Values

The strange phenomenon of the duplication of objects is not only found in the process of knowing, in the narrower sense of knowing nature or reality, but also in the intellectual function of "valuation," which may be considered as the cognition of values or norms, so far as it is expressed in "ought" statements. The cognition of values, as distinguished from the cognition of reality, is not concerned with explanation, but with justification. Also in this sphere it can be seen how the inquiry into the "why" (that is, here, the ground of any value expressible in an "ought") penetrates beyond that which is somehow given and attainable within the rational realm, analogous to that of natural experience, into a world of transcendent values. The immediately knowable empirical value must be represented as the emanation of that world of transcendent values in order to be value at all. There is a clear tendency, here again, to value an object, to justify some content by adding, so to speak, to the immediate object of the value judgment a second object which is in a sense behind and above it. The immediately given object must appear as the latter's copy or reproduction, so that it may be interpreted as valuable and seem justified. The positive morality, for instance, which is valid in any social community and specifically shaped according to time and place, is represented as the emanation of an eternal and divine law. Similarly in the doctrine of natural law, a natural order of human conduct arises behind the positive law of the State. The metaphysical philosophy of nature is particularly intent upon depicting the world of experience as but an inaccurate repetition of a transcendent reality and, by means of its specific image theory, it merely allows human cognition to reflect and not to create this empirical world. The natural-law philosophy characterized above maintains the same idea when it insists that, contrary to appearances, positive law is not the free creation of a human legislator and judge, but a mere reproduction of a natural law beyond this positive law, an inadequate copy of a "law in itself," and that, for this reason, positive law has validity and value. The difficulties into which the political and legal philosophy of natural law maneuvers itself, by means of this dualism of a positive and a natural order, are methodically analogous to those of the metaphysical philosophy of nature with its dualism of the "here" and the "beyond," of experience and transcendence. In both cases, there is the inaccessibility of the archetype and the hopeless attempt, in the one case to explain, in the other to justify, that which is given. In the one case as in the other, there is not only the constant threat of the insolvable contradiction between a somehow accepted ideal and a reality which does not conform to the ideal, but also the immanent tendency to overcome the dualism by complying with the postulate of the unity of knowledge. It is in this striving toward a science free from metaphysics that natural science emancipates itself from theology, legal and political science from natural-law doctrine.

This dualistic view of cosmos and life, as it runs through the philosophy of reality and value, nature and law, may manifest itself in different stages or grades of intensity, depending upon the degree to which the dualism has been carried. These stages will be further developed below. It is well to keep in mind that a certain stage of natural philosophy is not necessarily associated with the stage of legal philosophy which, epistemologically, corresponds to it. Legal philosophy meets, in its development to higher forms, much greater obstacles than natural philosophy, which is influenced by political, that is, governmental, interests either not at all or only indirectly. Above all, the following schematic presentation should not (or at least not primarily) be understood as a historical-genetic description of evolutionary stages succeeding one another according to a strict rule.

c. The Theory of Nature and Law among Primitives

Primitive man's conception of the structure of his natural environment is determined by the impotence which he experiences in the face of the mighty and overpowering manifestations of nature. This is especially true when his life is filled with the difficult and dangerous struggle with nature. The interpretation of nature by primitive man is determined by his characteristic lack of selfconsciousness; his natural philosophy, if it is possible to speak of one, is the expression of his sense of inferiority. Everything appears a god to him. For primitive man the tree is or harbors an effective spirit, a demon, who makes this tree grow and flower. He imagines the sun to be moved by a masculine, the moon by a feminine god. He regards animals, especially the animals of the chase which are important for his existence, as beings superior to himself which he dare not kill without asking their forgiveness. He is even convinced that he cannot kill them without their will, that they consent to be killed by him only if he acts in a manner of which they approve. This belief persists even though he himself has invented very effective weapons and has developed ingenious hunting methods. Nothing is more characteristic of the primitive's mythological conception of nature proceeding from his weak sense of self than the fact, observed in a savage tribe even very recently, that its members worshipped their home-made tools, their hammers and saws, as gods. Even where the primitive has created with his own hand, with the strength of his body and his spirit, he distrusts his own capacity. He believes he should revere his products as the products of supernatural forces, as the work of the gods. To him they are nothing "arbitrary," no "artificial" things or human handiwork; he interprets them, as we would say, as something "natural" which, to him, means something divine, something a god has created in him and through him.

Primitive man assumes the same attitude with regard to the social order in which he lives, with regard to the positive law which, as the command of the chieftain, medicine man, priest, judge, or other authority, requires his obedience, or, in the form of old custom, is applied by these same authorities. He does not regard these individual and general norms constituting his social community as human statutes, but as the direct expression of divine will. The primitive does not yet believe that there is beside or above this positive law a natural law, for he does not experience the positive law as such, but directly as something natural or divine. His legal theory is not yet properly dualistic, any more than his natural philosophy. It only contains the germ of this dualism. Primitive man does not yet imagine above nature, above his own world, a divine beyond, a supernatural sphere above the natural sphere. He merely duplicates the things of his experience by peopling the natural world with gods and demons. The conception of the immediately divine nature of the law which creates and maintains society is coupled with the conviction, springing from an underdeveloped consciousness of self, that this positive law is not an artificial handiwork of man. This manifests itself in the myth, still encountered in relatively advanced social conditions, that the legal order of the State has been created by the national deity through the mediation of a divinely worshipped leader, or that it goes ultimately back to such an act of divine lawmaking. Thus, Jehovah is said to have handed Moses the Tables of the Law on Mount Sinai, Allah or the Archangel Gabriel is said to have dictated the Koran to Mohammed, Hammurabi is said to have received his code from the Sun God; Dike, the deity of law, appeared to the ancient Greeks as the gift and daughter of Zeus, the old Frisian saga reports that the Asegen, the oldest speakers and finders of law, the first legislators, were instructed in law by a deity. It is only a variation of the same idea when the ruler who is empowered to make positive law is himself revered as a deity or as the son or more remote descendant of a divine ancestor. The political significance of this mythology is obvious. As a natural philosophy it has to explain nature, as an ideology of law and State it has to justify the positive order and to heighten, as far as possible, its effectiveness by creating an unconditional obedience founded upon the fear of the mysterious, omnipotent deity. Derived from a sense of inferiority, the myth has the function of reinforcing this sense, at least in the social sphere.

d. Metaphysical-Religious Dualism

As man grows in his knowledge of nature, he increasingly seeks and finds an immanent order in the chaos of things, he becomes more and more conscious of nature as a somehow coherent whole. He now ceases to duplicate every single thing and instead begins to duplicate nature as a whole. He sees that this tree stems from the little bush, the bush from a seedling, the seedling from a seed, which in turn comes from the fruit of the tree. Where was the dryad when the tree was still a seed? As man recognizes change in nature and through it the mutual connection of things, he removes the divine half from things, moves it out of the sphere of the interconnected things of his visible and tangible world and lets it coalesce in a second, supernatural world which is removed from both his senses and his reason. Only now has the metaphysical dualism been perfected, a dualism consisting of a beyond, which embraces the absolute truth, and the empirical world which alone is within the reach of erring man, of transcendence and experience, of idea and reality.

The same transformation of conceptions occurs with respect to positive law. As positive law increasingly reveals itself, to the more critical eye, as a changeable and ever-changing system of norms, created by a variety of legislators, varying in time and place, man recognizes this positive law as human handiwork. The personal connection between his own governmental order — which he now recognizes as. only one among many — and his individual national deity dissolves in his consciousness. Instead, he forms the conception of a permanent and unchangeable divine order, of a natural, absolute justice which reigns above any law which is positive and variable in time and place. The primitive conception of the divine nature of law has developed into the dualism of natural and positive law.

As we have seen, this metaphysical-religious dualism, as compared to the naive mythological natural and social philosophy, already represents the result of a certain critical contemplation. The human mind, however, cannot bear this terrible and, on principle, irreconcilable contrast of "here" and "beyond," of humanity and deity, of law and justice. Therefore, as the insight into this conflict develops, there is also born the unquenchable longing to overcome it. If it is possible to regard the history of the human spirit as the development of this metaphysical-religious dualism in its various forms, it is necessary to recognize it at the same time as the constantly renewed effort of the human spirit to liberate itself from this enormous conflict into which it has thrust itself, and which it seems tragically fated to enter forever anew.

According to the way in which the metaphysical-religious dualism seeks to resolve itself, one can distinguish essentially three fundamental types. Philosophical man may emphasize, within the dualistic system of his cosmic and moral philosophy, the beyond, the realm of the idea and of justice; or he may place the emphasis on the empirical world, the realm of experience and positive law. Or, thirdly, he may assume a compromise position and attempt somehow to balance the two ends of the scales, one of which would raise him heavenward, while the other would cast him to inferno. We may assume that there is an inner correspondence between the cosmic and moral philosophy of man and his character.* The first of these three types could, on this basis, be explained by the fundamentally pessimistic mood of a selfconsciousness, not weak in itself but directed, so-to-speak, against itself, a mood not of a really lessened, but of a self-deprecating consciousness. The second type originates in the optimism of an exalted and rising consciousness of self which even borders

* Cf. MÜLLER-FREIENFELS, PERSÖNLICHKEIT UND WELTANSCHAUUNG (2d ed. 1923).

on an exaggerated self-esteem. The third type is associated with the character whose fundamental mood is one of tired or cautious resignation, and which mediates between these extremes, sometimes leaning toward the one, sometimes toward the other side.

e. Pessimistic Dualism: Personality Type and Metaphysical Attitude

The dualism of the first type is obviously directed toward the transcendent sphere. In it are found the true, the really original images of all being, the *ideas* in a brightly radiant light which is not visible to man, at least during his bodily existence. Terrestrial things which have a shadowy existence in the dim twilight of the here and now hardly convey a glimmer of them. This whole world of experienced reality is, basically, not "real" at all, it is but appearance and deceit. True reality is only in the "beyond" which man hopes to enter after his death. This longing for the "beyond," which is merely an ideological concealment of fear and flight from present existence, makes man consider the entire world, as it is given him by the senses and reason, not only as worth nothing, but even as nothing. It is the very function of the "beyond" which his imagination has constructed, to destroy the given world of sensory and rational experience. "Pass the world by, it is nothing." It is the philosophical expression of this fundamental mood of pessimism. Its representative is the ascetic type, the saint.

It almost goes without saying that a dualism thus accentuated leads, in the field of political and legal philosophy, to a complete rejection of positive law and of the existent State, as superfluous and harmful, that it considers as "law" only that "natural" order which lies beyond all positive order and the State, and as the "true" State the community of the just, of the saints which can only exist in the beyond. It is the position of ideal anarchism with which we have already become familiar in another connection, that of the pure law of nature in whose perspective positive law does not appear as an order of valid normative rules, but merely as an ensemble of naked power relations, while the State is in no wise distinguished from a robber band. Here again, the transcendent order has solely the function of nullifying the positive-earthly one, that is, to make it appear as nothing. Whenever such a social pessimism develops in a personality with a strong volitional side, in a so-called "aggressive" type, the soil is prepared for the emergence of the revolutionary. It does not constitute an essential difference that the saint, more rooted in metaphysics, hopes for a celestial paradise beyond this life, while the utopian revolutionary dreams of an earthly paradise which, however, must be postponed to the no less inaccessible future.

f. Pessimistic Dualism: Its Social Theory; the Revolutionary Position

We use here the contrast of optimism and pessimism to characterize basic spiritual moods which provide a psychological explanation for two different types of metaphysical dualism. Yet this contrast, especially if it is to serve as a psychological and characterological qualification, must not be taken as absolute. Man can never be perfectly and wholly either optimistic or pessimistic. Either attitude would take him beyond the psychological boundaries within which psychological types have any meaning, because, beyond them, we can only speak of pathological phenomena. Even the basic types which have been used here merely show a preponderance of one of the contrasting elements over the other, and neither is entirely excluded. Certainly it is possible that with one part of his being and with one of the two attitudes a man may face the present, the actual conditions under which he lives and presumably will continue to live for a while, while with the other, he will face the more remote future as he desires or fears it. It is just this variable attitude which distinguishes the social pessimist from the social optimist. In this sense, a person may be called an outright pessimist if he is pessimistic only for the present, if he considers the present circumstances of society as thoroughly bad and even worth destroying because they conflict with his wishes and interests. He cannot remain contemplative, but must engage in activity toward this end: he becomes a revolutionary. This need not prevent him from visualizing the future, shaped in accordance with his desires and hopes, as the perfect opposite of the present. Just because he fears and flees the present, he lives in the future alone. At the same time, he must extend his attitude toward the present also into the past since it can appear to him only as the source of present ills. It follows that this type of ideal anarchist lacks the historical sense and confronts social conditions without attributing any importance to their organic development. Yet the belief in a golden age is often significantly associated with such social pessimism. True, this legend in its diverse intellectual connections and variations is exceedingly ambiguous. In a system of pessimistic metaphysical dualism, a paradise, transposed to the beginning of time (or, correspondingly, to the end of time), means this above all: because the good cannot be found in the present, it can only have existed in the immemorial past, if it is at all possible. In the legend it is a characteristic trait of the golden age that it seems separated by a fundamental barrier, by an unbridgeable abyss, from the historical development that leads to the present — just as the "beyond" is separated from the experienced world, the idea from reality, and divine truth from human error. Terrible crimes of man brought about the intervention of avenging and punishing gods and forever buried the paradise on earth. It has somehow been placed outside time's continuity. One speaks of paradise only in order to throw the evil present the more darkly into relief against this bright background. At bottom, this golden age is the idea of the just and natural order which is confronted with positive law and the real State to expose them in their essential nothingness. This reveals the radically pessimistic character of this type of metaphysical dualism.

g. Optimistic Dualism: Personality Type and Metaphysical Attitude

It is a decisive turn toward optimism, a symptom of the strengthened confidence of man in himself, in the perception of his senses and the achievements of his reason, when the metaphysical dualism is no longer taken to mean that all true reality and value can only be found in the beyond. No longer is reality denied to the world of experience; it is recognized as "real" or it becomes, at least, a postulate of knowledge to recognize, or of cognition to establish, its reality. The world beyond, with its archetypes of truth, no longer has the function of denying the "here and now," the world of human experience, but rather of explaining it. No longer does one try to overcome the conflict of these two worlds by having one annihilate the other, but by affirming their relatedness. Accordingly, earthly things are regarded as essentially similar emanations of supernatural archetypes. It is held to be the law of existence, of inner being, for each empirical entity that it strive to assimilate itself to its transcendent idea. While one cannot count on the perfect agreement of copy and archetype, one has the serene and even proud certainty that earthly things are not separated from the celestial by an abyss, but that the earth holds the heavens in a mysterious way; that man, in recognizing the world through his senses and reason, though he does not perceive the ultimate secret, still grasps "the deity's infinite robe." In his striving for knowledge man does not conceive of himself as an eternally blind creature groping in the dark. This optimism is particularly pronounced in epistemology, as it develops the belief in the possibility, if not of attaining, then at least of steadily approximating truth with the aid of human science. Optimistic dualism not only regards this world as "real," but also as valuable; it is even inclined to see in it the best, or, at any rate, the best possible of all empirical worlds.

It should not be forgotten, however, that the transcendent ideas, when they are not to deny but to explain experience, must adapt themselves to this experience. In the measure in which man, confident of his science, extends and deepens it as he obtains increasingly intimate knowledge of the "copies," the original images themselves, the ideas, must change their content in accordance with experience or, since such variability contradicts the essence of the ideas, they must gradually be emptied of their content and, more or less consciously and avowedly, turn into formal patterns. Thus man, who thinks of himself as the image of God, first shapes the deity in his own image and then, growing afraid of His likeness to man, formalizes God into an empty concept. This is the point at which metaphysical dualism begins to change into an entirely different type.

h. Optimistic Dualism; Its Political and Legal Philosophy; Conservatism

The metaphysical dualism of the optimistic type is ordinarily called "idealism," although the pessimistic type merits this designation no less. The term relates in particular to the value judgments of this system, to its ethic of which the legal and political philosophy forms an essential part. It is precisely in the ethical realm, in the realm of good and evil, that this idealism believes it fulfills itself most intimately, for here the terrestrial partakes most fully in the celestial, and man comes closest to the deity. The philosophy of State and law of this so-called "idealistic" dualism unfolds itself in complete parallel to its philosophy of nature. It is far removed from the assumption that justice resides only beyond positive law; it regards the political order of positive law as a system of perfectly valid "ought" norms and by no means as the mere expression of naked force. It recognizes State and law as a human makeshift, first of all. Yet the natural divine order which it assumes above the positive one is not assigned the function of nullifying it or even of questioning its validity. On the contrary, it declares that as the world of ideas has to lay the basis for the reality of the world of experience — that is, to explain natural reality — so it is the proper meaning of natural law to justify, and to lend a halo to, positive law. Positive law must accordingly be regarded, if not as perfect, yet as the best possible approximate reproduction of natural law, and any positive law must be admitted to have the innate tendency to resemble the original image. In another connection the essential elements of this legal philosophy have already been outlined. Within the system of idealistic dualism there is the obvious tendency to legitimize the positive law of the State as just, as that which is humanly possible, and to heighten, or even to render absolute, its claim to validity by regarding it as an emanation of divine-natural law.

The political character of this legal philosophy is that of conservatism. If we here assume this conservatism to be based upon a social optimism, it is in the sense that we regard as an optimist one to whom the present appears good because it agrees with his wishes and interests and is in accord with his ideal. He will affirm the present and live in it and, precisely for this reason, he will be pessimistic about the future, of which he has nothing further to expect. For he who is perfectly satisfied with the present is distrustful and apprehensive of the future. His motto is: "Nothing better will follow." The conservative, accordingly, while he seeks to preserve the present, also seeks to fend off any change. His opinion of the present, viewed as the necessary product of the past, is easily and gladly extended into the past. The conservative is a *laudator temporis acti*. Yet, he does not speak of the "good old times" in contrast to the bad present, but only as something to remember with gratitude. Pious devotion to the past as the cradle and source of the present, reverence for one's history and worship of the heroes to whose divinely blessed deeds one traces it back, and historic sense: these are characteristic traits of a conservatism which rests on social optimism. It corresponds — and this deserves particular emphasis here — to the same tendency in the philosophy of nature which founds empirical reality upon transcendent ideas and thus seeks the confirmation and not the denial of its true realness.

This conservative principle which defends positive law and the State as it is, and even strengthens their validity and effectiveness, is therefore understandable even without a political motive. We must not underestimate, however, the significance of this motive, that is, of the emphatic interest of those who, directly or indirectly, rule the State, in the existence and widest possible acceptance of such a legal and political philosophy. The connection between such a natural-law legal philosophy and the idealistic, that is, religious-metaphysical natural philosophy with optimistic tendencies, makes one understand why the ruling groups invariably favor an "idealistic" conception of the world. It is a strange fact that a metaphysical-dualistic natural philosophy can maintain itself with impressive persistence despite its growing clash with the rapidly progressing natural sciences. This phenomenon can be adequately explained only if the characteristic political interest of the ruling groups in an "idealistic" philosophy is taken into account.

With the increasing development of the natural sciences the transcendent ideas of natural philosophy — as we have pointed out — must change or turn into empty formulas; similarly, in the realm of legal philosophy, natural law must either become a more or less faithful replica of positive law or, when it can no longer fulfill its purpose because it has thus been "seen through," it also must evaporate into empty formulas which fit any legal order, conflict with none, and justify all of them. From formalized metaphysics and such a natural-law theory there is only one short step to an entirely different legal and political theory which completely discards the metaphysical dualism.

i. The Compromise Type of Metaphysical Dualism

Before attempting to sketch the basic pattern of this philosophy, we should consider the third type which is still possible within metaphysical dualism. It is characterized by the attempt to find a middle way between the pessimistic and the optimistic forms of metaphysical dualism. Its aim is a compromise between the two extremes. Therefore, it takes on features of both the philosophies between which it seeks to mediate. Its total picture is not at all unified, but at times rather contradictory, precisely because of this compromise character which, at the outset, distinguishes it from the intransigence of the other two. Here again, the basis is a metaphysical dualism of the empirical "here" and the transcendental "beyond." Its natural philosophy has no distinguishing note. While it more or less fits in with optimistic dualism, it modifies it in sensing more strongly the conflict between the pure idea and the blurred reality, between the perfect, divine spirit and the imperfect, human spirit; it therefore has less confidence in its capacity to grasp divine truth with the means of the human spirit, in the realm of experience. A certain skepticism pervades it, even though, unlike pessimistic dualism, it does not completely despair of the possibility of human understanding and does not believe in the nothingness and vanity of all earthly things.

The peculiarity and also the historical significance of this compromise type do not lie so much in the field of natural philosophy (which it need not even develop) as in that of ethics and, in particular, of legal and political philosophy. It, too, starts with the conception of a divine-natural order above the positive law of the State. Here again, it senses more strongly than social optimism the conflict of ideal and reality, of justice and law. It is characteristic of the personality type which corresponds to this particular dualistic optimism that it should suffer from this conflict. And how does it try to cope with this dilemma? The answer to this question reveals the lack of a homogeneous, consistent and purposive thinking within this type of system. It is especially at this point that we become more than ever aware of its relatedness to the temperament of the men who develop the system. More intensely than ever does one perceive that behind each "book" there is a man with his conflicts.

j. The Compromise Type: Personality and Metaphysics

The two varieties of metaphysical dualism developed above can be attributed to the pessimism of a lowered and to the optimism of a heightened sense of self or self-confidence. It can be assumed, then, that the system of legal and natural philosophy which holds the balance between the two extremes by establishing a compromise, corresponds to a personality type which similarly vacillates between pessimistic self-contempt and optimistic conceit, whose somewhat unstable spiritual pendulum easily wavers in either direction, and which therefore longs above all for the balance, for the peace, of the spirit. Its basic mood is one of noble resignation, the result neither of constitutional weakness nor of related cowardice, which seeks to keep as far aloof from passionate despair and violent hatred as from blind love and heaven-shaking hope. It does not blind itself to the fact that this is not the best of all possible worlds; it faces facts firmly; its reason, no weaker than its sentiment, is strong enough not to be deceived by its desires and interests. So it sees that positive law and the order of the State have grave shortcomings which make them appear almost unbearable. But it does not share the reaction of pessimism to this insight, which optimism refuses to face at all. It is merely resolved to accept the world as it is and to bear it bravely, despite all the sorrow it holds. This means that one has to comply with the commands, especially of positive law and political authority, as with the valid norms of competent lawgivers, even when they appear to be unjust. And while one seeks to bear this world, the world becomes bearable in the process. Whoever yields to it discovers that it is not as bad as it seemed, that beneath its very apparent defects, harshnesses, and injustices there lies hidden something of the right, of the good and just, whether its evils are found to be due to one's own guilt or whether one learns to understand them as punishments for such guilt. The empirical, and especially the social, world are interpreted as relatively good because they are not absolutely bad. Because good and evil, just and unjust, are made relative terms, a very significant change occurs in this system. In the field of political and legal theory, it is expressed by the doctrine of the relative law of nature. Also the compromising type endeavors to recognize positive law as just and therefore as natural law, precisely as in the system of social optimism. Yet critical insight into the actual condition of this law does not permit one to justify it in general by reference to natural law. An intermediate stage is introduced, as it were, between idea and reality. The idea of a relative natural law is injected between the absolute natural law of divine justice and the inadequate human handiwork of positive law, of a natural law adjusted to the particular circumstances and especially to the inadequacy of human nature, a secondary beneath the primary, natural law. From this stage, it is easier to justify positive law than from the highest stage in the pyramid of values. Evidently this relativism, which corresponds to the striving for compromise and the tendency to skepticism, conflicts with the metaphysical foundations of this system which still holds to the dualism and culminates in the assumption of an absolute truth, of an absolute value. The absolute tolerates no gradations; it is the perfect "either — or." The conception that the absolute good constitutes one end of a continuous series of values whose opposite end is represented by the absolute evil is, in truth, a discarding of the absolute. This is true not only because both good and evil are moved into the infinite distance and are thus given up as inaccessible to action and cognition, but also because any empirical position between these extremes appears as good and bad at the same time. This is possible only if good and bad are taken to be merely relative or if their opposition is made quantitative. Yet a consistent adherence to a once-chosen fundamental principle cannot constitute the strength of a doctrine which seeks to mediate between opposites. Such a doctrine is not so much concerned with a radical solution of an insoluble problem as with the decent avoidance of that problem. It does not yet have the energy to rid itself altogether of the whole problem of metaphysical dualism. But there is a way which leads from this attitude of compromise and almost skeptical relativism to the discarding of the metaphysical dualism, a solution to which we have already referred.

k. The Compromise Type: Its Legal-Political Attitude.
` Compromise and Evolutionary Position

The adherent of such a compromise philosophy has resigned himself to the present, especially to the given social conditions. He considers them by no means so bad that they have to be denied epistemologically or destroyed politically as the pessimistic dualist is inclined to demand. His attitude, which approves of the world in general and of positive law and the given State on principle, is hostile to any revolution. As he is not as perfectly satisfied with the present as the social optimist, he is not as distrustful of the future as the latter; he does not oppose every change of existing conditions; he is not so extremely conservative. He considers existing conditions capable of improvement; he believes in the possibility of an evolution toward higher stages and does not reject necessary reforms. At the same time, unlike the revolutionary utopian of the pessimistic type, he does not believe in a future paradise which is *toto coelo* different from the hell of the present. His relativism, with its sympathy for the idea of gradual development, makes that impossible. He rather seeks the realization of the social ideal in the past. He is too critical and conscientious to burden himself with the promise of an expected golden age. Therefore, a paradise placed at the beginning of time is particularly characteristic for him. "Once upon a time" — this lovely tale plays a most prominent role in his system. It is not the expression of hopeless dreams and of a permanently submerged earthly happiness which has been lost forever. The legend of a time when gods walked among men or directly spoke to them is, for him, rather the consoling symbol of the reconcilability of the earthly and the celestial. This image of the *aurea aetas* is not contrasted, as in the system of utopian revolutionism, with the counter-image of a future perfect society which could only arise from the ruins of a present so thoroughly evil that it must therefore be destroyed. Nor is the realization of the social ideal in the past represented as separated by an unbridgeable gulf from the present, as the system of pessimistic idealism would have it. On the contrary, an attempt is made to find a bridge which leads from the happy past to the less happy present by disclosing that all essential elements of the existing order may be found, at least in their germinal form, in the primeval paradise of humanity. It is in this version, particularly, which belongs to the compromise type of system, that the assumption of a golden age or an original state of paradisiacal human innocence has gained its great significance for the natural-law theory. It is precisely in this form that it makes possible a justification of the positive order of the State.

B. The Scientific-Critical Philosophy

a. The End of Metaphysical Dualism

The metaphysical-religious dualism of heaven and earth, of God and world, is overcome when man, especially through the advance of empirical science, finds the courage to discard the realm of the transcendent, which is beyond his experience, because it is an unknowable, uncontrollable, and therefore scientifically useless hypothesis. His confidence in the vigor of his own senses and his reason has now become sufficiently strong to confine his scientific view of the world to empirical reality. We cannot here survey the various forms of transition which lead from one system to another. One might single out the pantheistic system, which places God in the world, because it is the one which plays a great role in the history of natural-law theory. The typical picture of a philosophy which seeks to free itself from all metaphysics can be sketched here only to the extent to which it serves to elucidate the parallel to a legal and political doctrine emancipated from all natural-law theory.

The philosophy here described as scientific rejects metaphysical dualism, that is, any statement on an object beyond experience. This is not done on the assumption that the specifically metaphysical tendency, which aims beyond this limit, is wholly groundless. Even a philosophy which is free of metaphysics and based only on scientific experience must remain conscious of the eternal secret which surrounds the world of experience on all sides. Only blindness or delusion could presume to deny the riddle of the universe, or declare it scientifically soluble. It is the attitude of the philosophical ideal type under discussion, which alone deserves to be called "scientific," that it stops before the ultimate enigma which it freely recognizes, because it is conscious of the limitations of human knowledge. It is a self-discipline of the human mind which is as conscious of its vigor as of its unsurpassable limitations. The adherent of this philosophical outlook does not know whether the things of this world and their relationships are "really" as his senses and reason represent them, yet he declines any speculation on the ideas or archetypes of these things, the "things in themselves," as entirely fruitless and vain. Nevertheless, he retains this concept of the "thing in itself" as a symbol, as it were, of the limits of experience. He considers himself as incapable of straying beyond and as being therefore not entitled to do so. The "thing in itself" is, to him, not the expression of a transcendent reality, but the impasse in the infinite process of experience. He cannot degrade the data of experience to mere "phenomena" and take reality out of this world, which would then become merely one of appearance. For the world as it appears to us, because there is and can be no other for us, is the only world, and therefore the only real one.

b. The Epistemology of the Scientific Outlook; Its Psychological Foundation

The image theory of knowledge falls with metaphysical dualism. Cognition cannot be merely passive in relation to its objects; it cannot be confined to reflecting things which are somehow given in themselves, which exist in a transcendent sphere. As soon as we cease to believe that these things have a transcendent existence, independent of our cognition, cognition must assume an active, productive role in relation to its objects. Cognition itself creates its objects, out of materials provided by the senses and in accordance with its immanent laws. It is this conformity to laws which guarantees the objective validity of the results of the process of cognition. True, the ontological judgments no longer claim absolute truth; for they can no longer sustain themselves upon their relationship to a transcendent absolute. The truth which is affirmed within the system is never more than a relative truth, and it appears, therefore, in comparison with the metaphysical-absolute truth, as a merely formal one. It might appear that a cognition which produces its own objects can only claim subjective validity for its judgments. Actually there is the danger that, if we fail to anchor truth in a transcendent realm above all human cognition, we fall into the bottomless depth of subjectivism, into a boundless solipsism. Our type firmly wards off this danger by constant emphasis on a knowing which creates its objects in conformity to laws, and by considering the demonstration of this conformity as one of its main tasks. In place of metaphysical speculation we have a determination of the laws, that is, of the objective conditions under which the process of cognition occurs. Man can penetrate up to this point and no further in his striving beyond the sphere of material empirical science. A critical theory of knowledge takes the place of metaphysics, the "transcendental" (in the sense of Kant's philosophy) that of the transcendent. Yet this philosophy, too, is dualistic; only it is no longer a metaphysical, but an epistemological, critical dualism on which it rests. In contrast to the metaphysical we may call this the philosophy of criticism.

In characterizing the personality type which corresponds to this anti-metaphysical, critical attitude, we may assume that intellectual energy and a striving for knowledge prevail in it. It is more concerned with comprehending this world, with experiencing it by knowing, than with grasping it with the will and shaping, reshaping, or even ruling it in accordance with desires that tend to gratify instinctive cravings. The rational component of the consciousness is stronger than the emotional one. The spiritual well from which all metaphysical speculation is nourished, the wish-fulfilling imagination, flows only sparingly here, where a skeptical reason predominates. Accordingly, the contrast of optimism and pessimism is no longer applicable to this type. For the pictures which both the optimist and the pessimist draw of the world are above all determined by the effect upon their volitions and desires, upon their interests. The type of scientific, critical philosophy is, however, primarily characterized by the forced endeavor to keep knowledge free from the influences which all too easily spring from subjective wishes and interests. Because there exists in this case a balance between self-abnegation and conceit, an effort may be made to eliminate the self from the process of cognition. The ideal of objectivity emerges as dominant. Therefore we also find the prevalence of logic and the tendency to relativism. The idea of the absolute has its psychological roots more in the realm of volition than of cognition.

c. Legal Positivism; Law and Power

This is the philosophical and psychological basis of the legal theory which seriously rejects the assumption of a natural law and is called legal positivism. Its epistemological character may be sketched here in its essentials. While positivism denies to itself any natural-law speculation, that is to say, any attempt to recognize a "law in itself," it confines itself to a theory of positive law. Thus positive law is taken solely as a human product, and a natural order inaccessible to human cognition is in no wise considered as necessary for its justification. At the same time, no absolute value is claimed for the law. It is taken to have an entirely hypothetical-relative validity which has already been examined in a different context above. This hypothetical-relative character of the law does not prevent one from conceiving positive law as a system of valid "ought" norms. Juridical positivism declines to regard positive law as a mere complex of empirical facts, and the State as but an aggregate of factual power relationships. It differs from individualistic anarchism, the anarchism without ideal which views the supposed objective and normative validity of the politico-legal order as a mere fiction or ideology, just as the critical natural philosophy rejects the analogous subjectivist solipsism. From the point of view of juridical positivism natural law alone is regarded as such an ideology. The system of legal positivism discards the attempt to deduce from nature or reason substantial norms which, being beyond positive law, can serve as its model, an attempt which forever is only apparently successful and ends in formulas only pretending to have a content. Instead it deliberately examines the hypothetical assumptions of all positive and, in substance, infinitely variable law, that is, its merely "formal" conditions. We have already encountered the basic norm which, from the point of view of legal positivism, constitutes the ultimate assumption and hypothetical basis of any positive legal order and delegates the supreme law-making authority. Just as the transcendental logical principles of cognition (in the sense of Kant) are not empirical laws, but merely the conditions of all experience, the basic norm itself is no positive legal rule, no positive statute, because it has not been made, but is simply presupposed as the condition of all positive legal norms. And as one cannot know the empirical world from the transcendental logical principles, but merely by means of them, so positive law cannot be derived from the basic norm, but can merely be understood by means of it. The content of the basic norm, that is, the particular historical fact qualified by the basic norm as the original law-making fact, depends entirely upon the material to be taken as positive law, on the wealth of empirically given acts subjectively claiming to be legal acts. Objectively, they are only valid by virtue of their relatedness to the basic act which, thanks to the basic norm, is presupposed as the original law-making fact. Any legal order, therefore, to be positive, has to coincide in some measure with the actual human conduct which it seeks to regulate. The possibility of acts violating the legal order can never be wholly excluded; they will always occur to some extent. An order devoid of conflict with actual conduct would only be possible if it confined itself to prescribing as norm only that which actually occurs or will occur. Such an order would be meaningless as a normative order. The tension between norm and existence, between the "ought" and the "is," must not sink below a certain minimum. The contrast between the legal norm and the corresponding actuality of social existence must not, on the other hand, go beyond a certain maximum. Actual conduct must not completely contradict the legal order which regulates it. This can also be expressed in another way: the basic norm can only establish a law-making authority whose norms are, by and large, observed, so that social life broadly conforms to the legal order based on the hypothetical norm. The positivistic jurist, when he establishes the basic norm, is guided by the tendency to recognize as objective law the greatest possible number of empirically given acts the subjective meaning of which is to be legal acts. These acts — law creating and law executing acts — form the so-called historical-political reality. Thus, the basic norm, in a certain sense, means the transformation of power into law.

d. The Transcendental-Logical Natural-Law Doctrine. The Political Indifference of Legal Positivism

It has already been pointed out that it is the function of the basic norm not only to recognize a historically given material as law, but also to comprehend it as a meaningful whole. It must be frankly admitted (and it has already been stated) that such an accomplishment would not be possible by means of pure positivism, that is, merely by means of the dynamic principle of delegation as expressed in the basic norm of positive law. With the postulate of a meaningful, that is, non-contradictory order, juridical science oversteps the boundary of pure positivism. To abandon this postulate would at the same time entail the self-abandonment of juridical science. The basic norm has here been described as the essential presupposition of any positivistic legal cognition. If one wishes to regard it as an element of a natural-law doctrine despite its renunciation of any element of material justice, very little objection can be raised; just as little, in fact, as against calling the categories of Kant's transcendental philosophy metaphysics because they are not data of experience, but conditions of experience. What is involved is simply the minimum, there of metaphysics, here of natural law, without which neither a cognition of nature nor of law is possible. The hypothetical basic norm answers the question: how is positive law possible as an object of cognition, as an object of juridical science; and, consequently, how is a juridical science possible? Accordingly, the theory of the basic norm may be considered a natural-law doctrine in keeping with Kant's transcendental logic. There still remains the enormous difference which separates, and must forever separate, the transcendental conditions of all empirical knowledge and consequently the laws prevailing in nature on the one side from the transcendent metaphysics beyond all experience on the other. There is a similar difference between the basic norm which merely makes possible the cognition of positive law as a meaningful order and a natural-law doctrine which proposes to establish a just order beyond, and independent of, all positive law. It is the difference between critical philosophy as a theory of experience and subjective speculation.* It is therefore preferable to call this theory of positive law, which is aware of its assumptions and limitations, a critical positivism.

Just as the critical philosophy of nature above all seeks to conform to the postulate of objectivity, so it is the ideal of juridical positivism to preserve the theory of positive law from the influence of any political tendency or, which amounts to the same, from any subjective judgment of value. The purity of its knowledge in the sense of political indifference is its characteristic aim. This merely means that it accepts the given legal order without evaluating it as such, and endeavors to be most unbiassed in the presentation and interpretation of the legal material. In particular, it refuses to stand for any political interests under the pretext of interpreting the positive law or of providing its necessary correction through a norm of natural law, by pretending that such a norm is positive law, while in reality it conflicts with it. Just the same, the critical positivist remains entirely conscious of how much the content of the legal order with which he is concerned is itself the result of political efforts. The question as to where the content of the positive legal order has originated, as to what factors have caused this content, is beyond this cognition, which is limited to the given system of positive legal norms in its "ought" quality. If the question is raised, the answer lies in this none too fruitful insight: every legal order which has the degree of effectiveness necessary to make it positive is more or less of a compromise between conflicting interest-groups in their struggle for power, in their antagonistic tendencies to determine the content of the social order. This struggle for power invariably presents itself as a struggle for "justice"; all the fighting groups use the ideology of "natural law." They never represent the interests which they seek to realize as mere group-interests, but as the "true," the "common," the "general"

---

* Metaphysics, when it wants to leave the realm of subjective imagination, invariably enters the dogmatism of revealed religion; natural-law speculation, when it looks for certainty somewhere, flows into positive legal norms, constituted under the authority of a church, that is, of a power organization, which claims to represent an order with a validity superior to that of the State's law whose sphere it limits or whose content it determines in a certain way. Ordinarily these ecclesiastic norms present themselves as natural law, even if only to demonstrate their superiority to the State's positive law. In reality, they are only positive law, as the church is only a particular kind of State. The parallel of revealed religion and positive law is evident. The desire for objectivity enforces positivity.

interest. The result of this struggle determines the temporary content of the legal order. It is, just as little as its component parts, the expression of the general interest, of a higher "interest of the State," "above" interest-groups and beyond political parties. Furthermore, this concept of the "interest of the State" conceals the idea of the absolute value of justice, the idea of a natural law as the absolute justification of the positive legal order personified as the State. The conception of an order which realizes the "common" or "general" interest and constitutes a perfectly solidary society is identical with the utopia of pure natural law. The content of the positive legal order is no more than the compromise of conflicting interests, which leaves none of them wholly satisfied or dissatisfied. It is the expression of a social equilibrium manifested in the very effectiveness of the legal order, in that it is obeyed in general and encounters no serious resistance. In this sense, critical positivism recognizes every positive legal order as an order of peace.

e. The Ideal of Justice Becomes a Logical Pattern

If, as stated above, it is the function of the hypothetical basic norm to shape the empirical legal material into a meaningful, that is, a non-contradictory order, the result of legal positivism seems to approach rather closely that of the doctrine of natural law. It is not decisive that they both provide a basis for positive law; positivism directly and consciously, the natural-law doctrine indirectly and, for the most part, unconsciously. The decisive point is this: all the endeavors of natural-law doctrine to determine an absolute value measurement for positive law, to define justice as its archetype, ultimately converge in the idea of a formal order, in the idea of a non-contradictory system, in a formula, in other words, which is reconcilable with any positive law. The ideal of justice has ultimately no other meaning than the hypothetical basic norm of critical positivism with its function of constituting the empirical legal material as an order.

The idea of equality, for instance, which adherents of natural law most frequently affirm to be the essence of justice, the principle that equal things must be treated equally or, in other words, that equals deserve equally, *suum cuique*, does not actually proclaim anything more than the logical principle of identity or the principle of contradiction. It conveys no more than the idea of order, of unity within the system. An examination of the conceptual treatment of the principle of equality by natural-law theorists, who find in it the essence of justice, shows that they never have been able to determine what or who is equal. It has always been simply held that if A equals B both are to be treated alike. Since in reality there are no two individuals perfectly equal, equality as a principle of justice means that certain differences between individuals are to be considered as irrelevant. The question, however, whether, in a given case, A and B are "equal" or not, and that means, which differences, actually existing between A and B, are irrelevant, cannot be answered by natural-law doctrine. The answer is given exclusively by positive law. The principle of equality as a principle of justice implies only that if A is to be treated in a certain way and B equals A, it follows that B must be treated in the same way. Otherwise there would be a logical contradiction; the principle of identity would be violated and the idea of the unity of system destroyed. To reduce the idea of justice to the idea of equality or unity of order means no more and no less than the replacement of the ethical by the logical ideal. It means the rationalization of the originally irrational idea of justice, the "logification" of an ideal originally alien to the *logos*. It is the inevitable result of an attempt to transmute justice, a value of volition and action, into a problem of cognition which by necessity is subject to the value of truth, that is to the idea of a non-contradictory unity.

Since natural-law doctrine in the end comes to the same point as critical positivism, the latter might be induced to assume an affirmative attitude with reference to the problem of justice. The natural-law doctrine affirms, with all conceivable emphasis, that there is an absolute justice above positive law; yet it cannot produce more than the formal idea of order or equality. Under these circumstances, critical positivism, which need not be more papal than the pope, may claim that it, too, has grasped the essence of justice in its basic norm which constitutes the positive law as a non-contradictory order, especially if it comprehends the positive law, by means of this basic norm, as an order of peace. This is a temptation, particularly for the present with its thirst for metaphysical pathos. Nonetheless, though it may be more gratifying to give a sham answer to humanity's eternal quest for justice than none at all, critical positivism has to renounce such an advantage. As a science it is above all concerned with the cognitive value. The duty of truthfulness compels it to state that the scientific conception of justice has nothing in common with the ideal to which volition originally aspired. The real problem has been shifted by the truism that equals demand equal treatment. The answer to the main question as to what and who are equal, that is, as to the content of the just order is tacitly presupposed. The solution of the problem, which differences between individuals are irrelevant, has to be determined by the positive legislator. The old truth is thus confirmed that science is unable, and therefore not entitled, to offer value judgments. This applies equally to the science of law, even if it is considered to be a science of values. Like every science of values, it consists in the cognition of values, but it cannot produce these values. It can

understand norms, but it cannot create them.* Cognition, in the form
of natural science, cannot produce the empirical material, it can merely
construct from the material yielded by the senses a specific object.
In the field of legal science, it cannot properly produce material values;
it can only establish the values and acts of valuation yielded by volition as a specific object, a non-contradictory system of norms. It is
irrelevant for the pursuit of the original ideal of justice that, once an
order has been established, it exacts conformity from those to whom it
applies. Yet the idea of formal equality claims no more. From the point
of view of a material justice, it matters only what content the order must
have in order to be just. Even the least contradictory legal order and the
most perfect realization of the formal idea of equality may constitute a
condition of supreme injustice. Even an order of peace may be no more.
"Peace" need not mean "justice," not even in the sense of a solidarity of
interests. Only one group may be interested in "peace," namely the one
whose interests are better preserved by this order than those of other
groups. These other groups may also fail to violate the order. They may
maintain the state of peace not because they consider it just, but because,
in view of their own weakness, they must be satisfied with the minimum
of protection which this order affords to their interests. The longing for
peace means, as a rule, a renunciation of the original ideal of justice.
Yet any conception of justice obtained by cognition will justify any state
of peace as constituted by any order at all, consequently any order of
positive law. This is the deepest root, independent of all political tendencies, of the conservative function of legal philosophy as a doctrine of
justice.

Once justice becomes its object, cognition, by virtue of its immanent
tendency, cannot help denaturing the ethical ideal of justice to the logical
idea of order as the non-contradictory unity of system, a conception
quite alien to that ideal. Nonetheless, science will forever persist in
attempting to answer the question of justice, and politics in demanding
the answer to this question from science. In effect, cognition, that is
the science or philosophy of law, while pretending to prescribe justice to
volition, that is, to power, will, in the end, subsequently legitimate the
product of power by declaring positive law to be just. It is precisely this
abuse of cognition which critical positivism wishes to avoid.

f. The Method of the Ideal Type

The philosophical types of the preceding discussion are ideal types.
They have been constructed from a particular point of view, namely, that
of the relatedness of a view of the universe and a philosophy of life, of

* For this reason, positivism decidedly rejects the specific natural-law doctrine
of juridical science as a source of law.

natural and social philosophy. This makes, from the outset, for a certain one-sidedness of the scheme. It is not surprising that none of the actual philosophical systems in intellectual history completely fits into our scheme. Just as there is no living man who is the complete embodiment of a personality type, no matter how constructed, no historically known thinker has created a system of natural or social philosophy which would at all points correspond to our ideal types. These historical systems merely display more or less of a tendency toward an ideal type. This is why the ideal-type method is so questionable in the opinion of many. It still has the virtues of its vices, if we do not lose sight of its true character. Better than any description of the concrete philosophical-juridical systems, it demonstrates the far-reaching parallel between the problems of natural and social philosophy and the possible connection between their respective solutions. And this is of particular importance for us. In comparison, it matters less that reality does not always coincide with this possibility, if only the real tendency can be adequately interpreted with the aid of the ideal scheme. It should be remembered in particular that the connection between the natural and social philosophy of the same individual may be disturbed by various factors, and that, under certain circumstances, it may even be completely severed. This is where the social position of the thinker plays a great role; his membership in a class and his conscious or unconscious respect for the powers that be, especially the political authorities of his society: all these are significant. It is neither impossible nor improbable that a basic philosophical character, such as that of pessimistic dualism, will more clearly manifest itself in natural than in moral philosophy, since, in the latter, its manifestation might meet very serious external obstacles. In political and legal philosophy, for instance, such a character may actually reverse itself. On the other hand, it is undeniable that it is precisely the position of a thinker in political and legal philosophy, even as determined by external circumstances, which influence his metaphysics and epistemology. In a sense somewhat different from its original meaning, one could actually speak here of a primacy of practical over theoretical reason. But there are other factors important for the shaping of a social, especially a political and legal, philosophy which are strong enough to redirect and even to obstruct the orientation proceeding from a given view of the universe. The strongest incentive to assume an attitude directly the opposite of an orientation deeply rooted in personality may be where the mutual relations of men are involved and, with them, the place of law and political authority, both of which profoundly affect the thinker's personal interests. Such a departure from the original orientation is more than likely to occur under certain conditions, especially in the case of noble and proud natures. Lastly, one may not be able to establish such a connection between natural and ethical philosophy in a particular thinker, because he has only evolved a natural and not a political and legal philosophy, possibly for reasons not unrelated to these factors. He may also, from the outset, have confined his system to social philosophy, as can quite frequently be seen in recent times.

g. The Realization of Ideal Types in Intellectual History

With all these reservations in mind, we may now attempt to answer the question as to which of the actual historical doctrines corresponds most closely to our ideal types. Contempt for the world and escape from it inspire pessimistic dualism, whose radical negation of natural reality and positive law will generally prevent its adoption except as an esoteric doctrine. It is, accordingly, out of the question for any system which desires to gain the support of even the majority of the educated. Consequently, a legal and political theory which corresponds to this type can be actually found only in opposition to the dominant trend of natural-law doctrine, which in every respect presents itself as the natural-law theory of the ruling group or class. Original Christianity and later ascetic monasticism, as well as the teachings of certain sects, revolutionary liberalism, can all be taken as carriers of that opposition which expounds the pure idea of natural law against its actuality in the dominant dogma. Also the revolutionary anarcho-socialism of today displays essential traits of this type of natural-law doctrine, at least as long as it is the view of a minority and an opposition on principle.*

Only that type of optimistic dualism is destined to become a "prevailing" doctrine which serenely affirms the reality of nature as well as the given order of social life. The same is true of the compromise type of resigned dualism, whose ultimate wisdom it is to give in to reality. The optimistic type is relatively most clearly developed in the Platonic-Aristotelian philosophy, that of the compromise type in the Stoic system. It is one of the most significant facts in the intellectual history of mankind that Christianity through the Pauline development evolved from a strictly pessimistic type, primarily in the field of political and legal philosophy, towards the compromise type by leaning, in part consciously, upon Stoic philosophy. When this young and vigorously rising movement of Pauline Christianity, largely recruited as it was from the lower groups of the people, resigned itself to the Roman State and its positive law with Stoic indifference, this resignation had a complexion

* On the change which occurs in the theory of liberalism and socialism as soon as one or the other becomes the ideology of a group which rules or approaches rulership, cf. my study MARX ODER LASSALLE (1924) 1ff.

somewhat different from that which motivated the teachings of its classical models in Greece and Rome. Not by accident did the social philosophy of the Stoa culminate in the work of a Roman emperor; its resignation is the fruit of an old civilization which has run through all the phases of philosophical speculation and political struggle, and is safeguarded against any excess of pessimism or optimism by a certain fatigue. The resignation of early Christianity, while it sympathizes with Stoic philosophy, is not only, or not so much, the result of religious humility; it is rather the symptom of a vitality, hampered by extraneous circumstances, and prudently inclined toward caution in the face of the powers that be. This caution is the more easily exercised as it is inspired by the confidence that the future belongs to a strength thus reserved. Accordingly, as soon as the Christian doctrine had conquered this Roman State, with which it had first prudently and cautiously complied, it changed from the compromise type to that of optimistic dualism by adding to its Platonic-Aristotelian metaphysics a perfectly harmonizing natural-law theory. In the doctrine of Protestant Christianity, this change led, especially in the field of political and legal theory, to an unsurpassable climax. Considering the dominant importance which this Protestant theory has for the classical natural-law doctrine of the seventeenth and eighteenth centuries, it is no coincidence that the final point in the development of the whole natural-law doctrine is also found on the line which passes through this climax.

h. Kant's Critical Idealism and Legal Positivism

The last of the types we have here developed, which in contrast to the metaphysical, has been described as critical dualism, evidently bears the features of Kant's philosophy of critical idealism. Yet it will be immediately observed that Kant's philosophical system differs somewhat from our ideal picture. This is already the case in his natural philosophy. The struggle which this philosophical genius, supported by science, waged against metaphysics, which earned him the title of the "all-destroyer," was not actually pushed by him to the ultimate conclusion. In character, he was probably no real fighter but rather disposed to compromise conflicts. The role which the "thing-in-itself" plays in his system reveals a good deal of metaphysical transcendence. For this reason, we do not find in him a frank and uncompromising confession of relativism, which is the inescapable consequence of any real elimination of metaphysics. A complete emancipation from metaphysics was probably impossible for a personality still as deeply rooted in Christianity as Kant's. This is most evident in his practical philosophy. Just here, where the emphasis of the Christian doctrine rests, its metaphysical dualism has completely invaded his system, the same dualism which Kant fought so persistently in his theoretical philosophy. At this point, Kant abandoned his method of transcendental logic. This contradiction within the system of critical idealism has been noted often enough. So it happens that Kant, whose philosophy of transcendental logic was preëminently destined to provide the groundwork for a positivistic legal and political doctrine, stayed, as a legal philosopher, in the rut of the natural-law doctrine. Indeed, his *Principles of the Metaphysics of Ethics* can be regarded as the most perfect expression of the classical doctrine of natural law as it evolved in the seventeenth and eighteenth centuries on the basis of Protestant Christianity. No attempted explanation of this fact must overlook how closely the natural-law theory of the optimistic metaphysical dualism approaches a positivistic doctrine of law and State. Elsewhere we have already seen that both are primarily concerned with the validity of the positive legal order and the authority of government. As a matter of fact, this natural-law doctrine admits the validity of no other than the positive legal order. It is distinguishable from positivism merely by its mode of establishing its validity, which is absolute in the one case and only relative in the other. Ultimately, positivism proves itself only in discarding the particular ideology which the natural-law theory uses in its justification of positive law.

However, to eliminate a legitimizing ideology is extremely difficult, not only for epistemological, but even more for political reasons; the desire for an absolute foundation of the given social order is so potent that even the so-called positivistic legal and political theory of the nineteenth and twentieth centuries has never completely renounced it and therefore is, at times, quite thoroughly, though unavowedly, shot through with natural-law elements. Just at the time when it was thought that positivism had definitely defeated natural-law speculation, in the second decade of the twentieth century, a deliberate natural-law movement was inaugurated. It coincided with a turning away of natural philosophy from the direction of the Kantian criticism toward a new metaphysics and a rebirth of religious feeling. The eternal undular movement of the human spirit, which carries it from self-abasement or self-exaltation to the elimination of the self, from pessimism or optimism to the ideal of objectivity, from metaphysics to the critique of knowledge and back again, seems to have been accelerated by the overwhelming experience of the Great War. An anti-metaphysical, scientific-critical philosophy with objectivity as its ideal, like legal positivism, seems to thrive only in relatively quiet times; in periods of social balance. The social foundations and, with them, the self-confidence of the individual, have been deeply shaken in our time. Most values thus far taken for granted are questioned; the conflict between interest groups has been tremendously intensified, and with it the struggle for a new order is under way. In such times, a greatly deepened need for the absolute justification of the postulates put forth in the struggle will manifest itself. If even the individual naively experiences his temporary interest as a "right," how much more will every interest-group want to invoke "justice" in the realization of its demands! Before we had reason to expect it, the reaction has set in which augurs a renaissance of metaphysics and, thereby, of natural-law theory.

At this moment of our intellectual history, the present essay attempts to explore the foundations of natural-law theory and of positivism. It will have succeeded if it has been able to show that the contrast between these two elementary tendencies of legal science is rooted in the ultimate depths of philosophy and personality; and that it involves a never-ending conflict.

LIST OF PUBLICATIONS

BOOKS

Die Staatslehre des Dante Alighieri (Wien, Leipzig, 1905). 149 pp.

Kommentar zur österreichischen Reichsratswahlordnung (Wien, 1907). 217 pp.

Hauptprobleme der Staatsrechtslehre, entwickelt aus der Lehre vom Rechtssatze. 2nd ed. (Tübingen, 1923). xxxvi + 709 pp.

Ueber Grenzen zwischen juristischer und soziologischer Methode (Tübingen, 1911). 64 pp.

Das Problem der Souveränität und die Theorie des Völkerrechts. Beitrag zu einer reinen Rechtslehre. 2nd ed. (Tübingen, 1928). xii + 320 pp.

Sozialismus und Staat. Eine Untersuchung der politischen Theorie des Marxismus. 2nd ed. (Leipzig, 1923). viii + 208 pp.

Vom Wesen und Wert der Demokratie. 2nd ed. (Tübingen, 1929). viii + 119 pp.

Die Verfassungsgesetze der Republik Deutsch-Oesterreich, mit einer historischen Uebersicht und kritischen Erläuterungen (a commentary). 5 vols. (Wien, Leipzig, 1919–22).

Der soziologische und der juristische Staatsbegriff. Kritische Untersuchung des Verhältnisses zwischen Staat und Recht. 2nd ed. (Tübingen, 1928). viii + 253 pp.

Rechtswissenschaft und Recht. Erledigung eines Versuches zur Ueberwindung der "Rechtsdogmatik" (Wien, Leipzig, 1922). 135 pp.

Oesterreichisches Staatsrecht; ein Grundriss entwicklungsgeschichtlich dargestellt (Tübingen, 1923). 256 pp.

Marx oder Lassalle? (Leipzig, 1924). 50 pp.

Allgemeine Staatslehre (Berlin, 1925). xiv + 433 pp.

Der Staat als Uebermensch. Eine Erwiderung (Wien, 1926). 24 pp.

Das Problem des Parlamentarismus (Wien, Leipzig, 1925). 44 pp.

Grundriss einer allgemeinen Theorie des Staates (Wien, 1926). 64 pp.

Les Rapports de système entre le droit interne et le droit international public, Académie de droit international, Recueil des cours, vol. 14 (1926), part IV, pp. 231–331.

Rechtsgeschichte gegen Rechtsphilosophie? Eine Erwiderung (Wien, 1928). 31 pp.

Die philosophischen Grundlagen der Naturrechtslehre und des Rechtspositivismus (Charlottenburg, 1928). 78 pp.

Der Staat als Integration. Eine prinzipielle Auseinandersetzung (Wien, 1930). 91 pp.

Wer soll Hüter der Verfassung sein? (Berlin, 1931). 53 pp.

Théorie générale du droit international public. Problèmes choisis. Académie de droit international, Recueil des cours, vol. 42 (1932), part iv, pp. 116–351.

Staatsform und Weltanschauung (Tübingen, 1933). 30 pp.

Reine Rechtslehre, Einleitung in die rechtswissenschaftliche Problematik (Leipzig, Wien, 1934). xv + 236 pp.

The Legal Process and International Order: The New Commonwealth. Research Bureau Publications, Series A, no. 1 (London, 1934). 27 pp.

La Dictature de parti. Institut International de droit public (Paris, 1934). 19 pp.

Legal Technique in International Law, A Textual Critique of the League Covenant. Geneva Studies, vol. X, no. 6 (Geneva, 1939). 178 pp.

Law and Peace in International Relations (Cambridge: Harvard University Press, 1942). xi + 181 pp.

El Contrato y el Tratado. Analizados desde el punto de vista de la Teoría Pura del Derecho (Mexico: Imprenta Universitaria, 1943). xiii + 164 pp.

Society and Nature. A Sociological Inquiry (Chicago: The University of Chicago Press, 1943). viii + 391 pp.

Peace Through Law (Chapel Hill: The University of North Carolina Press, 1944). xii + 155 pp.

ARTICLES

"Zur Soziologie des Rechts. Kritische Betrachtungen," *Archiv für Sozialwissenschaft und Sozialpolitik*, 34: 601–614 (1912).

"Ueber Staatsunrecht. Zugleich ein Beitrag zur Frage der Deliktsfähigkeit juristischer Personen und zur Lehre vom fehlerhaften Staatsakt," *Zeitschrift für das Privat- und öffentliche Recht der Gegenwart*, 40: 1–114 (1913).

"Politische Weltanschauung und Erziehung," *Annalen für soziale Politik und Gesetzgebung*, 2: 1–26 (1913).

"Zur Lehre vom öffentlichen Rechtsgeschäft," *Archiv des öffentlichen Rechts*, 31: 53–98, 190–249 (1913).

"Rechtsstaat und Staatsrecht," *Oesterreichische Rundschau*, 36: 88–94 (1913).

"Zur Lehre vom Gesetz im formellen und materiellen Sinn, mit besonderer Berücksichtigung der österreichischen Verfassung," *Juristische Blätter*, 42: 229–232 (1913).

"Reichsgesetz und Landesgesetz nach der österreichischen Verfassung," *Archiv des öffentlichen Rechts*, 32: 202–245, 390–438 (1914).

"Eine Grundlegung der Rechtssoziologie," *Archiv für Sozialwissenschaft und Sozialpolitik*, 39: 839–876 (1915).

"Die Rechtswissenschaft als Norm- oder als Kulturwissenschaft. Eine methodenkritische Untersuchung," *Schmollers Jahrbuch für Gesetzgebung, Verwaltung und Volkswirtschaft im Deutschen Reiche*, 40: 1181–1239 (1916).

"Zur Theorie der juristischen Fiktionen. Mit besonderer Berücksichtigung von Vaihingers Philosophie des Als-Ob," *Annalen der Philosophie*, 1: 630–658 (1919).

"Der Staatsbegriff der 'verstehenden Soziologie'," *Zeitschrift für Volkswirtschaft und Sozialpolitik, Neue Folge*, 1: 104–119 (1921).

"Das Verhältnis von Staat und Recht im Lichte der Erkenntniskritik," *Zeitschrift für öffentliches Recht*, 2: 453–510 (1921).

"Staat und Recht. Zum Problem der soziologischen oder juristischen Erkenntnis des Staates," *Kölner Vierteljahrsschrift für Soziologie. Reihe A: Soziologische Hefte*, 2: 18–37 (1922).

"Der Begriff des Staates und die Sozialpsychologie. Mit besonderer Berücksichtigung von Freuds Theorie der Masse," *Imago, Zeitschrift für Anwendung der Psychoanalyse auf die Geisteswissenschaften*, 8: 97–141 (1922).

"Gott und Staat," *Logos, Internationale Zeitschrift für Philosophie der Kultur*, 11: 261–284 (1922/23).

"Die Lehre von den drei Gewalten oder Funktionen des Staates," Kant-Festschrift zu Kants 200. Geburtstag am 22. April 1924, *Archiv für Rechts- und Wirtschaftsphilosophie*, 17: 374–408 (1924).

"The Conception of the State and Social Psychology. With Special Reference to Freud's Group Theory," *The International Journal of Psycho-Analysis*, 5:1–38 (1924).

"Souveränität, völkerrechtliche," *Wörterbuch des Völkerrechts und der Diplomatie*, 2: 554–559 (Berlin, 1925).

"Staat und Völkerrecht," *Zeitschrift für öffentliches Recht*, 4: 207–222 (1925).

"Das Wesen des Staates," 1: *Internationale Zeitschrift für Theorie des Rechts*: 5–17 (1926).

"Staatsform als Rechtsform," *Zeitschrift für öffentliches Recht*, 5: 73–93 (1926).

"Die Bundesexekution. Ein Beitrag zur Theorie und Praxis des Bundesstaates, unter besonderer Berücksichtigung der Deutschen Reichs- und der österreichischen Bundesverfassung," *Festgabe für Fritz Fleiner* (Tübingen, 1927). 61 pp.

"Naturrecht und positives Recht. Eine Untersuchung ihres gegenseitigen Verhältnisses," *Internationale Zeitschrift für Theorie des Rechts*, 2: 71–94 (1927/28).

"Die Idee des Naturrechts," *Zeitschrift für öffentliches Recht*, 7: 221–250 (1927).

"Wesen und Entwicklung der Staatsgerichtsbarkeit, Bericht, erstattet der Tagung der Deutschen Staatsrechtslehrer zu Wien am 23. und 24. April 1928," *Veröffentlichungen der Vereinigung der Deutschen Staatsrechtslehrer*, Heft 5 (Berlin, Leipzig, 1929): 30–88, 117–123.

"Zum Begriff des Kompetenzkonfliktes," *Zeitschrift für öffentliches Recht*, 7: 583–599 (1928).

"Der Begriff des Kompetenzkonfliktes nach geltendem österreichischen Recht," *Juristische Blätter*, 57: 105–110 (1928).

"La Garantie juridictionnelle de la Constitution (La Justice Constitutionnelle)," *Revue du droit public et de la science politique en France et à l'étranger*, 45: 197–257 (1928); *Annuaire de l'Institut International de Droit Public*, 1929, pp. 52–143.

"Justiz und Verwaltung," *Zeitschrift für soziales Recht*: 1: 80–93 (1929). Wien, 1929. 25 pp.

"Souveränität," *Die neue Rundschau*, 40: 433–446 (1929).

"Juristischer Formalismus und Reine Rechtslehre," *Juristische Wochenschrift*, 58: 1723–1726 (1929).

"La Naissance de l'État et la formation de sa nationalité, les principes, leur application au cas de la Tchécoslovaquie," *Revue de droit international*, 4: 613–641 (1929).

Publications de la Cour Permanente de Justice Internationale, Série C. no. 68 (Leyden, 1933), pp. 71–102.

"Der Wandel des Souveränitätsbegriffes," *Studi filosofico-giuridici dedicati al Prof. Giorgio Del Vecchio* (Modena: Società Tipografica Modenese, 1931), 2: 1–11.

"Allgemeine Rechtslehre im Lichte materialistischer Geschichtsauffassung," *Archiv für Sozialwissenschaft und Sozialpolitik*, 66: 449–521 (1932).

"Unrecht und Unrechtsfolge im Völkerrecht," *Zeitschrift für öffentliches Recht*, 12: 481–608 (1932).

"Die platonische Gerechtigkeit," *Kant-Studien*, 38: 91–117 (1933).

"Die platonische Liebe," *Imago, Zeitschrift für psychoanalytische Psychologie, ihre Grenzgebiete und Anwendungen*, 19: 34–98, 225–255 (1933).

"Die hellenisch-makedonische Politik und die 'Politik' des Aristoteles," *Zeitschrift für öffentliches Recht*, 13: 625–678 (1933).

"Zur Theorie der Interpretation," *Internationale Zeitschrift für Theorie des Rechts*, 8: 9–17 (1934).

"La Méthode et la notion fondamentale de la théorie pure du droit," *Revue de Métaphysique et de Morale*, 41: 183–204 (1934).

"Die Technik des Völkerrechts und die Organisation des Friedens," *Zeitschrift für öffentliches Recht*, 14: 240–255 (1934).

"Völkerrechtliche Verträge zu Lasten Dritter," *Prager Juristische Zeitschrift*, 14: Spalte 419–431 (1934).

"The Pure Theory of Law, its Method and Fundamental Concepts," *The Law Quarterly Review*, 50: 474–498 (1934); 51: 517–535 (1935).

"Traités internationaux à la charge d'États tiers," *Mélanges offerts à Ernest Mahaim* (Paris: Sirey, 1935) II, 164–172.

"La Transformation du droit international en droit interne," *Revue générale de droit international public*, 43: 5–49 (1936).

"The Party-Dictatorship," *Politica*, 2: 19–32 (London, 1936).

"L'âme et le droit," *IIe Annuaire de l'Institut International de Philosophie de Droit et de Sociologie Juridique* (Paris: Sirey, 1936), pp. 60–82.

"Droit et État du point de vue d'une théorie pure," *Annales de l'Institut de Droit comparé de l'Université de Paris* (Paris: Sirey, 1936), pp. 17–59.

"Contribution à la théorie du traité international," *Revue internationale de la théorie du droit*, 10: 253–292 (1936).

"Die Ziele der Reinen Rechtslehre," Pocta k sesdesiatym narodeninam dr. Karla Lastovku, *Knihovna pravnickej fakulty university Komenskeho* (Bratislava), sv. 45 (1936), pp. 203–212.

"Centralization and Decentralization," A paper delivered at the Harvard Tercentenary Conference of Arts and Sciences, *Authority and the Individual*, Harvard Tercentenary Publications (Cambridge: Harvard University Press, 1937), pp. 210–239.

"Wissenschaft und Demokratie," *Neue Zürcher Zeitung*, 23./24.2. (1937), no. 321, no. 327.

"Die Parteidiktatur," *Festschrift für. Dolenc, Krek, Kusej und Skerlj* (Lublana: Jugoslovanska Tsikarna, 1937), pp. 421–430.

"The Soul and the Law," *The Review of Religion*, 1: 357–360 (1937).

"Zur rechtstechnischen Revision des Völkerbundstatuts," *Zeitschrift für öffentliches Recht*, 17: 401–490, 590–622 (1937).

"The Philosophy of Aristotle and the Hellenic-Macedonian Policy," *Ethics, An International Journal of Social, Political, and Legal Philosophy*, 48: 1–64 (1937).

"The Function of the Pure Theory of Law," *Law, A Century of Progress 1835–1935*. Contributions in Celebration of the 100th Anniversary of the Founding of the School of Law of the New York University (New York: New York University Press, 1937, II, 231–241.

"Platonic Justice," *Ethics, An International Journal of Social, Political, and Legal Philosophy*, 48: 367–400 (1937/38).

"De la séparation du pacte de la Société des Nations et des traités de paix," *La Crise Mondiale*, collection d'études publiée à l'occasion du 10ᵉ anniversaire de l'Institut Universitaire de Hautes Études Internationales, Zurich (Editions Polygraphiques, Paris: Sirey, 1938), pp. 143–173.

"The Separation of the Covenant of the League of Nations from the Peace Treaties," *The World Crisis*, Symposium of Studies published on the occasion of the Tenth Anniversary of the Graduate Institute of International Studies (London, New York, Toronto: Longmans Green & Co., 1938), pp. 133–159.

"Contributions à l'étude de la révision juridico-technique du Statut de la Société des Nations," *Revue générale du droit international public*, 44: 625–680 (1937); 45: 5–43, 161–240 (1938).

"Zur Reform des Völkerbundes" (Prag: Pax Edition, 1938). 10 pp.

"Zur Lehre vom Primat des Völkerrechts," *Revue internationale de la théorie du droit*, 12: 211–216 (1938).

"Die Entstehung des Kausalgesetzes aus dem Vergeltungsprinzip," *The Journal of Unified Science (Erkenntnis)*, 8: 69–130 (1939).

"International Peace — by Court or Government?" *The American Journal of Sociology*, 46: 571–581 (1941).

"The Essential Conditions of International Justice," *Proceedings of the 35th Annual Meeting of the American Society of International Law* (Washington, 1941), 70–86.

"Pure Theory of Law and Analytical Jurisprudence," *Harvard Law Review*, 40: 44–70 (1941).

"Causality and Retribution," *Philosophy of Science*, 8: 533–556 (1941).

"Recognition in International Law," *The American Journal of International Law*, 35: 605–617 (1941).

"The Law as a Specific Social Technique," *The University of Chicago Law Review*, 9: 75–97 (1941).

"Judicial Review of Legislation. A Comparative Study of the Austrian and the American Constitution," *The Journal of Politics*, 4: 183–200 (1942).

"Value Judgments in the Science of Law," *Journal of Social Philosophy and Jurisprudence*, 7: 312–333 (1942).

"Revision of the Covenant of the League of Nations," *World Organization*, 1942, pp. 392–412.

"Platonic Love," *The American Imago*, 3: 1–112 (1942).

"Post-War Problems," *Proceedings of the American Academy of Arts and Sciences*, 75: 11–13 (1942).

"Compulsory Adjudication of International Disputes," *The American Journal of International Law*, 37: 397–406 (1943).

"Quincy Wright's A Study of War and the Bellum Justum Theory," *Ethics, An International Journal of Social, Political, and Legal Philosophy*, 53: 208–211 (1943).

"Peace Through Law," *Journal of Legal and Political Sociology*, 2: 52–67 (1943).

"La Paz por el Derecho. Una Liga Permanente para el Mantenimiento de la Paz," *Rivista del Colegio de Abogados de Buenos Aires*, 21: 1–39 (1943).

"Collective and Individual Responsibility in International Law with Particular Regard to the Punishment of War Criminals," *California Law Review*, 31: 530–571 (1943).

"The Principle of Sovereign Equality of States as a Basis for International Organization," *Yale Law Journal*, 53: 207–220 (1944).

"The Strategy of Peace," *The American Journal of Sociology*, 49: 381–389 (1944).

"The International Legal Status of Germany to be established immediately upon Termination of the War," *The American Journal of International Law*, 39: 689–694 (1944).

"The Old and the New League," *The American Journal of International Law*, 40: 45–83 (1945).

TRANSLATIONS

FRENCH

La Démocratie. Sa nature — sa valeur, Bibliothèque constitutionnelle et parlementaire contemporaine, III (Paris: Recueil Sirey, 1932). x + 121 pp.

"Aperçu d'une théorie générale de l'État," *Revue du droit public et de la science politique en France et à l'étranger*, 43: 561–646 (1926). Paris, 1927. 94 pp.

"La Justice platonicienne," *Revue philosophique de la France et de l'étranger*, 57° année, 104: 364–396 (1932).

"La Technique du droit international et l'organisation de la paix," *Revue de droit international et de législation comparée*, 61° année (1934), pp. 5–24.

SPANISH

Teoría General del Estado, Enciclopedia de ciencias jurídicas y sociales (Barcelona, Madrid, Buenos Aires: Editorial Labor S.A., 1934). xix + 544 pp.

Compendio esquemático de una teoría general del estado (Barcelona, 1928). Nunez y Comp., xxvi + 131 pp.

La Teoría Pura del Derecho (Madrid, 1933). 83 pp.

Esencia y valor de la democracia (Barcelona: Labor, 1935). 159 pp.

"La técnica del derecho internacional y la organización de la paz," *Revista general de legislación y jurisprudencia*, año 84 (1935), 146: 769–789.

"Dictaturas de Partido," *Universidad de Panamá*, vol. 1, no. 4 (1936), pp. 1–12.

La Teoría Pura del Derecho; Introducción a la Problemática científica del Derecho, Biblioteca del Instituto Argentino de Filosofía Jurídica y Social (Buenos Aires: Editorial Losado, s.a., 1941). 213 pp.

"La Teoría Pura del Derecho y la Jurisprudencia Analitica," *La Ley*, Buenos Aires, Diciembre, 1941, pp. 1–6.

Derecho y Paz en las relaciones internacionales (Mexico: Fondo de cultura economica, 1943). 209 pp.

"La Idea del Derecho Natural," Boletín de la Facultad de Derecho y Ciencias Sociales de Córdoba, 6: no. 5 (1943).

"La responsabilidad colectiva e individual en Derecho internacional, con especial consideración al castigo de los criminales de guerra," *Revista de la Universidad Nacional de Córdoba*, 31 (1944). 54 pp.

"El principio de igualdad de soberanía entre los Estados, como base de la organización internacional," *Revista de la Universidad Nacional de Córdoba*, 31 (1944). 22 pp.

PORTUGUESE

Teoria geral do Estado (São Paulo: Livraria Academica, Saraiva, 1938), 159 pp.

Teoria geral do Estado, Colecção Studium Temas Filosóficos, Jurídicos e Sociais (Coimbra, 1938). 159 pp.

Teoria pura do direito (São Paulo: Livraria Academica, Saraiva, 1939). 112 pp.

Teoria pura do direito, Colecção Studium Temas Filosóficos, Jurídicos e Sociais (Coimbra, 1939). 112 pp.

ITALIAN

"Intorno alla natura ed al valore della democrazia," Lineamenti di una teoria generale dello Stato e altri scritti, a cura di Arnaldo Volpicelli, Roma, 1933, A.R.E., pp. 69–99.

"Diritto publico e privato," *Rivista internazionale di filosofia del diritto*, 4° anno, 1924, pp. 340–357.

"Il problema del parlamentarismo," *Nuovi Studi di diritto, economia e politica*, 2: 182–204 (1929), Lineamenti di una teoria generale dello Stato e altri scritti, a cura di A. Volpicelli, Roma, 1933, A.R.E., pp. 101–125.

"Lineamenti di una teoria generale dello Stato," *Nuovi Studi di diritto, economia e politica*, 2: 267–281, 368–376 (1929); 3: 208–228, 325–341 (1930). Roma, 1933, A.R.E., pp. 173.

"Concetto del diritto naturale," *Nuovi Studi di diritto, economia e politica*, 3: 392–421 (1930). Lineamenti di una teoria generale dello Stato e altri scritti, a cura di A. Volpicelli. Roma, 1933, A.R.E., pp. 127–159.

"Formalismo giuridico e dottrina pura del diritto," *Nuovi studi di diritto, economia e politica*, 4: 124–135 (1931). Lineamenti di una teoria generale dello Stato e altri scritti, a cura di A. Volpicelli, Roma, 1933, A.R.E., pp. 161–173.

La dottrina pura del diritto. Metodo e concetti fondamentali (Modena: Società tipografica Modenese, 1933). 53 pp.

CZECH

"Sociologická a právnická idea státní," *Sborník věd právních a státních*, 14: 69–101 (1913/14).

O podstatě a hodnotě demokracie (Praha: Orbis, 1933). 108 pp.

Základy obecní teorie státní (Brno: Barvic a Novotny, 1926). 84 pp.

"Juristický formalismus a ryzí nauka právní," *Časopis pro právní a státní vědu*, 12: 163–168, 207–211 (1929).

Ryzí nauka právní. Metoda a základní pojmy (Brno, Praha: Orbis, 1933). 55 pp.

Státní forma a světový názor (Praha: Fr. Borovy, 1937). 28 pp.

O reformě společnosti národu (Praha: Edice Pax, 1938). 14 pp.

POLISH

Zagadnienie Parlamentaryzmu (Warszawa: F. Hoesick, 1929). 32 pp.

Czysta teorja prawa. Metoda i pojecia zasadnicze (Warszawa: Gazeta administracji i policji panstwowej, 1934). 70 pp.

"Technika prawa narodow a organizacja pokoju," *Przeglad Wspolczesny*, vol. 14, no. 153 (1935), pp. 36–55.

Podstawowe zagadnienia nauki prawa panstwowego. Wrozwinieciu nauki o normie prawnej (Wilno: Universytat St. Batorego, 1935). 390 pp.

"Dyktatura Partji," *Ruch Prawniczy, ekonomiczny i socjologiezny*, vol. 16, nr. 1 (1936), pp. 1–12.

O istocie i wartosci demokracji (Warszawa: Ksiegarnia Powazechna, 1937). 138 pp.

SERB

"O granicama izmedju pravničke i sociološke metode," Beograd, 1928, Bibliothek der Rechts- und Gesellschaftswissenschaften, vol. 17, pp. 47.

ROUMANIAN

"Impartirea teritoriala a statului. Teorie asupra centralizarei si descentralizarei precum si legaturilor dintre State," *Revista de drept public*, 1: 375–395 (1926).

Teoria generala a statului, Biblioteca Institului Stiinte administrative, no. 12 (Bucuresti: Oltenia, 1928). 104 pp.

HUNGARIAN

Az államelmélet alapvonolai (Szeged: Szegedi Tudományos Könyvtár, 1927). xiii + 90 pp.

A szuverénitás fogalmának változása (Budapest: Zs. Politzer, 1931). 23 pp.

GREEK

"Stoicheia genikes theorias tes politeias," *Archeion philosophias kai theorias ton epistemon*, first year, 1929, pp. 281–297, 441–497.

"He kommatike diktatoria, Symbole eis ten kritiken analysin politikon ideon," *Archeion philosophias kai theorias ton epistemon*, 1934, pp. 322–345.

BULGARIAN

Technistoto utschenje za prawoto. Uwod w problematikata na prawnata nauka (Sofia: Prawna Misl, 1937). 111 pp.

SWEDISH

"Den rena rättsläran. Dess metod och grundbegrepp," *Statsvetenskaplig Tidskrift*, thirty-sixth year, 1933, pp. 193–244.

JAPANESE

Kihangaku matawa Bunkakagaku to shiteno Horitsugaku. Scientific treatises published by the Omura Press, vol. 19 (Tokyo, 1923). xvi + 149 pp.

Minshu Seiji to Dokusai Seiji. Demokurashii no Honshitsu to Kachi (Tokyo: Iwanami Shoten, 1932). 181 pp.

Kokka Gainen Kenkyu (Tokyo: Shunjusha, 1924). vii + 400 pp. 2nd ed., *Shakaigakuteki Kokka Gainen to Horisugakuteki Kokka Gainen* (Tokyo: Shunjusha, 1929). 268 pp.

" 'Kihanteki Taikei' to shiteno Kokka," *Hogaku Ronso*, 11: 117–134, 260–270, 387–396, 528–550 (Kyoto, 1924).

"Kokka Genri Teiyo," *Waseda Law Review*, 7: 1–118 (1927).

"Hōritsugakuteki Kokka Gainen," *Wien Gakuha Horitsugaku to sono Shomondai* (Tokyo: Taitokaku, 1927), pp. 169–243.

"Junsui Hōgaku no Hatten to sono Bunken," *Shogaku Ronso, Wakayama*, 2: 68–96 (1927).

Wien Gakuha no Horitsugaku to sono Shomondai (Tokyo: Taitokaku, 1927), pp. 153–168.

Shizen Hōgaku to Ho Jisshoshugi (Tokyo: Ohata Shoten, 1932). 133 pp.

Ippan Kokka Gainen (Tokyo: Iwanami, 1936). xiii + 823 pp.

CHINESE

I Pun Kuo Kia Hsio Ta Kan (Peiping: Koue Yo, 1935). 92 pp.

PUBLICATIONS ON THE PURE THEORY OF LAW

(This list is not complete. It contains only the more important contributions to the discussion of the problems concerned.)

Akzin, Benjamin, "L'école autrichienne et le droit des gens," *Revue de droit international*, 1: 342–372 (1927).

Amézaga Alvardo, Armando M., *Algunas consideraciones sobre el concepto del Derecho de la Escuela Vienesa* (México: 1935). 26 pp.

Budnik, Josef, "Kelsenovy námitky proti možnosti dualistické konstrukce mezinárodního práva," *Časopis pro právní a státní vědu*, 16: 303–315 (1933).

Campbell, A. H., "Some Reflections of an English Lawyer on Kelsen's Theory of Law and the State," in: R. Höhn, Th. Maunz, E. Swoboda, *Grundfragen der Rechtsauffassung* (München: 1938). pp. 31–43.

Castiglia, Tommaso Antonio, *Stato e diritto in Hans Kelsen* (1932). 195 pp.

Cohen, Hyman E., *Recent Theories of Sovereignty* (1937): Chapter: Pure Jurisprudence and International Law — Kelsen, pp. 224–234.

Condorelli, Orazio, "Il rapporto fra Stato e diritto secondo il Kelsen," *Rivista internazionale di filosofia del diritto*, 3: 307–315 (1923).

Cossio, Carlos, *Hans Kelsen, El jurista de la época contempóranea* (Buenos Aires: 1941). 20 pp.

Davy, Georges, "Le problème de l'obligation chez Duguit et Kelsen," *Archives de philosophie du droit et de sociologie juridique*, no. 1–2: 7–46 (1933).

Druks, Stanislaw, *Z zagadnien filozofji prawa. Kelsen i jego szkola* (1924).

Ebenstein, W., *Die rechtsphilosophische Schule der Reinen Rechtslehre* (1938). 180 pp.

————, *The Pure Theory of Law* (Madison, Univ. of Wisconsin Press: 1945). 211 pp.

Ereky, István, "A jogtudomány módszerei. A Duguit- és Kelsen-féle módszertani álláspontok birálata," *Városi Szemle*, 14: 1–64 (1929).

Fernández Llano, Ataulfo, *Teoría general del Estado: la doctrina normativista de Kelsen* (Habana: 1937). 63 pp.

Gómez Arias, Alejandro, *Al margen de Kelsen, notas sobre el sentido estético del Derecho* (México: 1938). 50 pp.

Hägerström, Axel, "Hans Kelsen, Allgemeine Staatslehre," *Litteris*, 5: 20–40, 83–99 (1928).

Heck, Philipp, "Die Reine Rechtslehre und die jungösterreichische Schule der Rechtswissenschaft," *Archiv für die zivilistische Praxis*, N. F. 2: 173–194 (1924).

Henrich, Walter, "Der Primat der Völkerrechtsordnung. Kritische Bemerkungen zu Kelsens Konstruktion des Völkerrechts," *Philosophie und Recht*, 1: 126–128 (1922).

Hintze, Otto, "Kelsens Staatslehre," *Historische Zeitschrift*, 135: 66–75 (1926).

Hippel, E., "Zur Kritik einiger Grundbegriffe in der 'Reinen Rechtslehre' Kelsens," *Archiv des öffentlichen Rechts*, N. F. 5: 327–346 (1923).

Horneffer, Reinhold, *Hans Kelsens Lehre von der Demokratie* (1926), 80 pp.

Husik, I., "The Legal Philosophy of Hans Kelsen," *Journal of Social Philosophy*, 3: 297–324 (1938).

Jaeger, F., *Le problème de la souveraineté dans la doctrine de Kelsen* (1932). 170 pp.

Janzen, Henry, "Kelsen's Theory of Law," *American Political Science Review*, 31: 205–226 (1937).

Jerusalem, F. W., "Die Staatslehre Hans Kelsens," *Zeitschrift für die gesamte Staatswissenschaft*, 80: 664–679 (1925–26).

Jöckel, Wilhelm, *Hans Kelsens rechtstheoretische Methode* (1930). viii + 213 pp.

Jones, J. Walter, *Historical Introduction to the Theory of Law* (1940): Chapter: Kelsen's Pure Theory of Law, pp. 224–234.

Kallab, Jaroslav, "Poznamky o vyznamu normativni teorie pro teorii prava trestniho," *Vedecka rocenka pravnicke faculty Masarykovy university*, 11: 41–65 (1932).

Kimura, Kameji, "Kelsen no Horitsu Shakaigaku no Hohoron," *Hogaku Shirin*, 24: no. 1, 46–75; no. 2, 70–107 (1922).

———, "Wien Gakuha to Horitsu no Kaishaku oyobi Tekiyo," *Hogaku Shirin*, 34: no. 4, 36–66 (1932).

Klinghoffer, Hans, "Direito Público e Direito Privado. Resumo da Teoria de Hans Kelsen," *Revista Forense*, 397–399 (1942).

Kockler, Claus, *Begriff der Souveränität und die Wiener Rechtsschule*. Kölner jur. Dissertation (1930). iv + 79 pp.

Koettgen, Arnold, "Kelsen und die Demokratie," Zeitschrift für die gesamte Staatswissenschaft, 90: 97–107 (1931).

Kraft-Fuchs, Margit, "Kelsens Staatstheorie und die Soziologie des Staates," *Zeitschrift für öffentliches Recht*, 11: 402–415 (1931).

Kunz, Josef L., *Völkerrechtswissenschaft und Reine Rechtslehre* (1923). 86 pp.

———, "The 'Vienna School' and International Law," *New York University Law Quarterly Review*, 11: no. 3, 1–52 (1934).

Kuroda, Satoru, *Wien Gakuha no Horitsugaku to sono Shomondai* (1927). 417 pp.

———, "Tagen teki Kokkaron to Wien Hogaku," *Hogakuronso*, 25: no. 1, 57–74; no. 3, 87–107; no. 4, 96–111 (1931).

Lagerroth, Fredrik, "Boström och Kelsen. En Jämförelse," *Statsvetenskaplig Tidskrift*, 28: 1–37 (1925).

Lande, Jerzy, "Norma a zjawisko prawne. Rozważania nad podstawami teorji prawa na tle krytyki systemu Kelsena," *Czasopismo prawnicze i ekonomiczne*, 23: 235–348 (1925).

Lauterpacht, H., "Kelsen's Pure Science of Law," *Modern Theories of Law*, 105–138 (Oxford, 1933).

Legaz y Lacambra, Luis, *Kelsen. Estudio crítico de la teoría pura del Derecho y del Estado de la Escuela de Viena* (1933). 371 pp.

———, *Prologo a la traducción española del libro del Prof. Kelsen* (1934). 5 pp.

———, "Notas sobre el valor actual de la teoría pura del Derecho," *La Ley* (Buenos Aires, Sept. 5, 1944), pp. 1–5.

Lenz, Heinrich, "Autorität und Demokratie in der Staatslehre von Hans Kelsen," *Schmollers Jahrbuch für Gesetzgebung, Verwaltung und Volkswirtschaft im Deutschen Reiche*, 50: 589–620 (1926).

Lüttger, Heinz, "Die Lehre von den Grundrechten und Grundpflichten der Staaten im Völkerrecht. Ein kritischer Beitrag im Sinne der Kelsenschen Rechtslehre," *Zeitschrift für öffentliches Recht*, 6: 203–212 (1926–27).

Makino, Eiichi, "Horitsuteki Shokyokushugi. Junsui Horitsu Riron to Keiho," *Hogaku Shirin*, 35: 1–47 (1932).

Man, Georges, *L'École de Vienne et le développement du droit des gens* (Paris: 1938). 146 pp.

Markovic, Ceda, "Dr. Hans Kelsen o ispitivanju ustavnosti zakona," *Archiv za pravne i društvene nauke*, 11: 250–251 (1925).

Mattern, Johannes, *Concepts of State, Sovereignty and International Law* (1928): Chapter: The State and the Civitas Maxima according to the Austrian School, pp. 121–139.

Maury, J., "Observations sur les idées du prof. Kelsen," *Revue critique de législation et de jurisprudence*, 49: no. 11/12, 537–563.

———, "Observaciones sobre las ideas del professor H. Kelsen," *Revista de Derecho Privado*, 16: 305–320 (1929).

Mayer, Hans, "Staatstheorie und Staatspolitik. Bemerkungen zu Hans Kelsens Schrift 'Der Staat als Integration,'" *Die Justiz*, 7: 249–259 (1932).

Menzel, Adolf, "Kelsens 'Allgemeine Staatslehre' und die Soziologie," *Jahrbuch für Soziologie*, 2: 261–275 (1926).

Merkl, Adolf, "Hans Kelsens System einer Reinen Rechtslehre," *Archiv des öffentlichen Rechts*, 41: 171–201 (1921).

———, "Neue Wege der Rechtswissenschaft. Zu Hans Kelsens Rechtstheorie," *Schweizerische Juristen-Zeitung*, 18: 303–307 (1922).

———, "Hans Kelsen als Verfassungspolitiker," *Juristische Blätter*, 60: 385–388 (1931).

Métall, Rudolf A., "Hans Kelsens Bedeutung für das österreichische Recht," *Österreichische Anwalts-Zeitung*, 8: 362–365 (1931).

———, "O Plano Kelsen de Organização Jurídica da Paz," *Direito*, n. XXIV, Ano IV (1943). 24 pp.

Minobe, Tatsukichi, "Kelsen Kyoju no Kokuho oyobi Kokusaiho Riron no Hihyo," *Kokkagakukai Zasshi*, 44: no. 8, 1–36; no. 9, 47–78 (1930).

Missong, Alfred, "Die juristische Grundlegung des Pazifismus durch den Souveränitätsbegriff der Reinen Rechtslehre," *Die Menschheit*, 15: 216–217 (1928).

Mokre, Hans, "Gegenstandstheorie und Reine Rechtslehre," *Zeitschrift für öffentliches Recht*, 9: 321–356 (1930).

Moór, Julius, "Reine Rechtslehre, Naturrecht und Rechtspositivismus," *Gesellschaft, Staat und Recht, Festschrift für Hans Kelsen*, 58–105 (1931).

Morawetz, Carl, "Challenge to Ostriches. Kelsen's Normative Theory of Law," *The School of Law Review*. University of Toronto, 2: no. 2; 1, 8 (1944).

Müller, Hellmut, *Über das Dogma der Einheit des Erkenntnisstandpunktes in der Kelsenschen Rechtslehre.* Breslauer jur. Dissertation (1933). 55 pp.

Mycielski, Andrzej, *O przestrzennych granicach pánstwa w świetle krytyki Kelsena* (1933). 21 pp.

Nakamura, Yasoji, "Note on Professor Kelsen's New Work 'Allgemeine Staatslehre,'" *Waseda Law Review*, 5: 1–11 (1925).

Neubauer, Zdenek, "O pojem prava," *Všehrd*, 3: 68–71 (1922).

———, "T. G. Masaryk o normativní teorii," *Časopis pro pravni a státni vĕdu*, 9: 53–60 (1926).

Olsson, Gustaf, *Det statsrealistiska problemet. Med särskild hänsyn till den rättsfilosofiska Skolan i Wien* (1925). ii + 271 pp.

Otaka, Tomoo, "Künftige Aufgaben der Reinen Rechtslehre," *Gesellschaft, Staat und Recht, Festschrift für Hans Kelsen*, 106–135 (1931).

Pagano, Antonio, "Per la critica di alcuni concetti fondamentali della 'Reine Rechtslehre' del Kelsen," *Rivista internazionale di filosofia del diritto*, 4: 80–81 (1924).

Pallares, Eduardo, *El Derecho deshumanizado* (México: 1941). 141 pp.

Pitamic, Leonidas, "Plato, Aristoteles und die Reine Rechtslehre," *Zeitschrift für öffentliches Recht*, 2: 683–700 (1920–21).

———, "Kritische Bemerkungen zum Gesellschafts-, Staats- und Gottesbegriff bei Kelsen," *Zeitschrift für öffentliches Recht*, 3: 531–554 (1921/22).

Pohl, W., "Kelsens Parallele: Gott und Staat," *Zeitschrift für öffentliches Recht*, 4: 571–609 (1924–25).

Pound, Roscoe, "Fifty Years of Jurisprudence," *Harvard Law Review*, 51: 449–450 (1938).

Prochazka, Adolf, "Normativní teorie a tvorba práva," *Sbornik Karla Engliše*, 436–455 (1930).

Rangel Frias, Raúl, *Identidad des Estado y Derecho en la teoría jurídica pura de Hans Kelsen* (México: 1938). 80 pp.

Rapisardi-Mirabelli, Andrea, "Fastigi nuovi del diritto internazionale celebrati dalla 'Reine Rechtslehre,' " *Rivista internazionale di filosofia del diritto*, 5: 236–247 (1925).

Recaséns Siches, Luis, *Prólogo a la traducción española del Compendio esquemático de una Teoría general del Estado, del Prof. Hans Kelsen* (1928). xxii pp.

———, *Direcciones contemporáneas del Pensamiento jurídico* (1929). Capítulo V: "La teoría pura del Derecho (Filosofía de la Ciencia jurídica o del Derecho positivo) según Kelsen," pp. 108–164.

———, "Estado y Derecho. El problema acerca de si son distintos o bien una sola e idéntica entidad," *Studi Filosofico-giuridici dedicati al Prof. Giorgio Del Vecchio*, 2: 314–345 (1931).

Roffenstein, Gaston, "Kelsens Staatsbegriff und die Soziologie," *Zeitschrift für öffentliches Recht*, 4: 539–561 (1924–25).

Rohatyn, Sigmund, "Die reine Normtheorie des Rechts," *Revue internationale de la théorie du droit*, 7: 171–179 (1932–33).

Sander, Fritz, "Rechtsdogmatik oder Theorie der Rechtserfahrung? Kritische Studie zur Rechtslehre Hans Kelsens," *Zeitschrift für öffentliches Recht*, 2: 511–670 (1920–21).

———, *Kelsens Rechtslehre* (1923). 177 pp.

Sauerländer, J. D., "Zum Kampf um die Reine Rechtslehre," *Zentralblatt für die Juristische Praxis*, 47: 175–186 (1929).

van Schaik, H. L. M., *Beschouwingen naar Aanleiding van Kelsens Gelijkstelling van Staat en Recht* (1930). viii + 127 pp.

Scheuner, Ulrich, "Dynamik und Statik in der Staatsrechtslehre. Eine Untersuchung zur Staats- und Rechtstheorie Léon Duguits und Hans Kelsens," Internationale Zeitschrift für Theorie des Rechts, 3: 220–246 (1928–29).

Schreier, Fritz, "Die Wiener rechtsphilosophische Schule," *Logos*, 11: 309–328 (1923).

———, "Reine Rechtslehre und Privatrecht," *Gesellschaft, Staat und Recht, Festschrift für Hans Kelsen*, 309–343 (1931).

Simon, Walter, "Die Grundlagen der Staatslehre Professor Kelsens," *Volkswohl*, 17: 106–111, 148–153, 191–196, 221–228 (1926).

Soler, Sebastian, "Algunas observaciones a la doctrina de Hans Kelsen," *Boletin de la Facultad de Derecho y Ciencias Sociales, Universidad de Córdoba* (julio-agosto 1943), 286–311.

Spiegel, Ludwig, "Kelsens Rechtslehre," *Prager Juristische Zeitschrift*, 1: 1–21 (1921).

Stark, Bernhard, "Eine Paraphrase Hans Kelsens 'Das Verhältnis von Staat und Recht im Lichte der Erkenntniskritik,'" *Juristische Blätter*, 51: 4–6 (1922).

Stern, W. B., "Kelsen's Theory of International Law," *American Political Science Review*, 30: 736–741 (1936).

Stockhammer, Moritz, "Kelsen und die Opposition," *Internationale Zeitschrift für Theorie des Rechts*, 8: 201–213 (1934).

Svens Uppslagsbok, Article "Kelsen," vol. 15: 228–230 (1933).

Tasić, Djordje, "O kritičkim primedbama professora Pitamica na Kelsenove pojmove društva, države i Boga," *Archiv za pravne i društvene nauke*, 7: 330–345 (1923).

———, "Jedan kritički pogled na pokušaj moderne kritičke državnopravne teorije: Duguit-Kelsen," *Slowenski pravnik*, 41: 219–234 (1926).

———, "Le principe de légalité dans les doctrines de Duguit et Kelsen," *Revue internationale de la théorie*, 4: 55–69 (1929–30).

Tezner, Friedrich, "Betrachtungen über Kelsens Lehre vom Rechtssatz," *Archiv des öffentlichen Rechts*, 28: 325–344 (1912).

Treves, Renato, *Il fondamento filosofico della dottrina pura del diritto di Hans Kelsen*, Atti della R. Academia delle Scienze di Torino (1934). 41 pp.

Uhde, Theodor, "Kelsenova konstrukce logické formy právní normy," *Všehrd*, 6: 155–168 (1925).

Ulloa Ortiz, Manuel, *Estado y Derecho: El problema de sus relaciones* (México: 1933). xii + 49 pp.

Verdross, Alfred, "Völkerrecht und einheitliches Rechtssystem. Kritische Studie zu den Völkerrechtstheorien von Max Wenzel, Hans Kelsen und Fritz Sander," *Zeitschrift für Völkerrecht*, 12: 405–438 (1923).

———, "Die Rechtstheorie Hans Kelsens," *Juristische Blätter*, 59: 421–423 (1930).

Victor, René, *Gerecht en Bestuur in het werk van Hans Kelsen* (1930). 24 pp.

———, "Hans Kelsen en de Intellectueele Vrijheid," *Rechtskundig Weekblad*, 2: 633–638 (1933).

Virsík, Jul., "Teleologický princip a normativna teoria," *Všehrd*, 13: 234–238 (1932).

Voegelin, Erich, "Reine Rechtslehre und Staatslehre," *Zeitschrift für öffentliches Recht*, 4: 80–131 (1924–25).

——, "Kelsen's Pure Theory of Law," *Political Science Quarterly*, 42: 268–276 (1927).

——, "Die Souveränitätstheorie Dickinsons und die Reine Rechtslehre," *Zeitschrift für öffentliches Recht*, 8: 413–434 (1928–29).

Volpicelli, Arnaldo, "Dalla democrazia al corporativismo. Polemizzando con H. Kelsen," *Nuovi studi di diritto, economia e politica*, 3: 1–20 (1930).

Walz, Gustav Adolf, "Zum Problem der 'monistischen' oder 'dualistischen' Konstruktion des Völkerrechts," *Zeitschrift für öffentliches Recht*, 10: 538–557 (1930).

Weyr, František, "Über zwei Hauptprobleme der Kelsenschen Staatsrechtslehre," *Zeitschrift für das Privat- und öffentliche Recht der Gegenwart*, 40: 175–188 (1914).

——, "Hans Kelsen," *Časopis pro právní a státní vědu*, 15: 1–18 (1932).

Wilk, Kurt, "Law and the State as Pure Ideas. Critical Notes on the Basic Concepts of Kelsen's Legal Philosophy," *Ethics*, 51: 158–184 (1941).

Wilson, Charles H., "The Basis of Kelsen's Theory of Law," *Politica*, no. 1: 54–82 (1934).

Winternitz, Emanuel, "Zum Streit um Kelsens Rechtslehre," *Juristische Blätter*, 52: 120–122 (1923).

Yokota, Kisaburo, *Kelsen no Junsui Hogaku* (1932), 429 pp.

——, "Junsui Hogaku no Jissai teki Kino," *Kokkagakukai Zasshi*, 47: no. 7, 1–35 (1933).

Zech, Herbert, *Die Rechtfertigung des Staates in der normativen Staatstheorie und der Integrationslehre* (1934). x + 76 pp.

INDEX

INDEX

Abroad, jurisdiction over citizens, 238
Absolute liability, *see* Liability, absolute
Absolute monarchy, 264f., 281, 300, 311
Absolute nullity, 160f.
Absolute responsibility, *see* Responsibility, absolute
Absolute and relative duty, 85f.
Absolute and relative natural law, 397, 431
Absolute and relative right, 85f.
Absolute and relative truth, 434
Absolute and relative validity, 393ff.
Absolute and suspensive veto, 271f.
Absolutism, metaphysical, and natural-law doctrine, 396
political, and natural-law doctrine, 417
Abstract (general) legal norms, concretization (individualization), 135, 397
Accession to treaty, 228
Accretion, 215
Acquisition and loss
of citizenship, 234, 238ff.
of territory, 213ff., 216, *see also* Territory
Acquisition of no State's land, 211f., 214f.
Act, *see also* Administrative, Coercive, Illegal, Judicial, Juristic, Law-applying, Law-creating, Legal, Legislative act
and norm, 39
partial and total, 195ff.
of State, *see* State, act of
Acting person, *see* Person, acting
Action and omission as delict, 54, 59
Additional and substitute duty, 139f., 329f., 357

Adjective law, judicial act determined only by, 144f., 152f.
and substantive law 129, 152f.
and substantive law, in application of law, 129
Administration, coercive acts of, 278f.
direct and indirect, 279f.
as execution (executive power), 256
judicial control of, 276f., 280
judicial function of, 274f.
and judiciary
connection between, 277f.
determined by constitution, 262
as law-applying function, 129ff.
legality of, and democracy, 299f.
by local autonomy, and State administration, 315f.
summary procedure of, 278
Administrative act, 114f., 128ff., 205, 275f.
as law-creating act, 114f.
and legal transaction, 276
and judicial act, determined by general legal norm, 128ff.
Administrative coercive act and sanction, 279
Administrative authority: independence of, 314
as law-creating organ, 130f.
Administrative contract, 276
Administrative court, 280
Administrative decentralization, 313f.
Administrative function: specific, 275f.
and political (governmental) function of State, 256
Administrative international law, 244, 248
Administrative law, 274
general rule (norm) of, 277

Renaissance of metaphysics and nattural-law doctrine, 446
Reparation: as purpose of civil law, 50f.
and sanction in international law, 357f.
and war-indemnity, 334
Reparation, duty of, 56, 70, 138ff., 200
in international law, 357ff.
and sanction, 329f.
Representation: concept of, 289f.
consensual and non-consensual, 83, 108
fiction of, 289ff.
functional (organic), 297f., 303
and juristic person, 101, 107f.
and legal right, 83f.
of minority, 296
proportional, see Proportional representation
Representative body, and electorate, 295f.
Representative (indirect) and direct democracy, 88, 235, 288ff.
Representative government, 289
Representative, organ of corporation as its representative, 107f.
Reprisals and war as sanctions of international law, 57, 106, 327, 330ff., 340, 344ff., 355
Republic: with cabinet government, 301
with collegiate government, 301
and monarchy, 283
president of, 301
presidential, 301
Reputation, right of, 249
Res judicata (force of law), 136, 154f., 158f., 403
Residence, right of, 236
Resignation, philosophy of, 443f.
Responsibility, see also Liability
absolute, 65ff., 361f.
absolute, in primitive law, 67
of cabinet ministers to parliament, 300

collective
and absolute liability, 70f.
and individual, 68ff., 106, 344
and individual, in international law, 344f., 355ff.
and juristic person, 106
of corporation, see Corporation
direct and indirect (vicarious), 107, 358ff.
and duty (obligation), 65ff., 71, 200
based on fault, 65ff.
legal, 65ff.
personal, of norm-creating organ as guarantee of legality of norm created by organ, 157f., 300
and sanction, 65
of State, see State, responsibility of
Retaliation, see Revenge
Retribution, 15f., 22, 55
divine, 16, 18
in hereafter, 17f.
or prevention as purpose of criminal law, 50f.
principle of
legal norm as prototype of, 47
nature interpreted according to, 16, 47
as origin of law of causality, 47
Retroactive force: annulment with, 159ff.
in international law, 226
recognition with, 226f.
Retroactive law, 43ff., 73, 146, 149, 226
and ignorantia juris, 44, 72
Revenge, 17, 56f., 338f.
war as act of, 334f.
Review, judicial, see Judicial review
Revolution: and coup d'Etat, 117, 219ff., 368f., 372
juristic criterion of, 117ff.
Revolutionary character of natural-law doctrine, 11, 47ff.
Revolutionism and pessimism, 425ff., 433
Reward and punishment, 15ff., 47